Practical Skills in

Biomolecular Sciences

Practical Skills in
Biomolecular Sciences

ROB REED

DAVID HOLMES

JONATHAN WEYERS

ALLAN JONES

Second edition

PEARSON
Prentice
Hall

Harlow, England • London • New York • Boston • San Francisco • Toronto
Sydney • Tokyo • Singapore • Hong Kong • Seoul • Taipei • New Delhi
Cape Town • Madrid • Mexico City • Amsterdam • Munich • Paris • Milan

Pearson Education Limited
Edinburgh Gate
Harlow
Essex CM20 2JE
England

and Associated Companies throughout the World

Visit us on the World Wide Web at:
www.pearsoneduc.com

First published 1998 by Addison Wesley Longman Limited
Second edition 2003

ISBN 0 130 45142 8

British Library Cataloguing-in-Publication Data
A catalogue record for this book is available from the British Library

Library of Congress Cataloging-in-Publication Data
Practical skills in biomolecular sciences / David Holmes ... [et al.].-- 2nd ed.
    p. cm.
  Includes bibliographical references (p.).
  ISBN 0-13-045142-8
  1. Molecular biology--Laboratory manuals. I. Holmes, David, 1946-

QH506 .P73 2003
572.8--dc21   2002035564

10 9 8 7 6 5 4 3 2 1
06 05 04 03

Typeset in 10/12pt Times by 25
Printed and bound by Henry Ling in Great Britain

The publisher's policy is to use paper manufactured from sustainable forests.

Contents

Contents

List of Boxes

List of Boxes

Preface to the Second Edition

Practical work forms the cornerstone of scientific knowledge: our understanding of the natural world has been shaped by the observations and experiments of earlier scientists, using a wide range of techniques and methods to investigate biological systems at the cellular and molecular levels. As a result, the training required for practical work in cellular and molecular biosciences is diverse: successful students must develop a number of specific practical skills, ranging from those required to observe, measure and record accurately to those associated with operating up-to-date analytical equipment, alongside broader skills involved in teamwork and effective study. In creating the second edition of *Practical Skills in Biomolecular Sciences*, we have maintained the approach of the previous edition, with the aim of providing support to students taking courses where cellular and molecular biosciences form a major component of the syllabus, e.g. microbiology, biochemistry, genetics, molecular biology, biomedical sciences, physiology and paramedical subjects. As before, this support is provided in a concise but user-friendly manner, with key points and definitions, illustrations and worked examples, tips and hints, 'how to' boxes and checklists where appropriate. However, we have also used the opportunity of the new edition to restructure the layout, to add to the content and to emphasise some of the broader aspects of transferable skills. As a result, this edition contains a new section at the front of the book dealing with study and examination skills, with additional chapters on transferable skills, time management, working with others, note-taking and revising, as well as assessments and exams. A chapter has been added on preparing a CV, since we feel that this provides a focus on the outcome of undergraduate study from the outset. In creating these new chapters, we have been mindful of the Quality Assurance Agency UK Subject Benchmarking Statements for Biosciences and Biomedical Sciences, published in 2002, and have endeavoured to cover all of the generic skills, along with practical aspects of many of the subject-specific topics in cellular and molecular biosciences. Perhaps the most important skill required of a modern science degree student is the ability to evaluate information, and we have added a new chapter on this key aspect, within an expanded section dealing with information technology and library resources.

We have also taken the opportunity to revise the subject-specific content of the text, mostly in response to feedback from students and staff. Thus, we have added new chapters on (i) the preparation and use of calibration curves and (ii) bioinformatics. We have significantly updated and added further material to many other chapters, especially in fast-moving aspects such as the use of the Internet/World Wide Web, along with topics such as photosynthetic physiology, fluorogenic enzyme substrates, etc. We have provided new material within the numeracy and statistics chapters, often in response to requests from students for greater support and guidance in these areas, and based on our own perceptions of the needs of students. Every chapter is now supported by a section giving key sources for further study – these include conventional printed texts, as well as electronic and Web-based resources and number over 300 in total. Another novel aspect is the provision of study exercises for each chapter – over 250 in total. Here, our aim is to reinforce learning with problems and practical exercises and these are further discussed in the section headed 'For the Student'. As a result of these changes and innovations, the new edition contains 8 more chapters and almost 200 additional pages. There are also 40 new figures, twice as many tables and 13 additional boxes compared with the previous edition. This edition also contains over 150 additional citations for relevant websites, enabling students to locate and use electronic resources *via* the Internet.

We would like to take this opportunity to thank our wives and families for their continued support, and to recognise the following colleagues and friends who have provided assistance, comment and food for thought at various points during the production of both editions: James Abbott, Chris Baldwin, Gary Black, Jon Bookham, Geoff Bosson, Eldridge Buultjens, Simon Charnock, Bob Cherry, Mirela Cucuclescu, Mark Daniels, Martin Davies, John Dean, Jackie Eager, Brian Eddy, Howard Griffiths, Nicola Hall, Claire Halpin, Rod Herbert, Steve Hitchin, Derek Holmes, Helen Hooper, Arthur James, Andy Johnston, Alan Jones, Ian Kill, Rhonda Knox, Ed Ludkin, Pete Maskrey, Steve Millam, Rachel Morris, John Raven, Steve Reed, Zoë Reed, Pete Rowell, Tom Marshall, David Sillars, Liz Smith, Nicola Smith, Bill Tomlinson, Paul Weyers, Will Whitfield, Katherine Williams, Ian

Winship, Ros Woodward, Peter Wright, Bob Young and Hilary-Kay Young. We would also like to thank the staff of Pearson Education for their support over the years, and would wish to acknowledge Alex Seabrook and Simon Lake for their encouragement and commitment to the *Practical Skills* series. As with the previous edition, we would be grateful to hear of any errors you might notice, so that these can be put right at the earliest opportunity.

ROB REED (rob.reed@unn.ac.uk)
DAVID HOLMES (david.holmes@unn.ac.uk)
JONATHAN WEYERS (j.d.b.weyers@dundee.ac.uk)
ALLAN JONES (a.m.jones@dundee.ac.uk)

For the Student

This book aims to provide guidance and support over the broad range of your undergraduate course, including laboratory classes, project work, lectures, tutorials, seminars and examinations, as outlined below.

Chapters 1–7 cover general skills

These include a number of transferable skills that you will develop during your course, for example: self-evaluation; time management; teamwork; preparing for exams; creating a CV.

Chapters 8–19 deal with IT, library resources and communication

These chapters will help you get the most out of the resources and information available in your library, and on the World Wide Web, as well as providing helpful guidance on the use of software packages for data analysis, preparing assignments, essays and laboratory reports, alongside support in relation to oral, visual and written forms of communication The ability to evaluate information is an increasingly important skill in contemporary society, and practical guidance is provided here, as well as more specific advice, e.g. on bioinformatics resources available *via* the Internet.

Chapters 20–62 cover a wide range of specific practical skills required in biomolecular sciences

These are based on the authors' experience of the questions students often ask in practical classes, and the support that is needed in order to get the most out of particular exercises. The text includes tips, hints, definitions, worked examples and 'how to' boxes that set out the key procedures in a step-by-step manner, with appropriate comments on safe working practice. The material ranges from basic laboratory procedures, such as preparing solutions, through specimen collection, identification and manipulation to the more advanced practical procedures that you might use during a final year project, e.g. radioisotope work and more advanced analytical methods.

Chapters 63–67 explain data analysis and presentation

This will be an important component of your course and you will find that these chapters guide you through the skills and techniques required, ranging from the presentation of results as graphs or tables through to the application of statistical tests. Worked examples are used to reinforce the numerical aspects wherever possible.

Study exercises and problems

We have added these as a new feature in the second edition, following comments from students and staff at UK universities, who felt that this would provide a useful opportunity to practise some of the skills covered in the book and a check on the understanding of the material. We hope that the exercises will be useful both to learners and to their tutors: some of the exercises are based on material contained within the corresponding chapter, while others provide opportunities to further develop understanding in a particular topic area. In general, the more straightforward exercises have been placed first, with more advanced problems at the end of each section.

Most of the problems assume students are working on their own, using the information supplied; however, tutors might wish to provide alternative starting material (e.g. a set of data from a practical class). We have also assumed that students will have access to a scientific calculator and, sometimes, to a networked PC with typical 'office' programs (especially word processor and spreadsheet), plus Internet access *via* a modem and browser. Where a library is mentioned, this is assumed to include access to standard reference works and a selection of scientific journals.

Answers are given at the back of the book for all exercises. For numerical problems, the working out is also shown along with the final answer, while the non-numerical exercises also have 'answers' in the form of tips, general guidance or illustrative examples, etc. We recommend that students work together for some exercises – this is a valuable means of learning and, where there is no single correct answer to a problem, teamwork provides a mechanism for checking and discussing your answers.

We hope that you will find this book a helpful guide throughout your course, and beyond.

Acknowledgements

We are grateful to the following for permission to reproduce copyright material:

Figure 11.3 from Dr. G. Black, Northumbria University; Figure 12.1 from screen shot of Microsoft® Excel 2002, *http://www.microsoft.com/office/excel/evaluation/tour/page2.asp*, Copyright © 2001 Microsoft Corporation. Screen shot reprinted by permission from Microsoft Corporation; Figure 23.1 from 'Monograph No. 8671 Sodium Chloride' from *The Merck Index: an Encyclopedia of Chemicals, Drugs and Biologicals*, 13th edn., O'Neil, M.J., Smith, A., Heckelman, P.E. and Obenchain, J.R., Eds. (Merck & Co, Inc., Whitehouse Station, NJ, USA, 2001). Reproduced with permission from *The Merck Index*, 13th edn., Copyright © 2001 by Merck & Co., Inc., Whitehouse Station, NJ, USA. All rights reserved; Figure 27.2 from photograph of *Olympus Model CX41* binocular microscope, supplied by Olympus Microscopes, Olympus Optical Company (UK) Limited, published courtesy of Olympus Optical Co (UK) Ltd; Table 40.1 based on data from Lüning, K.J. (1981) 'Light', in *The Biology of Seaweeds*, Botanical Monographs, Vol. 17, Blackwell Scientific, (Lobban, C.S., and Wynne, M.J. (eds.)), reproduced by kind permission of Blackwell Publishing Ltd.; Figure 40.3 from figure from *Methods for Physical and Chemical Analysis of Fresh Waters*, 2nd edn., International Biological Programme, No. 8, Blackwell Scientific, (Golterman, H.L., Clymo, R.S., and Ohnstad, M.A.M., 1978), reproduced by kind permission of Blackwell Publishing Ltd.; Figure 43.1 and Table 43.1 from diagram and table of properties of low-speed centrifuge *Model MSE Centaur 2*, supplied by Fisher Scientific UK Ltd., reproduced by kind permission of Fisher Scientific UK Ltd.; Figure 47.4 from Dr. T. Marshall and Dr. K.M. Williams, University of Sunderland; Figure 47.6 from figure of *Highly Sulphated Cyclodextrins*; Figure 47.7 from graph of *Amphetamine Absorbance* from website *http://www.beckmancoulter.com/products/splashpage/chiral38/default.asp*, Copyright © 1999–2002 Beckman Coulter, Inc.; Figure 54.3 from Dr. S. Chamock, Northumbria University.

In some instances we have been unable to trace the owners of copyright material, and we would appreciate any information that would enable us to do so.

We would especially like to thank the following people whose feedback on *Practical Skills in Biomolecular Sciences* has been valuable in the planning of this text:

Dr M. Miller (University of Odense, Denmark)
Dr A. Radford (University of Leeds, UK)
Dr C. Smith (Manchester Metropolitan University, UK)

List of Abbreviations

A	absorbance (e.g. A_{260} = absorbance at 260 nm)
AC	affinity chromatography
ACDP	Advisory Committee on Dangerous Pathogens
ADP	adenosine diphosphate
ANOVA	analysis of variance
ATP	adenosine triphosphate
BSA	bovine serum albumin
CCCP	carbonylcyanide m-chlorophenylhydrazine
CE	capillary electrophoresis
CFU	colony-forming unit
CGE	capillary gel electrophoresis
COSHH	Control of Substances Hazardous to Health
CTP	cytosine triphosphate
CZE	capillary zone electrophoresis
ddNTP	dideoxyribonucleotide triphosphate
DMSO	dimethyl sulphoxide
DNA	deoxyribonucleic acid
d.p.m.	disintegrations per minute
dsDNA	double stranded DNA
dNTP	deoxyribonucleoside triphosphate
ECD	electron capture detector
EDTA	ethylenediaminetetraacetic acid
EI	electron impact ionisation
EIA	enzyme immunoassay
ELISA	enzyme-linked immunosorbent assay
EMR	electromagnetic radiation
EOF	electro-osmotic flow
ESR	electron spin resonance
F	Faraday constant
FIA	fluorescence immunoassay
FID	flame ionisation detector
FPLC®	fast protein liquid chromatography
FT	Fourier transformation
GC	gas chromatography
GPC	gel permeation chromatography
HEPES	N-[2-hydroxyethyl]piperazine-N'-[ethanesulphonic acid]
HIC	hydrophobic interaction chromatography
HPLC	high performance liquid chromatography
IEC	ion-exchange chromatography
IEF	isoelectric focusing
Ig	immunoglobulin
IMAC	immobilised metal affinity chromatography
IR	infra-red (radiation)
IRGA	infra-red gas analyser
IRMA	immunoradiometric assay
IRMS	isotope ratio mass spectroscopy
ISE	ion selective electrode
K_m	Michaelis constant
K_w	ionisation constant of water

LDH	lactate dehydrogenase
LSD	least significant difference
MEKC	micellar electrokinetic chromatography
MPN	most probable number
M_r	relative molecular mass
MRI	magnetic resonance imaging
MS	mass spectrometry
NAD^+	nicotinamide adenine dinucleotide (oxidised form)
NADH	nicotinamide adenine dinucleotide (reduced form)
$NADP^+$	nicotinamide adenine dinucleotide phosphate (oxidised form)
NADPH	nicotinamide adenine dinucleotide phosphate (reduced form)
NH	null hypothesis
NMR	nuclear magnetic resonance
PAGE	polyacrylamide gel electrophoresis
PAR	photosynthetically active radiation
PCR	polymerase chain reaction
PEG	polyethylene glycol
PFD	photon flux density
PFU	plaque-forming unit
PGFE	pulsed field gel electrophoresis
pH	$-\log_{10}$ proton concentration (activity), in $mol\,l^{-1}$
PI	photosynthetic irradiance
PPFD	photosynthetic photon flux density
PPi	pyrophosphate (inorganic)
PVA	polyvinyl alcohol
PY-MS	pyrolysis-mass spectroscopy
R	universal gas constant
RCF	relative centrifugal field
R_F	relative frontal mobility
RIA	radioimmunoassay
RID	radioimmunodiffusion
RNA	ribonucleic acid
RP-HPLC	reverse phase high performance liquid chromatography
r.p.m.	revolutions per minute
RT	reverse transcriptase
SDS	sodium dodecyl sulphate
SE	standard error (of the sample mean)
SEM	scanning electron microscopy
SI	Système International d'Unités
ssRNA	single stranded RNA
STP	standard temperature and pressure
TCA	trichloracetic acid
TCD	thermal conductivity detector
TEM	transmission electron microscopy
TEMED	N,N,N',N'-tetramethylethylenediamine
TLC	thin layer chromatography
TRIS	tris(hydroxymethyl)aminomethane
TTP	thymidine triphosphate
UNG	uracil-N-glycosylase
URL	uniform resource locator
UV	ultraviolet (radiation)
V_{max}	maximum velocity
z	net charge on an ion

Study and examination skills

1 The importance of transferable skills

Skills terminology – *different phrases may be used to describe transferable skills, depending on place or context. These include: 'personal transferable skills' (PTS), 'key skills', 'core skills' and 'competences'.*

This chapter outlines the range of transferable skills and their significance to biomolecular scientists. It also indicates where practical skills fit into this scheme. Having a good understanding of this topic will help you place your work at university in a wider context. You will also gain an insight into the qualities that employers expect you to have developed by the time you graduate.

The range of transferable skills

Table 1.1 provides a comprehensive listing of university-level transferable skills under six skill categories. There are many possible classifications – and a different one may be used in your institution or field of study. Note particularly that 'study skills', while important, and rightly emphasised at the start of many courses, constitute only a subset of the skills acquired by most university students.

Using course materials – *study your course handbook and the schedules for each practical session to find out what skills you are expected to develop at each point in the curriculum.*

The phrase '*Practical Skills*' in the title of this book indicates that there is a special subset of transferable skills related to work in the laboratory. However, although this text deals primarily with skills and techniques required for laboratory practicals and associated studies, a broader range of material is included. This is because the skills concerned are important, not only in the biosciences but also in the wider world. Examples include time management, evaluating information and communicating effectively.

KEY POINT Biomolecular sciences are essentially practical subjects, and therefore involve highly developed laboratory skills. The importance that your lecturers place on practical skills will probably be evident from the large proportion of curriculum time you will spend on practical work in your course.

The word 'skill' implies much more than the robotic learning of, for example, a laboratory routine. Of course, some of the tasks you will be asked to carry out in practical classes *will* be repetitive. Certain techniques require manual dexterity and attention to detail if accuracy and precision are to be attained, and the necessary competence often requires practice to make perfect. However, a deeper understanding of the context of a technique is important if the skill is to be appreciated fully and then transferred to a new situation. That is why this text is not simply a 'recipe book' of methods and protocols and why it includes background information, tips and worked examples, as well as study exercises to test your understanding.

Example The skills involved in teamwork cannot be developed without a deeper understanding of the interrelationships involved in successful groups. The context will be different for every group and a flexible approach will always be required, according to the individuals involved and the nature of the task.

Transferability of skills

Transferable skills are those which allow someone with knowledge, understanding or ability gained in one situation to adapt or extend this for application in a different context. In some cases, the transfer of a skill is immediately obvious. Take, for example, the ability to use a spreadsheet to summarise biological data and create a graph to illustrate results. Once the key concepts and commands are learned

Table 1.1 Transferable skills identified as important in the biosciences. The list has been compiled from several sources, including the UK Quality Assurance Agency for Higher Education *Subject Benchmark Statement for the Biosciences and for Biomedical Sciences*. Particularly relevant chapters are shown for the skills covered by this book (numbers in **bold coloured** text indicate a deeper, or more extensive, treatment)

Skill category	Examples of skills and competences	Relevant chapters in this textbook
Generic skills for bioscientists	Having an appreciation of the complexity and diversity of life and life processes	11 28 29 33 36 56–59
	Reading and evaluating biological literature with a full and critical understanding	4 8 9
	Ability to communicate a clear and accurate account of a biological topic, both verbally and in writing	**14 15 16** 17–19
	Applying critical and analytical skills to evaluate evidence regarding theories and hypotheses	9 30
	Using a variety of methods for studying the biosciences	32–62
	Having the ability to think independently, set personal tasks and solve problems	30 31 **65**
Intellectual skills	Recognising and applying biological theories, concepts and principles	9 30
	Analysing, synthesising and summarising information critically	9 19 63–67
	Obtaining evidence to formulate and test hypotheses; applying knowledge to address familiar and unfamiliar problems	28 29 30 31 67
	Recognising and explaining moral, ethical and legal issues in biological research	20 21 32 33 34
Experimental and observational skills	Carrying out basic laboratory techniques and understanding the principles that underlie them	20 21–30 32 41 43 49 60
	Working in the laboratory safely, responsibly and legally, with due attention to ethical aspects	20 21 31–34
	Designing, planning, conducting and reporting on biological investigations and data arising from them	14 15 18 30 31
	Obtaining, recording, collating and analysing biological data	28–34 35 36 37 63–67
	Carrying out basic techniques relevant to core subjects in biomedical science (biochemistry, molecular genetics, immunology, microbiology)	20–26 27 28–31 32 33 34 35 36 37 38 39 41 42 43 44–48 49 50–59 60 61 62–67
Numeracy, communication and IT skills	Understanding and using data in several forms (e.g. numerical, textual, verbal and graphical)	4 9 63–66
	Communicating in written, verbal, graphical and visual forms	**14 15 16** 17–19 63 64 **65**
	Citing and referencing the work of others in an appropriate manner	8 9 19
	Obtaining data, including the concepts behind sampling and sampling errors, calibration and types of error	27 28 30 31 37 65–67
	Processing, interpreting and presenting data, and applying appropriate statistical methods for summarising and analysing data	11 63–65 **66 67**
	Solving problems with calculators and computers, including the use of tools such as spreadsheets	10 11 12 20 **65**
	Using computer technology to communicate and as a source of biological information	10 11 12 13
Interpersonal and teamwork skills	Working individually or in teams as appropriate; identifying individual and group goals and acting responsibly and appropriately to achieve them	3
	Recognising and respecting the views and opinions of others	3
	Evaluating your own performance and that of others	3 7
	Appreciating the interdisciplinary nature of contemporary biosciences	1 19
Self-management and professional development skills	Working independently, managing time and organising activities	2 30 31
	Identifying and working towards targets for personal, academic and career development	1 7
	Developing an adaptable and effective approach to study and work (including revision and exam technique)	2 4 5 6

(Chapter 12), they can be applied to many instances outside the biosciences where this type of output is used. This is not only true for similar data sets, but also in unrelated situations, such as making up a financial balance sheet and creating a pie chart to show sources of expenditure. Similarly, knowing the requirements for good graph drawing and tabulation (Chapters 63 and 64), perhaps practised by hand in earlier work, might help you use spreadsheet commands to make the output suit your needs.

Other cases may be less clear but equally valid. For example, towards the end of your undergraduate studies you may be involved in designing experiments as part of your project work. This task will draw on several skills gained at earlier stages in your course, such as preparing solutions (Chapters 22–25), deciding about numbers of replicates and experimental layout (Chapters 30 and 31) and perhaps carrying out some particular method of observation, measurement or analysis (Chapters 37–62). How and when might you transfer this complex set of skills? In the workplace, it is unlikely that you would be asked to repeat the same process, but in critically evaluating a problem or in planning a complex project for a new employer, you will need to use many of the time management, organisational and analytical skills developed when designing and carrying out experiments. The same applies to information retrieval and evaluation and writing essays and dissertations, when transferred to the task of analysing or writing a business report.

Opportunities to develop and practise skills in your private or social life – you could, for example, practise spreadsheet skills by organising personal or club finances using Microsoft® Excel, or teamwork skills within any university clubs or societies you may join (see Chapter 7).

What your future employer will be looking for

At the end of your course, which may seem some time away, you will aim to get a job and start on your chosen career path. You will need to sell yourself to your future employer, firstly in your application form and curriculum vitae (Chapter 7), and perhaps later at interview. Companies rarely employ bioscience graduates simply because they know how to carry out a particular lab routine or because they can remember specific facts about their chosen degree subject. Instead, employers tend to look for a range of qualities and transferable skills that together define an attribute known as 'graduateness'. This encompasses, for example, the ability to work in a team, to speak effectively and write clearly about your work, to understand complex data and to manage a project to completion. All of these skills can be developed at different stages during your University studies.

KEY POINT **Factual knowledge is important in degrees with a strong vocational element, but understanding how to find and evaluate information is usually rated more highly by employers than the ability to memorise facts.**

Most likely, your future employer(s) will seek someone with a organised yet flexible mind, capable of demonstrating a logical approach to problems – someone who has a range of skills and who can transfer these skills to new situations. Many competing applicants will probably have similar qualifications. If you want the job, you will have to show that your additional skills place you above the other candidates.

Sources for further study

Drew, S. and Bingham, R. (1997) *The Student Skills Guide*. Gower Publishing Ltd, Aldershot.

Race, P. (1999) *How to Get a Good Degree: Making the Most of Your Time at University*. Open University Press, Buckingham.

Study exercises

1.1 Evaluate your skills. Examine the list of skill topics shown in Table 1.1. Now create a new table with two columns, like the one below. The first half of this table should indicate *five* skills you feel confident about in column 1 and show where you demonstrated this skill in column 2 (for example, 'working in a team' and 'in a first year group project in molecular biology'). The second half of the table should show *five* skills you do not feel confident about, or you recognise need development (e.g. 'communicating in verbal form'). List these in column 1 and in column 2 list ways in which you think the course material for your current modules will provide you with the opportunity to develop these skills, or what activities you might take to improve them (e.g 'forming a study group with colleagues').

Skills I feel confident about	Where demonstrated
1.	
2.	
3.	
4.	
5.	
Skills that I could develop	Opportunities for development
6.	
7.	
8.	
9.	
10.	

1.2 Find skills resources. For at least one of the skills in the second half of the Table in 1.1, check your University's library database to see if there are any texts on that subject. Borrow an appropriate book and read the relevant sections. Alternatively, carry out a search for relevant websites (there are many); decide which are useful and 'bookmark' them for future use (see Chapter 10).

1.3 Analyse your goals and aspirations. Spend a little time thinking what you hope to gain from university. See if your friends have the same aspirations. Think about and/or discuss how these goals can be achieved, while keeping the necessary balance between university work, paid employment and your social life.

2

Managing your time

One of the most important activities that you can do is to organise your personal and working time effectively. There is a lot to do at university and a common complaint is that there isn't enough time to accomplish everything. In fact, research shows that most people use up a lot of their time without realising it through ineffective study or activities such as extended coffee breaks. Developing your time management skills will help you achieve more in work, rest and play, but it is important to remember that putting time management techniques into practice is an individual matter, requiring a level of self-discipline not unlike that required for dieting. A new system won't always work perfectly straight away, but through time you can develop a system that is effective for you.

The advantages of a good time management system include:

- a much greater feeling of control over your activities;
- avoidance of stress;
- improved productivity – achieve more in a shorter period;
- improved performance levels – work to higher standards because you are in charge;
- an increase in time available for non-work matters – work hard, but play hard too.

An inability to organise your time effectively, of course, results in the opposite of the above, especially feelings of failure, frustration, guilt and being out of control in your life.

Setting your goals

The first step is to identify clearly what you want to achieve, both in work and in your personal life. We all have a general idea of what we are aiming for, but to be effective, your goals must be clearly identified and priorities allocated. Clear concise objectives can provide you with a framework in which to make these choices. Try using the 'SMART' approach, in which objectives should be:

- Specific – clear and unambiguous, including what, when, where, how and why.
- Measurable – having quantified targets and benefits to provide an understanding of progress.
- Achievable – being attainable within your resources.
- Realistic – being within your abilities and expectations.
- Timed – stating the time period for completion.

Having identified your goals, you can now move on to answer four very important questions:

1. Where does your time go?
2. Where should your time go?
3. What are your time-wasting activities?
4. What strategies can help you?

Time slots	Activity								Notes
7.00–7.15									
7.15–7.30									
7.30–7.45									
7.45–8.00									
8.00–8.15									
8.15–8.30									
8.30–8.45									
8.45–9.00									
9.00–9.15									

Fig. 2.1 Example of how to lay out a time log. Write activities along the top of the page, and divide the day into 15-minute segments as shown. Think beforehand how you will categorise the different things you do, from the mundane (laundry, having a shower, drinking coffee, etc.) to the well-timetabled (tutorial meeting, sports club meeting) and add supplementary notes if required. At the end of each day, place a dot in the relevant column for each activity and sum the dots to give a total at the bottom of the page. You will need to keep a diary like this for at least a week before you see patterns emerging.

Analysing your current activities

The key to successful development of time management is a realistic knowledge of how you currently spend your time. Start by keeping a detailed time log for a typical week (Fig. 2.1), but you will need to be truthful in this process. Once you have completed the log, consider the following questions:

- How many hours do I work in total and how many hours do I use for relaxation?
- What range of activities do I do?
- How long do I spend on each activity?
- What do I spend most of my time doing?
- What do I spend the least amount of my time doing?
- Are my allocations of time in proportion to the importance of my activities?
- How much of my time is ineffectively used, e.g. for uncontrolled socialising or interruptions?

If you wish, you could use a spreadsheet (Chapter 12) to produce graphical summaries of time allocations in different categories as an aid to analysis and management. Divide your time into:

- Committed time – timetabled activities involving your main objectives/goals.
- Maintenance time – time spent supporting your general life activities (shopping, cleaning, laundry, etc.).
- Discretionary time – time for you to use as you wish, e.g. recreation, sport, hobbies, socialising.

Quality in time management – avoid spending a lot of time doing unproductive studying, e.g. reading a textbook without specific objectives for that reading. Make sure you test your recall of the material, if you are working towards an examination (p. 21).

Avoiding time-wasting activities

Look carefully at those tasks that could be identified as time-wasting activities. They include gossiping, over-long breaks, uninvited interruptions and even ineffective study periods. Try to reduce these to a minimum, but do not count on eliminating them entirely. Remember also that some relaxation *should* be programmed into your daily schedule.

Being assertive – if friends and colleagues continually interrupt you, find a way of controlling them, before they control you. Indicate clearly on your door that you do not wish to be disturbed and explain why. Otherwise, try to work away from disturbance.

Organising your tasks

Having analysed your time usage, you can now use this information, together with your objectives and prioritised goals, to organise your activities, both on a short-term and a long-term basis. Consider using a diary-based system (such as those produced by Filofax®, TMI® and Day-Timer®) that will help you plan ahead and analyse your progress.

Divide your tasks into several categories, such as:

● Urgent – must be done as a top priority and at short notice (e.g. doctor's appointment).
● Routine – predictable and regular and therefore easily scheduled (e.g. attending lectures or playing sport).
● One-off activities – usually with rather shorter deadlines and which may be of high priority (e.g. a tutorial assignment or seeking advice on a specific issue).
● Long-term tasks – sometimes referred to as 'elephant tasks' that are too large to 'eat' in one go (e.g. learning a language). These are best managed by scheduling frequent small 'bites' to achieve the task over a longer timescale.

Use checklists as often as possible – post your lists in places where they are easily and frequently visible, such as in front of your desk. Ticking things off as they are completed gives you a feeling of accomplishment and progress, increasing motivation.

You should make a weekly plan (Fig. 2.2) for the routine activities, with gaps for less predictable tasks. This should be supplemented by individual daily checklists, preferably written at the end of the previous working day. Such plans and checklists should be flexible, forming the basis for most of your activities except when exceptional circumstances intervene. The planning must be kept brief, however, and should be scheduled into your activities.

WEEKLY DIARY — Week beginning:

DATE	Sunday	Monday	Tuesday	Wednesday	Thursday	Friday	Saturday
7–8 am		Breakfast	Breakfast	Breakfast	Breakfast	Breakfast	
8–9		Preparation	Preparation	Preparation	Preparation	Preparation	Breakfast
9–10	Breakfast	PE112(L)	PE112(L)	PE112(L)	PE112(L)	BIOL(P)	Travel
10–11	FREE	CHEM(L)	CHEM(L)	CHEM(L)	CHEM(L)	BIOL(P)	WORK
11–12	STUDY	STUDY	STUDY	STUDY	STUDY	BIOL(P)	WORK
12–1 pm	STUDY	BIOL(L)	BIOL(L)	BIOL(L)	BIOL(L)	TUTORIAL	WORK
1–2	Lunch	Lunch	Lunch	Lunch	Lunch	Lunch	Lunch
2–3	(VOLLEY-	CHEM(P)	STUDY	SPORT	PE112(P)	STUDY	WORK
3–4	BALL	CHEM(P)	STUDY	(VOLLEY-	PE112(P)	STUDY	WORK
4–5	MATCH)	CHEM(P)	STUDY	BALL	PE112(P)	SHOPPING	WORK
5–6	FREE	STUDY	STUDY	CLUB)	STUDY	TEA ROTA	WORK
6–7	Tea	Tea	Tea	Tea	Tea	Tea	Tea
7–8	FREE*	STUDY	STUDY	FREE*	STUDY	FREE*	FREE
8–9	FREE*	STUDY	STUDY	FREE*	STUDY	FREE*	FREE
9–10	FREE*	FREE*	STUDY	FREE*	STUDY	FREE*	FREE

	Sunday	Monday	Tuesday	Wednesday	Thursday	Friday	Saturday
Study (h)	2	10	11	4	11	6	0
Other (h)	13	5	4	11	4	9	15

Total study time = 44 h

Fig. 2.2 A weekly diary with example of entries for a first year science student with a Saturday job and active membership of a volleyball club. Note that 'free time' changes to 'study time', e.g. for periods when assessed work is to be produced or during revision for exams. Study time (including attendance at lectures, practicals and tutorials) thus represents between 42 and 50 per cent of the total time.

KEY POINT Review each day's plan at the end of the previous day, making such modifications as are required by circumstances, e.g. adding an uncompleted task from the previous day or a new and urgent task.

Tips for effective planning and working

- Set guidelines and review expectations regularly.
- Don't procrastinate: don't keep putting off doing things you know are important – they will not go away but they will increase to crisis point.
- Don't be a perfectionist – perfection is paralysing.
- Learn from past experience – review your management system regularly.
- Don't set yourself unrealistic goals and objectives – this will lead to procrastination and feelings of failure.
- Avoid recurring crises – they are telling you that something is not working properly and needs to be changed.
- Learn to concentrate effectively and don't let yourself be distracted by casual interruptions.
- Learn to say 'no' firmly but graciously when appropriate.
- Know your own body rhythms: e.g. are you a morning person or an evening person?
- Learn to recognise the benefits of rest and relaxation at appropriate times.
- Take short but complete breaks from your tasks – come back feeling refreshed in mind and body.
- Work in suitable study areas and keep your own workspace organised.
- Avoid clutter (physical and mental).
- Learn to access and use information effectively (Chapter 9).
- Learn to read and write accurately and quickly (Chapters 4 and 16).

Matching your work to your body's rhythm – everyone has times of day when they feel more alert and able to work. Decide when these times are for you and programme your work accordingly. Plan relaxation events for periods when you tend to be less alert.

Sources for further study

Anon. *Day-Timer*. Available: http://www.daytimer.co.uk
Last accessed 08/01/03.
[Website for products of Day-Timers Europe Ltd., Chene Court, Poundwell Street, Modbury, Devon PL21 0QJ.]

Anon. *Filofax*. Available: http://www.filofax.co.uk
Last accessed 08/01/03.
[Website for products of Filofax UK, Unit 3, Victoria Gardens, Burgess Hill, West Sussex, RH15 9NB.]

Anon. *TMI Website*. Available: http://www.tmi.co.uk
Last accessed 08/01/03.
[Website for products of TMI (Time Manager International A/S), 50 High Street, Henley-in-Arden, Solihull, West Midlands B95 5AN.]

Mayer, J.L. (1999) *Time Management for Dummies*, 2nd edn. IDG Books Worldwide, Inc., Foster City.

Study exercises

2.1 Evaluate your time usage. Compile a spreadsheet to keep a record of your daily activities in 15-minute segments for a week. Analyse this graphically and identify areas for improvement.

2.2 List your short-, medium- and long-term tasks and allocate priorities. Produce several lists, one for each of the three timescales and prioritise each item. Use this list to plan your time management, by scheduling high priority tasks and leave low priority activities to 'fill in' the spare time that you may identify. This task should be done on a regular (monthly) basis to allow for changing situations.

2.3 Plan an 'elephant' task. Spend some time planning how to carry out a large or difficult task (learning a language or learning to use a complex computer program) by breaking it down into achievable segments ('bites').

3   Working with others

It is highly likely that you will be expected to work with fellow students during practicals. This might take the form of sharing tasks or casual collaboration through discussion, or it might be formally directed teamwork such as problem-based learning (Box 6.1) or preparing a poster (Chapter 14). Interacting with others can be extremely rewarding and realistically represents the professional world, where teamworking is common. The advantages of working with others include:

- Teamworking is usually synergistic in effect – it often results in better ideas, produced by the interchange of views.
- Working in teams can provide support for individuals within the team.
- Levels of personal commitment can be enhanced through concern about letting the team down.
- Responsibilities for tasks can be shared.

However, you can also feel both threatened and exposed if teamwork is not managed properly. Some of the main reasons for negative feelings towards working in groups include:

- Fear of strangers – uncertainty as to how others will react.
- Worries over rejection – a perception of being unpopular or being chosen last by the group.
- Anxiety about having nothing to contribute – letting the group down by a perceived lack of skills.
- Fear of being held back by others – especially for those who have been successful in individual work already.
- Lack of previous experience – worries about the kinds of personal interactions likely to occur and the team role likely to suit you best.

Confidence from experience – the more you take part in teamwork, the more you know how teams operate and how to make teamwork effective for you.

Teamwork skills

Some of the key skills you will need to develop to maximise the success of your teamworking activities include:

- Interpersonal skills. How do you react to new people? Are you able to both listen and communicate easily with them? How do you deal with conflicts and disagreements?
- Delegation/sharing of tasks. The primary advantage of teamwork is the sharing of effort and responsibility. Are you willing/able to do this? It involves trusting your team members. How will you deal with those group members who don't contribute fully?
- Effective listening. Successful listening is a skill that usually needs developing, e.g. during the exchange of ideas within a group.
- Speaking clearly and concisely. Without effective verbal communication, your ability to contribute to the group will be extremely limited. If you feel you are weak in this area, find ways of developing your skills through learning and practice.
- Providing constructive criticism. It is all too easy to be negative but only constructive criticism will have a positive effect on interactions with others.

Collaboration for learning

Much collaboration is informal and consists of pairs or groups of individuals getting together to exchange materials and ideas while studying. It may consist of a 'brainstorming' session for a topic or piece of work, or sharing efforts to research a topic. This has much to commend it and is generally encouraged. However, it is vital that this collaborative learning is distinguished from the collaborative writing of assessed documents: the latter is not usually acceptable and, in its most extreme form, is plagiarism, usually with a heavy potential punishment in university assessment systems. Make sure you know what plagiarism is, what unacceptable collaboration is, and how they are treated within your institution (see p. 47).

Web-based resources and support for brainstorming – websites such as http:// www.brainstorming.co.uk give further information and practical advice for teamworking.

KEY POINT **Collaboration is inappropriate during the final phase of an assessed piece of work unless you have been directed to produce a group report. Collaboration is encouraged during research and learning activities but the final write-up must normally be your own work. The extreme of producing copycat write-ups is regarded as plagiarism (p. 47) and will be punished accordingly.**

The dynamics of teamworking

It is important that team activities are properly structured so that each member knows what is expected of them. Allocation of responsibilities usually requires the clear identification of a leader. Several studies of groups have identified different team roles that derive from differences in personality. You should be aware of such categorisations, both in terms of your own predispositions and those of your fellow team members, as it will help the group to interact more productively. Belbin (1993) identified eight such roles, recently extended to nine, as shown in Table 3.1. Several of the categories shown in Table 3.1 are suitable for a leader, including 'co-ordinator' and 'shaper'.

Recording group discussions – make sure you structure meetings (including writing agendas) and note their outcomes (taking minutes and noting action points).

In formal team situations, your course organiser may deal with these issues; even if they do not, it is important that you are aware of these roles and their potential impact on the success or failure of teamwork. You should try to identify your own 'natural' role: if asked to form a team, bear these different roles in mind during your selection of colleagues and your interactions with them. The ideal team should contain members capable of adopting most of these roles. However, you should also note the following points:

- People will probably best fit one of these roles naturally as a function of their personality and skills.
- Group members may be suited to more than one role.
- In some circumstances, team members may be required to adapt and take a different role from the one that they feel suits them.
- No one role is 'better' than any other. For good teamwork, the group should have a balance of personality types present.
- If the number of team members is fewer than nine, people may have to cover multiple roles.

KEY POINT **In formal teamwork situations, be clear as to how individual contributions are to be identified and recognised. This might require discussion with the course organiser. Make sure that recognition, including assessment, is truly reflective of effort. Failure to ensure that this is the case can lead to disputes and feelings of unfairness.**

Table 3.1 A summary of the team roles described by Belbin (1993). A good team requires members who are able to undertake appropriate roles at different times. Each role provides important strengths to a team, and its compensatory weaknesses should be accepted within the group framework

Team role	Personality characteristics	Typical function in a team	Strengths	Allowable weaknesses
Co-ordinator	Self-confident, calm and controlled	Causing others to work towards shared goals	Good at spotting others' talents and delegating activities	Often less creative or intellectual than others in the group
Shaper	Strong need for achievement; outgoing; dynamic; highly strung	Generating action within team; imposing shape and pattern to work	Providing drive and realism to group activities	Can be headstrong, emotional and less patient than others
Innovator	Individualistic, serious-minded; often unorthodox	Generating new proposals and solving problems	Creative, innovative and knowledgeable	Tendency to work in isolation; ideas may not always be practical
Monitor–evaluator	Sober, unemotional and prudent	Analysing problems and evaluating ideas	Shrewd judgement	May work slowly; not usually a good motivator
Implementer	Well-organised and self-disciplined, with practical common sense	Doing what needs to be done	Organising abilities and common sense	Lack of flexibility and tendency to resist new ideas
Teamworker	Sociable, mild and sensitive	Being supportive, perceptive and diplomatic; keeping the team going	Good listener; reliable and flexible; promotes team spirit	Not comfortable when leading; may be indecisive
Resource investigator	Extrovert, enthusiastic, curious and communicative	Exploiting opportunities; finding resources; external relations	Quick thinking; good at developing others' ideas	May lose interest rapidly
Completer–finisher	Introvert and anxious; painstaking, orderly and conscientious	Ensuring completion of activity to high standard	Good focus on fulfilling objectives and goals	Obsessive about details; may wish to do all the work to control quality
Specialist	Professional, self-motivated and dedicated	Providing essential skills	Commitment and technical knowledge	Contribute on a narrow aspect of project; tend to be single-minded

Text reference

Belbin, R.M. (1993) *Team Roles at Work*. Butterworth-Heinemann, Oxford.

Source for further study

Belbin, R.M. *The Belbin Website*. Available: http://www.belbin.com/frames.html Last accessed 08/01/03.

Study exercises

3.1 Evaluate your 'natural' team role(s). Using Table 3.1 as a source, decide which team role best fits your personality.

3.2 Keep a journal during a group activity. Record your feelings and observations about experiences of working with other students. After the event, review the journal, then draw up a strategy for developing aspects where you feel you might have done better.

3.3 **Reflect upon your teamwork abilities**. Draw up a list of your reactions to previous efforts at collaboration or teamwork and analyse your strengths and weaknesses. How could these interactions have been improved or supported more effectively?

4 Taking notes from lectures and texts

Note-taking is an essential skill that you will require in many different situations, such as:

- listening to lectures and seminars;
- attending meetings and tutorials;
- reading texts and research papers;
- finding information on the World Wide Web.

KEY POINT Good performance in assessments and exams is built on effective learning and revision (Chapters 5 and 6). However, both ultimately depend on the quality of your notes.

Taking notes from lectures

Taking legible and meaningful lecture notes is essential if you are to make sense of them later, but many students find it difficult when starting their university studies. Begin by noting the date, course, topic and lecturer on the first page of each day's notes. Number every page in case they get mixed up later. The most popular way of taking notes is to write in a linear sequence down the page, emphasising the underlying structure via headings, as in Fig. 16.2. However, the 'pattern' and 'Mind Map®' methods (Figs 4.1 and 4.2) have their advocates: experiment, to see which method you prefer.

Whatever technique you use, don't try to take down all of the lecturer's words, except when an important definition or example is being given, or when the lecturer has made it clear that he/she is dictating. Listen first, then write. Your goal should be to take down the structure and reasoning behind the lecturer's approach in as few words and phrases as possible. At this stage, follow the lecturer's sequence of delivery. Use headings and leave plenty of space, but don't worry too much about being tidy – it is more important that you get down the appropriate information in a readable form. Use abbreviations to save

Compare lecture notes with a colleague – looking at different sets of notes for the same lecture may reveal interesting differences in approach, depth and detail.

Choose note-taking methods appropriately – the method you choose to take notes might depend on the subject; the lecturer and their style of delivery; and your own preference.

Fig. 4.1 An example of 'pattern' notes, an alternative to the more commonly used 'linear' format. Note the similarity to the 'spider diagram' method of brainstorming ideas (Fig. 16.1).

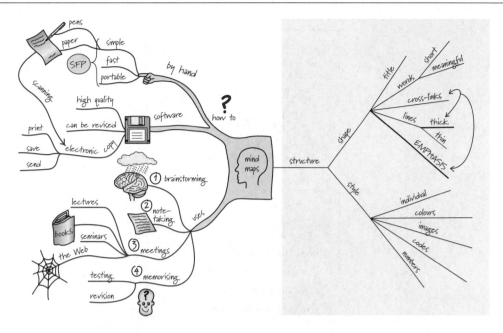

Fig. 4.2 Example of the 'Mind Map®' approach to note-taking and 'brainstorming'. Start at the centre with the overall topic title, adding branches and sub-branches for themes and subsidiary topics. 'Basic' maps consist of a branched hierarchy overwritten with key words (e.g. shaded portion). Connections should be indicated with arrows; numbering and abbreviations are encouraged. To aid recall and creativity, Buzan and Buzan (1993) recommend use of colour, different fonts, 3-dimensional doodles and other forms of emphasis (e.g. non-shaded portion).

Example Commonly used abbreviations include:

$\exists$	there are, there exist(s)
$\therefore$	therefore
$\because$	because
$\propto$	is proportional to
$\rightarrow$	leads to, into
$\leftarrow$	comes from, from
$\rightarrowtail$	involves several processes in a sequence
$1°, 2°$	primary, secondary (etc.)
$\approx, \cong$	approximately, roughly equal to
$=, \neq$	equals, not equal to
$\equiv, \not\equiv$	equivalent, not equivalent to
$<, >$	smaller than, bigger than
$\gg$	much bigger than
$[X]$	concentration of X
$\sum$	sum
Δ	change
f	function
$\#$	number
∞	infinity, infinite

You should also make up your own abbreviations relevant to the context, e.g. if a lecturer is talking about photosynthesis, you could write 'PS' instead, etc.

time. Recognise that you may need to alter your note-taking technique to suit different lecturers' styles.

Make sure you note down references to texts and take special care to ensure accuracy of definitions and numerical examples. If the lecturer repeats or otherwise emphasises a point, highlight (e.g. by underlining) or make a margin note of this – it could come in useful when revising. If there is something you don't understand, ask at the end of the lecture, or make an appointment to discuss the matter if there isn't time to deal with it then. Tutorials may provide an additional forum for discussing course topics.

Lectures delivered by PowerPoint® or similar presentation programs

Some students make the mistake of thinking that lectures delivered as computer-based presentations with an accompanying handout or Web-resource require little or no effort by way of note-taking. While it is true that you may be freed from the need to copy out large diagrams and the basic text may provide structure, you will still need to adapt and add to the lecturer's points. Much of the important detail and crucial emphasis will still be delivered verbally. Furthermore, if you simply listen passively to the lecture, or worse, try to work from the handout alone, it will be far more difficult to understand and remember the content.

If you are not supplied with handouts, you may be given access to the electronic file, so that you can print out the presentation beforehand, perhaps in the '3 slides per page' format that allows space for notes alongside each slide (Fig. 4.3). Scan through this before the lecture if you can; then, during the presentation, focus on listening to what the lecturer has to say. Note down any extra details, points of emphasis and examples. After lectures, you could also add notes from supplementary

Fig. 4.3 An example of a printout from PowerPoint® in 'Handouts (3 slides per page)' format.

Printing PowerPoint® slides – use the 'Black and White' option on the Print menu to avoid wasting ink on printing of coloured backgrounds. If you wish to use colour, remember that slides can be difficult to read if printed in small format. Always print a sample page before printing the whole lecture.

reading. The text in presentations can be converted to word processor format if you have access to the electronic file. In PowerPoint®, this can be achieved from the *Outline View* option on the *View* menu. You can copy and paste text between programs in the normal fashion, then modify font size and colour as appropriate.

'Making up' your notes

As soon as possible after each lecture, work through your notes, tidying them up and adding detail where necessary. Add emphasis to any headings you have made, so that the structure is clearer. If you feel it would be more logical for your purposes, change the order. Compare your notes with material in a textbook and correct any inconsistencies. Make notes from, or copy, any useful material you see in textbooks, ready for revision.

Taking notes from books and journal papers

Scanning and skimming are useful techniques to find sections to read in detail and to make notes from.

Scanning effectively – *you need to stay focused on your key words, otherwise you may be distracted by apparently interesting but peripheral material.*

Scanning

This involves searching for relevant content. Useful techniques are to:

- decide on key words relevant to your search;
- check that the book or journal title indicates relevance;
- look through the contents page (either paper titles in a journal volume, or chapter titles in a textbook);
- look at the index, if present.

Spotting sequences – *writers often number their points (firstly, secondly, thirdly, etc.) and looking for these words in the text can help you skim it quickly.*

Skimming

This is a valuable way to gain the maximum amount of information in the minimum amount of time, by reading as little of a text as is required. Essentially, the technique (also termed 'surveying') requires you to look at the structure of the text, rather than the detail. In a sense, you are trying to see the writer's original plan and the purpose behind each part of the text. Look through the whole of the piece first, to gain an overview of its scope and structure. Headings provide an obvious clue to structure, if present. Next, look for the 'topic sentence' in each paragraph (p. 96), which is often the first. You might then decide that the paragraph contains a definition that is important to note, or it may contain examples, so may not be worth reading for your purpose.

Making sure you have all the details of a source – *when taking notes from a text or journal paper: (a) always take full details (Chapter 8); (b) if copying word-for-word make sure you indicate this using quotes and take special care to ensure you do not alter the original wording.*

When you have found relevant material, note-taking fulfils the vital purpose of helping you understand and remember the information. If you simply read it, either directly or from a photocopy, you risk accomplishing neither. The act of paraphrasing (using different words to give the same meaning) makes you think about the meaning and forces you to express this for yourself. It is an important active learning technique. A popular method of skimming and note-taking is called the SQ3R technique (Box. 4.1).

Box 4.1 The SQ3R technique for skimming texts

Survey   Get a quick overview of the contents of the book or chapter, perhaps by rapidly reading the contents page or headings.

Question   Ask yourself what the material covers and how precisely it relates to your study objectives.

Read   Now read the text, paying attention to the ways it addresses your key questions.

Recall   Recite to yourself what has been stated every few paragraphs. Write notes of this if appropriate, paraphrasing the text rather than copying it.

Review   Think about what you have read and/or review your notes as a whole. Consider where it all fits in.

KEY POINT   **Finding information is not the same as understanding or learning it!**

Methods for finding and evaluating texts and articles are discussed further in Chapters 8 and 9.

Sources for further study

Buzan, T. and Buzan, B. (2000) *The Mind Map Book: Radiant Thinking (Millennium Edition)*. BBC Books, London.

Morris, S. and Smith, J. (1998) *Understanding Mind Maps ... in a Week*. Hodder and Stoughton, London.

Buzan, A. *Buzan Centres*. Available: http://www.mind-map.com
Last accessed 08/01/03.
[The official Mindmap® Website.]

Study exercises

4.1 Experiment with a new note-taking technique. If you haven't tried the pattern or mind-mapping methods (Figs 4.1 and 4.2), carry out a trial to see how they work for you. Research the methods first by consulting appropriate books or websites.

4.2 Carry out a 'spring clean' of your desk area and notes. Make a concerted effort to organise your notes and handouts, investing if necessary in files and folders. This will be especially valuable at the start of a revision period.

4.3 Try out the SQ3R technique. The next time you need to obtain information from a text, compare this method (Box 4.1) with others you may have adopted in the past. Is it faster, and does it aid your ability to recall the information?

5 Revising

Before you start revising, find out as much as you can about each exam, including:

- format and duration;
- date and location;
- types of question;
- whether any questions/sections are compulsory;
- whether the questions are internally or externally set or assessed;
- whether the exam is 'open book', and if so, which texts or notes are allowed.

Your course tutor is likely to give you details of exam structure and timing well beforehand, so that you can plan your revision; the course handbook and past papers (if available) can provide further useful details. Always check that the nature of the exam has not changed before you consult past papers.

> **KEY POINT** Use the learning objectives for your course (normally published in the handbook) as a fundamental part of your revision planning. These indicate what you will be expected to be able to do after taking part in the course, so exam questions are often based on them. Check this by reference to past papers.

Organising and using lecture notes, assignments and practical reports

Filing lecture notes – make sure your notes are kept neatly and in sequence by using a ring binder system. File the notes in lecture or practical sequence, adding any supplementary notes or photocopies alongside.

Given their importance as a source of material for revision, you should have sorted out any deficiencies or omissions in your lecture notes and practical reports at an early stage. For example, you may have missed a lecture or practical due to illness, etc., but the exam is likely to assume attendance throughout the year. Make sure you attend classes whenever possible and keep your notes up to date. Your practical reports and any assignment work will contain specific comments from the teaching staff, indicating where marks were lost, corrections, mistakes, inadequacies, etc. It is always worth reading these comments as soon as your work is returned, to improve the standard of your subsequent reports. If you are unsure about why you lost marks in an assignment, or about some particular aspects of a topic, ask the appropriate member of staff for further explanation. Most lecturers are quite happy to discuss such details with students on a one-to-one basis and this information may provide you with clues to the expectations of individual lecturers that may be useful in exams set by the same members of staff. However, you should never 'fish' for specific information on possible exam questions, as this is likely to be counter-productive.

Revision

Begin early, to avoid last-minute panic. Start in earnest several weeks beforehand, and plan your work carefully:

- Prepare a revision timetable – an 'action plan' that gives details of specific topics to be covered (Box 5.1). Plan your revision around

---

Box 5.1   Drawing up a revision timetable

1. **Make up a grid showing the number of days until your exams are finished.** Divide each day into several sections. If you like revising in large blocks of time, use am, pm and evening slots, but if you prefer shorter periods, divide each of these in two, or use hourly divisions (see also the table in study exercise 5.1).

2. **Write in your non-revision commitments,** including any time off you plan to allocate and physical activity at frequent intervals. Try to have about one-third or a quarter of the time off in any one day. Plan this in relation to your best times for useful work – for example, some people work best in the mornings, while others prefer evenings. If you wish, use a system where your relaxation time is a bonus to be worked for; this may help you motivate yourself.

3. **Decide on how you wish to subdivide your subjects** for revision purposes. This might be among

subjects, according to difficulty (with the hardest getting the most time), or within subjects, according to topics. Make sure there is an adequate balance of time among topics and especially that you do not avoid working on the subject(s) you find least interesting or most difficult.

4. **Allocate the work to the different slots available on your timetable.** You should work backwards from the exams, making sure that you cover every exam topic adequately in the period just before each exam. You may wish to colour-code the subjects.

5. **As you revise, mark off the slots completed** – this has a positive psychological effect and will boost your self-confidence.

6. **After the exams, revisit your timetable** and decide whether you would do anything differently next time.

Recognise when your concentration powers are dwindling – take a short break when this happens and return to work refreshed and ready to learn. Remember that 20 minutes is often quoted as a typical limit to full concentration effort.

when (and where) your examinations are to be held. Try to keep to your timetable. Time management during this period is as important as keeping to time during the exam itself.

- Use past papers as a guide to the form of exam and the type of question likely to be asked (Box 5.2).
- Remember to have several short (5 minute) breaks during each hour of revision and a longer break every few hours. In any day, try to work for a maximum of three-quarters of the time.
- Include recreation within your schedule: there is little point in tiring yourself with too much revision, as this is unlikely to be profitable.
- Make your revision as active and interesting as possible (see below): the least productive approach is simply to read and reread your notes.
- Ease back on the revision near the exam: plan your revision to avoid last-minute cramming and overload fatigue.

Active revision

The following techniques may prove useful in devising an active revision strategy:

Aiding recall through effective notes – the Mind Map® technique (pp. 16–17), when used to organise ideas, is claimed to enhance recall by connecting the material to visual images or linking it to the physical senses.

- 'Distil' your lecture notes to show the main headings and examples. Prepare revision sheets with details for a particular topic on a single sheet of paper, arranged as a numbered checklist. Wall posters are another useful revision aid.
- Confirm that you know the material by testing yourself – take a blank sheet of paper and write down all you know. Check your full notes to see if you missed anything out. If you did, go back immediately to a fresh blank sheet and redo the example. Repeat, as required.
- Memorise definitions and key phrases: definitions can be a useful starting point for many exam answers. Make up lists of relevant facts

Box 5.2 Using past exam papers

Past exam papers are a valuable resource for targeting your revision.

1. **Find out where the past exam papers are kept.** Copies may be lodged in your department or the library; or they may be accessible on-line.

2. **Locate and copy relevant papers for your module(s).** Check with your tutor or course handbook that the style of paper will not change for the next set of examinations.

3. **Analyse the design of the exam paper.** Taking into account the length in weeks of your module, and the different lecturers and/or topics for those weeks, note any patterns that emerge. For example, can you translate weeks of lectures/ practicals into numbers of questions or sections of the paper? Consider how this might affect your revision plans and exam tactics, taking into account (a) any choices or restrictions offered in the paper, and (b) the different types of questions asked (i.e. multiple choice, short-answer or essay).

4. **Examine carefully the style of questions.** Can you identify the expectations of your lecturers? Can you relate the questions to the learning objectives? How much extra reading do they seem to expect? Are the questions fact-based? Do they require a synthesis based on other knowledge? Can you

identify different styles for different lecturers? Consider how the answers to these questions might affect your revision effort and exam strategy.

5. **Practise answering questions.** Perhaps with friends, set up your own mock exam once you have done a fair amount of revision, but not too close to the exams. Use a relevant past exam paper and don't study it beforehand. You need not attempt all of the paper at one sitting. You'll need a quiet room in a place where you will not be interrupted (e.g. a library). Keep close track of time during the mock exam and try to do each question in the length of time you would normally assign to it (see p. 26) – this gives you a feel for the speed of thought and writing required and the scope of answer possible. Mark each other's papers and discuss how each of you interpreted the question and laid out your answers and your individual marking schemes.

6. **Practise writing answer plans and starting answers.** This can save time compared to the 'mock exam' approach. Practise in starting answers can help you get over stalling at the start and wasting valuable time. Writing essay plans gets you used to organising your thoughts quickly and putting your thoughts into a logical sequence.

or definitions associated with particular topics. Test yourself repeatedly on these, or get a friend to do this. Try to remember *how many* facts or definitions you need to know in each case – this will help you recall them all during the exam.

- Use mnemonics and acronyms to commit specific factual information to memory. Sometimes, the dafter they are, the better they seem to work.
- Use pattern diagrams or mind maps as a means of testing your powers of recall on a particular topic (p. 16).
- Draw diagrams from memory: make sure you can label them fully.
- Try recitation as an alternative to written recall. Talk about your topic to another person, preferably someone in your class. Talk to yourself if necessary. Explaining something out loud is an excellent test of your understanding.
- Associate facts with images or journeys if you find this method works.
- Use a wide variety of approaches to avoid boredom during revision (e.g. record information on audio tape, use cartoons, or any other method, as long as it's not just reading).
- Form a revision group to share ideas and discuss topics with other students.
- Prepare answers to past papers, e.g. write essays or, if time is limited, write essay plans (see Box 5.2).

Revision checks – it is important to test yourself frequently during revision, to ensure that you have retained the information you are revising.

- If your subject involves numerical calculations, work through representative problems.
- Make up your own questions: the act of putting yourself in the examiner's mind-set by inventing questions can help revision. However, you should not rely on 'question spotting': this is risky!

Final preparations – try to get a good night's sleep before an exam. Last-minute cramming will be counter-productive if you are too tired during the exam.

The evening before your exam should be spent in consolidating material, and checking through summary lists and plans. Avoid introducing new material at this late stage: your aim should be to boost your confidence, putting yourself in the right frame of mind for the exam itself.

Sources for further study

Burns, R. (1997) *The Student's Guide to Passing Exams*. Kogan Page, London.

Hamilton, D. (1999) *Passing Exams: A Guide for Maximum Stress and Minimum Stress.* Cassell, London.

Many universities host study skills websites; these can be found using 'study skills', 'revision' or 'exams' as key words in a search engine.

Study exercises

5.1 Draw up a revision timetable. Use the techniques discussed in Box 5.1 to create a revision timetable for your forthcoming exams. You may wish to use or adapt the following arrangement, either on paper or within a spreadsheet.

A revison timetable planner

Date	Morning		Lunch	Afternoon		Tea/Dinner	Evening	
	Session 1	Session 2		Session 1	Session 2		Session 1	Session 2

5.2 Make use of past exam papers. Use the techniques discussed in Box 5.2 to improve your revision strategy: assess their effectiveness in a particular exam, or series of exams.

5.3 Try out new active revision techniques. Try any or all of the methods mentioned on pages 22–4 when revising. Compare notes with a colleague – which seems to be the most successful technique for you and for the topic you are revising?

6 Assessments and exams

You are unlikely to have reached this stage in your education without being exposed to the examination process. You may not enjoy being assessed, but you probably want to do well in your course. It is therefore important to understand why and how you are being tested. Identifying and improving on the skills required for exam success will allow you to perform to the best of your ability.

In-course assessments

There are many forms of course work that are assessed. The main types covered at various points in this book are:

- practical exercises (Chapters 20–67);
- essays (Chapters 16 and 17);
- numerical problems (Chapter 65);
- data analysis (Chapters 65–67);
- poster and spoken presentations (Chapters 14 and 15);
- literature surveys and reviews (Chapter 19);
- project work (Chapters 18 and 31);
- problem-based learning (Box 6.1).

At the start of each year or module, read the course handbook or module guide carefully to find out when any assessed work needs to be submitted. Note relevant dates in your diary, and use this information to plan your work. Take special note if deadlines for different modules clash, or if they coincide with social or sporting commitments.

KEY POINT If, for some valid reason (e.g. illness), you will be late with an assessment, speak to your tutors as soon as possible. They may be able to take extenuating circumstances into account by not applying a marking penalty. They will let you know what paperwork you may be required to submit to support your claim.

Summative exams – general points

Summative exams normally involve you answering questions without being able to consult other students or your notes. Invigilators are present to ensure appropriate conduct, but departmental representatives may be present for some of the exam. Their role is to sort out any subject-related problems, so if you think something is wrong, ask at the earliest opportunity. It is not unknown for parts of questions to be omitted in error, or for double meanings to arise, for example.

Planning

When preparing for an exam, make a checklist of the items you'll need (e.g. pens, pencils, sharpener and eraser, calculator, paper tissues, watch, ID card). On the day of the exam, give yourself sufficient time to arrive at the correct room, without the risk of being late. Double-check the times and places of your exams, both well before the exam, and also on arrival. If you arrive at the exam venue early, you can always rectify a mistake if you find you've gone to the wrong place.

Formative assessments – these may be mid-term or mid-semester tests and are often in the same format as later exams. They are intended to give you exam practice, plus feedback on your performance. You should use the results to measure your performance against the work you put in, and to find out, either from grades or tutor's comments, how you could do better in future. If you don't understand the reason for your grade, talk to your tutor.

Summative assessments – these include end-of-year or end-of-module exams. They inform others about the standard of your work. In continuous or 'in-course' assessment, the summative elements are spread out over the course. Sometimes these exams may involve a formative aspect, if feedback is given.

Box 6.1   Problem-based learning (PBL)

In this relatively new teaching method, you are likely to be presented with a 'real world' problem or issue, often working within a team. As you tackle the problem, you will gain factual knowledge, develop skills and exercise critical thinking (Chapter 9). Because there is a direct and relevant context for your work, and because you have to employ active learning techniques, the knowledge and skills you gain are likely to be more readily assimilated and remembered. This approach also more closely mimics workplace practices. PBL usually proceeds as follows:

1. **You are presented with a problem** (e.g. a case study, a hypothetical patient, a topical issue).

2. **You consider what issues and topics you need to research,** by discussion with others if necessary. You may need to identify where relevant resources can be found (Chapters 8–11).

3. **You then need to rank the issues and topics in importance,** allocating tasks to group members, if appropriate. A structured approach is an important aspect of PBL.

4. **Having carried out the necessary research, you should review what information has been obtained.** As a result, new issues may need to be explored and, where appropriate, allocated to group members.

5. **You will be asked to produce an outcome, such as a report, diagnosis, seminar presentation or poster.** An outline structure will be required, and for groups, further allocation of tasks will be needed to accomplish this goal.

If asked to carry out PBL as part of your course, it is important to get off to a good start. At first, the problem may seem unfamiliar. However, once you become involved in the work, you will quickly gain confidence. If working as part of a group, make sure that your group meets as early as possible, that you attend all sessions and that you do the necessary background reading. When working in a team, a degree of self-awareness is necessary regarding your 'natural' role in group situations (Table 3.1). Various methods are used for assessing PBL, including written, oral and poster presentations, and the assessment may involve peer marking.

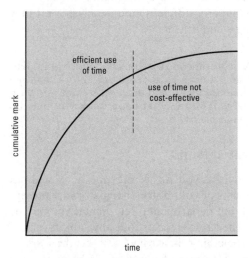

Fig. 6.1 Exam marks as a function of time. The marks awarded in a single answer will follow the law of diminishing returns – it will be far more difficult to achieve the final 25% of the available marks than the initial 25%. Do not spend too long on any one question.

Using the question paper – unless this is specifically forbidden, you should *write on the question paper to plan your strategy, keep to time and organise answers.*

Tackling the paper

Begin by reading the instructions at the top of the exam paper carefully, so that you do not make any errors based on lack of understanding of the exam structure. Make sure that you know:

- how many questions are set;
- how many must be answered;
- whether the paper is divided into sections;
- whether any parts are compulsory;
- what each question/section is worth, as a proportion of the total mark;
- whether different questions should be answered in different books.

Do not be tempted to spend too long on any one question or section: the return in terms of marks will not justify the loss of time from other questions (see Fig. 6.1). Take the first 10 minutes or so to read the paper and plan your strategy, before you begin writing. Do not be put off by those who begin immediately; it is almost certain they are producing unplanned work of a poor standard.

Underline the key phrases in the instructions, to reinforce their message. Next, read through the set of questions. If there is a choice, decide on those questions to be answered and decide on the order in which you will tackle them. Prepare a timetable which takes into account the amount of time required to complete each section and which reflects the allocation of marks – there is little point in spending one-quarter of the exam period on a question worth only 5 per cent of the total marks. Use the exam paper to mark the sequence in which the questions will be answered and write the finishing times alongside; refer to this timetable during the exam to keep yourself on course.

Reviewing your answers

At the end of the exam, you should allow at least 10 minutes to read through your script, to check for:

- errors of fact;
- missing information;
- grammatical and spelling errors;
- errors of scale and units;
- errors in calculations.

Make sure your name and/or ID number is on each exam book as required and on all other sheets of paper, including graph paper, even if securely attached to your script, as it is in your interest to ensure that your work does not go astray.

KEY POINT *Never* leave any exam early. Most exams assess work carried out over several months within a time period of 2–3 hours and there is always something constructive you can do with the remaining time to improve your script.

Special considerations for different types of exam question

Essay questions

Essay questions let examiners test the depth of your comprehension and understanding as well as your recall of facts. Essay questions give you

---

Box 6.2 Writing under exam conditions

Make sure you go into an exam with a strategy for managing the available time.

- **Allocate some time (say 5 per cent of the total) to consider which questions to answer and in which order.**

- **Share the rest of the time among the questions, according to the marks available.** Aim to optimise the marks obtained. A potentially good answer should be allocated slightly more time than one you don't feel so happy about. However, don't concentrate on any one answer (see Fig. 6.1).

- **For each question divide the time into planning, writing and revision phases** (see p. 99).

Employ time-saving techniques as much as possible:

- **Use spider diagrams** (Fig. 16.1) **or mind maps** (Fig. 4.2) to organise and plan your answer.

- **Use diagrams and tables** to save time in making difficult and lengthy explanations, but make sure you refer to each one in the text.

- **Use standard abbreviations** to save time repeating text but always explain them at the first point of use (e.g. PCR, polymerase chain reaction).

- **Consider speed of writing and neatness** – especially when selecting the type of pen to use – ballpoint pens are fastest, but they can tend to smudge. You can only gain marks if the examiner can read your script.

- **Keep your answer simple and to the point**, with clear explanations of your reasoning.

Make sure your answer is relevant.

- **Don't include irrelevant facts** just because you memorised them during revision, as this may do you more harm than good. You must answer the specific question that has been set.

- **Time taken to write irrelevant material is time lost from another question.**

Adopting different tactics according to the exam – *you should adjust your exam strategy (and revision methods) to allow for the differences in question types used in each exam paper.*

plenty of scope to show what you know. They suit those with a good grasp of principles but who perhaps have less ability to recall individual details.

Before you tackle a particular question, you must be sure of what is required in your answer. Ask yourself 'What is the examiner looking for in this particular question?' and then set about providing a *relevant* answer. Consider each word in the question and highlight, underline or circle the key words. Make sure you know the meaning of the terms given in Table 17.1 (p. 99) so that you can provide the appropriate information, where necessary. Spend some time planning your writing (see Chapter 16). Refer back to the question frequently as you write, to confirm that you are keeping to the subject matter. Box 6.2 gives advice on writing essays under exam conditions.

It is usually a good idea to begin with the question that you are most confident about. This will reassure you before tackling more difficult parts of the paper. If you run out of time, write in note form. Examiners are usually understanding, as long as the main components of the question have been addressed and the intended structure of the answer is clear. Common reasons for poor exam answers in essay-style questions are listed in Box 6.3.

Box 6.3 Reasons for poor exam answers to essay-style questions

The following are reasons that lecturers often cite when they give low marks for essay answers:

- **Not answering the exact question set.** Either failing to recognise the specialist terms used in the question, failing to demonstrate an understanding of the terms by not providing definitions, failing to carry out the precise instruction in a question, or failing to address all aspects of the question.

- **Running out of time.** Not matching the time allocated to the extent of the answer. Frequently, this results in spending too long on one question and not enough on the others, or even failing to complete the paper.

- **Not answering all parts** of a multiple part question, or not recognising that one part (perhaps involving more complex ideas) may carry more marks than another.

- **Failing to provide evidence** to support an answer. Forgetting to state the 'obvious' – either basic facts or definitions.

- **Failing to illustrate an answer appropriately**, either by not including a relevant diagram, or by providing a diagram that does not aid communication, or by not including examples.

- **Incomplete answer(s).** Failing to answer appropriately due to lack of knowledge.

- **Providing irrelevant evidence** to support an answer. 'Waffling' to fill space.

- **Illegible handwriting**.

- **Poor English**, such that facts and ideas are not expressed clearly.

- **Lack of logic** or structure to the answer.

- **Factual errors**, indicating poor note-taking, poor revision or poor recall.

- **Failing to correct obvious mistakes** by re-reading an answer before submitting the script.

At higher levels, the following aspects are especially important:

- **Not providing enough in-depth information.**

- **Providing a descriptive rather than an analytical answer** – focusing on facts, rather than deeper aspects of a topic.

- **Not setting a problem in context**, or not demonstrating a wider understanding of the topic. However, make sure you don't overdo this, or you may risk not answering the question set.

- **Not giving enough evidence of reading around the subject.** Wider reading can be demonstrated by quoting relevant papers and reviews and by giving author names and dates of publication.

- **Not considering both sides of a topic/debate, or not arriving at a conclusion.**

Multiple-choice and short-answer questions

Multiple-choice questions (MCQs) and short-answer questions (SAQs) are generally used to test the breadth and detail of your knowledge. The various styles that can be encompassed within the SAQ format allow for more demanding questions than MCQs, which may emphasise memory work and specific factual information.

A good approach for MCQ papers is as follows:

1. First trawl: read through the questions fairly rapidly, noting the 'correct' answer in those you can attempt immediately, perhaps in pencil.
2. Second trawl: go through the paper again, checking your original answers and this time marking up the answer sheet properly.
3. Third trawl: now tackle the difficult questions and those that require longer to answer (e.g. those based on numerical problems).

One reason for adopting this three-phase approach is that you may be prompted to recall facts relevant to questions looked at earlier. You can also spend more time per question on the difficult ones.

When unsure of an answer, the first stage is to rule out options that are clearly absurd or have obviously been placed there to distract you. Next, looking at the remaining options, can you judge between contrasting pairs with alternative answers? Logically, both cannot be correct, so you should see if you can rule one of the pair out. Watch out, however, in case *both* may be irrelevant to the answer. If the question involves a calculation, try to do this independently from the answers, so you are not influenced by them.

In SAQ papers, there may be a choice of questions. Choose your options carefully – it may be better to gain half marks for a correct answer to half a question, than to provide a largely irrelevant answer that apparently covers the whole question but lacks the necessary detail. For the SAQ form of question, few if any marks are given for writing style. Think in 'bullet points' and list the crucial points only. The time for answering SAQ questions may be tight, so get down to work fast, starting with answers that demand remembered facts. Stick to your timetable by moving on to the next question as soon as possible. Strategically, it is probably better to get part-marks for the full number of questions than good marks for only a few.

Practical and information-processing exams

The prospect of a practical or information-processing exam may cause you more concern than a theory exam. This may be due to a limited experience of practical examinations, or to the fact that practical and observational skills are tested, as well as recall, description and analysis of factual information. Your first thoughts may be that it is not possible to prepare for such exams but, in fact, you can improve your performance by mastering the various practical techniques described in this book.

You may be allowed to take your laboratory reports and other texts into the practical exam. Don't assume that this is a soft option, or that revision is unnecessary: you will not have time to read large sections of your reports or to familiarise yourself with basic principles, etc. The main advantage of 'open book' exams is that you can check specific details of methodology, reducing your reliance on memory, provided you know your way around your practical manual and notes. In all other respects, your revision and preparation for such exams should be similar to theory

Examples These are principal types of question you are likely to encounter in a practical or information processing exam:

Manipulative exercises Often based on work carried out during your practical course. Tests dexterity, specific techniques (e.g. sterile technique).

'Spot' tests Short questions requiring an identification, or brief descriptive notes on a specific item (e.g. a prepared slide). Tests knowledge of seen material or ability to transfer this to a new example.

Calculations May include the preparation of aqueous solutions at particular concentrations (p. 137) and statistical exercises (p. 483). Tests numeracy.

Data analyses May include the preparation and interpretation of graphs (p. 460) and numerical information, from data either obtained during the exam or provided by the examiner. Tests problem-solving skills.

Preparing specimens for examination with a microscope Tests staining technique and light microscopy technique.

Interpreting images Sometimes used when it is not possible to provide living specimens, e.g. in relation to electron microscopy. Can test a variety of skills.

Allow yourself to relax in oral exams – external examiners are experienced at putting students at ease. They will start by asking 'simple-to-answer' questions, such as what modules you did, how your project research went, and what your career aspirations are. Look on the external as a friend rather than a foe.

Terminology – the oral exams are sometimes known simply as 'orals' or, borrowing Latin, as 'viva voce' (by the living voice) exams or 'vivas'.

exams. Make sure you are familiar with all of the practical exercises, including any work carried out in class by your partner (since exams are assessed on individual performance). If necessary, check with the teaching staff to see whether you can be given access to the laboratory, to complete any exercises that you have missed.

At the outset of the practical exam, determine or decide on the order in which you will tackle the questions. A question in the latter half of the paper may need to be started early on in the exam period (e.g. an enzyme assay requiring 2 hour incubation in a 3 hour exam). Such questions are included to test your forward-planning and time-management skills. You may need to make additional decisions on the allocation of material, e.g. if you are given 30 sterile test tubes, there is little value in designing an experiment that uses 25 of these to answer question 1, only to find that you need at least 15 tubes for subsequent questions.

Make sure you explain your choice of apparatus and experimental design. Calculations should be set out in a stepwise manner, so that credit can be given, even if the final answer is incorrect (see p. 466). If there are any questions that rely on recall of factual information and you are unable to remember specific details, make sure that you describe the item fully, so that you gain credit for observational skills. Alternatively, leave a gap and return to the question at a later stage.

Oral exams and interviews

An oral interview is sometimes a part of final degree exams, representing a chance for the external examiner(s) to meet individual students and to test their abilities directly and interactively. In some departments, orals are used to validate the exam standard, or to test students on the borderline between exam grades. Sometimes an interview may form part of an assessment, as with project work or posters. This type of exam is often intimidating – many students say they don't know how to revise for an oral – and many candidates worry that they will be so nervous they won't be able to do themselves justice.

Preparation is just as important for oral exams as it is for written exams:

- Think about your earlier performances – if the oral follows written papers, it may be that you will be asked about questions you did not do so well on. These topics should be revised thoroughly. Be prepared to say how you would approach the questions if given a second chance.
- Read up a little about the examiner – he or she may focus their questions in their area of expertise.
- Get used to giving spoken answers – it is often difficult to transfer between written and spoken modes. Write down a few questions and get a friend to ask you them, possibly with unscripted follow-up queries.
- Research and think about topical issues in your subject area – some examiners will feel this reflects how interested you are in your subject.

Your conduct during the oral exam is important, too:

- Arrive promptly and wear reasonably smart clothing. Not to do either might be considered disrespectful by the examiner.
- Take your time before answering questions. Even if you think you know the answer immediately, take a little while to check mentally

whether you have considered all angles. A considered, logical approach will be more impressive than a quick but ill-considered response.

- Start answers with the basics, then develop into deeper aspects. There may be both surface and deeper aspects to a topic and more credit will be given to a student who mentions the latter.
- When your answer is finished, stop speaking. A short, crisp answer is better than a rambling one.
- If you don't know the answer, say so. To waffle and talk about irrelevant material is more damaging than admitting that you don't know.
- Make sure your answer is balanced. Talk about the evidence and opinions on both sides of a contentious issue.
- Don't disagree violently with the examiner. Politely put your point of view, detailing the evidence behind it. Examiners will be impressed by students who know their own mind and subject area. However, they will expect you to support a position at odds with the conventional viewpoint.
- Finally, be positive and enthusiastic about your topic.

Counteracting anxiety before and during exams

Adverse effects of anxiety need to be overcome by anticipation and preparation well in advance (Box 6.4). Exams, with their tight time limits, are especially stressful for perfectionists. To counteract this tendency, focus on the following points during the exam:

- Don't expect to produce a perfect essay – this won't be possible in the time available.
- Don't spend too long planning your answer – once you have an outline plan, get started.
- Don't spend too much time on the initial parts of an answer, at the expense of the main message.
- Concentrate on getting all of the basic points across – markers are looking for the main points first, before allocating extra marks for the detail.
- Don't be obsessed with neatness, either in handwriting, or in the diagrams you draw, but make sure your answers are legible.
- Don't worry if you forget something. You can't be expected to know everything. Most marking schemes give a first class grade to work that misses out on up to 30 per cent of the marks available.

KEY POINT Everyone worries about exams. Anxiety is a perfectly natural feeling. It works to your advantage, as it helps provide motivation and the adrenaline that can help you 'raise your game' on the day.

After the exam *– try to avoid becoming involved in prolonged analyses with other students over the 'ideal' answers to the questions; after all, it is too late to change anything at this stage. Go for a walk, watch TV for a while, or do something else that helps you relax, so that you are ready to face the next exam with confidence.*

There is a lot to be said for treating exams as a game. After all, they are artificial situations contrived to ensure that large numbers of candidates can be assessed together, with little risk of cheating. They have conventions and rules, just like games. If you understand the rationale behind them and follow the rules, this will aid your performance.

Sources for further study

Acres, D. (1995) *How to Pass Exams without Anxiety: Every Candidate's Guide to Success.* How To Books, London.

Box 6.4 Strategies for combating the symptoms of exam anxiety

Sleeplessness – this is common and does little harm in the short term. Get up, have a snack, do some light reading or other activity, then return to bed. Avoid caffeine (e.g. tea, coffee and cola) for several hours before going to bed.

Lack of appetite – again commonplace. Eat what you can, and take sugary sweets into the exam to keep energy levels up in case you become tired.

Fear of the unknown – it can be a good idea to visit the exam room, so you can become familiar with the location. Confirm dates and times of exams. Go through your pre-exam checklist (p. 25). Check any paperwork you have been given regarding the format and timing of the exam. Take a mascot or lucky charm with you if this helps.

Worries about timekeeping – get a *reliable* alarm clock or a new battery for an old one. Arrange for an alarm phone call; ask a friend or relative to make sure you are awake on time. Make reliable travel arrangements, to arrive on time. If your exam is early in the morning, it may be a good idea to get up early for a few days beforehand.

Blind panic during an exam – explain how you feel to an invigilator. Ask to go for a supervised walk outside. Do some relaxation exercises (see below), then return to your work. If you are having problems with a specific question, it may be appropriate to speak to the departmental representative at the exam, to check that you are not misinterpreting the question.

Feeling tense – shut your eyes, take several slow, deep breaths, do some stretching and relaxing muscle movements. During exams, it can be a good idea to do this between questions, and possibly to have a complete rest for a minute or so. Before exams, try some exercise activity or escape temporarily from your worries by watching TV or a movie.

Running out of time – don't panic when the invigilator says 'five minutes left'. It is surprising how much you can write in this time. Write note-style answers or state the areas you would have covered: you may get some credit.

Burns, R. (1997) *The Student's Guide to Passing Exams*. Kogan Page, London.

Hamilton, D. (1999) *Passing Exams: A Guide for Maximum Stress and Minimum Stress*. Cassell, London.

Many universities host study skills websites; these can be found using 'study skills', 'revision' or 'exams' as key words in a search engine.

Study exercises

6.1 Analyse your past performances. Think back to past exams and any feedback you received from them. How might you improve your performance? Consider ways in which you might approach the forthcoming exam differently. If you have kept past papers and answers to continuous assessment exercises, look at any specific comments your lecturers may have made.

6.2 Share revision notes with other students. Make a revision plan (see pp. 9 and 22) and then allocate some time to discussing your revision notes with a colleague. Try to learn from his or her approach. Discuss any issues you do not agree upon.

6.3 Plan your exam tactics. Find out from your module handbook or past papers what the format of each paper will be. Confirm this if necessary with staff. Decide how you will tackle each paper, allocating time to each section and to each question within the sections (see p. 99). Write a personal checklist of requirements for the exam (see p. 25).

Preparing your curriculum vitae

Many students only think about their curriculum vitae immediately before applying for a job. Reflecting this, chapters on preparing a CV are usually placed near the end of texts of this type. Putting the chapter near the beginning of this book emphasises the importance of focusing your thoughts on your CV at an early stage in your studies. There are four main reasons why this can be valuable:

1. Considering your CV and how it will look to a future employer will help you think more deeply about the direction and value of your academic studies.
2. Creating a draft CV will prompt you to assess your skills and personal qualities and how these fit into your career aspirations.
3. Your CV can be used as a record of all the relevant things you have done at university and then, later, will help you communicate these to a potential employer.
4. Your developing CV can be used when you apply for vacation or part-time employment.

KEY POINT Developing your skills and qualities needs to be treated as a long-term project. It makes sense to think early about your career aspirations so that you can make the most of opportunities to build up relevant experience. A good focus for such thoughts is your developing curriculum vitae, so it is useful to work on this from a very early stage.

Skills and personal qualities

Understanding skills and qualities – it may be helpful to think about how the skills and qualities in Tables 1.1 and 7.1 apply to particular activities during your studies, since this will give them a greater relevance.

Skills (sometimes called competences) are generally what you have learned to do and have improved with practice. Table 1.1 summarises some important skills for bioscientists. This list might seem quite daunting, but your tutors will have designed your courses to give you plenty of opportunities to develop your expertise. Personal qualities, on the other hand, are predominately innate. Examples include honesty, determination and thoroughness (Table 7.1). These qualities need not remain static, however, and can be developed or changed according to your experiences. By consciously deciding to take on new challenges and responsibilities, not only can you develop your personal qualities, but you can also provide supporting evidence for your CV.

Personal qualities and skills are inter-related because your personal qualities can influence the skills you gain. For example, you may become highly proficient at a skill requiring manual dexterity if you are particularly adept with your hands. Being able to transfer your skills is highly important (Chapter 1) – many employers take a long-term view and look for evidence of the adaptability that will allow you to be a flexible employee and one who will continue to develop skills.

Developing your curriculum vitae

The initial stage involves making an audit of the skills and qualities you already have, and thinking about those you might need to develop.

Table 7.1 *Some positive personal qualities*

Adaptability
Conscientiousness
Curiosity
Determination
Drive
Energy
Enthusiasm
Fitness and health
Flexible approach
Honesty
Innovation
Integrity
Leadership
Logical approach
Motivation
Patience
Performance under stress
Perseverance
Prudence
Quickness of thought
Seeing others' viewpoints
Self-confidence
Self-discipline
Sense of purpose
Shrewd judgement
Social skills (sociability)
Taking initiative
Tenacity
Tidiness
Thoroughness
Tolerance
Unemotional approach
Willingness to take on challenges

Seeing yourself as others see you – *you may not recognise all of your personal qualities and you may need someone else to give you an honest appraisal. This could be anyone whose opinion you value: a friend, a member of your family, a tutor, or a careers adviser.*

Setting your own agenda – *you have the capability to widen your experience and to demonstrate relevant personal qualities through both curricular and extracurricular activities.*

Paying attention to the quality of your CV – *your potential employer will regard your CV as an example of your very best work and will not be impressed if it is full of mistakes or badly presented, especially if you claim 'good written communication' as a skill!*

Tables 7.1 and 1.1 could form a basis of this self-appraisal. Assessing your skills may be easier than critically analysing your personal characteristics. In judging your qualities, try to take a positive view and avoid being overly modest. It is important to think of your qualities in a specific context, e.g. 'I have shown that I am trustworthy, by acting as treasurer for the Biochemistry Society', as this evidence will form a vital part of your CV and job applications.

If you can identify gaps in your skills, or qualities that you would like to develop, especially in relation to the needs of your intended career, the next step is to think about ways of improving them. This will be reasonably easy in some cases, but may require some creative thinking in others. A relatively simple example would be if you decided to learn a new language or to keep up with one you learned at school. There are likely to be many local college and university courses dealing with foreign languages at many different levels, so it would be a straightforward matter to join one of these. A rather more difficult case might be if you wished to demonstrate 'responsibility', because there are no courses available on this. One route to demonstrate this quality might be to put yourself up for election as an officer in a student society or club; another could be to take a leading role in a relevant activity within your community (e.g. voluntary work such as hospital radio). If you already take part in activities like these, your CV should relate them to this context.

Basic CV structures and their presentation

Box 7.1 illustrates the typical parts of a CV and explains the purpose of each part. Employers are more likely to take notice of a well-organised and well-presented CV, in contrast to one that is difficult to read and assimilate. They will expect it to be concise, complete and accurate. There are many ways of presenting information in a CV, and you will be assessed partly on your choices.

- **Order**. There is some flexibility as to the order in which you can present the different parts (see Box 7.1). A chronological approach within sections helps employers gain a picture of your experience.
- **Personality and 'colour'**. Make your CV different by avoiding standard or dull phrasing. Try not to focus solely on academic aspects: you will probably work in a team, and the social aspects of teamwork will be enhanced by your outside interests. However, make sure that the reader does not get the impression that these interests dominate your life.
- **Style**. Your CV should reflect *your* personality, but not in such a way that it indicates too idiosyncratic an approach. It is probably better to be formal in both language and presentation, as flippant or chatty expressions will not be well received.
- **Neatness**. Producing a well-presented, word-processed CV is very important. Use a laser-quality printer and good-quality paper; avoid poor-quality photocopying at all costs.
- **Layout**. Use headings for different aspects, such as personal details, education, etc. Emphasise words (e.g. with capitals, bold, italics or underlining) sparingly and with the primary aim of making the structure clearer. Remember that careful use of white space is important in design.

There is no right or wrong way to write a CV, and no single format applies. It is probably best to avoid software templates and CV 'wizards' as they can create a bland, standardised result, rather than something that demonstrates your individuality.

You should include the following components, with appropriate sub-headings, generally in the order given below:

1. **Personal details**. This section *must* include your full name and date of birth, your address (both home and term-time, with dates, if appropriate) and a contact telephone number at each address. If you have an e-mail account, you might also include this. You need only mention sex if your name could be either male or female.

2. **Education**. Choose either chronological order, or reverse chronological order and make sure you take the same approach in all other sections. Give educational institutions and dates (month, year) and provide more detail for your degree course than for your previous education. Remember to mention any prizes, scholarships or other academic achievements. Include your overall mark for the most recent year of your course, if it seems appropriate. Make sure you explain any gap years.

3. **Work experience**. Include all temporary, part-time, full-time or voluntary jobs. Details include dates, employer, job title and major duties involved.

4. **Skills and personal qualities**. Tables 1.1 and 7.1 give examples of the aspects you might include under this heading. Emphasise your strengths, and tailor this section to the specific requirements of the post (the 'job description'): for example, you might emphasise the practical skills you have gained during your degree studies if the post is a biological one, but concentrate on generic transferable skills and personal qualities for other jobs. Provide supporting evidence for your statements in all cases.

5. **Interests and activities**. This is an opportunity to bring out the positive aspects of your personality, and explain their relevance to the post you are applying for. Aim to keep this section short, or it may seem that your social life is more important than your education and work experience. Include up to four separate items, and provide sufficient detail to highlight the *positive* aspects of your interests (e.g. positions of responsibility, working with others, communication, etc.). Use sections 4 and 5 to demonstrate that you have the necessary attributes to fulfil the major requirements of the post.

6. **Referees**. Include the names (and titles), job descriptions, full postal addresses, contact telephone numbers and e-mail addresses of two referees (rarely, some employers may ask for three). It is usual to include your personal tutor or course leader at university (who among other things will verify your marks), plus another person – perhaps a current or former employer, or someone who runs a club or society and who knows your personal interests and activities. Unless you have kept in touch with a particular teacher since starting university, it is probably best to choose current contacts, rather than those from your previous education.

Some other points to consider:

- Try to avoid jargon and over-complicated phrases in your CV: aim for direct, active words and phrases (see Box 16.1, p. 96).

- Most employers will expect your CV to be word-processed (and spell-checked). Errors in style, grammar and presentation will count against you, so be sure to check through your final version (and ask a reliable person to second-check it for you).

- Aim for a *maximum* length of two pages, printed single-sided on A4 paper, using a 'formal' font (e.g. Times Roman or Arial) of no less than 12 point for the main text. Always print onto good quality white paper. Avoid fussy use of colour, borders, fonts or icons.

- Don't try to cram in too much detail. Use a clear and succinct approach with short sentences and lists to improve 'readability' and create structure. Remember that your aim is to catch the eye of your potential employer, who may have many applications to work through.

- It is polite to check that people are willing to act as a referee for you and to provide them with an up-to-date copy of your CV.

Your single-page covering letter should have four major components:

1. **Letterhead**. Include your contact details, the recipient's name and title (if known) and address, plus any job reference number.

2. **Introductory paragraph**. Explain who you are and state the post you are applying for.

3. **Main message**. This is your opportunity to sell yourself to a potential employer, highlighting particular attributes and experience. Keep it to three or four sentences at the most and relate it to the particular skills and qualities demanded in the job or person specification.

4. **Concluding paragraph**. A brief statement that you look forward to hearing the outcome of your application is sufficient.

Finally, add either 'Yours sincerely' (where the recipient's name is known) or 'Yours faithfully' (in a letter beginning 'Dear Sir or Madam') and then end with your signature.

- **Grammar and proofreading**. Look at your CV carefully before you submit it, as sloppy errors give a very poor impression. Even if you use a spell-checker, some errors may creep in. Ask someone whom you regard as a reliable proofreader to comment on it (many tutors will do this, if asked in advance).
- **Relevance**. If you can, slant your CV towards the job description and the qualifications required (see below). Make sure you provide evidence to back up your assertions about skills, qualities and experience.
- **Accuracy and completeness**. Check that all your dates tally; otherwise, you will seem careless. It is better to be honest about your grades and (say) a period of unemployment, than to cover this up or omit details that an employer will want to know. They may be suspicious if you leave things out.

Adjusting your CV

You should fine-tune your CV for each post. Employers frequently use a 'person specification' to define the skills and qualities demanded in a job, often under headings such as 'essential' and 'desirable'. This will help you decide whether to apply for a position and it assists the selection panel to filter the applicants. Highlight relevant qualifications as early in your CV as possible. Be selective – don't include every detail about yourself. Emphasise relevant parts and leave out irrelevant details, according to the job. Similarly, your letter of application is not merely a formal document but is also an opportunity for persuasion (Box 7.1). You can use it to state your ambitions and highlight particular qualifications and experience. However, don't go over the top – always keep the letter to a single page.

Creating a generic CV – as you may apply for several jobs, it is useful to construct a CV in electronic format (e.g. as a Word® file) which includes all information of potential relevance. This can then be modified to fit each post. Having a prepared CV on file will reduce the work each time you apply, while modifying this will help you focus on relevant skills and attributes for the particular job.

KEY POINT   A well-constructed and relevant CV won't necessarily guarantee you a job, but it may well get you onto the short list for interview. A poor-quality CV is a sure route to failure.

Sources for further study

Anon. (2000) *How to Write a Curriculum Vitae*. University of London Careers Service, London.

Anon. *Doctorjob.com Website*. Available: http://doctorjob.com
Last accessed 08/01/03.
[Created by GTI Specialist Publishers.]

Anon. *Prospects Website*. Available:
http://www.prospects.ac.uk/cms/showpage/home_page/p!elaxi
Last accessed 08/01/03.
[Created and maintained by the Higher Education Careers Services Unit, and containing good examples of typical CVs.]

Phillips, C. (1999) *Making Wizard Applications*. GTI Specialist Publishers Ltd, Wallingford.

Study exercises

7.1 Evaluate your personal attributes. Using Table 7.1 as a source, list *five* qualities that you feel that you would best use to describe yourself, and cite the evidence you might give to a potential employer to convince them that this was the case. List *five* attributes you could develop, then indicate how you might do this.

7.2 **Create a generic CV**. Drawing on your school record of achievement or similar, or any CV you may already have prepared, e.g. for a summer or part-time job, create a word-processed generic CV. Save the file in an appropriate (computer) folder and make a back-up copy. Print out a copy for filing. Periodically update the word-processed version. If necessary, keep or save different versions to be used in different contexts (e.g. when you apply for a vacation job).

7.3 **Think about your future career and ask for advice**. Make an appointment with one of the advisors in your University's careers service. Ask what the career options might be for people with your intended degree, or determine what qualifications or module options might be appropriate for occupations that attract you.

Information technology and library resources

8 Finding and citing published information

The ability to find scientific information is a skill required for many exercises in your degree programme. You will need to research facts and published findings as part of writing essays, literature reviews and project introductions, and when amplifying your lecture notes (p. 18) and revising for exams (p. 21). You must also learn how to follow scientific convention in citing source material as the authority for the statements you have made.

Sources of information

For essays and revision

You are unlikely to delve into the primary literature (p. 48) for these purposes – books and reviews are much more readable. If a lecturer or tutor specifies a particular book, then it should not be difficult to find out where it is shelved in your library, using the computerised index system. Library staff will generally be happy to assist with any queries. If you want to find out which books your library holds on a specified topic, use the system's subject index. You will also be able to search by author or by key words.

There are two main systems used by libraries to classify books: the Dewey Decimal system and the Library of Congress system. Libraries differ in the way they employ these systems, especially by adding further numbers and letters after the standard classification marks, e.g. to signify shelving position or edition number. Enquire at your library for a full explanation of local usage.

The World Wide Web is an expanding resource for gathering both general and specific information (see Chapters 10 and 11). Sites fall into analogous categories to those in the printed literature: there are sites with original information, sites that review information and bibliographic sites. One considerable problem is that websites may be frequently updated, so information present when you first looked may be altered or even absent when the site is next consulted. Further, very little of the information on the Web has been monitored or refereed. Another disadvantage is that the site information may not state the origin of the material, who wrote it or when it was written. This is considered in more detail in Box 10.3, p. 57.

For literature surveys and project work

You will probably need to consult the primary literature. If you are starting a new research project or writing a report from scratch, you can build up a core of relevant papers by using the following methods:

- Asking around: supervisors or their postgraduate students will almost certainly be able to supply you with a reference or two that will start you off.
- Searching a computer database, either via the Internet (see Chapter 10) or on CD-ROM: these cover very wide areas and are a convenient way to start a reference collection, although a charge is often made for access and sending out a listing of the papers selected (your library may or may not pass this on to you).
- Consulting the bibliography of other papers in your collection – an important way of finding the key papers in your field. In effect, you

---

Browsing in a library – this may turn up interesting material, but remember the books on the shelves are those not currently out on loan. Almost by definition, the latter may be more up-to-date and useful. To find out a library's full holding of books in any subject area, you need to search its catalogue (normally available as a computerised database).

Example The book *The Selfish Gene* by Richard Dawkins (1976; Oxford University Press) is likely to be classified as follows:

Dewey Decimal system: 591.51
where	591	refers to zoology
	591.5	refers to ecology of animals
	591.51	refers to habits and behaviour patterns

Library of Congress system: QL751
where	Q	refers to science
	QL	refers to zoology
	QL75	refers to animal behaviour
	QL751	refers to general works and treatises

Computer databases – several databases are now produced on CD-ROM for open use in libraries (e.g. Applied Science and Technology Index). Especially useful to bioscientists is the BIOSIS Previews® Database based on Biological Abstracts, accessed via Dialog Information Services, Inc. (Palo Alto, California, USA). Some databases can be accessed via the Internet, such as BIDS (Bath Information and Data Service) and the Web of Science database (username and password required via your library). Each of these databases usually has its own easy-to-follow menu instructions. It is worthwhile to consider keywords for your search beforehand, to focus your search and save time.

Definitions

Definitions

Journal/periodical/serial – any publication issued at regular intervals. In biosciences, usually containing papers describing original research findings and reviews of literature.
The primary literature – this comprises original research papers, published in specialist scientific periodicals. Certain prestigious general journals (e.g. *Nature*) contain important new advances from a wide subject area.
Monograph – a specialised book covering a single topic.
Review – an article in which recent advances in a specific area are outlined and discussed.
Proceedings – volume compiling written versions of papers read at a scientific meeting on a specific topic.
Abstracts – shortened versions of papers, often those read at scientific meetings. These may later appear in the literature as full papers.
Bibliography – a summary of the published work in a defined subject area.

Copyright law – *In Europe, copyright regulations were harmonised in 1993 (Directive 93/98/EEC) to allow literary copyright for 70 years after the death of an author and typographical copyright for 25 years after publication. This was implemented in the UK in 1996, where, in addition, the Copyright, Designs and Patents Act (1988) allows the Copyright Licensing Agency to license institutions so that lecturers, students and researchers may take copies for teaching and personal research purposes – no more than a single article per journal issue, one chapter of a book, or extracts to a total of 10 per cent of a book.*

are taking advantage of the fact that another researcher has already done all the hard work!

- Referring to 'current awareness' journals or computer databases: these are useful for keeping you up to date with current research; they usually provide a monthly listing of article details (title, authors, source, author address) arranged by subject and cross-referenced by subject and author. Current awareness journals cover a wider range of primary journals than could ever be available in any one library. Examples include:
  (a) *Current Contents*, published by the Institute of Scientific Information, Philadelphia, USA, which reproduces the contents pages of journals of a particular subject area and presents an analysis by author and subject.
  (b) *Current Advances*, published by Pergamon Press, Oxford, UK, which subdivides papers by subject within research areas and cross-references by subject and author.
  (c) *Biological Abstracts*, in which each paper's abstract is also reproduced. Papers may be cross-referenced according to various taxa, which is useful in allowing you to find out what work has been done on a particular organism.
- Using the *Science Citation Index* (SCI): this is a very valuable source of new references, because it lets you see who has cited a given paper; in effect, SCI allows you to move forward through the literature from an existing reference. The Index is also available on-line *via* ISI® Web of Science: this allows rapid access and output of selected information. Some libraries have copies on CD-ROM.

For specialised information

You may need to consult reference works, such as encyclopaedias, maps and books providing specialised information. Some of this is now available on the Web, or on CD-ROM or on-line (consult your library's information service Web pages). Three sources worth noting are:

- The *Handbook of Chemistry and Physics* (Lide, 2002; on-line via CHEMnetBASE): the Chemical Rubber Company's publication (affectionately known as the 'Rubber Bible') giving all manner of physical constants, radioisotope half-lives, etc.
- *The Merck Index* (O'Neil *et al.*, 2001), which gives useful information about organic chemicals, e.g. solubility, whether poisonous, etc., now also available on-line.
- The *Geigy Scientific Tables* (8th edition), a series of six volumes (Lentner, 1981; 1984; 1986; 1990; 1992; Lentner *et al.*, 1982) provides a wide range of information centred on biochemistry, e.g. buffer formulae, properties of constituents of living matter.

Obtaining and organising research papers

Obtaining a copy

It is usually more convenient to have personal copies of key research articles for direct consultation when working in a laboratory or writing. The simplest way of obtaining these is to photocopy the originals. For academic purposes, this is normally acceptable within copyright law. If your library does not take the journal, it may be possible for them to borrow it from a nearby institute or obtain a copy via a national borrowing centre (an 'inter-library loan'). If the latter, you will have to fill in a form giving full bibliographic details of the paper and where it was cited, as well as signing a copyright clearance statement concerning your use of the copy.

Your department might be able to supply 'reprint request' postcards to be sent to the designated author of a paper. This is an unreliable method of obtaining a copy because it may take some time (allow at least a month) and some requests will not receive a reply. Taking into account the waste involved in postage and printing, it is probably best simply to photocopy or send for a copy *via* inter-library loan.

Organising papers

Although the number of papers you accumulate may be small to start with, it is worth putting some thought into their storage and indexing before your collection becomes disorganised and unmanageable. Few things are more frustrating than not being able to lay your hands on a vital piece of information, and this can seriously disrupt your flow when writing or revising.

Card index systems

Index cards (Fig. 8.1) are a useful adjunct to any filing system. Firstly, you may not have a copy of the paper to file yet may still wish the reference information to be recorded somewhere for later use. Secondly, a selected pile of cards can be used when typing out different bibliographies. Thirdly, the cards can help when organising a review (see p. 108). Fourthly, the card can be used to record key points and comments on the paper. The priority rule for storage in card boxes is again first author name, subsequent author name(s), date. Computerised bibliographic databases, e.g. EndNote®, simplify cross-referencing and provide files for direct insertion into word-processed documents; however, they are very time-consuming to set up, so you should only consider using one if the time invested will prove worthwhile.

Making citations in text

There are two main ways of citing articles and creating a Bibliography (also referred to as 'References' or 'Literature Cited').

The Harvard system

For each citation, the author name(s) and the date of publication are given at the relevant point in the text. The Bibliography is organised alphabetically and by date of publication for papers with the same authors. Formats normally adopted are, for example, 'Smith and Jones (1983) stated that ...' or 'it has been shown that ... (Smith and Jones, 1983)'. Lists of references within parentheses are separated by semi-colons, e.g. '(Smith and Jones, 1983; Jones and Smith, 1985)', normally in order of date of publication. To avoid repetition within the same paragraph, an approach such as 'the investigations of Smith and Jones indicated that' could be used following an initial citation of the paper. Where there are more than two authors it is usual to write 'et al.' (or *et al.* if an italic font is available); this stands for the Latin *et alia* meaning 'and others'. If citing more than one paper with the same authors, put, for example, 'Smith and Jones (1987; 1990)' and if papers by a given set of authors appeared in the same year, letter them (e.g. Smith and Jones, 1989a; 1989b).

Storing research papers – these can easily be kept in alphabetical order within filing boxes or drawers, but if your collection is likely to grow large, it will need to be refiled as it outgrows the storage space. An alternative is to keep an alphabetical card index system (useful when typing out lists of references) and file the papers by 'accession number' as they accumulate. New filing space is only required at the end and you can use the accession numbers to form the basis of a simple cross-referencing system.

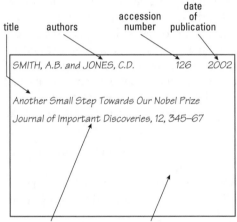

Fig. 8.1 A typical reference card. Make sure the index card carries all the bibliographic information of potential relevance.

The numerical or Vancouver system

Papers are cited via a superscript or bracketed reference number inserted at the appropriate point. Normal format would be, for example: 'DNA sequences[4,5] have shown that ...' or 'Jones [55,82] has claimed that ...'. Repeated citations use the number from the first citation. In the true numerical method (e.g. as in *Nature*), numbers are allocated by order of citation in the text, but in the alpha-numerical method (e.g. the *Annual Review* series), the references are first ordered alphabetically in the Bibliography, then numbered, and it is this number which is used in the text. Note that with this latter method, adding or removing references is tedious, so the numbering should be done only when the text has been finalised.

KEY POINT The main advantages of the Harvard system are that the reader might recognise the paper being referred to and that it is easily expanded if extra references are added. The main advantages of the Vancouver system are that it aids text flow and reduces length.

How to list your citations in a bibliography

Whichever citation method is used in the text, comprehensive details are required for the bibliography so that the reader has enough information to find the reference easily. Citations should be listed in alphabetical order with the priority: first author, subsequent author(s), date. Unfortunately, in terms of punctuation and layout, there are almost as many ways of citing papers as there are journals! Your department may specify an exact format for project work; if not, decide on a style and be consistent – if you do not pay attention to the details of citation you may lose marks. Take special care with the following aspects:

- Authors and editors: give details of *all* authors and editors in your bibliography, even if given as *et al.* in the text.
- Abbreviations for journals: while there are standard abbreviations for the titles of journals (consult library staff), it is a good idea to give the whole title, if possible.
- Books: the edition should always be specified as contents may change between editions. Add, for example, '(5th edition)' after the title of the book. You may be asked to give the International Standard Book Number (ISBN), a unique reference number for each book published.
- Unsigned articles, e.g. unattributed newspaper articles and instruction manuals – refer to the author(s) in text and bibliography as 'Anon.'.
- Unread articles: you may be forced to refer to a paper *via* another without having seen it. If possible, refer to another authority who has cited the paper, e.g. '... Jones (1980), cited in Smith (1990), claimed that ...'. Alternatively, you could denote such references in the bibliography by an asterisk and add a short note to explain at the start of the reference list.
- Personal communications: information received in a letter, seminar or conversation can be referred to in the text as, for example, '... (Smith, pers. comm.)'. These citations are not generally listed in the bibliography of papers, though in a thesis you could give a list of personal communicants and their addresses.

An example of how to cite a scientific paper available on-line is given on p. 109.

Examples

Paper in journal:
Smith, A. B., Jones, C.D. and Professor, A. (1998). Innovative results concerning our research interest. Journal of New Results, **11**, 234–5.

Book:
Smith, A. B. (1998). Summary of my life's work. Megadosh Publishing Corp., Bigcity. ISBN 0-123-45678-9.

Chapter in edited book:
Jones, C. D. and Smith, A. B. (1998). Earth-shattering research from our laboratory. In: Research Compendium 1998 (ed. A. Professor), pp. 123–456. Bigbucks Press, Booktown.

Thesis:
Smith, A. B. (1995). Investigations on my favourite topic. PhD thesis, University of Life, Fulchester.

Note that underlining used here specifies italics in print: use an italic font if working with a word processor (see examples in the 'text references' section of this chapter).

Citing websites – there is no widely accepted format at present. We suggest providing author name(s) and date in the text if using the Harvard system, (e.g. Hacker, 2003), while in the bibliography giving the URL details in the following format: Hacker, A. University of Anytown Homepage on Aardvarks. Available: http://www.myserver.ac.uk/homepage). Last accessed 08/01/03.

Text references

Budavari, S., O'Neil, M.J., Smith, A., Heckelman, P.E. and Obenchain, J.R. (2001) *The Merck Index: An Encyclopedia of Chemicals, Drugs and Biologicals*, 13th edn. Merck & Co., Inc., Whitehouse Station.

Lentner, C. (ed.) (1981) *Geigy Scientific Tables*, Vol. 1: *Units of Measurement, Body Fluids, Composition of the Body. Nutrition*, 8th edn. Ciba-Geigy, Basel.

Lentner, C. (ed.) (1984) *Geigy Scientific Tables*, Vol. 3: *Physical Chemistry, Composition of Blood, Hematology, Somatometric Data*, 8th edn. Ciba-Geigy, Basel.

Lentner, C. (ed.) (1986) *Geigy Scientific Tables*, Vol. 4: *Biochemistry, Metabolism of Xenobiotics, Inborn Errors of Metabolism, Pharmacogenetics, Ecogenetics*, 8th edn. Ciba-Geigy, Basel.

Lentner, C. (ed.) (1990) *Geigy Scientific Tables*, Vol. 5: *Heart and Circulation*, 8th edn. Ciba-Geigy, Basel.

Lentner, C. (ed.) (1992) *Geigy Scientific Tables*, Vol. 6: *Bacteria, Fungi, Protozoa, Helminths*, 8th edn. Ciba-Geigy, Basel.

Lentner, C., Diem, K. and Seldrup, J. (eds) (1982) *Geigy Scientific Tables*, Vol. 2: *Introduction to Statistics, Statistical Tables, Mathematical Formulae*, 8th edn. Ciba-Geigy, Basel.

Lide, D.R. (ed.) (2002) *CRC Handbook of Chemistry and Physics*, 83rd edn. CRC Press, Boca Raton.

Sources for further study

Anon. *BIDS UK: The BIDS 'for users' Page*. Available:
http://www.bids.ac.uk/info/fs_forusers.htm
Last accessed 08/01/03.

Anon. *BIOSIS® Resources*. Available:
http://www.biosis.org/free_resources/index.html
Last accessed 08/01/03.

Anon. *CHEMnetBASE*. Available:
http://www.chemnetbase.com
Last accessed 08/01/03.
[On-line access to the *Handbook of Chemistry and Physics*.]

Anon. Dialog®: *The Merck Index Online®*. Available:
http://library.dialog.com/bluesheets/html/bl0304.html
Last accessed 08/01/03.

Anon. *ISI Web of Science*. Available:
http://wos.mimas.ac.uk
Last accessed 08/01/03.
[Requires Athens password – consult University library staff for local details.]

Sheild, G. and Walton, G. *Cite Them Right! How to Organise Bibiographical References*. Available:
http://www.unn.ac.uk/central/isd/cite
Last accessed 08/01/03.

Study exercises

8.1 Test your library skills. This exercise relies on the fact that most university-level libraries serving bioscience departments will take the scientific journal *Nature*. To help you answer these questions, it may be beneficial to attend a library induction session, if you haven't already. Alternatively, the library's help or enquiry desks may be able to assist you if you are having problems.

(a) First, find out and provide the name of the classification system that your University uses for cataloguing its books and periodicals.

(b) Using your library's cataloguing system (on-line, preferably) find out the appropriate local classification number for the journal *Nature*.

(c) Where precisely is *Nature* shelved in your library? (Your answer need refer only to most recent issues if some have been archived.)

(d) What is the exact title of the landmark papers in the following two volumes? (i) *Nature* **171**, 737–738 (1953); (ii) *Nature* **408**, 796–815 (2000).

8.2 Explore different methods of citing references. Go to your library and seek out the journal area for biology or life sciences. Choose *three* different journals in your subject area and from a recent edition write down how they would print a typical citation for a multi-author journal paper in the 'references' or 'literature cited' section. Where used, indicate italicised text with normal underline and bold text with wavy underline. Pay attention to punctuation. Compare these methods with each other, with the methods recommended on pp. 43–4 of this book and with the recommendations your Department or your course handbook makes. Are they all the same?

8.3 Make website citations. Use a search engine (pp. 56–8) to find an informative website that covers each of the following:

(a) The use of SI units.

(b) Information about the bacterial culture collection of the Pasteur Institute (l'Institut Pasteur).

(c) The different types of blood cells.

Indicate how you would cite each website at the end of an essay (follow your Department's guidelines or use those in this chapter).

8.4 Compare the Harvard and Vancouver methods of citation. Pair up with a partner in your class. Each person should then pick one of the two main methods of citation and consider its pros and cons independently. Meet together and compare your lists. Given the choice, which method would you choose for (a) a handwritten essay; (b) a word-processed review; (c) an article in an academic journal, and why?

9 **Evaluating information**

Checking the reliability of information, assessing the relative value of different ideas and thinking critically are skills essential to the scientific approach (p. 182). You will need to develop your abilities to evaluate information in this way because:

- you will be faced with many sources of information, from which you will need to select the most appropriate material;
- you may come across conflicting sources of evidence and may have to decide which is the more reliable;
- the accuracy and validity of a specific fact may be vital to your work;
- you may doubt the quality of the information from a particular source;
- you may wish to check the original source because you are not sure whether someone else is quoting it correctly.

KEY POINT Advances in communications and information technology mean that we can now access almost limitless knowledge. Consequently, the ability to *evaluate* information has become an extremely important skill.

The process of evaluating and using information can be broken down into four stages:

1. Selecting and obtaining material. Library books and journals remain a prime source of information (Chapter 8). This can lead to difficulties because not every source is instantly available, and you may have to wait for weeks for an inter-library loan or photocopy to arrive. Nowadays, the Internet is increasingly a first port of call if you want to find something out. This has the advantage of being faster, but the authenticity of information on the Web can be more difficult to establish than for a conventional printed source (see Box 10.3).
2. Assessing the content. You will need to understand fully what has been written, including any technical terms and jargon used. Establish the relevance of the information to your needs and assure yourself that the data or conclusions have been presented in an unbiased way.
3. Modifying the information. In order to use the information, you may need to alter it to suit your needs. This may require you to make comparisons, interpret or summarise. Some sources may require translation. Some data may require mathematical transformation before they are useful. There is a chance of error in any of these processes and also a risk of plagiarism.
4. Analysis. This may be your own interpretation of the information presented, or an examination of the way the original author has used the information.

KEY POINT Avoiding plagiarism – when modifying information, avoid copying or modifying data or information without citing the source. Plagiarism is regarded as a serious academic offence and will always be penalised severely.

Example A Web search for the letters 'DNA' (e.g. using the search engine Google®, p. 57), will reveal that this acronym appears in over 5 million websites. Not all of these deal with deoxyribonucleic acid – the listed websites include: *Doctors' Net Access*, a web resource for American physicians; the website of the *Dermatology Nurses Association*; and that of *Delta Nu Alpha*, an international organisation for those working in the professions. These examples are easy to identify as irrelevant to research on 'DNA, the molecule', but considering the many websites that do actually cover this topic, which might contain the exact information you seek? How valid is the information? Is it biased towards one viewpoint or hypothesis? Does it represent current mainstream thinking on the topic? These are some of the issues that an evaluation of the information sources might deal with.

Definition

Plagiarism – the unacknowledged use of another's work as if it were one's own. In this definition, the concept of 'work' includes ideas, writing, data or inventions and not simply words; and the notion of 'use' does not only mean copy 'word-for-word', but also 'in substance' (i.e. a copy of the ideas involved). Use of another's work is acceptable, if you acknowledge the source. Therefore, to avoid unintentional plagiarism, if you think a particular author has said something particularly well, then quote him or her directly (using inverted commas) and provide a reference to the relevant article or book beside the quote. For example:

'Plagiarize \'pla-je-,riz also j - -\ vb -rized; -riz·ing vt [plagiary] : to steal and pass off (the ideas or words of another) as one's own : use (a created production) without crediting the source viz: to commit literary theft: present as new and original an idea or product derived from an existing source – **pla·gia·riz·er** *n'*

From: *Webster's New Collegiate Dictionary*, 9th edn (Merriam, Springfield: 1981, p. 870).

Note that this is not plagiarism because the source has been cited.

Evaluating sources of information

One way of assessing the reliability of a piece of scientific information is to think about how it was obtained in the first place. Essentially, 'facts' originate from someone's research or scholarship, whether they are numerical data, descriptions, concepts or interpretations. Sources are divided into two main types:

1. Primary sources – those in which ideas and data are first communicated. The primary literature is generally published in the form of 'papers' (articles) in journals. These are usually refereed by experts in the academic peer group of the author, and they will check the accuracy and originality of the work and report their opinions back to the editors of the journal. This peer review system helps to maintain reliability, but it is not perfect. Books and, more rarely, articles in magazines and newspapers, can also be primary sources but this depends on the nature of the information published rather than the medium. These sources are not formally refereed, although they may be read by editors and lawyers, to check for errors and unsubstantiated or libellous allegations.

2. Secondary sources – those which quote, adapt, interpret, translate, develop or otherwise use information drawn from primary sources. It is the act of quoting or paraphrasing that makes the source secondary, rather than the medium. Reviews are examples of secondary scientific sources, and books and magazine articles are often of this type.

When information is modified for use in a secondary source, alterations are likely to occur, whether intentional or unintentional. Most authors do not deliberately set out to change the meaning of the primary source, but they may unwittingly do so, e.g. in changing text to avoid plagiarism. Others may consciously or unconsciously exert bias in their reporting, for example, by quoting evidence that supports only one side of a debate. Therefore, the closer you can get to the primary source, the more reliable the information is likely to be. On the other hand, modification while creating a secondary source could involve correcting errors, or synthesising ideas and content from multiple sources.

Authorship and provenance

Clearly, much depends on who is writing the source and on what basis (e.g. who paid them?). Consequently, an important way of assessing sources is to investigate the ownership and provenance of the work (who and where it originated from, and why).

Can you identify who wrote the information? If it is signed or there is a 'by-line' showing who wrote it, you might be able to make a judgement on the quality of what you are reading. This may be a simple decision, if you know or can assume that the writer is an authority in the area; otherwise a little research might help (for example, by putting the name into a search engine for the Web). Of course, just because Professor X thinks something does not make it true. However, if you know that this opinion is backed up by years of research and experience, then you might take it a little more seriously than the thoughts of a school pupil. If an author is not cited, effectively nobody is taking responsibility for the content. Could there be a reason for this?

Distinguishing between primary and secondary sources – try the 'IMRaD test'. Many primary sources contain information in the order: Introduction, Materials and Methods, Results and Discussion. If you see this format, and particularly if data from an experiment, study or observation are presented, then you are probably reading a primary source.

Example If a journalist wrote an article about a new 'flesh-eating bug' for the *New York Times* that was based on an article in the *British Medical Journal*, the *New York Times* article would be the secondary source, while the *British Medical Journal* article would be the primary source.

Finding out about authors and provenance – these pieces of information are easy to find in most printed sources and may even be presented just below the title, for convenience. In the case of the Web, it may not be so easy to find what you want. Relevant clues can be obtained from 'home page' links and the header, body and footer information. For example, the domain (p. 54) may be useful, while the use of the tilde symbol (~) in a URL usually indicates a personal, rather than an institutional, website.

Is the author's place of work cited? This might tell you whether the facts or opinions given are based on an academic study. Is there a company with a vested interest behind the content? If the author works for a public body, there may be publication rules to follow and they may even have to submit their work to a publications committee before it is disseminated. They are certainly more likely to get into trouble if they include controversial material.

Evaluating facts and ideas

However reliable the source of a piece of information seems to be, it is probably a good idea to retain a slight degree of scepticism about the facts or ideas involved. Even information from impeccable primary sources may not be perfect – different approaches can give different outcomes, and interpretations can change with time and with further advances in knowledge.

Critically examining facts and ideas is a complex task depending on the particular issues involved and a number of different general approaches can be applied. You will need to decide which of the following general tips are useful in your specific case:

Assessing substance over presentation – just because the information is presented well (e.g. in a glossy magazine or a particularly well-constructed website), this does not necessarily tell you much about its quality. Try to look below the surface, using the methods mentioned in this chapter.

Different types of source/citation – this is covered in Chapter 8.

- Make cross-referencing checks – look at more than one source and compare what is said in each. The cross-referenced sources should be as independent as possible (for example, do not compare a primary source together with a secondary review based on it). If you find that all the sources give a similar picture, then you can be more confident about the reliability of the information.
- Look at the extent and quality of citations – if references are quoted, these indicate that a certain amount of research has been carried out beforehand, and that the ideas or results are based on genuine scholarship. If you are doubtful about the quality of the work, these references might be worth looking at. How up to date are they? Do they cite independent work, or is the author exclusively quoting their own work, or solely the work of one person?
- Consider the age of the source – the fact that a source is old is not necessarily a barrier to truth, but ideas and facts may have altered since the date of publication, and methods may have improved. Can you trace changes through time in the sources available to you? What key events or publications have forced any changes in the conclusions?
- Try to distinguish fact from opinion – to what extent has the author supported a given viewpoint? Have relevant facts been quoted, *via* literature citations or the author's own researches? Are numerical data used to substantiate the points used? Are these reliable and can you verify the information, for example, by looking at the sources cited? Might the author have a reason for putting forward biased evidence to support a personal opinion?
- Analyse the language used – words and their use can be very revealing. Subjective wording might indicate a personal opinion rather than an objective conclusion. Propaganda and personal bias might be indicated by absolute terms, such as 'everyone knows ...'; 'It can be guaranteed that ...' or, a seemingly one-sided consideration of the evidence. How carefully has the author considered the topic? A less studious approach might be indicated by exaggeration, ambiguity or

Table 9.1 Checklist for assessing information in science. How reliable is the information you have been reading? The more 'yes' answers you can give below, the more trustworthy you can assume it to be

Assessing sources

- ❏ Can you identify the author's name?
- ❏ Can you determine what relevant qualifications he/she holds?
- ❏ Can you say who employs the author?
- ❏ Do you know who paid for the work to be done?
- ❏ Is this a primary or secondary source?
- ❏ Is the content original or derived from another source?

Evaluating information

- ❏ Have you checked a range of sources?
- ❏ Is the information supported by relevant literature citation?
- ❏ Is the age of the source likely to be important regarding the accuracy of the information?
- ❏ Have you focused on the substance of the information presented rather than its packaging?
- ❏ Is the information fact or opinion?
- ❏ Have you checked for any logical fallacies in the arguments?
- ❏ Does the language used indicate anything about the status of the information?
- ❏ Have the errors associated with any numbers been taken into account?
- ❏ Have the data been analysed using appropriate statistics?
- ❏ Are any graphs constructed fairly?

Learning from examples – as your lecturers introduce you to case studies, you will see how life scientists have applied critical thinking to understand the nature of biomolecules, cells and organisms. Some of your laboratory sessions may mimic the processes involved – observation, hypothesis, experimental design, data gathering, analysis and formulating a conclusion (see Chapter 30). These skills and approaches can be applied in your degree programme, e.g. when writing about a biological issue or carrying out a research project.

the use of 'journalese' and slang. Always remember, however, that content should be judged above presentation.

- Look closely at any numbers – if the information you are looking at is numerical in form, have statistical errors been taken into consideration, and, where appropriate, quantified? If so, does this help you arrive at a conclusion about how genuine the differences are between important values?
- Think carefully about any hypothesis-testing statistics used – are the methods appropriate? Are the underlying hypotheses the right ones? Have the results of any tests been interpreted correctly in arriving at the conclusion? To deal with these matters, you will need at least a basic understanding of the 'statistical approach' and of commonly used techniques (see Chapters 66 and 67).

Table 9.1 provides a checklist to use when evaluating sources.

Critical thinking

Critical thinking involves the application of logic to a problem or issue. It requires a wide range of skills. Key processes involved include: acquiring and processing information; creating appropriate hypotheses and formulating conclusions; and acting on the conclusions towards a specific objective.

KEY POINT **Critical thinking needs reliable knowledge, but it requires you to use this appropriately to analyse a problem. It can be contrasted with rote learning – where you might memorise facts without an explicit purpose other than building your knowledge base.**

Critical thinking is particularly important in the biosciences, because the subject deals with complex and dynamic systems. These can be difficult to understand for several reasons:

- they are often multi-faceted, involving many interactions;
- it can be difficult to alter one variable in an experiment without producing confounding variables (see p. 184);
- many variables may be unmeasured or unmeasurable;
- heterogeneity (variability) is encountered at all scales from the molecular scale to the whole organism;
- perturbation of the system can lead to unexpected ('counter-intuitive') results.

As a result, conclusions in biological research are seldom clear-cut. Critical thinking allows you to arrive at the most probable conclusion from the results at hand; however, it also involves acknowledging that other conclusions might be possible. It allows you to weigh up these possibilities and find a working hypothesis or explanation, but also to understand that your conclusions are essentially dynamic and might alter when new facts are known. Hypothesis-testing with statistics (Chapter 67) is an important adjunct to critical thinking because it demands the formulation of simple hypotheses and provides rational reasons for making conclusions.

Recognising fallacies in arguments is an important aspect of critical thinking. Philosophers and logicians recognise different forms of argument and many different fallacies in each form. Damer (2000) provides an overview of this wide-ranging and complex topic.

'*You can prove anything with statistics*' – leaving aside the issue that statistical methods deal with probability, not certainty (Chapter 67), it is often possible to analyse and present data in such a way that they support one chosen argument or hypothesis rather than another. Detecting a bias of this kind can be difficult, but the critical thinking skills involved are essential for all life scientists (see e.g. Box 63.2).

Interpreting data

Numerical data

Information presented in public, whether as a written publication or a spoken presentation, is rarely in the same form as it was when first obtained. Chapters 28 and 37 deal with processes in which data are recorded and manipulated – take particular care over percentages and proportions (p. 469), while Chapter 66 describes the standard descriptive statistics used to 'encapsulate' large data sets. Chapter 65 covers some relevant mathematical techniques. Sampling (essentially, obtaining representative measurements) is at the heart of many observational and experimental approaches in the biosciences (see Chapters 28 and 30), and analysis of samples is a key component of hypothesis-testing statistics (Chapter 67). Understanding these topics and carrying out the associated study exercises will help you improve your ability to interpret numerical data.

Graphs

Frequently, understanding and analysis in science depend on your ability to interpret data presented in graphical form. The process of analysing a graph can be split into five phases:

1. Consider the context and aims.
2. Recognise the graph form and examine the axes.
3. Look closely at the scale of each axis.
4. Examine the symbols and curves.
5. Evaluate errors and statistics.

These processes are amplified in Chapter 63.

Sometimes, graphs may mislead. This may be unwitting, as in an unconscious effort to favour a 'pet' hypothesis of the author. Graphs may be used to 'sell' a product, e.g. in advertising, or to favour a viewpoint as, perhaps, in politics. Experience in drawing and interpreting graphs will help you spot these flawed presentations, and understanding how graphs can be erroneously presented (Box 63.2, p. 458) will help you avoid the same pitfalls.

Tables

Tables, especially large ones, can appear as a mass of numbers and thus be more daunting at first sight than graphs. In essence, however, most tables are simpler than most graphs. The process of analysing a table is similar to that of analysing graphs:

1. Consider the context and aims.
2. Examine what information is contained in the rows and columns.
3. Consider the units used and check any footnotes.
4. Compare the data values across rows and/or down columns. Look for patterns, trends, unusual values, etc.
5. Take into account any statistics that are presented.

The construction of tables is dealt with in Chapter 64.

Text reference

Damer, T.E. (2000) *Attacking Faulty Reasoning: A Practical Guide to Fallacy-Free Arguments*, 4th edn. Wadsworth, Belmont.

Sources for further study

Barnard, C.J., Gilbert, F.S. and MacGregor, P.K. (2001) *Asking Questions in Biology: Key Skills for Practical Assessments and Project Work*, 2nd edn. Prentice Hall, Harlow.

Smith, A. *Evaluation of Information Sources*. Available:
http://www.vuw.ac.nz/~agsmith/evaln/evaln.htm
Last accessed 08/01/03.
[Part of the Web-based Information Quality Virtual Library.]

Study exercises

9.1 Distinguish between primary and secondary literature. Based on their titles and any research you can do in your library, determine whether the following journals are primary or secondary sources:

(a) *British Journal of Haematology*
(b) *Proceedings of the National Academy of Sciences*
(c) *Annual Review of Molecular Biology*
(d) *Essays in Biochemistry*
(e) *Microbiological Research*
(f) *Trends in Biotechnology*
(g) *The Lancet*
(h) *Oecologia*
(i) *Scientific American*
(j) *Food Safety News*

9.2 Consider a controversial issue from both sides. Select a current biological topic being discussed in the newspapers or other media. A relatively controversial issue such as 'genetically modified crops' would be a good example. Next, write out a statement that you might use for a motion in a debate, such as 'Genetic modification of crops is a good thing'. Then write at least five points in support of either side of the argument, which you should organise in tabular form. If you can find more than five points, add these to your table, but for each point that you add to one side, you should add one to the other side.

9.3 Analyse graphic presentations in the media. Many newspapers provide graphic presentations related to current issues, and graphs are frequently used in television news reports. Practise critical thinking skills by determining whether the graphs presented are a fair representation of the facts.

10

Using the Internet and World Wide Web

Definitions

Browser – a program to display Web pages and other Internet resources.
FAQ – Frequently Asked Question; a file or Web page giving information on common queries, sometimes used as a file extension (.faq).
FTP – File Transfer Protocol; a mechanism of downloading files.
URL – Uniform Resource Locator; the 'address' for Web resources.

To make the most of information technology (IT) you will need to develop computer-based skills, especially in relation to the Internet and the World Wide Web (the Web). These skills include:

- searching databases and Internet resources, e.g. using a Web browser such as Internet Explorer®, Netscape® or Opera®;
- retrieving networked resources, e.g. to obtain copies of files;
- storing, modifying and analysing information from the Web, e.g. using databases; and
- communicating information over the Internet, e.g. by e-mail.

You will probably receive an introduction to your University's networked IT systems and you will be required to follow rules and regulations that are important for the operation of these systems. Whatever your level of experience with PCs and the Internet, you should also follow the basic guidelines shown in Box 10.1. Reminding yourself of these from time to time will reduce your chances of losing data.

The Internet as a global resource

The key to the rapid development of the Internet was the evolution and expansion of networks – collections of computers that can communicate with each other. They operate at various scales such as Local Area Networks (LANs) and Wide Area Networks (WANs) and these are connected to the Internet, which is thus a complex network of networks (Fig. 10.1). The Internet is loosely organised; no one group runs it or owns it. Instead, many private organisations, universities and government organisations fund and operate discrete parts of it.

The Web is the most popular application of the Internet. It allows easy links to information and files which may be located on networked computers across the world. The Web enables you to access millions of 'home pages' or 'websites' – the initial point of reference with many individuals, institutions and companies. Besides text and images, these sites may contain 'hypertext links', highlighted words or phrases that take you to another Internet location *via* a single mouse click.

You can gain access to the Internet either through a network at your University, at most public libraries, at a commercial 'Internet cafe', or from home via a modem connected to a telephone line, through a dial-in service provider (e.g. America On-line® or CompuServe®). You do not need to understand the technology of the network to use it – most of it is invisible to the user. White and Downs (2001) and Gralla (2001) give further details if you wish to understand more about computers and networks. You need to know the facilities available to you and their relative merits or disadvantages (e.g. speed of data transfer). You also need to understand a little about the nature of Internet addresses.

desktop PC

local area network

Internet service provider

router

Internet networks

Fig. 10.1 Diagram of a network system.

KEY POINT **Most material on the Internet has not been subject to peer review or vetting. Information obtained from the Web or posted on newsgroups may be inaccurate, biased or spoof; do not assume that everything you read is true or even legal.**

Box 10.1 Important guidelines for using PCs and networks

Hardware
- Don't drink or smoke around the computer.
- Try not to turn the computer off more than is necessary.
- Never turn off the electricity supply to the machine while in use.
- Rest your eyes at frequent intervals if working for extended periods at a computer monitor.
- Never try to re-format the hard disk without the help of an expert.

Floppy disks and CDs
- Protect floppy disks and CDs when not in use by keeping them in holders or boxes.
- Never touch the recording surface of a floppy disk or CD.
- Keep disks away from moisture, excess heat or cold.
- Keep disks well away from magnets; remember that these are present in loudspeakers, TVs, etc.
- Don't use disks from others, unless you first check them for viruses.
- Don't insert or remove a disk from the drive when it is operating (drive light on).
- Try not to leave a disk in the drive when you switch the computer off.

File management
- Organise your files in an appropriate set of folders.
- Always use virus-checking programs on copied or imported files before running them.
- Make backups of all important files at frequent intervals (say, every 10 minutes), e.g. when using a word processor or spreadsheet.
- Periodically clear out redundant files.

Network rules
- Never attempt to 'hack' into other people's files.
- Do not give out any of your passwords to others.
- Remember to log out of the network when finished; others can access your files if you forget to log out.
- Be polite when sending e-mail messages.
- Periodically reorganise your e-mail folder(s). These rapidly become filled with acknowledgements and redundant messages that reduce server efficiency and take up your allocated filespace.
- Do not play games without approval – they can affect the operation of the system.

The Golden Rule – always make backup copies of important files and store them well away from your working copies. Ensure that the same accident cannot happen to both copies.

Communicating on the Internet: e-mail, newsgroups and mailing lists

Junk and chain mail on the Internet *– do not redistribute junk or chain mail (the electronic equivalent of chain letters). This activity is likely to be against your University's rules for the use of its computer facilities because it can overload network operations.*

Using e-mail, you can send messages to anyone who is connected to the Internet. The messages themselves are usually simple in format but suitable for straightforward text communication. You can also attach text files, data files, pictures, video clips, sounds and executable files to your messages. The system can be used for personal, commercial and academic purposes, e.g. the submission of work to a tutor. Note, however, that e-mail is not always secure (confidential) and you should be careful about the transmission of sensitive information. Downsides of e-mail include the junk mail (sometimes termed 'spam') that you may receive once your e-mail address is known, and the possibility of receiving a virus in an e-mail attachment.

Specific address information is required to exchange information and e-mail between computers. Although the computer actually uses a complex series of numbers for this purpose, the Domain Name System/Service (DNS) was developed to make this easier for users. Each computer on the Internet is given a domain name (= Internet address) which is a hierarchy of lists and addresses. Thus, 'unn.ac.uk' is the DNS-registered name of Northumbria University: the top (root) level domain is 'uk', identifying its country as United Kingdom, and the next is 'ac', identifying the academic community sub-domain. The final sub-domain is 'unn' identifying the specific academic institution (University of Northumbria at Newcastle). For the purposes of e-mail, the names of individuals at that site may be added

Examples Common domains and sub-domains include:

.com	commercial (USA mainly)
.co	commercial (UK)
.edu	education (USA mainly)
.gov	government (USA and UK)
.mil	military (USA only)
.net	Internet-based companies
.org	organisation
.uk	United Kingdom

before the domain name and the @sign is used to separate them. Thus, the e-mail address of the first author of this book is 'rob.reed@unn.ac.uk'.

The Usenet Newsgroup service is an electronic discussion facility, and there are thousands of newsgroups representing different interests and topics. Any user can contribute to the discussion within a topic by posting their own message; it is like e-mail, but without privacy, since your message becomes available to all other subscribers. To access a newsgroup, your system must be running, or have access to, a newsgroup server which has subscribed to the newsgroup of interest.

With mailing lists, messages sent to the list address are distributed automatically to all members of the mailing list, via their personal e-mailbox, keeping them up to date on the particular topic of the mailing list. To receive such messages, you will need to join the mailing list. Relevant mailing lists for biological sciences can be found at http://www.jiscmail.ac.uk/. Take care not to join too many lists, as you will receive a large number of messages, and many are likely to be of only marginal interest. A number of mailing lists also have archived files, offering a more selective means of locating relevant material.

Internet tools

The specific programs you will use for accessing the Internet will depend on what has been installed locally, on the network you are using, and on your Internet service provider. The best way to learn the features of the programs is to try them out, making full use of whatever help services are available.

Internet browsers

These are software programs that interact with remote server computers around the world to carry out the tasks of requesting, retrieving and displaying the information you require. Many different browsers exist, but the most popular are Internet Explorer® (Microsoft) and Netscape Navigator® (Netscape Communications Corporation), both of which are available for PC and Apple Mac®. These two browsers dominate the market and have plug-ins and add-on programs available that allow, for example, video sequences to be seen on-line. Many browsers incorporate e-mail and newsgroup functions. The standard functions of browsers include:

- accessing Web documents;
- following links to other documents;
- printing the current document;
- maintaining a history of visited URLs (including 'bookmarks' for key sites);
- searching for a term in a document;
- viewing images and image maps.

Browsers provide access to millions of websites. Certain sites specialise in providing catalogued links to other sites; these are known as portals and can be of enormous help when searching within a particular area of interest. Your University's library website will almost certainly provide a useful portal to catalogues and search services, often arranged by subject area and this is often the first port of call for electronic resources; get to know your way around this part of the website as early as possible during your course.

Using newsgroups – these can be useful for getting answers to a specific problem: just post a query to the appropriate group and wait for someone to reply. Bear in mind that this may be the view of an individual person.

Definition

Bookmark – a feature of browsers that allows you to save details of websites you have visited. This is termed 'add to favorites' in Internet Explorer®. Bookmarks save you the trouble of remembering complex URL names and of typing them into the browser's address window.

Examples Useful web portals
BIOME – Internet Resources for the Health and Life Sciences, at: http://biome.ac.uk/
BioMedNet – for Biomedical Research, at: http://www.bmn.com/
OMIM – on-line Mendelian inheritance in man – http://www.ncbi.nlm.nih.gov/omim/

When using a browser program to get to a particular page of information on the Web, all you require is the location of that page, i.e. the URL (Uniform Resource Locator). The URL always takes the same format, beginning with http:// and followed by the various terms that direct the system to the appropriate site. If you don't have a specific URL in mind but wish to explore appropriate sites, you will need to use a search tool with the browser.

Locating information on the Web – *useful searching systems are located at the following URLs (some may be directly accessible from your browser):*
http://www.altavista.com/sites/search/ webadv (advanced search)
http://www.google.com/advanced_search (advanced search) http://www.scirus.com (subject-specific searching in science/ engineering) http://uk.searchengine.com (UK-restricted search engine)

Search tools

With the proliferation of information on the Web, one of the main problems is finding the exact information you require. There are a variety of information services that you can use to filter the material on the network. These include:

- search engines;
- meta-search engines;
- subject directories;
- subject gateways (portals).

Box 10.2 Useful tips for using search engines

- **Keywords should be chosen with care.** Try to make them as specific as possible, e.g. search for 'archaebacteria' 'or Archaea', rather than 'bacteria' or 'micro-organisms'.

- **Most search engines are case-insensitive.** Thus 'Nobel Prize' will return the same number of hits as 'nobel prize'. If in doubt, use lower case throughout.

- **Putting keyword phrases in double quotes (e.g. "capillary electrophoresis") will result in a search for sites with the phrase as a whole** rather than sites with both (all) parts of the phrase as separate words (i.e. 'capillary' and 'electrophoresis' at different places within a site). This feature allows you to include common words normally excluded in the search, such as 'the'.

- **Use multiple words/phrases plus similar words to improve your search,** for example 'terrestrial crustacean "land crab" Australia'. If you can, use scientific terms, as you are likely to find more relevant sites, e.g. search for the name of a particular species such as *Coenobita compressus*.

- **Adding words preceded with + or − will add or exclude sites with that word present** (e.g. 'blood diseases −leukaemia' will search for all blood diseases excluding those mentioning leukaemia). This feature can also be used to include common words normally excluded by the search engine.

- **Check that your search terms have the correct spelling**, otherwise you may only find sites with the same mis-spelled word. In some cases, the search engine may prompt you with an alternative

(correct) spelling. Remember that US and UK spellings may differ (e.g. hemolysis/haemolysis) and a search may only find hits from sites that use the spelling you can specify.

- **Boolean operators (AND, OR, NOT) can be used to specify combinations of keywords** to more precisely filter the sites identified (e.g. 'plant NOT engineering' will avoid sites about engineering plant and focus on biological material – though this combination might omit genetic engineering of plants).

- **Some search engines allow 'wildcards' to be introduced with the symbol** *. For example, this will allow you to specify the root of a word and include all possible endings, as with anthropomorph*, which would find anthropomorphic, anthropomorphism, etc. If the search engine does not allow wildcards (e.g. Google®), then you will need to be especially careful with the keywords used, including all possible words of relevance.

- **Numbers can be surprisingly useful in search engines.** For example, typing in EC 1.1.1.1 will find sites concerned with alcohol dehydrogenase, as this is its Enzyme Commission code number (p. 378). If you know the phone number for a person, institute or company or the ISBN of the book, this can often help you find relevant pages quickly.

- **If you arrive at a large site and cannot find the point at which your searched word or phrase appears, press** Control **and** F **together** and a 'local' search window will appear, allowing you to find the point(s) where it is mentioned.

Search engines such as Google® (http://www.google.com), AltaVista® (http://uk.altavista.com) and Lycos® (http://www.lycos.com) are tools designed to search, gather, index and classify Web-based information. Searching is usually by keyword(s), although specific phrases can be defined. Many search engines offer advanced searching tools such as the use of Boolean operators to specify combinations of keywords to more precisely filter the sites. Box 10.2 provides tips for refining keyword searches.

It is important to realise that each search engine will cover at most about 40 per cent of the available sites and if you want to carry out an exhaustive search it is necessary to use several to cover as much of the Web as possible. Meta-search engines make this easier. These operate by combining collections of search engines. Examples include Mamma (http://www.mamma.com/), Dogpile (http://www.dogpile.com/index.gsp/) and Metacrawler (http://www.metacrawler.com/index.html/).

Box 10.3 How to evaluate information on the World Wide Web

It is often said that 'you can find anything on the Web'. The two main disadvantages of this are, firstly, that you may need to sift through many sources before you find what you are looking for and, secondly, that the sources you find will vary in their quality and validity. *It is important to realise that evaluating sources is a key aspect of using the Internet for academic purposes, and one that you will need to develop during the course of your studies* (see also Chapter 9). The ease with which you can 'point and click' to reach various sources should not make you complacent about evaluating their information content. The following questions can help you to assess the quality of a website – the more times you can answer 'yes', the more credible the source is likely to be, and *vice versa*:

Authority
- Is the author identified?
- Are the author's qualifications or credentials given?
- Is the owner, publisher or sponsoring organisation identified?
- Is an address given (postal and/or e-mail)?

It is sometimes possible to get information on authority from the site's metadata (try the 'View' 'Source' option in Internet Explorer, or look at the URL to see if it gives any clues as to the organisation, e.g. whether the domain name ends in .ac, .edu, .gov or .org, rather than .co or .com).

Content
- Is there any evidence that the information has been peer-reviewed (p. 106), edited or otherwise validated, or is it based on such sources?
- Is the information factual or based on personal opinion?
- Is the factual data original (primary) or derived from other sources (secondary)?

- Are the sources of specific factual information detailed in full (Chapter 8)?
- Is there any indication that the information is up to date, or that the site has been recently updated?
- What is the purpose of the site and who is it aimed at?
- Is the content relevant to the question you are trying to answer?
- Is there any evidence of a potential conflict of interest, or bias? (Is the information comprehensive and balanced, or narrowly focused?)
- Did you find the information via a subject-specific website (e.g. a bioscience gateway such as BIOME), or through a more general source, such as a search engine (e.g. Google®)?

The above questions are similar to those that you would use in assessing the value of a printed resource (pp. 48–49), and similar criteria should be applied to Web-based information. You should be especially wary of sites containing unattributed factual information or data whose primary source is not given.

Presentation
- What is your overall impression of how well the site has been put together?
- Are there any grammatical or spelling mistakes?
- Are there links to other websites, to support statements and factual information?

The care with which a site has been constructed can give you an indication of the credibility of the author/organisation. However, while a poorly-presented site may cause you to question the credibility of the information, the reverse is not always necessarily true: don't be taken in by a slick, well-presented website – authority and content are *always* more important than presentation.

Some useful approaches to searching include the following:

- For a comprehensive search, use a variety of tools including search engines, meta-search engines and portals or directories.
- For a complex, finely specified search, employ Boolean operators and other tools to refine your keywords as fully as possible (Box 10.2). Some search engines allow you to include and exclude terms or restrict by date.
- Use 'cascading' searching when available – this is searching within the results of a previous search.
- Use advanced search facilities to limit your search, where possible, to the type of medium you are looking for (e.g. graphics, video), language, sites in a specific country (e.g. UK) or to a subject area (e.g. news only).

However well defined your search is, you will still need to evaluate the information obtained. Chapter 9 covers general aspects of this topic while Box 10.3 provides specific advice on assessing the quality of information provided on websites.

Directories

A directory is a list of Web resources organised by subject. It can usually be browsed and may or may not have a search facility. Directories often contain better quality information than the lists produced by search engines, as they have been evaluated, often by subject specialists or librarians. The BUBL information service life sciences directory of links, at: http://bubl.ac.uk/link/lif.html, is a good example.

FTP (File Transfer Protocol) and file transmission

FTP is a method of transferring files across the Internet. In many cases the files are made available for 'anonymous' FTP access, i.e. you do not need a previously arranged password. Log in as 'anonymous' and give your e-mail address as the password. Use your Web browser to locate the file you want and then use its FTP software to transfer it to your computer.

KEY POINT The transfer of files can result in the transfer of associated viruses. Always check new files for viruses before running them. Make frequent updates to your virus-checking software.

Using the Internet as a resource

A common way of finding information on the Web is by browsing or 'surfing'. However, this can be time-consuming; try to restrict yourself to sites known to be relevant to the topic of interest. Some of the most useful sites are those that provide hypertext links to other locations. Some other resources you can use on the Web are:

- Libraries, publishers and commercial organisations. Your University library is likely to subscribe to one or more databases providing access to scientific articles; these include BIDS (Bath Information and Database Services (http://www.bids.ac.uk), ISI® Web of Science (http://wos.mimas.ac.uk), and Science Direct (http://www.sciencedirect.com). A password is usually required, especially for off-campus use; consult your library staff for further details. Some scientific database sites give free access, without subscription or password; these include

---

'Dissecting' a Web address – you can often find out more about a particular site by progressively deleting sections of the URL from the right-hand side. This will often take you to the home page of the organisation or company involved.

Using traditional sources – remember that using the Internet to find information is not a substitute for visiting your University library. Internet resources complement rather than replace CD-ROM and more traditional printed sources.

Examples Selected websites of biological interest:
Biochemical Society:
http://www.biochemsoc.org.uk/default.htm
Genetics Society:
http://www.genetics.org.uk
Human Genome Organisation (HUGO):
http://www.gene.ucl.ac.uk/hugo
LTSN Bioscience Imagebank:
http://bio.ltsn.ac.uk/resources/bioscience/ibank/ibankhome.htm
Society for General Microbiology Web resources: http://www.socgenmicrobiol.org.uk/links.htm
UK university library catalogues: http://www.niss.ac.uk/lis/obi/obi.html
World Wide Web Virtual Library (Science): http://vlib.org/Science.html

PubMed/Medline (http://www.ncbi.nlm.nih.gov) and the Highwire Library of Sciences and Medicine (http://highwire.stanford.edu). Others allow free searching, but require payment for certain articles, e.g. SciBase (http://www.thescientificworld.com/scibase/) and Infotrieve (http://www4.infotrieve.com). Publishers such as Pearson and booksellers such as Amazon.com® provide on-line catalogues and e-commerce sites that can be useful sources of information (see http://www.pearsoneduc.com and http://www.amazon.com).

- On-line journals and e-books. A number of traditional journals have websites. You can keep up to date by visiting the websites of *Nature* (http://www.nature.com), *New Scientist* (http://www.newscientist.com) and *Scientific American* (http://www.sciam.com), or ScienceDirect journals (at http://www.sciencedirect.com/science/journals). Some scientific societies make their journals and other publications available via their websites, e.g. the American Society for Microbiology, at: http://www.asmusa.org. Journals solely published in electronic format are also available (e.g. *Molecular Vision*, http://www.molvis.org/molvis) but some require a subscription password for access; check whether your institute is a subscriber.

- Data and images. Archives of text material, video clips and photographs can be accessed, and much of the material is readily available. The Biological Image Gallery (http://www.academicinfo.net/bioimage.html) is a good example. When downloading such material, you should (i) check that you are not breaching copyright and (ii) avoid potential plagiarism by giving a full citation of the source, if you use such images in an assignment (see p. 47).

- Biological institutions. Many culture collections, scientific societies and other biological institutions around the world are now on-line. Use their sites to obtain specific information about collections, resources, etc. They frequently provide lists of other relevant sites or topics, e.g. the Society for General Microbiology (http://www.socgenmicrobiol.org.uk).

- Databases. In addition to those covering the scientific literature (e.g. ISI® Web of Science, or the PubMed service of the US National Library of Medicine), others focus on specific topics (e.g. biodiversity on the Internet, http://www.biodiversity.org.uk/ibs/; or academic employment, http://www.jobs.ac.uk). Chapter 11 provides further guidance on using databases for the analysis of biomolecular structure (bioinformatics).

Text references

Gralla, P. (2001) *How the Internet Works*, 6th edn. Que, Indianapolis.

White, R. and Downs, T. (2001) *How Computers Work*, 6th edn. Que, Indianapolis.

Sources for further study

Anon. *Search Basics*. Available:
http://www.frame-uk.demon.co.uk/guide/search_basics.htm
Last accessed 01/08/03.
[Demon Internet pages on browser searching.]

Anon. *Using the Internet*. Available:
http://www.sofweb.vic.edu.au/Internet/research.htm
Last accessed 08/01/03.
[Provided by the State of Victoria, Department of Education and Training.]

Brandt, D.S. *Why We Need to Evaluate What We Find on the Internet*. Available: http://thorplus.lib.purdue.edu/~techman/eval.html
Last accessed 08/01/03.

Dussart, G. (2002) *Biosciences on the Internet*. Wiley, Chichester.

Grassian, E. *Thinking Critically about World Wide Web Resources*. Available:
http://www.library.ucla.edu/libraries/college/help/critical/index.htm
Last accessed 08/01/03.

Isaacs, T. and Isaacs, M. (2000) *Internet Users Guide to Network Resource Tools*, 2000 edn. Addison-Wesley, Harlow.

Winship, I. and McNab, A. (2000) *Students' Guide to the Internet 2000–2001*. Library Association, London.

Study exercises

10.1 Explore the resources of the Web using a search engine. Pick a search engine (p. 56) and use it to find the answers to the following questions:

(a) Who is Barbara McClintock, and what is she famous for? What prize did she win and when?

(b) What is the common name for *Arabidopsis thaliana*?

(c) What is the postal address of the UK Biochemical Society?

10.2 Compare results from a variety of search engines. First, think of an appropriate biological keyword or phrase (e.g. a species name) and enter this into several search engines. Make sure that you include meta-search engines such as Mamma. Compare the outcomes to reveal the strengths and weaknesses of the individual search engines. Work with a colleague to compare different searches on a quantitative (i.e. number of hits) and qualitative (quality of hits) basis.

10.3 Organise your bookmarks. Enter the *'Organize favorites'* menu for your preferred browser and create folders with appropriate headings. Move existing bookmarks to these folders and save any new ones appropriately. Doing this will help you find bookmarks more easily, rather than searching through long lists.

11 Bioinformatics – Internet resources

Bioinformatics is a term used to describe the application of computer-based techniques in the biological sciences and, in particular, to the analysis of nucleic acid sequences (genomics, transcriptomics) and to the protein sequences predicted from nucleic acid sequence data (proteomics). These complex molecules contain a large amount of information within their structures: analysis of this information by visual examination is impractical for all but the smallest polynucleotide or polypeptide fragments.

KEY POINT The only practical approach to understanding the information in complex macromolecules is to use a computer – typically, by comparing sequence data for all or part of a specific biomolecule with that of others in a database.

Table 11.1 gives details of some of the most important databases accessible *via* the Internet.

A range of programs and packages can be used to analyse nucleic acid and protein sequences. Many programs can be used on-line, *via* the Internet, while others can be downloaded using FTP (p. 58), for local operation. In most instances, the information and software are freely available. Alternatively, commercial packages can be used, with database information either downloaded *via* the Internet, or supplied on CD-ROM, e.g. for use with a group of students. The large number of different programs available is a reflection of the various algorithms used for analysis, and such programs are likely to be updated in parallel with advances in computer hardware/software. When using a new program, make use of the help facilities to familiarise yourself with the operating principles.

Primary sequence databases

The major databases holding primary sequence information for nucleic acids and proteins are operated by the European Bioinformatics Institute (EBI, at http://www.ebi.ac.uk), the National Center for Biotechnology Information (NCBI, at http://www.ncbi.nlm.nih.gov) and the DNA Data Bank of Japan (DDBJ, at http://www.ddbj.nig.ac.jp). These databases hold comprehensive information submitted by researchers and sequencing groups across the world, with collaborative data-sharing on a daily basis, as part of the International Nucleotide Sequence Database Consortium.

Nucleic acid analysis
A typical application would be to investigate whether a nucleic acid sequence obtained, for example, as part of a cloning project (p. 443), has been reported previously. Table 11.1 gives details of URLs for the nucleic acid databases of the European Molecular Biology Laboratory (EMBL) and the NCBI. These databases allow you to:

- enter a particular nucleic acid sequence and edit the sequence, if required;
- find and retrieve a nucleotide sequence from the database using a keyword, author name, organism name or accession number, where known;

Table 11.1 Some useful databases and other Internet locations relevant to bioinformatics

Major nucleic acid sequence databases

EMBL nucleotide sequence database	http://www.ebi.ac.uk/embl/Access/index.html
NCBL GenBank®	http://www.ncbi.nlm.nih.gov/Genbank

Major protein sequence databases

SWISS-PROT (EBI protein sequence database)	http://ca.expasy.org/
TrEMBL (translated sequence database)	http://www.ebi.ac.uk/trembl
PIR (protein information resource)	http://pir.georgetown.edu

Other bioinformatics databases

PROSITE (protein motifs)	http://ca.expasy.org/prosite/
PRINTS	http://www.bioinf.man.ac.uk/dbbrowser/PRINTS
ExPaSy proteomics resource	http://ca.expasy.org
PDB (Protein Data Bank)	http://www.rcsb.org/pdb
CAZy (carbohydrate-active enzymes)	http://afmb.cnrs-mrs.fr/CAZY/index.html
MEROPS (proteases database)	http://metrops.sanger.ac.uk
Transport protein database	http://tcdb.ucsd.edu/tcdb/tcfamily.php?superfam=1.B
DOLOP (database of bacterial lipoproteins)	http://www.mrc-lmb.cam.ac.uk/genomes/dolop/class/ad.htm

Searching primary databases – *a search of the EMBL nucleic acid database can be carried out using BLAST (Fig. 11.1) to locate related sequences.*

- translate a nucleotide sequence into an amino acid sequence and *vice versa*;
- search for any resemblance between a particular sequence and sequences within the database, e.g. by comparing and aligning the sequence for several nucleic acids or proteins, to identify regions of sequence similarity (see Fig. 11.1);
- carry out phylogenetic analysis, constructing 'ancestry trees' to show the most likely evolutionary relationships between sequences from various organisms.

Other programs allow you to analyse nucleic acid sequence information in more detail, for example:

- to assemble/align sequence fragments into contiguous sequences, also known as 'contigs'. This type of alignment is particularly useful for sets of nucleic acid fragments from a clone library (p. 447);
- to simulate *in vitro* manipulation and cloning procedures, including the preparation of restriction digests, designing oligonucleotide probes and primers, and simulating PCR (p. 437).

Palindrome – *a sequence reading the same in both directions, e.g. GACCAG. These are often sites at which restriction enzymes cleave DNA (see p. 429).*

- to search for structural and functional 'motifs' within the nucleic acid sequence, including palindromes, restriction sites (p. 428), likely promoter or control sites and regions that might form secondary structures, such as hairpin loops;
- to identify likely coding regions (e.g. open reading frames, exons) and non-coding regions (e.g. introns, repeat sequences) in eukaryotic DNA, 'start' and 'stop' codons, etc. The starting point for this analysis is the creation of a 'six frame translation' of the target sequence (see Fig. 11.2).

```
H. sapiens    atgtatggcattgagaatgaagtcttcctgagccttccatgtatcctcaatgcccggggg
              ||||| ||||| ||||| |||||||||| || || || ||||| ||||| |||||
R. norvegicus atgtacggcatcgagaacgaagtcttcctcagtctcccgtgcatccttaatgctcggggg
```

Fig. 11.1 Representative output from a BLAST (basic local alignment search tool) alignment search for DNA sequences from part of the lactate dehydrogenase genes of *Homo sapiens* and *Rattus norvegicus*. Here, identical bases are shown in black, and non-identical bases are shown in blue. This region shows 49 identical bases out of 59, i.e. $49 \div 59 \times 100 = 83\%$ similarity (to the nearest integer).

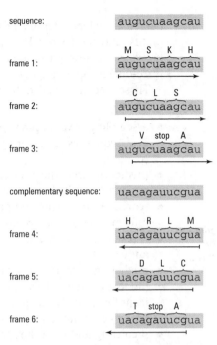

sequence: augucuaagcau

frame 1:
M S K H
augucuaagcau

frame 2:
C L S
augucuaagcau

frame 3:
V stop A
augucuaagcau

complementary sequence: uacagauucgua

frame 4:
H R L M
uacagauucgua

frame 5:
D L C
uacagauucgua

frame 6:
T stop A
uacagauucgua

Fig. 11.2 'Six frame translation' of a DNA sequence. The triplet codons corresponding to each amino acid are given in Table 60.1 (p. 427) and the single letter amino acid code is explained in Table 50.1 (p. 347). Note that the complementary sequence is translated in the reverse direction to the original sequence.

Analysis of proteins and polypeptides

The principal protein sequence databases are SWISSPROT and TrEMBL in Europe, together with PIR in the USA: Table 11.1 gives their current Internet locations. These databases can be searched using a range of programs equivalent to those described above for nucleic acid analysis, allowing the operator to:

- locate and retrieve a particular protein or amino acid sequence from the database by keyword, author name, organism name or accession number;
- enter and edit (cut and paste) a particular amino acid sequence, or convert a nucleotide sequence into an amino acid sequence, and *vice versa*;
- search the database for sequences with a perfect match, or for similarities in primary or secondary structure at a specified level of homology; such searches may be more informative than those based on DNA homology, since protein sequence information (based on 20 different amino acid residues) is more complex than nucleic acid sequence information (based on four different nucleotides);
- compare and align the amino acid sequences of several proteins, to identify particular regions of similarity and dissimilarity.

Other bioinformatics databases

Pattern recognition databases for proteins

These have been created using primary sequence data, to provide information on the patterns identified within proteins. The representative examples given in Table 11.1 include the PROSITE and PRINTS

Using databases – *many of the database websites are rather complex and newcomers may find them a little difficult to navigate, especially if you are just browsing. The best approach is to try out the on-line tutorials, to get a feel for how the website operates. If the URL changes, use a search engine (p. 56) to locate the new website.*

databases, which identify protein families by their diagnostic 'signature' motifs, and the <u>Ex</u>pert <u>P</u>rotein <u>A</u>nalysis <u>Sy</u>stem (ExPaSy) website, which provides a gateway to the general analysis of protein structure, including three-dimensional imaging.

These 'second-level' databases can be used for a range of purposes, including:

- assembling overlapping peptide fragments, based on their amino acid sequences, e.g. during sequence analysis of an individual protein (p. 350);
- predicting secondary structure from a primary sequence, identifying regions most likely to exist as α-helices or β-sheets, etc.;
- searching for motifs and patterns within a sequence that might provide information on the origins and/or possible function(s) of the protein;
- investigating properties such as hydropathy, solvent accessibility and antigenicity;
- predicting potential sites of post-translational modification;
- modelling the likely three-dimensional structure of the protein, identifying likely membrane-spanning regions, active sites and other tertiary and quaternary features;
- predicting and modelling the effects of changes in primary or secondary structure on protein characteristics and three-dimensional organisation.

Protein-specific databases

Several databases have been created to collect together information on a particular class of proteins – many are devoted to particular enzymes or groups of enzymes. An example of a second-level protein database is that devoted to the analysis of enzymes that degrade, modify or create glycosidic bonds, the <u>c</u>arbohydrate-<u>a</u>ctive en<u>zy</u>mes (CAZy database, Table 11.1). This website brings together information on the various families of enzymes that interact with carbohydrates, enabling researchers to compare sequences against known catalytic and carbohydrate-binding modules, arranged by enzyme class and by organism. Links to related websites are also included. Another example is the MEROPS protease database, which provides a structure-based catalogue of proteases and peptidases, giving amino acid and nucleotide sequences, classification and nomenclature, plus links to relevant literature through the NCBI Entrez/ PubMed search engine (p. 65). If you are looking for information on a particular enzyme or other protein, it may be worth using a search engine (p. 56) to see whether a specific database has been created (additional examples are given in Table 11.1).

Protein structure

The Protein Data Bank (PDB) is the worldwide repository for three-dimensional structures of proteins (Table 11.1), also serving as a general portal for structural information on biological macromolecules. The database can be searched by identity number (e.g. 1ALB is the code for an adipocyte lipid-binding protein) or by name (note that this is a US resource, so using the US spelling 'hemoglobin' locates more structures than using the UK spelling). Structures can be viewed in a variety of formats, including those compatible with molecular graphics software such as RasMol and Chime. Additional information includes secondary structure (helices, sheets, hairpins, etc.), crystallographic data, geometry, etc., plus links to related sites. Figure 11.3 shows an example of a typical

Hydropathy – hydrophobic interactions within a biomolecule; often important in determining folding and three-dimensional structure.

Example   RasMol is a molecular graphics program that enables the user to visualise the structure of proteins, nucleic acids and small biomolecules – it can be obtained by anonymous FTP (p. 58) from ftp://ftp.dcs.ed.ac.uk/pub/rasmol

Table 11.2   Other Internet locations relevant to bioinformatics

Databases and resources for particular organisms

Arabidopsis information resource	http://www.arabidopsis.org
Drosophila database (flybase)	http://flybase.bio.indiana.edu
Caenorhabditis genetics centre	http://biosci.umn.edu/CGC/CGChomepage.htm
E. coli genome project	http://www.genome.wisc.edu
Human genome project (US site)	http://www.ornl.gov/hgmis
HIV sequence database	http://hiv-web.lanl.gov/content/index
Plant genome data and information centre	http://www.nal.usda.gov/pgdic
Saccharomyces genome database	http://genome-www.stanford.edu/Saccharomyces
Mosquito genomics server	http://klab.agsci.colostate.edu

Portals and directories

The bioinformatics resource	http://www.hgmp.mrc.ac.uk/CCP11/index.jsp
Bioinformatics resource centre	http://www.hgmp.mrc.ac.uk/Bioinformatics
Molecular biology on-line	http://www.r9corporation.fsnet.co.uk/index.htm

Fig. 11.3. Representation of the three-dimensional structure of a pectate lyase from *Cellvibrio japonicus*. This is a solid ribbon display, with helices and sheets shown in blue. The cleft, in which the plant polysaccharide is bound, is clearly visible on the left of the structure. Image courtesy of G. Black.

output – in this instance, for the 3D structure of the enzyme pectate lyase, a virulence factor in some plant pathogenic bacteria.

Other Internet resources

Several websites have been constructed to bring together bioinformatic data and related information for a single organism – many of these sites have been produced as a result of a genome-sequencing project for a particular organism, e.g. the human genome mapping project (UK website at http://www.hgmp.mrc.ac.uk). In addition to the nucleic acid and/or protein sequence data available in the primary databases, the organism-specific websites provide a broader range of information and resources, often including links to other Web locations. As such, they can be a useful means of accessing relevant Internet sites: Table 11.2 gives examples, along with the locations of several portals and directories: these may be useful when researching a topic, e.g. as part of an assignment, or when planning a project (p. 191).

Sources for further study

(Note also the websites given in Tables 11.1 and 11.2.)

Anon. *PubMed Homepage*. Available:
http://www.ncbi.nlm.nih.gov/entrez/query.fcgi?db = PubMed
Last accessed 08/01/03.
[On-line access to details of biomedical papers and publications.]

Baxevanis, A.D. (ed.) (2001) *Bioinformatics: A Practical Guide to the Analysis of Genes and Proteins*, 2nd edn. Wiley-Liss, New York.

Brown, T.A. and Brown, A. (1999) *Genomes*. Wiley-Liss, New York.
[This book focuses on genomics, in contrast to more traditional molecular biology textbooks, which emphasise individual genes.]

Dennis, C., Gallagher, R. and Watson, J. (2002) *The Human Genome*. Palgrave Macmillan, New York.

Durbin, R. (ed.) (1999) *Biological Sequence Analysis: Probabilistic Models of Proteins and Nucleic Acids*. Cambridge University Press, Cambridge.

Mount, D.W. (2001) *Bioinformatics: Sequence and Genome Analysis.* Cold Spring Harbor Laboratory, Cold Spring Harbor. [Provides a good introduction and overview of bioinformatics.]

Rashidi, H. and Buehler, L.K. (2000) *Bioinformatics Basics: Applications in Biological Science and Medicine.* CRC Press, Boca Raton.

Study exercises

11.1 Investigate the potential of the Internet for locating information relevant to bioinformatics. Using the Web, answer the following questions:
  (a) How many nucleotide sequences are currently held by GenBank®?
  (b) What and where is Hinxton Hall?
  (c) Where is the European Molecular Biology Laboratory (EMBL) Mouse Biology Program located?
  (d) What is the total number of protein structures currently held by the Protein Data Bank?
  (e) What is the full postal address of the US National Center for Biotechnology Information?

11.2 Search GenBank® nucleotide database using a DNA sequence. Carry out a BLASTN search of GenBank® (at: http://www.ncbi.nlm.nih.gov/BLAST) for the following nucleotide sequence: **actgactcatagagtacccaccgtggtgct**. How many 'hits' do you find? What is the length of the sequence showing complete identity?

11.3 Search the NCBI database using a protein sequence. Carry out a BLASTP search (at: http://www.ncbi.nlm.nih.gov/BLAST) for the following amino acid sequence: **NVKAAWGKVGAHAGEYGAE** (note – p. 347 gives details of the code letters corresponding to each amino acid). (a) What protein is this sequence most likely to correspond to? (b) Which sequence gives the highest alignment score? (c) What is the highest score for a sequence from *Homo sapiens*?

11.4 Convert a DNA base sequence to an amino acid sequence. Using the 'DNA→protein translate tool' of the ExPaSy server (at: http://ca.expasy.org/tools/dna.html), carry out a six-frame translation of the following nucleotide sequence: **tcagagagaacccaccat**. Which of the six frames contains both a start and stop codon and what is the predicted amino acid sequence for this frame?

11.5 Use the Protein Data Bank to investigate the structure of an enzyme. Search the PDB archive (at: http://www.rcsb.org/pdb/) using 'beta-galactosidase' as the keyword in the SearchLite search tool, and locate the entry for the β-galactosidase ($= \beta$-glycosidase) enzyme of *Sulfolobus solfataricus*, deposited on 19 September 1996. Use the 'explore' command to find out: (a) the number of sub-units in the holoenzyme; (b) the number of amino acids residues in each chain; (c) the number of helices in each chain. Next, use the 'view structure' option to look at the 3D configuration (either in quick PDB format, or using Rasmol, if this program is available on your PC, or network): (d) save an image as a file and then incorporate it into a Word® document, as you might in an assignment.

Using spreadsheets

Spreadsheet – a display of a grid of cells into which numbers, text or formulae can be typed to form a worksheet. Each cell is uniquely identifiable by its column and row number combination (i.e. its 2-D coordinates) and can contain a formula which makes it possible for an entry to one cell to alter the contents of one or more other cells.

Template – a pre-designed spreadsheet without data but including all formulae necessary for (repeated) data analysis.

Macro – a sequence of user-defined instructions carried out by the spreadsheet, allowing complex repeated tasks to be 'automated'.

Office suite – a package of complementary and integrated programs such as a word processor, a spreadsheet and a database.

The spreadsheet is one of the most powerful and flexible microcomputer applications. It can be described as the electronic equivalent of a paper-based longhand calculation, where the sums are carried out automatically. Spreadsheets provide a dynamic method of storing, manipulating and analysing data sets. Advantages of spreadsheets include:

- Ease and convenience – especially when complex calculations are repeated on different sets of data.
- Improved presentation – data can be produced in graphical or tabular form to a very high quality.
- Integration with other programs – graphs and tables can be exported to other compatible programs, such as a word processor in the same office suite.
- Useful tools – advanced features include hypothesis-testing statistics, database features and macros.

Spreadsheets can be used to:

- store and manipulate raw data by removing the drudgery of repeated calculations, allowing easy transformation of data and calculation of statistics;
- graph out your data rapidly to get an instant evaluation of results. Printouts can be used in practical and project reports;
- carry out statistical analysis by built-in procedures or by allowing construction of formulae for specific tasks;
- model 'what if' situations where the consequences of changes in data can be seen and evaluated.

The spreadsheet (Fig. 12.1) is divided into rows (identified by numbers) and columns (identified by alphabetic characters). Each individual combination of column and row forms a cell which can contain either a

Fig. 12.1 The appearance of a typical spreadsheet, showing cells, rows and columns, toolbars, etc. Screen shot of Microsoft Excel 2002 reprinted by permission from Microsoft Corporation. Copyright © 2001 Microsoft Corporation.

data item, a formula, or a piece of text called a label. Formulae can include scientific and/or statistical functions and/or a reference to other cells or groups of cells (often called a range). Complex systems of data input and analysis can be constructed (models). The analysis, in part or complete, can be printed out. New data can be added at any time and the sheet recalculated. You can construct templates, pre-designed spreadsheets containing the formulae required for repeated data analyses, adding the data when they become available.

The power a spreadsheet offers is directly related to your ability to create models that are accurate and templates that are easy to use. The sequence of operations required is:

1. Determine what information/statistics you want to produce.
2. Identify the variables you will need to use, both for original data that will be entered and for any intermediate calculations that might be required.
3. Set up areas of the spreadsheet for data entry, calculation of intermediate values (statistical values such as sums of squares, etc.), calculation of final statistics and, if necessary, a summary area.
4. Establish the format of the numeric data if this is different from the default values. This can be done globally (affecting the entire spreadsheet) or locally (affecting only a specified part of the spreadsheet).
5. Establish the column widths required for the various activities.
6. Enter labels: use extensively for annotation.
7. Enter a test set of values to use during formula entry: use a fully worked example to check that formulae are working correctly.
8. Enter the formulae required to make all the calculations, both intermediate and final. Check that results are correct using the test data.

The spreadsheet is then ready for use. Delete all the test data values and you have created your template. Save the template to a disk and it is then available for repeated operations.

Data entry

Spreadsheets have built-in commands which allow you to control the layout of data in the cells. These include number format, the number of decimal places to be shown (the spreadsheet always calculates using eight or more places), the cell width and the location of the entry within the cell (left, right or centre). An auto-entry facility assists greatly in entering large amounts of data by moving the entry cursor either vertically or horizontally as data are entered. Recalculation default is usually automatic so that when a new data value is entered the entire sheet is recalculated immediately.

The parts of a spreadsheet

Labels

These identify the contents of rows and columns. They are text characters, and cannot be used in calculations. Separate them from the

Using templates – *these should contain:*
- *a data input section*
- *data transformation and/or calculation sections*
- *a results section, which can include graphics*
- *text in the form of headings and annotations*
- *a summary section.*

Constructing a spreadsheet – *start with a simple model and extend it gradually, checking for correct operation as you go.*

Using hidden (or zero-width) columns – *these are useful for storing intermediate calculations which you do not wish to be displayed on the screen or printout.*

data cells by drawing lines, if this feature is available. Programs make assumptions about the nature of the entry being made: most assume that if the first character is a number, then the entry is a number or formula. If it is a letter, then it will be a label. If you want to start a label with a number, you must override this assumption by typing a designated character before the number to tell the program that this is a label; check your program manual for details (e.g. in Excel® it is a single quote mark preceding the number).

Numbers

You can also enter numbers (values) in cells for use in calculations. Many programs let you enter numbers in more than one way and you must decide which method you prefer. The way you enter the number does not affect the way it is displayed on the screen as this is controlled by the cell format at the point of entry. There are usually special ways to enter data for percentages, currency and scientific notation for very large and small numbers.

Formulae

These are the 'power tools' of the spreadsheet because they do the calculations. A cell can be referred to by its alphanumeric code, e.g. A5 (column A, row 5) and the value contained in that cell manipulated within a formula, e.g. $=(A5+10)$ or $=(A5+B22)$ in another cell. Formulae can include various pre-programmed functions which can refer to a cell, so that if the value of that cell is changed, so is the result of the formula calculation. They may also include limited branching options through the use of logical operators (IF, TRUE, FALSE, OR, etc.).

Functions

A variety of functions is usually offered, but only mathematical and statistical functions will be considered here.

Mathematical functions

Spreadsheets have program-specific sets of predetermined functions but they almost all include trigonometrical functions, angle functions, logarithms and random number functions. Functions are invaluable for transforming sets of data rapidly and can be used in formulae required for more complex analyses. Spreadsheets work with an order of preference of the mathematical operators in much the same way as a standard calculator and this must always be taken into account when operators are used in formulae. They also require a very precise syntax – the program should warn you if you break this!

Statistical functions

Modern spreadsheets incorporate many sophisticated statistical functions, and if these are not appropriate, the spreadsheet can be used to carry out the calculations required for most of the statistical tests found in textbooks. The descriptive statistics normally available include:

- the sum of all data present in a column, row or block;
- the minimum and maximum of a defined range of cells;

Operators and brackets in spreadsheets – the standard mathematical operators $\div$ and $\times$ are usually replaced by / and * respectively, while ^ signifies 'to the power' (e.g. $10 \wedge 4 = 10^4$). In complex formulae, brackets should be used to separate the elements, otherwise the results may not be what you expect. For example, Excel® will calculate $=A1*B1/C1-D1$ differently from $(A1*B1)/(C1-D1)$.

Definition

Function – a pre-programmed code for the transformation of values (mathematical or statistical functions) or selection of text characters (string functions).

Example $= \sin(A5)$ is an example of a function in Excel®. If you write this in a cell, the spreadsheet will calculate the sine of the number in cell A5 (assuming it to be an angle in radians) and write it in the cell. Different programs may use a slightly different syntax.

Empty cells – note that these may be given the value 0 by the spreadsheet for certain functions. This may cause errors, e.g. by rendering a minimum value inappropriate. Also, an error return may result for certain functions if the cell content is zero.

- counts of cells – a useful operation if you have an unknown or variable number of data values;
- averages and other statistics describing location;
- standard deviations and other statistics describing dispersion.

A useful function where you have large numbers of data allows you to create frequency distributions using pre-defined class intervals.

The hypothesis-testing statistical functions are usually reasonably powerful (e.g. t-test, ANOVA, regression) and they often return the *probability* (P) of obtaining the test statistic (where $0 < P < 1$), so there may be no need to refer to statistical tables. Again, check on the effects of including empty cells within the statistical calculations.

Copying

All programs provide a means of copying (replicating) formulae or cell contents when required and this is a very useful feature. When copying, references to cells may be either relative, changing with the row/column as they are copied or absolute, remaining a fixed cell reference and not changing as the formulae are copied (Fig. 12.2).

> **KEY POINT** The distinction between relative and absolute cell references is very important and must be understood; it provides one of the most common forms of error when copying formulae.

In Excel®, copying is normally *relative* and if you wish a cell reference to be *absolute* when copied, this is done by putting a dollar ($) sign before and after the column reference letter e.g. $C$56.

Naming blocks

When a group of cells (a block) is carrying out a particular function, it is often easier to give the block a name which can then be used in all formulae referring to that block. This powerful feature also allows the spreadsheet to be more readable.

Graphics display

Most spreadsheets now offer a wide range of graphics facilities which are easy to use, and this represents an ideal way to examine your data sets rapidly and comprehensively. The quality of the final graphics output (to a printer) is variable but is usually perfectly sufficient for data exploration and analysis. Many of the options are business graphics styles but there are usually histogram, bar chart, X-Y plotting, line and area graphics options available. Note that some spreadsheet graphics may not come up to the standards expected for the formal presentation of scientific data, unless you manipulate the initial output appropriately.

Printing spreadsheets

This is usually a straightforward, menu-controlled procedure, made difficult only by the fact that your spreadsheet may be too big to fit on one piece of paper. Try to develop an area of the sheet which contains only the data that you will be printing, i.e. perhaps a summary area. Remember

Statistical calculations – *make sure you understand whether the functions you employ apply to populations or samples (see p. 480).*

(a)

	Cell	Formula	
Original → cell	A1	=B1+C1	← Original formula
Copied cells	A2	=B2+C2	Copied formulae (relative)
	A3	=B3+C3	
	A4	=B4+C4	

(b)

	Cell	Formula	
Original → cell	A1	=B1/$C$1	← Original formula
Copied cells	A2	=B2/$C$1	Copied formulae (mixed relative and absolute)
	A3	=B3/$C$1	
	A4	=B4/$C$1	

Fig. 12.2 Illustration of relative (a) and absolute (b) copying. In Excel®, the $ sign before and after the column letter makes the cell reference absolute, as shown in (b).

that columns can usually be hidden for printing purposes and you can control whether the printout is in portrait or landscape mode, and for continuous paper or single sheets (depending on printer capabilities). Use a screen preview option, if available, to check your layout before printing. A 'print to fit' option is also available in some programs, making the output fit the page dimensions.

Using a spreadsheet as a database

Many spreadsheets can be used as databases, using rows and columns to represent the fields and records (see Chapter 13). For many biological purposes, this form of database is perfectly adequate and should be considered before using a full-feature database program.

Sources for further study

Harvey, G. (1997) *Excel 97® for Windows® for Dummies®*. John Wiley, New York.

Harvey, G. (1997) *More Excel 97® for Dummies®*. John Wiley, New York.

(And similar texts for other release versions.)

Using string functions – these allow you to manipulate text within your spreadsheet and include functions such as 'find and replace' and alphabetical or numerical 'sort'.

Study exercises

The instructions and tips for these problems assume that you have Excel® (97 or later) available. If not, they should be readily modified for most advanced spreadsheet programs. If you have problems with any of the tasks, try using the program's *Help* facility.

12.1 Create a spreadsheet and graph (introductory).
    (i) Copy the information in the table below into a spreadsheet. Name and save the spreadsheet file appropriately.
    (ii) From the copied information, create a pie chart using the *Chart Wizard* function.
    (iii) Adjust the colours selected so the chart will print out in black and white. Save the final version of your spreadsheet. Print the chart out directly from Excel®.

Relative percentages of the major types of leukocytes in a blood sample

Cell type	Percentage
Neutrophils	60
Eosinophils	4
Basophils	1
Monocytes	7
Lymphocytes	28
Total	100

12.2 Create a spreadsheet and graph (advanced).
    (i) Copy the data in the table overleaf into a spreadsheet. Name and save the file appropriately.

Time course of cell population growth

Time (hours)	Cell count (per unit volume)
1	2.00
2	6.00
6	50.0
12	6.00×10^3
18	2.20×10^5
24	1.65×10^7

(ii) Use the spreadsheet and chart-making facilities to explore by eye which of the following transformations would result in the best linear fit for these data: reciprocal, square root, cube root or log.

(iii) Add a linear trend-line to the chart for the most appropriate transformation.

(iv) Copy the graph to a file in Word® and print out.

12.3 Use a spreadsheet as a simple database. Copy the data in the table below into cells within a spreadsheet. Modify the column widths so you can see all of the text on a single screen. Now sort the data in the following ways:

(a) by subject, in alphabetical order;

(b) by date and then by time of day;

(c) by topic, in reverse alphabetical order.

Exam timetable

Subject	Date	Time	Paper	Location	Topic
Biochemistry	3 Jun	Morning	1	Great Hall	Multiple choice
Biochemistry	17 Jun	Morning	2	Exam Hall 5	Essay paper
Biochemistry	2 Jun	Afternoon	3	Main Laboratory	Information processing
Genetics	3 Jun	Afternoon	A	Small Hall	Short answer questions
Genetics	14 Jun	Afternoon	B	Exam Hall 5	Essay paper
Cell Biology A	4 Jun	Morning	1	Small Hall	Short answer questions
Cell Biology B	1 Jul	Afternoon	1	Exam Hall 3	Short answer questions
Cell Biology A	13 Jun	Afternoon	2	Exam Hall 5	Essay paper
Cell Biology B	2 Jun	Morning	2	Main Laboratory	Practical exam

Word processors, databases and other packages

Word processors

The word processor has improved the process of writing because of the ease of revising text. Word processing is a transferable skill valuable beyond the immediate requirements of your course. Using a word processor should enhance your writing skills and speed because you can create, check and change your text on the screen before printing it as 'hard copy' on paper. Once entered and saved, multiple uses can be made of a piece of text with little effort.

When using a word processor you can:

- refine material many times before submission;
- insert material easily, allowing writing to take place in any sequence;
- use a spell-checker to check your text;
- use a thesaurus when composing your text;
- produce high quality final copies;
- reuse part or all of the text in other documents.

The potential disadvantages of using a word processor include:

- lack of ready access to a computer, software and/or a printer;
- time taken to learn the operational details of the program;
- the temptation to make 'trivial' revisions;
- loss of files due to computer breakdown, or disk loss, or failure.

Word processors come as 'packages' comprising the program and a manual, often with a tutorial program. Examples are Microsoft® Word® and WordPerfect®. Most word processors have similar general features but differ in operational detail; it is best to pick one and stick to it as far as possible so that you become familiar with it. Learning to use the package is like learning to drive a car – you need only to know how to drive the computer and its program, not to understand how the engine (program) and transmission (data transfer) work, although a little background knowledge is often helpful and will allow you to get the most from the program.

In most word processors, the appearance of the screen realistically represents what the printout on paper will look like. Word processing files actually contain large amounts of code relating to text format, etc., but these can clutter the screen if visible. Some word processors are menu-driven, others require keyboard entry of codes: menus are easier to start with and the more sophisticated programs allow you to choose between these options.

Because of variation in operational details, only general and strategic information is provided in this chapter: you must learn the details of your word processor through use of the appropriate manual and 'help' facilities.

Before starting you will need:

- the program (usually installed on a hard disk or available *via* a network);
- a floppy disk for storage, retrieval and back-up of your own files when created;

The computerised office – *many word processors are sold as part of an integrated office suite, e.g. PerfectOffice® and Microsoft® Office, with the advantage that they share a common interface in the different components (word processor, spreadsheet, database, etc.) and allow ready exchange of information (e.g. text, graphics) between component programs.*

Using textbooks, manuals and tutorials – *the manuals that come with some programs may not be very user-friendly and it is often worth investing in one of the textbooks that are available for most word processing programs. Alternatively, use an on-line 'help' tutorial.*

- the appropriate manual or textbook giving operational details;
- a draft page layout design: in particular you should have decided on page size, page margins, typeface (font) and size, type of text justification, and format of page numbering;
- an outline of the text content;
- access to a suitable printer: this need not be attached to the computer you are using since your file can be taken to an office where a printer is available, providing that it has the same word processing program.

Laying out (formatting) your document

Although you can format your text at any time, it is good practice to enter the basic commands at the start of your document: entering them later can lead to considerable problems due to reorganisation of the text layout. If you use a particular set of layout criteria regularly, e.g. an A4 page with space for a letterhead, make a template containing the appropriate codes that can be called up whenever you start a new document. Note that various printers may respond differently to particular codes, resulting in a different spacing and layout.

Typing the text

Think of the screen as a piece of typing paper. The cursor marks the position where your text/data will be entered and can be moved around the screen by use of the cursor-control keys. When you type, don't worry about running out of space on the line because the text will wrap around to the next line automatically. Do not use a carriage return (usually the ENTER or ↵ key) unless you wish to force a new line, e.g. when a new paragraph is wanted. If you make a mistake when typing, correction is easy. You can usually delete characters or words or lines and the space is closed automatically. You can also insert new text in the middle of a line or word. You can insert special codes to carry out a variety of tasks, including changing text appearance such as underlining, **emboldening** and *italics*. Paragraph indentations can be automated using TAB or ⇥ as on a typewriter but you can also indent or bullet whole blocks of text using special menu options. The function keys are usually pre-programmed to assist in many of these operations.

Editing features

Word processors usually have an array of features designed to make editing documents easy. In addition to the simple editing procedures described above, the program usually offers facilities to allow blocks of text to be moved ('cut and paste'), copied or deleted.

An extremely valuable editing facility is the find or search procedure: this can rapidly scan through a document looking for a specified word, phrase or punctuation. This is particularly valuable when combined with a replace facility so that, for example, you could find the word 'test' and replace it with 'trial' throughout your document simply and rapidly.

Most word processors have a command which reveals the normally hidden codes controlling the layout and appearance of the printed text. When editing, this can be a very useful feature, since some changes to your text will cause difficulties if these hidden codes are not taken into account; in particular, make sure that the cursor is at the correct point

---

Using a word processor – take full advantage of the differences between word processing and 'normal' writing (which necessarily follows a linear sequence and requires more planning):

- Simply jot down your initial ideas for a plan, preferably at paragraph topic level. The order can be altered easily and if a paragraph grows too much it can easily be split.
- Start writing wherever you wish and fill in the rest later.
- Just put down your ideas as you think, confident in the knowledge that it is the concepts that are important to note; their order and the way you express them can be adjusted later.
- Don't worry about spelling and use of synonyms – these can (and should) be checked during a separate revision run through your text, using the spell checker first to correct obvious mistakes, then the thesaurus to change words for style or to find the mot juste.
- Don't forget that a draft printout may be required to check (a) for pace and spacing – difficult to correct for on-screen; and (b) to ensure that words checked for spelling fit the required sense.

Deleting and restoring text – because deletion can sometimes be made in error, there is usually an 'undelete' or 'restore' feature which allows the last deletion to be recovered, usually available through the program's 'Edit' menu.

before making changes to text containing hidden code, otherwise your text will sometimes change in apparently mystifying ways.

Fonts and line spacing

Most word processors offer a variety of fonts depending upon the printer being used. Fonts come in a wide variety of types and sizes, but they are defined in particular ways as follows:

Presenting your documents – it is good practice not to mix typefaces too much in a formal document; also the font size should not differ greatly for different headings, subheadings and the text.

- Typeface: the term for a family of characters of a particular design, each of which is given a particular name. The most commonly used for normal text is Times Roman (as used here for the main text) but many others are widely available, particularly for the better quality printers. They fall into three broad groups: serif fonts with curves and flourishes at the ends of the characters (e.g. Times Roman); sans serif fonts without such flourishes, providing a clean, modern appearance (e.g. Helvetica or Arial); and decorative fonts used for special purposes only, such as the production of newsletters and notices.

Preparing draft documents – use double line spacing to allow room for your editing comments on the printed page.

- Size: measured in points. A point is the smallest typographical unit of measurement, there being 72 points to the inch (about 28 points per cm). The standard sizes for text are 10, 11 and 12 point, but typefaces are often available up to 72 point or more.
- Appearance: many typefaces are available in a variety of styles and weights. Many of these are not designed for use in scientific literature but for desk-top publishing.

Using fixed space fonts – proportional fonts can create problems of base letter misalignment when representing DNA sequences (p. 62), so you should use a fixed space font, e.g. Courier.

- Spacing: can be either fixed, where every character is the same width, or proportional, where the width of every character, including spaces, is varied. Typewriter fonts such as Elite and Prestige use fixed spacing and are useful for filling in forms or tables, but proportional fonts make the overall appearance of text more pleasing and readable.
- Pitch: specifies the number of characters per horizontal inch of text. Typewriter fonts are usually 10 or 12 pitch, but proportional fonts are never given a pitch value since it is inherently variable.
- Justification is the term describing the way in which text is aligned vertically. Left justification is normal, but for some documents, both left and right justification may be used (as here).

You should also consider the vertical spacing of lines in your document. Drafts and manuscripts are frequently double-spaced. If your document has unusual font sizes, this may well affect line spacing, although most word processors will cope with this automatically.

Preparing final documents – for most work, use a 12 point proportional serif typeface with spacing dependent upon the specifications for the work.

Table construction

Tables can be produced by a variety of methods:

- Using the tab key ⇥ as on a typewriter: this moves the cursor to predetermined positions on the page, equivalent to the start of each tabular column. You can define the positions of these tabs as required at the start of each table.
- Using special table-constructing procedures. Here the table construction is largely done for you and it is much easier than using tabs, providing you enter the correct information when you set up the table.
- Using a spreadsheet to construct the table and then copying it to the word processor. This procedure requires considerably more

manipulation than using the word processor directly and is best reserved for special circumstances, such as the presentation of a very large or complex table of data, especially if the data are already stored as a spreadsheet.

Graphics and special characters

Many word processors can incorporate graphics from other programs into the text of a document. Files must be compatible (see your manual) but if this is so, it is a relatively straightforward procedure. For professional documents this is a valuable facility, but for most undergraduate work it is probably better to produce and use graphics as a separate operation, e.g. using a spreadsheet.

You can draw lines and other graphical features directly within most word processors and special characters (e.g. Greek characters) may be available, dependent upon your printer's capabilities.

Inserting special characters – Greek letters and other characters are available using the 'Insert' and 'Symbol' features in Word®.

Tools

Many word processors also offer you special tools, the most important of which are:

- Macros: special sets of files you can create when you have a frequently repeated set of keystrokes to make. You can record these keystrokes as a 'macro' so that it can provide a short-cut for repeated operations.
- Thesaurus: used to look up alternative words of similar or opposite meaning while composing text at the keyboard.
- Spell-checker: a very useful facility which will check your spellings against a dictionary provided by the program. This dictionary is often expandable to include specialist words which you use in your work. The danger lies in becoming too dependent upon such facilities as they all have limitations: in particular, they will not pick up incorrect words which happen to be correct in a different context (i.e. 'was' typed as 'saw' or 'see' rather than 'sea'). Be aware of American spellings in programs from the USA, e.g. 'color' instead of 'colour'. The rule, therefore, is to use the spell-check first and then carefully read the text for errors which have slipped through.
- Word count: useful when you are writing to a prescribed limit.

Using a spell-check facility – do not rely on this to spot all errors. Remember that spell-check programs do not correct grammatical errors.

Printing from your program

Word processors require you to specify precisely the type of printer and/or other style details you wish to use. Most printers also offer choices as to text and graphics quality, so choose draft (low) quality for all but your final copy since this will save both time and materials.

Use a print preview option to show the page layout, if this is available. Assuming that you have entered appropriate layout and font commands, printing is a straightforward operation carried out by the word processor at your command. Problems usually arise because of some incompatibility between the criteria you have entered and the printer's own capabilities. Make sure that you know what your printer offers before starting to type: although specified details are modifiable at any time, changing the page size, margin size, font size, etc., all cause your text to be rearranged, and this can be frustrating if you have spent time carefully laying out the pages.

Using the print preview mode – this can reveal errors of several kinds, e.g. spacing between pages, that can prevent you wasting paper and printer ink unnecessarily.

Word processors, databases and other packages

Databases

Choosing between a database and a spreadsheet – use a database only after careful consideration. Can the task be done better within a spreadsheet? A database program can be complex to set up and usually needs to be updated regularly.

A database is an electronic filing system whose structure is similar to a manual record card collection. Its collection of records is termed a file. The individual items of information on each record are termed fields. Once the database is constructed, search criteria can be used to view files through various filters according to your requirements. The computerised catalogues in your library are just such a system; you enter the filter requirements in the form of author or subject keywords.

You can use a database to catalogue, search, sort and relate collections of information. The benefits of a computerised database over a manual card-file system are:

- The information content is easily amended/updated.
- Printout of relevant items can be obtained.
- It is quick and easy to organise through sorting and searching/selection criteria, to produce sub-groups of relevant records.
- Record displays can easily be redesigned, allowing flexible methods of presenting records according to interest.
- Relational databases can be combined, giving the whole system immense flexibility. The older 'flat-file' databases store information in files which can be searched and sorted, but cannot be linked to other databases.

Using databases in bioformatics – this is covered in Chapter 11.

Relatively simple database files can be constructed within spreadsheets using the columns and rows as fields and records respectively. These are capable of reasonably advanced sorting and searching operations and are probably sufficient for most types of databases you are likely to require as an undergraduate. You may also make use of a bibliographic database specially constructed for that purpose (p. 43).

Statistical analysis packages

Statistical packages vary from small programs designed to carry out very specific statistical tasks to larger packages (Statgraphics®, Minitab®, etc.) intended to provide statistical assistance, from experimental design to the analysis of results. Consider the following features when selecting a package:

- The data entry and editing section should be user-friendly, with options for transforming data.
- Data exploration options should include descriptive statistics and exploratory data analysis techniques.
- Hypothesis-testing techniques should include ANOVA, regression analysis, multivariate techniques, parametric and non-parametric statistics (see Chapter 67).
- The program may provide assistance with experimental design.
- Output facilities should be suitable for graphical and tabular formats.

Some programs have very complex data entry systems, limiting the ease of using data in different tests. The data entry and storage system should be based on a spreadsheet system, so that subsequent editing and transformation operations are straightforward.

KEY POINT **Make sure that you understand the statistical basis for your test and the computational techniques involved** *before* **using a particular program.**

Graphics/presentation packages

Many of these packages are specifically designed for business graphics rather than life sciences. They do, however, have considerable value in the preparation of materials for posters and talks where visual quality is an important factor. There are many packages available for microcomputers such as Sigmaplot®, Harvard Graphics® and Microsoft® PowerPoint® (p. 17), which provide templates for the preparation of overhead transparencies, slide transparencies and paper copy, both black and white and in colour. They usually incorporate a 'freehand' drawing option, allowing you to make your own designs.

Although the facilities offered are often attractive, the learning time required for some of the more complex operations is considerable and they should be considered only for specific purposes: routine graphical presentation of data sets is best done from within a spreadsheet or statistical package.

The most important points regarding the use of graphics packages are:

- Graphics quality: the built-in graphics are sometimes of only moderate quality. Use of annotation facilities can improve graphics considerably. Do not use inappropriate graphics for scientific presentation.
- The production of colour graphics: this requires a good quality colour printer/plotter.
- Importing of graphics files: graphs produced by spreadsheets or other statistical programs can usually be imported into graphics programs – this is useful for adding legends, annotations, etc., when the facilities offered by the original programs are inadequate. Check that the format of files produced by your statistics/spreadsheet program can be recognised by your graphics program. The different types of file are distinguished by the three-character filename extension.

KEY POINT **Computer graphics are not always satisfactory for scientific presentation. While they may be useful for exploratory procedures, they may need to be redrawn, e.g. for a handwritten final report. It may be helpful to use a computer-generated graph as a template for the final version.**

Sources for further study

Barrows, A. (1997) *Access 97® for Windows® for Dummies® Quick Reference*. John Wiley, New York.

Gookin, D. (1996) *Word 97® for Windows® for Dummies®*. John Wiley, New York.

Presentation using computer packages – while many computer programs enhance presentational aspects of your work, there are occasions when they can make your presentation worse. Take care to avoid the following common pitfalls:

- Default or 'chart wizard' settings for graphs may result in output that is non-standard for the sciences (e.g. shaded background, gridlines, coloured symbols), or is missing key elements. Use the same criteria for producing graphs by computer as you would for hand-drawn ones (see Chapter 63).
- Selecting the wrong chart type can result in non-linear axes, or evenly spaced data on the x-axis, when they are not evenly spaced numerically.
- Fonts in labels and legends may not be consistent with other parts of your presentation.
- Some programs cannot produce Greek symbols (e.g. μ; do not use 'u' as a substitute). The same applies to scientific notation and superscripts: do not use e.g. $1.4E+09$ for 1.4×10^9 or 14C for ^{14}C. It is better to draw the proper symbol or superscript by hand on the printed version.
- Do not rely on spell-checkers. You should always proofread your work carefully in draft form.
- Do not rely on grammar checkers. These often operate by making 'suggestions' for changes. This does not mean they are correct. You will need to make a grammatically based decision yourself.

Wang, W. and Parker R.C. (1997) *Microsoft Office 97® for Windows® for Dummies®*. John Wiley, New York.

(And similar texts for other packages and release versions.)

Study exercises

13.1 Investigate intermediate/advanced Word® features. The tasks in the following list are likely to useful in preparing assignments and report writing within the life sciences. Can you carry out all of the tasks? If not, use either a manual or the on-line *Help* feature to find out how to accomplish them. Tips are given in the answer section.

(a) Sort information in a list into alphabetical order.

(b) Replace a text string word or phrase with a new text string throughout your document.

(c) Replace a text string in normal font with the same text string in italics throughout your document.

(d) Add a 'header' and 'footer' to your document, the former showing the document's title and the latter containing page numbers in the bottom centre of the page.

(e) Adjust the margins of the page to give a 5 cm margin on the left and a 2 cm margin on the right.

(f) Change the type of bullets used in a list from standard (● or ■) to a different form (e.g. –, ◆ or ☑).

(g) Use the 'thesaurus' option to find a different or more suitable word to express your meaning. Try, for example, to find alternatives to the word 'alternative'.

(h) Carry out a spell-check on your document.

(i) Carry out a word count on your document and on a selected part of it.

(j) Open two documents and switch between them.

13.2 Make precise copies of tables. Copy the following tables using a word processor such as Word®

Test organism	Results of analysis (units)		
	August	September	October
X			
Y			
Z			

Test organism	Results of analysis (units)		
	August	September	October
X			
Y			
Z			

13.3 Investigate what programs and packages are available to you as a student. Test each program with appropriate data, images, etc.

Communicating information

14 Organising a poster display

A scientific poster is a visual display of the results of an investigation, usually mounted on a rectangular board. Posters are used at scientific meetings, to communicate research findings, and in undergraduate courses, to display project results or assignment work.

In a written report you can include a reasonable amount of specific detail and the reader can go back and reread difficult passages. However, if a poster is long-winded or contains too much detail, your reader is likely to lose interest.

KEY POINT A poster session is like a competition – you are competing for the attention of people in a room. Because you need to attract and hold the attention of your audience, make your poster as interesting as possible. Think of it as an advertisement for your work and you will not go far wrong.

Preliminaries

Before considering the content of your poster, you should find out:

- the linear dimensions of your poster area, typically up to 1.5 m wide by 1.0 m high;
- the composition of the poster board and the method of attachment, whether drawing pins, Velcro® tape, or some other form of adhesive; and whether these will be provided – in any case, it's safer to bring your own;
- the time(s) when the poster should be set up and when you should attend;
- the room where the poster session will be held.

Design

Plan your poster with your audience in mind, as this will dictate the appropriate level for your presentation. Aim to make your poster as accessible as possible to a broad audience. Since a poster is a *visual* display, you must pay particular attention to the presentation of information: work that may have taken hours to prepare can be ruined in a few minutes by the ill-considered arrangement of items (Fig. 14.1). Begin by making a draft sketch of the major elements of your poster. It is worth discussing your intended design with someone else, as constructive advice at the draft stage will save a lot of time and effort when you prepare the final version (or consult Simmonds and Reynolds, 1994).

Layout
Usually the best approach is to divide the poster into several smaller areas, perhaps six or eight in all, and prepare each as a separate item on a piece of thick card. Some people prefer to produce a single large poster on one sheet of paper or card and store it inside a protective cardboard tube. However, a single large poster will bend and crease, making it difficult to flatten out. In addition, photographs and text attached to the backing sheet often work loose.

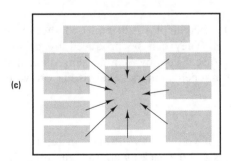

Fig. 14.1 Poster design. (a) An uninspiring design: sub-units of equal area, reading left to right, are not recommended. (b) This design is more interesting and the text will be easier to read (column format). (c) An alternative approach, with a central focus and arrows/tapes to guide the reader.

Subdividing your poster means that each smaller area can be prepared on a separate piece of paper or card, of A4 size or slightly larger, making transport and storage easier. It also breaks the reading matter up into smaller pieces, looking less formidable to a potential reader. By using pieces of card of different colours you can provide emphasis for key aspects, or link text with figures or photographs.

You will need to guide your reader through the poster. It is often appropriate to use either a numbering system, with large, clear numbers at the top of each piece of card, or a system of arrows (or thin tapes), to show the relationship of sections within the poster (see Fig. 14.1). Make sure that the relationship is clear and that the arrows or tapes do not cross.

Presenting a poster at a formal conference – it can be useful to include a photograph of the contributor for identification purposes.

Title

Your chosen title should be concise (no more than eight words), specific and interesting, to encourage people to read the poster. Make the title large and bold – it should run across the top of your poster, in letters at least 4 cm high, so that it can be read from the other side of the room. Coloured spirit-based marker and block capitals drawn with a ruler work well, as long as your writing is readable and neat (the colour can be used to add emphasis). Alternatively, you can use Letraset®, or similar lettering. Details of authors, together with their addresses (if appropriate), should be given, usually in the top right-hand corner in somewhat smaller lettering than the title.

Text

Keep text to a minimum – aim to have a maximum of 500 words in your poster. Write in short sentences and avoid verbosity. Keep your poster as visual as possible and make effective use of the spaces between the blocks of text. Your final text should be double-spaced and should have a minimum capital letter height of 8 mm (minimum font size 36 point), preferably greater, so that the poster can be read at a distance of 1 m. One method of obtaining text of the required size is to photo-enlarge standard typescript (using a good-quality photocopier), or use a high-quality (laser) printer. It is best to avoid continuous use of text in capitals, since it slows reading and makes the text less interesting to the reader. Also avoid italic, 'balloon' or decorative styles of lettering.

Making up your poster – text and graphics printed on good-quality paper can be glued directly onto a contrasting mounting card: use photographic spray mountant or Pritt® rather than liquid glue. Trim carefully using a guillotine to give equal margins, parallel with the paper. Photographs should be scanned into an electronic format, or placed in a window mount to avoid the tendency for their corners to curl. Another approach is to trim pages or photographs to their correct size, then encapsulate in plastic film: this gives a highly professional finish and is less weighty to transport.

Subtitles and headings

These should have a capital letter height of 15–20 mm, and should be restricted to two or three words. They can be produced by photo-enlargement, by stencilling, Letraset® or by hand, using pencilled guidelines (but make sure that no pencil marks are visible on your finished poster).

Colour

Consider the overall visual effect of your chosen display, including the relationship between text, diagrams and the backing board. Colour can be used to highlight key aspects of your poster. However, it is very easy to ruin a poster by the inappropriate choice and application of colour. Careful use of two, or at most three, complementary colours will be easier on the eye and may aid comprehension. Colour can be used to link the text with the visual images (e.g. by picking out a colour in a photograph and using the same colour on the mounting board for the accompanying text).

Producing composite material for posters – PowerPoint® is generally more useful than Word® when you wish to include text, graphics and/or images on the same page. It is even possible to use PowerPoint® to produce a complete poster, although is can be expensive to have this printed out commercially to A1 or A0 size.

Use coloured inks or water-based paints to provide colour in diagrams and figures, as felt pens rarely give satisfactory results.

Content

The typical format is that of a scientific report (see Box 18.1), i.e. with the same headings, but with a considerably reduced content. Never be tempted to spend the minimum amount of time converting a piece of scientific writing into poster format. At scientific meetings, the least interesting posters are those where the author simply displays pages from a written communication (e.g. a journal article) on the poster board. Keep references within the text to a minimum – interested parties can always ask you for further information.

Introduction

This should give the reader background information on the broad field of study and the aims of your own work. It is vital that this section is as interesting as possible, to capture the interest of your audience. It is often worth listing your objectives as a series of numbered points.

Materials and methods

Keep this short, and describe only the principal techniques used. You might mention any special techniques, or problems of general interest.

Results

Don't present your raw data: use data reduction wherever possible, i.e. figures and simple statistical comparisons. Graphs, diagrams, histograms and pie charts give clear visual images of trends and relationships and should be used in place of tabulated data (see p. 453). Final copies of all figures should be produced so that the numbers can be read from a distance of 1 m. Each should have a concise title and legend, so that it is self-contained: if appropriate, a series of numbered points can be used to link a diagram with the accompanying text. Where symbols are used, provide a key on each graph (symbol size should be at least 5 mm). Avoid using graphs straight from a written version, e.g. a project report, textbook, or a paper, without considering whether they need modification to meet your requirements.

Conclusions

This is where many readers will begin, and they may go no further unless you make this section sufficiently interesting. This part needs to be the strongest section of your poster. Refer to your figures here to draw the reader into the main part of your poster. A slightly larger or bolder typeface may add emphasis, though too many different typefaces can look messy.

The poster session

If you stand at the side of your poster throughout the session, you are likely to discourage some readers, who may not wish to become involved in a detailed conversation about the poster. Stand nearby. Find something to do – talk to someone else, or browse among the other posters, but remain aware of people reading your poster and be ready to answer any queries they may raise. Do not be too discouraged if you aren't asked lots

Designing the materials and methods section – photographs or diagrams of apparatus can help to break up the text of the Materials and Methods section and provide visual interest. It is sometimes worth preparing this section in a smaller typeface.

Keeping graphs and diagrams simple – avoid composite graphs with different scales for the same axis, or with several trend lines (use a maximum of three trend lines per graph).

Listing your conclusions – a series of numbered points is a useful approach, if your findings fit this pattern.

Consider providing a handout – this is a useful way to summarise the main points of your poster, so that your readers have a permanent record of the information you have presented.

of questions: remember, the poster is meant to be a self-contained, visual story, without need for further explanation.

A poster display will never feel like an oral presentation, where the nervousness beforehand is replaced by a combination of satisfaction and relief as you unwind after the event. However, it can be a very satisfying means of communication, particularly if you follow these guidelines.

Text reference

Simmonds, D. and Reynolds, L. (1994) *Data Presentation and Visual Literacy in Medicine and Science*. Butterworth-Heinemann, London.

Sources for further study

Briscoe, M.H. (1996) *Preparing Scientific Illustrations: A Guide to Better Posters, Presentations and Publications*. Springer-Verlag, New York.

Davis, M. (1997) *Scientific Papers and Presentations*. Academic Press, New York.

Gosling, P.J. (1999) *Scientist's Guide to Poster Presentations*. Kluwer, New York.

Hess, G. and Liegel, L. *Creating Effective Poster Presentations*. Available: http://www.ncsu.edu/project/posters
Last accessed 08/01/03.

Study exercises

14.1 **Design a poster**. Either working with a partner, or with a few others from your year group, decide on a suitable poster topic (perhaps something linked to your current teaching programme). Working individually, make an outline plan of the major elements of the poster, with appropriate sub-headings and a brief indication of the content and relative size of each element (including figures, diagrams and images). Exchange draft plans with your partner, or among the group members and arrange a session where you can discuss the merits and disadvantages of the various designs.

14.2 **Prepare a checklist for assessing the quality of a poster presentation**. After reading through the material in this chapter, prepare a 10-point checklist of assessment criteria under the heading 'What makes a good poster presentation?' Compare your list with the one that we have provided (p. 501) – do you agree with our criteria, or do you prefer your own checklist (and can you justify your preferences)?

14.3 **Evaluate the posters in your University**. Most universities have a wide range of academic posters on display. Some of these cover general topics (e.g. course structures within your Department), while others may deal with specific research topics (e.g. poster presentations from past conferences). Consider their good and bad features (if you wish to make this a group exercise, you might compare your evaluation with that of other students, e.g. in a group discussion session).

15 Giving a spoken presentation

Opportunities for practising speaking skills – these include:
- answering lecturers' questions;
- contributing in tutorials;
- talking to informal groups;
- stating your views at formal (committee) meetings;
- demonstrating or explaining to other students, e.g. during a practical;
- asking questions at seminars;
- answering an examiner's questions in an oral exam.

Most students feel very nervous about giving talks. This is natural, since very few people are sufficiently confident and outgoing that they look forward to speaking in public. Additionally, the technical nature of your subject matter may give you cause for concern, especially if you feel that some members of the audience have a greater knowledge than you have, e.g. your tutors. However, this is a fundamental method of scientific communication and it therefore forms an important component of many courses.

The comments in this chapter apply equally to informal talks, e.g. those based on assignments and project work, and to more formal conference presentations. It is hoped that the advice and guidance given below will encourage you to make the most of your opportunities for public speaking, but there is no substitute for practice. Do not expect to find all of the answers from this, or any other, book. Rehearse, and learn from your own experience.

KEY POINT The three 'Rs' of successful public speaking are: reflect – give sufficient thought to all aspects of your presentation, particularly at the planning stage; rehearse – to improve your delivery; rewrite – modify the content and style of your material in response to your own ideas and to the comments of others.

Preparation

Preliminary information

Begin by marshalling the details needed to plan your presentation, including:

- the duration of the talk;
- whether time for questions is included;
- the size and location of the room;
- the projection/lighting facilities provided, and whether pointers or similar aids are available.

Learning from experience – use your own experience of good and bad lecturers to shape your performance. Some of the more common errors include:

- speaking too quickly;
- reading to notes and ignoring the audience;
- inexpressive, impersonal or indistinct speech;
- distracting mannerisms;
- poorly structured material with little emphasis on key information;
- factual information too complex and detailed;
- too few visual aids.

It is especially important to find out whether the room has the necessary equipment for slide projection (slide projector and screen, black-out curtains or blinds, appropriate lighting), overhead projection, or has a digital projection system before you prepare your audio-visual aids. If you concentrate only on the spoken part of your presentation at this stage, you are inviting trouble later on. Have a look around the room and try out the equipment at the earliest opportunity, so that you are able to use the lights, projector, etc., with confidence.

Audio-visual aids

Testing the room – if possible, try to rehearse your talk in the room in which it will be presented. This will help you to make allowance for layout of equipment, lighting, acoustics and sight lines that might affect the way you deliver your talk. It will also put you at ease on the day, because of the familiarity of the surroundings.

Find out whether your department has facilities for preparing overhead transparencies and slides, whether these facilities are available for your use and the cost of materials. Adopt the following guidelines:

- Keep text to a minimum: present only the key points, with up to 20 words per slide/transparency.
- Make sure the text is readable: try out your material beforehand.
- Use several simpler figures rather than a single complex graph.

- Avoid too much colour on overhead transparencies: blue and black are easier to read than red or green.
- Don't mix slides and transparencies as this is often distracting.
- Use spirit-based pens for transparencies: use alcohol for corrections.
- Transparencies can be produced from typewritten or printed text using a photocopier, often giving a better product than pens. Note that you must use special heat-resistant acetate sheets for photocopying.

Electronic presentation software (e.g. PowerPoint®) can replace these specialist requirements, as long as the necessary facilities are available for your talk (see below).

Audience

You should consider your audience at the earliest stage, since they will determine the appropriate level for your presentation. If you are talking to fellow students you may be able to assume a common level of background knowledge. In contrast, a research lecture given to your Department, or a paper at a meeting of a scientific society, will be presented to an audience from a broader range of backgrounds. An oral presentation is not the place for a complex discussion of specialised information: build up your talk from a low level. The speed at which this can be done will vary according to your audience. As long as you are not boring or patronising, you can cover basic information without losing the attention of the more knowledgeable members in your audience.

Using PowerPoint® to deliver a talk

The PowerPoint® presentation program can be used to produce high quality aids for a spoken presentation, assuming a computer and digital projector are available where you intend to speak. PowerPoint® can also be used to create high quality overheads and handouts. The program is relatively easy to use if you are familiar with others in the Microsoft Office® suite. Your presentation is produced as a series of slides with a choice of backgrounds onto which you can insert headings, bullet points, digital images (e.g. in 'jpg' format), clipart and diagrams. An 'animation' (or 'build') feature allows you to reveal parts of slides in sequence and this will help you pace your talk.

When creating a PowerPoint® talk, you should bear the following points in mind:

- Background – choose whether you wish to present your talk as a light font on a dark background (more restful) or a dark font on a light background (more lively). Avoid flat and dull backgrounds, as these will seem uninteresting, or brightly coloured ones, as these will distract. A number of pre-set backgrounds are available (*Format* menu, *Apply design* option), but bear in mind that your audience may have seen these before.
- Layout – as you create each new slide, you can choose different layouts for the material. Areas designated for text or images can easily be modified later.
- Font – the default fonts for headings and bullet points are large (intentionally so, for clarity). Do not be tempted to reduce to less than 28 point to cram more words into the slide. If you have too much material, create a new slide and divide your information. Aim

Pitching your talk at the right level – the general rule should be: 'do not overestimate the background knowledge of your audience'. This sometimes happens in student presentations, where fears about the presence of 'experts' can encourage the speaker to include too much detail, overloading the audience with facts.

Consider providing your audience with a handout of your PowerPoint® talk – there are several options available, including some that provide space for notes (see Fig. 4.3).

Using the Slide Master – this useful feature of PowerPoint® allows you to specify the background and default font size for all slides in your presentation (accessed from the View menu, Master option). For instance, you can adjust the background and font colour, create a logo or 'footer' that identifies each slide in the talk as yours, and add slide numbers.

Using headings to structure your talk – when delivering a presentation given with overheads or PowerPoint® slides, keep the text to a minimum. Use these as prompts to structure what you have to say and if necessary, keep a separate set of notes to remind you of points you wish to raise. PowerPoint® incorporates a 'notes' option that allows you to record these easily.

for no more than 40 words per slide, preferably fewer. Try to use more than one font colour, perhaps to fit with levels of hierarchy in the material. Ensure the colours are complementary with each other and with the background.

- Text – use keywords and short phrases, rather than whole sentences. Do not simply read out the text from the screen during your presentation, as you will rapidly lose the attention of your audience.
- Images – slides simply made up of text alone can be very uninteresting. Adding images or diagrams can brighten up your talk considerably (use the *Insert* menu, *Picture* option). Images can be taken with a digital camera, scanned or copied from the Web, but you should take care not to break copyright regulations. Clipart is copyright-free, but use it sparingly, as most people will have seen the images before, and they are rarely wholly relevant. Diagrams can be made from components created using the *Drawing* menu.
- Animation – avoid excessive use of animation features such as movement of text onto the slide and sound effects, as these will distract both you and your listeners. However, you should consider revealing different topic points as you talk using the *Appear* command on the *Custom Animation, Effects* menu. This will prevent the audience trying to read ahead and will help you gain and keep their attention.

When delivering your talk using PowerPoint®, don't forget to engage the audience. Don't let the computer gadgetry distract you from the essential rules of good speaking, as discussed elsewhere in this chapter.

Content

While the specific details in your talk will be for you to decide, most spoken presentations share some common features of structure, as described below.

Introductory remarks

It is vital to capture the interest of your audience at the outset. Consequently, you must make sure your opening comments are strong, otherwise your audience will lose interest before you reach the main message. Remember it takes a sentence or two for an audience to establish a relationship with a new speaker. Your opening sentence should be some form of preamble and should not contain any key information. For a formal lecture, you might begin with 'Thank you for that introduction. My talk today is about …' then restate the title and acknowledge other contributors, etc. You might show a transparency or slide with the title printed on it, or an introductory photograph, if appropriate. This should provide the necessary settling-in period.

Getting the introduction right – a good idea is to have an initial slide giving your personal details and the title of your talk, and a second slide telling the audience how your presentation will be structured.

After these preliminaries, you should introduce your topic. Begin your story on a strong note – this is no place for timid or apologetic phrases. You should:

- explain the structure of your talk;
- set out the aims and objectives of your work;
- explain your approach to the topic.

Opening remarks are unlikely to occupy more than 10% of the talk. However, because of their significance, you might reasonably spend up to 25% of your preparation time on them. Make sure you have practised this section, so that you can deliver the material in a flowing style, with less chance of mistakes.

The main message

This section should include the bulk of your experimental results or literature findings, depending on the type of presentation. Keep details of methods to the minimum needed to explain your data. This is *not* the place for a detailed description of equipment and experimental protocol (unless it is a talk about methodology). Results should be presented in an easily digested format.

Do not expect your audience to cope with large amounts of data; use a maximum of six numbers per slide. Present summary statistics (Chapter 66) rather than individual results. Show the final results of any analyses in terms of the statistics calculated, and their significance (p. 486), rather than dwelling on details of the procedures used. Remember that graphs and diagrams are usually better than tables of raw data, since the audience will be able to see the trends and relationships in your data (p. 453). However, figures should not be crowded with unnecessary detail. Every diagram should have a concise title and the symbols and trend lines should be clearly labelled, with an explanatory key where necessary. When presenting graphical data always 'introduce' each graph by stating the units for each axis and describing the relationship for each trend line or data set. Summary slides can be used at regular intervals, to maintain the flow of the presentation and to emphasise the key points.

Take the audience through your story step-by-step at a reasonable pace. Try not to rush the delivery of your main message due to nervousness. Avoid complex, convoluted story-lines – one of the most distracting things you can do is to fumble backwards through slides or overhead transparencies. If you need to use the same diagram or graph more than once then you should make two (or more) copies. In a presentation of experimental results, you should discuss each point as it is raised, in contrast to written text, where the results and discussion may be in separate sections. The main message typically occupies approximately 80% of the time allocated to an oral presentation.

Concluding remarks

Having captured the interest of your audience in the introduction and given them the details of your story in the middle section, you must now bring your talk to a conclusion. At all costs, do not end weakly, e.g. by running out of steam on the last slide. Provide your audience with a clear 'take-home message', by returning to the key points in your presentation. It is often appropriate to prepare a slide or overhead transparency listing your main conclusions as a numbered series.

Signal the end of your talk by saying 'finally . . .', 'in conclusion . . .', or a similar comment and then finish speaking after that sentence. Your audience will lose interest if you extend your closing remarks beyond this point. You may add a simple end phrase (for example, 'thank you') as you put your notes into your folder, but do not say 'that's all folks!', or make any similar offhand remark. Finish as strongly and as clearly as you started.

Allowing time for slides – *as a rough guide you should allow at least two minutes per illustration, although some diagrams may need longer, depending on content.*

Final remarks – *make sure you give the audience sufficient time to assimilate your final slide: some of them may wish to write down the key points. Alternatively, you might provide a handout, with a brief outline of the aims of your study and the major conclusions.*

Hints on presentation

Notes

Many accomplished speakers use abbreviated notes for guidance, rather than reading from a prepared script. When writing your talk:

- Prepare a first draft as a full script: write in spoken English, keeping the text simple and avoiding an impersonal style. Aim to *talk* to your audience, not read to them.
- Use note cards with key phrases and words: it is best to avoid using a full script at the final presentation. As you rehearse and your confidence improves, a set of cards may be a more appropriate format for your notes.
- Consider the structure of your talk: keep it as simple as possible and announce each subdivision, so your audience is aware of the structure.
- Mark the position of slides/key points, etc.: each note card should contain details of structure, as well as content.
- Memorise your introductory/closing remarks: you may prefer to rely on a full written version for these sections, in case your memory fails.
- Use notes: write on only one side of the card/paper, in handwriting large enough to be read easily during the presentation. Each card or sheet must be clearly numbered, so that you do not lose your place.
- Rehearse your presentation: ask a friend to listen and to comment constructively on parts that were difficult to follow.
- Use 'split times' to pace yourself: following rehearsal, note the time at which you should arrive at key points of your talk. These timing marks will help you keep to time during the 'real thing'.

Using slides or PowerPoint® – check that the lecture theatre has a lectern light, otherwise you may have problems reading your notes when the lights are dimmed.

Image

Ensure that the image you project is appropriate for the occasion:

- Consider what to wear: aim to be respectable without 'dressing up', otherwise your message may be diminished.
- Develop a good posture: it will help your voice projection if you stand upright, rather than slouching or leaning over the lectern.
- Project your voice: speak towards the back of the room.
- Make eye contact: look at members of the audience in all parts of the room. Avoid talking to your notes, or to only one section of the audience.
- Deliver your material with expression: arm movements and subdued body language will help maintain the interest of your audience. However, you should avoid extreme gestures (it may work for some TV personalities, but it isn't recommended for the beginner!).
- Try to identify and control any distracting repetitive mannerisms, e.g. repeated empty phrases, fidgeting with pens, keys, etc., as this will distract your audience. Practising in front of a mirror may help.
- Practise your delivery: use the comments of your friends to improve your performance.

Managing your time when speaking – avoid looking at your watch as it gives a negative signal to the audience. Use a wall clock, if one is provided, or take off your watch and put it beside your notes, so you can glance at it without distracting your audience.

Questions

Many speakers are worried by the prospect of questions after their oral presentation. Once again, the best approach is to prepare beforehand:

- Consider what questions you may be asked: prepare brief answers.

- Do not be afraid to say 'I don't know': your audience will appreciate honesty, rather than vacillation, if you don't have an answer for a particular question.
- Avoid arguing with a questioner: suggest a discussion afterwards rather than becoming involved in a debate about specific details.
- If no questions are forthcoming you may pose a question yourself, and then ask for opinions from the audience: if you use this approach you should be prepared to comment briefly if your audience has no suggestions. This will prevent the presentation from ending in an embarrassing silence.

Sources for further study

Capp, C.C. and Capp, G.R. (1989) *Basic Oral Communication*, 5th edn. Prentice Hall, Harlow.

Matthews, C. and Marino, J. (1999) *Professional Interactions: Oral Communication Skills of Science, Technology and Medicine*. Pearson, Harlow.

Radel, J. *Oral Presentations*. Available:
http://www.biology.eku.edu/RITCHISO/oralpres.html
Last accessed 08/01/03.

Study exercises

15.1 **Prepare a checklist for assessing the quality of an oral presentation**. After reading through the material in this chapter, prepare a 10-point checklist of assessment criteria under the heading 'What makes a good oral presentation?' Compare your list with the one that we have provided (p. 501) – do you agree with our criteria, or do you prefer your own checklist (and can you justify your preferences)?

15.2 **Evaluate the presentation styles of other speakers**. There are many opportunities to assess the strengths and weaknesses of academic 'public speakers', including your lecturers, seminar speakers, presenters of TV documentaries, etc. Decide in advance how you are going to tackle the evaluation (e.g. with a quantitative marking scheme, or a less formal procedure).

15.3 **Rehearse a talk and get feedback on your performance**. There are a number of approaches you might take, including: (i) recording and reviewing your presentation on 'video'; or (ii) giving your talk to a small group of fellow students and asking them to provide constructive feedback.

16   General aspects of scientific writing

Written communication is an essential component of all sciences. Most courses include writing exercises in which you will learn to describe ideas and results accurately, succinctly and in an appropriate style and format. The following are features common to all forms of scientific writing.

Organising time

Time management – practical advice is given in Chapter 2, pp. 7–11.

Making a timetable at the outset helps ensure that you give each stage adequate attention and complete the work on time. To create and use a timetable:

1. Break down the task into stages.
2. Decide on the proportion of the total time each stage should take.
3. Set realistic deadlines for completing each stage, allowing some time for slippage.
4. Refer to your timetable frequently as you work: if you fail to meet one of your deadlines, make a serious effort to catch up as soon as possible.

KEY POINT   The appropriate allocation of your time to reading, planning, writing and revising will differ according to the task in hand (see Chapters 17–19).

Organising information and ideas

Before you write, you need to gather and/or think about relevant material (Chapters 8 and 9). You must then decide:

- what needs to be included and what doesn't;
- in what order it should appear.

Start by jotting down headings for everything of potential relevance to the topic (this is sometimes called 'brainstorming'). A spider diagram (Fig. 16.1) or a Mind Map® (Fig. 4.2) will help you organise these ideas. The next stage is to create an outline of your text (Fig. 16.2). Outlines are valuable because they:

Creating an outline – an informal outline can be made simply by indicating the order of sections on a spider diagram (as in Fig. 16.1).

- force you to think about and plan the structure;
- provide a checklist so nothing is missed out;
- ensure the material is balanced in content and length;
- help you organise figures and tables by showing where they will be used.

In an essay or review, the structure of your writing should help the reader to assimilate and understand your main points. Subdivisions of the topic could simply be related to the physical nature of the subject matter (e.g. levels of organisation of a protein) and should proceed logically (e.g. primary structure then secondary, etc.).

A chronological approach is good for evaluation of past work (e.g. the development of the concept of DNA as the hereditary material), whereas a step-by-step comparison might be best for certain exam questions (e.g. 'Discuss the differences between prokaryotes and eukaryotes'). There is little choice about structure for practical and project reports (see p. 104).

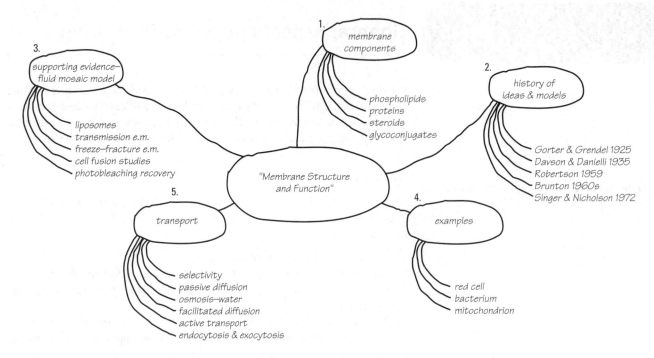

Fig. 16.1 Spider diagram showing how you might 'brainstorm' an essay with the title 'Membrane Structure and Function'. Write out the essay title in full to form the spider's body, and as you think of possible content, place headings around this to form its legs. Decide which headings are relevant and which are not and use arrows to note connections between subjects. This may influence your choice of order and may help to make your writing flow because the links between paragraphs will be natural. You can make an informal outline directly on a spider diagram by adding numbers indicating a sequence of paragraphs (as shown). This method is best when you must work quickly, as with an essay written under exam conditions.

Fig. 16.2 Formal outlines. These are useful for a long piece of work where you or the reader might otherwise lose track of the structure. The headings for sections and paragraphs are simply written in sequence with the type of lettering and level of indentation indicating their hierarchy. Two different forms of formal outline are shown, a minimal form (a) and a numbered form (b). Note that the headings used in an outline are often repeated within the essay to emphasise its structure. The content of an outline will depend on the time you have available and the nature of the work, but the most detailed hierarchy you should reasonably include is the subject of each paragraph.

Membrane structure and function

Introduction
   membrane components
      phospholipids
      proteins
      sterols
      glycoconjugates
   history of ideas & models
      Gorter & Grendel 1925
      Davson & Danielli 1935
      Robertson 1959
      Brunton 1960s
      Singer & Nicholson 1972
Supporting evidence – fluid mosaic model
   liposomes
   transmission e.m.
   freeze-fracture e.m.
   cell fusion studies
   photobleaching recovery
Transport
   selectivity
   passive diffusion
   osmosis – water
   facilitated diffusion
   active transport
   endocytosis & exocytosis
Examples
   red cell
   bacterium
   mitochondrion

(a)

Membrane structure and function

1. INTRODUCTION
   1.1 membrane components
      1.1.1 phospholipids
      1.1.2 proteins
      1.1.3 sterols
      1.1.4 glycoconjugates
   1.2 history of ideas & models
      1.2.1 Gorter & Grendel 1925
      1.2.2 Davson & Danielli 1935
      1.2.3 Robertson 1959
      1.2.4 Brunton 1960s
      1.2.5 Singer & Nicholson 1972
2. SUPPORTING EVIDENCE – FLUID MOSAIC MODEL
   2.1 liposomes
   2.2 transmission e.m.
   2.3 freeze-fracture e.m.
   2.4 cell fusion studies
   2.5 photobleaching recovery
3. TRANSPORT
   3.1 selectivity
   3.2 passive diffusion
   3.3 osmosis – water
   3.4 facilitated diffusion
   3.5 active transport
   3.5 endocytosis & exocytosis
4. EXAMPLES
   4.1 red cell
   4.2 bacterium
   4.3 mitochondrion

(b)

Writing

Adopting a scientific style

Your main aim in developing a scientific style should be to get your message across directly and unambiguously. While you can try to achieve this through a set of 'rules' (see Box 16.1), you may find other requirements driving your writing in a contradictory direction. For instance, the need to be accurate and complete may result in text littered with technical terms, and the flow may be continually interrupted by references to the literature. The need to be succinct also affects style and readability through the use of, for example, stacked noun-adjectives (e.g. 'restriction fragment length polymorphism') and acronyms (e.g. 'RFLP'). Finally, style is very much a matter of taste and each tutor, examiner, supervisor or editor will have pet loves and hates which you may have to accommodate.

Developing technique

Writing is a skill that can be improved, but not instantly. You should analyse your deficiencies with the help of feedback from your tutors, be prepared to change work habits (e.g. start planning your work more carefully), and willing to learn from some of the excellent texts that are available on scientific writing (p. 97–8).

Getting started

A common problem is 'writer's block' – inactivity or stalling brought on by a variety of causes. If blocked, ask yourself these questions:

- Are you comfortable with your surroundings? Make sure you are seated comfortably at a reasonably clear desk and have minimised the possibility of interruptions and distractions.
- Are you trying to write too soon? Have you clarified your thoughts on the subject? Have you done enough preliminary reading?
- Are you happy with the underlying structure of your work? If you haven't made an outline, try this. If you are unhappy because you can't think of a particular detail at the planning stage, just start writing – it is more likely to come to you while you are thinking of something else.
- Are you trying to be too clever? Your first sentence doesn't have to be earth-shattering in content or particularly smart in style. A short statement of fact or a definition is fine. If there will be time for revision, get your ideas down on paper and revise grammar, content and order later.
- Do you really need to start writing at the beginning? Try writing the opening remarks after a more straightforward part. With reports of experimental work, the Materials and Methods section may be the easiest to start at.
- Are you too tired to work? Don't try to 'sweat it out' by writing for long periods at a stretch: stop frequently for a rest.

Revising your text

Wholesale revision of your first draft is strongly advised for all writing, apart from in exams. If a word processor is available, this can be a simple process. Where possible, schedule your writing so you can leave the first

Improving your writing skills – you need to take a long-term view if you wish to improve your writing skills. An essential preliminary is to invest in and make full use of a personal reference library (see Box 16.2).

Talking about your work – discussing your topic with a friend or colleague might bring out ideas or reveal deficiencies in your knowledge.

Box 16.1   How to achieve a clear, readable style

Words and phrases

- Choose short clear words and phrases rather than long ones: e.g. use 'build' rather than 'fabricate'; 'now' rather than 'at the present time'. At certain times, technical terms must be used for precision, but don't use jargon if you don't have to.
- Don't worry too much about repeating words, especially when to introduce an alternative might subtly alter your meaning.
- Where appropriate, use the first person to describe your actions ('We decided to '; 'I conclude that '), but not if this is specifically discouraged by your supervisor or Department.
- Favour active forms of writing ('the observer completed the survey in ten minutes') rather than a passive style ('the survey was completed by the observer in ten minutes').
- Use tenses consistently. Past tense is always used for materials and methods ('samples were taken from...') and for reviewing past work ('Smith (1990) concluded that...'). The present tense is used when describing data ('Fig. 1 shows...'), for generalisations ('Most authorities agree that...') and conclusions ('It can be concluded that ...').
- Use statements in parentheses sparingly – they disrupt the reader's attention to your central theme.
- Avoid clichés and colloquialisms – they are usually inappropriate in a scientific context.

Punctuation

- Try to use a variety of types of punctuation, to make the text more interesting to read.
- Decide whether you wish to use 'closed' punctuation (frequent commas at the end of clauses) or 'open' punctuation (less frequent punctuation) and be consistent.
- Don't link two sentences with a comma. Use a full stop, this is an example of what *not* to do.
- Pay special attention to apostrophes, using the following rules:
  - To indicate possession, use an apostrophe before an 's' for a singular word (e.g. the rat's temperature was...') and after the s for a plural word ending in s (e.g. the rats' temperatures were = the temperatures of the rats were). If the word has a special plural (e.g. woman → women) then use the apostrophe before the s (the women's temperatures were ...).
  - When contracting words, use an apostrophe (e.g. do not = don't; it's = it is), but remember that contractions are generally *not* used in formal scientific writing.
  - Do *not* use an apostrophe for 'its' as the possessive form of 'it' (e.g. 'the university and its surroundings') Note that 'it's' is reserved for 'it is'. This is an exception to the general rule and a very common mistake.
  - Never use an apostrophe to indicate plurals. Even for abbreviations, the accepted style is now to omit the apostrophe for the plural (e.g. write 'the ELISAs were').

Sentences

- Don't make them over-long or complicated.
- Introduce variety in structure and length.
- If unhappy with the structure of a sentence, try chopping it into a series of shorter sentences.

Paragraphs

- Get the paragraph length right – five sentences or so. Do *not* submit an essay that consists of a single paragraph, nor one of single sentence paragraphs.
- Make sure each paragraph is logical, dealing with a single topic or theme.
- Take care with the first sentence in a paragraph (the 'topic' sentence); this introduces the theme of the paragraph. Further sentences should then develop this theme, e.g. by providing supporting information, examples or contrasting cases.
- Use 'linking' words or phrases to maintain the flow of the text within a paragraph (e.g. 'for example'; 'in contrast'; 'however'; 'on the other hand').
- Make your text more readable, by adopting modern layout style. The first paragraph in any section of text is usually *not* indented, but following paragraphs are (by the equivalent of three character spaces). In addition, the space between paragraphs should be slightly larger than the space between lines. Follow departmental guidelines if these specify a format.
- Group paragraphs in sections under appropriate headings and sub-headings to reinforce the structure underlying your writing.
- Think carefully about the first and last paragraphs in any piece of writing: these are often the most important as they respectively set the aims and report the conclusions.

Note: If you're not sure what is meant by any of the terms used here, consult a guide on writing (see sources for further study).

Box 16.2   Improve your writing ability by consulting a personal reference library

Using dictionaries

We all know that a dictionary helps with spelling and definitions, but how many of us use one effectively? You should:

- Keep a dictionary beside you when writing and always use it if in any doubt about spelling or definitions.
- Use it to prepare a list of words which you have difficulty in spelling: apart from speeding up the checking process, the act of writing out the words helps commit them to memory.
- Use it to write out a personal glossary of terms. This can help you memorise definitions. From time to time, test yourself.

Not all dictionaries are the same! Ask your tutor or supervisor whether he/she has a preference and why. Try out the *Oxford Advanced Learner's Dictionary*, which is particularly useful because it gives examples of use of all words and helps with grammar, e.g. by indicating which prepositions to use with verbs. Dictionaries of biology tend to be variable in quality, possibly because the subject is so wide and new terms are continually being coined. *Henderson's Dictionary of Biological Terms* is a useful example.

Using a thesaurus

A thesaurus contains lists of words of similar meaning grouped thematically; words of opposite meaning always appear nearby.

- Use a thesaurus to find a more precise and appropriate word to fit your meaning, but check definitions of unfamiliar words with a dictionary.
- Use it to find a word or phrase 'on the tip of your tongue' by looking up a word of similar meaning.
- Use it to increase your vocabulary.

Roget's Thesaurus is the standard. Collins also publish a combined dictionary and thesaurus.

Using guides for written English

These provide help with the use of words.

- Use guides to solve grammatical problems such as when to use 'shall' or 'will', 'which' or 'that', 'effect' or 'affect', etc.
- Use them for help with the paragraph concept and the correct use of punctuation.
- Use them to learn how to structure writing for different tasks.

---

draft to 'settle' for at least a couple of days. When you return to it fresh, you will see more easily where improvements can be made. Try the following structured revision process, each stage being covered in a separate scan of your text:

1. Examine content. Have you included everything you need to? Is all the material relevant?
2. Check the grammar and spelling. Can you spot any 'howlers'?
3. Focus on clarity. Is the text clear and unambiguous? Does each sentence really say what you want it to say?
4. Be succinct. What could be missed out without spoiling the essence of your work? It might help to imagine an editor has set you the target of reducing the text by 15%.
5. Improve style. Could the text read better? Consider the sentence and paragraph structure and the way your text develops to its conclusion.

Revising your text – to improve clarity and shorten your text, 'distil' each sentence by taking away unnecessary words and 'condense' words or phrases by choosing a shorter alternative.

Sources for further study

Burchfield, R.W. (ed.) (1996) *Fowler's Modern English Usage*, 3rd edn. Clarendon Press, Oxford.

Clark, R. *The English Style Book. A Guide to the Writing of Scholarly English*. Available:
http://www.uea.ac.uk/eas/People/clark/TheEnglishStyleBook.htm
Last accessed 08/01/03.

Kane, T.S. (1983) *The Oxford Guide to Writing*. Oxford University Press, New York.
[This is excellent for the basics of English – it covers grammar, usage and the construction of sentences and paragraphs.]

Lindsay, D. (1995) *A Guide to Scientific Writing*, 2nd edn. Longman, Harlow.

Partridge, E. (1990) *You Have a Point There*. Routledge and Kegan Paul, London.
[This covers punctuation in a very readable manner.]

Pechnick, J.A. and Lamb, B.C. (1994) *How to Write about Biology*. HarperCollins, London.

Tichy, H.J. (1988) *Effective Writing for Engineers, Managers and Scientists*. John Wiley and Sons, New York.
[This is strong on scientific style and clarity in writing.]

Study exercises

16.1 'Brainstorm' an essay title. Pair up with a partner in your class. Together, pick a suitable essay title from a past exam paper. Using the spider diagram or another technique, individually 'brainstorm' the title. Meet afterwards, compare your ideas, and discuss their relative merits and disadvantages.

16.2 Improve your writing technique. From the following checklist, identify the *three* weakest aspects of your writing, either in your own opinion or from essay/assignment feedback:

- grammar;
- paragraph organisation;
- presentation of work;
- punctuation;
- scientific style;
- sentence structure/variety;
- spelling;
- structure and flow;
- vocabulary.

Now visit a local library (or bookshop) and take out (or buy) a book or books that deal(s) with your weakest aspects of writing. Read the relevant chapters or sections and for each aspect write down some tips that should help you in future.

16.3 Improve your spelling and vocabulary with two lists. Create a pair of lists and pin these up beside your desk. One should be entitled *Spelling Mistakes* and the other *New Words*. Now, whenever you make a mistake in spelling or have to look up how to spell a word in a dictionary, add the problem word to your spelling list, showing where you made the mistake. Also, whenever you come across a word whose meaning is unclear to you, look it up in a dictionary and write the word and its meaning in the 'new words' vocabulary list.

Writing essays

The function of an essay is to show how much you understand about a topic and how well you can organise and express your knowledge.

Organising your time

The way you should divide your time when producing an essay depends on whether you are writing it for in-course assessment or under exam conditions (Fig. 17.1). Essays written over a long period with access to books and other resources will probably involve a research element, not only before the planning phase but also when writing (Fig. 17.1a). For exams, it is assumed that you have revised appropriately (Chapter 5) and essentially have all the information at your fingertips. To keep things uncomplicated, the time allocated for each essay should be divided into three components – planning, writing and reviewing (Fig. 17.1b), and you should adopt time-saving techniques whenever possible (Box 6.2).

Making a plan for your essay

Dissect the meaning of the essay question or title

Read the title very carefully and think about the topic before starting to write. Consider the definitions of each of the important nouns (this can

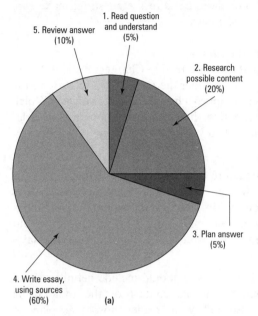

1. Read question and understand (5%)
5. Review answer (10%)
2. Research possible content (20%)
3. Plan answer (5%)
4. Write essay, using sources (60%)
(a)

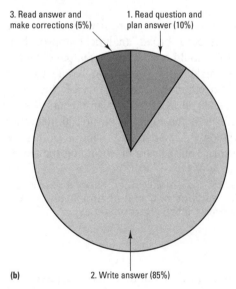

3. Read answer and make corrections (5%)
1. Read question and plan answer (10%)
2. Write answer (85%)
(b)

Fig. 17.1 Typical division of time for an essay written as part of an in-course assessment (a) or under exam conditions (b).

Table 17.1 Instructions often used in essay questions and their meanings. When more than one instruction is given (e.g. compare and contrast; describe and explain), make sure you carry out *both* or you may lose a large proportion of the available marks

Account for:	give the reasons for
Analyse:	examine in depth and describe the main characteristics of
Assess:	weigh up the elements of and arrive at a conclusion about
Comment:	give an opinion on and provide evidence for your views
Compare:	bring out the similarities between
Contrast:	bring out dissimilarities between
Criticise:	judge the worth of (give both positive and negative aspects)
Define:	explain the exact meaning of
Describe:	use words and diagrams to illustrate
Discuss:	provide evidence or opinions about, arriving at a balanced conclusion
Enumerate:	list in outline form
Evaluate:	weigh up or appraise; find a numerical value for
Explain:	make the meaning of something clear
Illustrate:	use diagrams or examples to make clear
Interpret:	express in simple terms, providing a judgement
Justify:	show that an idea or statement is correct
List:	provide an itemised series of statements about
Outline:	describe the essential parts only, stressing the classification
Prove:	establish the truth of
Relate:	show the connection between
Review:	examine critically, perhaps concentrating on the stages in the development of an idea or method
State:	express clearly
Summarise:	without illustrations, provide a brief account of
Trace:	describe a sequence of events from a defined point of origin

Essay content – it is rarely enough simply to lay down facts for the reader – you must analyse them and comment on their significance.

Ten Golden Rules for essay writing – these are framed for in-course assessments (p. 25), though many are also relevant for exams (see also Box 6.2).

1. Read the question carefully, and decide exactly what the assessor wants you to achieve in your answer.
2. Make sure you understand the question by considering all aspects – discuss your approach with colleagues or a tutor.
3. Carry out the necessary research (using books, journals, the Web), taking appropriate notes. Gain an overview of the topic before getting involved with the details.
4. Always plan your work in outline before you start writing. Check that your plan covers the main points and that it flows logically.
5. Introduce your essay by showing that you understand the topic and stating how you intend to approach it.
6. As you write the main content, ensure it is relevant by continually looking back at the question.
7. Use headings and sub-headings to organise and structure your essay.
8. Support your statements with relevant examples, diagrams and references where appropriate.
9. Conclude by summarising the key points of the topic, indicating the present state of knowledge, what we still need to find out and how this might be achieved.
10. Always review your essay before submitting it. Check grammar and spelling and confirm that you have answered all aspects of the question.

Using diagrams – give a title and legend to each diagram so that it makes sense in isolation and point out in the text when the reader should consult it (e.g. 'as shown in Fig. 1 ...' or 'as can be seen in the accompanying diagram, ...').

help in approaching the introductory section). Also think about the meaning of the verb(s) used and try to follow each instruction precisely (see Table 17.1). Don't get side-tracked because you know something about one word or phrase in the title: consider the whole title and all its ramifications. If there are two or more parts to the question, make sure you give adequate attention to each part.

Consider possible content and examples

Research content using the methods described in Chapters 8 and 9. If you have time to read several sources, consider their content in relation to the essay title. Can you spot different approaches to the same subject? Which do you prefer as a means of treating the topic in relation to your title? Which examples are most relevant to your case, and why?

Construct an outline

Every essay should have a structure related to its title. Most marks for essays are lost because the written material is badly organised or is irrelevant. An essay plan, by definition, creates order and, if thought about carefully, can ensure relevance. Your plan should be written down (but scored through later if written in an exam book). Think about an essay's content in three parts:

1. The introductory section, in which you should include definitions and some background information on the context of the topic being considered. You should also tell your reader how you plan to approach the subject.
2. The middle of the essay, where you develop your answer and provide relevant examples. Decide whether a broad analytical approach is appropriate or whether the essay should contain more factual detail.
3. The conclusion, which you can make quite short. You should use this part to summarise and draw together the components of the essay, without merely repeating previous phrases. You might mention such things as: the broader significance of the topic; its future; its relevance to other important areas of biology. Always try to mention both sides of any debate you have touched on, but beware of 'sitting on the fence'.

KEY POINT Use paragraphs to make the essay's structure obvious. Emphasise them with headings and sub-headings unless the material beneath the headings would be too short or trivial.

Now start writing!

- Never lose track of the importance of content and its relevance. Repeatedly ask yourself: 'Am I really answering this question?' Never waffle just to increase the length of an essay. Quality rather than quantity is important.
- Illustrate your answer appropriately. Use examples to make your points clear, but remember that too many similar examples can stifle the flow of an essay. Use diagrams where a written description would be difficult or take too long. Use tables to condense information.
- Take care with your handwriting. You can't get marks if your writing is illegible! Try to cultivate an open form of handwriting, making the individual letters large and distinct. If there is time, make out a rough draft from which a tidy version can be copied.

Reviewing your answer

Don't stop until you have:

- re-read the question to check that you have answered all points;
- re-read your essay to check for errors in punctuation, spelling and content. Make any corrections obvious. Don't panic if you suddenly realise you've missed a large chunk out as the reader can be redirected to a supplementary paragraph if necessary.

Sources for further study

Anon. (2000) *Essay and Report Writing Skills*. Open University, Milton Keynes.

Anon. *Yahoo! Directory: Writing > Essays and Research Papers*. Available:
http://d3.dir.dcx.yahoo.com/Social_Science/Communications/Writing/Essays_and_Research_Papers
Last accessed 08/01/03.
[An extensive directory of Web resources.]

Good, S. and Jensen, B. (1995) *The Student's Only Survival Guide to Essay Writing*. Orca Book Publishers, Victoria.

Study exercises

17.1 Practise dissecting essay titles. Use past exam papers, or make up questions based on learning objectives for your course and your lecture notes. Take each essay title and carefully 'dissect' the wording, working out exactly what you think the assessor expects you to do (see e.g. Table 17.1).

17.2 Write essay plans under self-imposed time limits. Continuing from 17.1, outline plans for essays from a past exam paper. Allow yourself a maximum of 5 minutes per outline. Within this time your main goal is to create an essay plan. To do this, you may need to 'brainstorm' the topic. Alternatively, if you allocate 10 minutes per essay, you may be able to provide more details, e.g. list the examples you could describe.

17.3 Practise reviewing your work carefully. For the next assignment you write, review it fully as part of the writing process. This will require you to finish the first draft about one week before the hand-in date, e.g. by setting yourself an earlier deadline than the submission date. This exercise is best done with a word processed essay. Do not worry if it is a little over the word limit at the draft stage.

(a) Print out a copy of the essay. Do not look at it for at least two days after finishing this version.

(b) Review 1: spelling, grammar and sense. Read through the draft critically (try to imagine it had been written by someone else) and correct any obvious errors that strike you. Does the text make sense? Do the sentences and paragraphs flow smoothly?

(c) Review 2: structure and relevance. Consider again the structure of the essay, asking yourself whether you have really

Learning from lecturers' and tutors' comments – ask for further explanations if you don't understand a comment or why an essay was less successful than you thought it should have been.

answered the question that was set (see Study Exercise 17.1). Are all the parts in the right order? Is anything missed out? Have you followed precisely the instruction(s) in the title? Are the different parts of the essay linked together well?

(d) Review 3: shorten and improve style. Check the word count. Shorten the essay if required. Look critically at the phrasing, and, even if the essay is within the word limit, ask yourself whether any of the words are unnecessary or whether the phrasing could be made more concise, more precise or more apt.

Reporting practical and project work

Typical structure of scientific reports – this follows the 'IMRaD' acronym: **I**ntroduction, **M**aterials and Methods, **R**esults and **D**iscussion.

Practical reports, project reports, theses and scientific papers differ greatly in depth, scope and size, but they all have the same basic structure. Some variation is permitted, however (see Box 18.1), and you should always follow the advice or rules provided by your Department.

Additional parts may be specified: for theses, a title page is often required and a List of Figures and Tables as part of the Contents section. When work is submitted for certain degrees, you may need to include certain declarations and statements made by the student and supervisor. In scientific papers, a list of Key Words is often added following the Abstract: this information may be combined with words in the title for computer cross-referencing systems.

KEY POINT Department or Faculty regulations may specify a precise format for producing your report or thesis. Obtain a copy of these rules at an early stage and follow them closely.

Practical and project reports

These are exercises designed to make you think more deeply about your experiments and to practise and test the skills necessary for writing up research work. Special features are:

- Introductory material is generally short and unless otherwise specified should outline the aims of the experiment(s) with a minimum of background material.
- Materials and methods may be provided by your supervisor for practical reports. If you make changes to this, you should state clearly what you did. With project work, your lab notebook (see p. 172) should provide the basis for writing this section.
- Great attention in assessment will be paid to presentation and analysis of data. Take special care over graphs (see p. 458). Make sure your conclusions are justified by the evidence.

Options for discussing data – the main optional variants of the general structure include combining Results and Discussion *into a single section* and adding a separate Conclusions *section*.

- *The main advantage of a joint* Results and Discussion *section is that you can link together different experiments, perhaps explaining why a particular result led to a new hypothesis and the next experiment.*
- *The main advantage of having a separate* Conclusions *section is to draw together and emphasise the chief points arising from your work, when these may have been 'buried' in an extensive* Discussion *section.*

Theses

Theses are submitted as part of the examination for a degree following an extended period of research. They act to place on record full details about your experimental work and will normally only be read by those with a direct interest in it – your examiners or colleagues. Note the following:

- You are allowed scope to expand on your findings and to include detail that might otherwise be omitted in a scientific paper.
- You may have problems with the volume of information that has to be organised. One method of coping with this is to divide your thesis into chapters, each having the standard format (as in Box 18.1). A General Introduction can be given at the start and a General Discussion at the end. Discuss this with your supervisor.
- There may be an oral exam (*viva*) associated with the submission of the thesis. The primary aim of the examiners will be to ensure that you understand what you did and why you did it.

Box 18.1 The structure of reports of experimental work

Undergraduate practical and project reports are generally modelled on this arrangement or a close variant of it, because this is the structure used for nearly all research papers and theses. The more common variations include Results and Discussion combined into a single section and Conclusions appearing separately as a series of points arising from the work. In scientific papers, a list of Key Words (for computer cross-referencing systems) may be included following the Abstract. Acknowledgements may appear after the Contents section, rather than near the end. Department or faculty regulations for producing theses and reports may specify a precise format; they often require a title page to be inserted at the start and a list of figures and tables as part of the Contents section, and may specify declarations and statements to be made by the student and supervisor.

Part (in order)	Contents/purpose	Checklist for reviewing content
Title	Explains what the project was about	Does it explain what the text is about succinctly?
Authors plus their institutions	Explains who did the work and where; also where they can be contacted now	Are all the details correct?
Abstract/Summary	Synopsis of methods, results and conclusion of work described. Allows the reader to grasp quickly the essence of the work	Does it explain why the work was done? Does it outline the whole of your work and your findings?
List of Contents	Shows the organisation of the text (not required for short papers)	Are all the sections covered? Are the page numbers correct?
Abbreviations	Lists all the abbreviations used (but not those of SI, chemical elements or standard biochemical terms)	Have they all been explained? Are they all in the accepted form? Are they in alphabetical order?
Introduction	Orientates the reader, explains why the work has been done and its context in the literature, why the methods used were chosen, why the experimental organisms were chosen. Indicates the central hypothesis behind the experiments	Does it provide enough background information and cite all the relevant references? Is it of the correct depth for the readership? Have all the technical terms been defined? Have you explained why you investigated the problem? Have you outlined your aims and objectives? Have you explained your methodological approach? Have you stated your hypothesis?
Materials and Methods	Explains how the work was done. Should contain sufficient detail to allow another competent worker to repeat the work	Is each experiment covered and have you avoided unnecessary duplication? Is there sufficient detail to allow repetition of the work? Are proper scientific names and authorities given for all organisms? Have you explained where you got them from? Are the correct names, sources and grades given for all chemicals?
Results	Displays and describes the data obtained. Should be presented in a form which is easily assimilated (graphs rather than tables, small tables rather than large ones)	Is the sequence of experiments logical? Are the parts adequately linked? Are the data presented in the clearest possible way? Have SI units been used properly throughout? Has adequate statistical analysis been carried out? Is all the material relevant? Are the figures and tables all numbered in the order of their appearance? Are their titles appropriate? Do the figure and table legends provide all the information necessary to interpret the data without reference to the text? Have you presented the same data more than once?
Discussion/ Conclusions	Discusses the results: their meaning, their importance; compares the results with those of others; suggests what to do next	Have you explained the significance of the results? Have you compared your data with other published work? Are your conclusions justified by the data presented?
Acknowledgements	Gives credit to those who helped carry out the work	Have you listed everyone that helped, including any grant-awarding bodies?
Literature Cited (Bibliography)	Lists all references cited in appropriate format: provides enough information to allow the reader to find the reference in a library	Do all the references in the text appear on the list? Do all the listed references appear in the text? Do the years of publications and authors match? Are the journal details complete and in the correct format? Is the list in alphabetical order, or correct numerical order?

Steps in the production of a practical report or thesis

Choose the experiments you wish to describe and decide how best to present them

Try to start this process before your lab work ends, because at the stage of reviewing your experiments, a gap may become apparent (e.g. a missing control) and you might still have time to rectify the deficiency. Irrelevant material should be ruthlessly eliminated, at the same time bearing in mind that negative results can be extremely important (see p. 182). Use as many different forms of data presentation as are appropriate, but avoid presenting the same data in more than one form. Graphs are generally easier for the reader to assimilate, while tables can be used to condense a lot of data into a small space. Relegate large tables of data to an appendix and summarise the important points. Make sure that the experiments you describe are representative: always state the number of times they were repeated and how consistent your findings were.

Repeating your experiments – remember, if you do an experiment twice, you have repeated it only once!

Make up plans or outlines for the component parts

The overall plan is well defined (see Box 18.1), but individual parts will need to be organised as with any other form of writing (see Chapter 16).

Write!

The Materials and Methods section is often the easiest to write once you have decided what to report. Remember to use the past tense and do not allow results or discussion to creep in. The Results section is the next easiest as it should only involve description. At this stage, you may benefit from jotting down ideas for the Discussion – this may be the hardest part to compose as you need an overview both of your own work and of the relevant literature. It is also liable to become wordy, so try hard to make it succinct. The Introduction shouldn't be too difficult if you have fully understood the aims of the experiments. Write the Abstract and complete the list of references at the end. To assist with the latter, it is a good idea as you write to jot down the references you use or to pull out their cards from your index system.

Presenting your results – remember that the order of results presented in a report need not correspond with the order in which you carried out the experiments: you are expected to rearrange them to provide a logical sequence of findings.

Revise the text

Once your first draft is complete, try to answer all the questions given in Box 18.1. Show your work to your supervisors and learn from their comments. Let a friend or colleague who is unfamiliar with your subject read your text; they may be able to pinpoint obscure wording and show where information or explanation is missing. If writing a thesis, double-check that you are adhering to your institution's thesis regulations.

Prepare the final version

Markers appreciate neatly produced work but a well-presented document will not disguise poor science! If using a word processor, print the final version with the best printer available. Make sure figures are clear and in the correct size and format.

Submit your work

Your department will specify when to submit a thesis or project report, so plan your work carefully to meet this deadline or you may lose marks. Tell your supervisor early of any circumstances that may cause delay.

Producing a scientific paper

Scientific papers are the means by which research findings are communicated to others. They are published in journals with a wide circulation among academics and are 'peer reviewed' by one or more referees before being accepted. Each journal covers a well-defined subject area and publishes details of the format they expect. It would be very unusual for an undergraduate to submit a paper on his or her own – this would normally be done in collaboration with your project supervisor and only then if your research has satisfied appropriate criteria. However, it is important to understand the process whereby a paper comes into being (Box 18.2), as this can help you when interpreting the primary literature.

Box 18.2 Steps in producing a scientific paper

Scientific papers are the lifeblood of any science and it is a major landmark in your scientific career to publish your first paper. The main steps in doing this should include the following:

Assessing potential content
The work must be of an appropriate standard to be published and should be 'new, true and meaningful'. Therefore, before starting, the authors need to review their work critically under these headings. The material included in a scientific paper will generally be a subset of the total work done during a project, so it must be carefully selected for relevance to a clear central hypothesis – if the authors won't prune, the referees and editors of the journal certainly will!

Choosing a journal
There are thousands of journals covering biology and each covers a specific area (which may change through time). The main factors in deciding on an appropriate journal are the range of subjects it covers, the quality of its content and the number and geographical distribution of its readers. The choice of journal always dictates the format of a paper since authors must follow to the letter the journal's 'Instructions to Authors'.

Deciding on authorship
In multi-author papers, a contentious issue is often who should appear as an author and in what order they should be cited. Where authors make an equal contribution, an alphabetical order of names may be used. Otherwise, each author should have made a substantial contribution to the paper and should be prepared to defend it in public. Ideally, the order of appearance will reflect the amount of work done rather than seniority. This may not always happen in practice!

Writing
The paper's format will be similar to that shown in Box 18.1 and the process of writing will include outlining, reviewing, etc., as discussed elsewhere in this chapter. Figures must be finished to an appropriate standard and this may involve preparing photographs or digital images of them.

Submitting
When completed, copies of the paper are submitted to the editor of the chosen journal with a simple covering letter. A delay of one to two months usually follows while the manuscript is sent to one or more anonymous referees who will be asked by the editor to check that the paper is novel, scientifically correct and that its length is fully justified.

Responding to referees' comments
The editor will send on the referees' comments to the authors who will then have a chance to respond. The editor will decide on the basis of the comments and replies to them whether the paper should be published. Sometimes quite heated correspondence can result if the authors and referees disagree!

Checking proofs and waiting for publication
If a paper is accepted, it will be sent off to the typesetters. The next the authors see of it is the proofs (first printed version in style of journal), which have to be corrected carefully for errors and returned. Eventually, the paper will appear in print, but a delay of six months following acceptance is not unusual. Most journals offer the authors reprints, which can be sent to other researchers in the field or to those who send in reprint request cards.

Sources for further study

Berry, R. (2000) *The Research Project: How to Write it*, 4th edn. Routledge, London.

Day, R.A. (1995) *How to Write and Publish a Scientific Paper*, 4th edn. Cambridge University Press, Cambridge.

Lobban, C.S. and Schefter, M. (1992) *Successful Lab Reports: A Manual for Science Students*. Cambridge University Press, Cambridge.

Luck, M. (1999) *Your Student Research Project*. Gower, London.

Luey, B. (2002) *Handbook for Academic Authors*, 4th edn. Cambridge University Press, Cambridge.

Study exercises

18.1 Write a formal 'Materials and Methods' section. Adopting the style of a research paper (e.g. past tense, all relevant detail reported such that a competent colleague could repeat your work), write out the Materials and Methods for a practical you have recently carried out. Ask a colleague or tutor to comment on what you have written.

18.2 Describe a set of results in words. Again adopting the style of a research paper, write a paragraph, describing the results contained in a particular table or graph. Ask a colleague or tutor to comment on your description.

18.3 Write an abstract for a paper. Pair up with a colleague. Each of you should independently choose a different research paper in a current journal. Copy the paper, but mask over the abstract section, having first counted the words used. Swap papers. Now, working to the same amount of words as in the original, read the paper and provide an abstract of its contents. Then, compare this with the real abstract. Compare your abstracts.

Writing literature surveys and reviews

The literature survey or review is a specialised form of essay which summarises and reviews the evidence and concepts concerning a particular area of research.

> **KEY POINT** A literature review should *not* be a simple recitation of facts. The best reviews are those which analyse information rather than simply describe it.

Making up a timetable

Figure 19.1 illustrates how you might divide up your time for writing a literature survey. There are many subdivisions in this chart because of the size of the task: in general, for lengthy tasks, it is best to divide up the work into manageable chunks. Note also that proportionately less time is allocated to writing itself than with an essay. In a literature survey, make sure that you spend adequate time on research and revision.

Selecting a topic

You may have no choice in the topic to be covered, but if you do, carry out your selection as a three-stage process:

1. Identify a broad subject area that interests you.
2. Find and read relevant literature in that area. Try to gain a broad impression of the field from books and general review articles. Discuss your ideas with your supervisor.
3. Select a relevant and concise title. The wording should be considered very carefully as it will define the content expected by the reader. A narrow subject area will cut down on the amount of literature you will be expected to review, but will also restrict the scope of the conclusions you can make (and *vice versa* for a wide subject area).

Scanning the literature and organising your references

You will need to carry out a thorough investigation of the literature before you start to write. The key problems are as follows:

- Getting an initial toehold in the literature. Seek help from your supervisor, who may be willing to supply a few key papers to get you started. Hints on expanding your collection of references are given on p. 41.
- Assessing the relevance and value of each article. This is the essence of writing a review, but it is difficult unless you already have a good understanding of the field (Catch 22). Try reading earlier reviews in your area.
- Clarifying your thoughts. Sometimes you can't see the wood for the trees! Subdividing the main topic and assigning your references to these smaller subject areas may help you gain a better overview of the literature.

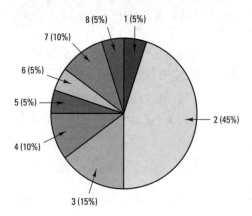

Fig. 19.1 Pie chart showing how you might allocate time for a literature survey:
1. select a topic;
2. scan the literature;
3. plan the review;
4. write first draft;
5. leave to settle;
6. prepare a structured review of text;
7. write final draft;
8. produce top copy.

Using index cards (see p. 43) – these can help you organise large numbers of references. Write key points on each card – this helps when considering where the reference fits into the literature. Arrange the cards in subject piles, eliminating irrelevant ones. Order the cards in the sequence you wish to write in.

Deciding on structure and content

The general structure and content of a literature survey are described below.

Introduction

Defining terms – the Introduction is a good place to explain the meaning of the key terms used in your survey or review.

The introduction should give the general background to the research area, concentrating on its development and importance. You should also make a statement about the scope of your survey; as well as defining the subject matter to be discussed, you may wish to restrict the period being considered.

Main body of text

The review itself should discuss the published work in the selected field and may be subdivided into appropriate sections. Within each portion of a review, the approach is usually chronological, with appropriate linking phrases (e.g. 'Following on from this, …'; 'Meanwhile, Bloggs (2002) tackled the problem from a different angle …'). However, a good review is much more than a chronological list of work done. It should:

Balancing opposing views – even if you favour one side of a disagreement in the literature, your review should provide a balanced and fair description of all the published views of the topic. Having done this, if you do wish to state a preference, give reasons for your opinion.

- allow the reader to obtain an overall view of the current state of the research area, identifying the key areas where knowledge is advancing;
- show how techniques are developing and discuss the benefits and disadvantages of using particular organisms or experimental systems;
- assess the relative worth of different types of evidence – this is the most important aspect (see Chapter 9). Do not be intimidated from taking a critical approach as the conclusions you may read in the primary literature aren't always correct;
- indicate where there is conflict in findings or theories, suggesting if possible which side has the stronger case;
- indicate gaps in current knowledge.

Conclusions

The conclusions should draw together the threads of the preceding parts and point the way forward, perhaps listing areas of ignorance or where the application of new techniques may lead to advances.

References, etc.

Making citations – a review of literature poses stylistic problems because of the need to cite large numbers of papers; in the Annual Review series this is overcome by using numbered references (see p. 44).

The References or Literature Cited section should provide full details of all papers referred to in the text (see p. 44). The regulations for your Department may also specify a format and position for the title page, list of contents, acknowledgements, etc.

Style of literature surveys

The *Annual Review* series (available in most university libraries) provides good examples of appropriate style for reviews of the biosciences.

Source for further study

Rudner, L.M. and Schafer, W.D. (1999) How to write a scholarly research report. *Practical Assessment, Research & Evaluation*, **6**(13). Available: http://ericae.net/pare/getvn.asp?v=6&n=13 Last accessed 08/01/03.

Study exercises

19.1 Summarise the main differences between a review and a scientific paper. From the many subject areas in the *Annual Review* series (find *via* your library's periodical indexing system), pick one that matches your subject interests, and within this find a review that seems relevant or interesting. Read the review and write down *five* ways in which the writing style and content differ from those that seen in primary scientific papers.

19.2 Gather a collection of primary sources for a topic. From the journal section of the library, select an interesting scientific paper published about 5–10 years ago. First, work *back* from the references cited by that paper: can you identify from the text or the article titles, which are the most important and relevant to the topic? List five of these, using the proper conventions for citing articles in a reference list (see Chapter 8). Note that each of these papers will also cite other articles, always going back in time. Now using the Science Citation Index or a similar system (e.g. the Web of Science website at http://wos.mimas.ac.uk), work *forward* and find out who has cited your selected article in the time since its publication. Again list the five most important articles found.

19.3 Write a synopsis of a review. Again using one of the *Annual Review* series as a source, allow yourself just *five* single-sentence bullet points to summarise the key points reported in a particular review.

Fundamental laboratory techniques

20 Your approach to practical work

Developing practical skills – these will include:

- *designing experiments*
- *observing and measuring*
- *recording data*
- *analysing and interpreting data*
- *reporting/presenting.*

All knowledge and theory in science have originated from practical observation and experimentation: this is equally true for disciplines as diverse as microscopy and molecular genetics. Practical work is an important part of most courses and often accounts for a significant proportion of the assessment marks. The abilities developed in practical classes will continue to be useful throughout your course and beyond, some within science and others in any career you choose (see Chapter 1).

Being prepared

KEY POINT You will get the most out of practicals if you prepare well in advance. Do not go into a practical session assuming that everything will be provided, without any input on your part.

The main points to remember are:

- Read any handouts in advance: make sure you understand the purpose of the practical and the particular skills involved. Does the practical relate to, or expand upon, a current topic in your lectures? Is there any additional preparatory reading that will help?
- Take along appropriate textbooks, to explain aspects in the practical.
- Consider what safety hazards might be involved, and any precautions you might need to take, before you begin (p. 118).
- Listen carefully to any introductory guidance and note any important points: adjust your schedule/handout as necessary.
- During the practical session, organise your bench space – make sure your lab book is adjacent to, but not within, your working area. You will often find it easiest to keep clean items of glassware, etc. on one side of your working space, with used equipment on the other side.
- Write up your work as soon as possible, and submit it on time, or you may lose marks.
- Catch up on any work you have missed as soon as possible – preferably, before the next practical session.

Using textbooks in the lab – take this book along to the relevant classes, so that you can make full use of the information during the practical sessions.

Ethical and legal aspects

You will need to consider the ethical and legal implications of biological work at several points during your studies:

- Safe working means following a code of safe practice, supported by legislation, alongside a moral obligation to avoid harm to yourself and others, as discussed in Chapter 21.
- Any laboratory work that involves working with animals must be carefully considered.
- Fieldwork can have a legal aspect, e.g. in relation to specimen collection, since legislation may protect particular habitats and/or species. Ethical and human aspects that must all be considered before any work is carried out include: possible damage to fauna and flora; safety of others within your group; implications of your work to others, e.g. landowners, or other users.

In addition to the above, life science research throws up moral and legal dilemmas, and students are increasingly likely to be asked to reflect on bioethical topics, e.g. in group discussions on current issues, including: environmental ethics (e.g. genetically modified plants; plant biotechnology); animal ethics (e.g. transgenic animals; factory farming) and medical ethics (e.g. cloning; human embryo research; genetic testing; xenotransplantation). In such topics, you will find that there is rarely a 'right' or 'wrong' answer, and it is important to be able to consider these issues in a rational and logical manner, and to provide reasoned argument in support of a particular viewpoint. Many of these topics are covered by websites, including:

- introductory bioethics (e.g. at http://www.accessexcellence.org/AE/AEPC/WWC/1992/bioethics_intro.html or http://bioethics.net/beginners.php);
- bioethics resources (e.g. http://www.nih.gov/sigs/bioethics/ or http://www.mcw.edu/bioethics/links.html);
- bioethics discussion groups (e.g. http://www-hsc.usc.edu/~mbernste/).

Basic requirements

Recording practical results

An A4 loose-leaf ring binder offers flexibility, since you can insert laboratory handouts or lined and graph paper at appropriate points. The danger of losing one or more pages from a loose-leaf system is the main drawback. Bound books avoid this problem, although those containing alternating lined/graph or lined/blank pages tend to be wasteful – it is often better to paste sheets of graph paper into a bound book, as required.

A good quality HB pencil or propelling pencil is recommended for recording your raw data, making diagrams, etc. as mistakes are easily corrected. Buy a black, spirit-based (permanent) marker for labelling experimental glassware, Petri plates, etc. Fibre-tipped fine line drawing/lettering pens are useful for preparing final versions of hand-drawn graphs and diagrams for assessment purposes. Use a see-through ruler (with an undamaged edge) for graph drawing, so that you can see data points and information below the ruler as you draw.

Calculators

These range from basic machines with no pre-programmed functions and only one memory, to sophisticated programmable minicomputers with many memories. The following may be helpful when using a calculator:

- Power sources. Choose a battery-powered machine, rather than a mains-operated or solar-powered type. You will need one with basic mathematical/scientific operations, including powers, logarithms (p. 470), roots and parentheses (brackets), together with statistical functions such as sample means and standard deviations (Chapter 66).
- Mode of operation. The older operating system used by e.g. Hewlett-Packard calculators is known as the reverse Polish notation: to calculate the sum of two numbers, the sequence is 2 [enter] 4 + and the answer 6 is displayed. The more usual method of calculating this equation is as $2 + 4 =$, which is the system used by the majority of modern calculators. Most newcomers find the latter approach to be

---

Definition

Xenotransplantation – the use of animal organs in humans – or, more strictly, one species' organs in another.

Presenting results – while you don't need to be a graphic designer to produce work of a satisfactory standard, presentation and layout are important and you will lose marks for poorly presented work.

Using inexpensive calculators – many unsophisticated calculators have a restricted display for exponential numbers and do not show the 'power of 10', e.g. displaying 2.4×10^{-5} as 2.4^{-05}, or $2.4E{-}05$, or $2.4{-}05$

---

more straightforward. Spend some time finding out how a calculator operates, e.g. does it have true algebraic logic ($\sqrt{}$ then number, rather than number then $\sqrt{}$)? How does it deal with scientific notation (p. 470)?

- Display. Some calculators will display an entire mathematical operation (e.g. '$2 + 4 = 6$'), while others simply display the last number/operation. The former type may offer advantages in tracing errors.
- Complexity. In the early stages, it is usually better to avoid the more complex machines, full of impressive-looking, but often unused pre-programmed functions – go for more memory, parentheses or statistical functions rather than engineering or mathematical constants. Programmable calculators may be worth considering for more advanced studies. However, it is important to note that such calculators are often unacceptable for exams.

Presenting more advanced practical work

In some practical reports and in project work, you may need to use more sophisticated presentation equipment. Computer-based graphics packages can be useful – choose easily read fonts such as Arial or Helvetica for posters and consider the layout and content carefully. Alternatively, you could use fine line drawing pens and dry-transfer lettering/symbols, such as those made by Letraset®, although this approach can be more time-consuming than computer-based systems.

To prepare overhead transparencies for spoken presentations, you can use spirit-based markers and acetate sheets. An alternative approach is to photocopy onto special acetates, or print directly from a computer-based package, using a laser printer and special acetates, or use a PC-based presentation package (e.g. PowerPoint®) and a suitable projector. Advice on content and presentation is given in Chapter 15.

Presenting graphs and diagrams – ensure these are large enough to be easily read: a common error is to present graphs or diagrams that are too small, with poorly chosen scales.

Printing on acetates – standard overhead transparencies are not suitable for use in laser printers or photocopiers: you need to make sure that you use the correct type.

Sources for further study

Barnard, C.J., Gilbert, F.S. and MacGregor, P.K. (2001) *Asking Questions in Biology: Key Skills for Practical Assessments and Project Work*, 2nd edn. Prentice Hall, Harlow.

Howell, J.H., Sale, W.F. and Callahan, D. (2000) *Life Choices: A Hastings Center Introduction to Bioethics*. Georgetown University Press, Washington, DC.

Jecker, N.S., Jonsen, A.R. and Pearlman, A.R. (1997) *Bioethics: An Introduction to the History, Methods and Practice*. Jones and Bartlett, Sudbury.

Kuhse, H. and Singer, P. (eds) (1998) *A Companion to Bioethics*. Blackwell, Oxford.

Mappes, T. and Degrazia, D. (2000) *Biomedical Ethics*, 5th edn. W.C. Brown/McGraw-Hill, New York.

Mier-Jedrzejowicz, W.A.C. (1999) *A Guide to HP Handheld Calculators and Computers*. Wilson-Barnett, Tustin. [Provides further guidance on the use of Hewlett-Packard calculators (reverse Polish notation).]

Study exercises

20.1 Consider the value of practical work. Spend a few minutes thinking about the purpose of practical work within a specific part of your course (e.g. a particular first year module) and then write a list of the six most important points. Compare your list with the generic list that we have provided on p. 502, which is based on our experience as lecturers – does it differ much from your list, which is drawn up from a student perspective?

20.2 Make a list of items required for a particular practical exercise. This exercise is likely to be most useful if you can relate it to an appropriate practical session on your course. However, we have given a model list for a tissue dissection as an example.

20.3 Check your calculator skills. Carry out the following mathematical operations, using either a hand-held calculator or a PC with appropriate 'calculator' software.
(a) $5 \times (2 + 6)$
(b) $(8.3 \div [6.4 - 1.9]) \times 24$ (to 4 significant figures)
(c) $(1 \div 32) \times (5 \div 8)$ (to 3 significant figures)
(d) $1.2 \times 10^5 + 4.0 \times 10^4$ in scientific notation (see p. 470)
(e) $3.4 \times 10^{-2} - 2.7 \times 10^{-3}$ in 'normal' notation (i.e. conventional notation, not scientific format) and to 3 decimal places.
(See also the numerical exercises in Chapter 65.)

Health and safety

In the UK, the **Health & Safety at Work, etc. Act 1974** provides the main legal framework for health and safety. The **Control of Substances Hazardous to Health (COSHH) Regulations 1999** impose specific legal requirements for risk assessment wherever hazardous chemicals or biological agents are used, with Approved Codes of Practice for the control of hazardous substances, carcinogens and biological agents, including pathogenic microbes.

Health and safety law requires academic institutions to provide a working environment that is safe and without risk to health. Where appropriate, training and information on safe working practices must be provided. Students and staff must take reasonable care to ensure the health and safety of themselves and of others, and must not misuse any safety equipment.

> **KEY POINT** All practical work must be carried out with safety in mind, to minimise the risk of harm to yourself and to others – safety is everyone's responsibility.

Risk assessment

The most widespread approach to safe working practice involves the use of risk assessment, which aims to establish:

1. The intrinsic chemical, biological and physical hazards, together with any maximum exposure limits (MELs) or occupational exposure standards (OESs), where appropriate. Chemical manufacturers provide data sheets listing the hazards associated with particular chemical compounds, while pathogenic (disease-causing) microbes are categorised according to their ability to cause illness (p. 199).
2. The risks involved, by taking into account the amount of substance to be used, the way in which it will be used and the possible routes of entry into the body (Fig. 21.1). In this regard, it is important to distinguish between the intrinsic hazards of a particular substance and the risks involved in its use in a particular exercise.
3. The persons at risk, and the ways in which they might be exposed to hazardous substances, including accidental exposure (spillage).
4. The steps required to prevent or control exposure. Ideally, a non-hazardous or less hazardous alternative should be used. If this is not feasible, adequate control measures must be used, e.g. a fume cupboard or other containment system. Personal protective equipment (e.g. lab coats, safety glasses) must be used in addition to such containment measures. A safe means of disposal will be required.

Definitions

Hazard – the ability of a substance or biological agent to cause harm.

Risk – the likelihood that a substance or biological agent might be harmful under specific circumstances.

Distinguishing between hazard and risk – one of the hazards associated with water is drowning. However, the risk of drowning in a few drops of water is minimal!

The outcome of the risk assessment process must be recorded and appropriate safety information must be passed on to those at risk. For most practical classes, risk assessments will have been carried out in advance by the person in charge: the information necessary to minimise the risks to students may be given in the practical schedule. Make sure you know how your Department provides such information and that you have read the appropriate material before you begin your practical work. You should also pay close attention to the person in charge at the beginning of the practical session, as they may emphasise the major hazards and risks. In project work, you will need to be involved in the risk assessment process along with your supervisor, before you carry out any practical work.

In addition to specific risk assessments, most institutions will have a safety handbook, giving general details of safe working practices, together with the names and telephone numbers of safety personnel, first aiders, hospitals, etc. Make sure you read this and abide by any instructions.

Fig. 21.1 Major routes of entry of harmful substances into the body.

inhalation

ingestion

inoculation or absorption

absorption from spillage

Fig. 21.2 Warning labels for specific chemical hazards. These appear on suppliers' containers and on tape used to label working vessels.

Basic rules for laboratory work

- Make sure you know what to do in case of fire, including exit routes, how to raise the alarm, and where to gather on leaving the building. Remember that the most important consideration at all times is human safety: do not attempt to fight a fire unless it is safe to do so.
- All laboratories display notices telling you where to find the first aid kit and who to contact in case of accident or emergency. Report all accidents, even those appearing insignificant – your Department will have a formal recording procedure to comply with safety legislation.
- Wear appropriate protective clothing at all times – a clean lab coat (buttoned up), plus safety glasses if there is any risk to the eyes.
- Never smoke, eat or drink in any laboratory, because of the risks of contamination by inhalation or ingestion (Fig. 21.1).
- Never mouth pipette any liquid. Use a pipette filler (see p. 21) or, if appropriate, a pipettor (p. 23).
- Take care when handling glassware – see p. 25 for details.
- Know the warning symbols for specific chemical hazards (see Fig. 21.2).
- Use a fume cupboard for hazardous chemicals. Make sure that it is working and then open the front only as far as is necessary: many fume cupboards are marked with a maximum opening.
- Always use the minimum quantity of any hazardous materials.
- Work in a logical, tidy manner and minimise risks by thinking ahead.
- Always clear up at the end of each session. This is an important aspect of safety, encouraging a responsible attitude towards laboratory work.
- Dispose of waste in appropriate containers. Most labs will have bins for sharps, glassware, hazardous solutions and radioactive waste.

Genetic engineering and molecular genetics

Additional legal constraints apply to practical work involving genetic manipulation. A specific risk assessment must be carried out for any experiment where a cell or organism is modified by genetic engineering techniques (Chapter 62) involving the insertion of DNA into a cell or organism in which it does not normally occur. Before any practical work can be carried out, it must be authorised by the establishment's genetic manipulation safety committee and notified to the relevant authority. Such work must be carried out with appropriate containment, to prevent the accidental release of genetically modified organisms into the environment.

Practicals in molecular genetics will involve some of the techniques of genetic manipulation. Typically, these will be examples of 'self-cloning' where recombinant DNA molecules are constructed from fragments of DNA which naturally occur in that organism, for example, the transformation of laboratory strains of *Escherichia coli* using a pUC plasmid (p. 445).

Sources for further study

Anon. (1989) *COSHH in Laboratories*. Royal Society of Chemistry, London.

Anon. *BUBL Link – Biochemical Safety*. Available:
http://bubl.ac.uk/link/b/biochemicalsafety.htm
Last accessed 08/01/03.
[Provides a single-step link to a number of databases giving information on chemical and microbiological hazards.]

Anon. *Howard Hughes Medical Institute On-line Safety Course*. Available:
http://www.practicingsafescience.org
Last accessed 08/01/03.
[This site, designed for laboratory workers, enables you to test your knowledge and understanding of laboratory safety.]

Picot, A. and Grenouillet, P. (1995) *Safety in the Chemistry and Biochemistry Laboratory*. Wiley, New York.

Study exercises

21.1 Test your knowledge of safe working procedures. After reading the appropriate sections of this book, can you remember the following:

(a) The four main steps involved in the process of risk assessment?
(b) The major routes of entry of harmful substances into the body?
(c) The warning labels for the major chemical hazard symbols (either describe them or draw them from memory)?
(d) The international symbol for a biohazard?
(e) The international symbol for radioactivity?

21.2 Locate relevant health and safety features in a laboratory. Find each of the following in one of the laboratories used as part of your course (draw a simple location map, if this seems appropriate):

(a) fire exit(s);
(b) fire-fighting equipment;
(c) first aid kit;
(d) 'sharps' container;
(e) container for disposal of broken glassware;
(f) eye wash station (where appropriate).

21.3 Investigate the health and safety procedures in operation at your University. Can you find out the following?

(a) your University's procedure in case of fire;
(b) the colour coding for fire extinguishers available in your Department and their recommendations for use;
(c) the accident reporting procedure used in your Department;
(d) your Department's Code of Practice relating to a specific aspect of bioscience, e.g. working with micro-organisms.

21.4 Carry out risk assessments for specific chemical hazards. Look up the hazards associated with the use of the following chemicals and list the appropriate protective measures required to minimise risk during use in a lab class:

(a) formaldehyde solution, used as a preservative for animal tissue, to be used for microscopic examination (Chapter 27);

(b) acetone, e.g. for use as a solvent for the quantitative analysis of plant pigments (Chapter 41);

(c) sodium hydroxide, used in solid form to prepare a dilute solution to be used for pH adjustment (Chapter 25).

22 **Working with liquids**

Measuring and dispensing liquids

The equipment you should choose to measure out liquids depends on the volumes being dispensed, the accuracy required and the number of times the job must be done (Table 22.1).

Table 22.1 Criteria for choosing a method for measuring out a liquid

Method	Best volume range	Accuracy	Usefulness for repetitive measurement
Pasteur pipette	30 μl to 2 ml	Low	Convenient
Conical flask/beaker	25–5000 ml	Very low	Convenient
Measuring cylinder	5–2000 ml	Medium	Convenient
Volumetric flask	5–2000 ml	High	Convenient
Burette	1–100 ml	High	Convenient
Glass pipette	1–100 ml	High	Convenient
Mechanical pipettor	5–1000 μl	High*	Convenient
Syringe	0.5–20 μl	Medium**	Convenient
Microsyringe	0.5–50 μl	High	Convenient
Weighing	Any (depends on accuracy of balance)	Very high	Inconvenient

* If correctly calibrated and used properly (see p. 23).
** Accuracy depends on width of barrel: large volumes less accurate.

Certain liquids may cause problems:

- High viscosity liquids are difficult to dispense: allow time for all the liquid to transfer.
- Organic solvents may evaporate rapidly, making measurements inaccurate: work quickly; seal containers without delay.
- Solutions prone to frothing (e.g. protein and detergent solutions) are difficult to measure and dispense: avoid forming bubbles due to overagitation; do not transfer quickly.
- Suspensions (e.g. cell cultures) may sediment: thoroughly mix them before dispensing.

Reading any volumetric scale – *make sure your eye is level with the bottom of the liquid's meniscus and take the reading from this point.*

Pasteur pipettes
Hold correctly during use (Fig. 22.1) – keep the pipette vertical, with the middle fingers gripping the barrel while the thumb and index finger provide controlled pressure on the bulb. Squeeze gently to dispense individual drops.

Pasteur pipettes should be used with care for hazardous solutions: remove the tip from the solution before fully releasing pressure on the bulb – the air taken up helps prevent spillage. To avoid the risk of cross-contamination, take care not to draw up solution into the bulb or to lie the pipette on its side. Plastic disposable 'Pastettes®' are safer and avoid cross-contamination.

Measuring cylinders and volumetric flasks
These must be used on a level surface so that the scale is horizontal; you should first fill with solution until just below the desired mark; then fill

thumb and index finger provide pressure on bulb

middle finger at side of pipette barrel supporting the pipette

Fig. 22.1 How to hold a Pasteur pipette.

Working with liquids

Fig. 22.2 Glass pipettes – graduated pipette, reading from zero to shoulder (a); graduated pipette, reading from maximum to tip, by gravity (b); bulb (volumetric) pipette, showing volume (calibration mark to tip, by gravity) on bulb (c).

Fig. 22.3 A pipettor – the Gilson Pipetman®.

slowly (e.g. using a Pasteur pipette) until the meniscus is level with the mark. Allow time for the solution to run down the walls of the vessel.

Burettes

Burettes should be mounted vertically on a clamp stand – don't overtighten the clamp. First ensure the tap is closed and fill the body with solution using a funnel. Open the tap and allow some liquid to fill the tubing below the tap before first use. Take a meniscus reading, noting the value in your notebook. Dispense the solution via the tap and measure the new meniscus reading. The volume dispensed is the difference between the two readings. Titrations are usually performed using a magnetic stirrer to ensure thorough mixing.

Pipettes

These come in various designs, including graduated and bulb (volumetric) pipettes (Fig. 22.2). Take care to look at the volume scale before use: some pipettes empty from full volume to zero, others from zero to full volume; some scales refer to the shoulder of the tip, others to the tip by gravity or to the tip after blowing out.

KEY POINT For safety reasons, it is no longer permissible to mouth pipette – various aids are available such as the Pi-pump®.

Pipettors (Autopipettors)

These come in two basic types:

- Air displacement pipettors. For routine work with dilute aqueous solutions. One of the most widely used examples is the Gilson Pipetman® (Fig. 22.3). Box 22.1 gives details on its use.
- Positive displacement pipettors. For non-standard applications, including dispensing viscous, dense or volatile liquids, or certain procedures in molecular genetics, e.g. the PCR (p. 437), where an air displacement pipettor might create aerosols, leading to errors.

Air displacement and positive displacement pipettors may be:

- Fixed volume: capable of delivering a single factory-set volume.
- Adjustable: where the volume is determined by the operator across a particular range of values.
- Pre-set: movable between a limited number of values.
- Multi-channel: able to deliver several replicate volumes at the same time.

Whichever type you use, you must ensure that you understand the operating principles of the volume scale and the method for changing the volume delivered – some pipettors are easily misread.

A pipettor must be fitted with the correct disposable tip before use: each manufacturer produces different tips to fit particular models. Specialised tips are available for particular applications.

Syringes

Syringes should be used by placing the tip of the needle in the solution and drawing the plunger up slowly to the required point on the scale. Check the barrel to make sure no air bubbles have been drawn up. Expel slowly and touch the syringe on the edge of the vessel to remove any liquid adhering to the end of the needle. Microsyringes should always be cleaned before and after use by repeatedly drawing up and expelling pure solvent. The dead

Box 22.1 Using a pipettor to deliver accurate, reproducible volumes of liquid

A pipettor can be used to dispense volumes with accuracy and precision, by following this stepwise procedure:

1. **Select a pipettor that operates over the appropriate range.** Most adjustable pipettors are accurate only over a particular working range and should not be used to deliver volumes below the manufacturer's specifications (minimum volume is usually 10–20% of maximum value). Do not attempt to set the volume above the maximum limit, or the pipettor may be damaged.

2. **Set the volume to be delivered.** In some pipettors, you 'dial up' the required volume. Types like the Gilson Pipetman® have a system where the scale (or 'volumeter') consists of three numbers, read from top to bottom of the barrel, and adjusted using the black knurled adjustment ring (Fig. 22.3). This number gives the first three digits of the volume scale and thus can only be understood by establishing the maximum volume of the Pipetman®, as shown on the push-button on the end of the plunger (Fig. 22.3). The following examples illustrate the principle for two common sizes of Pipetman®:

P1000 Pipetman®
(maximum volume 1000 μl)
if you dial up

| 1 |
| 0 |
| 0 |

the volume is set at 1000 μl

P20 Pipetman®
(maximum volume 20 μl)
if you dial up

| 1 |
| 0 |
| 0 |

the volume is set at 10.0 μl

3. **Fit a new disposable tip to the end of the barrel.** Make sure that it is the appropriate type for your pipettor and that it is correctly fitted. Press the tip on firmly using a slight twisting motion – if not, you will take up less than the set volume and liquid will drip from the tip during use. Tips are often supplied in boxes, for ease of use: if sterility is important, make sure you use appropriate sterile technique at all times (p. 197). *Never, ever, try to use a pipettor without its disposable tip.*

4. **Check your delivery.** Confirm that the pipettor delivers the correct volume by dispensing volumes of distilled water and weighing on a balance, assuming $1\,mg = 1\,\mu l = 1\,mm^3$. The value should be within 1% of the selected volume. For small volumes, measure several 'squirts' together, e.g. 20 'squirts' of $5\,\mu l = 100\,mg$. If the pipettor is inaccurate (p. 171) giving a biased result (e.g. delivering significantly more or less than the volume set), you can make a temporary correction by adjusting the volumeter scale down or up accordingly (the volume *delivered* is more important than the value *displayed* on the volumeter), or have the pipettor recalibrated. If the pipettor is imprecise (p. 171), delivering a variable amount of liquid each time, it may need to be serviced. After calibration, fit a clean (sterile) tip if necessary.

5. **Draw up the appropriate volume.** Holding the pipettor *vertically*, press down on the plunger/push-button until a resistance (spring-loaded stop) is met. Then place the end of the tip in the liquid. Keeping your thumb on the plunger/push-button, release the pressure slowly and evenly: watch the liquid being drawn up into the tip, to confirm that no air bubbles are present. Wait a second or so, to confirm that the liquid has been taken up, then withdraw the end of the tip from the liquid. Inexperienced users often have problems caused by drawing up the liquid too quickly/carelessly. If you accidentally draw liquid into the barrel, seek assistance from your demonstrator or supervisor as the barrel will need to be cleaned before further use.

6. **Make a quick visual check on the liquid in the tip.** Does the volume seem reasonable? (e.g. a $100\,\mu l$ volume should occupy approximately half the volume of a P200 tip). The liquid will remain in the tip, without dripping, as long as the tip is fitted correctly and the pipettor is not tilted too far from a vertical position.

7. **Deliver the liquid.** Place the end of the tip against the wall of the vessel at a slight angle (10–15° from vertical) and press the plunger/push-button slowly and smoothly to the first (spring-loaded) stop. Wait a second or two, to allow any residual liquid to run down the inside of the tip, then press again to the final stop, dispensing any remaining liquid. Remove from the vessel with the plunger/push-button still depressed.

8. **Eject the tip.** Press the tip ejector button if present (Fig. 22.3). If the tip is contaminated, eject directly into an appropriate container, e.g. a beaker of disinfectant, for microbiological work, or a labelled container for hazardous solutions (p. 118). For repeat delivery, fit a new tip if necessary and begin again at step 5 above. Always make sure that the tip is ejected before putting a pipettor on the bench.

space in the syringe needle can occupy up to 4% of the nominal syringe volume. A way of avoiding such problems is to fill the dead space with an inert substance (e.g. silicone oil) after sampling. An alternative is to use a syringe where the plunger occupies the needle space (available for small volumes only).

Balances

These can be used to weigh accurately (p. 33) how much liquid you have dispensed. Convert mass to volume using the equation:

$$\text{mass/density} = \text{volume} \tag{22.1}$$

Densities of common solvents can be found in Lide (2002). You will also need to know the liquid's temperature, as density is temperature dependent.

> **Example** Weighing 9 g of liquid with a density of 1.2 g ml^{-1} will give a volume of $9 \div 1.2 = 7.5$ ml

Holding and storing liquids

Test tubes

These are used for colour tests, small-scale reactions, holding cultures, etc. The tube can be sterilised by heating (p. 197) and maintained in this state with a cap or cotton wool plug.

Beakers

Beakers are used for general purposes, e.g. heating a solvent while the solute dissolves, carrying out a titration, etc. They may have volume gradations on the side: these are often inaccurate and should only be used where approximations will suffice.

Conical (Erlenmeyer) flasks

These are used for storage of solutions: their wide base makes them stable, while their small mouth reduces evaporation and makes them easier to seal. Volume gradations, where present, are often inaccurate.

Bottles and vials

These are used when the solution needs to be sealed for safety, sterility or to prevent evaporation or oxidation. They usually have a screw top or ground glass stopper to prevent evaporation and contamination. Many types are available, including 'bijou', 'McCartney', 'universal' and 'Winkler'.

You should clearly label all stored solutions (see p. 33), including relevant hazard information, preferably marking with hazard warning tape (p. 118). Seal vessels in an appropriate way, e.g. using a stopper or a sealing film such as Parafilm® or Nescofilm® to prevent evaporation. To avoid degradation store your solution in a fridge, but allow it to reach room temperature before use. Unless a solution containing organic constituents has been sterilised or is toxic, microbes will start growing, so older solutions may not give reliable results.

> *Storing light-sensitive chemicals* – use a coloured vessel or wrap aluminium foil around a clear vessel.

Creating specialised apparatus

Glassware systems incorporating ground glass connections such as Quickfit® are useful for setting up combinations of standard glass components, e.g. for chemical reactions. In project work, you may need to adapt standard forms of glassware for a special need. A glassblowing service (often available in chemistry departments) can make special items to order.

Choosing between glass and plastic

Bear in mind the following points:

- Reactivity. Plastic vessels often distort at relatively low temperatures; they may be inflammable, may dissolve in certain organic solvents and may be affected by prolonged exposure to ultraviolet (UV) light. Some plasticisers may leach from vessels and have been shown to have biological activity. Glass may adsorb ions and other molecules and then leach them into solutions, especially in alkaline conditions. Pyrex® glass is stronger than ordinary soda glass and can withstand temperatures up to 500 °C.
- Rigidity and resilience. Plastic vessels are not recommended where volume is critical as they may distort through time: use class A volumetric glassware for accurate work, e.g. preparing solutions (Chapter 24). Glass vessels are more easily broken than plastic, which is particularly important for centrifugation (see p. 293).
- Opacity. Both glass and plastic absorb light in the UV range of the EMR spectrum (Table 22.2). Quartz should be used where this is important, e.g. in cuvettes for UV spectrophotometry (see p. 271).
- Disposability. Plastic items may be cheap enough to make them disposable, an advantage where there is a risk of chemical or microbial contamination.

Table 22.2 Spectral cutoff values for glass and plastics (λ_{50} = wavelength at which transmission of EMR is reduced to 50%)

Material	λ_{50} (nm)
Routine glassware	340
Pyrex® glass	292
Polycarbonate	396
Acrylic	342
Polyester	318
Quartz	220

Special cleaning of glass – for an acid wash use dilute acid, e.g. 100 mmol l^{-1} (100 mol m^{-3}) HCl. Rinse thoroughly at least three times with distilled or deionised water. Glassware that must be exceptionally clean (e.g. for a micro-nutrient study) should be washed in a chromic acid bath, but this involves toxic and corrosive chemicals and should only be used under supervision.

Cleaning glass and plastic

Take care to avoid the possibility of contamination arising from prior use of chemicals or inadequate rinsing following washing. A thorough rinse with distilled or deionised water immediately before use will remove dust and other deposits and is good practice in quantitative work, but ensure that the rinsing solution is not left in the vessel. 'Strong' basic detergents (e.g. Pyroneg®) are good for solubilising acidic deposits. If there is a risk of basic deposits remaining, use an acid wash. If there is a risk of contamination from organic deposits, a rinse with Analar® grade ethanol is recommended. Glassware can be disinfected by washing with a sodium hypochlorite bleach such as Chloros®, with sodium metabisulphite or a blended commercial product such as Virkon® – dilute as recommended before use and rinse thoroughly with sterile water after use. Alternatively, to sterilise glassware, heat to at least 121 °C for 15 min in an autoclave or 160 °C for 3 h in an oven.

Safety with glass

Many minor accidents in the laboratory are due to lack of care with glassware. You should follow these general precautions:

- Wear safety glasses when there is *any* risk of glass breakage, e.g. when using low pressures or heating solutions.
- If heating glassware, use a 'soft' Bunsen flame – this avoids creating a hot spot where cracks may start. Always use tongs or special heat-resistant gloves when handling hot glassware.
- Don't use chipped or cracked glassware – it may break under very slight strains and should be disposed of in the broken glassware bin.
- Never carry large bottles by their necks – support them with a hand underneath or, better still, carry them in a basket.

Wrong

Right

Fig. 22.4 Handling glass pipettes tubing.

- Take care when attaching tubing to glass tubes and when putting glass tubes into bungs – always hold the tube and 'hole' close together (Fig. 22.4) and wear thick gloves when appropriate.
- Don't force bungs too firmly into bottles – they can be very difficult to remove. If you need a tight seal, use a screw top bottle with a rubber or plastic seal.
- Dispose of broken glass thoroughly and with great care – use disposable paper towels and wear thick gloves. Always put pieces of broken glass into the correct bin.

Text reference

Lide, D.R. (ed.) (2002) *CRC Handbook of Chemistry and Physics*, 83rd edn. CRC Press, Boca Raton.

Sources for further study

Anon. *CHEMnet BASE*. Available
http://www.chemnetbase.com
Last accessed 08/01/03.
[On-line access to the *Handbook of Chemistry and Physics*.]

Boyer, R. (2000) *Modern Experimental Biochemistry*, 3rd edn. Benjamin Cummings, San Francisco.

Henrikson, C., Byrd, L.C. and Hunter, N.W. (2000) *A Laboratory Manual for General, Organic and Biochemistry*. McGraw-Hill, New York.

Seidman, L.A. and Moore, C.J. (2000) *Basic Laboratory Methods for Biotechnology: Textbook and Laboratory Reference*. Prentice Hall, New Jersey.

Study exercises

22.1 Decide on the appropriate methods and equipment for the following procedures:

    (a) Preparing one litre of ethanol at approximately 70% v/v in water for use as a general-purpose reagent.

    (b) Adding $10\,\mu l$ of a sample to the well of an agarose gel during a molecular biology procedure.

    (c) Preparing a calibration standard of 100 ml of DNA, to contain $200.0\,\mu g\ ml^{-1}$, for spectrophotometry.

    (d) Carrying out a titration curve for a buffer solution.

22.2 Write a protocol for calibrating and using a pipettor. After reading this chapter, prepare a detailed stepwise protocol explaining how to use a pipettor to deliver a specific volume, say of $500\,\mu l$ (e.g. using a Gilson Pipetman®, or an alternative if your Department does not use this type). Ask another student to evaluate your protocol and provide you with written feedback – either simply by reading through your protocol, or by trying it out with a pipettor as part of a class exercise (check with a member of staff before you attempt this in a laboratory).

22.3 Determine the accuracy and precision of a pipette. Using the following data for three different models of pipettor, determine which pipettor is most *accurate* and which is most *precise* (check p. 153 if you are unsure of the definitions of these two terms). All three pipettors were set to deliver $1000\,\mu l$ (1.000 ml) and 10 repetitive measurements of the weight of the volume of water in grams delivered were made using a three-place balance:

Model A pipettor: 0.986; 0.971; 0.993; 0.964; 0.983; 0.996; 0.977; 0.969; 0.982; 0.974

Model B pipettor: 1.013; 1.011; 1.010; 1.009; 1.011; 1.010; 1.011; 1.009; 1.011; 1.012

Model C pipettor: 0.985; 1.022; 1.051; 1.067; 0.973; 0.982; 0.894; 1.045; 1.062; 0.928

In your answer, you should support your conclusions with appropriate numerical (statistical) evidence (see Chapter 66 for appropriate measures of location and dispersion).

Basic laboratory procedures

8671. Sodium Chloride. [7647-14-5] Salt; common salt. ClNa; mol wt 58.44. Cl 60.67%, Na 39.34%. NaCl. The article of commerce is also known as *table salt*, *rock salt* or *sea salt*. Occurs in nature as the mineral *halite*. Produced by mining (rock salt), by evaporation of brine from underground salt deposits and from sea water by solar evaporation: *Faith, Keyes & Clark's Industrial Chemicals*, F. A. Lowenheim, M. K. Moran, Eds. (Wiley-Interscience, New York, 4th ed., 1975) pp 722-730. Toxicity studies: E. M. Boyd, M. N. Shanas, *Arch. Int. Pharmacodyn.* **144**, 86 (1963). Comprehensive monograph: D. W. Kaufmann, *Sodium Chloride*, ACS Monograph Series no. **145** (Reinhold, New York, 1960) 743 pp.

Cubic, white crystals, granules, or powder; colorless and transparent or translucent when in large crystals. d 2.17. The salt of commerce usually contains some calcium and magnesium chlorides which absorb moisture and make it cake. mp 804° and begins to volatilize at a little above this temp. One gram dissolves in 2.8 ml water at 25°, in 2.6 ml boiling water, in 10 ml glycerol; very slightly sol in alcohol. Its soly in water is decreased by HCl. Almost insol in concd HCl. Its aq soln is neutral. pH: 6.7-7.3. d of satd aq soln at 25° is 1.202. A 23% aq soln of sodium chloride freezes at −20.5°C (5°F). LD_{50} orally in rats: 3.75 ±0.43 g/kg (Boyd, Shanas).

Note: **Blusalt**, a brand of sodium chloride contg trace amounts of cobalt, iodine, iron, copper, manganese, zinc is used in farm animals.

Caution: Not generally considered poisonous. Accidental substitution of NaCl for lactose in baby formulas has caused fatal poisoning.

USE: Natural salt is the source of chlorine and of sodium as well as of all, or practically all, their compds, e.g., hydrochloric acid, chlorates, sodium carbonate, hydroxide, etc.; for preserving foods; manuf soap, dyes—to salt them out; in freezing mixtures; for dyeing and printing fabrics, glazing pottery, curing hides; metallurgy of tin and other metals.

THERAP CAT: Electrolyte replenisher; emetic; topical anti-inflammatory.

THERAP CAT (VET): Essential nutrient factor. May be given orally as emetic, stomachic, laxative or to stimulate thirst (prevention of calculi). Intravenously as isotonic solution to raise blood volume, to combat dehydration. Locally as wound irrigant, rectal douche.

Fig. 23.1 Example of typical *Merck Index* entry showing type of information given for each chemical. From *The Merck Index: an Encyclopedia of Chemicals, Drugs and Biologicals,* Thirteenth edition, O'Neil, M.J., Smith, A., Heckelman, P.E. and Obenchain, J.R. (eds). Merck & Co, Inc, Whitehouse Station, NJ, USA, 2001. Reproduced with permission. Copyright © 2001 by Merck & Co, Inc. All rights reserved.

Using chemicals

Safety aspects

In practical classes, the person in charge has a responsibility to inform you of any hazards associated with the use of chemicals. In project work, your first duty when using an unfamiliar chemical is to find out about its properties, especially those relating to safety. For routine practical procedures, a risk assessment will have been carried out by a member of staff and relevant safety information will be included in the practical schedule: an example is shown in Table 23.1. Before you use any chemical you must find out whether safety precautions need to be taken and complete the appropriate forms confirming that you appreciate the risks involved. Your Department must provide the relevant information to allow you to do this. If your supervisor has filled out the form, read it carefully before signing.

Key safety points when handling chemicals are:

- Treat all chemicals as potentially dangerous.
- Wear a laboratory coat, with buttons fastened, at all times.
- Make sure you know where safety devices such as eye bath, fire extinguisher, first aid kit, are kept before you begin work in the lab.
- Wear gloves and safety glasses for toxic, irritant or corrosive chemicals and carry out procedures with them in a fume cupboard.
- Use aids such as pipette fillers to minimise risk of contact.
- Extinguish all naked flames when working with flammable substances.
- Never smoke, eat, drink or chew gum in a lab where chemicals are handled.
- Label solutions appropriately (see pp. 118, 133).
- Report all spillages and clean them up properly.
- Dispose of chemicals in the correct manner.

Table 23.1 Representative risk assessment information for a practical exercise in molecular biology, involving the isolation of DNA

Substance	Hazards	Comments
Sodium dodecyl sulphate (SDS)	Irritant Toxic	Wear gloves
Sodium hydroxide (NaOH)	Highly corrosive Severe irritant	Wear gloves
Isopropanol	Highly flammable Irritant/corrosive Potential carcinogen	No naked flames Wear gloves
Phenol	Highly toxic Causes skin burns Potential carcinogen	Use in fume hood Wear gloves
Chloroform	Volatile and toxic Irritant/corrosive Potential carcinogen	Use in fume hood Wear gloves

Using chemicals – be considerate to others: always return store room chemicals promptly to the correct place. Report when supplies are getting low to the person responsible for looking after the store. If you empty an aspirator or wash bottle, fill it up from the appropriate source!

Selection

Chemicals are supplied in various degrees of purity and this is always stated on the manufacturer's containers. Suppliers differ in the names given to the grades and there is no conformity in purity standards. Very pure chemicals cost more, sometimes a lot more, and should only be used if the situation demands. If you need to order a chemical, your Department will have a defined procedure for doing this.

Preparing solutions

Solutions are usually prepared with respect to their molar concentrations (e.g. $mmol\,l^{-1}$, or $mol\,m^{-3}$), or mass concentrations (e.g. $g\,l^{-1}$, or $kg\,m^{-3}$): both can be regarded as an amount of *substance* per unit volume of *solution*, in accordance with the relationship:

$$\text{Concentration} = \frac{\text{amount}}{\text{volume}} \qquad [23.1]$$

The most important aspect of Eqn [23.1] is to recognise clearly the units involved, and to prepare the solution accordingly: for molar concentrations, you will need the relative molecular mass of the compound, so that you can determine the mass of substance required. Further advice on concentrations and interconversion of units is given on pp. 138–9.

Box 23.1 shows the steps involved in making up a solution. The concentration you require is likely to be defined by a protocol you are following and the grade of chemical and supplier may also be specified. Success may depend on using the same source and quality, e.g. with enzyme work. To avoid waste, think carefully about the volume of solution you require, though it is always a good idea to err on the high side because you may spill some or make a mistake when dispensing it. Try to choose one of the standard volumes for vessels, as this will make measuring out easier.

Use distilled or deionised water to make up aqueous solutions and stir to make sure all the chemical is dissolved. Magnetic stirrers are the most convenient means of doing this: carefully drop a clean magnetic stirrer bar ('flea') in the beaker, avoiding splashing; place the beaker centrally on the stirrer plate, switch on the stirrer and gradually increase the speed of stirring. When the crystals or powder have completely dissolved, switch off and retrieve the flea with a magnet or another flea. Take care not to contaminate your solution when you do this and rinse the flea with distilled water.

'Obstinate' solutions may require heating but do this only if you know that the chemical will not be damaged at the temperature used. Use a stirrer-heater to keep the solution mixed as you heat it. Allow the solution to cool down before you measure its volume or pH as these are affected by temperature.

Solubility problems – if your chemical does not dissolve after a reasonable time:
- check the limits of solubility for your compound (see Merck Index, O'Neil et al. 2001),
- check the pH of the solution – solubility is sometimes low at pH extremes.

Stock solutions

Stock solutions are valuable when making up a range of solutions containing different concentrations of a reagent or if the solutions have some common ingredients. They also save work if the same solution is used over a prolonged period (e.g. a nutrient solution). The stock solution is more concentrated than the final requirement and is diluted as appropriate when the final solutions are made up. The principle is best illustrated with an example (Table 23.2).

Box 23.1 How to make up an aqueous solution of known concentration from solid material

1. **Find out or decide the concentration of chemical required** and the degree of purity necessary.

2. **Decide on the volume of solution required.**

3. **Find out the relative molecular mass of the chemical (M_r).** This is the sum of the atomic (elemental) masses of the component elements and can be found on the container. If the chemical is hydrated, i.e. has water molecules associated with it, these must be included when calculating the mass required.

4. **Work out the mass of chemical that will give the concentration desired in the volume required.**
   Suppose your procedure requires you to prepare 250 ml of 0.1 mol l^{-1} NaCl.

   (a) Begin by expressing all volumes in the same units, either millilitres or litres (e.g. 250 ml as 0.25 litres).

   (b) Calculate the number of moles required from Eqn. [23.1]: 0.1 = amount (mol) ÷ 0.25. By rearrangement, the required number of moles is thus $0.1 \times 0.25 = 0.025$ mol.

   (c) Convert from mol to g by multiplying by the relative molecular mass (M_r for NaCl = 58.44)

   (d) Therefore, you need to make up $0.025 \times 58.44 = 1.461$ g to 250 ml of solution, using distilled water.

   In some instances, it may be easier to work in SI units, though you must be careful when using exponential numbers (p. 470).
   Suppose your protocol states that you need 100 ml of 10 mmol l^{-1} KCl.

   (a) Start by converting this to 100×10^{-6} m^3 of 10 mol m^{-3} KCl.

   (b) The required number of mol is thus $(100 \times 10^{-6}) \times (10) = 10^{3}$.

   (c) Each mol of KCl weighs 72.56 g (M_r, the relative molecular mass).

   (d) Therefore you need to make up 72.56×10^{-3} g = 72.56 mg KCl to 100×10^{-6} m^3 (100 ml) with distilled water.

   See Box 24.1 for additional information.

5. **Weigh out the required mass of chemical to an appropriate accuracy.** If the mass is too small to weigh to the desired degree of accuracy, consider the following options:

   (a) Make up a greater volume of solution.

   (b) Make up a stock solution which can be diluted at a later stage (p. 129).

   (c) Weigh the mass first, and calculate what volume to make the solution up to afterwards using Eqn [23.1].

6. **Add the chemical to a beaker or conical flask then add a little less water than the final amount required.** If some of the chemical sticks to the paper, foil or weighing boat, use some of the water to wash it off.

7. **Stir and, if necessary, heat the solution to ensure all the chemical dissolves.** You can determine when this has happened visually by observing the disappearance of the crystals or powder.

8. **If required, check and adjust the pH of the solution when cool** (see p. 147).

9. **Make up the solution to the desired volume.** If the concentration needs to be accurate, use a class A volumetric flask; if a high degree of accuracy is not required, use a measuring cylinder (class B).

   (a) Pour the solution from the beaker into the measuring vessel using a funnel to avoid spillage.

   (b) Make up the volume so that the meniscus comes up to the appropriate measurement line (p. 121). For accurate work, rinse out the original vessel and use this liquid to make up the volume.

10. **Transfer the solution to a reagent bottle or a conical flask and label the vessel clearly.**

Preparing dilutions

Making a single dilution

In analytical work, you may need to dilute a stock solution to give a particular mass concentration, or molar concentration. Use the following procedure:

1. Transfer an accurate volume of stock solution to a volumetric flask, using appropriate equipment (Table 23.1).

Making a dilution – use the relationship $[C_1]V_1 = [C_2]V_2$ to determine volume or concentration (see p. 139).

Table 23.2 Use of stock solutions. Suppose you need a set of solutions 10 ml in volume containing differing concentrations of KCl, with and without reagent Q. You decide to make up a stock of KCl at twice the maximum required concentration (50 mmol l^{-1} = 50 mol m^{-3}) and a stock of reagent Q at twice its required concentration. The table shows how you might use these stocks to make up the media you require. Note that the total volumes of stock you require can be calculated from the table (end column)

Stock solutions	Volume of stock required to make required solutions (ml)						Total volume of stock required (ml)
	No KCl plus Q	No KCl minus Q	15 mmol l^{-1} KCl plus Q	15 mmol l^{-1} KCl minus Q	25 mmol l^{-1} KCl plus Q	25 mmol l^{-1} KCl minus Q	
50 mmol l^{-1} KCl	0	0	3	3	5	5	16
[reagent Q] × 2	5	0	5	0	5	0	15
Water	5	10	2	7	0	5	29
Total	10	10	10	10	10	10	60

2. Make up to the calibration mark with solvent – add the last few drops from a pipette or solvent bottle, until the meniscus is level with the calibration mark.
3. Mix thoroughly, either by repeated inversion (holding the stopper firmly) or by prolonged stirring, using a magnetic stirrer. Make sure you add the magnetic flea *after* the volume adjustment step.

For routine work using dilute aqueous solutions where the highest degree of accuracy is not required, it may be acceptable to substitute test tubes or conical flasks for volumetric flasks. In such cases, you would calculate the volumes of stock solution and diluent required, with the assumption that the final volume is determined by the sum of the individual volumes of stock and diluent used (e.g. Table 23.2). Thus, a twofold dilution would be prepared using 1 volume of stock solution and 1 volume of diluent. The dilution factor is obtained from the ratio of the initial concentration of the stock solution and the final concentration of the diluted solution. The dilution factor can be used to determine the volumes of stock and diluent required in a particular instance. For example, suppose you wanted to prepare 100 ml of a solution of NaCl at 0.2 mol l^{-1}. Using a stock solution containing 4.0 mol l^{-1} NaCl, the dilution factor is 0.2 ÷ 4.0 = 0.05 = 1/20 (a twentyfold dilution). Therefore, the amount of stock solution required is 1/20th of 100 ml = 5 ml and the amount of diluent needed is 19/20ths of 100 ml = 95 ml.

Preparing a dilution series

Dilution series are used in a wide range of procedures, including the preparation of standard curves for calibration of analytical instruments (Chapter 37), and in microbiology (Chapter 32) and immunoassay (Chapter 38), where a range of dilutions of a particular sample is often required. A variety of different approaches can be used:

Linear dilution series

Here, the concentrations are separated by an equal amount, e.g. a series containing protein at 0, 0.2, 0.4, 0.6, 0.8, 1.0 μg ml^{-1}. Such a dilution series might be used to prepare a calibration curve for spectrophotometric assay of protein concentration (Box 50.1), or an enzyme assay (p. 378). Use $[C_1]V_1 = [C_2]V_2$ to determine the amount of stock solution required for each member of the series, with the volume of diluent being determined by subtraction.

Removing a magnetic flea from a volumetric flask – use a strong magnet to bring the flea to the top of the flask, to avoid contamination during removal.

Using the correct volumes – it is important to distinguish between the volumes of the various liquids: a one-in-ten dilution is obtained using 1 volume of stock solution plus 9 volumes of diluent (1 + 9 = 10). Note that when this is shown as a ratio, it may represent the initial and final volumes (e.g. 1 : 10) or, sometimes, the volumes of stock solution and diluent (e.g. 1 : 9).

Using diluents – various liquids are used, including distilled or deionised water, salt solutions, buffers, Ringer's solution (p. 218), etc., according to the specific requirements of the procedure.

most
concentrated
solution
(in excess)

1 ml 1 ml 1 ml 1 ml 1 ml

9 ml
diluent

undiluted	$1/10$	$1/100$	$1/1000$	$1/10\,000$	$1/100\,000$
(10)	(10^{-1})	(10^{-2})	(10^{-3})	(10^{-4})	(10^{-5})

Fig. 23.2 Preparation of a dilution series. The example shown is a decimal dilution series, down to $1/100\,000$ (10^{-5}) of the solution in the first (left-hand) tube. Note that all solutions must be mixed thoroughly before transferring the volume to the next in the series. In microbiology and cell culture, sterile solutions and appropriate aseptic technique will be required (p. 197).

Preparing a dilution series using pipettes or pipettors – *use a fresh pipette or disposable tip for each dilution, to prevent carry-over of solutions.*

Logarithmic dilution series

Here, the concentrations are separated by a constant proportion, often referred to as the step interval. This type of serial dilution is useful when a broad range of concentrations is required, e.g. for titration of biologically active substances (p. 231), making a plate count of a suspension of microbes (p. 200), or when a process is logarithmically related to concentration.

The most common examples are:

- Doubling dilutions – where each concentration is half that of the previous one (twofold step interval, $\log_2$ dilution series). First, make up the most concentrated solution at twice the volume required. Measure out half of this volume into a vessel containing the same volume of diluent, mix thoroughly and repeat, for as many doubling dilutions as are required. The concentrations obtained will be $1/2$, $1/4$, $1/8$, $1/16$, etc. times the original (i.e. the dilutions will be two, four, eight and sixteenfold, etc.).
- Decimal dilutions – where each concentration is one-tenth that of the previous one (tenfold step interval, $\log_{10}$ dilution series). First, make up the most concentrated solution required, with at least a 10% excess. Measure out one-tenth of the volume required into a vessel containing nine times as much diluent, mix thoroughly and repeat. The concentrations obtained will be $1/10$, $1/100$, $1/1000$, etc. times the original (i.e. dilutions of 10^{-1}, 10^{-2}, 10^{-3}, etc.). To calculate the actual concentration of solute, multiply by the appropriate dilution factor.

When preparing serial doubling or decimal dilutions, it is often easiest to add the appropriate amount of diluent to several vessels beforehand, as shown in the worked example in Fig. 23.2. When preparing a dilution series, it is essential that all volumes are dispensed accurately, e.g. using calibrated pipettors (p. 123), otherwise any inaccuracies will be compounded, leading to gross errors in the most dilute solutions.

Harmonic dilution series

Here, the concentrations in the series take the values of the reciprocals of successive whole numbers, e.g. 1, $1/2$, $1/3$, $1/4$, $1/5$, etc. The individual dilutions are simply achieved by a stepwise increase in the volume of diluent in successive vessels, e.g. by adding 0, 1, 2, 3, 4 and 5 times the volume of diluent to a set of test tubes, then adding a constant unit volume of stock solution to each vessel. Although there is no dilution transfer error between individual dilutions, the main disadvantage is that the series is non-linear, with a step interval that becomes progressively smaller as the series is extended.

Solutions must be thoroughly mixed before measuring out volumes for the next dilution. Use a fresh measuring vessel for each dilution to avoid contamination, or wash your vessel thoroughly between dilutions. Clearly label the vessel containing each dilution when it is made: it is easy to get confused! When deciding on the volumes required, allow for the aliquot removed when making up the next member in the series. Remember to discard any excess from the last in the series if volumes are critical.

Mixing solutions and suspensions

Various devices may be used, including:

- Magnetic stirrers and fleas. Magnetic fleas come in a range of shapes and sizes, and some stirrers have integral heaters. During use, stirrer speed may increase as the instrument warms up.

Using a vortex mixer with open or capped test tubes – do not vortex too vigorously or liquid will spill from the top of the tube, creating a contamination risk.

- Vortex mixers. For vigorous mixing of small volumes of solution, e.g. when preparing a dilution series in test tubes. Take care when adjusting the mixing speed – if the setting is too low, the test tube will vibrate rather than creating a vortex, giving inadequate mixing. If the setting is too high, the test tube may slip from your hand.
- Orbital shakers and shaking water baths. These are used to provide controlled mixing at a particular temperature, e.g. for long-term incubation and cell growth studies (p. 226).
- Bottle rollers. For cell culture work, ensuring gentle, continuous mixing.

Storing chemicals and solutions

Labile chemicals may be stored in a fridge or freezer. Take special care when using chemicals that have been stored at low temperature: the container and its contents must be warmed up to room temperature before use, otherwise water vapour will condense on the chemical. This may render any weighing you do meaningless and it could ruin the chemical. Other chemicals may need to be kept in a desiccator, especially if they are deliquescent (water-absorbing).

Cleaning up chemical spillages – you must always clean up any spillages of chemicals, as you are the only person who knows the risks from the spilled material.

KEY POINT Label all stored chemicals clearly with the following information: the chemical name (if a solution, state solute(s), concentration(s) and pH if measured), plus any relevant hazard warning information, the date made up, and your name.

Separating components of mixtures and solutions

Particulate solids (e.g. soils) can be separated on the basis of size using sieves. These are available in stacking forms which fit on automatic shakers. Sieves with the largest pores are placed at the top and the assembly is shaken for a fixed time until the sample separates. Suspensions of solids in liquids may be separated out by centrifugation (see p. 289) or filtration. Various forms of filter paper are available having different porosities and purities. Vacuum-assisted filtration speeds up the process and is best carried out with a filter funnel attached to a filter flask. Filtration through pre-sterilised membranes with very small pores (e.g. the Millipore® type) is an excellent method of sterilising small volumes of solution. Solvents can be removed from solutes by heating, using rotary film evaporation under low pressure and, for water, by freeze drying. The last two are especially useful for heat-labile solutes – refer to the manufacturers' specific instructions for use.

Weighing – never weigh anything directly onto a balance's pan: you may contaminate it for other users. Use a weighing boat or a slip of aluminium foil. Otherwise, choose a suitable vessel like a beaker, conical flask or aluminium tray.

Using balances

Electronic balances with digital readouts are now favoured over mechanical types: they are easy to read and their self-taring feature means the mass of the weighing boat or container can be subtracted automatically before weighing an object. The most common type offers accuracy down to 1 mg over the range 1 mg to 160 g, which is suitable for most biological applications.

To operate a standard self-taring balance:

1. Check that it is level, using the adjustable feet to centre the bubble in the spirit level (usually at the back of the machine). For accurate work, make sure a draught shield is on the balance.

Deciding on which balance to use – select a balance that weighs to an appropriate number of decimal places. For example, you should use a top-loading balance weighing to one decimal place for less accurate work. Note that a weight of 6.4 g on such a balance may represent a true value of between 6.350 g and 6.449 g (to three decimal places).

Basic laboratory procedures

Using a balance – *it is poor technique to use a large container to weight out a small amount of a chemical: you are attempting to make accurate measurements of a small difference between two large numbers. Instead, use a small weighing container.*

2. Place an empty vessel in the middle of the balance pan and allow the reading to stabilise. *If the object is larger than the pan, take care that no part rests on the body of the balance or the draught shield as this will invalidate the reading.* Press the tare bar to bring the reading to zero.
3. Place the chemical or object carefully in the vessel (powdered chemicals should be dispensed with a suitably sized clean spatula). Take care to avoid spillages.
4. Allow the reading to stabilise and make a note of the value.
5. If you add excess chemical, take great care when removing it. Switch off if you need to clean any deposit accidentally left on or around the balance.

Larger masses should be weighed on a top-loading balance to an appropriate degree of accuracy. Take care to note the limits for the balance: while most have devices to protect against overloading, you may damage the mechanism. In the field, spring or battery-operated balances may be preferred. Try to find a place out of the wind to use them. For extremely small masses, there are electrical balances that can weigh down to $1\,\mu g$, but these are very delicate and must be used under supervision.

Measuring and controlling temperature

Heating samples

Care is required when heating samples – there is a danger of fire whenever organic material is heated and a danger of scalding from heated liquids. Safety glasses should always be worn. Use a thermostatically controlled electric stirrer-heater if possible. If using a Bunsen burner, keep the flame well away from yourself and your clothing (tie back long hair). Use a non-flammable mat beneath a Bunsen to protect the bench. Switch off when no longer required. To light a Bunsen, close the air hole first, then apply a lit match or lighter. Open the air hole if you need a hotter, more concentrated flame: the hottest part of the flame is just above the apex of the blue cone in its centre.

Ovens and drying cabinets may be used to dry specimens or glassware. They are normally thermostatically controlled. If drying organic material for dry weight measurement, do so at about $80\,°C$ to avoid caramelising the sample. Always state the actual temperature used as this affects results. Check that all water has been driven off by weighing until a constant mass is reached.

Cooling samples and specimens

Heating/cooling glass vessels – *take care if heating or cooling glass vessels rapidly as they may break when heat stressed. Freezing aqueous solutions in thin-walled glass vessels is risky because ice expansion may break the glass.*

Fridges and freezers are used for storing stock solutions and chemicals that would either break down or become contaminated at room temperature. Normal fridge and freezer temperatures are about $4\,°C$ and $-15\,°C$ respectively. Ice baths can be used when reactants must be kept close to $0\,°C$. Most bioscience departments will have a machine which provides flaked ice for use in these baths. If common salt is mixed with ice, temperatures below $0\,°C$ can be achieved. A mixture of ethanol and solid CO_2 will provide a temperature of $-72\,°C$ if required. To freeze a specimen quickly, immerse in liquid N_2 $(-196\,°C)$ using tongs and wearing an apron and thick gloves, as splashes will damage your skin. Always work in a well-ventilated room.

Maintaining constant temperature

Thermostatically controlled temperature rooms and incubators can be used to maintain temperature at a desired level. Always check with a thermometer or thermograph that the thermostat is accurate enough for your study. To achieve a controlled temperature on a smaller scale, e.g. for an oxygen electrode (pp. 334–8), use a water bath. These usually incorporate heating elements, a circulating mechanism and a thermostat. Baths for sub-ambient temperatures have a cooling element.

Controlling atmospheric conditions

Gas composition

The atmosphere may be 'scrubbed' of certain gases by passing through a U-tube or Dreschel bottle containing an appropriate chemical or solution.

For accurate control of gas concentrations, use cylinders of pure gas; the contents can be mixed to give specified concentrations by controlling individual flow rates. The cylinder head regulator (Fig. 23.3) allows you to control the pressure (and hence flow rate) of gas; adjust using the controls on the regulator or with spanners of appropriate size. Before use, ensure the regulator outlet tap is off (turn anticlockwise), then switch on at the cylinder (turn clockwise) – the cylinder dial will give you the pressure reading for the cylinder contents. Now switch on at the regulator outlet (turn clockwise) and adjust to desired pressure/flow setting. To switch off, carry out the above directions in reverse order.

To control dissolved gas composition in liquids, either 'degas' under vacuum or bubble with another gas, e.g. when preparing oxygen-free liquids for HPLC (p. 297) by bubbling with nitrogen.

Pressure

Many forms of pump are used to pressurise or provide partial vacuum, usually to force gas or liquid movement. Each has specific instructions for use. Many laboratories are supplied with 'vacuum' (suction) and pressurised air lines that are useful for procedures such as vacuum-assisted filtration. Make sure you switch off the taps after use. Take special care with glass items kept at very low or high pressures. These should be contained within a metal cage to minimise the risk of injury (e.g. a vacuum desiccator, as shown in Fig. 23.4).

Fig. 23.3 Parts of a cylinder head regulator. The regulator is normally attached by tightening the attachment nut clockwise; the exception is with cylinders of hydrogen, where the special regulator is tightened *anticlockwise* to avoid the chance of this potentially explosive gas being incorrectly used.

Fig. 23.4 Vacuum desiccator (with mesh safety cage).

Measuring time

Many experiments and observations need to be carefully timed. Large-faced stopclocks allow you to set and follow 'experimental time' and remove the potential difficulties in calculating this from 'real time' on a watch or clock. Some timers incorporate an alarm which you can set to warn when readings or operations must be carried out; 24-h timers are available for controlling light and temperature regimes.

Text references

O'Neil, M.J., Smith, A., Heckelman, P.E. and Obenchain, J.R. (2001) *The Merck Index: An Encyclopedia of Chemicals, Drugs and Biologicals*, 13th edn. Merck & Co., Inc., Whitehouse Station.

Lide, D.R. (ed.) (2002) *CRC Handbook of Chemistry and Physics*, 83rd edn. CRC Press, Boca Raton.

Sources for further study

Anon. *CHEMnet BASE*. Available:
http://www.chemnetbase.com
Last accessed 08/01/03.
[On-line access to the *Handbook of Chemistry and Physics*.]

Jack, C.R. (1995) *Basic Biochemical Laboratory Procedures and Computing*. Oxford University Press, Oxford.

Seidman, L.A. and Moore, C.J. (2000) *Basic Laboratory Methods for Biotechnology: Textbook and Laboratory Reference*. Prentice Hall, New Jersey.

Study exercises

23.1 Practise the calculations involved in preparing specific volumes of aqueous solutions (see also Study exercise 24.1). What mass of substance would be required to prepare each of the following (answer in each case to 3 significant figures):
  (a) 100 ml of NaCl at 50 mmol l^{-1} (M_r of NaCl = 58.44)?
  (b) 250 ml of mannitol at 0.10 mol l^{-1} (M_r of mannitol = 182.17)?
  (c) 200 ml of a bovine serum albumin solution at 800 $\mu g\,ml^{-1}$?
  (d) 0.5 litres of $MgCl_2$ prepared from the hexahydrate salt at 22.5 mmol l^{-1} (M_r of $MgCl_2 \cdot 6H_2O$ = 203.30)?
  (e) 400 ml of DNA at 20 ng μl^{-1}?

23.2 Practise the calculations involved in preparing dilutions (answer in each case to 3 significant figures).
  (a) If you added 1.0 ml of an aqueous solution of NaCl at 0.4 mol l^{-1} to 9.0 ml of water, what would be the final concentration of NaCl in mmol l^{-1}?
  (b) If you added 25 ml of an aqueous solution of DNA at 10 $\mu g\,ml^{-1}$ to a 500 ml volumetric flask and made it up to the specified volume with water, what would be the final concentration of DNA, in ng ml^{-1}?

(c) If you added $10\,\mu l$ of an aqueous solution of sucrose at $200\,\mathrm{mmol\,l^{-1}}$ to a 250 ml volumetric flask and made it up to the specified volume with water, what would be the final concentration of sucrose, in $\mathrm{nmol\,ml^{-1}}$?

(d) How would you prepare 250 ml of KCl at a final concentration of $20.0\,\mathrm{mmol\,l^{-1}}$ from a solution containing KCl at $0.2\,\mathrm{mol\,l^{-1}}$?

(e) How would you prepare $1\times10^{-3}\,\mathrm{m^3}$ of glucose at a final concentration of $50\,\mu\mathrm{mol\,m^{-3}}$ from a stock solution containing glucose at $20.0\,\mathrm{g\,m^{-3}}$ (M_r of glucose $=180.16$)?

23.3 **Practise the calculations involved in using stock solutions**. Suppose you had the following stock solutions: NaCl $100.0\,\mathrm{mmol\,l^{-1}}$; KCl $200.0\,\mathrm{mmol\,l^{-1}}$; $CaCl_2$ $160.0\,\mathrm{mmol\,l^{-1}}$; glucose $5.0\,\mathrm{mmol\,l^{-1}}$. Calculate the volumes of each stock solution and the volume of water required to prepare each of the following (answer in each case to 3 significant figures):

(a) 1.0 ml of a solution containing only KCl at $10.0\,\mathrm{mmol\,l^{-1}}$

(b) 50 ml of a solution containing NaCl at $2.5\,\mathrm{mmol\,l^{-1}}$ and glucose at $0.5\,\mathrm{mmol\,l^{-1}}$

(c) 100 ml of a solution containing NaCl at $5.0\,\mathrm{mmol\,l^{-1}}$, KCl at $2.5\,\mathrm{mmol\,l^{-1}}$, $CaCl_2$ at $40.0\,\mathrm{mmol\,l^{-1}}$ and glucose at $0.25\,\mathrm{mmol\,l^{-1}}$

(d) 10 ml of a solution containing NaCl, $CaCl_2$ and KCl, all at $20.0\,\mu\mathrm{mol\,ml^{-1}}$

(e) 25 ml of a solution containing $CaCl_2$ at $8.0\,\mathrm{mmol\,l^{-1}}$, KCl at $50.0\,\mathrm{mmol\,l^{-1}}$ and glucose at $20.0\,\mathrm{nmol\,ml^{-1}}$.

Principles of solution chemistry

Preparing solutions – practical advice is given on pp. 129–33, while O'Neil et al. (2001) gives you information on M_r, solubility, etc.

A solution is a homogeneous liquid, formed by the addition of solutes to a solvent (usually water in biological systems). The behaviour of solutions is determined by the type of solutes involved and by their proportions, relative to the solvent. Many laboratory exercises involve calculation of concentrations, e.g. when preparing an experimental solution at a particular concentration, or when expressing data in terms of solute concentration. Make sure that you understand the basic principles set out in this chapter before you tackle such exercises.

Solutes can affect the properties of solutions in several ways, including:

Electrolytic dissociation

This occurs where individual molecules of an electrolyte dissociate to give charged particles (ions). For a strong electrolyte, e.g. NaCl, dissociation is essentially complete. In contrast, a weak electrolyte, e.g. acetic acid, will be only partly dissociated, depending upon the pH and temperature of the solution (pp. 146–7).

Osmotic effects

These are the result of solute particles lowering the effective concentration of the solvent (water). These effects are particularly relevant to biological systems since membranes are far more permeable to water than to most solutes. Water moves across biological membranes from the solution with the higher effective water concentration to that with the lower effective water concentration (osmosis).

Ideal/non-ideal behaviour

This occurs because solutions of real substances do not necessarily conform to the theoretical relationships predicted for dilute solutions of so-called ideal solutes. It is often necessary to take account of the non-ideal behaviour of real solutions, especially at high solute concentrations (see Lide, 2002, and Robinson and Stokes, 2000, for appropriate data).

Concentration

In SI units (p. 176), the concentration of a solute in a solution is expressed in $mol\,m^{-3}$, which is convenient for most biological purposes. The concentration of a solute is usually symbolised by square brackets, e.g. [NaCl]. Details of how to prepare a solution using SI and non-SI units are given in Box 23.1 on p. 130.

A number of alternative ways of expressing the relative amounts of solute and solvent are in general use, and you may come across these terms in your practical work, or in the literature:

Molarity

This is the term used to denote molar concentration, $[C]$, expressed as moles of solute per litre volume of solution $(mol\,l^{-1})$. This non-SI term continues to find widespread usage, in part because of the familiarity of working scientists with the term, but also because laboratory glassware is calibrated in millilitres and litres, making the preparation of molar and

Expressing solute concentrations – you should use SI units wherever possible. However, you are likely to meet non-SI concentrations and you must be able to deal with these units too.

Example A 1.0 molar solution of NaCl would contain 58.44 g NaCl (the relative molecular mass) per litre of solution.

Box 24.1 Useful procedures for calculations involving molar concentrations

1. **Preparing a solution of defined molarity.** For a solute of known relative molecular mass, M_r, the following relationship can be applied:

$$[C] = \frac{\text{mass of solute/relative molecular mass}}{\text{volume of solution}} \quad [24.1]$$

So, if you wanted to make up 200 ml (0.2 l) of an aqueous solution of NaCl (M_r 58.44) at a concentration of 500 mmol l^{-1} (0.5 mol l^{-1}), you could calculate the amount of NaCl required by inserting these values into Eqn [24.1]:

$$0.5 = \frac{\text{mass of solute/58.44}}{0.2}$$

which can be rearranged to

$$\text{mass of solute} = 0.5 \times 0.2 \times 58.44 = 5.844 \text{ g}$$

The same relationship can be used to calculate the concentration of a solution containing a known amount of a solute, e.g. if 21.1 g of NaCl were made up to a volume of 100 ml (0.1 l), this would give

$$[NaCl] = \frac{21.1/58.44}{0.1} = 3.61 \text{ mol l}^{-1}$$

2. **Dilutions and concentrations.** The following relationship is very useful if you are diluting (or concentrating) a solution:

$$[C_1]V_1 = [C_2]V_2 \quad [24.2]$$

where $[C_1]$ and $[C_2]$ are the initial and final concentrations, while V_1 and V_2 are their respective volumes: each pair must be expressed in the same units. Thus, if you wanted to dilute 200 ml of 0.5 mol l^{-1} NaCl to give a final molarity of 0.1 mol l^{-1}, then, by substitution into Eqn [24.2]:

$$0.5 \times 200 = 0.1 \times V_2$$

Thus $V_2 = 1000$ ml (in other words, you would have to add water to 200 ml of 0.5 mol l^{-1} NaCl to give a final volume of 1000 ml to obtain a 0.1 mol l^{-1} solution).

3. **Interconversion.** A simple way of interconverting amounts and volumes of any particular solution is to divide the amount and volume by a factor of 10^3: thus a molar solution of a substance contains 1 mol l^{-1}, which is equivalent to 1 mmol ml^{-1}, or 1 μmol μl^{-1}, or 1 nmol nl^{-1}, etc. You may find this technique useful when calculating the amount of substance present in a small volume of solution of known concentration, e.g. to calculate the amount of NaCl present in 50 μl of a solution with a concentration (molarity) of 0.5 mol l^{-1} NaCl:

(a) this is equivalent to 0.5 μmol μl^{-1};

(b) therefore 50 μl will contain $50 \times 0.5 \mu$mol = 25 μmol.

Alternatively, you may prefer to convert to primary SI units, for ease of calculation (see Box 23.1).

The 'unitary method' (p. 472) is an alternative approach to these calculations.

---

millimolar solutions relatively straightforward. However, the symbols in common use for molar (M) and millimolar (mM) solutions are at odds with the SI system and many people now prefer to use mol l^{-1} and mmol l^{-1} respectively, to avoid confusion. Box 24.1 gives details of some useful approaches to calculations involving molarities.

Molality

This is used to express the concentration of solute relative to the *mass* of solvent, i.e. mol kg^{-1}. Molality is a temperature-independent means of expressing solute concentration, rarely used except when the osmotic properties of a solution are of interest (p. 142).

Example A 0.5 molal solution of NaCl would contain $58.44 \times 0.5 = 29.22$ g NaCl per kg of water.

Per cent composition (% w/w)

This is the solute mass (in g) per 100 g solution. The advantage of this expression is the ease with which a solution can be prepared, since it simply requires each component to be pre-weighed (for water, a volumetric measurement may be used, e.g. using a measuring cylinder) and then mixed together. Similar terms are parts per thousand (‰), e.g. mg g^{-1}, and parts per million (ppm), e.g. μg g^{-1} (see overleaf).

Example A 5% w/w sucrose solution contains 5 g sucrose and 95 g water (= 95 ml water, assuming a density of 1 g ml^{-1}) to give 100 g of solution.

Per cent concentration (% w/v and % v/v)

For solutes added in solid form, this is the number of grams of solute per 100 ml solution. This is more commonly used than per cent composition, since solutions can be accurately prepared by weighing out the required amount of solute and then making this up to a known volume using a volumetric flask. The equivalent expression for liquid solutes is % v/v.

The principal use of mass/mass or mass/volume terms (including $g\,l^{-1}$) is for solutes whose relative molecular mass is unknown (e.g. cellular proteins), or for mixtures of certain classes of substance (e.g. total salt in sea water). You should *never* use the per cent term without specifying how the solution was prepared, i.e. by using the qualifier w/w, w/v or v/v. For mass concentrations, it is simpler to use mass per unit volume, e.g. $mg\,l^{-1}$, $\mu g\,\mu l^{-1}$, etc.

> **Example**   A 5% w/v sucrose solution contains 5 g sucrose in 100 ml of solution. A 5% v/v glycerol solution would contain 5 ml glycerol in 100 ml of solution.
>
>   Note that when water is the solvent this is often not specified in the expression, e.g. a 20% v/v ethanol solution contains 20% ethanol made up to 100 ml of solution using water.

> **Alternative expressions** – *parts per thousand (‰) w/v can be used as an alternative to $g\,l^{-1}$*

Parts per million (ppm) and parts per billion (ppb) concentration

Ppm is a non-SI weight per volume (w/v) concentration term commonly used in quantitative analysis such as flame photometry, atomic absorption spectroscopy and gas chromatography, where low concentrations of solutes are analysed. The term ppm is equivalent to the expression of concentration as $\mu g\,ml^{-1}$ ($10^{-6}\,g\,ml^{-1}$) and a 1.0 ppm solution of a substance will have a concentration of 1.0 $\mu g\,ml^{-1}$ ($1.0 \times 10^{-6}\,g\,ml^{-1}$).

Parts per billion (ppb) is an extension of this concentration term as $ng\,ml^{-1}$ ($10^{-9}\,g\,ml^{-1}$) and is commonly used to express concentrations of very dilute solutions. For example, the allowable concentration of arsenic in water is 0.05 ppm, more conveniently expressed as 50 ppb. Also note that ppm and ppb are sometimes used as a weight per weight (w/w) term, e.g. $\mu g\,g^{-1}$ and $ng\,g^{-1}$ respectively.

Activity (a)

This is a term used to describe the *effective* concentration of a solute. In dilute solutions, solutes can be considered to behave according to ideal (thermodynamic) principles, i.e. they will have an effective concentration equivalent to the actual concentration. However, in concentrated solutions ($\geqslant 500\,mol\,m^{-3}$), the behaviour of solutes is often non-ideal, and their effective concentration (activity) will be less than the actual concentration [C]. The ratio between the effective concentration and the actual concentration is called the activity coefficient (γ) where

Table 24.1 Activity coefficient of NaCl solutions as a function of molality. Data from Robinson and Stokes (2000)

Molality	Activity coefficient at 25 °C
0.1	0.778
0.5	0.681
1.0	0.657
2.0	0.668
4.0	0.783
6.0	0.986

$$\gamma = \frac{a}{[C]} \qquad [24.3]$$

Equation [24.3] can be used for SI units ($mol\,m^{-3}$), molarity ($mol\,l^{-1}$) or molality ($mol\,kg^{-1}$). In all cases, γ is a dimensionless term, since a and [C] are expressed in the same units. The activity coefficient of a solute is effectively unity in dilute solution, decreasing as the solute concentration increases (Table 24.1). At high concentrations of certain ionic solutes, γ may increase to become greater than unity.

> **KEY POINT**   Activity is often the correct expression for theoretical relationships involving solute concentration (e.g. where a property of the solution is dependent on concentration). However, for most practical purposes, it is possible to use the *actual* concentration of a solute rather than the activity, since the difference between the two terms can be ignored for dilute solutions.

Example A solution of NaCl with a molality of 0.5 mol kg^{-1} has an activity coefficient of 0.681 at 25 °C and a molal activity of $0.5 \times 0.681 = 0.340$ mol kg^{-1}.

Examples For carbonate ions (CO_3^{2-}), with a relative molecular mass of 60.00 and a valency of 2, the equivalent mass is $60.00/2 = 30.00$ g eq^{-1}.

For sulphuric acid (H_2SO_4, relative molecular mass 98.08), where 2 hydrogen ions are available, the equivalent mass is $98.08/2 = 49.04$ g eq^{-1}.

Example A 0.5 N solution of sulphuric acid would contain $0.5 \times 49.04 = 24.52$ g l^{-1}.

Example Under ideal conditions, 1 mol of NaCl dissolved in water would give 1 mol of Na$^+$ ions and 1 mol of Cl$^-$ ions, equivalent to a theoretical osmolarity of 2 osmol l^{-1}.

Example A 1.0 mol kg^{-1} solution of NaCl has an osmotic coefficient of 0.936 at 25 °C and an osmolality of $1.0 \times 2 \times 0.936 = 1.872$ osmol kg^{-1}.

Table 24.2 Osmotic coefficients of NaCl solutions as a function of molality. Data from Robinson and Stokes (2000)

Molality	Osmotic coefficient at 25 °C
0.1	0.932
0.5	0.921
1.0	0.936
2.0	0.983
4.0	1.116
6.0	1.271

The particular use of the term 'water activity' is considered below, since it is based on the mole fraction of solvent, rather than the effective concentration of solute.

Equivalent mass (equivalent weight)
Equivalence and normality are outdated terms, although you may come across them in older texts. They apply to certain solutes whose reactions involve the transfer of charged ions, e.g. acids and alkalis (which may be involved in H$^+$ or OH$^-$ transfer), and electrolytes (which form cations and anions that may take part in further reactions). These two terms take into account the valency of the charged solutes. Thus the equivalent mass of an ion is its relative molecular mass divided by its valency (ignoring the sign), expressed in grams per equivalent (eq) according to the relationship:

$$\text{equivalent mass} = \frac{\text{relative molecular mass}}{\text{valency}} \quad [24.4]$$

For acids and alkalis, the equivalent mass is the mass of substance that will provide 1 mol of either H$^+$ or OH$^-$ ions in a reaction, obtained by dividing the molecular mass by the number of available ions (n), using n instead of valency as the denominator in eqn [24.4].

Normality
A 1 normal solution (1 N) is one that contains one equivalent mass of a substance per litre of solution. The general formula is:

$$\text{normality} = \frac{\text{mass of substance per litre}}{\text{equivalent mass}} \quad [24.5]$$

Osmolarity
This non-SI expression is used to describe the number of moles of osmotically active solute particles per litre of solution (osmol l^{-1}). The need for such a term arises because some molecules dissociate to give more than one osmotically active particle in aqueous solution.

Osmolality
This term describes the number of moles of osmotically active solute particles per unit mass of solvent (osmol kg^{-1}). For an ideal solute, the osmolality can be determined by multiplying the molality by n, the number of solute particles produced in solution (e.g. for NaCl, $n = 2$). However, for real (i.e. non-ideal) solutes, a correction factor (the osmotic coefficient, ϕ) is used:

$$\text{osmolality} = \text{molality} \times n \times \phi \quad [24.6]$$

If necessary, the osmotic coefficients of a particular solute can be obtained from tables (e.g. Table 24.2): non-ideal behaviour means that ϕ may have values >1 at high concentrations. Alternatively, the osmolality of a solution can be measured using an osmometer.

Colligative properties and their use in osmometry

Several properties vary in direct proportion to the effective number of osmotically active solute particles per unit mass of solvent and can be used

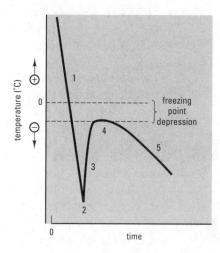

Fig. 24.1 Temperature responses of a cryoscopic osmometer. The response can be subdivided into:
1. initial supercooling
2. initiation of crystallisation
3. crystallisation/freezing
4. plateau, at the freezing point
5. slow temperature decrease.

to determine the osmolality of a solution. These colligative properties include freezing point, boiling point and vapour pressure.

An osmometer is an instrument which measures the osmolality of a solution, usually by determining the freezing point depression of the solution in relation to pure water, a technique known as cryoscopic osmometry. A small amount of sample is cooled rapidly and then brought to the freezing point (Fig. 24.1), which is measured by a temperature-sensitive thermistor probe calibrated in $mosmol\,kg^{-1}$. An alternative method is used in vapour pressure osmometry, which measures the relative decrease in the vapour pressure produced in the gas phase when a small sample of the solution is equilibrated within a chamber.

Using an osmometer – *it is vital that the sample holder and probe are clean, otherwise small droplets of the previous sample may be carried over, leading to inaccurate measurement.*

Osmotic properties of solutions

Several interrelated terms can be used to describe the osmotic status of a solution. In addition to osmolality, you may come across the following:

Osmotic pressure

This is based on the concept of a membrane permeable to water, but not to solute molecules. For example, if a sucrose solution is placed on one side and pure water on the other, then a passive driving force will be created and water will diffuse across the membrane into the sucrose solution, since the effective water concentration in the sucrose solution will be lower. The tendency for water to diffuse into the sucrose solution could be counteracted by applying a hydrostatic pressure equivalent to the passive driving force. Thus, the osmotic pressure of a solution is the excess hydrostatic pressure required to prevent the net flow of water into a vessel containing the solution. The SI unit of osmotic pressure is the pascal, Pa ($= kg\,m^{-1}\,s^{-2}$). Older sources may use atmospheres, or bars, and conversion factors are given in Table 29.1 (p. 178). Osmotic pressure and osmolality can be interconverted using the expression $1\,osmol\,kg^{-1}$ $= 2.479\,MPa$ at 25 °C.

Example A $1.0\,mol\,kg^{-1}$ solution of NaCl at 25 °C has an osmolality of $1.872\,osmol\,kg^{-1}$ and an osmotic pressure of $1.872 \times 2.479 = 4.641\,MPa$.

The use of osmotic pressure has been criticised as misleading, since a solution does not exhibit an 'osmotic pressure', unless it is placed on the other side of a selectively permeable membrane from pure water!

Table 24.3 Water activity (a_w) of NaCl solutions as a function of molality. Data from Robinson and Stokes (2000)

Molality	a_w
0.1	0.997
0.5	0.984
1.0	0.967
2.0	0.932
4.0	0.852
6.0	0.760

Water activity (a_w)

This is a term often used to describe the osmotic behaviour of microbial cells. It is a measure of the relative proportion of water in a solution, expressed in terms of its mole fraction, i.e. the ratio of the number of moles of water (n_w) to the total number of moles of all substances (i.e. water and solutes) in solution (n_t), taking into account the molal activity coefficient of the solvent, water (i.e. γ_w):

$$a_w = \gamma_w \frac{n_w}{n_t} \qquad [24.7]$$

The water activity of pure water is unity, decreasing as solutes are added. One disadvantage of a_w is the limited change which occurs in response to a change in solute concentration: a $1.0\,mol\,kg^{-1}$ solution of NaCl has a water activity of 0.967 (Table 24.3).

Osmolality, osmotic pressure and water activity are measurements based solely on the osmotic properties of a solution, with no regard for any other driving forces, e.g. hydrostatic and gravitational forces. In circumstances where such other forces are important, you will need to measure a variable that takes into account these aspects of water status, namely water potential.

Water potential (hydraulic potential) and its applications

Water potential, Ψ_w, is the most appropriate measure of osmotic status in many areas of the biosciences. It is a term derived from the chemical potential of water. It expresses the difference between the chemical potential of water in the test system and that of pure water under standard conditions and has units of pressure (i.e. Pa). It is a more appropriate term than osmotic pressure because it is based on sound theoretical principles and because it can be used to predict the direction of passive movement of water, since water will flow down a gradient of chemical potential (i.e. osmosis occurs from a solution with a higher water potential to one with a lower water potential). A solution of pure water at 20 °C and at 0.1 MPa pressure (i.e. $\approx$ atmospheric) has a water potential of zero. The addition of solutes will lower the water potential (i.e. make it negative), while the application of pressure, e.g. from hydrostatic or gravitational forces, will raise it (i.e. make it positive).

Often, the two principal components of water potential are referred to as the solute potential, or osmotic potential (Ψ_s, sometimes symbolised as Ψ_π or π) and the hydrostatic pressure potential (Ψ_p) respectively. For a solution at atmospheric pressure, the water potential is due solely to the presence of osmotically active solute molecules (osmotic potential) and may be calculated from the measured osmolality (osmol kg^{-1}) at 25 °C, using the relationship:

$$\Psi_w\,(MPa) = \Psi_s\,(MPa) = -2.479 \times osmolality \qquad [24.8]$$

For aquatic microbial cells, e.g. algae, fungi and bacteria, equilibrated in their growth medium at atmospheric pressure, the water potential of the external medium will be equal to the cellular water potential and the latter can be derived from the measured osmolality of the medium (eqn [24.8]) by osmometry (pp. 141–2). The water potential of such cells can be

Examples A $1.0\,mol\,kg^{-1}$ solution of NaCl has a (negative) water potential of -4.641 MPa.

A solution of pure water at 0.2 MPa pressure (about 0.1 MPa above atmospheric pressure) has a (positive) water potential of 0.1 MPa.

subdivided into two major parts, the cell solute potential (Ψ_s) and the cell turgor pressure (Ψ_p) as follows:

$$\Psi_w = \Psi_s + \Psi_p \qquad [24.9]$$

To calculate the relative contribution of the osmotic and pressure terms in eqn [24.9], an estimate of the internal osmolality is required, e.g. by measuring the freezing point depression of expressed intracellular fluid. Once you have values for Ψ_w and Ψ_s, the turgor pressure can be calculated by substitution into Eqn [24.9].

For terrestrial plant cells, the water potential may be determined directly using a vapour pressure osmometer, by placing a sample of the material within the osmometer chamber and allowing it to equilibrate. If Ψ_s of expressed sap is then measured, Ψ_p can be determined from Eqn [24.9].

The van't Hoff relationship can be used to estimate Ψ_s, by summation of the osmotic potentials due to the major solutes, determined from their concentrations, as:

$$\Psi_s = -RTn\phi[C] \qquad [24.10]$$

where RT is the product of the universal gas constant and absolute temperature ($2\,479$ J mol^{-1} at 25 °C), n and ϕ are as previously defined and $[C]$ is expressed in SI terms as mol m^{-3}.

Measuring water potential – eqn [24.9] ignores the effects of gravitational forces – for systems where gravitational effects are important an additional term is required (Nobel, 1999).

Text references

O'Neil, M.J., Smith, A., Heckelman, P.E. and Obenchain, J.R. (2001) *The Merck Index: An Encyclopedia of Chemicals, Drugs and Biologicals*, 13th edn. Merck & Co., Inc., Whitehouse Station.

Lide, D.R. (ed.) (2002) *CRC Handbook of Chemistry and Physics*, 83rd edn. CRC Press, Boca Raton.

Nobel, P.S. (1999) *Physicochemical and Environmental Plant Physiology*, 2nd edn. Academic Press, New York.

Robinson, R.A. and Stokes, R.H. (2000) *Electrolyte Solutions*. Dover Publications, New York.

Sources for further study

Burtis, C.A. and Ashwood, E.R. (2001) *Fundamentals of Clinical Chemistry*, 5th edn. Saunders, Philadelphia.

Chapman, C. (1998) *Basic Chemistry for Biology*. McGraw-Hill, New York.

Seidman, L.A. and Moore, C.J. (2000) *Basic Laboratory Methods for Biotechnology: Textbook and Laboratory Reference*. Prentice Hall, New Jersey.

Study exercises

24.1 Practise calculations involving molar concentrations (see also Study exercises 23.1 and 23.2). What mass of substance would be required to prepare each of the following aqueous solutions (answer in grams, to 3 decimal places in each case):

(a) 1 litre of NaCl at a concentration of 1 molar? (M_r of NaCl = 58.44.)

(b) 250 ml of $CaCl_2$ at 100 mmol l^{-1}? (M_r of $CaCl_2$ = 110.99.)

(c) 2.5 l of mannitol at 10 nmol μl^{-1}? (M_r of mannitol = 182.17.)

(d) 400 ml of KCl at 5% w/v?

(e) 250 ml of glucose at 2.50 mol m^{-3}? (M_r of glucose = 180.16.)

24.2 Practise expressing concentrations in different ways. Express all answers to 3 significant figures:

(a) What is 5 g l^{-1} sucrose, expressed in terms of molarity? (M_r of sucrose = 342.3.)

(b) What is 1.0 mol m^{-3} NaCl, expressed in g l^{-1}? (M_r of NaCl = 58.44.)

(c) What is 5% v/v ethanol, expressed in terms of molarity? (M_r of ethanol = 46.06 and density of ethanol at 25°C = 0.789 g ml^{-1}.)

(d) What is 150 mmol l^{-1} glucose, expressed in terms of per cent concentration (% w/v)? (M_r of glucose = 180.16.)

(e) What is a 1.0 molal solution of KCl, expressed as per cent composition (% w/w)? (M_r of KCl = 74.55.)

24.3 Calculate osmolality and osmotic potentials.

(a) Assuming NaCl, KCl and $CaCl_2$ behave according to ideal thermodynamic principles, what would be the predicted osmolality of a solution containing:

(i) NaCl alone, at 50 mmol kg^{-1}?

(ii) KCl at 200 mmol kg^{-1} and $CaCl_2$ at 40 mmol kg^{-1}?

(iii) NaCl at 100 mmol kg^{-1}, KCl at 60 mmol kg^{-1} and $CaCl_2$ at 75 mmol kg^{-1}?

(b) What is the predicted osmotic pressure and osmotic potential of each of the solutions in (a) at 25 °C? (Answer to 3 significant figures in all cases.)

pH and buffer solutions

Acid – a compound that acts as a proton donor in aqueous solution.

Base – a compound that acts as a proton acceptor in aqueous solution.

Conjugate pair – an acid together with its corresponding base.

Alkali – a compound that liberates hydroxyl ions when it dissociates. Since hydroxyl ions are strongly basic, this will reduce the proton concentration.

Ampholyte – a compound that can act as both an acid and a base. Water is an ampholyte since it may dissociate to give a proton and a hydroxyl ion (amphoteric behaviour).

pH is a measure of the amount of hydrogen ions (H^+) in a solution: this affects the solubility of many substances and the activity of most biological systems, from individual molecules to whole organisms. It is usual to think of aqueous solutions as containing H^+ ions (protons), though protons actually exist in their hydrated form, as hydronium ions (H_3O^+). The proton concentration of an aqueous solution $[H^+]$ is affected by several factors:

- Ionisation (dissociation) of water, which liberates protons and hydroxyl ions in equal quantities, according to the reversible relationship:

$$H_2O \rightleftharpoons H^+ + OH^- \qquad [25.1]$$

- Dissociation of acids, according to the equation:

$$H–A \rightleftharpoons H^+ + A^- \qquad [25.2]$$

where H–A represents the acid and A^- is the corresponding conjugate base. The dissociation of an acid in water will increase the amount of protons, reducing the amount of hydroxyl ions as water molecules are formed (eqn [25.1]). The addition of a base (usually, as its salt) to water will decrease the amount of H^+, due to the formation of the conjugate acid (eqn [25.2]).

- Dissociation of alkalis, according to the relationship:

$$X–OH \rightleftharpoons X^+ + OH^- \qquad [25.3]$$

where X–OH represents the undissociated alkali. Since the dissociation of water is reversible (eqn [25.1]), in an aqueous solution the production of hydroxyl ions will effectively act to 'mop up' protons, lowering the proton concentration.

Many compounds act as acids, bases or alkalis: those which are almost completely ionised in solution are usually called strong acids or bases, while weak acids or bases are only slightly ionised in solution.

In an aqueous solution, most of the water molecules are not ionised. In fact, the extent of ionisation of pure water is constant at any given temperature and is usually expressed in terms of the ion product (or ionisation constant) of water, K_w:

$$K_w = [H^+][OH^-] \qquad [25.4]$$

where $[H^+]$ and $[OH^-]$ represent the molar concentration (strictly, the activity) of protons and hydroxyl ions in solution, expressed as $mol\,l^{-1}$. At 25 °C, the ion product of pure water is $10^{-14}\,mol^2\,l^{-2}$ (i.e. $10^{-8}\,mol^2\,m^{-6}$). This means that the concentration of protons in solution will be $10^{-7}\,mol\,l^{-1}$ ($10^{-4}\,mol\,m^{-3}$), with an equivalent concentration of hydroxyl ions (eqn [25.1]). Since these values are very low and involve negative powers of 10, it is customary to use the pH scale, where:

$$pH = -\log_{10}[H^+] \qquad [25.5]$$

Example Human blood plasma has a typical H^+ concentration of approximately $0.4 \times 10^{-7}\,mol\,l^{-1}$ ($= 10^{-7.4}\,mol\,l^{-1}$), giving a pH of 7.4.

and $[H^+]$ is the proton activity in $mol\,l^{-1}$ (see p. 140).

Table 25.1 Effects of temperature on the ion product of water (K_w), H^+ ion concentration and pH at neutrality. Values calculated from Lide (2002)

Temp. (°C)	K_w (mol^2 l^{-2})	[H^+] at neutrality (nmol l^{-1})	pH at neutrality
0	0.11×10^{-14}	33.9	7.47
4	0.17×10^{-14}	40.7	7.39
10	0.29×10^{-14}	53.7	7.27
20	0.68×10^{-14}	83.2	7.08
25	1.01×10^{-14}	100.4	7.00
30	1.47×10^{-14}	120.2	6.92
37	2.39×10^{-14}	154.9	6.81
45	4.02×10^{-14}	199.5	6.70

KEY POINT While pH is strictly the negative logarithm (to the base 10) of H^+ activity, in practice H^+ concentration in mol l^{-1} (equivalent to kmol m^{-3} in SI terminology) is most often used in place of activity, since the two are virtually the same, given the limited dissociation of H_2O. The pH scale is not SI: nevertheless, it continues to be used widely in biological science.

The value where an equal amount of H^+ and OH^- ions are present is termed neutrality: at 25 °C the pH of pure water at neutrality is 7.0. At this temperature, pH values below 7.0 are acidic while values above 7.0 are alkaline. However, the pH of a neutral solution changes with temperature (Table 25.1), due to the enhanced dissociation of water with increasing temperature. This must be taken into account when measuring the pH of any solution and when interpreting your results.

Always remember that the pH scale is a logarithmic one, not a linear one: a solution with a pH of 3.0 is not twice as acidic as a solution of pH 6.0, but one thousand times as acidic (i.e. contains 1000 times the amount of H^+ ions). Therefore, you may need to convert pH values into proton concentrations before you carry out mathematical manipulations (see Box 66.2, p. 482). For similar reasons, it is important that pH change is expressed in terms of the original and final pH values, rather than simply quoting the difference between the values: a pH change of 0.1 has little meaning unless the initial or final pH is known.

Measuring pH

pH electrodes

Accurate pH measurements can be made using a pH electrode, coupled to a pH meter. The pH electrode is usually a combination electrode, comprising two separate systems: an H^+-sensitive glass electrode and a reference electrode which is unaffected by H^+ ion concentration (Fig. 25.1). When this is immersed in a solution, a pH-dependent voltage between the two electrodes can be measured using a potentiometer. In most cases, the pH electrode assembly (containing the glass and reference electrodes) is connected to a separate pH meter by a cable, although some hand-held instruments (pH probes) have the electrodes and meter within the same assembly, often using an H^+-sensitive field effect transistor in place of a glass electrode, to improve durability and portability.

Box 25.1 gives details of the steps involved in making a pH measurement with a glass pH electrode and meter.

pH indicator dyes

These compounds (usually weak acids) change colour in a pH-dependent manner. They may be added in small amounts to a solution, or they can be used in paper strip form. Each indicator dye usually changes colour over a restricted pH range, typically 1–2 pH units (Table 25.2): universal indicator dyes/papers make use of a combination of individual dyes to measure a wider pH range. Dyes are not suitable for accurate pH measurement as they are affected by other components of the solution including oxidising and reducing agents and salts. However, they are useful for:

- estimating the approximate pH of a solution;
- determining a change in pH, for example at the end-point of a titration or the production of acids during bacterial metabolism (pp. 212–13);
- establishing the approximate pH of intracellular compartments, for example the use of neutral red as a 'vital' stain (p. 163).

Table 25.2 Properties of some pH indicator dyes

Dye	Acid–base colour change	Useful pH range
Thymol blue (acid)	red–yellow	1.2–6.8
Bromophenol blue	yellow–blue	1.2–6.8
Congo red	blue–red	3.0–5.2
Bromocresol green	yellow–blue	3.8–5.4
Resazurin	orange–violet	3.8–6.5
Methyl red	red–yellow	4.3–6.1
Litmus	red–blue	4.5–8.3
Bromocresol purple	yellow–purple	5.8–6.8
Bromothymol blue	yellow–blue	6.0–7.6
Neutral red	red–yellow	6.8–8.0
Phenol red	yellow–red	6.8–8.2
Thymol blue (alkaline)	yellow–blue	8.0–9.6
Phenol-phthalein	none–red	8.3–10.0

Box 25.1 Using a glass pH electrode and meter to measure the pH of a solution

The following procedure should be used whenever you make a pH measurement: consult the manufacturer's handbook for specific information, where necessary. Do not be tempted to miss out any of the steps detailed below, particularly those relating to the effects of temperature, or your measurements are likely to be inaccurate.

Fig. 25.1 Measurement of pH using a combination pH electrode and meter. The electrical potential difference recorded by the potentiometer is directly proportional to the pH of the test solution.

1. **Stir the test solution thoroughly before you make any measurement**: it is often best to use a magnetic stirrer. Leave the solution for sufficient time to allow equilibration at lab temperature.

2. **Record the temperature of every solution you use**, including all calibration standards and samples, since this will affect K_w, neutrality and pH.

3. **Set the temperature compensator on the meter to the appropriate value.** This control makes an allowance for the effect of temperature on the electrical potential difference recorded by the meter: it does *not* allow for the other temperature-dependent effects mentioned elsewhere. Basic instruments have no temperature compensator, and should only be used at a specified temperature, either 20 °C or 25 °C, otherwise they will not give an accurate measurement. More sophisticated systems have automatic temperature compensation.

4. **Rinse the electrode assembly with distilled water** and gently dab off the excess water onto a clean tissue: check for visible damage or contamination of the glass electrode (consult a member of staff if the glass is broken or dirty). Also check that the solution within the glass assembly is covering the metal electrode.

5. **Calibrate the instrument:** set the meter to 'pH' mode, if appropriate, and then place the electrode assembly in a standard solution of known pH, usually pH 7.00. This solution may be supplied as a liquid, or may be prepared by dissolving a measured amount of a calibration standard in water: calibration standards are often provided in tablet form, to be dissolved in water to give a particular volume of solution. Adjust the calibration control to give the correct reading. Remember that your calibration standards will only give the specified pH at a particular temperature, usually either 20 °C or 25 °C. If you are working at a different temperature, you must establish the actual pH of your calibration standards, either from the supplier, or from literature information.

6. **Remove the electrode assembly from the calibration solution and rinse again with distilled water:** dab off the excess water. Basic instruments have no further calibration steps (single-point calibration), while the more refined pH meters have additional calibration procedures.

   If you are using a basic instrument, you should check that your apparatus is accurate over the appropriate pH range by measuring the pH of another standard whose pH is close to that expected for the test solution. If the standard does not give the expected reading, the instrument is not functioning correctly: consult a member of staff.

   If you are using an instrument with a slope control function, this will allow you to correct for any deviation in electrical potential from that predicted by the theoretical relationship (at 25 °C,

Box 25.1 (continued)

a change in pH of 1.00 unit should result in a change in electrical potential of 59.16 mV) by performing a two-point calibration. Having calibrated the instrument at pH 7.00, immerse in a second standard at the same temperature as that of the first standard, usually buffered to either pH 4.00 or pH 9.00, depending upon the expected pH of your samples. Adjust the slope control until the exact value of the second standard is achieved (Fig. 25.2). A pH electrode and meter calibrated using the two-point method will give accurate readings over the pH range from 3 to 11: laboratory pH electrodes are not accurate outside this range, since the theoretical relationship between electrical potential and pH is no longer valid.

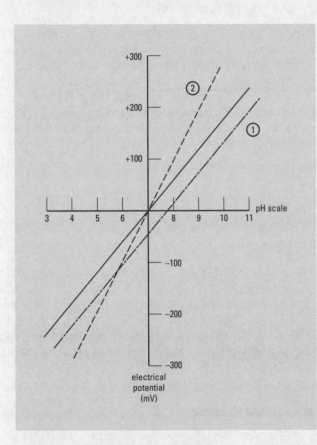

Fig. 25.2 The relationship between electrical potential and pH. The solid line shows the response of a calibrated electrode while the other plots are for instruments requiring calibration: 1 has the correct slope but incorrect isopotential point (calibration control adjustment is needed); 2 has the correct isopotential point but incorrect slope (slope control adjustment is needed).

7. **Once the instrument is calibrated, measure the pH of your solution(s)**, making sure that the electrode assembly is rinsed thoroughly between measurements. You should be particularly aware of this requirement if your solutions contain organic biological material, e.g. soil, tissue fluids, protein solutions, etc., since these may adhere to the glass electrode and affect the calibration of your instrument. If your electrode becomes contaminated during use, check with a member of staff before cleaning: avoid touching the surface of the glass electrode with abrasive material. Allow sufficient time for the pH reading to stabilise in each solution before taking a measurement: for unbuffered solutions, this may take several minutes, so do not take inaccurate pH readings due to impatience!

8. **After use, the electrode assembly must not be allowed to dry out.** Most pH electrodes should be stored in a neutral solution of KCl, either by suspending the assembly in a small beaker, or by using an electrode cap filled with the appropriate solution (typically $1.0 \, mol \, l^{-1}$ KCl buffered at pH 7.0). However, many labs simply use distilled water as a storage solution, leading to loss of ions from the interior of the electrode assembly. In practice, this means that pH electrodes stored in distilled water will take far longer to give a stable reading than those stored in KCl.

9. **Switch the meter to zero (where appropriate), but do not turn off the power:** pH meters give more stable readings if they are left on during normal working hours.

    Problems (and solutions) include: inaccurate and/or unstable pH readings caused by cross-contamination (rinse electrode assembly with distilled water and blot dry between measurements); development of a protein film on the surface of the electrode (soak in 1% w/v pepsin in $0.1 \, mol \, l^{-1}$ HCl for at least an hour); deposition of organic or inorganic contaminants on the glass bulb (use an organic solvent, such as acetone, or a solution of $0.1 \, mol \, l^{-1}$ disodium ethylenediaminetetraacetic acid, respectively); drying out of the internal reference solutions (drain, flush and refill with fresh solution, then allow to equilibrate in $0.1 \, mol \, l^{-1}$ HCl for at least an hour); cracks or chips to the surface of the glass bulb (use a replacement electrode).

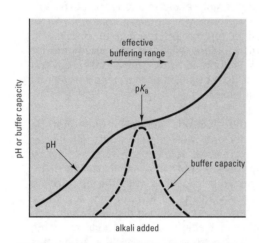

Fig. 25.3 Theoretical pH titration curve for a buffer solution. pH change is lowest and buffer capacity is greatest at the pK_a of the buffer solution.

An ideal buffer for biological purposes would possess the following characteristics:

- impermeability to biological membranes;
- biological stability and lack of interference with metabolic and biological processes;
- lack of significant absorption of ultraviolet or visible light;
- lack of formation of insoluble complexes with cations;
- minimal effect of ionic composition or salt concentration;
- limited pH change in response to temperature.

Buffers

Rather than simply measuring the pH of a solution, you may wish to *control* the pH, e.g. in metabolic experiments, or in a growth medium for cell culture (p. 226). In fact, you should consider whether you need to control pH in any experiment involving a biological system, whether whole organisms, isolated cells, subcellular components or biomolecules. One of the most effective ways to control pH is to use a buffer solution.

A buffer solution is usually a mixture of a weak acid and its conjugate base. Added protons will be neutralised by the anionic base while a reduction in protons, e.g. due to the addition of hydroxyl ions, will be counterbalanced by dissociation of the acid (eqn [25.2]); thus the conjugate pair acts as a 'buffer' to pH change. The innate resistance of most biological fluids to pH change is due to the presence of cellular constituents that act as buffers, e.g. proteins, which have a large number of weakly acidic and basic groups in their amino acid side chains.

Buffer capacity and the effects of pH

The extent of resistance to pH change is called the buffer capacity of a solution. The buffer capacity is measured experimentally at a particular pH by titration against a strong acid or alkali: the resultant curve will be strongly sigmoidal, with a plateau where the buffer capacity is greatest (Fig. 25.3). The mid-point of the plateau represents the pH where equal quantities of acid and conjugate base are present, and is given the symbol pK_a, which refers to the negative logarithm (to the base 10) of the acid dissociation constant, K_a, where

$$K_a = \frac{[H^+][A^-]}{[HA]} \qquad [25.6]$$

By rearranging eqn [25.6] and taking negative logarithms, we obtain:

$$pH = pK_a + \log_{10}\frac{[A^-]}{[HA]} \qquad [25.7]$$

This relationship is known as the Henderson–Hasselbalch equation and it shows that the pH will be equal to the pK_a when the ratio of conjugate base to acid is unity, since the final term in eqn [25.7] will be zero. Consequently, the pK_a of a buffer solution is an important factor in determining the buffer capacity at a particular pH. In practical terms, this means that a buffer solution will work most effectively at pH values about one unit either side of the pK_a.

Selecting an appropriate buffer

When selecting a buffer, you should be aware of certain limitations to their use. Citric acid and phosphate buffers readily form insoluble complexes with divalent cations, while phosphate can also act as a substrate, activator or inhibitor of certain enzymes. Both of these buffers contain biologically significant quantities of cations, e.g. Na^+ or K^+. TRIS (Table 25.3) is often toxic to biological systems: due to its high lipid solubility it can penetrate membranes, uncoupling electron transport reactions in whole cells and isolated organelles. In addition, it is markedly affected by temperature, with a tenfold increase in H^+ concentration from

Table 25.3 pK_a values at 25 °C and M_r of some acids and bases (upper section) and some large organic zwitterions (lower section) commonly used in buffer solutions. For polyprotic acids, where more than one proton may dissociate, the pK_a values are given for each ionisation step. Only the trivial acronyms of the larger molecules are provided: their full names can be obtained from the catalogues of most chemical suppliers.

Acid or base	pK_a value(s)	M_r
Acetic acid	4.8	60.1
Boric acid	9.2	61.8
Citric acid	3.1, 4.8, 5.4	191.2
Glycylglycine	3.1, 8.2	132.1
Phosphoric acid	2.1, 7.1, 12.3	98.0
Phthalic acid	2.9, 5.5	166.1
Succinic acid	4.2, 5.6	118.1
TRIS (base)*	8.3	121.1
CAPS (free acid)	10.4	221.3
CHES (free acid)	9.3	207.3
HEPES (free acid)	7.5	238.3
MES (free acid)	6.1	213.2
MOPS (free acid)	7.2	209.3
PIPES (free acid)	6.8	302.4
TAPS (free acid)	8.4	243.3
TRICINE (free acid)	8.1	179.2

*Note that this compound is hygroscopic and should be stored in a desiccator; also see text regarding its biological toxicity (p. 150).

4 °C to 37 °C. A number of zwitterionic molecules (possessing both positive and negative groups) have been introduced to overcome some of the disadvantages of the more traditional buffers. These newer compounds are often referred to as 'Good buffers', to acknowledge the early work of Dr N.E. Good and co-workers: HEPES is one of the most useful zwitterionic buffers, with a pK_a of 7.5 at 25 °C.

These zwitterionic substances are usually added to water as the free acid: the solution must then be adjusted to the correct pH with a strong alkali, usually NaOH or KOH. Alternatively, they may be used as their sodium or potassium salts, adjusted to the correct pH with a strong acid, e.g. HCl. Consequently, you may need to consider what effects such changes in ion concentration may have in a solution where zwitterions are used as buffers. In addition, zwitterionic buffers can interfere with protein determinations (e.g. Lowry method, p. 322).

Figure 25.4 shows a number of traditional and zwitterionic buffers and their effective pH ranges. When selecting one of these buffers, aim for a pK_a which is in the direction of the expected pH change (Table 25.3). For example, HEPES buffer would be a better choice of buffer than PIPES for use at pH 7.2 for experimental systems where a pH increase is anticipated, while PIPES would be a better choice where acidification is expected.

Preparation of buffer solutions

Having selected an appropriate buffer, you will need to make up your solution to give the desired pH. You will need to consider two factors:

- The ratio of acid and conjugate base required to give the correct pH.
- The amount of buffering required; buffer capacity depends upon the absolute quantities of acid and base, as well as their relative proportions.

In most instances, buffer solutions are prepared to contain between $10 \, \text{mmol} \, l^{-1}$ and $200 \, \text{mmol} \, l^{-1}$ of the conjugate pair. While it is possible to calculate the quantities required from first principles using the Henderson–Hasselbalch equation, there are several sources which tabulate the amount of substance required to give a particular volume of solution with a specific pH value for a wide range of traditional buffers

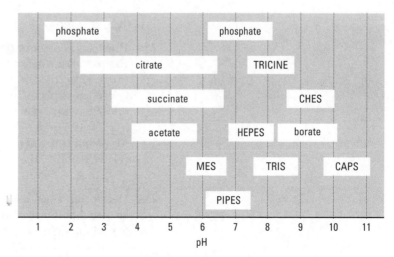

Fig. 25.4 Useful pH ranges of some commonly used buffers.

pH and buffer solutions

Table 25.4 Preparation of sodium phosphate buffer solutions for use at 25 °C. Prepare separate stock solutions of (a) disodium hydrogen phosphate ($M_r = 141.96$) and (b) sodium dihydrogen phosphate ($M_r = 156.01$), both at 200 mol m^{-3}. Buffer solutions (at 100 mol m^{-3}) are then prepared at the required pH by mixing together the volume of each stock solution shown in the table, then diluting to a final volume of 100 ml using distilled or deionised water

Required pH (at 25 °C)	Volume of stock (a) Na$_2$HPO$_4$ (ml)	Volume of stock (b) NaH$_2$PO$_4$ (ml)
6.0	6.2	43.8
6.2	9.3	40.7
6.4	13.3	36.7
6.6	18.8	31.2
6.8	24.5	25.5
7.0	30.5	19.5
7.2	36.0	14.0
7.4	40.5	9.5
7.6	43.5	6.5
7.8	45.8	4.2
8.0	47.4	2.6

(e.g. Perrin and Dempsey, 1974; Galster, 1991). For traditional buffers, it is customary to mix stock solutions of acidic and basic components in the correct proportions to give the required pH (Table 25.4). For zwitterionic acids, the usual procedure is to add the compound to water, then bring the solution to the required pH by adding a specific amount of strong alkali or acid (obtained from tables). Alternatively, the required pH can be obtained by dropwise addition of alkali or acid, using a meter to check the pH, until the correct value is reached. When preparing solutions of zwitterionic buffers, the acid may be relatively insoluble. Do not wait for it to dissolve fully before adding alkali to change the pH – the addition of alkali will help bring the acid into solution (but make sure it has all dissolved before the desired pH is reached).

Remember that buffer solutions will only work effectively if they have sufficient buffering capacity to resist the change in pH expected during the course of the experiment. Thus a weak solution of HEPES (e.g. 10 mmol l^{-1}, adjusted to pH 7.0 with NaOH) will not be able to buffer the growth medium of a dense suspension of cells for more than a few minutes.

Finally, when preparing a buffer solution based on tabulated information, always confirm the pH with a pH meter before use.

Text references

Galster, H. (1991) *pH Measurement: Fundamentals, Methods, Applications, Instrumentation.* Wiley, New York.

Lide, D.R. (ed.) (2002) *CRC Handbook of Chemistry and Physics*, 83rd edn. CRC Press, Boca Raton.

Perrin, D.D. and Dempsey, B. (1974) *Buffers for pH and Metal Ion Control.* Chapman and Hall, London.

Sources for further study

Rilbe, H. (1996) *pH and Buffer Theory – a New Approach.* Wiley, New York.

Westcott, C.C. (1978) *pH Measurements.* Academic Press, New York.

Study exercises

25.1 Practise interconverting pH values and proton concentrations. Express all answers to 3 significant figures.
   (a) What is pH 7.4 expressed as [H$^+$] in mol l^{-1}?
   (b) What is pH 4.1 expressed as [H$^+$] in mol m^{-3}?
   (c) What is the pH of a solution containing H$^+$ at 2×10^{-5} mol l^{-1}?
   (d) What is the pH of a solution containing H$^+$ at $10^{-12.5}$ mol l^{-1}?
   (e) What is the pH of a solution containing H$^+$ at 2.8×10^{-5} mol m^{-3}?

25.2 Decide on a suitable buffer to use. In the following instances, choose a buffer that would be suitable:
   (a) Maintaining the pH at 8.5 during an enzyme assay of a cell-free extract at 25 °C.

(b) Keeping a stable pH of 6.5 in an experiment to measure the uptake of radiolabelled glucose by a dense suspension of *E. coli*.

(c) Carrying out an assay of photosynthetic activity at pH 7.2 at temperatures of 10 °C, 20 °C and 30 °C.

(d) Stabilising pH at 5.5 during enzyme extraction, in a solution where you intend to measure total protein concentration at a later stage.

25.3 Practise using the Henderson–Hasselbalch equation. What are the relative proportions of deprotonated (A^-) and protonated (HA) forms of each substance at the following pH values:

(a) acetic acid ($pK_a = 4.8$) for use in an experiment at pH 3.8;

(b) boric acid ($pK_a = 9.2$) for use in an experiment at pH 9.5;

(c) HEPES ($pK_a = 7.5$) for use in an experiment at pH 8.1.

Introduction to microscopy

Many features of interest in biological systems are too small to be seen by the naked eye and can only be observed with a microscope. All microscopes consist of a coordinated system of lenses arranged so that a magnified image of a specimen is seen by the viewer (Figs 26.1 and 26.2). The main differences are the wavelengths of electromagnetic radiation used to produce the image, the nature and arrangement of the lens systems and the methods used to view the image.

Fig. 26.1 Simplified diagrams of light and electron microscopes. Note that the electron microscopes are drawn upside down to aid comparison with the light microscope.

Table 26.1 Comparison of microscope types. Resolution is that obtained by a skilled user. LM, light microscope; SEM, scanning electron microscope; TEM, transmission electron microscope

Property	Type of microscope		
	LM	SEM	TEM
Resolution	200 nm	10 nm	1 nm
Depth of focus	Low	High	Medium
Field of view	Good	Good	Limited
Specimen preparation (ease)	Easy	Easy	Skilled
Specimen preparation (speed)	Rapid	Quite rapid	Slow
Relative cost of instrument	Low	High	High

Microscopes allow objects to be viewed with increased resolution and contrast. Resolution is the ability to distinguish between two points on the specimen – the better the resolution, the 'sharper' the image. Resolution is affected by lens design and inversely related to the wavelength of radiation used. Contrast is the difference in intensity perceived between different parts of an image. This can be enhanced (a) by the use of stains, and (b) by adjusting microscope settings, usually at the expense of resolution.

The three main forms of microscopy are light microscopy, transmission electron microscopy (TEM) and scanning electron microscopy (SEM). Their main properties are compared in Table 26.1.

Light microscopy

Two forms of the standard light microscope are (i) the binocular (compound) microscope described in detail in Chapter 27, and (ii) the dissecting microscope. These are the instruments most likely to be used in routine practical work. Figure 26.2(a) shows a typical image of cells

(a)

(b)

(c)

Fig. 26.2 Examples of images of a similar specimen (the stomatal complex of *Commelina communis*) obtained using different microscopic techniques: (a) light microscopy (surface view); (b) transmission electron microscopy (transverse section through guard cell pair at mid pore); and (c) scanning electron microscopy (surface view). As an indication of scale, the width of a single guard cell is about 10 μm.

viewed with a light microscope. In more advanced project work, you may use one or more of the following more sophisticated variants of light microscopy to improve image quality:

- Dark field illumination involves a special condenser which causes reflected and diffracted light from the specimen to be seen against a dark background. The method is particularly useful for near-transparent specimens and for delicate structures like flagella. Care must be taken with the thickness of slides used – air bubbles and dust must be avoided and immersion oil must be used between the dark field condenser and the underside of the slide.
- Ultraviolet microscopy uses short-wavelength UV light to increase resolution. Fluorescence microscopy uses radiation at UV wavelengths to make certain fluorescent substances (e.g. chlorophyll or fluorescent dyes which bind to specific cell components) emit light of visible wavelengths. Special light sources, lenses and mountants are required for UV and fluorescence microscopy and filters must be used to prevent damage to users' eyes.
- Phase contrast microscopy is useful for increasing contrast when viewing transparent specimens. It is superior to dark field microscopy because a better image of the interior of specimens is obtained. Phase contrast operates by causing constructive and destructive interference effects in the image, visible as increased contrast. Adjustments must be made, using a phase telescope in place of the eyepiece, for each objective lens and a matching phase condenser, and the microscope must be set up carefully to give optimal results.
- Nomarski or differential interference contrast (DIC) microscopy gives an image with a three-dimensional quality. However, the relief seen is optical rather than morphological, and care should be taken in interpreting the result. One of the advantages of the technique is the extremely limited depth of focus which results: this allows 'optical sectioning' of a specimen.
- Polarised light microscopy can be used to reveal the presence and orientation of optically active components within specimens (e.g. starch grains, cellulose fibres), showing them brightly against a dark background.
- Confocal microscopy allows three-dimensional views of cells or thick sections. A finely focused laser is used to create electronic images of layered horizontal 'slices', usually after fluorescent staining. Images can be viewed individually or reconstructed to provide a 3D computer-generated image of the whole specimen.

Electron microscopes

Electron microscopes offer an image resolution up to 200 times better than light microscopes (Table 26.1) because they utilise radiation of shorter wavelength in the form of an electron beam. The electrons are produced by a tungsten filament operating in a vacuum and are focused by electromagnets. TEM and SEM differ in the way in which the electron beam interacts with the specimen: in TEM, the beam passes through the specimen (Fig. 26.1b), while in SEM the beam is scanned across the specimen and is reflected from the surface (Fig. 26.1c). In both cases, the beam must fall on a fluorescent screen before the image can be seen.

Permanent images ('electron micrographs') are produced after focusing the beam on photographic film (Figs 26.2b and c).

You are unlikely to use either type of electron microscope as part of undergraduate practical work because of the time required for specimen preparation and the need for detailed training before these complex machines can be operated correctly. However, electron microscopy is extremely important in understanding cellular and sub-cellular structures and you may be shown electron micrographs, with one or more of the following objectives:

- to demonstrate cell ultrastructure (TEM);
- to show surface features of organisms (SEM);
- to investigate changes in the number, size, shape and condition of cells and organelles (TEM);
- to carry out quantitative studies of cell and organelle disposition (TEM).

Preparative procedures

Without careful preparation of the material being studied, the biological structures viewed with any type of microscope can be rendered meaningless. Figure 26.3 summarises the processes involved for the main types of microscopy discussed above (see also Chapter 27 for light microscopy).

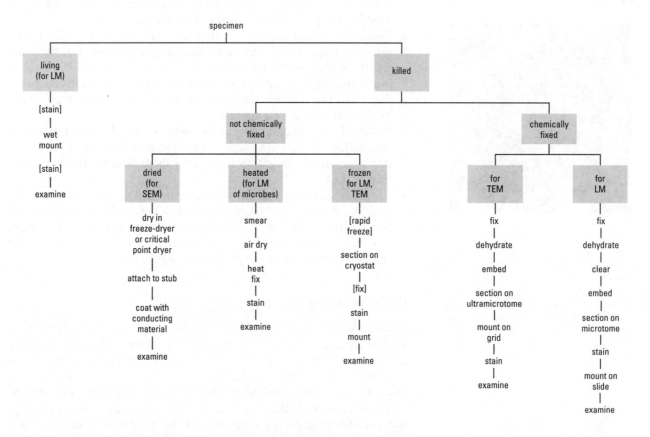

Fig. 26.3 Flowchart of procedures necessary to prepare specimens for different forms of microscopy. Steps enclosed in brackets are optional. LM, light microscope; SEM, scanning electron microscope; TEM, transmission electron microscope.

Sources for further study

Bradbury, S. (1976) *The Optical Microscope in Biology*. Edward Arnold, London.

Bradbury, S. (1984) *An Introduction to the Optical Microscope*. Oxford University Press, Oxford.

Davidson, M.W. and Abramowitz, M. *Molecular Expressions. Exploring the World of Optics and Microscopy*. Available:
http://micro.magnet.fsu.edu/index.html
Last accessed 08/01/03.
[Covers many areas of basic knowledge underlying microscopy. Includes a microscopy primer.]

Jeffries, C. *Microscopy Web Sites – by Organisation*. Available:
http://www.ou.edu/research/electron/mirror/web-org.html
Last accessed 08/01/03.
[Comprehensive set of links to microscopy websites.]

Murphy, D.B. (2001) *Fundamentals of Light Microscopy and Electronic Imaging*. Wiley-Liss, New York.

Study exercises

26.1 Test your microscopy knowledge. Indicate whether the following statements about light microscopy, scanning electron microscopy (SEM) or transmission electron microscopy (TEM) are true or false.
  (a) TEM allows you to see at finer resolution than light microscopy.
  (b) TEM allows you to see surface features of specimens.
  (c) SEM always requires staining of specimens.
  (d) The resolution of TEM is about 200 times better than that of light microscopy.
  (e) The resolution of a microscope is linked to the wavelength of electromagnetic radiation employed.
  (f) The specimen in both TEM and SEM is viewed under near-vacuum conditions.
  (g) Specimens for light microscopy can be living or dead.
  (h) SEM provides better resolution than TEM.
  (i) The depth of focus in light microscopy is greater than that in SEM.
  (j) Light microscopy, SEM and TEM all involve the use of a condenser lens within the microscope.

26.2 Fill in the blanks in the following paragraph. Dark field microscopy involves shining reflected and _____ light on the specimen against a dark background. It is particularly useful for _____ specimens. UV microscopy uses short wavelength UV light in order to increase image _____. Phase contrast microscopy utilises constructive and destructive _____ effects to increase image _____. Nomarski microscopy provides a pseudo ____ image, with a very small depth of _____, allowing _____ _____ to be carried out. _____ light microscopy allows visualisation of optically active components in the specimen. Confocal microscopy involves the use of a _____ light source and can yield computer-generated 3D images.

26.3 **Identify the missing preparative procedures**. In each sequence below, one or two steps have been missed out. Using Fig. 26.3, identify the missing procedures.

(a) For light microscopy on a killed and fixed specimen: fix – dehydrate – clear – _____ – section – _____ – mount – examine.

(b) For light microscopy on a heat-fixed microbial specimen: smear – _____ – heat fix – _____ – examine.

(c) For TEM on a killed and fixed specimen: fix – _____ – embed – section – mount – stain – examine.

Setting up and using a light microscope

Fig. 27.1 Objective lens parameters. Most lenses are inscribed to show the details labelled above. The numerical aperture is a measure of the light-gathering power of the lens.

Using binocular eyepieces – *if you do not know your interpupillary distance, ask someone to measure it with a ruler. You should stare at a fixed point in the distance while the measurement is taken. Take a note of the value for future use.*

Problems with spectacles – *those who wear glasses can remove them for viewing, as microscope adjustments will accommodate most deficiencies in eyesight (except astigmatism). This is more comfortable and stops the spectacle lenses being scratched by the eyepiece holders. However, it creates difficulties in focusing when drawing diagrams.*

Correct use of the light microscope is one of the basic and essential laboratory skills. A standard undergraduate binocular microscope consists of three main types of optical unit: eyepiece, objective (Fig. 27.1) and condenser. These are attached to a stand which holds the specimen on a stage (Fig. 27.2). A monocular microscope is constructed similarly but has one eyepiece lens rather than two.

Setting up a binocular light microscope

Before using any microscope, familiarise yourself with its component parts.

> **KEY POINT** Never assume that the previous person to use your microscope has left it set up correctly: apart from differences in users' eyes, the microscope needs to be properly set up for each lens combination used.

The procedures outlined below are simplified to allow you to set up microscopes like those of the Olympus CX series (Fig. 27.2). For monocular microscopes, disregard instructions for adjusting eyepiece lenses in (5).

1. Place the microscope at a convenient position on the bench. Adjust your seating so that you are comfortable operating the focus and stage controls. Unwind the power cable, plug in and switch on after first ensuring that the lamp setting is at a minimum. Then adjust the lamp setting to about two-thirds of the maximum.
2. Select a low-power (e.g. ×10) objective. Make sure that the lens clicks home.
3. Set the eyepiece (ocular) lenses to your interpupillary distance; this can usually be read off a scale on the turret. You should now see a single circular field of vision. If you do not, try adjusting in either direction.
4. Put a prepared slide on the stage. Examine it first against a light source and note the position, colour and rough size of the specimen. Place the slide on the stage (coverslip up) and, viewing from the side, position it with the stage adjustment controls so that the specimen is illuminated.
5. Focus the image of the specimen using first the coarse and then the fine focusing controls (Fig. 27.3). The image will be reversed and upside down compared to that seen by viewing the slide directly.
   (a) If both eyepiece lenses are adjustable, set your interpupillary distance on the scale on each lens. Close your left eye, look through the right eyepiece with your right eye and focus the image with the normal controls. Now close your right eye, look through the left eyepiece with your left eye and focus the image by rotating the eyepiece holder. Take a note of the setting for future use.
   (b) If only the left eyepiece is adjustable, close your left eye, look with the right eye through the static right eyepiece and focus the image with the normal controls. Now close your right eye, look through the left eyepiece with your left eye and focus the image by rotating the eyepiece holder. Take a note of the setting for future use.

6. Close the condenser–iris diaphragm (aperture–iris diaphragm), then open it to a position such that further opening has no effect on the brightness of the image (the 'threshold of darkening'). The edge of the diaphragm should not be in view. Turn down the lamp if it is too bright.

7. Focus the condenser. Place an opaque pointed object (the tip of a mounted needle or a sharp pencil point) on the centre of the light source. Adjust the condenser setting until both the specimen and needle tip/pencil point are in focus together. Check that the condenser–iris diaphragm is just outside the field of view.

8. For higher magnifications, swing in the relevant objective (e.g. ×40), carefully checking that there is space for it. Adjust the focus using the fine control only. If the object you wish to view is in the centre of the field with the ×10 objective, it should remain in view (magnified, of course) with the ×40. Adjust the condenser–iris diaphragm and condenser as before – the correct setting for each lens will be different.

9. When you have finished using the microscope, remove the last slide and clean the stage if necessary. Turn down the lamp setting to its minimum, then switch off. Clean the eyepiece lenses with lens tissue. Check that the objectives are clean. Unplug the microscope from the mains and wind the cable round the stand and under the stage. Replace the dust cover.

If you have problems in obtaining a satisfactory image, refer to Box 27.1; if this doesn't help, refer the problem to the class supervisor.

Adjusting a microscope with a field–iris diaphragm – adjust this before the condenser–iris diaphragm: close it until its image appears in view as a circle of light, if necessary focusing on the edge of the circle with the condenser controls and centring it with the centring screws. Now open it so the whole field is just illuminated.

Using high-power objectives – never remove a slide while a high power objective lens (i.e. ×40 or ×100) is in position. Always turn back to the ×10 first. Having done this, lower the stage and remove the slide.

Box 27.1 Problems in light microscopy and possible solutions

No image; very dark image; image dark and illuminated irregularly
- Microscope not switched on (check plug and base)
- Illumination control at low setting or off
- Objective nosepiece not clicked into place over a lens
- Diaphragm closed down too much or off-centre
- Lamp failure

Image visible and focused but pale and indistinct
- Diaphragm needs to be closed down further (see Fig. 27.4)
- Condenser requires adjustment

Image blurred and cannot be focused
- Dirty objective
- Dirty slide
- Slide upside down
- Slide not completely flat on stage
- Eyepiece lenses not set up properly for user's eyes
- Fine focus at end of travel
- Oil immersion objective in use, without oil

Dust and dirt in field of view
- Eyepiece lenses dirty
- Objective lens dirty
- Slide dirty
- Dirt on lamp glass or upper condenser lens

Procedure for observing transparent specimens

Some stained preparations and all colourless objects are difficult to see when the microscope is adjusted as above (Fig. 27.4). Contrast can be improved by closing down the condenser–iris diaphragm. Note that when you do this, diffraction haloes appear round the edges of objects. These obscure the image of the true structure of the specimen and may result in loss of resolution. Nevertheless, an image with increased contrast may be easier to interpret. Figure 27.5 shows several types of non-biological artefacts that you will come to recognise through practical experience.

Fig. 27.2 Diagram of the Olympus binocular microscope model CX41.

- The lamp in the base of the stand (**1**) supplies light; its brightness is controlled by an on–off switch and voltage control (**2**). Never use maximum voltage or the life of the bulb will be reduced – a setting two-thirds to three-quarters of maximum should be adequate for most specimens. A field–iris diaphragm may be fitted close to the lamp to control the area of illumination (**3**).
- The condenser control focuses light from the condenser lens system (**4**) onto the specimen and projects the specimen's image onto the front lens of the objective. Correctly used, it ensures optimal resolution.
- The condenser–iris diaphragm (**5**) controls the amount of light entering and leaving the condenser; its aperture can be adjusted using the condenser–iris diaphragm lever (**6**). Use this to reduce glare and enhance image contrast by cutting down the amount of stray light reaching the objective lens.
- The specimen (normally mounted on a slide) is fitted to a mechanical stage or slide holder (**7**) using a spring mechanism. Two controls allow you to move the slide in *x* and *y* planes. Vernier scales on the slide holder can be used to return to the same place on a slide. The fine and coarse focus controls (**8**) adjust the height of the stage relative to the lens systems. Take care when adjusting the focus controls to avoid hitting the lenses with the stage or slide.
- The objective lens (**9**) supplies the initial magnified image; it is the most important component of any microscope because its qualities determine resolution, depth of field and optical aberrations. The objective lenses are attached to a revolving nosepiece (**10**). Take care not to jam the longer lenses onto the stage or slide as you rotate the nosepiece. You should feel a distinct click as each lens is moved into position. The magnification of each objective is written on its side; a normal complement would be ×4, ×10, ×40 and ×100 (oil immersion).
- The eyepiece lens (**11**) is used to further magnify the image from the objective and to put it in a form and position suitable for viewing. Its magnification is written on the holder (normally ×10). By twisting the holder for one or both of the eyepiece lenses you can adjust their relative heights to take account of optical differences between your eyes. The interpupillary distance scale (**12**) and adjustment knob allow compensation to be made for differences in the distance between users' pupils.

From a photograph of Olympus Model CX41 binocular microscope, supplied by Olympus microscopes, Olympus Optical Company (UK) Limited, published courtesy of Olympus Optical Co (UK) Ltd.

Plantcells

(b)

Fig. 27.3 Importance of correct focus in light microscopy. Stomatal complex of *Commelina communis*, a specimen that is a monolayer of cells approximately 30–50 μm thick. (a) Focal plane is on 'internal' walls of the cells; (b) focal plane is on the 'external' walls and stomatal pore. The two images are different and while it would not be possible to measure the stomatal pore in (a), it would not be possible to see the vacuolar crystals in (b). When looking at specimens, always use the fine focus control to view different focal planes.

Fig. 27.4 Effect of closing the condenser–iris diaphragm on contrast. Head of human head louse, *Pediculus humanus capitus* (a) with condenser–iris diaphragm open; (b) with condenser–iris diaphragm closed (all other settings the same). Note the difference in detail that can be seen in (b), but also that image (b) is darker. When using the condenser–iris diaphragm in this way you may need to compensate by increasing the light setting.

Using an eyepiece graticule – *choose the eyepiece lens corresponding to your stronger eye (usually the same side as the hand you write with) and check that you have made the correct adjustments to the eyepiece lenses as detailed on p. 159.*

Procedure for oil immersion objectives

These provide the highest resolution of which the light microscope is capable. They must be used with immersion oil filling the space between the objective lens and the top of the slide. The oil has the same refractive index as the glass lenses, so loss of light by reflection and refraction at the glass/air interface is reduced. This increases the resolution, brightness and clarity of the image and reduces aberration. Use oil immersion objective(s) as follows:

1. Check that the object of interest is in the field of view using e.g. the ×10 or ×40 objective.
2. Apply a single small droplet of immersion oil to the illuminated spot on the top of the slide, having first swung the ×40 objective away. Never use too much oil: it can run off the slide and mess up the microscope.
3. Move the high power (×100) oil immersion objective into position carefully, checking first that there is space for it. Focus on the specimen using the fine control only. You may need a higher brightness setting.
4. Perform condenser–iris diaphragm and condenser focusing adjustments as for the other lenses.
5. When finished, clean the oil immersion lens by gently wiping it with clean lens tissue. If the slide is a prepared one, wipe the oil off with lens tissue.

You should take great care when working with oil immersion lenses as they are the most expensive to replace. Because the working distance between the lens and coverslip is so short (less than 2 mm), it is easy to damage the lens surface by inadvertently hitting the slide or coverslip surface. You must also remember that they need oil to work properly. If working with an unfamiliar microscope, you can easily recognise oil immersion lenses. They will either carry a black ring on the lens barrel near to the lens, or will state 'oil' clearly on the barrel.

Stains and staining procedures

Table 27.1 gives a number of widely used stains and their applications for animal, plant and microbial cells and tissues.

Establishing scale and measuring objects

The magnification of a light microscope image is calculated by multiplying the objective magnification by the eyepiece magnification. However, the magnification of the image bears no certain relation to the magnification of any drawing of the image – you may equally well choose to draw the same image 10 mm or 10 cm long. For this reason, *it is essential to add a scale to all your diagrams.* You can provide either a bar giving the estimated size of an object of interest, or a bar of defined length (e.g. 100 μm.

The simplest method of estimating linear dimensions is to compare the size of the image to the diameter of the field of view. You can make a rough estimate of the field diameter by focusing on the millimetre scale of a transparent ruler using the lowest power objective. Estimate the diameter of this field directly, then use the information to work out the

Table 27.1   A selection of stains for light microscopy

	Stain	What it stains	Comments
Plant cells	Chlorazol black	Cell walls: black Nuclei: black, yellow or green Suberin: amber	The solvent used (70% ethanol in water or water alone) affects colours developed
	Neutral red	Living cells: pink (pH < 7)	A 'vital' stain used to determine cell viability or to visualise plant protoplasts in plasmolysis experiments; best used at neutral external pH
	Phloroglucinol/HCl	Lignified cell walls: red	Care is required because the acid may damage microscope lenses
	Ruthenium red	Pectins: red	Shows up the middle lamella
	Safranin + Fast green	Nuclei, chromosomes, cuticle and lignin: red Other components: green	Stain in safranin first, then counterstain with fast green (light green will substitute). A differentiation step is required
	Toluidine blue	Lignified cell walls: blue Cellulose cell walls: purple	Best to apply dilute and allow progressive staining to occur
Fungi and bacteria	Giemsa	Bacterial chromosome: purple Bacterial cytoplasm: colourless	Also used in zoology to stain protozoa
	Gram	Gram-positive bacteria: violet/purple Gram-negative bacteria: red/pink Yeasts: violet/purple	See p. 211 for procedure
	Gray	Bacterial flagella: red	Uses toxic chemicals: mercuric chloride and formaldehyde. Leifson's stain is an alternative
	Lactophenol cotton blue	Fungal cytoplasm: blue (hyphal wall unstained)	Shrinkage may occur
	Nigrosin or India ink	Background: grey–black	Negative stains for visualisation of capsules: requires a very thin film
	Shaeffer and Fulton	Bacterial endospores: green Vegetative cells: pink/red	Malachite green is primary stain, heated for 5 min. Counterstained with safranin
	Ziehl–Neelsen	Actinomycetes: red Bacterial endospores: red Other microbes: blue	Requires heat treatment of fuchsin primary stain, decolorisation with ethanol–HCl and a methylene blue counterstain (acid-fast structures remain red)
Animal cells	Azure A/eosin B	Nuclei, RNA: blue Basophilic cells: blue–violet Most other cells: pale blue Muscle cells: pink Necrosing cells: pink Cartilage matrix: red–violet Bone: pink Red blood cells: orange–red Mucins: green–blue/blue–violet	Used in pathology – shows up bacteria as blue; must be fresh; care required over pH: Mann's methyl blue/eosin gives similar results
	Chlorazol black	Chitin: greenish-black Nuclei: black, yellow or green Glycogen: pink or red	Solvent (70% v/v ethanol in water or water alone) affects colours formed
	Iron haematoxylin	Nuclei, chromosomes and red blood cells: black Other structures: grey or blue–black	Good for resolving fine detail; iron alum used as mordant before haematoxylin to differentiate
	Mallory	Nuclei: red Nucleoli: yellow Collagen, mucus: blue Red blood cells: yellow Cytoplasm: pink or yellow	Simple, one stage stain; fades within a year; not to be used with osmium-containing fixatives. Heidenhain's azan gives similar results but does not fade. Cason's one-step Mallory is a rapidly applied stain which is particularly good for connective tissue
	Masson's trichrome	Collagen, mucus: green Cytoplasm: orange or pink	Used as a counterstain after, for example, iron haematoxylin which will have stained nuclei black. Not to be used after osmium fixation
	Mayer's (haemalum and eosin; 'H&E')	Nuclei: blue/purple Cytoplasm: pink	Alum used as mordant for haematoxylin; eosin is the counterstain. To show up collagen, use van Gieson's stain as counterstain

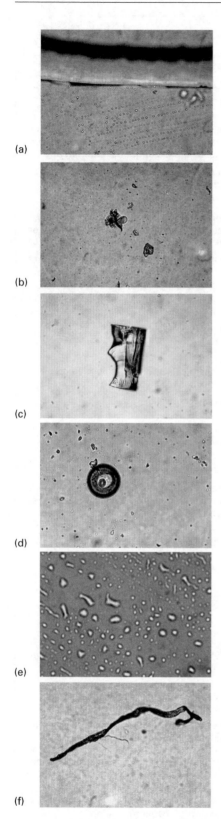

Fig. 27.5 Artefacts in light microscopy. Do not mistake any of the following for biological specimens: (a) edge of coverslip; (b) dust on slide; (c) shard of glass; (d) air bubble; (e) grease spots; (f) cellulose fibre.

field diameters at the higher powers *pro rata*. For example, if the field at an overall magnification of ×40 is 4 mm, at an overall magnification of ×100 it will be: $40/100 \times 4\,mm = 1.6\,mm\ (1600\,\mu m)$.

Greater accuracy can be obtained if an eyepiece micrometer (graticule) is used. This carries a fine scale and fits inside an eyepiece lens. The eyepiece micrometer is calibrated using a stage micrometer, basically a slide with a fine scale on it.

Figure 27.6 shows how to calibrate an eyepiece micrometer, along with a worked example. Once you have calibrate your eyepiece micrometer for each objective lens used, you can use it to measure objects: in the example shown in Fig. 27.6 the scale reading is multiplied by $2.65\,\mu m$ to give the value in micrometres. So, if you measured the width of a human hair at 34 eyepiece micrometer units, then this will be equal to $34 \times 2.65 = 90.1\,\mu m$. An alternative approach is to put a scale bar on a diagram, e.g. a $100\,\mu m$ scale bar would be equivalent to the length of almost 38 eyepiece micrometer divisions. You should avoid putting to many significant figures in any estimates of dimensions: there may be quite large errors involved, which could make the implied accuracy misleading (spurious accuracy, p. 171).

Care and maintenance of your microscope

Microscopes are delicate precision instruments. Handle them with care and never force any of the controls. Never touch any of the glass surfaces with anything other than clean, dry lens tissue. Bear in mind that a replacement would be very expensive.

If moving a microscope, hold the stand above the stage with one hand and rest the base of the stand on your other hand. Always keep the microscope vertical (or the eyepieces may fall out). Put the microscope down gently.

Fig. 27.6 Calibrating an eyepiece micrometer (graticule). Align two scales and read the number of stage micrometer divisions (shown in colour) for a particular number of eyepiece micrometer divisions (shown in colour) for a particular number of eyepiece micrometer divisions (shown in black). In this case 26.5 scale divisions of 0.01 mm are equivalent to 100 eyepiece divisions, so each eyepiece division $0.265 \div 100 = 0.002\,65\,mm = 2.65\,\mu m$. This is a typical value for a total magnification of ×400 (e.g. ×40 objective and ×10 eyepiece).

Measuring specimens using a dissecting microscope – because of the low magnification, sizes can generally be estimated by comparison with a ruler placed alongside the specimen. If accurate measurements are required, eyepiece graticules can be used.

Clean lenses by gently wiping with clean, dry lens tissue. Use each piece of tissue once only. Try not to touch lenses with your fingers as oily fingerprints are difficult to clean off. Do not allow any solvent (including water) to come into contact with a lens; sea water is particularly damaging.

Sources for further study

Bradbury. S. (1984) *An Introduction to the Optical Microscope*. Oxford University Press, Oxford.

Davidson, M.W. and Abramowitz, M. *Nikon Microscopy: Introduction to Microscope Objectives*. Available:
http://www.microscopyu.com/articles/optics/objectiveintro.html
Last accessed 08/01/03.
[Covers the optics of objective lenses.]

Study exercises

27.1 Test your knowledge of the parts of a binocular light microscope. Cover up the legend on the left of Fig. 27.2 with a piece of paper or card. Now identify the parts of the light microscope numbered on the diagram. Check your answers from the legend.

27.2 Identify roles of parts of a binocular light microscope. State briefly the *primary* role of each component of a standard binocular light microscope:
(a) condenser
(b) objective lens
(c) condenser–iris diaphragm
(d) interpupillary distance scale
(e) Vernier scales on the mechanical stage.

27.3 Identify the correct sequence of adjustments when setting up a light microscope.
(a) Focus specimen – set interpupillary distance – adjust condenser–iris diaphragm – make individual eyepiece adjustment – focus condenser – focus specimen.
(b) Make individual eyepiece adjustment – set interpupillary distance – focus condenser – focus specimen – adjust condenser–iris diaphragm – focus specimen.
(c) Set interpupillary distance – focus specimen – make individual eyepiece adjustment – adjust condenser–iris diaphragm – focus condenser – focus specimen.
(d) Make individual eyepiece adjustment – set interpupillary distance – focus specimen – adjust condenser–iris diaphragm – focus condenser – focus specimen.
(e) Focus specimen – make individual eyepiece adjustment – set interpupillary distance – focus condenser – adjust condenser–iris diaphragm.

27.4 Calculate the size of an object seen down a microscope using graticule readings. At 100× overall magnification, you find that 1 stage micrometer unit of 0.1 mm = 11 eyepiece micrometer units.

The length of a parasitic worm on a slide viewed at this magnification appears to be 25 eyepiece units. What is its estimated true length to the nearest μm?

27.5 Select appropriate stains. From Table 27.1, identify stains you could use to help indicate the presence of the following:

(a) glycogen in a liver section;

(b) woody (lignified) cells in a plant stem section;

(c) a fungal pathogen in a leaf section;

(d) living cells in an onion epidermal peel;

(e) mucus in a lung section;

(f) bacteria in a food sample.

The investigative approach

28 Making and recording measurements

The term data (singular = datum, or data value) refers to items of information, and you will use different types of data from a wide range of sources during your practical work. Consequently, it is important to appreciate the underlying features of data collection and measurement.

Variables

Biological variables (Fig. 28.1) can be classified as follows:

Quantitative variables

These are characteristics whose differing states can be described by means of a number. They are of two basic types:

- Continuous variables, such as length; these are usually measured against a numerical scale. Theoretically, they can take any value on the measurement scale. In practice, the number of significant figures of a measurement is directly related to the precision of your measuring system; for example, dimensions measured with Vernier callipers will provide readings of greater precision than a millimetre ruler. Many of the variables measured in biomolecular sciences are continuous and quantitative, e.g. mass, temperature, time, amount of product formed by an enzyme.
- Discontinuous (discrete) variables; these are always obtained by counting and therefore the data values must be whole numbers (integers), with no intermediate values.

Ranked variables

These provide data which can be listed in order of magnitude (i.e. ranked). A familiar example is the abundance of an organism in a sample, which is often expressed as a series of ranks, e.g. rare = 1, occasional = 2, frequent = 3, common = 4, and abundant = 5. When such data are given numerical ranks, rather than descriptive terms, they are sometimes called 'semi-quantitative data'. Note that the difference in magnitude between ranks need not be consistent. For example, regardless of whether there was a one-year or a five-year gap between offspring in a family; their ranks in order of birth would be the same.

Qualitative variables (attributes)

These are non-numerical and descriptive; they have no order of preference and, therefore, are not measured on a numerical scale nor ranked in order of magnitude, but are described in terms of categories. Examples include viability (i.e. dead or alive), shape (e.g. round, flat, elongated), presence/absence of a particular biomolecule in a sample (p. 343).

Variables may be independent or dependent. Usually, the variable under the control of the experimenter (e.g. time) is the independent variable, while the variable being measured is the dependent variable (p. 183). Sometimes it is inappropriate to describe variables in this way and they are then referred to as interdependent variables (e.g. the length and breadth of an organism).

The majority of data values are recorded as direct measurements, readings or counts, but there is an important group, called derived (or

***Working with discontinuous variables** – note that while the original data values must be integers, derived data and statistical values do not have to be whole numbers. Thus, it is perfectly acceptable to express the mean number of children per family as 2.4.*

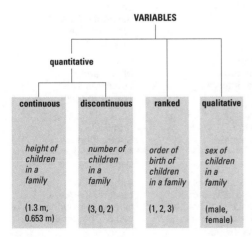

Fig. 28.1 Examples of the different types of variables as used to describe some characteristics of families.

computed), which result from calculations based on two or more data values, e.g. ratios, percentages, indices and rates.

Measurement scales

Variables may be measured on different types of scale:

- Nominal scale: this classifies objects into categories based on a descriptive characteristic. It is the only scale suitable for qualitative data.
- Ordinal scale: this classifies by rank. There is a logical order in any number scale used.
- Interval scale: this is used for quantitative variables. Numbers on an equal unit scale are related to an arbitrary zero point.
- Ratio scale: this is similar to the interval scale, except that the zero point now represents an absence of that character (i.e. it is an absolute zero).

The measurement scale is important in determining the mathematical and statistical methods used to analyse your data. Table 28.1 presents a summary of the important properties of these scales. Note that you may be able to measure a characteristic in more than one way, or you may be able to convert data collected in one form to a different form. For instance, you might measure light in terms of the photon flux density (p. 268) between particular wavelengths of the EMR spectrum (ratio scale), or simply as 'blue' or 'red' (nominal scale); you could find out the dates of birth of individuals (interval scale) but then use this information to rank them in order of birth (ordinal scale). Where there are no other

Examples A **nominal scale** for temperature is not feasible, since the relevant descriptive terms can be ranked in order of magnitude.

An **ordinal scale** for temperature measurement might use descriptive terms, ranked in ascending order, e.g. cold = 1, cool = 2, warm = 3, hot = 4.

The **Celsius scale** is an interval scale for temperature measurement, since the arbitrary zero corresponds to the freezing point of water (0 °C).

The **Kelvin scale** is a ratio scale for temperature measurement since 0 K represents a temperature of absolute zero (for information, the freezing point of water is 273.15 K on this scale).

Table 28.1 Some important features of scales of measurement

| | Measurement scale | | | |
	Nominal	Ordinal	Interval	Ratio
Type of variable	Qualitative (Ranked)* (Quantitative)*	Ranked (Quantitative)*	Quantitative	Quantitative
Examples	Species Sex Colour	Abundance scales Reproductive condition Optical assessment of colour development	Fahrenheit temperature scale Date (BC/AD)	Kelvin temperature scale Weight Length Response time Most physical measurements
Mathematical properties	Identity	Identity Magnitude	Identity Magnitude Equal intervals	Identity Magnitude Equal intervals True zero point
Mathematical operations possible on data	None	Rank	Rank Addition Subtraction	Rank Addition Subtraction Multiplication Division
Typical statistics used	Only those based on frequency of counts made: contingency tables, frequency distributions, etc. Chi-square test	Non-parametric methods, sign tests. Mann–Whitney U-test	Almost all types of test, t-test, analysis of variance (ANOVA), etc. (check distribution before using, Chapter 67)	Almost all types of test, t-test, ANOVA, etc. (check distribution before using, Chapter 67)

*In some instances (see text for examples).

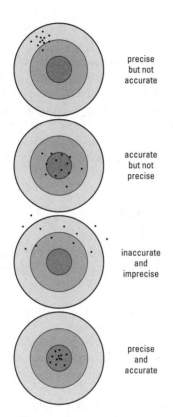

Fig. 28.2 'Target' diagrams illustrating precision and accuracy.

constraints, you should use a ratio scale to measure a quantitative variable, since this will allow you to use the broadest range of mathematical and statistical procedures (Table 28.1).

Accuracy and precision

Accuracy is the closeness of a measured or derived data value to its true value, while precision is the closeness of repeated measurements to each other (Fig. 28.2). A balance with a fault in it (i.e. a bias, see below) could give precise (i.e. very repeatable) but inaccurate (i.e. untrue) results. Unless there is bias in a measuring system, precision will lead to accuracy and it is precision that is generally the most important practical consideration, if there is no reason to suspect bias. You can investigate the precision of any measuring system by repeated measurements of individual samples.

Absolute accuracy and precision are impossible to achieve, due to both the limitations of measuring systems for continuous quantitative data and the fact that you are usually working with incomplete data sets (samples). It is particularly important to avoid spurious accuracy in the presentation of results; include only those digits that the accuracy of the measuring system implies. This type of error is common when changing units (e.g. inches to metres) and in derived data, especially when calculators give results to a large number of decimal places. Further advice is given on p. 467.

Bias (systematic error) and consistency

Bias is a systematic or non-random distortion and is one of the most troublesome difficulties in using numerical data. Biases may be associated with incorrectly calibrated instruments, e.g. a faulty pipettor, or with experimental manipulations, e.g. shrinkage during the preservation of a specimen. Bias in measurement can also be subjective, or personal, e.g. an experimenter's preconceived ideas about an 'expected' result.

Bias can be minimised by using a carefully standardised procedure, with fully calibrated instruments. You can investigate bias in 'trial runs' by measuring a single variable in several different ways, to see whether the same result is obtained.

To avoid personal bias, 'blind' measurements should be made where the identity of individual samples is not known to the operator, e.g. using a coding system.

Measurement error

Minimising errors – *determine early in your study what the dominant errors are likely to be and concentrate your time and effort on reducing these.*

All measurements are subject to error, but the dangers of misinterpretation are reduced by recognising and understanding the likely sources of error and by adopting appropriate protocols and calculation procedures.

A common source of measurement error is carelessness, e.g. reading a scale in the wrong direction or parallax errors. This can be reduced greatly by careful recording and may be detected by repeating the measurement. Other errors arise from faulty or inaccurate equipment, but even a perfectly functioning machine has distinct limits to the accuracy and precision of its measurements. These limits are often quoted in manufacturers' specifications and are applicable when an instrument is new; however, you should allow for some deterioration with age. Further errors are introduced when the subject being studied is open to influences outside your control. Resolving such

Working with derived data – *special effort should be made to reduce measurement errors because their effects can be magnified when differences, ratios, indices or rates are calculated.*

problems requires appropriate experimental design and representative sampling.

One major influence virtually impossible to eliminate is the effect of the investigation itself: even putting a thermometer in a liquid may change the temperature of the liquid. The very act of measurement may give rise to a confounding variable (p. 184) as discussed in Chapter 30. You should include descriptions of possible sources of errors and estimates of their likely importance in any report. However, do not use 'biological variability' as a catch-all excuse for poor technique or inadequacies in your experimental design.

Collecting and recording primary data

When carrying out advanced lab work or research projects, you will need to master the important skill of managing data and observations and learn how to keep a record of your studies in a lab book. This is important for the following reasons:

Recording primary data – never be tempted to jot down data on scraps of paper: you are likely to lose them, or to forget what individual values mean.

- An accurate and neat record helps when using information later, perhaps for exam purposes or when writing a report.
- It allows you to practise important skills such as scientific writing, drawing diagrams, preparing graphs and tables and interpreting results.
- Analysing and writing up your data as you go along prevents a backlog at the end of your study time.
- You can show your work to a future employer to prove you have developed the skills necessary for writing up properly; in industry, this is vital so that others in your team can interpret and develop your work.

KEY POINT A good set of lab notes should:

Recording numerical data – write down only those figures that can be justified by the measurement technique (significant figures).

- **outline the purpose of your experiment or observation;**
- **set down all the information required to describe your materials and methods;**
- **record all relevant information about your results or observations and provide a visual representation of the data;**
- **note your immediate conclusions and suggestions for further experiments.**

Individual observations (e.g. laboratory temperature) can be recorded in the text of your notes, but tables are often the most convenient way to collect large amounts of information. When preparing a table for data collection, you should:

1. Use a concise title or a numbered code for cross referencing.
2. Decide on the number of variables to be measured and their relationship with each other and lay out the table appropriately:

Designing a table for data collection – use a spreadsheet or the table-creating facility in a word processor to create your table. This will allow you to reorganise it easily if required. Make sure there is sufficient space in each column for the values – if in doubt, err on the generous side.

   (a) The first column of your table should show values of the independent (controlled) variable, with subsequent columns for the individual (measured) values for each replicate or sample.
   (b) If several variables are measured for the same organism or sample, each should be given a row.
   (c) In time-course studies, put the replicates as columns grouped according to treatment, with the rows relating to different times.
3. Make sure the arrangement reflects the order in which the values will be collected. Your table should be designed to make the recording

process as straightforward as possible, to minimise the possibility of mistakes. For final presentation, a different arrangement may be best (Chapter 64).

4. Consider whether additional columns are required for subsequent calculations. Create a separate column for each mathematical manipulation, so the step-by-step calculations are clearly visible. Use a computer spreadsheet (pp. 68–72) if you are manipulating lots of data.

5. Use a pencil to record data so that mistakes can be easily corrected.

6. Take sufficient time to record quantitative data unambiguously – use large clear numbers, making sure that individual numerals cannot be confused.

7. Record numerical data to an appropriate number of significant figures, reflecting the accuracy and precision of your measurement. Do not round off data values, as this might affect the subsequent analysis of your data.

8. Record discrete or grouped data as a tally chart, each row showing the possible values or classes of the variable. Provided that tally marks are of consistent size and spacing, this method has the advantage of providing an 'instant' frequency distribution chart.

9. Prepare duplicated recording tables if your experiments or observations will be repeated.

10. Explain any unusual data values or observations in a footnote. Don't rely on your memory.

Recording details of project and research work

The recommended system is one where you make a dual record.

Primary record

The primary record is made at the bench or in the field. In this, you must concentrate on the detail of materials, methods and results. Include information that would not be used elsewhere, but which might prove useful in error tracing: for example, if you note how a solution was made up (exact volumes and weights used rather than concentration alone), this could reveal whether a miscalculation had been the cause of a rogue result. Note the origin, type and state of the chemicals and organism(s) used. Make rough diagrams to show the arrangement of replicates, equipment, etc. If you are forced to use loose paper to record data, make sure each sheet is dated and taped to your lab book, collected in a ring binder, or attached together with a treasury tag. The same applies to traces, printouts and graphs.

The basic order of the primary record should mirror that of a research report (see p. 104), including: the title and date; brief introduction; comprehensive materials and methods; the data and short conclusions.

Secondary record

You should make a secondary record concurrently or later in a bound book and it ought to be neater, in both organisation and presentation. This book will be used when discussing results with your supervisor, and when writing up a report or thesis, and may be part of your course assessment. While these notes should retain the essential features of the primary record, they should be

Identifying your notes – always put a date and time on each of your primary record sheets. You may also wish to add your name and details of the type of observation or experiment.

Recording observations – write down the actual observation, not your interpretation of it. For example, the colour of a biochemical test, rather than whether the test was positive or negative.

Choosing a notebook for primary recording – a spiral-bound notebook is good for making a primary record – it lies conveniently open on the bench and provides a simple method of dealing with major mistakes!

Choosing a book for secondary recording – a hard-backed A4 size lined book is good because you will not lose pages. Graphs, printouts, etc. can be stuck in, as required.

more concise and the emphasis should move towards analysis of the experiment. Outline the aims more carefully at the start and link the experiment to others in a series (e.g. 'Following the results of Expt. D24, I decided to test whether . . .'). You should present data in an easily digested form, e.g. as tables of means or as summary graphs. Use appropriate statistical tests (Chapter 67) to support your analysis of the results. The choice of a bound book ensures that data are not easily lost.

Note that the dual method of recording deals with the inevitable untidiness of notes taken at the bench or in the field; these often have to be made rapidly, in awkward positions and in a generally complex environment. Writing a second, neater version forces you to consider again details that might have been overlooked in the primary record and provides a duplicate in case of loss or damage.

If you find it difficult to decide on the amount of detail required in Materials and Methods, the basic ground rule is to record enough information to allow a reasonably competent scientist to repeat your work exactly. You must tread a line between the extremes of pedantic, irrelevant detail and the omission of information essential for a proper interpretation of the data – better perhaps to err on the side of extra detail to begin with. An experienced worker can help you decide which subtle shifts in technique are important (e.g. batch numbers for an important chemical, or when a new stock solution is made up and used). Many important scientific advances have been made because of careful observation and record taking or because coincident data were recorded that did not seem of immediate value.

When creating a primary record, take care not to lose any of the information content of the data: for instance, if you only write down means and not individual values, this may affect your ability to carry out subsequent statistical analyses.

There are numerous ways to reduce the labour of keeping a record. Don't repeat Materials and Methods for a series of similar experiments; use devices such as 'method as for Expt. B4'. A photocopy might suffice if the method is derived from a text or article (check with supervisor). To save time, make up and copy a checklist in which details such as chemical batch numbers can be entered.

Using communal records

If working with a research team, you may need to use their communal databases. These avoid duplication of effort and ensure uniformity in techniques. They may also form part of the legal safety requirements for lab work. You will be expected to use the databases carefully and to contribute to them properly. They might include:

- a shared notebook of common techniques (e.g. how to make up media or solutions);
- a set of simplified step-by-step instructions for use of equipment. Manuals are often complex and poorly written and it may help to redraft them, incorporating any differences in procedure adopted by the group;
- an alphabetical list of suppliers of equipment and consumables (perhaps held on a card index system);
- a list of chemicals required by the group and where they are stored;
- the risk assessment sheets for dangerous procedures (p. 117);
- the record book detailing the use of radioisotopes and their disposal.

Sources for further study

Anon. *Suggestions for Keeping Laboratory Notebooks*. Available: http://otl.stanford.edu/inventors/resources/labnotebooks.html
Last accessed 08/01/03.
[A Stanford University Website which looks at the laboratory notebook from the patenting perspective.]

Friedrich, G.W. *Basic Principles of Measurement. Methods of Inquiry*. Available: http://www.scils.rutgers.edu/~gusf/measurement.html
Last accessed 08/01/03.
[Course notes covering valid aspects of measurement and inquiry.]

Kanare, H.M. (1985) *Writing the Laboratory Notebook*. American Chemical Society, Washington.

National Instruments. *Measurement Encyclopedia*. Available: http://zone.ni.com/devzone/nidzgloss.nsf/glossary
Last accessed 08/01/03.

Pechenik, J.A.A. (2001) *Short Guide to Writing about Biology*, 4th edn. Longman, Harlow.
[Chapter 8 is particularly relevant.]

Study exercises

28.1 Classify variables. Decide on the type of variables used for the following measures, indicating whether they are quantitative or qualitative, continuous or discontinuous, and the type of scale that would be used.
(a) Number of organisms in a sample.
(b) Height of individuals in a sample.
(c) Eye colour of individuals in a sample.
(d) Species present in a sample.
(e) Date of a sample.
(f) Reproductive status of an animal.

28.2 Investigate types of error. A student weighed a set of standard masses on two electronic balances and obtained the readings shown in the table below. Explain these results in terms of the type of error involved in each case.

Comparison of weights of masses on two balances

	Standard mass (g)				
	10	25	50	100	250
Reading (balance A)	10.050	25.049	50.051	100.048	250.052
Reading (balance B)	10.004	25.011	50.021	100.039	250.102

28.3 Design a secondary record sheet for the collection and analysis of a set of count data for the number of bacterial colonies developed in each of 10 replicates for each of 5 different treatments. Assume that you need to calculate means, variable, etc and then compare the results for each treatment.

SI units and their use

When describing a measurement, you normally state both a number and a unit (e.g. 'the length is 1.85 metres'). The number expresses the ratio of the measured quantity to a fixed standard, while the unit identifies that standard measure or dimension. Clearly, a single unified system of units is essential for efficient communication of such data within the scientific community. The Système International d'Unités (SI) is the internationally ratified form of the metre-kilogram-second system of measurement and represents the accepted scientific convention for measurements of physical quantities.

Another important reason for adopting consistent units is to simplify complex calculations where you may be dealing with several measured quantities (see p. 466). Although the rules of the SI are complex and the scale of the base units is sometimes inconvenient, to gain the full benefits of the system you should observe its conventions strictly.

The description of measurements in SI involves:

- seven base units and two supplementary units, each having a specified abbreviation or symbol (Table 29.1);
- derived units, obtained from combinations of base and supplementary units, which may also be given special symbols (Table 29.2);
- a set of prefixes to denote multiplication factors of 10^3, used for convenience to express multiples or fractions of units (Table 29.3).

Table 29.1 The base and supplementary SI units

Measured quantity	Name of SI unit	Symbol
Base units		
Length	metre	m
Mass	kilogram	kg
Amount of substance	mole	mol
Time	second	s
Electric current	ampere	A
Temperature	kelvin	K
Luminous intensity	candela	cd
Supplementary units		
Plane angle	radian	rad
Solid angle	steradian	sr

Table 29.2 Some important derived SI units

Measured quantity	Name of unit	Symbol	Definition in base units	Alternative in derived units
Energy	joule	J	$m^2\,kg\,s^{-2}$	N m
Force	newton	N	$m\,kg\,s^{-2}$	$J\,m^{-1}$
Pressure	pascal	Pa	$kg\,m^{-1}\,s^{-2}$	$N\,m^{-2}$
Power	watt	W	$m^2\,kg\,s^{-3}$	$J\,s^{-1}$
Electric charge	coulomb	C	A s	$J\,V^{-1}$
Electric potential difference	volt	V	$m^2\,kg\,A^{-1}\,s^{-3}$	$J\,C^{-1}$
Electric resistance	ohm	Ω	$m^2\,kg\,A^{-2}\,s^{-3}$	$V\,A^{-1}$
Electric conductance	siemens	S	$s^3\,A^2\,kg^{-1}\,m^{-2}$	$A\,V^{-1}$ or Ω^{-1}
Electric capacitance	farad	F	$s^4\,A^2\,kg^{-1}\,m^{-2}$	$C\,V^{-1}$
Luminous flux	lumen	lm	cd sr	
Illumination	lux	lx	$cd\,sr\,m^{-2}$	$lm\,m^{-2}$
Frequency	hertz	Hz	s^{-1}	
Radioactivity	becquerel	Bq	s^{-1}	
Enzyme activity	katal	kat	$mol\ substrate\ s^{-1}$	

Table 29.3 Prefixes used in the SI

Multiple	Prefix	Symbol	Multiple	Prefix	Symbol
10^{-3}	milli	m	10^3	kilo	k
10^{-6}	micro	μ	10^6	mega	M
10^{-9}	nano	n	10^9	giga	G
10^{-12}	pico	p	10^{12}	tera	T
10^{-15}	femto	f	10^{15}	peta	P
10^{-18}	atto	a	10^{18}	exa	E
10^{-21}	zepto	z	10^{21}	zetta	Z
10^{-24}	yocto	y	10^{24}	yotta	Y

Recommendations for describing measurements in SI units

Basic format

- Express each measurement as a number separated from its units by a space. If a prefix is required, no space is left between the prefix and the unit it refers to. Symbols for units are only written in their singular form and do not require full stops to show that they are abbreviated or that they are being multiplied together.

- Give symbols and prefixes appropriate upper or lower case initial letters as this may define their meaning. Upper case symbols are named after persons but when written out in full they are not given initial capital letters.
- Show the decimal sign as a full point on the line. Some metric countries continue to use the comma for this purpose and you may come across this in the literature: commas should not therefore be used to separate groups of thousands. In numbers that contain many significant figures, you should separate multiples of 10^3 by spaces rather than commas.

Example n stands for nano and N for newtons.

Example 1 982 963.192 309 kg (perhaps better expressed as 1.982 963 192 309 Gg).

Compound expressions for derived units

- Take care to separate symbols in compound expressions by a space to avoid the potential for confusion with prefixes. Note, for example, that 200 m s (metre-seconds) is different from 200 ms (milliseconds).
- Express compound units using negative powers rather than a solidus (/): for example, write $mol\,m^{-3}$ rather than mol/m^3. The solidus is reserved for separating a descriptive label from its units (see p. 453).
- Use parentheses to enclose expressions being raised to a power if this avoids confusion: for example, a photosynthetic rate might be given in $mol\,CO_2\,(mol\,photons)^{-1}\,s^{-1}$.
- Where there is a choice, select relevant (natural) combinations of derived and base units: e.g. you might choose units of $Pa\,m^{-1}$ to describe a hydrostatic pressure gradient rather than $kg\,m^{-2}\,s^{-1}$, even though these units are equivalent and the measurements are numerically the same.

Use of prefixes

- Use prefixes to denote multiples of 10^3 (Table 29.3) so that numbers are kept between 0.1 and 1000.
- Treat a combination of a prefix and a symbol as a single symbol. Thus, when a modified unit is raised to a power, this refers to the whole unit including the prefix.
- Avoid the prefixes deci (d) for 10^{-1}, centi (c) for 10^{-2}, deca (da) for 10 and hecto (h) for 100 as they are not strictly SI.
- Express very large or small numbers as a number between 1 and 10 multiplied by a power of 10 if they are outside the range of prefixes shown in Table 29.3.
- Do not use prefixes in the middle of derived units: they should be attached only to a unit in the numerator (the exception is in the unit for mass, kg).

Examples

- $10\,\mu m$ is preferred to 0.000 01 m or 0.010 mm.
- $1\,mm^2 = 10^{-6}\,m^2$ (not one-thousandth of a square metre).
- $1\,dm^3$ (1 litre) is more properly expressed in SI as $1 \times 10^{-3}\,m^3$.
- The mass of a neutrino is 10^{-36} kg.
- State as $MW\,m^{-2}$ rather than $W\,mm^{-2}$.

KEY POINT For the foreseeable future, you will need to make conversions from other units to SI units, as much of the literature quotes data using imperial, c.g.s. or other systems. You will need to recognise these units and find the conversion factors required. Examples relevant to biology are given in Box 29.1. Table 29.4 provides values of some important physical constants in SI units.

Table 29.4 Some physical constants in SI terms

Physical constant	Symbol	Value and units
Avogadro's constant	N_A	$6.022\,174 \times 10^{23}\,mol^{-1}$
Boltzmann's constant	k	$1.380\,626 \times 10^{-23}\,J\,K^{-1}$
Charge of electron	e	$1.602\,192 \times 10^{-19}\,C$
Gas constant	R	$8.314\,43\,J\,K^{-1}\,mol^{-1}$
Faraday's constant	F	$9.648\,675 \times 10^{4}\,C\,mol^{-1}$
Molar volume of ideal gas at STP	V_0	$0.022\,414\,m^3\,mol^{-1}$
Speed of light *in vacuo*	c	$2.997\,924 \times 10^{8}\,m\,s^{-1}$
Planck's constant	h	$6.626\,205 \times 10^{-34}\,J\,s$

Box 29.1 Conversion factors between some redundant units and the SI

Quantity	SI unit/symbol	Old unit/symbol	Multiply number in old unit by this factor for equivalent in SI unit*	Multiply number in SI unit by this factor for equivalent in old unit*
Area	square metre/m^2	acre	$4.046\,86 \times 10^3$	$0.247\,105 \times 10^{-3}$
		hectare/ha	10×10^3	0.1×10^{-3}
		square foot/ft^2	$0.092\,903$	$10.763\,9$
		square inch/in^2	645.16×10^{-9}	$1.550\,00 \times 10^6$
		square yard/yd^2	$0.836\,127$	$1.195\,99$
Angle	radian/rad	degree/°	$17.453\,2 \times 10^{-3}$	$57.295\,8$
Energy	joule/J	erg	0.1×10^{-6}	10×10^6
		kilowatt hour/kWh	3.6×10^6	$0.277\,778 \times 10^{-6}$
		calorie/cal	4.1868	0.2388
Length	metre/m	Ångstrom/Å	0.1×10^{-9}	10×10^9
		foot/ft	0.3048	$3.280\,84$
		inch/in	25.4×10^{-3}	$39.370\,1$
		mile	$1.609\,34 \times 10^3$	$0.621\,373 \times 10^{-3}$
		yard/yd	$0.914\,4$	$1.093\,61$
Mass	kilogram/kg	ounce/oz	$28.349\,5 \times 10^{-3}$	$35.274\,0$
		pound/lb	$0.453\,592$	$2.204\,62$
		stone	$6.350\,29$	$0.157\,473$
		hundredweight/cwt	$50.802\,4$	$19.684\,1 \times 10^{-3}$
		ton (UK)	$1.016\,05 \times 10^3$	$0.984\,203 \times 10^{-3}$
Pressure	pascal/Pa	atmosphere/atm	$101\,325$	$9.869\,23 \times 10^{-6}$
		bar/b	$100\,000$	10×10^{-6}
		millimetre of mercury/mmHg	133.322	$7.500\,64 \times 10^{-3}$
		torr/Torr	133.322	$7.500\,64 \times 10^{-3}$
Radioactivity	becquerel/Bq	curie/Ci	37×10^9	$27.027\,0 \times 10^{-12}$
Temperature	kelvin/K	centigrade (Celsius) degree/°C	°C $+ 273.15$	K $- 273.15$
		Fahrenheit degree/°F	(°F $+ 459.67) \times 5/9$	(K $\times 9/5) - 459.67$
Volume	cubic metre/m^3	cubic foot/ft^3	$0.028\,316\,8$	$35.314\,7$
		cubic inch/in^3	$16.387\,1 \times 10^{-6}$	$61.023\,6 \times 10^3$
		cubic yard/yd^3	$0.764\,555$	$1.307\,95$
		UK pint/pt	$0.568\,261 \times 10^{-3}$	$1\,759.75$
		US pint/liq pt	$0.473\,176 \times 10^{-3}$	$2\,113.38$
		UK gallon/gal	$4.546\,09 \times 10^{-3}$	219.969
		US gallon/gal	$3.785\,41 \times 10^{-3}$	264.172

*In the case of temperature measurements, use formulae shown.

Some implications of SI in bioscience

Volume

The SI unit of volume is the cubic metre, m^3, which is rather large for practical purposes. The litre (l) and the millilitre (ml) are technically obsolete, but are widely used and glassware is still calibrated using them. Note also that the US spelling is liter. In some instances you may find litre given the symbol L, rather than l to avoid confusion with the number 1 and with I, e.g. in certain font styles.

In this book, we use l and ml where you would normally find equipment calibrated in that way, but use SI units where this simplifies calculations. In formal scientific writing, constructions such as $1 \times 10^{-6} m^3$ $(= 1 ml)$ and $1 mm^3$ $(= 1 \mu l)$ may be used.

Mass

The SI unit for mass is the kilogram (kg) rather than the gram (g): this is unusual because the base unit has a prefix applied.

Amount of substance

Expressing enzyme activity – the derived SI unit is the katal (kat) which is the amount of enzyme that will transform 1 mol of substrate in 1 s (see Chapter 55).

You should use the mole (mol, i.e. Avogadro's constant, see Table 29.4) to express very large numbers. The mole gives the number of atoms in the atomic mass, a convenient constant. Always specify the elementary unit referred to in other situations (e.g. mol photons $m^{-2} s^{-1}$).

Concentration

The SI unit of concentration, $mol\,m^{-3}$, is quite convenient for biological systems. It is equivalent to the non-SI term 'millimolar' ($mM \equiv mmol\,l^{-1}$) while 'molar' (M) becomes $kmol\,m^{-3}$. Note that the symbol M in the SI is reserved for mega and hence should not be used for concentrations. If the solvent is not specified, then it is assumed to be water (see Chapter 24).

Time

In general, use the second (s) when reporting physical quantities having a time element (e.g. give photosynthetic rates in mol $CO_2\,m^{-2}\,s^{-1}$). Hours (h), days (d) and years should be used if seconds are clearly absurd (e.g. samples were taken over a 5-year period). Note, however, that you may have to convert these units to seconds when doing calculations.

Temperature

Definition

STP – Standard Temperature and Pressure = 293.15 K and 0.101 325 MPa.

The SI unit is the kelvin, K. The degree Celsius scale has units of the same magnitude, °C, but starts at 273.15 K, the melting point of ice at STP. Temperature is similar to time in that the Celsius scale is in widespread use, but note that conversions to K may be required for calculations. Note also that you must not use the degree sign (°) with K and that this symbol must be in upper case to avoid confusion with k for kilo; however, you *should* retain the degree sign with °C to avoid confusion with the coulomb, C.

Light

While the first six base units in Table 29.1 have standards of high precision, the SI base unit for luminous intensity, the candela (cd) and the derived units lm and lx (Table 29.2), are defined in 'human' terms. They are, in fact, based on the spectral responses of the eyes of 52 American GIs measured in 1923! Clearly, few organisms 'see' light in the same way as this sample of humans. Also, light sources differ in their spectral quality. For these reasons, it is better to use expressions based on energy or photon content (e.g. $W\,m^{-2}$ or mol photons $m^{-2}\,s^{-1}$), in studies other than those on human vision. Ideally you should specify the photon wavelength spectrum involved (see Chapter 40).

Sources for further study

Bell, R.J. (1993) *SI, The International System of Units*. HMSO, London.

Institute of Biology (1997) *Biological Nomenclature: Recommendations on Terms, Units and Symbols*, 2nd edn. Institute of Biology, London.

National Institute of Standards and Technology. *International System of Units (SI)*. Available: http://www.physics.nist.gov/cuu/Units/index.html Last accessed 08/01/03.

Pennycuick, C.J. (1988) *Conversion Factors: SI Units and Many Others: Over 2100 Conversion Factors for Biologists and Mechanical Engineers Arranged in 21 Quick-Reference Tables*. The University of Chicago Press, Chicago.

Rowlett, R. *How Many? A Dictionary of Units of Measurement*. Available: http://www.unc.edu/~rowlett/units Last accessed 08/01/03.

Tapson, F. *A Dictionary of Units*. Available: http://www.ex.ac.uk/cimt/dictunit/dictunit.htm Last accessed 08/01/03.

Study exercises

29.1 **Practise converting between units**. Using Box 29.1 as a source, convert the following amounts into the units shown. Give your answers to three significant figures.
   (a) 101 000 Pa into atmospheres
   (b) One square yard into square millimetres
   (c) One UK pint into millilitres
   (d) 37 °C into kelvin
   (e) 11 stone 6 pounds into kilograms.

29.2 **Practise using prefixes appropriately**. Simplify the following number/unit combinations using an appropriate prefix so that the number component lies between 0.1 and 1000.
   (a) 10 000 mm
   (b) 0.015 ml
   (c) 5×10^{9} J
   (d) 65 000 m s^{-1}
   (e) 0.000 000 000 1 g

29.3 **Check units in an equation**. The Hagan–Poiseuille equation describes water flux in smooth cylindrical pipes assuming laminar flow. This equation can be expressed as:

$$J_{\mathrm{v}} = \frac{r^2 \times \delta P}{8\eta \times \delta x}$$

where

r = the radius of the cylindrical pipe (m);
η ('eta') = the viscosity of the liquid (Pa s);
δP = the pressure difference across the ends of the pipe (Pa);
δx = the length of the pipe (m).

Verify, by putting relevant units in place of the variables in this equation and simplifying the resulting relationship, that appropriate units for J_v are $m\,s^{-1}$ (mean flow rate).

Scientific method and design of experiments

There are many interpretations of the following terms. For the purposes of this chapter, the following will be used.

Paradigm – theoretical framework so successful and well-confirmed that most research is carried out within its context and doesn't challenge it – even significant difficulties can be 'shelved' in favour of its retention.

Theory – a collection of hypotheses that covers a range of natural phenomena – a 'larger-scale' idea than a hypothesis. Note that a theory may be 'hypothetical', in the sense that it is a tentative explanation.

Hypothesis – an explanation tested in a specific experiment or by a set of observations. Tends to involve a 'small scale' idea.

(Scientific) Law – this concept can be summarised as an equation (law) that provides a succinct encapsulation of a system, often in the form of a mathematical relationship. The term is often used in the physical sciences (e.g. 'Beer's Law', p. 271).

Fig. 30.1 A model of scientific method as used when testing hypotheses on a small scale. Hypotheses can arise as a result of various thought-processes on the part of the scientist, and are consistent with the overlying paradigm. Each hypothesis is testable by experiment or observation, leading to its confirmation or rejection. Confirmed hypotheses act to strengthen the status of the paradigm, but rejected ones do not immediately result in the paradigm's replacement.

Science is a body of knowledge based on observation and experiment. Biological scientists attempt to explain life in terms of theories and hypotheses. They make predictions from these hypotheses and test them by experiment or further observations. The philosophy and sociology that underlie this process are complex topics (see e.g. Chalmers, 1999) and any brief description must involve simplifications.

Figure 30.1 models the scientific process you are most likely to be involved in – testing hypotheses on a small scale. These represent the sorts of explanation that can give rise to predictions which can be tested by an experiment or a series of observations. For example, you might put forward the hypothesis that the rate of K^+ efflux from a particular cell type is dependent on the intracellular concentration of calcium ions. This might then lead to a prediction that the application of a substance known to decrease the intracellular concentration of calcium ions, would reduce K^+ efflux from the cells. An experiment could be set up to test this hypothesis and the results would either confirm or falsify the hypothesis.

If confirmed, a hypothesis is retained with greater confidence. If falsified, it is either rejected outright as false, or modified and retested. Alternatively, it might be decided that the experiment was not a valid test of the hypothesis (perhaps because it was later found that the applied substance could not penetrate the cell membrane to a presumed site of action).

Nearly all scientific research deals with the testing of small-scale hypotheses. These hypotheses operate within a theoretical framework that has proven to be successful (i.e. is confirmed by many experiments and is consistently predictive). This operating model or 'paradigm' is not changed readily, and even if a result appears that seems to challenge the conventional view, would not be overturned immediately. The conflicting result would be 'shelved' until an explanation was found after further investigation. In the example used above, a relevant paradigm could be the notion that life processes are ultimately chemical in nature.

Although changes in paradigms are rare, they are important, and the scientists who recognise them become famous. For example, a 'paradigm shift' can be said to have occurred when Darwin's ideas about natural selection replaced special creation as an explanation for the origin of species. Generally, however, results from hypothesis-testing tend to support and develop ('articulate') the paradigm, enhancing its relevance and strengthening its status. Thus, research in the area of population genetics has developed and refined Darwinism.

Where do ideas for small-scale hypotheses come from? They arise from one or more thought-processes on the part of a scientist:

- analogy with other systems;
- recognition of a pattern;
- recognition of departure from a pattern;
- invention of new analytical methods;
- development of a mathematical model;
- intuition;
- imagination.

Recently, it has been recognised that the process of science is not an entirely objective one. For instance, the choice of analogy which led to a new hypothesis might well be subjective, depending on past knowledge or understanding. Also, science is a social activity, where researchers put forward and defend viewpoints against those who hold an opposing view; where groups may work together towards a common goal; and where effort may depend on externally dictated financial opportunities and constraints. As with any other human activity, science is bound to involve an element of subjectivity.

How are decisions made about whether to accept or reject a hypothesis? This is sometimes clear-cut, as in some areas of genetics, where experiments can be set up to result in a binary outcome (Chapter 58). In many other cases, the existence of 'biological variation' means that statistical techniques need to be employed (Chapters 66 and 67; Box 58.2).

No hypothesis can ever be rejected with certainty. Statistics allow us to quantify as vanishingly small the probability of an erroneous conclusion, but we are nevertheless left in the position of never being 100% certain that we have rejected all relevant alternative hypotheses, nor 100% certain that our decision to reject some alternative hypotheses was correct! However, despite these problems, experimental science has yielded and continues to yield many important findings.

KEY POINT The fallibility of scientific 'facts' is essential to grasp. No explanation can ever be 100% certain as it is always possible for a new alternative hypothesis to be generated. Our understanding of biology changes all the time as new observations and methods force old hypotheses to be retested.

Quantitative hypotheses involve a mathematical description of the biological system. They can be formulated concisely by mathematical models. Formulating models is often useful because it forces deeper thought about mechanisms and encourages simplification of the system. A mathematical model:

- is inherently testable through experiment;
- identifies areas where information is lacking or uncertain;
- encapsulates many observations;
- allows you to predict the behaviour of the system.

Remember, however, that assumptions and simplifications required to create a model may result in it being unrealistic. Further, the results obtained from any model are only as good as the information put into it.

The terminology of experimentation

In many experiments, the aim is to provide evidence for causality. If x causes y, we expect, repeatedly, to find that a change in x results in a change in y. Hence, the ideal experiment of this kind involves measurement of y, the dependent (measured) variable, at one or more values of x, the independent variable, and subsequent demonstration of some relationship between them. Experiments therefore involve comparisons of the results of treatments – changes in the independent variable as applied to an experimental subject. The change is engineered by the experimenter under controlled conditions.

Definition

Mathematical model – an algebraic summary of the relationship between the variables in a system.

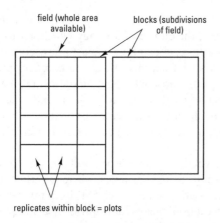

field (whole area available)   blocks (subdivisions of field)

replicates within block = plots

Fig. 30.2 Terminology and physical arrangement of elements in an experiment. Each block should contain the complete range of treatments (treatments may be replicated more than once in each block).

Subjects given the same treatment are known as replicates (they are also called plots in some situations). A block is a grouping of replicates or plots. The blocks are contained in a field, i.e. the whole area (or time) available for the experiment (Fig. 30.2). These terms originated from the statistical analysis of agricultural experiments, but they are now used across all areas of bioscience.

Why you need to control variables in experiments

Interpretation of experiments is seldom clear-cut because uncontrolled variables always change when treatments are given.

Confounding variables
These increase or decrease systematically as the independent variable increases or decreases. Their effects are known as systematic variation. This form of variation can be disentangled from that caused directly by treatments by incorporating appropriate controls in the experiment. A control is really just another treatment where a potentially confounding variable is adjusted so that its effects, if any, can be taken into account. The results from a control may therefore allow an alternative hypothesis to be rejected. There are often many potential controls for any experiment.

The consequence of systematic variation is that you can never be certain that the treatment, and the treatment alone, has caused an observed result. By careful design, you can, however, 'minimise the uncertainty' involved in your conclusion. Methods available include:

- Ensuring, through experimental design, that the independent variable is the only major factor that changes in any treatment.
- Incorporating appropriate controls to show that potential confounding variables have little or no effect.
- Selecting experimental subjects randomly to cancel out systematic variation arising from biased selection.
- Matching or pairing individuals among treatments so that differences in response due to their initial status are eliminated.
- Arranging subjects and treatments randomly so that responses to systematic differences in conditions do not influence the results.
- Ensuring that experimental conditions are uniform so that responses to systematic differences in conditions are minimised. When attempting this, beware 'edge effects' where subjects on the periphery of the layout receive substantially different conditions from those in the centre.

Reducing edge effects – one approach is to incorporate a 'buffer zone' of untreated subjects around the experiment proper.

Nuisance variables
These are uncontrolled variables which cause differences in the value of y independently of the value of x, resulting in random variation. Experimental biology is characterised by the high number of nuisance variables that are found and their relatively great influence on results: biological data tend to have large errors. To reduce and assess the consequences of nuisance variables:

- incorporate replicates to allow random variation to be quantified;
- choose subjects that are as similar as possible;
- control random fluctuations in environmental conditions.

Constraints on experimental design

Box 30.1 outlines the important stages in designing an experiment. At an early stage, you should find out how resources may constrain the design. For example, limits may be set by availability of subjects, cost of treatment, availability of a chemical or bench space. Logistics may be a factor (e.g. time taken to record or analyse data).

Your equipment or facilities may affect design because you cannot regulate conditions as well as you might desire. For example, you may be unable to ensure that temperature and lighting are equal over an experiment laid out in a glasshouse or you may have to accept a great deal of initial variability if your subjects are collected from the wild. This problem is especially acute for experiments carried out under field conditions.

Using replicates

Replicate results show how variable the response is within treatments. They allow you to compare the differences among treatments in the context of the variability within treatments – you can do this *via* statistical tests such as analysis of variance (Chapter 67). Larger sample sizes tend to increase the precision of estimates of parameters and increase the chances

---

Box 30.1 Checklist for designing and performing an experiment

1. **Preliminaries**

   (a) **Read background material** and decide on a subject area to investigate.

   (b) **Formulate a simple hypothesis to test.** It is preferable to have a clear answer to one question than to be uncertain about several questions.

   (c) **Decide which dependent variable you are going to measure and how:** is it relevant to the problem? Can you measure it accurately, precisely and without bias?

   (d) **Think about and plan the statistical analysis of your results.** Will this affect your design?

2. **Designing**

   (a) **Find out the limitations on your resources.**

   (b) **Choose treatments that alter the minimum of confounding variables.**

   (c) **Incorporate as many effective controls as possible.**

   (d) **Keep the number of replicates as high as is feasible.**

   (e) **Ensure that the same number of replicates is present in each treatment.**

   (f) **Use effective randomisation and blocking arrangements.**

3. **Planning**

   (a) **List all the materials you will need.** Order any chemicals and make up solutions; grow, collect or breed the experimental subjects you require; check equipment is available.

   (b) **Organise space and/or time** in which to do the experiment.

   (c) **Account for the time taken to apply treatments and record results.** Make out a timesheet if things will be hectic.

4. **Carrying out the experiment**

   (a) **Record the results and make careful notes of everything you do** (see p. 172–4). Make additional observations to those planned if interesting things happen.

   (b) **Repeat experiment** if time and resources allow.

5. **Analysing**

   (a) **Graph data as soon as possible** (during the experiment if you can). This will allow you to visualise what has happened and make adjustments to the design (e.g. timing of measurements).

   (b) **Carry out the planned statistical analysis.**

   (c) **Jot down conclusions and new hypotheses** arising from the experiment.

Deciding the number of replicates in each treatment – try to: maximise the number of replicates in each treatment within the constraints of time and resources available.

of showing a significant difference between treatments if one exists. For statistical reasons (weighting, ease of calculation, fitting data to certain tests), it is often best to keep the number of replicates even. Remember that the degree of independence of replicates is important: sub-samples cannot act as replicate samples – they tell you about variability in the measurement method but not in the quantity being measured.

If the total number of replicates available for an experiment is limited by resources, you may need to compromise between the number of treatments and the number of replicates per treatment. Statistics can help here, for it is possible to work out the minimum number of replicates you would need to show a certain difference between pairs of means (say 10%) at a specified level of significance (say $P = 0.05$). For this, you need to obtain a prior estimate of variability within treatments (see Sokal and Rohlf, 1994).

Randomisation of treatments

The two aspects of randomisation you must consider are:

- positioning of treatments within experimental blocks;
- allocation of treatments to the experimental subjects.

Box 30.2 How to use random number tables to assign subjects to positions and treatments

This is one method of many that could be used. It requires two sets of n random numbers – where n is the total number of subjects used.

1. **Number the subjects in any arbitrary order** but in such a way that you know which is which (i.e. mark or tag them).

2. **Decide how treatments will be assigned**, e.g. first five subjects selected treatment A; second five – treatment B, etc.

3. **Use the first set of random numbers in the sequence obtained to identify subjects and allocate them to treatment groups** in order of selection as decided in (2).

4. **Map the positions for subjects in the block or field. Assign numbers to these positions using the second set of random numbers**, working through the positions in some arbitrary order, e.g. top left to bottom right.

5. **Match the original numbers given to subjects with the position numbers.**

To obtain a sequence of random numbers:

1. **Decide on the range of random numbers you need.**

2. **Decide how you wish to sample the random number tables** (e.g. row-by-row and top to bottom) and your starting point.

3. **Moving in the selected manner, read the sequence of numbers until you come to a group that fits your needs** (e.g. in the sequence 978186, 18 represents a number between 1 and 20). Write this down and continue sampling until you get a new number. If a number is repeated, ignore it. Small numbers need to have the appropriate number of zeros preceding (e.g. $5 = 05$ for a range in the tens, $21 = 021$ for a range in the hundreds).

4. **When you come to the last number required, you don't need to sample any more:** simply write it down.

Example: You find the following random number sequence in a table and wish to select numbers between 1 and 10 from it.

9059146823	4862925166	1063260345
1277423810	9948040676	6430247598
8357945137	2490145183	5946242208
6588812379	2325701558	3260726568

Working left to right and top to bottom, the order of numbers found is 5, 10, 3, 9, 4, 6, 2, 1, 8, 7 as indicated by blue type. If the table is sampled by working row-by-row right to left from bottom to top, the order is 6, 10, 7, 2, 9, 3, 4, 8, 1, 5.

Fig. 30.3 Examples of Latin square arrangements for 3 and 4 treatments. Letters indicate treatments; the number of possible arrangements for each size of square increases greatly as the size increases.

Example If you knew that soil type varied in a graded fashion across a field, you might arrange blocks to be long thin rectangles at right angles to the gradient to ensure conditions within the block were as even as possible.

Example A Latin square format is used for agar bioassays of antibiotics and vitamins (p. 231). Replicates are arranged so that gradients across the plate are cancelled out.

For relatively simple experiments, you can adopt a completely randomised design; here, the position and treatment assigned to any subject are defined randomly. You can draw lots, use a random number generator on a calculator, or use the random number tables which can be found in most books of statistical tables (see Box 30.2).

A completely randomised layout has the advantage of simplicity but cannot show how confounding variables alter in space or time. This information can be obtained if you use a blocked design in which the degree of randomisation is restricted. Here, the experimental space or time is divided into blocks, each of which accommodates the complete set of treatments (Fig. 30.2). When analysed appropriately, the results for the blocks can be compared to test for differences in the confounding variables and these effects can be separated out from the effects of the treatments. The size and shape (or timing) of the block you choose is important: besides being able to accommodate the number of replicates desired, the suspected confounding variable should be relatively uniform within the block.

A Latin square is a method of placing treatments so that they appear in a balanced fashion within a square block or field. Treatments appear once in each column and row (see Fig. 30.3), so the effects of confounding variables can be 'cancelled out' in two directions at right angles to each other. This is effective if there is a smooth gradient in some confounding variable over the field. It is less useful if the variable has a patchy distribution, where a randomised block design might be better.

Latin square designs are useful in serial experiments where different treatments are given to the same subjects in a sequence (e.g. Fig. 30.4). A disadvantage of Latin squares is the fact that the number of plots is equal to the number of replicates, so increases in the number of replicates can only be made by the use of further Latin squares.

Pairing and matching subjects

The paired comparison is a special case of blocking used to reduce systematic variation when there are two treatments. Examples of its use are:

- 'Before and after' comparison. Here, the pairing removes variability arising from the initial state of the subjects, e.g. weight gain of mice on a diet, where the weight gain may depend on the initial weight.
- Application of a treatment and control to parts of the same subject or to closely related subjects. This allows comparison without complications arising from different origin of subjects, e.g. drug or placebo given to sibling rats, virus-containing or control solution swabbed on left or right halves of a leaf.
- Application of treatment and control under shared conditions. This allows comparison without complications arising from different environments of subjects, e.g. rats in a cage, plants in a pot.

Matched samples represent a restriction on randomisation where you make a balanced selection of subjects for treatments on the basis of some attribute or attributes that may influence results, e.g. age, sex, prior history. The effect of matching should be to 'cancel out' the unwanted source(s) of variation. Disadvantages include the subjective

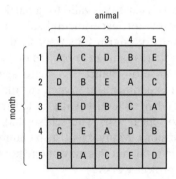

Fig. 30.4 Example of how to use a Latin square design to arrange sequential treatments. The experimenter wishes to test the effect of drugs A–E on weight gain, but only has five animals available. Each animal is fed on control diet for the first 3 weeks of each month, then on control diet plus drug for the last week. Weights are taken at start and finish of each treatment. Each animal receives all treatments.

element in choice of character(s) to be balanced, inexact matching of quantitative characteristics, the time matching takes and possible wastage of unmatched subjects.

When analysed statistically, both paired comparisons and matched samples can show up differences between treatments that might otherwise be rejected on the basis of a fully randomised design, but note that the statistical analysis may be different.

Multifactorial experiments

The simplest experiments are those in which one treatment (factor) is applied at a time to the subjects. This approach is likely to give clear-cut answers, but it could be criticised for lacking realism. In particular, it cannot take account of interactions among two or more conditions that are likely to occur in real life. A multifactorial experiment (Fig. 30.5) is an attempt to do this; the interactions among treatments can be analysed by specialised statistics.

Multifactorial experiments are economical on resources because of 'hidden replication'. This arises when two or more treatments are given to a subject because the result acts statistically as a replicate for each treatment. Choice of relevant treatments to combine is important in multifactorial experiments; for instance, an interaction may be present at certain concentrations of a chemical but not at others (perhaps because the response is saturated). It is also important that the measurement scale for the response is consistent, otherwise spurious interactions may occur. Beware when planning a multifactorial experiment that the numbers of replicates do not get out of hand: you may have to restrict the treatments to 'plus' or 'minus' the factor of interest (as in Fig. 30.5).

Repetition of experiments

Even if your experiment is well designed and analysed, only limited conclusions can be made. Firstly, what you can say is valid for a particular place and time, with a particular investigator, experimental subject and method of applying treatments. Secondly, if your results were significant at the 5% level of probability (p. 486), there is still an approximately one-in-twenty chance that the results did arise by chance. To guard against these possibilities, it is important that experiments are repeated. Ideally, this would be done by an independent scientist with independent materials. However, it makes sense to repeat work yourself so that you can have full confidence in your conclusions. Many scientists recommend that experiments are done three times in total, but this may not be possible in undergraduate practical classes or project work.

Text references

Chalmers, A.F. (1999) *What is This Thing Called Science?* Open University Press, Buckingham.

Sokal, R.R. and Rohlf, F.J. (1994) *Biometry*, 3rd edn. W.H. Freeman, San Francisco.

Definition

Interaction – where the effect of treatments given together is greater or less than the sum of their individual effects.

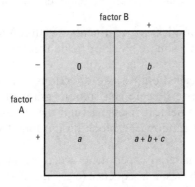

Fig. 30.5 Design of a simple multifactorial experiment. Factors A and B have effects a and b when applied alone. When both are applied together, the effect is denoted by $a + b + c$.

- If $c = 0$, there is no interaction (e.g. $2 + 2 + c = 4$).
- If c is positive, there is a positive interaction (synergism) between A and B (e.g. $2 + 2 + c = 5$).
- If c is negative, there is a negative interaction (antagonism) between A and B (e.g. $2 + 2 + c = 3$).

Reporting results – *it is good practice to report how many times your experiments were repeated (in Materials and Methods); in the Results section, you should add a statement saying that the illustrated experiment is representative, or one explaining any differences between results obtained.*

Sources for further study

Heath, D. (1995) *An Introduction to Experimental Design and Statistics for Biology*. UCL Press Ltd, London.

Maber, J. (1999) *Data Analysis for Biomolecular Sciences*. Longman, Harlow.

Quinn, G.P. and Keough, M.J. (2002) *Experimental Design and Data Analysis for Biologists*. Cambridge University Press, Cambridge.

Study exercises

30.1 Consider the application of a Latin square design. Treatments W, X, Y and Z are to be applied to potted plants in a glasshouse where the researcher suspects there may be a slight gradation in temperature and light over an oblong bench that can hold a total of 48 pots. You decide to use an experimental design consisting of three 4×4 blocks of plants, each arranged in a different Latin square design (see below). Assign treatments to the locations in the diagram below. Explain why this design will help to eliminate the effects of the confounding variables.

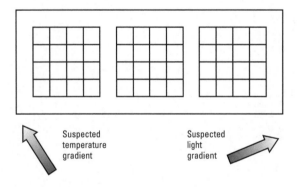

Layout for glasshouse experiment

30.2 Generate random numbers. Produce a list of 20 random whole numbers between 1 and 5 using a spreadsheet. If using MS Excel®, investigate the RAND() and INT functions. The RAND() function produces a random number between 0 and 1, so you will need to multiply by a constant factor to scale your final output appropriately. Copy your test formula(e) to several cells to test empirically whether it works.

30.3 Investigate possible interactions. Treatments A, B and C involve tests of three different nutrients on proliferation of cells in a culture of carrot cells. Analyse the results in the table overleaf to determine whether any interactions have occurred between the four possible combinations of treatments. No complex statistical analysis is required, simply a calculation of mean experimental effect (treatment minus controls) in each combined treatment and a comparison with the data for the relevant treatments on their own (in other words, assume that observed differences reflect true underlying differences). Classify the results as 'no interaction', 'antagonism' or 'synergism'.

Results of cell proliferation experiment

	Replicate (growth of callus in g)				
Treatment	1	2	3	4	5
Control	4.8	5.2	5.2	4.8	5.0
A	6.5	7.3	7.0	7.1	7.1
B	7.7	8.3	8.5	7.5	8.0
C	10.7	10.0	9.9	9.8	9.6
A+B	6.6	7.2	6.8	7.2	7.2
A+C	11.9	11.7	12.0	12.0	12.4
B+C	17.3	16.8	17.1	16.6	17.2
A+B+C	12.8	12.9	13.1	13.3	12.9

31 Project work

Research projects are an important component of the final year syllabus for most degree programmes in the biosciences, while shorter projects may also be carried out during courses in earlier years. Project work presents difficulties at many stages, but can be extremely rewarding. The assessment of your project is likely to contribute significantly to your degree grade, so all aspects of this work should be approached in a thorough manner.

Deciding on a topic to study

Assuming you have a choice, this important decision should be researched carefully. Make appointments to visit possible supervisors and ask them for advice on topics that you find interesting. Use library texts and research papers to obtain further background information. Perhaps the most important criterion is whether the topic will sustain your interest over the whole period of the project. Other things to look for include:

- Opportunities to learn new skills. Ideally, you should attempt to gain experience and skills that you might be able to 'sell' to a potential employer.
- Ease of obtaining valid results. An ideal project provides a means to obtain 'guaranteed' data for your report, but also the chance to extend knowledge by doing genuinely novel research.
- Assistance. What help will be available to you during the project? A busy lab with many research students might provide a supportive environment should your potential supervisor be too busy to meet you often; on the other hand, a smaller lab may provide the opportunity for more personal interaction with your supervisor.
- Impact. It is not outside the bounds of possibility for undergraduate work to contribute to research papers. Your prospective supervisor can alert you to such opportunities.

Planning your work

As with any lengthy exercise, planning is required to make the best use of the time allocated (p. 9). This is true on a daily basis as well as over the entire period of the project. It is especially important not to underestimate the time it will take to write and produce your thesis (see below). If you wish to benefit from feedback given by your supervisor, you should aim to have drafts in his/her hands in good time. Since a large proportion of marks will be allocated to the report, you should not rush its production.

If your department requires you to write an interim report, look on this as an opportunity to clarify your thoughts and get some of the time-consuming preparative work out of the way. If not, you should set your own deadlines for producing drafts of the introduction, materials and methods section, etc.

Project work can be very time-consuming at times. Try not to neglect other aspects of your course – make sure your lecture notes are up-to-date and collect relevant supporting information as you go along.

The Internet as an information source – since many university departments have home pages on the World Wide Web, searches using relevant key words may indicate where research in your area is currently being carried out. Academics usually respond positively to e-mailed questions about their area of expertise.

Asking around – one of the best sources of information about supervisors, laboratories and projects is past students. Some of the postgraduates in your department may be products of your own system and they could provide an alternative source of advice.

Liaising with your supervisor(s) – this is essential if your work is to proceed efficiently. Specific meetings may be timetabled, e.g. to discuss a term's progress, review your work plan or consider a draft introduction. Most supervisors also have an 'open-door' policy, allowing you to air current problems. Prepare well for all meetings: have a list of questions ready before the meeting; provide results in an easily digestible form (but take your lab notebook along); be clear about your future plans for work.

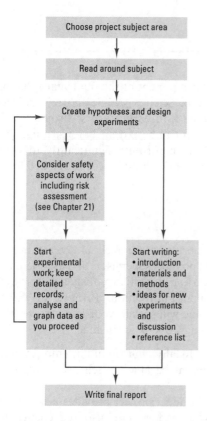

Fig. 31.1 Flowchart showing a recommended sequence of events in carrying out an undergraduate research project.

Getting started

Figure 31.1 is a flowchart illustrating how a project might proceed; at the start, don't spend too long reading the literature and working out a lengthy programme of research. Get stuck in and do an experiment. There's no substitute for 'getting your hands dirty' for stimulating new ideas:

- even a 'failed' experiment will provide some useful information which may allow you to create a new or modified hypothesis;
- pilot experiments may point out deficiencies in experimental technique that will need to be rectified;
- the experience will help you create a realistic plan of work.

Designing experiments or sampling procedures

Design of experiments and sampling procedure is covered in Chapter 30. Avoid being too ambitious at the start of your work. It is generally best to work with a simple hypothesis and design your experiments or sampling around this. A small pilot experiment or test sample will highlight potential stumbling blocks including resource limitations, whether in materials, or time, or both.

Working in a laboratory environment

During your time as a project student, you are effectively a guest in your supervisor's laboratory.

- Be considerate – keep your 'area' tidy and offer to do your share of lab duties such as calibrating the pH meter, replenishing stock solutions, distilled water, etc., maintaining cultures, tending plants or animals.
- Use instruments carefully – they could be worth more than you'd think. Careless use may invalidate calibration settings and ruin other people's work as well as your own.
- Do your homework on techniques you intend to use – there's less chance of making costly mistakes if you have a good background understanding of the methods you will be using.
- Always seek advice if you are unsure of what you are doing.

KEY POINT It is essential that you follow all the safety rules applying to the laboratory or field site. Make sure you know all relevant procedures – normally there will be prominent warnings about these. If in doubt, ask.

Keeping notes and analysing your results

Tidy record keeping is often associated with good research, and you should follow the advice and hints given in detail within Chapter 28. Try to keep copies of all files relating to your project. As you obtain results, you should always calculate, analyse and graph data as soon as you can (see Fig. 31.1). This can reveal aspects that may not be obvious in numerical or readout form. Don't be worried by negative results – these can sometimes be as useful as positive results if they allow you to eliminate hypotheses – and don't be too dispirited if things do not work first time. Thomas Edison's maxim 'Genius is one per cent inspiration and ninety-nine per cent perspiration' certainly applies to research work.

Writing your project report

The structure of scientific reports is dealt with in Chapter 18. The following advice concerns methods of accumulating relevant information.

Introduction This is a big piece of writing that can be very time-consuming. Therefore, the more work you can do on it early on, the better. You should allocate some time at the start for library work (without neglecting your lab work), so that you can build up a database of references (Chapter 8). While photocopying can be expensive, you will find it valuable to have copies of key reviews and references handy when writing away from the library. Discuss proposals for content and structure with your supervisor to make sure your effort is relevant. Leave space at the end for a section on aims and objectives. This is important to orientate readers (including assessors), but you may prefer to finalise the content after the results have been analysed.

Materials and methods You should note as many details as possible *when doing the experiment or making observations*. Don't rely on your memory or hope that the information will still be available when you come to write up. Even if it is, chasing these details can waste valuable time.

Results Show your supervisor graphed and tabulated versions of your data promptly. These can easily be produced using a spreadsheet (p. 68), but you should seek your supervisor's advice on whether the design and print quality is appropriate to be included in your report. You may wish to use a specialist graphics program to produce publishable-quality graphs and charts: allow some time for learning its idiosyncrasies. If you are producing a poster for assessment (Chapter 14), be sure to mock up the design well in advance. Similarly, think ahead about your needs for any seminar or poster you will present.

Discussion Because this comes at the end of your report, and some parts can only be written after you have all the results in place, the temptation is to leave the discussion to last. This means that it might be rushed – not a good idea because of the weight attached by assessors to your analysis of data and thoughts about future experiments. It will help greatly if you keep notes of aims, conclusions and ideas for future work as you go along (Fig. 31.1). Another useful tip is to make notes of comparable data and conclusions from the literature as you read papers and reviews.

Acknowledgements Make a special place in your notebook for noting all those who have helped you carry out the work, for use when writing this section of the report.

References Because of the complex formats involved (p. 44), these can be tricky to type. To save time, process them in batches as you go along.

> **KEY POINT** Make sure you are absolutely certain about the deadline for submitting your report and work towards submitting a day or so before it. If you leave things until the last moment, you may find access to printers, photocopiers and binding machines is difficult.

Brushing up on your IT skills – word processors and spreadsheets are extremely useful when producing a thesis. Chapters 12 and 13 detail key features of these programs. You might benefit from attending courses on the relevant programs or studying manuals or texts so that you can use them more efficiently.

Using drawings and photographs – these can provide valuable records of sampling sites or experimental set-ups and could be useful in your report. Plan ahead and do the relevant work at the time of carrying out your research rather than afterwards.

Sources for further study

Luck, M. (1999) *Your Student Research Project*. Gower, London.

Marshall, P. (1997) *Research Methods: How to Design & Conduct a Successful Project*. How To Books, Plymouth.

Study exercises

Note: These exercises assume that you have started a research project, or are about to start one, as part of your studies.

31.1 Prepare a project plan. Make a formal plan for your research project, incorporating any milestones dictated by your department, such as interim reports and final submission dates. Discuss your plan with your supervisor and incorporate his or her comments. Refer back to the plan frequently during your project, to see how well you are meeting your deadlines.

31.2 Resolve to write up your work as you go along. Each time you complete an experiment or observation, write up the materials and methods, analyse the data and draw up the graphs as soon as you can. While you may reject some of your work at a later stage, you may wish to modify it; this will spread out the majority of the effort and allow time for critical thinking close to the final submission date.

31.3 Devise a computer database or card-index system for keeping details of your references. Keeping these records up-to-date will save you a lot of time when writing up. You will need to decide on an appropriate format, or find out about that followed by your department.

Handling cells and tissues

Sterile technique and microbial culture

Achieving a sterile state – you should assume that all items of laboratory equipment have contaminating microbes on their surfaces, unless they have been destroyed by some form of sterilisation. Such items will only remain sterile if they do not come into contact with the non-sterile environment.

Sterile technique (aseptic technique) is the name given to the procedures used in cell culture. While the same general principles apply to all cell types, you are most likely to learn the basic procedures using bacteria and most of the examples given in this section refer to bacterial culture.

Sterile technique serves two main purposes:

1. To prevent accidental contamination of laboratory cultures due to microbes from external sources, e.g. skin, clothing or the surrounding environment.
2. To prevent microbial contamination of laboratory workers, in this instance you and your fellow students.

KEY POINT *All* microbial cell cultures should be treated as if they contained potentially harmful organisms. Sterile technique forms an important part of safety procedures, and must be followed whenever cell cultures are handled in the laboratory.

Care is required because:

- You may accidentally isolate a harmful microbe as a contaminant when culturing a relatively harmless strain.
- Some individuals are more susceptible to infection and disease than others – not everyone exposed to a particular microbe will become ill.
- Laboratory culture involves purifying and growing large numbers of microbial cells – this represents a greater risk than small numbers of the original microbe.
- A microbe may change its characteristics, perhaps as a result of gene exchange or mutation.

Fig. 32.1 International symbol for a biohazard. Usually red on a yellow background, or black on a red background.

The international biohazard symbol, shown in Fig. 32.1, is used to indicate a significant risk due to a pathogenic microbe (pp. 199–200).

Sterilisation procedures

Given the ubiquity of microbes, the only way to achieve a sterile state is by their destruction or removal. Several methods can be used to achieve this objective:

Heat treatment
This is the most widespread form of sterilisation and is used in several basic laboratory procedures including the following:

- Red heat sterilisation. Achieved by heating metal inoculating loops, forceps, needles, etc., in a Bunsen flame (Fig. 32.2). This is a simple and effective form of sterilisation as no microbe will survive even a brief exposure to a naked flame. Flame sterilisation using alcohol is used for glass rods and spreaders (see below).
- Dry heat sterilisation. Here, a hot air oven is used at a temperature of at least 160 °C for at least 2 h. This method is used for the routine sterilisation of laboratory glassware. Dry heat procedures are of little value for items requiring repeated sterilisation during use.

loop handle

wire

Bunsen burner

Fig. 32.2 'Flaming' a wire loop. Keep the loop in the hottest part of the Bunsen flame (just outside the blue 'cone') until the wire is red hot.

• Moist heat sterilisation. This is the method of choice for many laboratory items, including most fluids, apart from heat-sensitive media. It is also used to decontaminate liquid media and glassware after use. The laboratory autoclave is used for these purposes. Typically, most items will be sterile after 15 min at 121 °C, although large items may require a longer period. The rapid killing action results from the latent heat of condensation of the pressurised steam, released on contact with cool materials in the autoclave.

Radiation

Many disposable plastic items used in microbiology and cell biology are sterilised by exposure to UV or ionising radiation. They are supplied commercially in sterile packages, ready for use. Ultraviolet radiation has limited use in the laboratory, while ionising radiation (e.g. γ-rays) requires industrial facilities and cannot be operated on a laboratory scale.

Filtration

Heat-labile solutions (e.g. complex macromolecules, including proteins, antibiotics, serum) are particularly suited to this form of sterilisation. The filters come in a variety of shapes, sizes and materials, usually with a pore size of either 0.2 or 0.45 μm. The filtration apparatus and associated equipment are usually sterilised by autoclaving, or by dry heat. Passage of liquid through a sterile filter of pore size 0.2 μm into a sterile vessel is usually sufficient to remove bacteria but not viruses, so filtered liquids are not necessarily virus-free.

Chemical agents

These are known as disinfectants, or biocides, and are most often used for the disposal of contaminated items following laboratory use, e.g. glass slides and pipettes. They are also used to treat spillages. The term 'disinfection' implies destruction of disease-causing bacterial cells, although spores and viruses may not always be destroyed. Remember that disinfectants require time to exert their killing effect – any spillage should be covered with an appropriate disinfectant and left for at least 10 min before mopping up.

Use of laboratory equipment

Working area

One of the most important aspects of good sterile technique is to keep your working area as clean and tidy as possible. Start by clearing all items from your working surface, wipe the bench down with disinfectant and then arrange the items you need for a particular procedure so that they are close at hand, leaving a clear working space in the centre of your bench.

Media

Cells may be cultured in either a liquid medium (broth), or a solidified medium (p. 225). The gelling agent used in most solidified media is agar, a complex polysaccharide from red algae that produces a stiff transparent gel when used at 1–2% (w/v). Agar is used because it is relatively resistant to degradation by most bacteria and because of its rheological properties – an agar medium melts at 98 °C, remaining solid at all temperatures used for routine laboratory culture. However, once melted, it does not solidify

Using a sterile filter – most filters are supplied as pre-sterilised items. Make sure you follow a procedure that does not contaminate the filter on removal from its protective wrapping.

Using molten agar – a water bath (at 45–50°C) can be used to keep an agar-based medium in its molten state after autoclaving. Always dry the outside of the container on removal from the water bath, to reduce the risk of contamination from microbes in the water, e.g. during pour plating (p. 201).

again until the temperature falls to about 44 °C. This means that heat-sensitive constituents (e.g. vitamins, blood, cells) can be added aseptically to the medium after autoclaving.

Inoculating loops

The initial isolation and subsequent transfer of microbes between containers can be achieved using a sterile inoculating loop. Most teaching laboratories use nichrome wire loops in a metal handle. A wire loop can be repeatedly sterilised by heating the wire, loop downwards and almost vertical, in the hottest part of a Bunsen flame until the whole wire becomes red hot. Then the loop is removed from the flame to minimise heat transfer to the handle. After cooling for 8–10 s (without touching any other object), it is ready for use.

When resterilising a contaminated wire loop in a Bunsen flame after use, do not heat the loop too rapidly, as the sample may spatter, creating an aerosol: it is better to soak the loop for a few minutes in disinfectant than to risk heating a fully charged (contaminated) inoculating loop.

Containers

There is a risk of contamination whenever a sterile bottle, flask or test tube is opened. One method that reduces the chance of airborne contamination is quickly to pass the open mouth of the glass vessel through a flame. This destroys any microbes on the outer surfaces nearest to the mouth of the vessel. In addition, by heating the air within the neck of the vessel, an outwardly directed air flow is established, reducing the likelihood of microbial contamination.

It is general practice to flame the mouth of each vessel immediately after opening and then repeat the procedure just before replacing the top. Caps, lids and cotton wool plugs must not be placed on the bench during flaming and sampling: they should be removed and held using the smallest finger of one hand, to minimise the risk of contamination. This also leaves the remaining fingers free to carry out other manipulations. With practice, it is possible to remove the tops from two tubes, flame each tube and transfer material from one to the other while holding one top in each hand.

Laminar flow cabinets

These are designed to prevent airborne contamination, e.g. when preparing media or subculturing microbes or tissue cultures. Sterile air is produced by passage through a high efficiency particulate air (HEPA) filter: this is then directed over the working area, either horizontally (towards the operator) or downwards. The operator handles specimens, media, etc., through an opening at the front of the cabinet. Standard laminar flow cabinets do *not* protect the worker from contamination and must not be used with pathogenic microbes: special safety cabinets and laboratories are used for work with ACDP hazard group 3 and 4 microbes (Table 32.1) and for samples that might contain such pathogens.

Microbiological hazards

KEY POINT The most obvious risks when handling microbial cultures are those due to ingestion or entry via a cut in the skin – all cuts should be covered with a plaster or disposable plastic gloves. A less

---

Working with plastic disposable loops – these are used in many research laboratories: pre-sterilised and suitable for single use, they avoid the hazards of naked flames and the risk of aerosol formation during heating. Discard into a disinfectant solution after use.

Using glass pipettes – these are plugged with cotton wool at the top before being autoclaved inside a metal can. Flame the open end of the can on removal of a pipette, to prevent contamination of the remaining pipettes. Autopipettors and sterile disposable tips (p. 123) offer an alternative approach.

Using a Bunsen burner to reduce airborne contamination – working close to the updraught created by a Bunsen flame reduces the likelihood of particles falling from the air into an open vessel.

Table 32.1 Classification of microbes on the basis of hazard. The following categories are recommended by the UK Advisory Committee on Dangerous Pathogens (ACDP)

Hazard group	Comments
1	Unlikely to cause human disease
2	May cause disease: possible hazard to laboratory workers, minimal hazard to community
3	May cause severe disease: may be a serious hazard to laboratory workers, may spread to community
4	Causes severe disease: is a serious hazard to laboratory workers, high risk to community

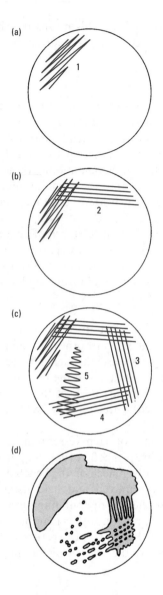

Fig. 32.3 Preparation of a streak plate for single colonies. (a) Using a sterile metal loop, take a small sample of the material to be streaked. Distribute the sample over a small sector of the plate (area 1), then flame the loop and allow to cool (approximately 8–10 s). (b) Make several small streaks from the initial sector into the adjacent sector (area 2), taking care not to allow the streaks to overlap. Flame the loop and allow to cool. (c) Repeat the procedure for areas 3 and 4, resterilising the loop between each step. Finally, make a single, long streak, as shown for area 5. (d) The expected result after incubation at the appropriate temperature (e.g. 37 °C for 24 h): each step should have diluted the inoculum, giving individual colonies within one or more sectors on the plate. Further subculture of an individual colony should give a pure (clonal) culture.

obvious source of hazard is the formation of aerosols of liquid droplets from microbial suspensions, with the risk of inhalation, or surface contamination of other objects.

The following steps will minimise the risk of aerosol formation:

- Use stoppered tubes when shaking, centrifuging or mixing microbial suspensions.
- Pour solutions gently, keeping the difference in height to a minimum.
- Discharge pipettes onto the side of the container.

Other general rules which apply in all laboratories include:

- Take care with sharp instruments, including needles and glass Pasteur pipettes.
- Do not pour waste cultures down the sink – they must be autoclaved.
- Put other contaminated items (e.g. slides, pipettes) into disinfectant after use.
- Wipe down your bench with disinfectant when practical work is complete.
- Always wash your hands before leaving the laboratory.

Plating methods

Many culture methods make use of a solidified medium within a Petri plate. A variety of techniques can be used to transfer and distribute the organisms prior to incubation. The three most important procedures are described below.

Streak dilution plate

Streaking a plate for single colonies is one of the most important basic skills in microbiology, since it is used in the initial isolation of a cell culture and in maintaining stock cultures, where a streak dilution plate with single colonies all of the same type confirms the purity of the strain. A sterile inoculating loop is used to streak the organisms over the surface of the medium, thereby diluting the sample (Fig. 32.3). The aim is to achieve single colonies at some point on the plate: ideally, such colonies are derived from single cells (e.g. in the case of unicellular bacteria, animal and plant cell lines) or from groups of cells of the same species (in filamentous or colonial forms). Single colonies, containing cells of a single species and derived from a single parental cell, form the basis of most pure culture methods (p. 206).

Note the following:

- Keep the lid of the Petri plate as close to the base as possible to reduce the risk of aerial contamination.
- Allow the loop to glide over the surface of the medium. Hold the handle at the balance point (near the centre) and use light, sweeping movements, as the agar surface is easily damaged and torn.
- Work quickly, but carefully. Do not breathe directly onto the exposed agar surface and replace the lid as soon as possible.

Spread plate

This method is used with cells in suspension, either in a liquid growth medium or in an appropriate sterile diluent. It is one method of quantifying the number of viable cells (or colony-forming units) in a sample, after appropriate dilution (p. 131).

An L-shaped glass spreader is sterilised by dipping the end of the spreader in a beaker containing a small amount of 70% v/v alcohol, allowing the excess to drain from the spreader and then igniting the remainder in a Bunsen flame. After cooling, the spreader is used to distribute a known volume of cell suspension across the plate (Fig. 32.4). *There is a significant fire risk associated with this technique,* so take care not to ignite the alcohol in the beaker, e.g. by returning an overheated glass rod to the beaker. The alcohol will burn with a pale blue flame that may be difficult to see, but will readily ignite other materials (e.g. a laboratory coat). Another source of risk comes from small droplets of flaming alcohol shed by an overloaded spreader onto the bench and this is why you *must* drain excess alcohol from the spreader *before* flaming. Some laboratories now provide plastic disposable spreaders for student use, to avoid the risk of fire.

Pour plate

This procedure also uses cells in suspension, but requires molten agar medium, usually in screw-capped bottles containing sufficient medium to prepare a single Petri plate (i.e. 15–20 ml), maintained in a water bath at 45–50 °C. A known volume of cell suspension is mixed with this molten agar, distributing the cells throughout the medium. This is then poured without delay into an empty sterile Petri plate and incubated, giving widely spaced colonies (Fig. 32.5). Furthermore, as most of the colonies are formed within the medium, they are far smaller than those of the surface streak method, allowing higher cell numbers to be counted (e.g. over 100 colonies per plate): some workers pour a thin layer of molten agar onto the surface of a pour plate after it has set, to ensure that no surface colonies are produced. Most bacteria and fungi are not killed by brief exposure to temperatures of 45–50 °C, though the procedure may be more damaging to microbes from low temperature conditions, e.g. psychrophilic bacteria.

One disadvantage of the pour plate method is that the typical colony morphology seen in surface-grown cultures will not be observed for those colonies that develop within the agar medium. A further disadvantage is that some of the suspension will be left behind in the screw-capped bottle. This can be avoided by transferring the suspension to the Petri plate, adding the molten agar, then swirling the plate to mix the two liquids. However, even when the plate is swirled repeatedly and in several directions, the liquids are not mixed as evenly as in the former procedure.

Working with molten agar – keep tubes and bottles of molten agar in the water bath until you are ready to use them, as they will begin to set within a couple of minutes at room temperature.

(a) (b) (c) (d)

Fig. 32.4 Preparation of a spread plate. (a) Transfer a small volume of cell suspension (0.05–0.5 ml) to the surface of a solidified medium in a Petri plate. (b) Flame sterilise a glass spreader and allow to cool (8–10 s). (c) Distribute the liquid over the surface of the plate using the sterile spreader. Make sure of an even coverage by rotating the plate as you spread: allow the liquid to be absorbed into the agar medium. Incubate under suitable conditions. (d) After incubation, the microbial colonies should be distributed over the surface of the plate.

(a)   (b)   (c)   (d)

Fig. 32.5 Preparation of a pour plate. (a) Add a known volume of cell suspension (0.05–1.0 ml) to a small bottle of molten agar medium from a 45 °C water bath. (b) Mix thoroughly, by rotating between the palms of the hands: do not shake or this will cause frothing of the medium. (c) Pour the mixture into an empty, sterile Petri plate and allow to set. Incubate under suitable conditions. (d) After incubation, the microbial colonies will be distributed throughout the medium: any cells deposited at the surface will give larger, spreading colonies.

Working with phages

Bacterial viruses ('bacteriophages', or simply 'phages') are often used to illustrate the general principles involved in the detection and enumeration of viruses. They also have a role in genome mapping of bacteria. Individual phage particles (virions) are too small to be seen by light microscopy, but are detected by their effects on susceptible host cells:

- Virulent phages will infect and replicate within actively growing host cells, causing cell lysis and releasing new infective phages – this 'lytic cycle' takes ≈30 min for T-even phages of *E. coli*, e.g. T4.
- Temperate phages are a specialised group, capable either of lytic growth or an alternative cycle, termed lysogeny – the phage becomes latent within a host cell (lysogen), typically by insertion of its genetic information into the host cell genome, becoming a 'prophage'. At a later stage, termed induction, the prophage may enter the lytic cycle. A widely used example is λ phage of *E. coli*.

The lytic cycle can be used to detect and quantify the number of phages in a sample. A known volume of sample is mixed with susceptible bacterial cells in molten soft agar medium (45–50 °C), then poured on top of a plate of the same medium, creating a thin layer of 'top agar'. The upper layer contains only half the normal amount of agar, to allow phages to diffuse through the medium and attach to susceptible cells. On incubation, the bacteria will grow throughout the agar to produce a homogeneous 'lawn' of cells, except in those parts of the plate where a phage particle has infected and lysed the cells to create a clear area, termed a plaque (Fig. 32.6). Each plaque is due to a single functional phage (i.e. a plaque-forming unit, or PFU). A count of the number of plaques can be used to give the number of phages in a particular sample (e.g. as $PFU\,ml^{-1}$), with appropriate correction for dilution and the volume of sample counted in an analogous manner to a bacterial plate count (p. 230). When counting plaques in phage assays you should view them against a black background to make them easier to see: mark each plaque with a spirit-based marker to ensure an accurate count. Temperate phages often produce cloudy plaques, because many of the infected cells will be lysogenised rather than lysed, creating turbidity within the plaque. Samples of material from within the plaque can be used to subculture the phage for further study,

(a) surface view

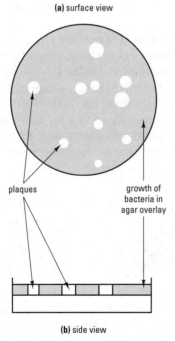

plaques   growth of bacteria in agar overlay

(b) side view

Fig. 32.6 Phage plaques in a 'lawn' of susceptible host bacterium.

perhaps in a broth culture where the phages will cause widespread cell lysis and a decrease in turbidity. Alternatively, phages can be stored by adding chloroform to aqueous suspensions – this will prevent contamination by cellular micro-organisms. A similar approach can be used to detect and count animal or human viruses, using a monolayer of a susceptible animal or human cells.

Electron microscopy (EM, p. 154) provides an alternative approach to the detection of viruses, avoiding the requirement for culture of infected host cells, and giving a faster result. However, it requires access to specialised equipment and expertise. EM counts are often higher than culture-based methods, for similar reasons to those described for bacteria (p. 230).

Labelling your plates and cultures

Petri plates should always be labelled on the *base*, rather than the lid, using a permanent marker. Restrict your labelling to the outermost region of the plate, to avoid problems when counting colonies, assessing growth, etc. After labelling, Petri plates usually are incubated upside-down in a temperature-controlled incubator (often at 37 °C) for an appropriate period (usually 18–72 h).

Labelling Petri plates – the following information should be recorded:

- *date*
- *the growth medium*
- *your name or initials*
- *brief details of the organism, experimental treatment, etc.*

Sources for further study

Anon. (1995) *Advisory Committee on Dangerous Pathogens: Categorisation of Biological Agents According to Hazard and Categories of Containment*, 4th edn. HSE Books, London.

Bartelt, M.A. (1999) *Diagnostic Bacteriology: A Study Guide*. Davis, New York.

Collins, C.H., Lyne, P.M. and Grange, J.M. (1995) *Collins and Lyne's Microbiological Methods*, 7th edn. Oxford University Press, Oxford.

Isenberg, H.D. (1998) *Essential Procedures for Clinical Microbiology*. American Society for Microbiology, Washington, DC.

Rhodes, P.M. and Stanbury, P.F. (1997) *Applied Microbial Physiology: a Practical Approach*. IRL Press, Oxford.

Study exercises

32.1 Check that you understand how to label a plate culture. List the key aspects and then compare your list against the one provided on p. 506.

32.2 Decide on the best method of sterilisation. What would be the most appropriate method of sterilisation for the following items?
(a) A box of 100 plastic tips to be used with a pipettor.
(b) A 50 ml batch of blood, for use in 5% v/v blood agar plates.
(c) A 1 litre batch of MacConkey agar.
(d) Ten 5 ml glass pipettes.
(e) A microbiological wire, used for 'stab' cultures.

(f) A 10 ml sample of a heat-sensitive solution of an antibiotic, to be used as a component of a selective agar-based medium for the isolation of a particular bacterium.

32.3 Find out the biohazard classification (UK ACDP categorisation – Table 32.1) for the following microbes:
(a) *Salmonella typhimurium*
(b) *Leptospira interrogans*
(c) *Shigella dysenteriae* (type 1)
(d) *E. coli* K12
(e) *E. coli* O157
(f) Human immunodeficiency virus (HIV)
(g) *Cryptococcus neoformans* var. *neoformans*
(h) *Mycobacterium tuberculosis*
(i) *Lactobacillus plantarum*
(j) Marburg virus.

32.4 Consider the advantages and disadvantages of spread plating and pour plating methods. Having read through this chapter, list up to six pros/cons of each plating method and compare your answers either with the list we have provided on pp. 506–7, or with those of other students, as a group exercise.

Isolating and identifying microbes

Micro-organisms have a broad range of applications in the life sciences:

- Microbes are widely used as model systems, as they are often easier to study under controlled laboratory conditions than 'higher' organisms.
- Bacteria and fungi are used as sources of particular biomolecules, e.g. for the characterisation of a specific enzyme *in vitro*.
- Pathogenic microbes are studied at the molecular level, to find new methods of identification using biochemical 'markers' and to investigate the molecular basis of their pathogenicity.
- Microbes are used in biotechnology and industrial microbiology as sources of particular biomolecules, e.g. production of blood-clotting factors using yeast cells.

In your practical classes, you are likely to gain experience of a wide range of laboratory exercises involving microbes, particularly bacteria such as *Escherichia coli* (*E. coli*), using the procedures of sterile technique described in Chapter 32.

Sampling microbes

Microbes can be studied by taking samples for analysis, usually in one of the following ways:

- by direct examination of individual cells of a particular microbe, e.g. using fluorescence microscopy (pp. 154–8);
- by isolating/purifying a particular species or related individuals of a taxonomic group, e.g. the faecal indicator bacterium *E. coli* in sea water;
- by studying microbial processes, rather than individual microbes, either *in situ*, or in the laboratory.

Sampling techniques include the use of swabs, Sellotape strips and agar contact methods for sampling surfaces, bottles for aquatic habitats, plastic bags and corers for soils and sediments. A wide range of complex apparatus is available for accurately sampling water or soil at particular depths.

Avoiding contamination during sampling – always remember that you are the most important source of contamination of field samples: components of the oral or skin microflora are the most likely contaminants.

KEY POINT An important feature of all sampling protocols is that the sampling apparatus must be sterile; strict aseptic technique must be used throughout the sampling process.

The sampling method must minimise the chance of contamination with microbes from other sources, especially the exterior of the sampling apparatus and the operator. For example, if you are sampling an aquatic habitat, stand downstream of the sampling site. A portable Bunsen burner or spirit lamp can be used to enable sterile technique during field sampling.

Process the sample as quickly as possible, to minimise any changes in microbiological status. As a general guideline, many procedures require samples to be analysed within 6 h of collection. Changes in aeration, pH

Subsampling – to minimise the effects of changes in temperature, aeration and water status during transportation, a primary sample may be returned to the laboratory, where the working sample (subsample) is then taken (e.g. from the centre of a large block of soil).

and water content may occur after collection. Some microbes are more susceptible to such effects, e.g. anaerobic bacteria may not survive if the sample is exposed to air.

Soil and water samples are often kept cool (at $0-5\,°C$) during transport to the laboratory. In contrast, microbes adapted to grow in association with warm-blooded animals may be damaged by low temperatures. An alternative approach is to keep the sample near the ambient sampling temperature using an insulated vessel (e.g. Thermos flask).

Isolating a particular microbe

Several different approaches may be used to obtain microbes in pure culture. The choice of method will depend upon the microbe to be isolated: some organisms are relatively easy to isolate, while others require more involved procedures.

Separation methods

Most microbial isolation procedures involve some form of separation to obtain individual microbial cells. The most common approach is to use an agar-based medium for primary isolation, with streak dilution, spread plating or pour plating to produce single colonies, each derived from an individual micro-organism (pp. 201–2). It is often necessary to dilute samples before isolation, so that a small number of individual microbial cells are transferred to the growth medium. Strict serial dilution (pp. 131–3) of a known amount of sample is needed for quantitative work.

Obtaining a pure culture – if a single colony from a primary isolation medium is used to prepare a streak dilution plate and all the colonies on the second plate appear identical, then a pure culture has been established. Otherwise, you cannot assume that your culture is pure.

KEY POINT If your aim is to isolate a particular microbe, perhaps for further investigation, you will need to subculture individual colonies from the primary isolation plate to establish a pure culture, also known as an axenic culture.

Pure cultures of most microbes can be maintained indefinitely, using sterile technique and microbial culture methods (Chapter 32).

Other separation techniques include:

Using a sonicator – minimise heat damage with short treatment 'bursts' (typically up to 1 min), cooling the sample between bursts.

- Dilution to extinction. This involves diluting the sample to such an extent that only one or two microbes are present per millilitre: small volumes of this dilution are then transferred to a liquid growth medium. After incubation, most of the tubes will show no growth, but some tubes may show growth, having been inoculated with a single viable microbe at the outset. This should give a pure culture, though it is wasteful of resources.

Definitions

Psychrophile – a microbe with an optimum temperature for growth of $<20\,°C$ (literally 'cold-loving').

Psychrotroph – a microbe with an optimum temperature for growth of $\geqslant 20\,°C$, but capable of growing at lower temperature, typically $0-5\,°C$ (literally 'cold-feeding').

Thermophile – a microbe with an optimum growth temperature of $>45\,°C$ (literally 'heat-loving').

Mesophile – a microbe with an optimum growth temperature of $20-45\,°C$ (literally 'middle-loving').

- Sonication/homogenisation. Useful for separating individual microbial cells from each other and from inert particles, prior to isolation. However, some decrease in viability is likely.
- Filtration. This can be useful where the number of microbes is low. Samples can be passed through a sterile cellulose ester filter (pore size $0.2\,\mu m$), which is then incubated on the surface of an appropriate solidified medium. Sieving and filtration techniques (p. 133) are often used in soil microbiology to subdivide a sample on the basis of particle size.
- Micromanipulation. It may be possible to separate the microbe from contaminants using a micropipette and dissecting microscope. The microbe can then be transferred to an appropriate growth medium,

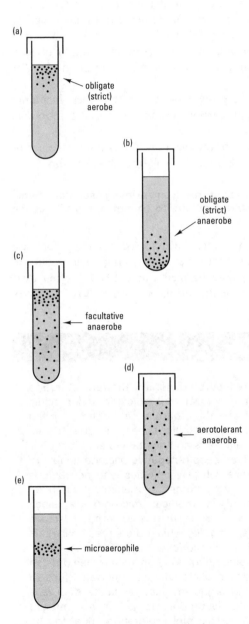

(a) obligate (strict) aerobe

(b) obligate (strict) anaerobe

(c) facultative anaerobe

(d) aerotolerant anaerobe

(e) microaerophile

Fig. 33.1 Agar shake tubes. Bacteria are suspended in molten agar at 45–50 °C and allowed to cool. The growth pattern after incubation reflects the atmospheric (oxygen) requirements of the bacterium.

to give a pure culture. However, this is rarely an easy task for the novice.

- Motility. Phototactic microbes (including photosynthetic flagellates and motile cyanobacteria) will move towards a light source, while heterotrophic flagellate bacteria will move through a filter of appropriate pore size into a nutrient solution, or away from unfavourable conditions.

Selective and enrichment methods

Selective methods are based on the use of conditions that will permit the growth of a particular group of microbes while inhibiting others. Laboratory incubation under selective conditions will allow the particular microbes to be isolated in pure culture. Enrichment techniques encourage the growth of certain bacteria, usually by providing additional nutrients in the growth medium. The difference between selective and enrichment techniques is that the former use growth conditions unfavourable for competitors while the latter provide improved growth conditions for the chosen microbes.

Selective and enrichment techniques can be considered together, since they both enhance the growth of a particular microbe when compared with its competitors. Methods based on specific physical conditions include:

- Temperature. Psychrophilic and psychrotrophic microbes can be isolated by incubating the growth medium at 4 °C, while thermophilic microbes require temperatures above 45 °C for isolation. Short-term heat treatment of samples can be used to select for endospore-forming bacteria, e.g. 70–80 °C for 5–15 min, prior to isolation.
- Atmosphere. Many eukaryotic microbes are obligate aerobes, requiring an adequate supply of oxygen to grow. Bacteria vary in their responses to oxygen: obligate anaerobes are the most demanding, growing only under anaerobic conditions (e.g. in an anaerobic cabinet or jar). Oxygen requirements can be determined using the agar shake tube method as part of the isolation procedure (Fig. 33.1). Some pathogenic bacteria grow best in an atmosphere with a reduced oxygen status and increased CO_2 concentration: such carboxyphilic bacteria (capnophiles) are grown in an incubator where the gas composition can be adjusted.
- Centrifugation. This can be used to separate buoyant microbes from their non-buoyant counterparts – on centrifugation, such organisms will collect at the surface while the remaining microbes will sediment. Alternatively, density gradient methods may be used (p. 290). Centrifugation can be combined with repeated washing, to separate microbes from contaminants.
- Ultraviolet irradiation. Some microbes are tolerant of UV treatment and can be selected by exposing samples to UV light. However, the survivors may show a greater rate of mutation.
- Illumination. Samples may be enriched for cyanobacteria and microalgae by incubation under a suitable light regime. For dilute samples, where the number of photosynthetic microbes is too low to give the sample any visible green coloration, there is a risk of photoinhibition and loss of viability if the irradiance is too high. Such samples need shading during initial growth.

Chemical methods form the mainstay of bacteriological isolation techniques and various media have been developed for the isolation of specific groups of bacteria. The chemicals involved can be subdivided into the following groups:

- Selectively toxic substances: for example, salt-tolerant, Gram-positive cocci can be grown in a medium containing 7.5% w/v NaCl, which prevents the growth of most common heterotrophic bacteria. Several media include dyes as selective agents, particularly against Gram-positive bacteria.
- Antibiotics: for example, the use of antibacterial agents (penicillin, streptomycin, chloramphenicol) in media designed to isolate fungi, or the use of antifungal agents (cycloheximide, nystatin) in bacterial media. Some antibacterial agents show a narrow spectrum of toxicity and these can be incorporated into selective isolation media for resistant bacteria.
- Nutrients that encourage the growth of certain microbes: including the addition of a particular carbon source, or specific inorganic nutrients.
- Substances that affect the pH of the medium: for example, the use of alkaline peptone water at pH 8.6 for the isolation of *Vibrio* spp.

Example Slow-growing *Legionella pneumophila* can be isolated from water samples using media containing the antibiotics vancomycin, polymyxin and cycloheximide, to suppress other microbes.

KEY POINT Note that subcultures from primary isolation media must be grown in a non-selective medium, to confirm the purity of the isolate.

Many of the selective and enrichment media used in bacteriology are able to distinguish between different types of bacteria: such media are termed differential media or diagnostic media and they are often used in the preliminary stages of an identification procedure. Box 33.1 gives

Box 33.1 Differential media for bacterial isolation: an example

MacConkey agar is both a selective and a differential medium, useful for the isolation and identification of intestinal Gram-negative bacteria. Each component in the medium has a particular role:

- **Peptone:** (a meat digest) provides a rich source of complex organic nutrients, to support the growth of non-exacting bacteria.
- **Bile salts:** toxic to most microbes apart from those growing in the intestinal tract.
- **Lactose:** present as an additional, specific carbon source.
- **Neutral red:** a pH indicator dye, to show the decrease in pH which accompanies the breakdown of lactose.
- **Crystal violet:** selectively inhibits the growth of Gram-positive bacteria. (This component is only present in certain formations.)

Any intestinal Gram-negative bacterium capable of fermenting lactose will grow on MacConkey agar to produce large red–purple colonies, the red coloration being due to the neutral red indicator under acidic conditions while the purple coloration, often accompanied by a metallic sheen, is due to the precipitation of bile salts and crystal violet at low pH.

In contrast, enteric Gram-negative bacteria unable to metabolise lactose will give colonies with no obvious pigmentation. This differential medium has been particularly useful in medical microbiology, since many enteric bacteria are unable to ferment lactose (e.g. *Salmonella*, *Shigella*) while others metabolise this carbohydrate (e.g. *Escherichia coli*, *Klebsiella* spp.). Colonial morphology (Fig. 33.2) on such a medium can give an experienced bacteriologist important clues to the identity of an organism, e.g. capsulate *Klebsiella* spp. characteristically produce large, convex, mucoid colonies with a weak pink coloration, due to the fermentation of lactose, while *E. coli* produces smaller, flattened colonies with a stronger red coloration and a metallic sheen.

Table 33.1 Selective agents in bacteriological media

Substance	Selective for
Azide salts	*Enterococcus* spp.
Bile salts	Intestinal bacteria
Brilliant green	Gram-negative bacteria
Gentian violet	Gram-negative bacteria
Lauryl sulphate	Gram-negative bacteria
Methyl violet	*Vibrio* spp.
Malachite green	*Mycobacterium*
Polymyxin	*Bacillus* spp.
Sodium selenite	*Salmonella* spp.
Sodium chloride	Halotolerant bacteria *Staphylococcus aureus*
Sodium tetrathionate	*Salmonella* spp.
Trypan blue	*Streptococcus* spp.

details of the constituents of MacConkey medium, a selective, differential medium used in clinical microbiology (e.g. for the isolation of certain faecal bacteria), while Table 33.1 gives details of selective agents used.

Further details on methods can be found in Gerhardt (1994), Collins *et al.* (1995) or Hurst *et al.* (2002). Note that isolation procedures for a particular microbe often combine several of the techniques described above. For instance, a protocol for isolating a food-poisoning bacterium from a foodstuff might involve:

1. homogenisation of a known amount of sample in a suitable diluent;
2. serial decimal dilution;
3. separation procedures using spread or pour plates to quantify the number of bacteria of a particular type in the foodstuff and provide a plate count (p. 230);
4. selective/enrichment procedures, e.g. specific media/temperatures/atmospheric conditions, depending on the bacteria to be isolated;
5. confirmation of identity: any organism growing on a primary isolation medium would require subculture and further tests, to confirm the preliminary identification as discussed below.

Identifying a particular microbe

Most of the methods described in this chapter were developed for the identification of bacteria, and bacterial examples are used to illustrate the principles involved. While the basic techniques are equally applicable to other types of microbe, the identification systems for some protozoa, fungi and algae rely predominantly on microscopic appearance. Identification of viruses requires electron microscopy or immunological techniques.

KEY POINT Identification of bacteria is often based on a combination of a number of different features, including growth characteristics, microscopic examination, physiological or biochemical characterisation, and, where necessary, immunological tests.

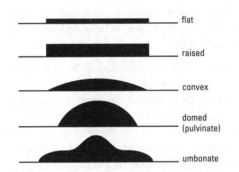

Fig. 33.2 Colony elevations (cross-sectional profile).

flat

raised

convex

domed (pulvinate)

umbonate

Direct observation

Once a microbe has been isolated and cultured in the laboratory (Chapter 32), the visual appearance of individual colonies on the surface of a solidified medium may provide useful information. Bacteria typically produce smooth, glistening colonies, varying in diameter from <1 mm to >1 cm. Actinomycete colonies are often <1 cm, with a shrivelled, powdery surface. Filamentous fungi usually grow as large, spreading mycelia with a matt appearance and are identified by microscopy, using the morphological characteristics of their reproductive structures. Yeasts produce small, glistening colonies: identification usually involves microscopy, combined with physiological and biochemical tests similar to those used for bacteria.

Colony characteristics

When measuring colony size, choose a typical colony, well spaced from any others, as colony size is affected by competition for nutrients. The characteristics of a microbial colony on a particular medium include:

- Size: some bacteria produce punctiform colonies, with a diameter of less than 1 mm, while motile bacteria may spread over the entire plate.

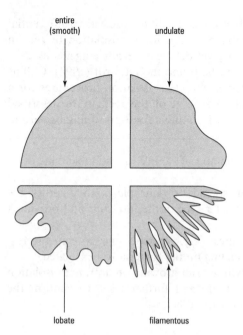

entire
(smooth)

undulate

lobate

filamentous

Fig. 33.3 Colony margins (surface view).

Using cell shape in microbial identification – *many bacteria are pleomorphic, varying in size and shape according to the growth conditions and the age of the culture: thus, other characteristics are required for identification.*

Assessing the Gram status of an unknown bacterium – *if a pure culture gives both Gram-positive and Gram-negative cells, identical in size and shape, it can be regarded as a Gram-positive organism that is demonstrating Gram-variability.*

- Form: colonies may be circular, irregular, lenticular (spindle-shaped) or filamentous.
- Elevation: colonies may be flat, raised, convex, etc. (see Fig. 33.2).
- Margin: the edge of a colony may be entire (smooth) or more distinctive, e.g. undulate, lobate or filamentous (Fig. 33.3).
- Consistency: colonies may be viscous (or mucoid), butyrous (of similar consistency to butter) or friable (dry and granular), etc.
- Colour: some bacteria produce characteristic pigments. A few pigments are fluorescent under UV light.
- Optical properties: colonies may be translucent or opaque.
- Haemolytic reactions on blood agar: many pathogenic bacteria produce characteristic zones of haemolysis. Alpha haemolysis is a partial breakdown of the haemoglobin from the erythrocytes, producing a green zone around the colony, while beta haemolysis is the complete destruction of haemoglobin, producing a clear zone.
- Odour: some actinomycetes and cyanobacteria produce earthy odours, while certain bacteria and yeasts produce fruity or 'off' odours. However, odour is not a reliable characteristic in bacterial identification and smelling plates creates a risk of inhaling microbes (pp. 199–200).

Microscopic examination – cell shape

Bacteria are usually observed using an oil immersion objective at a total magnification of ×1000 (p. 259). Bacteria are subdivided into the following groups, based on their cell shape:

- Cocci (singular, coccus): spherical, or almost spherical, cells, sometimes growing in pairs (diplococci), chains or clumps.
- Rods: straight, cylindrical cells with flattened, tapered or rounded ends, termed bacilli. Short rods are sometimes called cocco-bacilli.
- Curved rods: the curvature varies according to the organism, from short curved rods, sometimes tapered at one end, to spiral shapes.
- Branched filaments: characteristic of actinomycete bacteria.

Gram staining

This is the most important differential staining technique in bacteriology (Box 33.2 gives details). It enables us to divide bacteria into two distinct groups, Gram-positive and Gram-negative, according to a particular staining procedure (the technique is given a capital letter, since it is named after its originator, H.C. Gram). The basis of the staining reaction is the different structure of the cell walls of Gram-positive and Gram-negative bacteria. Heat fixation of air-dried bacteria causes some shrinkage, but cells retain their shape: to measure cell dimensions use a chemical fixative.

Gram staining should be carried out using light smears of young, active cultures, since older cultures may give variable results. In particular, certain Gram-positive bacteria may stain Gram-negative if older cultures are used. This Gram-variability is due to autolytic changes in the cell wall of Gram-positive bacteria. Developing spores are often visible as unstained areas within older vegetative cells of *Bacillus* and *Clostridium*. Other stains are required to demonstrate spores, capsules or flagella (p. 163).

Motility

Wet mounts can be prepared by placing a small drop of bacterial suspension on a clean, degreased slide, adding a coverslip and examining

Box 33.2 Preparation of a heat-fixed, Gram-stained smear

Preparation of a heat-fixed smear
The following procedure will provide you with a thin film of bacteria on a microscope slide, for staining.

1. **Take a clean microscope slide and pass it through a Bunsen flame twice**, to ensure it is free of grease. Allow to cool.
2. **Using a sterile inoculating loop, place a single drop of water in the centre of the slide and then mix in a small amount of sample** from a single bacterial colony with the drop, until the suspension is slightly turbid. Smear the suspension over the central area of the slide, to form a thin film. For liquid cultures, use a single drop of culture fluid, spread in a similar manner.
3. **Allow to air-dry at room temperature**, or high above a Bunsen flame: air-drying must proceed gently, or the cells will shrink and become distorted.
4. **Fix the air-dried film by passage through a Bunsen flame.** Using a slide holder or forceps, pass the slide, film side up, rapidly through the hottest part of the flame (just above the blue cone). The temperature of the slide should be just too hot for comfort on the back of your hand: note that you must not overheat the slide or you may burn yourself (you will also ruin the preparation).
5. **Allow to cool**: the smear is now ready for staining.

Gram-staining procedure
The version given here is a modification of the Hucker method, since acetone is used to decolorise the smear. Note that some of the staining solutions used are flammable, especially the acetone decolorising solvent: you must make sure that all Bunsens are turned off during staining. The procedure should be carried out with the slides suspended over a sink, using a staining rack.

1. **Flood a heat-fixed smear with 2% w/v crystal violet in 20% v/v ethanol : water** and leave for 1 min.
2. **Pour off the crystal violet and rinse briefly with tap water. Flood with Gram's iodine** (2 g KI and 1 g I_2 in 300 ml water) for 1 min.
3. **Rinse briefly with tap water** and leave the tap running gently.
4. **Tilt the slide and decolorise with acetone** for 2–3 s: acetone should be added dropwise to the slide until no colour appears in the effluent. This step is critical, since acetone is a powerful decolorising solvent and must not be left in contact with the slide for too long.
5. **Immediately immerse the smear in a gentle stream of tap water**, to remove the acetone.
6. **Pour off the water and counterstain for 10–15 s using 2.5% w/v safranin** in 95% v/v ethanol : water.
7. **Pour off the counterstain, rinse briefly with tap water, then dry the smear** by blotting gently with absorbent paper: all traces of water must be removed before the stained smear is examined microscopically.
8. **Place a small drop of immersion oil on the stained smear: examine directly** (without a coverslip) using an oil-immersion objective (p. 162).

Gram-positive bacteria retain the crystal violet (primary stain) and appear purple, while Gram-negative bacteria are decolorised by acetone and counterstained by the safranin, appearing pink or red when viewed microscopically.

Other decolorising solvents are sometimes used, including ethanol : water, ethyl ether : acetone and acetone : alcohol mixtures. The time of decolorisation must be adjusted, depending upon the strength of the solvents used, e.g. 95% v/v ethanol : water is less powerful than acetone, requiring around 30 s to decolorise a smear.

Hanging drop technique – place a drop of bacterial suspension on a coverslip and invert over a cavity slide so that the drop does not make contact with the slide: motile aerobes are observed at the edge of the droplet, where oxygen is most abundant.

the film by light microscopy without delay. For aerobes, areas near air bubbles or by the edge of the coverslip give best results, while anaerobes show greatest motility in the centre of the preparation, with rapid loss of motility due to oxygen toxicity.

Prepare wet mounts using young cultures in exponential growth in a liquid medium (p. 226). It is best to work with cultures grown at 20 or 25 °C, since those grown at 37 °C may not be actively motile on cooling to room temperature. It is essential to distinguish between the following:

- True motility, due to the presence of flagella: bacteria dart around the field of view, changing direction in zigzag, tumbling movements.
- Brownian motion: non-motile bacteria show a localised, vibratory, random motion, due to bombardment of bacterial cells by molecules in the solution.

- Passive motion, due to currents within the suspension: all cells will be swept in the same direction at a similar rate of movement.
- Gliding motility: a slower, intermittent movement, parallel to the longitudinal axis of the cell, requiring contact with a solid surface.

Basic laboratory tests

At least two simple biochemical tests are usually performed:

1. Oxidase test This identifies cytochrome c oxidase, an enzyme found in obligate aerobic bacteria. Soak a small piece of filter paper in a fresh solution of 1% (w/v) N-N-N'-N'-tetramethyl-p-phenylenediamine dihydrochloride on a microscope slide. Rub a small amount from the surface of a young, active colony onto the filter paper using a glass rod or *plastic* loop: a purple-blue colour within 10 s is a positive result.

2. Catalase test This identifies catalase, an enzyme found in obligate aerobes and in most facultative anaerobes, which catalyses the breakdown of hydrogen peroxide into water and oxygen. Transfer a small sample of your unknown bacterium onto a coverslip using a disposable plastic loop or glass rod. Invert onto a drop of hydrogen peroxide: the appearance of bubbles within 30 s is a positive reaction. This method minimises the dangers from aerosols formed when gas bubbles burst.

The oxidase and catalase tests effectively allow us to subdivide bacteria on the basis of their oxygen requirements, without using agar shake cultures (p. 207) and overnight incubation, since, for the most part:

- obligate aerobes will be oxidase and catalase positive;
- facultative anaerobes are generally oxidase negative and catalase positive;
- microaerophilic bacteria, aerotolerant anaerobes and strict (obligate) anaerobes will be oxidase and catalase negative – the latter group will grow only under anaerobic conditions (p. 207).

Once you have reached this stage (colony characteristics, motility, shape, Gram reaction, oxidase and catalase status) it may be possible to make a tentative identification, at least for certain Gram-positive bacteria, at the generic level. To identify Gram-negative bacteria, particularly the oxidase-negative, catalase-positive rods, further tests are required.

Identification tables: further laboratory tests

Bacteria are asexual organisms and strains of the same species may give different results for individual biochemical/physiological tests. This variation is allowed for in identification tables, based on the results of a large number of tests. Identification tables are often used for particular subgroups of bacteria, after Gram staining and basic laboratory tests have been performed: an example is shown in Table 33.2.

A large number of specific biochemical and physiological tests are used in bacterial identification including:

- Carbohydrate utilisation tests. Some bacteria can use a particular carbohydrate as a carbon and energy source. Acidic end-products can be identified using a pH indicator dye (p. 147) while CO_2 is detected in liquid culture using an inverted small test tube (Durham tube,

Table 33.2 Identification table for selected Gram-negative rods

Bacterium	Biochemical test								
	1	2	3	4	5	6	7	8	9
Escherichia coli	v	+	−	+	−	v	v	+	−
Proteus mirabilis	−	−	v	−	+	−	+	−	+
Morganella morganii	−	−	−	−	+	−	+	+	−
Vibrio parahaemolyticus	−	+	v	−	−	+	+	+	−
Salmonella spp.	−	+	v	−	−	+	+	−	+

Key to biochemical tests and symbols
1. sucrose utilisation
2. mannitol utilisation
3. citrate utilisation
4. β-galactosidase activity
5. urease activity
6. lysine decarboxylase activity
7. ornithine decarboxylase activity
8. indole production
9. H_2S production
+, >90% of strains tested positive
−, <10% of strains tested positive
v, 10–90% of strains tested positive

broth
gas collects here
Durham tube

Fig. 33.4 Durham tube in carbohydrate utilisation broth. Air within the Durham tube is replaced by broth during the autoclaving procedure.

Molecular approaches to microbial identification – *several novel methods of detection and identification are based on nucleic acid techniques, including use of the PCR and Southern blotting to detect particular microbes (pp. 431–2).*

Fig. 33.4). Aerobic breakdown is termed oxidation while anaerobic breakdown is known as fermentation. Identification tables usually incorporate tests for several different carbohydrates, e.g. Table 33.2.

- Enzyme tests. Most of these incorporate a substance which changes colour if the enzyme is present, e.g. a pH indicator, or a chromogenic or fluorogenic substrate (p. 379).
- Tests for specific end-products of metabolism, e.g. the production of indole due to the metabolic breakdown of the amino acid tryptophan, or H_2S from sulphur-containing amino acids.

Identification kits

Some biochemical tests are now supplied in kit form, e.g. the API 20E system incorporates 20 tests within a sterile plastic strip. After inoculation and overnight incubation, the results of the tests are converted into a seven-digit code, for comparison with known bacteria using either a reference book (the Analytical Profile Index), or a computer program. While kit identification systems save time and labour, they are more expensive and less flexible than conventional biochemical tests.

Immunological tests

Tests used in diagnostic microbiology include:

- Agglutination tests: based on the reaction between specific antibodies and a particular bacterium (p. 251). These tests are particularly useful for subdividing biochemically similar bacteria.
- Fluorescent antibody tests: the reaction between a labelled antibody and a particular bacterium can be visualised using UV microscopy. The direct fluorescent antibody test uses fluorescein isothiocyanate as the label.
- Enzyme-linked immunoassay tests using antibodies labelled with a particular enzyme, e.g. the double antibody sandwich ELISA test (p. 254).

While such tests can give specific and accurate confirmation of the identity of a bacterium under controlled laboratory conditions, they are too expensive and time-consuming for routine identification purposes.

Typing methods

The identification of bacteria at subspecies level is known as typing: this is usually done in a specialist laboratory, e.g. as part of an epidemiological study to establish the source of an infection. Various methods are used:

- Antigen typing or serotyping is based on immunological tests.
- Phage typing is based on the susceptibility of different strains to certain bacterial viruses (phages).
- Biotyping is based on biochemical differences between different strains, e.g. enzyme profiles or antibiotic resistance screening ('antibiograms').
- Bacteriocin typing: bacteriocins are proteins released by bacteria which inhibit the growth of other members of the same species.

Naming microbes

The use of scientific names is fundamental to all aspects of biological science since it aims to provide a system of identification which is precise, fixed and of universal application. Without such a system, comparative studies would be impossible.

There are two bases for such classification:

- Phenetic taxonomy, which involves grouping on the basis of phenotypic similarity, frequently using complex statistical techniques to obtain objective measures of similarity. The characters used have been largely morphological and anatomical, but biochemical, cytological and other characters are increasingly used.
- Phyletic taxonomy, which involves grouping on the basis of presumed evolutionary, and therefore genetic, relationships.

These two systems usually are fairly similar in outcome, since closely related organisms are usually fairly similar to each other and because judgements of evolutionary relationships are usually themselves based upon similarities. The situation is made more complex by phenomena such as convergent and divergent evolution; phyletic classifications are also liable to subjective bias.

The basis of classification

The basic unit of classification is the species, which represents a group of recognisably similar individuals, clearly distinct from other such groups. No simple definition of a species is possible, but there are two generally used definitions:

- A group of organisms capable of interbreeding and producing fertile offspring – this, however, excludes all asexual forms, such as bacteria and some other microbes.
- A group of organisms showing a close similarity in phenotypic characteristics – this would include morphological, anatomical, biochemical, ecological and life history characters or, increasingly, similarities in nucleic acid sequence.

When species are compared, groups of species may show a number of features in common; they are then arranged into larger groupings known as genera (singular genus). Cellular microbes (e.g. bacteria, archaea, fungi, protozoa and algae) are given two Latin terms to identify their genus and species (a Latin 'binomial'), for example *Escherichia coli*. All scientific

---

Practical applications of bacterial typing – E. coli *O157:H7 is a serotype of this bacterium that is capable of causing severe human disease: it can be identified on the basis of an agglutination reaction with an appropriate antiserum.*

Definitions

Systematics – the study of the diversity of living organisms and of the evolutionary relationships between them.

Classification (taxonomy) – the study of the theory and methods of organisation of taxa and therefore, a part of systematics.

Taxon (plural taxa) – an assemblage of organisms sharing some basic features.

Nomenclature – the allocation of names to taxa.

Identification – the placing of organisms into taxa.

Writing taxonomic names – *always underline or italicise generic and species names to avoid confusion: thus bacillus is a descriptive term for rod-shaped bacteria, while* Bacillus *is a generic name.*

names of organisms are either Latin or are treated as Latin, written in the Latin alphabet and subject to the rules of Latin grammar. Consequently, you must be very precise in your use of such names. When used in a formal scientific context, the specific name may be followed by the authority on which that name is based, i.e. the name of the person describing that species and the date of the description, e.g. *Escherichia coli* (Migula) Castelleni and Chalmers. Where specified, additional terms may follow the species name to indicate the type or subspecies, e.g. *Shigella dysenteriae* type 1. Many micro-organisms are now referred to by their generic and specific names followed by a culture collection reference number, e.g. *Bacillus subtilis* NCTC 10400, where NCTC stands for the National Collection of Type Cultures and 10400 is the reference number of that strain in the collection.

After first use in a text, the genus name may be abbreviated to a single letter, e.g. *E. coli*, as long as this does not cause confusion with other genera. Where the species name is unknown, the (non-italicised) abbreviation 'sp.' (singular) or 'spp.' (plural) should be used, e.g. *Enterococcus* sp.

The classification and nomenclature of viruses are less advanced than for cellular organisms and the current nomenclature has been arrived at on a piecemeal, *ad hoc* basis. The International Committee for Virus Taxonomy proposed a unified classification system, dividing viruses into 50 families on the basis of: host preference, nucleic acid type (i.e. DNA or RNA), whether the nucleic acid is single or double stranded and the presence or absence of a surrounding envelope. Many viruses are still referred to by trivial names or by code-names (sigla), e.g. the bacterial viruses ϕX174, T4, etc. Many of the names used reflect the diseases caused by the virus. Often, a three-letter abbreviation is used, e.g. HIV (for human immunodeficiency virus), TMV (for tobacco mosaic virus).

Strains – the term 'strain' is now more widely used, particularly in the context of the practice of lodging microbiological strains with culture collections. Cell lines (Chapter 34) are often given code names and/or reference numbers.

Example The virus that causes tobacco mosaic disease belongs to the *Tobamovirus* group and can be referred to as tobacco mosaic tobamovirus, tobacco mosaic virus or TMV.

Text references

Collins, C.H., Lyne, P.M. and Grange, J.M. (1995) *Microbiological Methods*, 7th edn. Butterworth-Heinemann, London.

Gerhardt, P. (ed.) (1994) *Manual of Methods for General and Molecular Bacteriology*. American Society for Microbiology, Washington, DC.

Hurst, C.J., Crawford, R.L. and Knudsen, G.R. (2002) *Manual of Environmental Microbiology*, 2nd edn. American Society for Microbiology, Washington, DC.

Sources for further study

Barrow, G.I. and Feltham, R.K.A. (1993) *Cowan and Steel's Manual for the Identification of Medical Bacteria*, 3rd edn. Cambridge University Press, Cambridge.
[A standard reference work for the identification of clinically important bacteria.]

Boone, D.R. *Naming a New Procaryotic Taxon*. Available: http://methanogens.pdx.edu/naming.html
Last accessed 08/01/03.
[Succinct indication of procedures for naming a new prokaryote species.]

Clesceri, L.S., Eaton, A.D. and Greenberg, A.E. (1999) *Standard Methods for Examination of Water and Wastewater*. American Public Health Association, Washington DC.
[Gives standard US protocols for a range of indicator bacteria.]

Cullimore, D.R. (2000) *Practical Atlas for Bacterial Identification*. CRC Press, Boca Raton.
[Detailed coverage of practical methods applicable to a wide range of bacteria.]

Fisher, F., Cook, N.B., Fisher, F.W. and Kaszczuk, S. (1998) *Fundamentals of Diagnostic Mycology*. Saunders, Philadelphia.
[Covers identification techniques for medically important fungi.]

Institute of Biology (2000) *Biological Nomenclature: Recommendations on Terms, Units and Symbols*. Institute of Biology, London.
[Includes sections on taxonomy and classification of organisms.]

Jeffrey, C. (1989) *Biological Nomenclature*, 3rd edn. Edward Arnold, London.

Levett, P.N. (ed.) (1991) *Anaerobic Microbiology: A Practical Approach*. IRL Press, Oxford.
[Provides practical details of the methods used to isolate and culture anaerobic micro-organisms.]

Macfaddin, J.F. (2000) *Biochemical Tests for the Identification of Medical Bacteria*, 3rd edn. Williams and Wilkins, Philadelphia.
[Explains the operating principles underlying most of the biochemical tests in routine use in diagnostic bacteriology.]

Pepper, I.L., Gerba, C.P. and Brendecke, J.W. (1995) *Environmental Microbiology: A Laboratory Manual*. Academic Press, New York.

Rochelle, P.A. (2001) *Environmental Molecular Microbiology: Protocols and Applications*. Bios, Oxford.
[Covers newer approaches to the detection and identification of microbes in environmental samples.]

Study exercises

33.1 Plan a collection/sampling strategy for a target group of microbes. What approaches might you take in the following instances?
(a) Collecting representatives of the normal skin microflora.
(b) Sampling psychrotrophic anaerobes from the subsurface mud of an estuary.
(c) Collecting a sample of sea water to enumerate faecal indicator bacteria.
(d) Mapping the microflora on the surface of a leaf.

33.2 Decide on an appropriate isolation procedure for a particular microbe. How might you isolate the following microbes from a sample?
(a) Photosynthetic flagellate algae in a sample of pond water.
(b) Bacteria growing as a biofilm on the surface of sand particles.
(c) Faecal streptococci (enterococci) present at low density (<1 per ml) in a sample of river water.

(d) A distinctively shaped bacterium present at very low numbers in a sample containing a high number of other microbes of different shape but with similar nutritional requirements.

33.3 **Investigate the selective basis of microbiological media**. Using textbooks on bacteriological methods or the Web, research how each of the following media operates, in terms of their selective and diagnostic (differential) features:

(a) Mannitol salt agar for *Staphylococcus aureus*.

(b) Membrane lauryl sulphate broth for coliforms and *E. coli*.

(c) Slanetz and Bartley medium for faecal streptococci (enterococci).

(d) Mannitol pyruvate egg yolk polymyxin (MPYP) medium for *Bacillus cereus*.

33.4 **Describe the colonial characteristics of selected microbes**. Either research the features of the following microbes (e.g. *via* the Web), or look at well-isolated individual colonies in the laboratory, following overnight growth on a suitable medium:

(a) *Escherichia coli*;

(b) *Pseudomonas aerogenes*;

(c) *Staphylococcus aureus*;

(d) *Streptococcus pneumoniae*;

(e) *Bacillus subtilis*;

(f) *Saccharomyces cerevisiae*.

33.5 **Find out how some of the tests used in microbial identification work**. Research the operating principles that underpin the following tests, using microbiological textbooks or the Web and prepare brief notes explaining how each of the following tests works:

(a) oxidase test;

(b) indole test;

(c) β-galactosidase test;

(d) urease test;

(e) lysine decarboxylase test;

(f) H_2S production.

33.6 **Identify the following oxidase-negative, catalase-positive, Gram-negative rod-shaped bacteria, using Table 33.2**.

(a) Positive for citrate, urease, ornithine decarboxylase and H_2S only.

(b) Positive for sucrose, mannitol, β-galactosidase, lysine decarboxylase and indole only.

(c) Positive for mannitol, citrate, lysine decarboxylase, ornithine decarboxylase and H_2S only.

(d) Positive for urease, ornithine decarboxylase and indole only.

(e) Positive for mannitol, β-galactosidase and indole only.

Working with animal and plant tissues and cells

In vivo – occurring within a living organism (literally 'in life').

In vitro – occurring outside a living organism, in an artificial environment (literally 'in glass').

In silico – occurring within a computer system (literally 'in silicon').

While the aim of many studies is to isolate, quantify and characterise individual molecules from a biological system, e.g. the purification of a particular enzyme (p. 370), this is not always the most appropriate course of action. Depending on the purpose of the investigation, it may be more relevant to study the functioning of biomolecules within more complex systems, in order to understand their role in a particular biological process. At one extreme this may be carried out *in vivo*, using whole multicellular organisms (e.g. individual animals or plants), while the other extreme is represented by *in vitro* studies, using subcellular 'cell-free' extracts. Between these two extremes, a range of tissue and cell culture techniques offers some of the biological complexity of the intact organism combined with a degree of experimental control that may not be obtainable *in vivo*. The ethics and costs of whole animal experimentation have provided an additional stimulus to the development of *in vitro* methods, e.g. toxicity tests using mammalian cell culture rather than laboratory animals, while developments in molecular genetics lead to further applications of cell and tissue culture.

Animal tissues and organs

Working with vertebrate animals and their organs/tissues – remember that procedures must be consistent with the law, i.e. in the UK, the **Animals Scientific Procedures Act 1986**.

Physiological experiments are carried out using either whole organisms, or a range of animal organs and tissues, including heart, liver, muscle, etc.

KEY POINT A major practical consideration is that the tissue should be studied as soon as possible after the death of the animal, typically under laboratory conditions that mimic the *in vivo* environment as closely as possible.

In most instances, the experiments are relatively short term (<24 h) and the aim is to maintain the tissue in a physiological state similar to that within the living organism. For metabolic studies, the whole organ or a tissue slice (typically 1–10 mm thick) will be bathed in an appropriate perfusion fluid, supplied either by gravity or by peristaltic pump. Practical considerations include:

- Inorganic solute requirements – the chemical composition of the perfusion fluid is usually chosen to reflect the major inorganic ion requirements of the tissue. For short-term studies, a number of so-called 'physiological salt solutions' may be used, e.g. Ringer's solution, one formulation of which is given in Table 34.1.
- Oxygen requirements – it may be necessary to increase the O_2 content of the perfusion fluid by bubbling with O_2, in order to meet the oxygen demand of the innermost parts of the tissue. However, this can lead to oxygen toxicity in the outermost parts and an alternative approach is simply to increase the rate of perfusion.
- Physicochemical conditions – including temperature (usually controlled to $\pm 1\,°C$ of normal body temperature), water status (the perfusion fluid should be isotonic with the tissue), pH and buffering

Table 34.1 Composition of Ringer's solution (simplified formulation, for amphibians, etc.)

Compound	Amount per litre (g)
NaCl	6.0
KCl	0.075
CaCl$_2$	0.1
NaHCO$_3$	0.1

Plasmodesmata – transverse connections through the cell wall, linking the cytoplasm of adjacent plant cells and creating a symplasm.

Apoplasm – that part of the plant body outside the symplasm.

Light compensation point – the amount of photosynthetically active radiation (PAR) where photosynthetic CO_2 uptake is balanced by CO_2 production due to respiration and photorespiration (p. 398).

Table 34.2 Components of Long Ashton medium (nitrate version)

Stock solution: mass required per litre of solution (g)	Volume of stock solution to make 1 litre of medium (ml)
Major nutrients	
KNO_3: 50.60	8
$Ca(NO_3)_2$: 80.25	8
$MgSO_4 \cdot 7H_2O$: 46.00	8
$NaH_2PO_4 \cdot 2H_2O$: 52.00	4
Micronutrients	
FeKEDTA: 3.30	5
$MnSO_4 \cdot 4H_2O$: 2.23	1
$ZnSO_4 \cdot 7H_2O$: 0.29	1
$CuSO_4 \cdot 5H_2O$: 0.25	1
H_3BO_3: 3.10	1
$Na_2MoO_4 \cdot 2H_2O$: 0.12	1
NaCl: 5.85	1
$CoSO_4 \cdot 7H_2O$: 0.056	1

Effects of humans on plants – remember that your exhaled breath will be nearly saturated with water vapour and will contain CO_2 at 3–4% v/v, some 100 times more concentrated than atmospheric CO_2: your breath can thus affect rates of transpiration and photosynthesis.

capacity (e.g. some perfusion fluids have elevated an $NaHCO_3$ concentration, to mimic the buffering capacity of mammalian serum).

- Organic nutrient requirements – for longer-term studies, suitable organic nutrients will be required: these may be chemically defined additives, e.g. vitamins, amino acids, proteins, etc., or biological fluids such as plasma or serum. Glucose is often added as a carbon and energy source (Freshney, 2000).

Plant tissues and organs

Individual plant components (e.g. leaves, leaf slices and epidermal strips) can be isolated from the main plant body for study under controlled conditions. Since photosynthetic plant parts are autotrophic, they may be maintained *in vitro* for longer than animal organs, given adequate light and CO_2. However, most plant cells are joined via plasmodesmata, and the separation of such cells when the component is removed from the plant often leads to death when these connections are broken. Plants also show wound responses that may affect the metabolic processes under study. For these reasons, the most suitable systems for longer-term studies are often whole organs, e.g. whole leaves or entire root systems. Water culture (e.g. in Long Ashton medium, Table 34.2) is an alternative approach, offering greater control over the root environment (Dodds and Robert, 1995).

It is best to use vigorous, healthy stock plants and to follow a well-established procedure, taking account of the following:

- Sterility – strict attention to sterile technique can be essential to the success of many longer-term experiments. Decontamination of plant organs may be especially difficult where specimens are obtained from soil: to achieve this, use a surface wash with disinfectant (e.g. 10% w/v sodium hypochlorite), followed by several rinses with sterile water.
- Gaseous environment – in general, the experimental system should be well ventilated. Actively photosynthetic tissues will rapidly deplete the atmospheric CO_2 in a closed vessel: plant parts may also produce physiologically active gases, such as ethylene, especially at wound sites. Turgor loss may occur in isolated plant parts unless a high humidity is maintained.
- Nutrition – plant tissues may benefit from a supply of inorganic ions, including K^+, SO_4^{2-}, etc. and may require certain vitamins, micronutrients and plant hormones for prolonged studies.
- Physicochemical conditions – light is the most important environmental requirement for green plant parts. At atmospheric CO_2 concentrations, the light compensation point is about 5–10 μmol photons PAR $m^{-2} s^{-1}$ (p. 268) and photosynthesis is usually saturated between 500 and 2000 μmol photons PAR $m^{-2} s^{-1}$, depending on the plant type. Light quality and photoperiod (daylength) are also important: fluorescent tubes and incandescent bulbs that mimic the photosynthetic spectrum of sunlight are available (see p. 268), while photoperiod can be controlled using an electric timer. The water potential of aqueous media can be adjusted using an impermeant osmoticum such as mannitol, and pH values are often kept close to those of the apoplasm ($\approx$pH 6) using appropriate buffers, if necessary (p. 150).

Cell and tissue cultures

KEY POINT One of the main differences between organ and tissue incubation techniques and those used in cell/tissue culture is that the former aim simply to maintain metabolic and physiological activity for a limited period, while the latter provide conditions suitable for cell growth, division and development *in vitro* over an extended timescale, from a few days to several months.

The basic principles involved in culturing animal and plant cells are broadly similar to those described for microbial cell culture (p. 197). Definitions for several key terms are given in the margin.

Applications of cell and tissue culture

The main uses of animal and plant cell culture systems include:

- Experimental model systems in biochemistry, pharmacology and physiology: cell culture offers certain advantages over whole organism studies, with greater control over environmental conditions and biological variability. The use of genetically defined clones of cells may simplify the analysis of experimental data. Conversely, results obtained with specialised cell-based systems might be unrepresentative of a broader range of cell types and may be more difficult to interpret in terms of the whole organism.
- Studies of the growth requirements of particular cells: including studies of the positive effects of growth factors or growth-promoting substances, and the negative effects of xenobiotics or cytotoxic compounds. The use of cell culture in bioassays and mutagenicity testing is considered in Chapter 35.
- Studies of cell development and differentiation: including aspects of the cell cycle and gene expression. Cell cultures retaining their ability to differentiate *in vitro* are particularly interesting to researchers, while the lack of differentiation and uncontrolled growth of many animal cell lines makes them useful models of tumour development and neoplasia.
- Pathological studies: including the culture of foetal cells for karyotyping and the detection of genetic abnormality, e.g. trisomy, translocation, etc.
- Genetic manipulation: cell culture techniques have played an essential role in the development of molecular biology, including the production of transgenic animals and plants by techniques such as transfection, etc.
- Biotechnology: including the industrial production of therapeutic proteins, vaccines, monoclonal antibodies, etc. using large-scale batch and continuous culture techniques similar to those used in microbiology (pp. 226–8).

Animal cell culture systems

These may be established either from whole organisms (e.g. chick embryo), discrete organs (e.g. rat liver) or from blood (e.g. lymphocytes), typically using *mild* enzymic tissue disruption techniques, where necessary. While, in theory, it is possible to culture nucleated cells from virtually any source, in practice, the highest rates of success are most often achieved with young, actively growing tissues. The principal

---

Definitions

Primary culture – a cell culture derived from tissue or organ fragments (explants). Primary culture ends on first subculture.

Passage – an alternative term for subculture.

Cell line – a cell culture derived by passage of a primary culture.

Finite cell line – a culture with a limited capacity for growth *in vitro* (maximum number of cell doublings).

Continuous cell line – a culture with the capacity for unlimited multiplication *in vitro*. Sometimes termed an established cell line.

Clone – a population of cells derived from a single original cell, i.e. sharing the same genotype.

Transformation – a permanent alteration in the growth characteristics of a finite cell line that may include (i) changes in morphology, (ii) an increased growth rate and/or (iii) the acquisition of an infinite lifespan, often termed immortalisation. Transformation may be spontaneous or may be induced by chemical agents or viruses, and often involves a change in chromosome number.

Senescence – the end-point in the limited lifespan of a finite cell line, characterised by the lack of proliferation. Conversion to an established (continuous) cell line requires 'escape' from senescence.

considerations in animal cell culture are:

- Safety: it is important to be aware of the potential dangers of infection from cell cultures. Although avian and rodent cells present a reduced risk of disease transmission compared to human cells, all animal cell cultures must be regarded as a potential source of pathogenic microbes, and appropriate sterile technique should be used at all times (see p. 197). Work involving animal tissues and cell cultures must be carried out in a safety cabinet by trained, experienced personnel – you are unlikely to gain practical experience with such cultures in the early stages of your course. For other cell cultures, you will need to follow the code of safe practice of your Department – consult your Departmental Safety Officer if you have any doubts about safe working procedures.

- Whether to use a primary culture or a continuous cell line: freshly isolated cells are more likely to reflect the biochemical activities of cells *in vivo*, though they will have a limited lifespan in culture, requiring repeated isolation for longer-term projects. Continuous cell lines are more easily cultured and offer the advantage that their growth requirements in culture may be known in some detail, especially for the more widely used cell lines (e.g. BHK, HeLa).

- The requirements for a solid substratum: some cells must be attached to a solid surface in order to grow. Anchorage dependence is a typical feature of primary cultures and finite cell lines – such cultures show density-dependent growth inhibition once the cells have formed a confluent monolayer on the surface of the substratum. An alternative approach is to grow such cells on a particulate support using 'microcarrier' beads. In contrast, many continuous cell lines can be maintained in suspension culture, as individual cells or aggregates.

- The physicochemical conditions, including pH (typically 7.2–7.5) and buffering capacity, osmolality (usually $300 \pm 20 \, \text{mosmol kg}^{-1}$) and temperature (e.g. 35–37 °C for mammalian cells).

- The requirements of the culture medium: these will include the provision of inorganic ions (as a balanced salt solution), a carbon/energy source plus other organic nutrients, and a supplement containing antimicrobial agents to counter the risks of contamination. For example, Dulbecco's modified Eagle's medium is used for many mammalian cell types that grow as adherent monolayers, while suspension cultures of continuous cell lines can be maintained using less stringent media. To support growth, the basal medium is usually supplemented with serum (usually foetal calf serum, at up to 20% v/v), or a chemically defined serum-like supplement containing a mixture of proteins, polypeptides, hormones, lipids and trace components. A typical antimicrobial supplement might include antibacterial agents, e.g. penicillin and streptomycin, an antifungal agent, e.g. griseofulvin, and an antimycoplasmal agent, e.g. gentamicin, The *in vitro* level of CO_2 and O_2 must also be considered: many cell cultures are buffered using bicarbonate, and must be maintained in an atmosphere of elevated CO_2, either in a sealed culture vessel or in a CO_2 incubator, to maintain pH balance. In some cases, a pH-sensitive dye (e.g. phenol red, p. 147) may be incorporated into the growth medium, to provide

Working with tissue cultures safely – do not confuse laminar flow hoods (p. 199) with safety cabinets, as they perform completely different functions.

Example Dulbecco's modified Eagle's medium contains Ca^{2+}, Fe^{3+}, Mg^{2+}, K^+, Na^+, Cl^-, SO_4^{2-}, PO_4^{2-}, glucose, 20 amino acids, 10 vitamins, inositol and glutathione. Foetal calf serum is usually added at up to 20% v/v.

Using a horizontal laminar flow hood – note that this is designed to minimise contamination of the culture, rather than the worker.

Working with animal and plant tissues and cells

a visual check on pH status during growth – a colour change indicates acidification of the medium and the growth medium should be renewed.

- The equipment required: this may include a laminar flow hood or safety cabinet to reduce the possibility of microbial contamination, suitable culture vessels (typically presterilised, disposable polystyrene dishes, bottles and flasks, treated to create a negatively charged, hydrophilic surface), a supply of high purity water (typically distilled, deionised and carbon filtered), a suitable incubator with temperature control of $\pm 0.5\,°C$ or better, often with CO_2 control and mechanical mixing, and an inverted microscope to examine adherent cell monolayers during growth.

The successive stages of isolation of animal components are shown in Fig. 34.1a.

Plant tissue and cell culture systems

Plant tissue cultures can be established by growing explants of sterilised tissue on the surface of an agar-based growth medium to give a callus of undifferentiated cells. Initial sterilisation is usually achieved by incubation for 15–20 min in 10% w/v sodium hypochlorite.

KEY POINT For most plants, cell cultures can be established from a broad range of tissue types, reflecting the totipotency of many plant cells.

Fig. 34.1 Isolation of animal (a) and plant (b) components for *in vitro* study (note decreasing scale, from organisms to cells).

Embryogenic callus may be induced to differentiate, forming tissues and organs on a medium containing appropriate plant hormones: in many cases, these cultures will develop to form plantlets that can be grown on to mature plants, or encapsulated to produce so-called 'artificial seeds'. This approach can be used to study the conditions necessary for differentiation and development, or to propagate rare plants and other valuable stock (e.g. virus-free stock, or genetically altered plants). Callus derived from anthers can be used to provide haploid cell cultures and haploid plants – these are often useful for experimental genetics and breeding purposes.

Plant cell suspension cultures (Fig. 34.1b) are usually obtained by transferring fragments of actively growing callus to a 'shake' flask containing liquid medium in an orbital incubator: gentle agitation causes fragmentation of the callus tissue, to give a suspension culture that will contain individual plant cells and cell aggregates. This culture can be maintained by repeated subculturing of material from the upper layers of the liquid, encouraging the growth of small aggregates. However, in contrast to animal cell suspension cultures, it is rare for plant suspension cultures to be entirely unicellular, due to the presence of plasmodesmata and plant cell walls. Suspension cultures often require a minimum inoculum size on subculture – an inoculum volume of 10% v/v may be necessary to ensure successful subculture. It may also be helpful to add a small amount of 'conditioned' medium from a previous culture. Commercial-scale suspension cultures are used to produce certain plant pigments and secondary metabolites such as flavourings and high value pharmaceutical compounds.

The growth media used for callus and suspension cultures are more complex than those required for intact plant organs and tissues, with organic nutrient supplements in addition to a balanced salt solution. Such organic supplements often include a major carbon and energy source, e.g. sucrose, plus various vitamins and growth regulators (typically, at least one auxin and a cytokinin), together with undefined components such as yeast extract and hydrolysed casein in some instances. Otherwise, the techniques are broadly similar to those described for microbial systems (pp. 197–202).

Plant protoplasts

Some experimental procedures using plant cells require the enzymatic removal of their cell walls, creating protoplasts that can be manipulated *in vitro*, then maintained under conditions that allow the regeneration of cell walls, with subsequent growth and differentiation to give genetically modified plants. Protoplast isolation often involves pretreatment in a concentrated osmoticum (e.g. sucrose or mannitol, at 300–500 mmol l^{-1}) to plasmolyse the cells, weakening the linkage between cell wall and plasma membrane. Enzymatic treatment is often prolonged, taking several hours in a suitable mixture of enzymes, e.g. cellulase and Macerozyme®. The resulting material can be sieved through fine nylon mesh, centrifuged at low speed and then re-suspended, to remove subcellular debris and cell aggregates. The protoplast preparation can be checked for fragments of cell wall using a suitable stain, e.g. 0.1% w/v calcofluor white and a fluorescence microscope.

The fusion of protoplasts from different plants can be used to produce a somatic hybrid: this process can be used to circumvent inter-species reproductive barriers, creating novel plants. Protoplast fusion can be induced by chemical 'fusogens', e.g. using polyethylene glycol (PEG) at

Example Murashige and Skoog's medium contains a balanced mixture of the principal inorganic ions, plus 7 trace element compounds, 3 vitamins, inositol, glycine and sucrose (at 30 g l^{-1}) as the major carbon source.

Working with protoplasts – remember that all solutions must contain a suitable osmoticum, to prevent bursting. Mannitol is widely used at ≈ 400 mmol l^{-1}.

Assessing cell and protoplast viability – cytochemical techniques are often used, e.g. exclusion of the mortal stain Trypan blue or Evan's blue. The fluorogenic vital stain fluorescein diacetate is an alternative: it is cleaved by esterases within living cells, liberating fluorescein and giving green–yellow fluorescent cells when viewed by UV fluorescence microscopy.

high concentration, or by electrofusion (incubation under low alternating current to encourage aggregation, then brief exposure to a high voltage electrical field – typically $1000\,\mathrm{V\,cm^{-1}}$ for 1–2 ms – causing protoplast fusion). The successive stages of isolation of plant components are illustrated in Fig. 34.1b.

Text references

Dodds, J.H. and Robert, L.W. (1995) *Experiments in Plant Tissue Culture*, 3rd edn. Cambridge University Press, Cambridge.

Freshney, R.I. (2000) *Culture of Animal Cells: A Manual of Basic Technique*, 4th edn. Wiley, New York.

Sources for further study

Butler, M. (1997) *Animal Cell Culture and Technology: The Basics*. IRL Press, Oxford.

Dixon, R.A. and Gonzales, R.A. (1995) *Plant Cell Culture: A Practical Approach*. IRL Press, Oxford.

Doyle, A., Griffiths, J.B. and Newell, D.G. (1998) *Cell and Tissue Culture: Laboratory Procedures*. Wiley, New York.

Hall, R.D. (1999) *Plant Cell Culture Protocols. Methods in Molecular Biology Series*. Humana Press, New Jersey.

Harrison, M.A. and Rae, I.F. (1997) *General Techniques of Cell Culture*. Cambridge University Press, Cambridge.

Study exercises

34.1 Calculate the osmolarity of Ringer's solution from its individual constituents. Use the data in Table 34.1 and the information in Chapter 24, and assume that each constituent behaves according to ideal thermodynamic principles. Note the following M_r values: NaCl 58.44; KCl 74.55; $CaCl_2$ 110.99; $NaHCO_3$ 84.01, required to convert the data in Table 34.1 to molar concentrations (see p. 130 if you are unsure about this conversion). Give your final answer in $\mathrm{mosmol\,kg^{-1}}$, to 1 decimal place.

34.2 Find out about the availability of cell cultures using the Web. Research the culture collections of particular countries via their websites. How useful is each site in terms of features such as: ease of use; access to catalogues; information on individual strains, e.g. culture media; details of costs?

34.3 Research the origins of the code names used for individual cell lines. In many instances, the code names given to individual cell lines are derived from their original source. Use the Web to find out the origin of the following descriptors for cell lines:
(a) HeLa
(b) Vero
(c) BHK
(d) CHO
(e) TBY-2

Culture systems and growth measurement

Definitions

Heterotroph – an organism that uses complex organic carbon compounds as a source of carbon and energy.

Photoautotroph – an organism that uses light as a source of energy and CO_2 as a carbon source (photosynthetic metabolism).

Chemoautotroph – an organism that acquires energy from the oxidation of simple inorganic compounds, fixing CO_2 as a source of carbon (chemosynthetic metabolism).

Microbial, animal and plant cell culture methods are based on the same general principles, requiring:

- a pure culture (also known as an axenic culture), perhaps isolated as part of an earlier procedure, or from a culture collection;
- a suitable nutrient medium to provide the necessary components for growth. This medium must be sterilised before use;
- satisfactory growth conditions including temperature, pH, atmospheric requirements, ionic and osmotic conditions;
- sterile technique (p. 197) to maintain the culture in pure form.

Heterotrophic animal cells, fungi and many bacteria require appropriate organic compounds as sources of carbon and energy. Non-exacting bacteria can utilise a wide range of compounds and they are often grown in media containing complex natural substances (including meat extract, yeast extract, soil, blood). Animal cells have more stringent growth requirements (p. 220).

Photoautotrophic bacteria, cyanobacteria and algae are grown in a mineral medium containing inorganic ions including chelated iron, with a light source and CO_2 supply. Plant cells may require additional vitamins and hormones (p. 222). For chemoautotrophic bacteria, the light source is replaced by a suitable inorganic energy source, e.g. H_2S for sulphur-oxidising bacteria, NH_3/NH_4^+ for nitrifying bacteria, etc.

Growth on solidified media

Many organisms can be cultured on an agar-based medium (p. 198). An important benefit is that an individual cell inoculated onto the surface can develop to form a visible colony: this is the basis of most microbial isolation and purification methods, including the streak dilution, spread plate and pour plate procedures (p. 200).

Animal cells are often grown as an adherent monolayer on the surface of a plastic or glass culture vessel (p. 221), rather than on an agar-based medium.

Several types of culture vessel are used:

Harvesting bacteria from a plate – colonies can be harvested using a sterile loop, providing large numbers of cells without the need for centrifugation. The cells are relatively free from components of the growth medium; this is useful if the medium contains substances that interfere with subsequent procedures.

- Petri plates (Petri dishes): usually the presterilised, disposable plastic type, providing a large surface area for growth.
- Glass bottles or test tubes: these provide sufficient depth of agar medium for prolonged growth of bacterial and fungal cultures, avoiding problems of dehydration and salt crystallisation. Inoculate aerobes on the surface and anaerobes by stabbing down the centre, into the base (stab culture).
- Flat-sided bottles: these are used for animal cell culture, to provide an increased surface area for attachment and allow growth of cells as a surface monolayer. Usually plastic and disposable.

Subculturing – when subculturing microbes from a colony on an agar medium, take your sample from the growing edge, so that viable cells are transferred.

The dynamics of growth are usually studied in liquid culture, apart from certain rapidly growing filamentous fungi, where increases in colony diameter can be measured accurately, e.g. using Vernier callipers.

Growth in liquid media

Many cells, apart from primary cultures of animal cells, can be grown as a homogeneous unicellular suspension in a suitable liquid medium, where growth is usually considered in terms of cell number (population growth) rather than cell size. Most liquid culture systems need agitation, to ensure adequate mixing and to keep the cells in suspension. An Erlenmeyer flask (100–2000 ml capacity) can be used to grow a batch culture on an orbital shaker, operating at 20–250 cycles per minute. For aerobic organisms, the surface area of such a culture should be as large as possible: restrict the volume of medium to not more than 20% of the flask volume. Larger cultures may need to be gassed with sterile air and mixed using a magnetic stirrer rather than an orbital shaker. The simplest method of air sterilisation is filtration, using glass wool, non-absorbent cotton wool or a commercial filter unit of appropriate pore size (usually $0.2 \, \mu m$). Air is introduced via a sparger (a glass tube with many small holes, so that small bubbles are produced) near the bottom of the culture vessel to increase the surface area and enhance gas exchange. More complex systems have baffles and paddles to further improve mixing and gas exchange.

Liquid culture systems may be subdivided under two broad headings:

Batch culture

This is the most common approach for routine liquid culture. Cells are inoculated into a sterile vessel containing a fixed amount of growth medium. Your choice of vessel will depend upon the volume of culture required: larger-scale vessels (e.g. 1 litre and above) are often called 'fermenters' or 'bioreactors', particularly in biotechnology. Growth within the vessel usually follows a predictable S-shaped (sinusoidal) curve when plotted in log–linear format (Fig. 35.1), divided into four components:

1. Lag phase: the initial period when no increase in cell number is seen. The larger the inoculum of active cells the shorter the lag phase will be, provided the cells are transferred from similar growth conditions.
2. Log phase, or exponential phase: where cells are growing at their maximum rate. This may be quantified by the specific growth rate (μ), where:

$$\mu = \frac{2.303 \, (\log N_x - \log N_0)}{(t_x - t_0)} \qquad [35.1]$$

where N_0 is the initial number of cells at time t_0 and N_x is the number of cells at time t_x. For times specified in hours, μ is expressed as h^{-1}.

Prokaryotes grow by binary fission while eukaryotes grow by mitotic cell division; in both cases each cell divides to give two identical offspring. Consequently, the doubling time or generation time (g, or T_2) is:

$$g = \frac{0.301 \, (t_x - t_0)}{\log N_x - \log N_0} \qquad [35.2]$$

Cells grow at different rates, with doubling times ranging from under 20 min for some bacteria to 24 h or more for animal and plant cells. Exponential phase cells are often used in laboratory experiments, since growth and metabolism are nearly uniform.

Fig. 35.1 Population growth curve for cells in batch culture (liquid medium).

Example Suppose you counted 2×10^3 cells ($\log_{10} = 3.30$) per unit volume at t_0 and 6.3×10^4 cells ($\log_{10} = 4.80$) after 2 h (t_x).

Substitution into Eqn [35.1] gives $[2.303(4.8 - 3.3)] \div 2 = 1.727 \, h^{-1}$ (or $0.0288 \, min^{-1}$).

Substituting the same values into Eqn [35.2] gives: $[0.301 \times 2] \div [4.8 - 3.3] = 0.40 \, h$ (or 24 min).

3. Stationary phase: growth decreases as nutrients are depleted and waste products accumulate. Any increase in cell number is offset by death. This phase is usually termed the 'plateau' in animal cell culture.

4. Decline phase, or death phase: this is the result of prolonged starvation and toxicity, unless the cells are subcultured. Like growth, death often shows an exponential relationship with time, which can be characterised by a rate (specific death rate), equivalent to that used to express growth or, more often, as the decimal reduction time (d, or T_{90}), the time required to reduce the population by 90%:

$$d = \frac{t_x - t_0}{\log N_x - \log N_0} \qquad [35.3]$$

Some cells undergo rapid autolysis at the end of the stationary period while others show a slower decline.

Batch culture methods can be used to maintain stocks of particular organisms; cells are subcultured onto fresh medium before they enter the decline phase. However, primary cultures of animal cells have a finite life unless transformed to give a continuous cell line, capable of indefinite growth (p. 220).

Continuous culture

This is a method of maintaining cells in exponential growth for an extended period by continuously adding fresh growth medium to a culture vessel of fixed capacity. The new medium replaces nutrients and displaces some of the culture, diluting the remaining cells and allowing further growth.

After inoculating the vessel, the culture is allowed to grow for a short time as a batch culture, until a suitable population size is reached. Then medium is pumped into the vessel: the system is usually set up so that any increase in cell number due to growth will be offset by an equivalent loss due to dilution, i.e. the cell number within the vessel is maintained at a steady state. The cells will be growing at a particular rate (μ), counterbalanced by dilution at an equivalent rate (D):

$$D = \frac{\text{flow rate}}{\text{vessel volume}} \qquad [35.4]$$

where D is expressed per unit time (e.g. h^{-1}). In a chemostat, the growth rate is limited by the availability of some nutrient in the inflowing medium, usually either carbon or nitrogen (see Fig. 35.2). In a turbidostat, the input of medium is controlled by the turbidity of the culture, measured using a photocell. A turbidostat is more complex than a chemostat, with additional equipment and controls.

To determine the specific growth rate (μ) of a continuous culture:

1. Measure the flow of medium through the vessel over a known time interval (e.g. connect a sterile measuring cylinder or similar volumetric device to the outlet), to calculate the flow rate.
2. Divide the flow rate by the vessel volume (Eqn [35.4]) to give the dilution rate (D).
3. This equals the specific growth rate, since $D = \mu$ at steady state.

Fig. 35.2 Example of a two-dimensional lab equipment diagram of components of a chemostat.

air filter
reservoir of sterile medium
flow-regulating clamp
air input
air filters
inoculation port
culture vessel
magnetic stirrer   sampling port
reservoir of spent medium

4. If you want to know the doubling time (g), calculate using the relationship:

$$g = \frac{0.693}{\mu} \qquad [35.5]$$

(Note that Eqn [35.5] also applies to exponential phase cells in batch culture and is useful for interconverting g and μ.)

Continuous culture systems are more complex to set up than batch cultures. They are prone to contamination, having additional vessels for fresh medium and waste culture: strict aseptic technique is necessary when the medium reservoir is replaced, and during sampling and harvesting. However, they offer several advantages over batch cultures, including the following:

- The physiological state of the cells is more clearly defined, since actively growing cells at the same stage of growth are provided over an extended time period. This is useful for biochemical and physiological studies.
- Monitoring and control can be automated and computerised.
- Modelling can be carried out for biotechnology/fermentation technology.

Measuring growth in cell cultures

The most widely used methods of measuring growth are based on cell number:

Direct microscopic counts

One of the simplest methods is to count the cells in a known volume of medium using a microscope and a counting chamber or haemocytometer (Box 35.1). While this gives a rapid assessment of the total cell number, it does not discriminate between living and dead cells. It is also time-consuming as a large number of cells must be counted for accurate measurement. It may be difficult to distinguish individual cells, e.g. for cells growing as clumps.

Electronic particle counters

These instruments can be used to give a direct (total) count of a suspension of microbial cells. The Coulter® counter detects particles due to change in electrical resistance when they pass through a small aperture in a glass tube (Fig. 35.3). It gives a rapid count based on a larger number of cells than direct microscopy. It is well-suited for repeat measurements or large sample numbers and can be linked to a microcomputer for data processing. If correctly calibrated, the counter can also measure cell sizes. A major limitation of electronic counters is the lack of discrimination between living cells, dead cells, cell clumps and other particles (e.g. dust). In addition, the instrument must be set up and calibrated by trained personnel. Flow cytometry is a more specialised alternative, since particles can be sorted as well as counted.

Culture-based counting methods

A variety of culture-based techniques can be used to determine the number of microbes in a sample. A major assumption of such methods is

Fig. 35.3 Components of an electronic particle counter. During operation, the cell suspension is drawn through the aperture by the vacuum, creating a 'pulse' of resistance between the two electrodes as each cell passes through the aperture.

Box 35.1 How to use a counting chamber or haemocytometer

A counting chamber is a specially designed slide containing a chamber of known depth with a grid etched onto its lower surface. When a flat coverslip is placed over the chamber, the depth is uniform. Use as follows:

1. **Place the special coverslip over the chamber.** Press the edges firmly, to ensure that the coverslip makes contact with the surface of the slide, but take care that you do not break the slide or coverslip by using too much force. When correctly positioned, you should be able to see interference rings (Newton's rings) at the edge of the coverslip.

2. **Add a small amount of your cell suspension to fill the central space above the grid.** Place on the microscope stage and allow the cells to settle (2–3 min).

3. **Examine the grid microscopically,** using the ×10 objective lens first, since the counting chamber is far thicker than a standard microscope slide. Then switch to the ×40 objective: take care not to scratch the surface of the objective lens, as the special coverslip is thicker than a normal coverslip. For a dense culture, the small squares are used, while the larger squares are used for dilute suspensions. You may need to dilute your suspension if it contains more than 30 cells per small square.

4. **Count the number of cells in several squares:** at least 600 cells should be counted for accurate measurements. Include those cells that cross the upper and left-hand boundaries, but not those that cross the lower or right-hand rulings (p. 180). A hand tally may be used to aid counting. Motile cells must be immobilised prior to counting (e.g. by killing with a suitable biocide).

5. **Divide the total number of cells (C) by the number of squares counted (S),** to give the mean cell count per square.

6. **Determine the volume (in ml) of liquid corresponding to a single square (V),** e.g. a Petroff–Hausser chamber has small squares of linear dimension 0.2 mm, giving an area of 0.04 mm^2; since the depth of the chamber is 0.02 mm, the volume is $0.04 \times 0.02 = 0.0008$ mm^3; as there are 1000 mm^3 in 1 ml, the volume of a small square is 8×10^{-7} ml; similarly, the volume of a large square (equal to 25 small squares) is 2×10^{-5} ml. Note that other types of counting chamber will have different volumes: check the manufacturer's instructions. For example, the improved Neubauer chamber has small squares of volume 0.000 25 mm$^3 = 2.5 \times 10^{-7}$ ml.

7. **Calculate the cell number per ml by dividing the mean cell count per square by the volume of a single square (in ml).**

8. **Remember to take account of any dilution of your original suspension** in your final calculation by multiplying by the reciprocal of the dilution (M), e.g. if you counted a 1 in 20 dilution of your sample, multiply by 20, or if you diluted to 10^{-5}, multiply by 10^5.

The complete equation for calculating the total microscopic count is:

$$\text{Total cell count (per ml)} = (C \div S \div V) \times M \quad [35.6]$$

e.g. if the mean cell count for a 100-fold dilution of a cell suspension, counted using a Petroff–Hausser chamber, was 12.4 cells in 10 small squares, the total count would be

$$(12.4 \div 10 \div 8 \times 10^{-7}) \times 10^2 = 1.55 \times 10^8 \, \text{ml}^{-1}$$

A simpler, less accurate approach is to use a known volume of sample under a coverslip of known area on a standard glass slide, counting the number of cells per field of view using a calibrated microscope of known field diameter, then multiplying up to give the cell number per ml.

Definition

CFU – colony-forming unit: a cell or group of cells giving rise to a single colony on a solidified medium.

that, under suitable conditions, an individual viable microbial cell will be able to multiply and grow to give a visible change in the growth medium, i.e. a colony on an agar-based medium, or turbidity ('cloudiness') in a liquid medium. You are most likely to gain practical experience using bacterial cultures, counted by one or more of the following methods:

- Spread or pour plate methods ('plate counts', p. 200). The most widespread approach is to transfer a suitable amount of the sample to an agar medium, incubate under appropriate conditions and then count the resulting colonies (Box 35.2).
- Membrane filtration. For bacterial samples where the expected cell number is lower than 10 CFU ml^{-1}, pass the sample through a sterile filter (pore size 0.2 or 0.45 μm). The filter is then incubated on a

Box 35.2 How to make a plate count of bacteria using an agar-based medium

1. **Prepare serial decimal dilutions of the sample in a sterile diluent (pp. 131–2).** The most widely used diluents are 0.1% w/v peptone water or 0.9% w/v NaCl, buffered at pH 7.3. Take care that you mix each dilution before making the next one. For soil, food or other solid samples, make the initial decimal dilution by taking 1 g of sample and making this up to 10 ml using a suitable diluent. Gentle shaking or homogenisation may be required for organisms growing in clumps. The number of decimal dilutions required for a particular sample will be governed by your expected count: dilute until the expected number of viable cells is around 100–1000 ml^{-1}.

2. **Transfer an appropriate volume (e.g. 0.05–0.5 ml) of the lowest dilution to an agar plate** using either the spread plate method or the pour plate procedure (p. 200). At least two, and preferably more, replicate plates should be prepared for each sample. You may also wish to prepare plates for more than one dilution, if you are unsure of the expected number of viable cells.

3. **Incubate under suitable conditions for 18–72 h, then count the number of colonies on each replicate plate at the most appropriate dilution.** The most accurate results will be obtained for plates containing 30–300 colonies. Mark the base of the plate with a spirit-based pen each time you count a colony. Determine the mean colony count per plate at this dilution (C).

4. **Calculate the colony count per ml of that particular dilution** by dividing by the volume (in ml) of liquid transferred to each plate (V).

5. **Now calculate the count per ml of the original sample** by multiplying by the reciprocal of the dilution: this is the multiplication factor (M); e.g. for a dilution of 10^{-3}, the multiplication factor would be 10^3. For soil, food or other solid samples, the count should be expressed per g of sample.

The complete equation for calculating the viable count is:

$$\text{Count per ml (or per g)} = (C \div V) \times M \text{ [35.7]}$$

e.g. for a sample with a mean colony count of 5.5 colonies per plate for a volume of 0.05 ml at a dilution of 10^{-7}, the count would be:

$$(5.5 \div 0.05) \times 10^7 = 1.1 \times 10^9 \text{ CFU ml}^{-1}$$

The count should be reported as colony-forming units (CFU) per ml, rather than as cells per ml, since a colony may be the product of more than one cell, particularly in filamentous microbes or in organisms with a tendency to aggregate. You should also be aware of the problems associated with counts of zero – these are best recorded as '<1', and you should then apply the appropriate correction factors for dilution and volume to obtain the detection limit. For example, a zero count (<1) of 100 μl of a fivefold dilution gives a detection limit of (<1 $\div$ 0.1) $\times$ 5 = <50 CFU ml^{-1}.

---

suitable medium until colonies are produced, giving a count by dividing the mean colony count per filter by the volume of sample filtered.

- Multiple tube count, or most probable number (MPN). A bacteriological technique where the sample is diluted and known volumes are transferred to several tubes of liquid medium (typically, five tubes at three volumes), chosen so that there is a low probability of the smallest volumes containing a viable cell. After incubation, the number of tubes showing growth (turbidity) is compared to tabulated values to give the most probable number (MPN per ml).

The principal advantage of culture-based counting procedures is that dead cells will not be counted. However, for such techniques, the incubation conditions and media used may not allow growth of all cells, underestimating the true viable count. Further problems are caused by cell clumping and dilution errors. In addition, such methods require sterile apparatus and media and the incubation period is lengthy before results are obtained. An alternative approach is to use direct microscopy, combined with 'vital' or 'mortal' staining. For example, the direct

Counting injured or stressed microbes – a resuscitation stage may be required, to allow cells to grow under selective conditions, p. 207.

epifluorescence technique (DEFT) uses acridine orange and UV epifluorescence microscopy to separate living and dead bacteria, while neutral red is a vital stain used for plant cells. Chapter 27 gives examples of vital/mortal stains for other cell types. A further approach is to use DNA-based methods, such as the polymerase chain reaction (PCR, p. 437).

Bioassays and their applications

A bioassay is a method of quantifying a chemical substance (analyte) by measuring its effect on a biological system under controlled conditions. The hypothetical underlying phenomena are summarised by the relationship:

$$A + Rec \rightleftharpoons ARec \rightarrow\rightarrow R \qquad [35.8]$$

where A is the analyte, Rec the receptor, ARec the analyte–receptor complex and R the response. This relation is analogous to the formation of product from an enzyme–substrate complex and, using similar mathematical arguments to those of enzyme kinetics (p. 383), it can be shown that the expected relationship between [A] and rate of response is hyperbolic (sigmoidal in a log–linear plot like Fig. 35.4). This pattern of response is usually observed in practice if a wide enough range of [A] is tested.

To carry out the assay, the response elicited by the unknown sample is compared to the response obtained for differing concentrations of the substance, as shown in Fig. 35.4. When fitting a curve to standard points and estimating unknowns, the available methods, in order of increasing accuracy, are:

1. fitting by eye;
2. using linear regression on a restricted 'linear' portion of the assay curve;
3. linearisation followed by regression (e.g. by probit transformation);
4. non-linear regression (e.g. to the Morgan–Mercer–Flodin equation).

In general, bioassay techniques have more potential faults than physicochemical assay techniques. These may include the following:

- A greater level of variability: error in the estimate of the unknown compound will result because no two organisms will respond in exactly the same way. Assay curves vary through time, and because they are non-linear, a full standard curve is required each time the assay is carried out.
- Lack of chemical information: bioassays provide information about *biological* activity; they say little about the chemical structure of an unknown compound. The presence of a specific compound may need to be confirmed by a physicochemical method (e.g. mass spectrometry).
- Possibility of interference: while many bioassays are very specific, it is possible that different chemicals in the extract may influence the results.

Despite these problems, bioassays are still much used. They are 'low-tech' and generally cheap to set up. They often allow detection at very low concentrations. Bioassays also provide the means to assess the biological activity of chemicals and to study changes in sensitivity to a chemical, which physicochemical techniques cannot do. Changes in sensitivity may

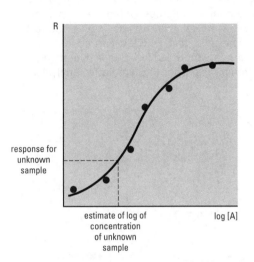

Fig. 35.4 Typical bioassay response curve, showing estimation of an unknown sample. Closed circles represent responses with standard samples.

Examples The following are typical bioassays:

- measuring the amount of a plant growth substance in a plant extract using the coleoptile straight growth assay;
- measuring the effect of a drug on the dilation of a person's pupils;
- measuring the mutagenic properties of a chemical compound in the Ames test (see Box 35.3).

Box 35.3 Mutagenicity testing using the Ames test – an example of a widely used bioassay

Chemical carcinogens can be identified by the formation of tumours in laboratory animals exposed to the compound under controlled conditions. However, such animal bioassays are time-consuming and expensive. Dr B.N. Ames and co-workers have shown that most carcinogens are also mutagens, i.e. they will induce mutational changes in DNA. The Ames test makes use of this correlation to provide a simple, rapid and inexpensive bioassay for the initial screening of potential carcinogens. The test makes use of particular strains of *Salmonella typhimurium* with the following characteristics:

- histidine auxotrophy – the tester strains are unable to grow on a minimal medium without added histidine: this characteristic is the result of specific mutational changes to the DNA of these strains, including base substitutions and frame shifts;
- increased cell envelope permeability, to permit access of the test compound to the cell interior;
- defects in excision repair systems and enhanced error-prone repair systems, to reduce the likelihood of DNA repair after treatment with a potential mutagen.

When grown in the presence of a chemical mutagen, the bacteria may revert to prototrophy as a result of back mutations that restore the wild-type phenotype: such revertants grow independently of external histidine and are able to form colonies on minimal medium, unlike the original test strains. The extent of reversion can be used to assess the mutagenic potential of a particular chemical compound. Since many chemicals must be activated *in vivo*, the test incorporates a rat liver homogenate (so-called 'S-9 activator', containing microsomal enzymes) to simulate the metabolic events within the liver. The tester strains are mixed with S-9 activator and a small amount of molten soft agar, then poured as a thin agar overlay (top agar) on a minimal medium plate. The top agar layer contains a very small amount of histidine, to allow the tester strains to divide a few times and express any mutational changes (i.e. prototrophy).

The test can be performed in one of two ways:

1. **Spot test:** a concentrated drop of the test compound is placed at the centre of the plate, either directly on the agar surface, or on a small filter paper disc. The test compound will diffuse into the agar and revertants appear as a ring of colonies around the site of inoculation, as shown in Fig. 35.5. The distance of the ring of colonies from this site provides a measure of the toxicity of the compound, while the number of colonies within the ring gives an indication of the relative mutagenicity of the test substance. The spot test is often carried out in a simplified form, without added S-9 activator, as a rapid preliminary test prior to quantitative analysis.

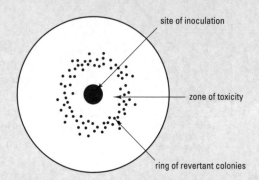

Fig. 35.5 Typical outcome of spot test (Ames test).

2. **Agar incorporation test:** known amounts of the test compound are mixed separately with molten top agar and the other constituents and poured onto separate minimal agar plates. After incubation for 48 h, revertants will appear as evenly dispersed colonies throughout the agar overlay. The number of colonies reflects the relative mutagenicity of the test compounds, with a direct relationship between colony count and the amount of mutagen. Agar incorporation tests can be used to generate dose–response curves similar to that shown in Fig. 35.4. The simplicity, sensitivity and reproducibility of the Ames test has resulted in its widespread use for screening potential carcinogens in many countries, though it is not an infallible test for carcinogenicity.

N.B. Safe handling procedures *must* be followed at all times, as the test substances may be carcinogenic – testers should wear gloves and avoid skin contact or ingestion.

be evident in the shape of the dose–response curve and its position on the concentration axis.

Bioassays can involve responses of whole organisms or parts of organisms. 'Isolated' responding systems (e.g. excised tissues or cells, Chapter 34) decrease the possibility of interference from other parts of the organism. Disadvantages include disruption of nutrition and wound damage during excision. Isolation can continue down to the molecular level, as in immunoassays (Chapter 38).

Bioassays are the basis for characterising the efficacy of drugs and the toxicity of chemicals. Here, response is often treated as a quantal (all-or-nothing) event. The E_{50} is defined as that concentration of a compound causing 50% of the organisms to respond. Where death is the observed response, the LD_{50} describes the concentration of a chemical that would cause 50% of the test organisms to die within a specified period under a specified set of conditions. Box 35.3 presents details of the Ames test, a widely used bioassay used to assess the mutagenicity of chemicals.

Considerations when setting up a bioassay

- The response should be easily measured and as metabolically 'close' to the initial binding event as possible.
- The experimental conditions should mimic the *in vivo* environment.
- The standards should be chemically identical to the compound being measured and spread over the expected concentration range being tested.
- The samples should be purified if interfering compounds are present and diluted so the response will be on the 'linear' portion of the assay curve.

To check for interference, the bioassay may be standardised against another method (preferably physicochemical). Related compounds known to be present in the analyte solution should be shown to have minimal activity in the bioassay. If an interfering compound is present, this may show up if a known amount of standard is added to sample vials – the result will not be the sum of independently determined results for the standard and sample.

Sources for further study

Ball, A.S. (1997) *Bacterial Cell Culture: Essential Data*. Wiley, New York.

Cartledge, T.G. (ed.) (1992) *In Vitro Cultivation of Micro-organisms*. Butterworth-Heinemann, Oxford.
[Includes in-depth coverage of the mathematical principles underlying growth in batch and continuous culture.]

Hewitt, W. and Vincent, S. (1989) *Theory and Application of Microbiological Assay*. Academic Press, New York.

Jennings, D.H. and Isaac, S. (1995) *Microbial Culture*. Bios, Oxford.

Rhodes, P.M. and Stanbury, P.F. (1997) *Applied Microbial Physiology: A Practical Approach*. IRL Press, Oxford.
[Provides details of growth requirements and culture methods applicable to a range of different microbes.]

Salanki, J., Jeffrey, D. and Hughes, G.M. (1994) *Biological Monitoring of the Environment: A Manual of Methods*. CAB, Wallingford.

Study exercises

35.1 Calculate the specific growth rate and doubling time of cells in culture. What are the specific growth rates and doubling times of the following? (Give all answers to 3 significant figures.)

Legal use of bioassays – in the UK, where bioassays involving 'higher' (vertebrate) animals are controlled by the **Animals Scientific Procedures Act (1986)**, they can only be carried out under the direct supervision of a scientist licensed by the Home Office.

(a) A broth culture of the yeast *Saccharomyces cerevisiae* growing in exponential phase and containing 5.2×10^4 cells at 10 am and 3.4×10^6 cells at 7 pm.

(b) A log phase culture of *E. coli* containing 3.0×10^4 CFU ml^{-1} at the start of the experiment and 6.7×10^7 CFU ml^{-1} at the end of the experiment, 200 minutes later.

(c) An actively growing culture of *Bacillus subtilis* containing 32 bacteria in 25 squares of a haemocytometer chamber at 13.00 hours and 250 bacteria in 25 squares of the same haemocytometer chamber at 15.30 hours.

35.2 Practise the calculations involved in using a haemocytometer to make a direct microscopic count. Express your answers to 3 significant figures in all cases.

(a) The mean cell count of a yeast suspension per small square of an improved Neubauer counting chamber was 6.42. If the volume of a small square is 2.5×10^{-7} ml, what is the cell count per ml?

(b) The following counts were obtained for bacteria in 20 individual small squares of a Petroff–Hauser counting chamber: 26, 36, 42, 35, 27, 16, 29, 50, 24, 43, 41, 35, 18, 36, 33, 47, 25, 46, 32, 57. If the volume of each small square is 8×10^{-7} ml, what is the cell count per ml?

(c) A 10^{-2} dilution of a dense suspension of *E. coli* was examined microscopically using an improved Neubauer counting chamber, giving a total of 78 cells in a total of 25 small squares. If the volume of each small square is 2.5×10^{-7} ml what is the cell count per ml of the original (undiluted) suspension?

(d) A dilute suspension of yeast cells was concentrated tenfold by centrifuging 10 ml and resuspending the pellet in 1 ml. The mean cell count of the concentrated yeast suspension per large square of a Petroff–Hauser counting chamber was 6.8. If the volume of the large square is 2×10^{-5} ml, what is the cell count per ml of the original suspension?

35.3 Practise the calculations involved in making a plate count. Express your answers to 3 significant figures.

(a) The mean spread plate count for 100 µl of a 10^{-5} dilution of a culture of *E. coli* was 54.4 CFU. What is the mean plate count per ml of the original suspension?

(b) Three replicate plates of nutrient agar were each spread with 200 µl of a 10^{-3} dilution of a bacterial suspension, giving colony counts of 34, 40 and 37 after 24 h incubation. What is the mean plate count per ml of the original suspension?

(c) A 20-fold dilution of a yeast suspension was used to prepare four replicate pour plates, each containing 500 µl of this dilution and giving counts of 211, 186, 194 and 202 after incubation. What is the mean plate count per ml of the original suspension?

(d) A sample of 50 g of raw seafood was homogenised and diluted to 2% w/v in sterile saline solution. Three replicate pour plates were prepared using 1 ml of the diluted sample, giving counts for *E. coli* of 35, 41 and 32. What is the average count of *E. coli* per 100 g of raw seafood?

(e) Duplicate samples of 250 ml of river water were filtered through separate sterile membranes of pore size 0.2 μm. The membranes were then transferred to the surface of an agar-based medium and incubated for 48 h at 37 °C, giving colony counts of 45 and 32 respectively. What is the mean count per 100 ml of river water?

(f) A sample of bottled drinking water was processed by serial decimal dilution and 500 μl samples of each dilution were pour plated and incubated at 22 °C for 72 h. The colony counts obtained for the three replicate plates of the 10^{-1} dilution were 28, 32 and 39. Does this water meet the EU regulations for mineral water, which specify a maximum average plate count at 22 °C of 100 CFU ml^{-1}?

35.4 **Use bioassay data to estimate the amount of analyte in unknown samples.** Bioassay data obtained by exposing water fleas (*Daphnia* sp.) to a purified algal toxin are shown in the following table.

(a) Graph the data and use the graph to estimate the toxin contents of two samples obtained from two lochs which gave (i) a heart rate of 130 beats per minute and (ii) a heart rate of 25 beats per minute.

(b) Which one of the two estimates would be the least reliable and why?

(c) How could you improve the reliability of this estimate, if you had more of the sample?

(d) What unmeasured factors might limit the usefulness of this assay?

Responses of *Daphnia* to toxin

Toxin concentration (mmol l^{-1})	Mean heart rate of *Daphnia* sp. (beats per minute)
1.00×10^{-3}	20
3.16×10^{-4}	23
1.00×10^{-4}	26
3.16×10^{-5}	50
1.00×10^{-5}	180
3.16×10^{-6}	192
1.00×10^{-6}	195

35.5 **Use agar diffusion bioassay data to quantify a growth inhibitor in a sample.** Agar diffusion bioassay is a simple means of estimating the amount of an inhibitory substance in a test sample, by adding the substance, in aqueous solution, to wells cut in a Petri plate of agar medium seeded with a microbe sensitive to the substance and then incubating the plate at an appropriate growth temperature. Diffusion of the inhibitory substance gives a zone of growth inhibition proportional to $\log_{10}$ of the concentration of substance. In the following example and table (overleaf), the amount of the antibiotic nisin in a test sample can be determined by comparing the degree of growth inhibition of *Bacillus subtilis* for the test solution and a series of standards containing known concentrations of nisin. Prepare a calibration curve and determine the nisin concentration of solution 5 (unknown). Express your answer in $\mu\text{g}\,\text{ml}^{-1}$, to one decimal place.

Growth inhibition of *B. subtilis* in solutions containing different amounts of nisin

Solution	Nisin content ($\mu\text{g}\,\text{ml}^{-1}$)	Zone of growth inhibition (mm)
1	40	26.5
2	20	23
3	10	19.5
4	5	17
5	unknown (test solution)	22.5

Homogenisation and fractionation of cells and tissues

Disruption – *a process involving structural damage to cells and tissues, to an extent where the biomolecule or complex of interest is released.*

Homogenisation – *a process where cells and tissues are broken into fragments small enough to create a uniform, stable emulsion (the homogenate).*

Homogeniser – *a general term for any equipment used to disrupt or homogenise cells and tissues.*

Most biological molecules and subcellular complexes must be isolated from their source material in order to be studied in detail. Unless the biomolecule is already a component of an aqueous medium (e.g. plasma, tissue exudate), the first step will be to disrupt the structure of the appropriate cells or tissues. Following disruption and/or homogenisation, the *in vitro* environment will be very different from that of the intact cell, and it is important that the integrity of the biomolecule or subcellular complex is preserved as far as possible during the isolation procedure.

KEY POINT Disruption may be achieved by chemical, physical or mechanical procedures – the rigour of the technique(s) required will depend on the intracellular location of the molecule and the nature of the source material.

Types of cell and their susceptibility to disruption

Cell walls are a major obstacle to disruption in many organisms and the technique used for a given application must take into account this aspect. With animal cells, there is no cell wall and the plasma membrane and cytoskeleton are relatively weak: unicellular suspensions of animal cells (e.g. blood cells) can be disrupted by gentle techniques. Animal cells within tissues are more difficult to disrupt, due to the presence of connective tissue. Muscle requires vigorous techniques, as a result of additional contractile proteins. For plant cells, the plasma membrane is surrounded by a cellulose cell wall, sometimes with additional components, e.g. lignin or waxes. As a result, large shear forces are often required to disrupt plant cells.

Most Gram-positive and Gram-negative bacteria are surrounded by a rigid, protective cell wall. Peptidoglycan is a major structural component and this may be degraded by the enzyme lysozyme, particularly in certain Gram-positive organisms. In contrast, the outer membrane of Gram-negative bacteria (Fig. 36.1b) protects against lysozyme: however, prior treatment of Gram-negative bacteria with EDTA destabilises the outer membrane by removing Ca^{2+}, making the cell sensitive to lysozyme. In an osmotically buffered solution, the cells will be converted to sphaeroplasts (p. 223), since components the Gram-negative envelope will remain after lysozyme treatment. Note also that some Gram-positive bacteria may be insensitive to lysozyme, due either to a modified peptidoglycan structure or to additional protective outer layers (proteinaceous S-layers: Fig. 36.1a).

The cell walls of filamentous fungi and yeasts are very robust, containing up to 90% polysaccharide (e.g. chitin, mannan), with embedded protein microfibrils – they are often difficult to disrupt, requiring enzymic digestion and/or mechanical homogenisation.

(a)

(b)

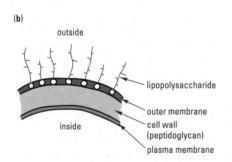

Fig. 36.1 Cell envelopes of (a) Gram-positive and (b) Gram-negative bacteria.

Homogenising media

The solution used for homogenisation serves several purposes, since it acts as a solvent or suspension medium for the released components; it serves as a cooling medium (since many biological macromolecules are denatured by heat); and it contains various reagents that may help to preserve the biological integrity of components. A typical medium will contain:

- Buffer. This replaces the intracellular buffer systems and is needed to prevent pH changes that might denature proteins. TRIS and phosphate buffers are often used for 'physiological' pH values (7.0–8.0); alternatives include various zwitterionic buffers (p. 151).

- Inorganic salts. The intracellular ionic strength is quite high, so KCl and NaCl are often included to maintain the ionic strength of the homogenate. However, the total concentration of inorganic salts should be kept below $100 \, \text{mmol} \, l^{-1}$, to avoid thickening of the homogenate due to solubilisation of structural proteins.

- Sucrose. This is used to prevent osmotic lysis of organelles (e.g. mitochondria, lysosomes), and stabilises proteins from hydrophobic intracellular environments by reducing the polarity of the aqueous medium.

- Mg^{2+}. This helps to preserve the integrity of membrane systems by counteracting the fixed negative charges of membrane phospholipids.

- EDTA. This chelates divalent cations and removes metal ions (e.g. Cu^{2+}, Pb^{2+}, Hg^{2+}) that inactivate proteins by binding to thiol groups. In addition, it removes Ca^{2+} which could activate certain proteases, nucleases and lipases in the homogenate.

- Protease inhibitors (e.g. phenylmethanesulphonylfluoride, PMSF; L-trans-epoxysuccinylleucylamido-(4-guanodino)-butane, E-64; leupeptin). These protect solubilised proteins from digestion by intracellular proteases, mainly released from lysosomes on disruption of the cell. Lysosomal proteases have acid pH optima, another reason for maintaining the pH of the medium close to neutrality.

- Reducing agents (e.g. 2-mercaptoethanol, dithiothreitol, cysteine at $\approx 1 \, \text{mmol} \, l^{-1}$). These reagents prevent oxidation of certain proteins, particularly those with free thiol groups that may be oxidised to disulphide bonds when released from the cell under aerobic conditions.

- Detergents (e.g. Triton X-100, SDS). These cause dissociation of proteins and lipoproteins from the cell membrane, aiding the release of membrane-bound and intracellular components.

Methods of disrupting cells and tissues

Prior to disruption, animal tissues will need to be freed of any visible fat deposits and connective components, and then randomly sliced with fine scissors or a scalpel. Any fibrous and vascular tissue should be removed from plant material. Disruption can be achieved by mechanical and non-mechanical means: the principal applications of various methods are described in Table 36.1 for the major cell and tissue types.

Non-mechanical methods

- Osmotic shock: cells are first placed in a hypertonic solution of high osmolality (p. 141), e.g. 20% w/v sucrose, leading to loss of water. On dilution of this solution (e.g. by addition of water or transfer to a hypotonic solution), the cells will burst due to water influx. Osmotic

Using chelating agents – EDTA (ethylenediaminetetraacetic acid) and EGTA (ethylenebis(oxethylenenitrilo)-tetraacetic acid). If Mg^{2+} is an important component of the medium, use EGTA, which does not chelate Mg^{2+}.

Extracting proteins from plants – carry out all post-homogenisation procedures as quickly as possible, because plant cell vacuoles may contain phenols that will inactivate proteins when released.

Definitions

Isotonic – *a medium with the same water potential (p. 143) as the cells or tissues.*

Hypertonic – *a medium with a more negative water potential, compared with the cells or medium.*

Hypotonic – *a medium with a less negative water potential, compared with the cells or medium.*

shock treatment is effective for wall-less cells, sphaeroplasts (p. 223) or protoplasts.

- Freezing and thawing: causing leakage of intracellular material, following cell wall and membrane damage and internal disruption due to ice crystal formation.
- Lytic enzymes: damaging the cell wall and/or plasma membrane. Cells can then be disrupted by osmotic shock or gentle mechanical treatment.

Mechanical methods

All mechanical procedures for cell disruption generate heat, and this may denature proteins. Therefore it is very important to cool the starting material, the homogenising medium, and, if possible, the homogeniser itself (to ≈4 °C). The homogenisation should be carried out in short bursts, and the homogenate should be cooled in an ice bath between each burst. Cooling will also reduce the activity of any degradative enzymes in the homogenate. Ideally, carry out homogenisation in a walk-in cooler ('cold room').

Equipment commonly used includes:

- Mixers and blenders. These are similar to domestic liquidisers, with a static vessel and rotating blades. The Waring blender is widely used: it has a stainless steel vessel that will stay cool if pre-chilled. The vessel and blades are designed to maximise turbulence, both disrupting and homogenising tissues and cells.

Avoiding protein denaturation during homogenisation – excessive frothing of the homogenate indicates denaturation of proteins (think of whipping egg whites for meringue).

Table 36.1 Summary of techniques for the disruption of tissues and cells – note that safety glasses should be worn for all procedures

Technique	Suitability	Comments
Non-mechanical methods		
Osmotic shock	Animal soft tissues Some plant cells	Small scale only
Freeze/thaw	Animal soft tissues Some bacteria	Time consuming; small scale; closed system – suitable for pathogens with appropriate safety measures; some enzymes are cold-labile
Lytic enzymes, e.g. lipases; proteases pectinase; cellulase	Animal cells Plant cells	Mild and selective; small scale; expensive; enzymes must be removed once lysis is complete
Lysozyme	Some bacteria	Gram-negative bacteria must be pretreated with EDTA. Suitable for some organisms resistant to mechanical disruption.
Mechanical methods		
Pestle and mortar + abrasives	Tough tissues	Not suitable for delicate tissues
Ball mills + glass beads	Bacteria and fungi	May cause organelle damage in eukaryotes
Blenders and rotor-stators	Plant and animal tissues	Ineffective for microbes
Homogenisers (glass and Teflon)	Soft, delicate tissues e.g. white blood cells, liver	Glass may shatter – wear safety glasses during use
Solid extrusion (Hughes press)	Tough plant material; bacteria; yeasts	Small scale
Liquid extrusion (French pressure cell)	Microbial cells	Small scale
Ultrasonication	Microbial cells	Cooling required; small scale; may cause damage to organelles, especially in eukaryotic cells.

Fig. 36.2 Components of a rotor-stator homogeniser.

Fig. 36.3 Ground-glass homogeniser.

- Ball mills (e.g. Retch mixer mill, Mickle mill). These devices contain glass beads that vibrate and collide with each other and with tissues/cells, leading to disruption.

- Liquid extrusion devices (e.g. French pressure cell). Cells are forced from a vessel to the outside, through a very narrow orifice at high pressures ($\approx$100 MPa). The resulting pressure changes are a powerful means of disrupting cells.

- Solid extrusion (e.g. Hughes press). Here, a frozen cell paste is forced through a narrow orifice, where the shear forces and the abrasive properties of the ice crystals cause cell disruption.

- Rotor-stators (e.g. Ultra-turrax® homogeniser). These have a rotor (a set of stainless steel blades) and a stator (a slotted stainless steel cylinder) at the tip of a stainless steel shaft, immersed in the homogenising medium: the arrangement is illustrated in Fig. 36.2. The high speed of the rotor blades causes material in the homogenising fluid to be sucked into the dispersing head, where it is pressed radially through the slots in the stator. Along with the cutting action of the rotor blades, the material is subjected to very high shear and thrust and the resulting turbulence in the gap between rotor and stator gives effective mixing. The vigour of the homogenisation process can be altered by varying the rotor speed setting. Various sizes of rotor-stator are available, with typical diameters in the range 8–65 mm: the smaller sizes are particularly useful for small-scale preparations.

- Sonicators. Ultrasonic waves are transmitted to an aqueous suspension of cells via a metal probe. The ultrasound creates bubbles within the liquid and these produce shock waves when they collapse. Successful disruption depends on the correct choice of power and incubation time, together with pH, temperature and ionic strength of the suspension medium, often obtained by trial and error. You can reduce the effects of heating during ultrasonication by using short 'bursts' of power (10–30 s), with rests of 30–60 s in between, and by keeping your cell suspension on ice during disruption. An ultrasonic water bath provides a more gentle means of disrupting certain types of cells, e.g. some bacterial and animal cells.

- Homogenisers. These involve the reciprocating movement of a ground glass or Teflon® pestle within a glass tube (Fig. 36.3). Cells are forced against the walls of the tube, releasing their contents. For glass pestles, the tubes also have ground glass homogenising surfaces and may have an overflow chamber. The homogeniser can either be hand operated (e.g. Dounce), or motorised (e.g. Potter-Elvejham). The clearance between the pestle and the tube (range 0.05–0.5 mm) must be chosen to suit the particular application.

Cell fractionation and the isolation of organelles

The fractionation and separation of organelles from a cell homogenate by differential centrifugation are described in Chapter 43. Particular organelles can be obtained by appropriate choice of source tissue and homogenisation method, as illustrated in Table 36.2 for the major types of organelle.

Table 36.2 Isolation and fractionation procedures for various organelles

Stage	Nuclei	Mitochondria	Microsomes	Chloroplasts*
Source	Thymus tissue, which has little cytoplasm, giving high yields.	Beef heart, with fat and connective tissue removed, then cubed and minced. Keep at pH 7.5 using TRIS buffer.	Rat liver, stored overnight to reduce glycogen content.	Spinach leaves, de-ribbed and cut into 1 cm strips.
Pretreatment	Rinse with buffered physiological saline. Suspend in homogenising medium.	Suspend in 2× volume of ice-cold homogenising medium. Squeeze through muslin.	Chop finely with scissors and wash in 2× volume of homogenising medium.	Rinse, then suspend in 3× volume of prechilled homogenising medium.
Homogenising medium	250 mmol l^{-1} sucrose; 10 mmol l^{-1} TRIS/HCl buffer, pH 7.6; 5 mmol l^{-1} $MgCl_2$; 0.2–0.5% v/v Triton X-100	250 mmol l^{-1} sucrose; 10 mmol l^{-1} TRIS/HCl buffer pH 7.7, containing 1 mmol l^{-1} succinic acid and 0.2 mmol l^{-1} EDTA.	250 mmol l^{-1} sucrose; 50 mmol l^{-1} TRIS/HCl buffer, pH 7.5; 25 mmol l^{-1} KCl; 5 mmol l^{-1} $MgCl_2$.	400 mmol l^{-1} sucrose; 25 mmol l^{-1} HEPES/NaOH buffer at pH 7.6; 2 mmol l^{-1} EDTA.
Homogenisation	Waring blender, low speed, 3 min.	Bring to pH 7.8 using 2 mol l^{-1} TRIS base: Waring blender, high speed, 15 s: check and adjust pH to 7.8 and repeat blending step, 5 s.	Potter-Elvejham glass homogeniser with a Teflon pestle – 3 × 5 min at 800 rpm.	Prechilled Waring blender or rotor-stator.
Filtration/ centrifugation	Filter through gauze. Spin at 2000 *g* for 10 min; discard supernatant. Repeat the homogenisation, filtration and centrifugation stages to improve purity of organelles.	Spin at 1200 *g* for 20 min: filter supernatant through muslin: centrifuge at 26 000 *g* for 15 min. Remove and discard upper (lighter) layer of pellet. Resuspend lower layer and rehomogenise (2 × 5 s). Centrifuge at 26 000 *g* for 15 min.	Centrifuge at 680 *g* for 10 min – discard pellet; centrifuge at 10 000 *g* for 10 min – discard pellet; centrifuge at 100 000 *g* for 60 min – retain pellet. Resuspend in buffer, pH 8.0 and re-centrifuge at 100 000 *g* for 60 min.	Pass through several layers of muslin (wear gloves); centrifuge at 2500 *g* for 60 s; resuspend pellet in buffer, pH 7.6; recentrifuge at 2500 *g* for 60 s. The colour of the supernatants gives a visual indication of chloroplast damage (e.g. if green).
Before use	Resuspend in homogenisation medium without Triton X-100.	Resuspend pellet in buffer, pH 7.8 and either use immediately, or store at −20 °C overnight.	Resuspend in buffer solution at pH 8.0.	Resuspend pellet in appropriate incubation medium, containing sucrose, e.g. for CO_2/O_2 studies, p. 398.

*An alternative approach is to use plant protoplasts (p. 223) as the starting material, releasing the chloroplasts by gentle lysis – diluting the medium with water.

Sources for further study

Anon. *Ultrasonic Homogenizers.* Available: http://www.biologics-inc.com/ultrasonic_homogenizers.htm Last accessed 08/01/03.
[One of many websites dealing with commercial products]

Boyer, R. (2000) *Modern Experimental Biochemistry*, 3rd edn. Benjamin Cummings, San Francisco.
[Also covers centrifugation, spectroscopy, etc.]

Graham, J.M. and Rickwood, D. (1997) *Subcellular Fractionation: A Practical Approach.* IRL, Oxford.

Hopkins, T. *Review of Laboratory Cell Disrupters.* Available: http://www.biospec.com/HomePage/Review.html

Last accessed 08/01/03.
[Provides a brief overview of methods.]

Wilson, K. and Walker, J. (eds) (2000) *Principles and Techniques of Practical Biochemistry*, 5th edn. Cambridge University Press, Cambridge. [Also covers a range of other topics, including spectroscopy and chromatography.]

Study exercises

36.1 Consider suitable disruption procedures for particular types of cell or tissue. After reading this chapter, identify the major problems associated with disrupting each of the following, and list suitable practical procedures to overcome these problems:
(a) Gram-negative bacteria;
(b) skeletal muscle;
(c) plant tissue.

36.2 Select a suitable disruption technique for the preparation of intracellular components. How might the procedure used to prepare a soluble cytoplasmic protein from fresh liver differ from that required for the isolation of intact organelles?

36.3 Test your understanding of the function of homogenisation medium components. The following list provides a number of possible components that might be used in a homogenisation medium:
(a) sucrose;
(b) low ionic strength buffer;
(c) dithiothreitol;
(d) detergent (e.g. Triton X-100).
Select one of these components to include in a medium for preparing:
 (i) a membrane protein from liver tissue;
 (ii) a mitochondrial suspension from liver tissue;
(iii) an oxygen-sensitive enzyme from pancreatic tissue;
(iv) a protein from the sarcolemma (cytoplasm) of skeletal muscle.
Give a brief explanation for your selection in each case.

Analytical techniques

Calibration and its application to quantitative analysis

There are many instances where it is necessary to measure the quantity of a test substance using a calibrated procedure. You are most likely to encounter this approach in one or more of the following practical exercises:

- Quantitative spectrophotometric assay of biomolecules (Chapter 41).
- Flame or atomic absorption spectroscopic analysis of metal ions in biological solutions (pp. 276–7).
- Using a chromogenic or fluorogenic substrate to determine the activity of an enzyme (p. 397).
- Quantitative chromatographic analysis, e.g. GC or HPLC (Chapter 45).
- Using a bioassay system (p. 231) to quantify a test substance: examples include immunodiffusion (Chapter 38) and radioimmunoassay (p. 253).

In all of these instances, calibration involves the establishment of a relationship between the measured response (the 'signal') and one or more 'standards' containing a known amount of substance. In some instances, you can measure a signal due to an inherent property of the substance, e.g. the absorption of UV light by nucleic acids (p. 366), whereas in other cases you will need to react it with another substance to see the result (e.g. molecular weight measurements of DNA fragments after electrophoresis, visualised using ethidium bromide (p. 367), or to produce a measurable response (e.g. the reaction of cupric ions and peptide bonds in the biuret assay for proteins, p. 348).

The different types of calibration curve

By preparing a set of solutions (termed 'standards'), each containing either (i) a known *amount* or (ii) a specific *concentration* of the substance, and then measuring the response of each standard solution, the underlying relationship can be established in graphical form as a 'calibration curve', or 'standard curve'. This can then be used to determine either (i) the amount or (ii) the concentration of the substance in one or more test samples. Alternatively, the response can be expressed solely in mathematical terms: an example of this approach is the determination of chlorophyll pigments in plant extracts by measuring absorption at particular wavelengths, and then applying a formula based on previous (published) measurements for purified pigments (p. 273).

There are various types of standard curve: in the simplest cases, the relationship between signal and substance will be linear, or nearly so, and the calibration will be represented best by a straight-line graph (see Box 37.1). In some instances (Fig. 37.1a), you will need to transform either the *x* values or *y* values, in order to produce a linear graph (e.g. in radial immunodiffusion bioassay, where the *y* values are squared, pp. 313–5. In other instances, the straight-line relationship may only hold up to a certain value (the 'linear dynamic range') and beyond this point the graph may curve (e.g. in quantitative spectrophotometry, the

Understanding quantitative measurement – Chapters 28 and 49 contain details of the basic principles of valid measurement, while Chapters 38–48 deal with some of the specific analytical techniques used in biomolecular science. The use of internal standards is covered on p. 311.

Calibrating laboratory apparatus – this is important in relation to validation of equipment, e.g. when determining the accuracy and precision of a pipettor by the weighing method: see p. 118.

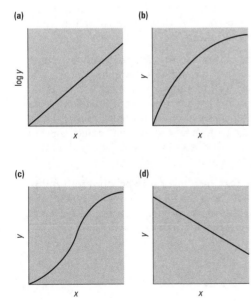

Fig. 37.1 Calibration curves: (a) log-linear; (b) curvilinear; (c) sigmoid, or S-shaped; (d) inverse.

Box 37.1 The stages involved in preparing and using a calibration curve

1. **Decide on an appropriate test method** – for example, in a project, you may need to research the best approach to the analysis of a particular metabolite in your biological material.

2. **Select either (a) amount or (b) concentration, and an appropriate range and number of standards** – in practical classes, this may be given in your schedule, along with detailed instructions on how to make up the standard solutions. In other cases, you may be expected to work this out from first principles (Chapters 22–24 give worked examples) – aim to have evenly spaced values along the x axis.

3. **Prepare your standards very carefully** – due attention to detail is required: for example, you should ensure that you check the calibration of pipettors beforehand, using the weighing method (p. 123). Don't forget the 'zero standard' plus any other controls required, e.g. to test for interference due to other chemical substances. Your standards should cover the range of values expected in your test samples.

4. **Assay the standards and the unknown (test) samples** – preferably all at the same time, to avoid introducing error due to changes in the sensitivity or drift in the zero setting of the instrument with time. It is a good idea to measure all of your standard solutions at the outset, and then measure your test solutions, checking that the 'zero standard' and 'top standard' give the same values after, say, every six test measurements. If the re-measured standards do not fall within a reasonable margin of the previous value, then you will have to go back and recalibrate the instrument, and repeat the last six test measurements. If your test samples lie outside the range of your standards, you may need to repeat the assay using diluted test samples (extrapolation of your curve may not be valid, see p. 456).

5. **Draw the standard curve, or determine the underlying relationship** – Figure 37.2 gives an example of a typical linear calibration curve, where the spectrophotometric absorbance of a series of standard solutions is related to the amount of substance. When using Excel® or graphics packages (pp. 68–79), it is often appropriate to use

Fig. 37.2 Typical calibration curve for spectrophotometric analysis.

Model I linear regression (p. 494) to produce a linear trend line (also termed the 'line of best fit') and you can then quote the value of r^2, which is a measure of the 'fit' of the measurements to the line (see pp. 493–4). However, you should take care not to use a linear plot when the underlying relationship is clearly non-linear (Fig. 63.12) and you must consider whether the assumptions of the regression analysis are valid (e.g. for transformed data).

6. **Determine the amount or concentration in each unknown sample** – either by reading the appropriate value from the calibration curve, or by using the underlying mathematical relationship, i.e. $y = a + bx$ (pp. 471–2). Make sure you draw any horizontal and vertical construction lines very carefully – students often lose marks unnecessarily by submitting poorly drawn construction lines within practical reports.

7. **Correct for dilution or concentration, where appropriate** – for example, if you diluted each test sample by 10-fold, then you would need to multiply by 10 to determine the value for the undiluted test sample. As another example, if you assayed 0.2 ml of test sample, you would need to multiply the value obtained from the calibration curve by 5, to give the value per ml.

8. **Quote your test results to an appropriate number of significant figures** – this should reflect the accuracy of the method used (see pp. 467–9), not the size of your calculator's display.

Beer–Lambert relationship often becomes invalid at high absorbance, giving a curve, Fig. 37.1b). Some calibration curves are sigmoid (Fig. 37.1c). Finally, the signal may *decrease* in response to an increase in the substance (Fig. 37.1d), e.g. radioimmunoassay, where an inverse sigmoid calibration curve is obtained (p. 253). In some practical classes, you may be told that the relationship is expected to be linear, curvilinear, or whatever, while in others you may have to decide the form of the standard curve as part of the exercise.

Practical considerations

Amount or concentration?

This first step is often the most confusing for new students. It is vital that you understand the difference between *amount* of substance (e.g. mg, ng), and *concentration* (the amount of substance per unit volume, e.g. $mmol\,l^{-1}$, $mol\,m^{-3}$, % w/v) before you begin your practical work. Essentially, you have to choose whether to work in terms of either (i) the total amount of substance in your assay vessel (e.g. test tube, or cuvette) or (ii) the final concentration of the substance in your assay vessel, which is independent of the volume used (see worked examples, p. 130). Either way, this is usually plotted on the x (horizontal) axis and the measured response on the y (vertical) axis.

Choice of standards

In your early practical classes, you may be provided with a stock solution (p. 131), from which you then have to prepare a specified number of standard solutions. In such cases, you will need to understand how to use dilutions to achieve the required amounts or concentrations (pp. 131–2). In later work and projects, you may need to prepare your standards from chemical reagents in solid form, where the important considerations are purity and solubility (p. 129). For professional analysis (e.g. in forensic science, or clinical biochemistry), it is often important to be able to trace the original standard or stock solution back to national or international standards (Chapter 49).

How many standards are required?

This may be given in your practical schedule, or you may have to decide what is appropriate (e.g. in project work and research). If the form and working range of the standard curve are known in advance, this may influence your choice – for example, linear calibration curves can be established with fewer standards than curvilinear relationships. In some instances, analytical instruments can be calibrated using a single standard solution, often termed a 'calibrator'. Replication of each standard solution is a good idea, since it will give you some information on the variability involved in preparing and assaying the standards. Consider whether it is best to plot mean values on your standard curve, or whether you should plot the individual values (if one value appears to be well off the line, you are likely to have made an error, and you may need to check and repeat).

Preparing your standards

It is extremely important to take the greatest care to measure out all chemicals and liquids very accurately, to achieve the best possible

Example A test tube containing 8 ml of water plus 2 ml of 1% w/v NaCl ($M_r = 58.44$) would have a *mass concentration* of 0.2% w/v NaCl (a five-fold dilution of the original NaCl solution), which can also be expressed as $2\,g\,l^{-1}$; in terms of *molar concentration* (p. 138), this would be equivalent to $2 \div 58.44 = 0.0342\,mol\,l^{-1}$ (to 3 significant figures). Expressed in terms of the *amount* of NaCl test tube, this would be 0.02 g in *mass*, or $0.02 \div 58.44 = 3.42 \times 10^{-4}$ in the mol ($342\,\mu$mol) in *moles*.

Plotting a standard curve – do not force your calibration line to pass through zero if it clearly does not. There is no reason to assume that the zero value is any more accurate than any other reading you have made.

Dealing with interfering substances – one approach is to use the method of 'standard additions', where the standards all contain a fixed additional amount of the sample (see e.g. Dean, 1997). Internal standards (pp. 310–11) can also be used to detect such problems.

standard curve. The grade of volumetric flask used and temperature of the solution also affect accuracy (grade A apparatus is best). You may also consider what other additives might be required in your standard solutions. For example, do your test samples have high levels of potentially interfering substances, and should these also be added to your standards? Also consider what controls and blank solutions to prepare.

KEY POINT The validity of your standard curve depends upon careful preparation of standards, especially in relation to accurate dispensing of the volumes of any stock solution and diluting liquid – the results for your test samples can only be as good as your standard curve!

Preparing the calibration curve and determinining the amount of the unknown (test) sample(s)

This is described in stepwise fashion within Box 37.1. Check you understand the requirements of graph drawing, especially in relation to plotted curves (p. 455) and the mathematics of straight-line graphs (p. 471).

Text reference

Dean, J.D. (1997) *Atomic Absorption and Plasma Spectroscopy*, 2nd edn. Wiley, Chichester.
[Chapter 1 deals with calibration, and covers the principle of standard additions.]

Sources for further study

Anon. Statlets-Data Analysis.
Available: http://www.sgcorp.com/statlets.htm
Last accessed 08/01/03.
[On-line access to Java applet software for calibration curves.]

Brown, P.J. (1994) *Measurement, Regression, and Calibration*. Clarendon Press, Oxford.
[Covers advanced methods, including curve fitting and multivariate methods.]

Mark, H. (1991) *Principles and Practice of Spectroscopic Calibration*. Wiley, New York.

Miller, J.N. and Miller, J.C. (2000) *Statistics and Chemometrics for Analytical Chemistry*, 4th edn. Prentice Hall, Harlow.
[Gives detailed coverage of calibration methods and the validity of analytical measurements.]

Study exercises

37.1 Determine unknowns from a hand-drawn calibration curve. The following data are for a set of calibration standards for Zn, measured by atomic absorption spectrophotometry.

Absorbance measurements for a series of standard solutions containing different amounts of zinc

Zinc concentration ($\mu g\,ml^{-1}$)	Absorbance
0	0.000
1	0.082
2	0.174
3	0.257
4	0.340
5	0.408
6	0.463
7	0.511
8	0.543
9	0.561
10	0.575

Draw a calibration curve by hand using graph paper and estimate the concentration of zinc in the following water samples:
(a) an undiluted sample, giving an absorbance of 0.157
(b) a 20-fold dilution, giving an absorbance of 0.304
(c) a fivefold dilution, giving an absorbance of 0.550.
Give your answer to 3 significant figures in each case.

37.2 Determine unknowns from a calibration curve produced in Excel®. The following data are for a set of calibration standards for protein content, measured by the Lowry (Folin–Ciocalteau) method (p. 349).

Absorbance measurements for a series of protein standards

Protein (mg per tube)	Absorbance (A_{600})
0.00	0.000
0.02	0.161
0.04	0.284
0.06	0.438
0.08	0.572
0.10	0.762

Using PC-based software (e.g. Excel®), fit a trend line (linear regression) and determine the protein content of solutions with the following absorbances:
(a) 0.225   (b) 0.465   (c) 0.682
Give your answers to 3 significant figures in each case.

37.3 Identify the errors in a calibration curve. The margin figure shows a calibration curve of the type that might be submitted in a practical write-up. List the errors and compare your observations with the list given on p. 511.

Calibration graph

Immunological methods

Antibody – a protein produced in response to an antigen (an *anti*body-*gen*erating foreign macromolecule).

Epitope – a site on the antigen that determines its interaction with a particular antibody.

Hapten – a substance that contains at least one epitope, but is too small to induce antibody formation unless it is linked to a macromolecule.

Ligand – a molecule or chemical group that binds to a particular site on another molecule.

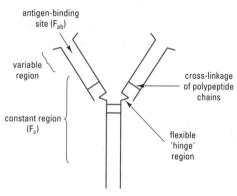

Fig. 38.1 Diagrammatic representation of IgG (antibody).

Producing polyclonal antibodies – in the UK, this is controlled by Government regulations, since it involves vertebrate animals: personnel must be licensed by the Home Office and must operate in accordance with the Animals Scientific Procedures Act (1986).

Antibodies are an important component of the immune system, which protects animals against certain diseases (see Roitt and Delves, 2001). They are produced in response to foreign macromolecules (antigens). A particular antibody will bind to a site on a specific antigen, forming an antigen–antibody complex (immune complex). Immunological bioassays use the specificity of this interaction for:

- identifying macromolecules, cellular components or whole cells;
- quantifying a particular substance.

Antibody structure

An antibody is a complex globular protein, or immunoglobulin (Ig). While there are several types, IgG is the major soluble antibody in vertebrates and is used in most immunological assays. Its main features are:

- Shape: IgG is a Y-shaped molecule (Fig. 38.1), with two antigen-binding sites.
- Specificity: variation in amino acid composition at the antigen-binding sites explains the specificity of the antigen–antibody interaction.
- Flexibility: each IgG molecule can interact with epitopes which are different distances apart, including those on different antigen molecules.
- Labelling: regions other than the antigen-binding sites can be labelled, e.g. using a radioisotope or an enzyme with fluorogenic or chromogenic detection (p. 379).

KEY POINT The presence of two antigen-binding sites on a single flexible antibody molecule is relevant to many immunological assays, especially the agglutination and precipitation reactions.

Antibody production

Polyclonal antibodies
These are commonly used at undergraduate level. They are produced by repeated injection of antigen into a laboratory animal. After a suitable period (3–4 weeks) blood is removed and allowed to clot, leaving a liquid phase (polyclonal antiserum) containing many different IgG antibodies, resulting in:

- cross-reaction with other antigens or haptens;
- batch variation, as individual animals produce slightly different antibodies in response to the same antigen;
- non-specificity, as the antiserum will contain many other antibodies.

Standardisation of polyclonal antisera therefore is difficult. You may need to assess the amount of cross-reaction, inter-batch variation or non-specific binding using appropriate controls, assayed at the same time as the test samples.

Monoclonal antibodies
These are specific to a single epitope and are produced from individual clones of cells, grown using cell culture techniques (p. 225). Such cultures

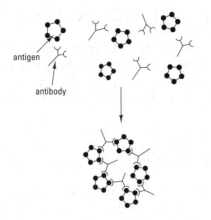

Fig. 38.2 Formation of an antigen–antibody complex (immune complex).

provide a stable source of antibodies of known, uniform specificity. While monoclonal antibodies are likely to be used increasingly in future years, polyclonal antisera are currently employed for most routine immunological assays.

Agglutination tests

When antibodies interact with a suspension of a particulate antigen, e.g. cells or latex particles, the formation of immune complexes (Fig. 38.2) causes visible clumping, termed agglutination. A positive haemagglutination reaction gives an even 'carpet' of red cells over the base of the tube, while a negative reaction gives a tightly packed 'button' of red cells at the bottom of the tube. Agglutination tests are used in several ways:

- Microbial identification: at the species or subspecies level (serotyping), e.g. mixing an unknown bacterium with the appropriate antiserum will cause the cells to agglutinate.
- Latex agglutination (bound antigens): by coating soluble (non-particulate) antigens onto microscopic latex spheres, their reaction with a particular antibody can be visualised.
- Latex agglutination (bound antibodies): antibodies can be bound to latex microspheres, leaving their antigen-binding sites free to react with soluble antigen.
- Haemagglutination: red blood cells can be used as agglutinating particles. However, in some instances, such reactions do not involve antibody interactions (e.g. some animal viruses may haemagglutinate unmodified red blood cells).

Precipitin tests

Immune complexes of antibodies and soluble antigens (or haptens) usually settle out of solution as a visible precipitate: this is termed a precipitin test, or precipitation test. The formation of visible immune complexes in agglutination and precipitation reactions only occurs if antibody and antigen are present in an optimal ratio (Fig. 38.3). It is important to appreciate the shape of this curve: cross-linkage is maximal in the zone of equivalence, decreasing if either component is present in excess. The quantitative precipitin test can be used to measure the antibody content of a solution (Hay *et al.*, 2002 give details). Visual assessment of precipitation reactions forms the basis of several other techniques, described below.

Fig. 38.3 Precipitation curve for an antigen titrated against a fixed amount of antibody.

[Figure 38.3: graph with y-axis labelled "antigen–antibody precipitate" and x-axis labelled "antigen added"; regions marked "antibody excess (prozone)", "zone of equivalence", "antigen excess (postzone)"]

Immunodiffusion assays

These techniques are easier to perform and interpret than the quantitative precipitin test. Precipitation of antibody and antigen occurs within an agarose gel, giving a visible line corresponding to the zone of equivalence (Fig. 38.3). The two most widespread techniques are detailed below.

Single radial immunodiffusion (RID) (Mancini technique)
This is used to quantify the amount of antigen in a test solution, as follows:

1. Prepare an agarose gel (1.5% w/v), containing a fixed amount of antibody: allow to set on a glass slide or plate, on a level surface.

Preparing wells for RID – cut your wells carefully. They should have straight sides and the agarose must not be torn or lifted from the glass plate. All wells should be filled to the top, with a flat meniscus, to ensure identical diffusion characteristics. Non-circular precipitin rings, resulting from poor technique, should not be included in your analysis.

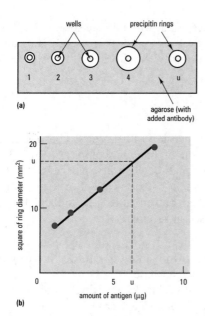

Fig. 38.4 Single radial immunodiffusion (RID). (a) Assay: four standards are shown (wells 1 to 4, each one double the strength of the previous standard), and an unknown (u), run at the same time. (b) Calibration curve. The unknown contains $6.25\,\mu g$ of antigen. Note the non-zero intercept of the calibration curve, corresponding to the square of the well diameter: do not force such calibration lines through the origin.

2. Cut several circular wells in the gel. These should be of a fixed size between 2 and 4 mm in diameter (see Fig. 38.4a).
3. Add a known amount of the antigen or test solution to each well.
4. Incubate on a level surface at room temperature in a moist chamber: diffusion of antigen into the gel produces a precipitin ring. This is usually measured after 2–7 days, depending on the molecular mass of the antigen.
5. Examine the plates against a black background (with side illumination), or stain using a protein dye (e.g. Coomassie blue).
6. Measure the diameter of the precipitin ring, e.g. using Vernier callipers.
7. Prepare a calibration curve (Chapter 37) from the samples containing known amounts of antigen (Fig. 38.4b): the squared diameter of the precipitin ring is directly proportional to the amount of antigen in the well.
8. Use the calibration curve to quantify the amount of antigen in your test solutions, assayed at the same time.

Double diffusion immunoassay (Ouchterlony technique)

This technique is widely used to detect particular antigens in a test solution, or to look for cross-reaction between different antigens.

1. Prepare an agarose gel (1.5% w/v) on a level glass slide or plate: allow to set.
2. Cut several circular wells in the gel.
3. Add test solutions of antigen or polyclonal antiserum to adjacent wells. Both solutions diffuse outwards, forming visible precipitin lines where antigen and corresponding antibody are present in optimal ratio (Fig. 38.5).

The various reactions between antigen and antiserum are:

- Identity: two wells containing the same antigen, or antigens with identical epitopes, will give a fused precipitin line (identical interaction between the antiserum and the test antigens, Fig. 38.5a).
- Non-identity: where the antiserum contains antibodies to two different antigens, each with its own distinct epitopes, giving two precipitin lines which intersect without any interaction (no cross-reaction, Fig. 38.5b).
- Partial identity: where two antigens have at least one epitope in common, but where other epitopes are present, giving a fused precipitin line with a spur (cross-reaction, Fig. 38.5c).

Immunoelectrophoretic assays

These methods combine the precipitin reaction with electrophoretic migration, providing sensitive, rapid assays with increased separation and resolution. The principal techniques are:

Cross-over electrophoresis (counter-current electrophoresis)

Similar to the Ouchterlony technique, since antigen and antibody are in separate wells. However, the movement of antigen and antibody towards each other is driven by a voltage gradient (p. 313): most antigens migrate towards the anode, while IgG migrates towards the cathode. This method

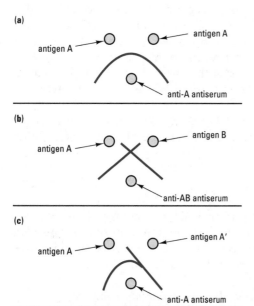

Fig. 38.5 Precipitin reactions in double diffusion immunoassay: (a) identity; (b) non-identity; (c) partial identity.

Fig. 38.6 Laurell rocket immunoelectrophoresis. (a) Assay: precipitin rockets are formed by electrophoresis of five standards of increasing concentration (wells 1 to 5) and an unknown (u). (b) Calibration curve: the unknown sample contains 7.7 μg of antigen.

is faster and more sensitive than double immunodiffusio..
20 min to reach completion.

Quantitative immunoelectrophoresis (Laurell rocket immunoelectrophoresis)

Similar to RID, as the antibody is incorporated into an agarose ...ate while the antigen is placed in a well. However, a voltage gradient moves the antigen into the gel, usually towards the anode, while the antibody moves towards the cathode, giving a sharply peaked, rocket-shaped precipitin line, once equivalence is reached (within 2–10 h). The height of each rocket shape at equivalence is directly proportional to the amount of antigen added to each well. A calibration curve for samples containing a known amount of antigen can be used to quantify the amount of antigen present in test samples (Fig. 38.6).

Radioimmunological methods

These methods use radioisotopes to detect and quantify the antigen–antibody interaction, giving improved sensitivity over agglutination and precipitation methods. The principal techniques are:

Radioimmunoassay (RIA)

This is based on competition between a radioactively labelled antigen (or hapten) and an unlabelled antigen for the binding sites on a limited amount of antibody. The quantity of antigen in a test solution can be determined using a known amount of radiolabelled antigen and a fixed amount of antibody (Fig. 38.7). As with other immunoassay methods, it is important to perform appropriate controls, to screen for potentially interfering compounds. The basic procedure for RIA is:

1. Add appropriate volumes of a sample to a series of small test tubes. Prepare a further set of tubes containing known quantities of the substance to be assayed to provide a standard curve.
2. Add a known amount of radiolabelled antigen (or hapten) to each tube (sample and standard).
3. Add a fixed amount of antibody to each tube (the antibody must be present in limited quantity).
4. Leave at constant temperature for a fixed time (usually 24 h), to allow antigen–antibody complexes to form.
5. Precipitate the antibody and bound antigen using saturated ammonium sulphate, followed by centrifugation.
6. Determine the radioactivity of the supernatant or the precipitate (pp. 260–3).
7. Prepare a calibration curve of radioactivity against $\log_{10}$ antigen (Fig. 38.7). The curve is most accurate in the central region, so adjust the amount of antigen in your test sample to fall within this range.

Note the following:

- You must be registered to work with radioactivity: check with the Departmental Safety Officer, if necessary (p. 265).
- Measure all volumes as accurately as possible as the end result depends on the volumetric quantities of unlabelled (sample) antigen,

Fig. 38.7 Radioimmunoassay calibration curve. Note that the assay is insensitive at very low and very high antigen levels.

radiolabelled antigen and antibody: an error in any of these reagents will invalidate the assay.

- Incorporate replicates, so that errors can be quantified.
- Seek your supervisor's advice about fitting a curve to your data: this can be a complex process.

Immunoradiometric assay (IRMA)

This technique uses radiolabelled antibody, rather than antigen, for direct measurement of the amount of antigen (or hapten) in a sample. Most immunoradiometric assays are similar to the double antibody sandwich method described below, except that the second antibody is labelled using a radioisotope. The important advantages over RIA are:

- linear relationship between amount of radioactivity and test antigen;
- wider working range for test substance;
- improved stability/longer shelf-life.

Enzyme immunoassays (EIA)

These techniques are also known as enzyme-linked immunosorbent assays (ELISA). They combine the specificity of the antibody–antigen interaction with the sensitivity of enzyme assays using either an antibody or an antigen conjugated (linked) to an enzyme at a site which does not affect the activity of either component. The enzyme is measured by adding an appropriate chromogenic substrate (p. 379), which yields a coloured product. Enzymes offer the following advantages over radioisotopic labels:

- Increased sensitivity: a single enzyme molecule can produce many product molecules, amplifying the signal.
- Simplified assay: enzyme assays are usually easier than radioisotope assays (p. 378).
- Improved stability of reagents: components are generally more stable than their radiolabelled counterparts, giving them a longer shelf-life.
- No radiological hazard: no requirement for specialised containment/disposal facilities.
- Automation is straightforward: using disposable microtitre plates and an optical scanner.

The principal techniques are:

Double antibody sandwich ELISA

This is used to detect specific antigens, involving a three-component complex between a capture antibody linked to a solid support, the antigen, and a second, enzyme-linked antibody (Fig. 38.8). This can be used to detect a particular antigen, e.g. a virus in a clinical sample, or to quantify the amount of antigen.

Indirect ELISA

This is used for antibody detection, with a specific antigen attached to a solid support. When the appropriate antibody is added, it binds to the antigen and will not be washed away during rinsing. Bound antibody is then detected using an enzyme-linked anti-immunoglobulin, e.g. a rabbit IgG antibody raised against human IgG (Fig. 38.9). One advantage of the indirect assay is that a single enzyme-linked anti-immunoglobulin can be

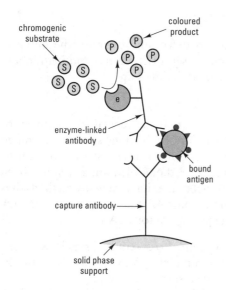

Fig. 38.8   Double antibody sandwich ELISA.

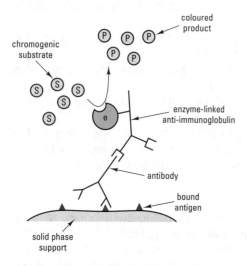

Fig. 38.9   Indirect ELISA.

used to detect several different antibodies, since the specificity is provided by the bound antigen.

Complement-based assays

Complement is a term applied to a group of around 20 different proteins which are involved in various aspects of immune function, including (i) control of inflammation, (ii) preparation of microbial cells for phagocytosis (opsonisation), (iii) lysis of target cells (e.g. antibody-coated cells) and (iv) activation of leucocytes (for details see Roitt *et al.*, 2001). At a practical level, the complement system can be used to detect (i) antibodies, (ii) antigens or (iii) antibody–antigen complexes, often *via* its lytic action on antibody-coated ('sensitised') cells. Its principal benefit is that it operates as an amplifying cascade of reactions, providing higher sensitivity than assays based on agglutination or precipitin reactions. For example, antibodies can be detected at concentrations of less than $1\,\mu g\,ml^{-1}$. The operating principles of a complement fixation assay are illustrated in Fig. 38.10 for antibody detection, with the following steps:

1. Prepare serial doubling dilutions (pp. 131–2) of a test sample containing an unknown amount of antibody.
2. Add a standard amount of antigen: antigen–antibody complexes will be formed in direct proportion to the amount of antibody present in the sample.
3. Then, add a known amount of complement to the mixture: if immune complexes (Fig. 38.2) are present, they will 'fix' complement (i.e. the complement components will be consumed and no longer 'free' in solution), whereas if immune complexes are not present, or are at low concentration, complement will remain 'free' in solution, and available for subsequent reaction.
4. In the final step, an indicator system for unbound complement is added – sensitised sheep red blood cells (sSRBCs) coated with rabbit anti-erythrocyte antibodies are often used. Unfixed complement is detected by lysis of the sensitised erythrocytes. The lowest dilution showing complement fixation (i.e. no erythrocyte lysis) gives the titre of antibody in the test sample.

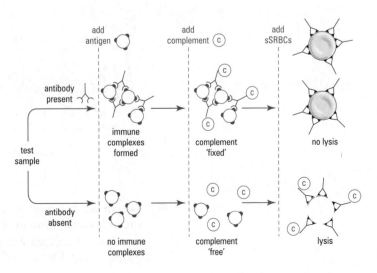

Fig. 38.10 Complement fixation test for antibody.

Example Complement fixation tests are the basis of the Wasserman test to detect anti-treponemal antibodies in the serum of patients with syphilis.

The test can be modified to test for antigens in a sample, by titration against a fixed amount of added antibody. In all cases, suitable controls are required, to check for non-specific reactions and to confirm that immune complexes are not already present in the sample, since these will fix complement and invalidate the titration. Complement fixation tests are useful for many classes of IgG and for IgM, but not for most other antibody types.

Text references

Hay, F.C., Westwood, O.M.R. and Nelson, P.N. (2002) *Practical Immunology*. Blackwell, Oxford.

Roitt, I.M., Broscoff, J. and Male, D.K. (eds) (2001) *Immunology*, 6th edn. Mosby, New York.

Roitt, I. and Delves, P.J. (2001) *Roitt's Essential Immunology*, 10th edn. Blackwell, Oxford.

Sources for further study

Clausen, J. (1989) *Immunochemical Techniques for the Identification and Estimation of Macromolecules*, 3rd edn. Elsevier, Amsterdam.

Diamandis, E.P. and Christopoulos, T.K. (1997) *Immunoassay*. Academic Press, New York.

Lefkovits, I. (1997) *Immunology Methods Manual: The Comprehensive Sourcebook of Techniques*. Academic Press, New York.

Study exercises

38.1 Determine the amount of antigen in a test solution using Laurell rocket immunoelectrophoresis. The figure below represents the results from a rocket immunoelectrophoresis assay for a series of standards. Determine the amount of antigen in a test solution giving a rocket (precipitin line) height of 18.5 mm.

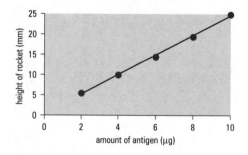

38.2 Determine the amount of antigen in a test solution using single radial immunodiffusion (RID). Using the following data for a series of standards, determine the amount of antigen in a test solution giving a ring diameter of 6.5 mm.

Single radial immunodiffusion results for a series of standards containing 4–20 μg antigen

Amount of antigen (μg)	Ring diameter (mm)
4	3.5
8	5.5
12	7.0
16	8.0
20	9.0

38.3 **Interpret data from a haemagglutination test.** In some conditions, such as Hashimoto's disease, autoantibodies to the thyroid protein thyroglobulin are produced in large amounts. The level of these antibodies in serum can be measured by indirect haemagglutination: red blood cells coated with thyroglobulin are mixed with serial doubling dilutions of the test serum. The titre of antithyroglobulin autoantibodies is the lowest dilution at which haemagglutination occurs. The figure represents the outcome of an antithyroglobulin haemagglutination test on a serum sample. The first well – numbered 1 – represents a 10-fold dilution of the serum sample, with serial doubling dilutions in subsequent wells.

(a) Write a brief explanation of the test results shown in the figure.

(b) Determine the autoantibody titre.

(c) Score the sample as 'positive' if the titre is more dilute than 1 in 5000 (i.e. 1 : >5000) and 'negative' if it is less dilute than 1 in 5000 (i.e. 1 : <5000).

Radioactive isotopes and their uses

The isotopes of a particular element have the same number of protons in the nucleus but a different number of neutrons, giving them the same proton number (atomic number) but a different nucleon number (mass number, i.e. number of protons + number of neutrons). Isotopes may be stable or radioactive. Radioactive isotopes (radioisotopes) disintegrate spontaneously at random to yield radiation and a decay product.

Radioactive decay

There are three forms of radioactivity (Table 39.1) arising from three main types of nuclear decay:

Table 39.1 Types of radioactivity and their properties

Radiation	Range of maximum energies (MeV*)	Penetration range in air (m)	Suitable shielding material
Alpha (α)	4–8	0.025–0.080	Unnecessary
Beta (β)	0.01–3	0.150–16	Plastic (e.g. Perspex®)
Gamma (γ)	0.03–3	1.3–13†	Lead

*Note that 1 MeV = 1.6×10^{-13} J
† Distance at which radiation intensity is reduced to half

- Alpha decay involves the loss of a particle equivalent to a helium nucleus. Alpha (α) particles, being large and positively charged, do not penetrate far in living tissue, but they do cause ionisation damage and this makes them generally unsuitable for tracer studies.
- Beta decay involves the loss or gain of an electron or its positive counterpart, the positron. There are three subtypes:
  (a) Negatron (β^{-}) emission: loss of an electron from the nucleus when a neutron transforms into a proton. This is the most important form of decay for radioactive tracers used in biology. Negatron-emitting isotopes of biological importance include ^{3}H, ^{14}C, ^{32}P and ^{35}S.
  (b) Positron (β^{+}) emission: loss of a positron when a proton transforms into a neutron. This only occurs when sufficient energy is available from the transition and may involve the production of gamma rays when the positron is later annihilated by collision with an electron.
  (c) Electron capture (EC): when a proton 'captures' an electron and transforms into a neutron. This may involve the production of X-rays as electrons 'shuffle' about in the atom (as with ^{125}I) and it frequently involves electron emission.
- Internal transition involves the emission of electromagnetic radiation in the form of gamma (γ) rays from a nucleus in a metastable state and always follows initial alpha or beta decay. Emission of gamma radiation leads to no further change in atomic number or mass.

Note from the above that more than one type of radiation may be emitted when a radioisotope decays. The main radioisotopes used in biology and their properties are listed in Table 39.2.

Table 39.2 Properties of some isotopes used commonly in the life sciences. Physical data obtained from Lide (2002)

Isotope	Emission(s)	Maximum energy (MeV)	Half-life	Main uses	Advantages	Disadvantages
^{3}H	β^-	0.01861	12.3 years	Suitable for labelling organic molecules in wide range of positions at high specific activity	Relatively safe	Low efficiency of detection, high isotope effect, high rate of exchange with environment
^{14}C	β^-	0.15648	5715 years	Suitable for labelling organic molecules in a wide range of positions	Relatively safe, low rate of exchange with environment	Low specific activity
^{22}Na	β^+ (90%) + γ, EC	2.842 (β^+)	2.60 years	Transport studies	High specific activity	Hazardous
^{32}P	β^-	1.710	14.3 days	Labelling proteins and nucleotides (e.g. DNA)	High specific activity, ease of detection	Short half-life, hazardous
^{33}P	β^-	0.248	25 days	Labelling nucleotides and proteins	Safer than ^{32}P	Moderate half-life
^{35}S	β^-	0.167	87.2 days	Labelling proteins and nucleotides	Low isotope effect	Low specific activity
^{36}Cl	β^-, β^+, EC	0.709 (β^-) 1.142 (β^+, EC)	300000 years	Transport studies	Low isotope effect	Low specific activity, hazardous
^{125}I	EC + γ	0.178 (EC)	59.9 days	Labelling proteins and nucleotides	High specific activity	Hazardous
^{131}I	β^- + γ	0.971 (β^-)	8.04 days	Labelling proteins and nucleotides	High specific activity	Hazardous

Fig. 39.1 Decay of a radioactive isotope with time. The time taken for the radioactivity to decline from x to $0.5x$ is the same as the time taken for the radioactivity to decline from $0.5x$ to $0.25x$, and so on. This time is the half-life ($t_{1/2}$) of the isotope.

Each radioactive particle or ray carries energy, usually measured in electron volts (eV). The particles or rays emitted by a particular radioisotope exhibit a range of energies, termed an energy spectrum, characterised by the maximum energy of the radiation produced, E_{max} (Table 39.2). The energy spectrum of a particular radioisotope is relevant to the following:

- Safety: isotopes with the highest maximum energies will have the greatest penetrating power, requiring appropriate shielding (Table 39.1).
- Detection: different instruments vary in their ability to detect isotopes with different energies.
- Discrimination: some instruments can distinguish between isotopes, based on the energy spectrum of the radiation produced (p. 263).

The decay of an individual atom (a 'disintegration') occurs at random, but that of a population of atoms occurs in a predictable manner. The radioactivity decays exponentially, having a characteristic half-life ($t_{1/2}$). This is the time taken for the radioactivity to fall from a given value to half that value (Fig. 39.1). The $t_{1/2}$ values of different radioisotopes range from fractions of a second to more than 10^{19} years (see also Table 39.2). If the $t_{1/2}$ is very short, as with ^{15}O ($t_{1/2} \approx 2\,\text{min}$), then it is generally impractical to use the isotope in experiments because you would need to account for the decay during the experiment and counting period.

To calculate the fraction (f) of the original radioactivity left after a particular time (t), use the following relationship:

$$f = e^x, \text{ where } x = -0.693t/t_{\frac{1}{2}}$$ [39.1]

Note that the same units must be used for t and $t_{1/2}$ in the above equation.

Table 39.3 Relationships between units of radioactivity

1 Bq = 1 d.p.s.
1 Bq = 60 d.p.m.
1 Bq = 27 pCi
1 d.p.s. = 1 Bq
1 d.p.m. = 0.016 7 Bq
1 Ci = 37 GBq
1 mCi = 37 MBq
1 μCi = 37 kBq
1 Sv = 100 rem
1 Gy = 100 rad
1 Gy $\approx$ 100 roentgen
1 rem = 0.01 Sv
1 rad = 0.01 Gy
1 roentgen $\approx$ 0.01 Gy

Measuring radioactivity

The SI unit of radioactivity is the becquerel (Bq), equivalent to one disintegration per second (d.p.s.), but disintegrations per minute (d.p.m.) are also used. The curie (Ci) is a non-SI unit equivalent to the number of disintegrations produced by 1 g of radium (37 GBq). Table 39.3 shows the relationships between these units. In practice, most instruments are not able to detect all of the disintegrations from a particular sample, i.e. their efficiency is less than 100% and the rate of decay may be presented as counts min^{-1} (c.p.m.) or counts s^{-1} (c.p.s.). Most modern instruments correct for background radiation and inefficiencies in counting, converting count data to d.p.m. Alternatively, the results may be presented as the measured count rate, although this is only valid where the efficiency of counting does not vary greatly among samples.

> **KEY POINT** The specific activity is a measure of the quantity of radioactivity present in a known amount of the substance:

$$\text{specific activity} = \frac{\text{radioactivity (Bq, Ci, d.p.m., etc.)}}{\text{amount of substance (mol, g, etc.)}} \quad [39.2]$$

This is an important concept in practical work involving radioisotopes, since it allows inter-conversion of disintegrations (activity) and amount of substance (see Box 39.1).

Two SI units refer to doses of radioactivity and these are used when calculating exposure levels for a particular source. The sievert (Sv) is the amount of radioactivity giving a dose in man equivalent to 1 gray (Gy) of X-rays: 1 Gy = an energy absorption of 1 J kg^{-1}. The dose received in most biological experiments is a negligible fraction of the maximum permitted exposure limit. Conversion factors from older units are given in Table 39.3.

The most important methods of measuring radioactivity for biological purposes are described below.

The Geiger–Müller (G–M) tube

This operates by detecting radiation when it ionises gas between a pair of electrodes across which a voltage has been applied. You should use a hand-held Geiger–Müller tube for routine checking for contamination (although it will not pick up ^{3}H activity).

The scintillation counter

This operates by detecting the scintillations (fluorescence 'flashes') produced when radiation interacts with certain chemicals called fluors (Fig. 39.2). In solid (or external) scintillation counters (often referred to as 'gamma counters') the radioactivity causes scintillations in a crystal of fluorescent material held close to the sample. This method is only suitable for radioisotopes producing penetrating radiation.

Liquid scintillation counters are mainly used for detecting beta decay and they are especially useful in biology. The sample is dispersed or dissolved in a suitable solvent containing the fluor(s) – the 'scintillation cocktail'. The radiation first interacts with the solvent, and the energy from this interaction is passed to the fluors which produce detectable light. The scintillations are measured by photomultiplier tubes (Fig. 39.2) which turn the light pulses into electronic pulses, the magnitude of which is directly related to the energy of the original radioactive event. The spectrum of electronic pulses is thus related to the energy spectrum of the radioisotope.

Fig. 39.2 Components of a scintillation counter. Note that in most modern instruments, all components are enclosed within a single cabinet.

Box 39.1 How to determine the specific activity of an experimental solution

Suppose you need to make up a certain volume of an experimental solution, to contain a particular amount of radioactivity. For example, 50 ml of a mannitol solution at a concentration of 25 mmol l^{-1}, to contain 5 Bq μl^{-1} – using a manufacturer's stock solution of ^{14}C-labelled mannitol (specific activity = 0.1 Ci mmol^{-1}).

1. **Calculate the total amount of radioactivity in the experimental solution**, in this example 5 × 1000 (to convert μl to ml) × 50 (50 ml required) = 2.5 × 10^5 Bq (i.e. 250 kBq).

2. **Establish the volume of stock radioisotope solution required**: for example, a manufacturer's stock solution of ^{14}C-labelled mannitol contains 50 μCi of radioisotope in 1 ml of 90% v/v ethanol: water. Using Table 39.3, this is equivalent to an activity of 50 × 37 = 1850 kBq. So, the volume of solution required is 250/1850 of the stock volume, i.e. 0.135 1 ml (135 μl).

3. **Calculate the amount of non-radioactive substance required** as for any calculation involving concentration (see pp. 130, 139), e.g. 50 ml (0.05 l) of a 25 mmol l^{-1} (0.025 mol l^{-1}) mannitol (relative molecular mass 182.17) will contain 0.05 × 0.025 × 182.17 = 0.227 7 g.

4. **Check the amount of radioactive isotope to be added.** In most cases, this represents a negligible amount of substance, e.g. in this instance, 250 kBq of stock solution at a specific activity of 14.8 × 10^6 kBq mmol^{-1} (converted from 0.4 Ci mmol^{-1} using Table 39.3) is equal to 250/14 800 000 = 16.89 nmol, equivalent to approximately 3 μg mannitol. This can be ignored in calculating the mannitol concentration of the experimental solution.

5. **Make up the experimental solution** by adding the appropriate amount of non-radioactive substance and the correct volume of stock solution.

6. **Measure the radioactivity in a known volume of the experimental solution**. If you are using an instrument with automatic correction to Bq, your sample should contain the predicted amount of radioactivity, e.g. an accurately dispensed volume of 100 μl of the mannitol solution should give a corrected count of 100 × 5 = 500 Bq (or 500 × 60 = 30 000 d.p.m.).

7. **Note the specific activity of the experimental solution**: in this case, 100 μl (1 × 10^{-4} l) of the mannitol solution at a concentration of 0.025 mol l^{-1} will contain 25 × 10^{-7} mol (2.5 μmol) mannitol. Dividing the radioactivity in this volume (30 000 d.p.m.) by the amount of substance (eqn [39.2]) gives a specific activity of 30 000/2.5 = 12 000 d.p.m. μmol^{-1}, or 12 d.p.m. nmol^{-1}. This value can be used:

(a) To assess the accuracy of your protocol for preparing the experimental solution: if the measured activity is substantially different from the predicted value, you may have made an error in making up the solution.

(b) To determine the counting efficiency of an instrument; by comparing the measured count rate with the value predicted by your calculations.

(c) To interconvert activity and amount of substance: the most important practical application of specific activity is the conversion of experimental data from counts (activity) into amounts of substance. This is only possible where the substance has not been metabolised or otherwise converted into another form; e.g. a tissue sample incubated in the experimental solution described above with a measured activity of 245 d.p.m. can be converted to nmol mannitol by dividing by the specific activity, expressed in the correct form. Thus 245/12 = 20.417 nmol mannitol.

Correcting for quenching – find out how your instrument corrects for quenching and check the quench indication parameter (QIP) on the printout, which measures the extent of quenching of each sample. Large differences in the QIP would indicate that quenching is variable among samples and might give you cause for concern.

Modern liquid scintillation counters use a series of electronic 'windows' to split the pulse spectrum into two or three components. This may allow more than one isotope to be detected in a single sample, provided their energy spectra are sufficiently different (Fig. 39.3). A complication of this approach is that the energy spectrum can be altered by pigments and chemicals in the sample, which absorb scintillations or interfere with the transfer of energy to the fluor; this is known as quenching (Fig. 39.3). Most instruments have computer-operated quench correction facilities (based on measurements of standards of known activity and energy spectrum) which correct for such changes in counting efficiency.

Box 39.2 Tips for preparing samples for liquid scintillation counting

Modern scintillation counters are very simple to operate; problems are more likely to be due to inadequate sample preparation than to incorrect operation of the machine. Common pitfalls are the following:

- **Incomplete dispersal of the radioactive compound in the scintillation cocktail.** This may lead to underestimation of the true amount of radioactivity present:

  (a) Water-based samples may not mix with the scintillation cocktail – change to an emulsifier-based cocktail. Take care to observe the recommended limits, upper and lower, for amounts of water to be added or the cocktail may not emulsify properly.

  (b) Solid specimens may absorb disintegrations or scintillations: extract radiochemicals using an intermediate solvent like ethanol (ideally within the scintillation vial) and then add the cocktail. Tissue-solubilising compounds such as Soluene® are effective, particularly for animal material, but extremely toxic, so the manufacturer's instructions must be followed closely. Radioactive compounds on slices of agarose or polyacrylamide gels may be extracted using a product such as Protosol®. Agarose gels can be dissolved in a small volume of boiling water.

  (c) Particulate samples may sediment to the bottom of the scintillation vial – suspend them by forming a gel. This can be done with certain emulsifier-based cocktails by adding a specific amount of water.

- **Chemiluminescence.** This is where a chemical reacts with the fluors in the scintillation cocktail causing spurious scintillations, a particular risk with solutions containing strong bases or oxidising agents. Symptoms include very high initial counts which decrease through time. Possible remedies are:

  (a) Leave the vials at room temperature for a time before counting. Check with a suitable blank that counts have dropped to an acceptable level.

  (b) Neutralise basic samples with acid (e.g. acetic acid or HCl).

  (c) Use a scintillation cocktail that resists chemiluminescence such as Hiconicfluor®.

  (d) Raise the energy of the lower counts detected to about 8 keV – most chemiluminescence pulses are weak (0–7 keV). This approach is not suitable for weak emitters, e.g. ^{3}H.

Liquid scintillation counting of high energy β-emitters – β-particles with energies greater than 1 MeV can be counted in water (Čerencov radiation), with no requirement for additional fluors (e.g. ^{32}P).

Many liquid scintillation counters treat the first sample as a 'background', subtracting whatever value is obtained from the subsequent measurements as part of the procedure for converting to d.p.m. If not, you will need to subtract the background count from all other samples. Make sure that you use an appropriate background sample, identical in all respects to your radioactive sample but with no added radioisotope, in the correct position within the machine. Check that the background reading is reasonable (15–30 c.p.m.). Tips for preparing samples for liquid scintillation counting are given in Box 39.2.

Gamma-ray (γ-ray) spectrometry

This is a method by which a mixture of γ-ray-emitting radionuclides can be resolved quantitatively by pulse-height analysis. It is based on the fact that pulse heights (voltages) produced by a photomultiplier tube are proportional to the amounts of γ-ray energy arriving at the scintillant or a lithium-drifted germanium detector. The lithium-drifted germanium detector, which is abbreviated to Ge(Li) – pronounced 'jelly' – provides high resolution (narrow peaks), essential in the analysis of complex mixtures.

Autoradiography

This is a method where photographic film is exposed to the isotope. It is used mainly to locate radioactive tracers in thin sections of an organism or

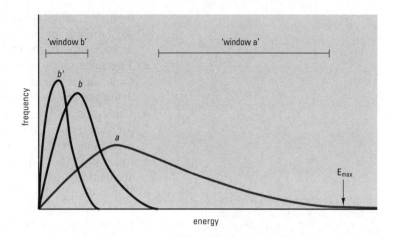

Fig. 39.3 Energy spectra for three radioactive samples, detected using a scintillation counter. Sample *a* is a high energy β-emitter while *b* contains a low energy β-emitter, giving a lower spectral range. Sample *b'* contains the same amount of low energy β-emitter, but with quenching, shifting the spectral distribution to a lower energy band. The counter can be set up to record disintegrations within a selected range (a 'window'). Here, 'window a' could be used to count isotope *a* while 'window b' could give a value of isotope *b*, by applying a correction for the counts due to isotope *a*, based on the results from 'window a'. Dual counting allows experiments to be carried out using two isotopes (double labelling).

on chromatography papers and gels, but quantitative work is possible. The radiation interacts with the film in a similar way to light, silver grains being formed in the developed film where the particles or rays have passed through. The radiation must have enough energy to penetrate into the film, but if it has too much energy the grain formation may be too distant from the point where the isotope was located to identify precisely the point of origin (e.g. high energy β-emitters). Autoradiography is a relatively specialised method and individual lab protocols should be followed for particular isotopes/applications.

Biological applications for radioactive isotopes

The main advantages of using radioactive isotopes in biological experiments are:

- Radioactivity is readily detected. Methods of detection are sufficiently sensitive to measure extremely small amounts of radioactive substances.
- Studies can be carried out on intact, living organisms. If care is taken, minimal disruption of normal conditions will occur when radiolabelled compounds are introduced.
- Protocols are simple compared to equivalent methods for chemical analysis.

The main disadvantages are:

- The 'isotope effect'. Molecules containing different isotopes of the same atom may react at slightly different rates and behave in slightly different ways from the natural isotope. The isotope effect is more extreme the smaller the atom and is most important for ^{3}H-labelled compounds of low molecular mass.
- The possibility of mistaken identity. The presence of radioactivity does not tell you anything about the compound in which the radioactivity is present: it could be different from the one in which it was applied, due to metabolism or spontaneous breakdown of a ^{14}C-containing organic compound.

The main types of experiments are:

- Investigations of metabolic pathways: a radioactively labelled substrate is added (often to an *in vitro* experimental 'system' rather than a whole

Metabolism of radiolabelled compounds *– you may need to separate individual metabolites before counting, e.g. using chromatography (Chapter 44), or electrophoresis (Chapter 46).*

organism) and samples taken at different time intervals. By identifying the labelled compounds and plotting their appearance through time, an indication of the pathway of metabolism can be obtained.

- Translocation studies: radioisotopes are used to follow the fate of molecules within an organism. Uptake and translocation rates can be determined with relative ease.
- Ecological studies: radioisotopic tracers provide a convenient method for determining food web inter-relationships and for investigating behaviour patterns, while environmental monitoring may involve following the 'spectral signature' of isotopes deliberately or accidentally released.
- Radio-dating: the age of plant or mineral samples can be determined by measuring the amount of a radioisotope in the sample. The age of the specimen can be found using the $t_{1/2}$ by assuming how much was originally incorporated.
- Mutagenesis and sterilisation: radioactive sources can be used to induce mutations, particularly in micro-organisms. Gamma emitters of high energy will kill microbes and are used to sterilise equipment such as disposable Petri dishes.
- Assays: radioisotopes are used in several quantitative detection methods of value to biologists. Radioimmunoassay is described on p. 315. Isotope dilution analysis works on the assumption that introduced radiolabelled molecules will equilibrate with unlabelled molecules present in the specimen. The amount of substance initially present can be worked out from the change in specific activity of the radioisotope when it is diluted by the 'cold' material. A method is required whereby the substance can be purified from the sample and sufficient substance must be present for its mass to be measured accurately.

Billington *et al.* (1992) give further details and practical advice on using radioisotopes in biological experiments.

Working practices when using radioactive isotopes

By law, undergraduate work with radioactive isotopes must be very closely supervised. In practical classes, the protocols will be clearly outlined, but in project work you may have the opportunity to plan and carry out your own experiments, albeit under supervision. Some of the factors that you should take into account, based on the assumption that your Department and laboratory are registered for radioisotope use, are discussed below:

1. Must you use radioactivity? If not, it may be legal requirement that you use an alternative method.
2. Have you registered for radioactive work? Normal practice is for all users to register with a local Radiation Protection Supervisor. Details of the project may have to be approved by the appropriate administrator(s). You may have to have a short medical examination before you can start work.
3. What labelled compound will you use? Radioactive isotopes must be ordered well in advance through your Department's Radiation Protection Supervisor. Aspects that need to be considered include:
   (a) The radionuclide. With many organic compounds this will be confined to ^3H and ^{14}C (but see Table 39.2). The risk of a significant 'isotope effect' may influence this decision (see p. 263).

Example Carbon dating – living organisms have essentially the same ratio of ^{14}C to ^{12}C as the atmosphere; however, when an organism dies, its $^{14}C/^{12}C$ falls because the radioactive ^{14}C isotope decays. Since we know the half-life of ^{14}C (5715 years), a sample's $^{14}C/^{12}C$ ratio will allow us to estimate its age; e.g. if the ratio were exactly 1/8 of that in the atmosphere, the sample is three half-lives old and was formed 17 145 years before present. Such estimates carry an error of the order of 10% and are unreliable for samples older than 50 000 years, for which longer-lived isotopes can be used.

Registering for radioisotope work – in the UK, institutions must be registered for work with specific radioisotopes under the **Radioactive Substances Act (1993).**

Supervision of work with radioisotopes – in the UK, the **Ionising Radiations Act (1985)** provides details of local arrangements for the supervision of radioisotope work.

(b) The labelling position. This may be a crucial part of a metabolic study. Specifically labelled compounds are normally more expensive than those that are uniformly ('generally') labelled.

(c) The specific activity. The upper limit for this is defined by the isotope's half-life, but below this the higher the specific activity, the more expensive the compound.

4. Are suitable facilities available? You'll need a suitable work area, preferably out of the way of general lab traffic and within a fume cupboard for those cases where volatile radioactive substances are used or may be produced.

Each new experiment should be planned carefully and experimental protocols laid down in advance so you work as safely as possible and do not waste expensive radioactively labelled compounds. In conjunction with your supervisor, decide whether your method of application will introduce enough radioactivity into the system, how you will account for any loss of radioactivity during recovery of the isotope and whether there will be enough activity to count at the end. You should be able to predict approximately the amount of radioactivity in your samples, based on the specific activity of the isotope used, the expected rate of uptake/exchange and the amount of sample to be counted. Use the isotope's specific activity to estimate whether the non-radioactive ('cold') compound introduced with the radiolabelled ('hot') compound may lead to excessive concentrations being administered. Advice for handling data is given in Box 39.1.

Carrying out a 'dry run' – *consider doing this before working with radioactive compounds, perhaps using a dye to show the movement or dilution of introduced liquids, as this will lessen the risks of accident and improve your technique.*

Using Benchkote® – *the correct way to use Benchkote® and similar products is with the waxed surface down (to protect the bench or tray surface) and the absorbent surface up (to absorb any spillage). Write the date in the corner when you put down a new piece. Monitor using a G–M tube and replace regularly under normal circumstances. If you are aware of spillage, replace immediately and dispose of correctly.*

Safety and procedural aspects

Make sure the bench surface is one that can be easily decontaminated by washing (e.g. Formica®) and always use a disposable surfacing material such as Benchkote®. It is good practice to carry out as many operations as possible within a Benchkote®-lined plastic tray so that any spillages are contained. You will need a lab coat to be used exclusively for work with radioactivity, safety spectacles and a supply of thin latex or vinyl disposable gloves. Suitable vessels for liquid waste disposal will be required and special plastic bags for solids – make sure you know beforehand the disposal procedures for liquid and solid wastes. Wash your hands after handling a vessel containing a radioactive solution and again before removing your gloves. Gloves should be placed in the appropriate disposal bag as soon as your experimental procedures are complete.

It is important to comply with the following guidelines:

- Read and obey the local rules for safe usage of radiochemicals.
- Maximise the distance between you and the source as much as possible.
- Minimise the duration of exposure.
- Wear protective clothing (properly fastened lab coat, safety glasses, gloves) at all times.
- Use appropriate shielding at all times (Table 39.1).
- Monitor your working area for contamination frequently.
- Mark all glassware, trays, bench work areas, etc., with tape incorporating the international symbol for radioactivity (Fig. 39.4).
- Keep adequate records of what you have done with a radioisotope – the stock remaining and that disposed of in waste form must agree.

CAUTION
RADIOACTIVE
MATERIAL

Fig. 39.4 Tape showing the international symbol for radioactivity.

- Store radiolabelled compounds appropriately and return them to storage areas immediately after use.
- Dispose of waste promptly and with due regard for local rules.
- Make the necessary reports about waste disposal, etc., to your Departmental Radiation Protection Supervisor.
- Clear up after you have finished each experiment.
- Wash thoroughly after using radioactivity.
- Monitor the work area and your body when finished.

Text references and sources for further study

Billington, D., Jayson, G.G. and Maltby, P.J. (1992) *Radioisotopes*. Bios, Oxford.

L'Annunziata, M.F. (ed.) (1998) *Handbook of Radioactivity Analysis*. Academic Press, New York.

Lide, D.R. (ed.) (2002) *CRC Handbook of Chemistry and Physics*, 83rd edn. CRC Press, Boca Raton.

Study exercises

39.1 Carry out a half-life calculation. A rat dropping found in a pyramid in Egypt had a $^{14}C:^{12}C$ ratio that was 57.25% of a modern-day standard. Use this value to estimate the approximate date when the rat visited the pyramid, to the nearest century.

39.2 Practise radioactivity interconversions. Express the following values in the alternative units indicated, with appropriate prefixes as necessary. Answer to 3 significant figures.
   (a) 72 000 d.p.m. as Bq;
   (b) 20 μCi as d.p.m.;
   (c) 44 400 Bq as μCi;
   (d) 6.3×10^5 d.p.m. mol^{-1} as Bq g^{-1}, for a compound with a relative molecular mass of 350;
   (e) 3108 d.p.m. as pmol, for a sample of a standard where the specific activity is stated as 50 Ci mol^{-1}.

39.3 Use the concept of specific activity in calculations. A researcher wishes to estimate the rate of uptake of the sugar galactose by carrot cells in a suspension culture. She prepares 250 ml of the cell culture medium containing 10^7 cells per ml and unlabelled galactose at a concentration of 5 mmol l^{-1}. She then 'spikes' this with 5 μl (regard this as an insignificant volume) of radioactive standard containing 55 MBq of ^{14}C-labelled galactose (regard as an insignificant concentration). Answer to 2 significant figures.
   (a) Calculate the specific activity of the galactose in the culture solution in Bq mol^{-1}.
   (b) If the total cell sample takes up 79.2×10^5 Bq in a 2-hour period, calculate the galactose uptake rate in mol s^{-1} cell^{-1}.

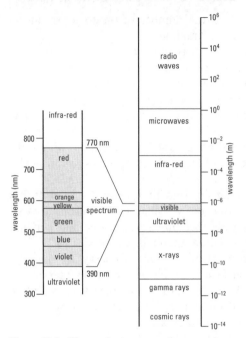

Fig. 40.1 The electromagnetic spectrum, *Methods for Physical and Chemical Analysis of Fresh Waters*, second edition, International Biological Programme, No. 8, Blackwell Scientific (Golterman, H.L., Clymo, R.S. and Ohnstad, M.A.M., 1978), reproduced by kind permission of Fisher Scientific UK Ltd..

Table 40.1 Wavelength ranges for UV, visible and IR radiation, compiled from several sources

Type	Wavelength range (nm)
UVC	100–290*
UVB	290–320
UVA	320–400
Violet	390–450
Blue	450–500
Green	500–560
Yellow	560–600
Orange	600–620
Red	620–770
IR	>770

* Note that UVC is absorbed by the earth's ozone layer.

40   Light measurement

The measurement of light is directly relevant to several aspects of biology, including: photosynthesis, photomorphogenesis and photoperiodism in plants; perception and thermoregulation in animals; and aspects of aquatic biology.

The nature of light

Light is most strictly defined as that part of the spectrum of electromagnetic radiation detected by the human eye. However, the term is also applied to radiation just outside that visible range (e.g. UV and infra-red 'light'). Electromagnetic radiation is emitted by the sun and by other sources (e.g. an incandescent lamp) and the electromagnetic spectrum is a broad band of radiation, ranging from cosmic rays to radio waves (Fig. 40.1). Most biological experiments involve measurements within the UV, visible and infra-red (IR) regions (generally, within the wavelength range 200–1000 nm; see Table 40.1).

Radiation has the characteristics of a particle and of a vibrating wave, travelling in discrete particulate units, or 'packets', termed photons. A quantum is the amount of energy contained within a single photon (it is important not to confuse these two terms, although they are sometimes used interchangeably in the literature). In some circumstances, it is appropriate to measure light in terms of the number of photons, usually expressed directly in moles (6.02×10^{23} photons = 1 mol); older textbooks may use the redundant term Einstein as the unit of measurement, where 1 Einstein = 1 mol photons. Alternatively, the energy content (power) may be measured (e.g. in $W\,m^{-2}$). Radiation also behaves as a vibrating electrical and magnetic field moving in a particular direction, with the magnetic and electrical components vibrating perpendicular to one another and perpendicular to the direction of travel. The wave nature of radiation gives rise to the concepts of wavelength (λ, usually measured in nm), frequency (v, measured in s^{-1}), speed (c, the speed of electromagnetic radiation, which is $3 \times 10^8\,m\,s^{-1}$ in a vacuum), and direction. In other words, radiation is a vector quantity, where

$$c = \lambda v \qquad\qquad [40.1]$$

Photometric and radiometric measurements

Photometric measurements

These are based on the energy perceived by a 'standard' human eye, with maximum sensitivity in the yellow–green region, around 555 nm (Fig. 40.2). The unit of measurement is the candela, a base unit in the SI system, defined in terms of the visual appearance of a specific quantity of platinum at its freezing point. Derived units are used for the luminous flow (lumen) and luminous flow per unit area (lux). These units were once used in photobiology and you may come across them in older literature. However, it is now recognised that such measurements are of little direct relevance to biologists, including even those who may wish to study visual responses, because they are not based on fundamental physical principles.

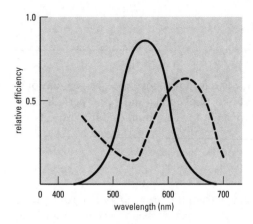

Fig. 40.2 Relative efficiency of vision (solid line) and photosynthesis (dotted line) as a function of wavelength.

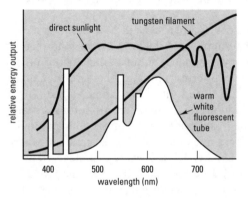

Fig. 40.3 Spectral distribution of energy output from various sources. (Adapted from Golterman *et al.*, 1978. Reproduced by kind permission of Blackwell Publishing Ltd.)

Table 40.2 Approximate conversion factors for a photosynthetic irradiance (PI) of $1\,W\,m^{-2}$ to photosynthetic photon flux density (PPFD)

Source	PPFD (μmol photons $m^{-2}\,s^{-1}$)
Sunlight	4.6
'Cool white' fluorescent tube	4.6
Osram 'daylight' fluorescent tube	4.6
Quartz-iodine lamp	5.0
Tungsten bulb	5.0

(*Source*: Lüning, 1981. Reproduced by kind permission of Blackwell Publishing Ltd.)

Radiometric measurements

The radiometric system is based on physical properties of the electromagnetic radiation itself, expressed either as the number of photons, or their energy content. The following terms are used (units of measurement in parentheses):

- Photon flux (mol photons s^{-1}) is the number of photons arriving at an object within the specified time interval.
- Photon exposure (mol photons m^{-2}) is the total number of photons received by an object, usually expressed per unit surface area.
- Photon flux density (mol photons $m^{-2}\,s^{-1}$) or PFD is the most commonly used term to describe the number of photons arriving at a particular surface, expressed per unit surface area and per unit time interval.
- Photosynthetically active radiation or PAR is radiation within the waveband 400–700 nm, since the photosynthetic pigments (chlorophylls, carotenoids, etc.) show maximum absorption within this band.
- Photosynthetic photon flux density (mol photons $m^{-2}\,s^{-1}$) or PPFD is the number of photons within the waveband 400–700 nm arriving at a particular surface, expressed per unit surface area and per unit time interval. Often this term is used interchangeably with PFD.
- Irradiance ($J\,m^{-2}\,s^{-1} = W\,m^{-2}$) is the amount of energy arriving at a surface, expressed per unit surface area and per unit time interval.
- Photosynthetic irradiance ($W\,m^{-2}$) or PI is the energy of radiation within the waveband 400–700 nm arriving at a surface, expressed per unit surface area and per unit time interval.

Choice of measurement scale

Photon flux density

This is often the most appropriate unit of measurement for biological systems where individual photons are involved in the underlying process, e.g. in photosynthetic studies, where PPFD is measured, since each photochemical reaction involves the absorption of a single photon by a pigment molecule. Most modern light-measuring instruments (radiometers) can measure this quantity, giving a reading in μmol photons $m^{-2}\,s^{-1}$.

Irradiance

This is appropriate if you are interested in the energy content of the light, e.g. if you are studying energy balance, or thermal effects. Many radiometers measure photosynthetic irradiance within the waveband 400–700 nm, giving a reading in $W\,m^{-2}$. It is possible to make an approximate conversion between PPFD and PI measurements, providing the spectral properties of the light source are known (see Table 40.2).

Spectral distribution

This can be determined using a spectroradiometer, e.g. to compare different light sources (Fig. 40.3). A spectroradiometer measures irradiance or photon flux density in specific wavebands. This instrument consists of a monochromator (p. 272) to allow separate narrow wavebands (5–25 nm bandwidth) to be measured by a detector; some instruments provide a plot of the spectral characteristics of the source.

Using a radiometer ('light meter')

The main components of a radiometer are:

- Receiver: either flat-plate, hemispherical or spherical, depending upon requirements. Most incorporate a protective diffuser, to reduce reflection.
- Detector: either thermoelectric or photoelectric. Some photoelectric detectors suffer from fatigue, with a decreasing response on prolonged exposure: check the manufacturer's handbook for exposure times.
- Processor and readout device to convert the output from the detector into a visible reading, in analogue or digital form.

Box 40.1 gives practical details of the steps involved in using a radiometer.

Box 40.1   Measuring photon flux density or irradiance using a battery-powered radiometer

1. **Check the battery.** Most instruments have a setting that gives a direct readout of battery voltage. Recharge if necessary before use.

2. **Select the appropriate type of measurement** (e.g. photon flux density or irradiance over the PAR waveband, or an alternative range): the simpler instruments have a selection dial for this purpose.

3. **Place the sensor in the correct location and position** for the measurement: it may be appropriate to make several measurements at different positions, and take an average.

4. **Choose the most appropriate scale** for the readout device: for needle-type meters, the choice of maximum reading is usually selected by a dial, within the range 0.3 to 30 000. Start at a high range and work down until the reading is on the scale. Your final scale should be chosen to provide the most accurate reading, e.g. a reading of

15 μmol photons $m^{-2}\,s^{-1}$ should be made using the 0–30 scale, rather than a higher range.

5. **Read the value from the meter.** For needle-type instruments there may be two scales, the upper one marked from 0 to 10 and the lower one from 0 to 3: make sure you use the correct one, e.g. a half-scale deflection on the 0–30 scale is 1.5.

6. **Check that the answer is realistic**, e.g. full sunlight has a PPFD of up to 2 000 μmol photons $m^{-2}\,s^{-1}$ (PI $\equiv$ 400 W m^{-2}), though the value will be far lower on a dull or cloudy day, while the PPFD at a distance of 1 m from a mercury lamp is around 150 μmol photons $m^{-2}\,s^{-1}$, and 50 μmol photons $m^{-2}\,s^{-1}$ at the same distance from a fluorescent lamp.

In your write-up give full details of how the measurement was made, e.g. the type of light source, instrument used, where the sensor was placed, whether an average was calculated, etc.

Text references

Golterman, H.L., Clymo, R.S. and Ohnstad, M.A.M. (1978) *Methods for Physical and Chemical Analysis of Fresh Waters*. Blackwell Scientific Publications, Oxford.

Lüning, K.J. (1981) 'Light', in C.S. Lobban and M.J. Wynne (eds), *The Biology of Seaweeds*, pp. 326–55, Blackwell Scientific, Oxford.

Sources for further study

Anon. *International Light Homepage*.
Available: http://www.intl-light.com
Last accessed 08/01/03.
[Information on products including several types of detector and meter. Also includes access to a light measurement handbook.]

Boyd, R.W. (1983) *Radiometry and the Detection of Optical Radiation.* Wiley, New York.

Study exercises

40.1 Carry out a calculation involving interconversion of photosynthetic photon flux and photosynthetic irradiance. For sunlight with a photosynthetic photon flux density (PPFD) of $1610\,\text{mol}\,\text{m}^{-2}$, what is the total amount of photosynthetic energy (in joules) falling on a leaf of area $45\,\text{cm}^2$ over a 30-minute experimental period?

40.2 Compare the photosynthetic photon flux densities (PPFD) of different locations. The following values represent typical light levels for a range of different situations, expressed either as photosynthetic irradiance (PI) or PPFD:

(a) outside, on a sunny day: $\text{PI} = 300\,\text{W}\,\text{m}^{-2}$;

(b) in a room lit by 'cool white' fluorescent tubes: $\text{PPFD} = 6.50\,\text{nmol photons}\,\text{cm}^{-2}\,\text{s}^{-1}$;

(c) under the leaf canopy in a forest: $\text{PPFD} = 275\,\mu\text{mol photons}\,\text{m}^{-2}\,\text{s}^{-1}$;

(d) in a growth cabinet lit by a bank of 'daylight' fluorescent lights: $\text{PI} = 35.2\,\text{W}\,\text{m}^{-2}$;

(e) in a room lit by a tungsten bulb: $\text{PI} = 1.15\,\text{mW}\,\text{cm}^{-2}$.

Convert all to PPFD in the same units (expressed to 3 significant figures) and then rank the locations in order of decreasing PPFD.

40.3 Research the various types of commercial radiometers (light meters) available on the Web. Make a list of the features that you might want to find out about and see how much information you can find.

41 Basic spectroscopy

Spectroscopic techniques can be used to:

- *tentatively identify compounds, by determining their absorption or emission spectra;*
- *quantify substances, either singly or in the presence of other compounds, by measuring the signal strength at an appropriate wavelength;*
- *determine molecular structure;*
- *follow reactions, by measuring the disappearance of a substance, or the appearance of a product as a function of time.*

The absorption and emission of electromagnetic radiation of specific energy (wavelength) are characteristic features of many molecules, involving the movement of electrons between different energy states, in accordance with the laws of quantum mechanics. Electrons in atoms or molecules are distributed at various energy levels, but are mainly at the lowest energy level, usually termed the ground state. When exposed to energy (e.g. from electromagnetic radiation), electrons may be excited to higher energy levels (excited states), with the associated absorption of energy at specific wavelengths giving rise to an absorption spectrum. One quantum of energy is absorbed for a single electron transition from the ground state to an excited state. On the other hand, when an electron returns to its ground state, one quantum of energy is released; this may be dissipated to the surrounding molecules (as heat) or may give rise to an emission spectrum. The energy change (ΔE) for an electron moving between two energy states, E_1 and E_2, is given by the equation:

$$\Delta E = E_1 - E_2 = h\nu \qquad [41.1]$$

where h is the Planck constant (p. 178) and ν is the frequency of the electromagnetic radiation expressed in Hz or s^{-1}). Frequency is related to wavelength (λ, usually expressed in nm) and the speed of electromagnetic radiation, c (p. 178) by the expression:

$$\nu = c \div \lambda \qquad [41.2]$$

UV/visible spectrophotometry

This is a widely used technique for measuring the absorption of radiation in the visible and UV regions of the spectrum. A spectrophotometer is an instrument designed to allow precise measurement at a particular wavelength, while a colorimeter is a simpler instrument, using filters to measure broader wavebands (e.g. light in the green, red or blue regions of the visible spectrum).

Principles of light absorption
Two fundamental principles govern the absorption of light passing through a solution:

- The absorption of light is exponentially related to the number of molecules of the absorbing solute that are encountered, i.e. the solute concentration [C].
- The absorption of light is exponentially related to the length of the light path through the absorbing solution, l.

These two principles are combined in the Beer–Lambert relationship (sometimes referred to simply as "Beer's Law"), which is usually expressed in terms of absorbance (A) – the logarithm of the ratio of the incident light (I_0) to the emergent light (I):

$$A = \varepsilon l [C] \qquad [41.3]$$

where A is absorbance, ε is a constant for the absorbing substance and the wavelength, termed the absorption coefficient or absorptivity, and [C] is

Definition

Absorbance (A) – this is given by:

$A = \log_{10}(I_0/I)$.

Usually shown as A_x where 'x' is the wavelength, in nanometres.

Basic spectroscopy

Transmittance (T) – this is usually expressed as a percentage, where

$T = (I/I_0) \times 100\,(\%)$.

expressed either as mol l^{-1} or g l^{-1} (see p. 129) and l is given in cm. This relationship is extremely useful, since most spectrophotometers are constructed to give a direct measurement of absorbance (A), sometimes also termed extinction (E), of a solution (older texts may use the outdated term optical density, OD). Note that for substances obeying the Beer–Lambert relationship, A is linearly related to [C]. Absorbance at a particular wavelength is often shown as a subscript, e.g. A_{550} represents the absorbance at 550 nm. The proportion of light passing through the solution is known as the transmittance (T), and is calculated as the ratio of the emergent and incident light intensities.

Some instruments have two scales:

- an exponential scale from zero to infinity, measuring absorbance;
- a linear scale from 0 to 100, measuring (per cent) transmittance.

For most practical purposes, the Beer–Lambert relationship applies and you should use the absorbance scale.

UV/visible spectrophotometer

The principal components of a UV/visible spectrophotometer are shown in Fig. 41.1. High intensity tungsten bulbs are used as the light source in basic instruments, capable of operating in the visible region (i.e. 400–700 nm). Deuterium lamps are used for UV spectrophotometry (200–400 nm); these lamps are fitted with quartz envelopes, since glass does not transmit UV radiation.

A major improvement over the simple colorimeter is the use of a diffraction grating to produce a parallel beam of monochromatic light from the (polychromatic) light source. In practice the light emerging from such a monochromator is not of a single wavelength, but is a narrow band of wavelengths. This bandwidth is an important characteristic, since it determines the wavelengths used in absorption measurements – the bandwidth of basic spectrophotometers is around 5–10 nm while research instruments have bandwidths of less than 1 nm.

Bandwidth is affected by the width of the exit slit (the slit width), since the bandwidth will be reduced by decreasing the slit width. To obtain accurate data at a particular wavelength setting, the narrowest possible slit width should be used. However, decreasing the slit width also reduces the amount of light reaching the detector, decreasing the signal-to-noise ratio. The extent to which the slit width can be reduced depends upon the sensitivity and stability of the detection/amplification system and the presence of stray light.

Most UV/visible spectrophotometers are designed to take cuvettes with an optical path length of 10 mm. Disposable plastic cuvettes are suitable for routine work in the visible range using aqueous and alcohol-based solvents, while glass cuvettes are useful for other organic solvents. Glass cuvettes are manufactured to more exacting standards, so use optically matched glass cuvettes for accurate work, especially at low absorbances (< 0.1), where any differences in the optical properties of cuvettes for reference and test samples will be pronounced. Glass and plastic absorb UV light and quartz cuvettes must be used at wavelengths below 300 nm.

Before taking a measurement, make sure that cuvettes are clean, unscratched, dry on the outside, filled to the correct level and in the correct position in their sample holders. Proteins and nucleic acids in biological samples can accumulate on the inside faces of glass/quartz

Fig. 41.1 Components of a UV/visible spectrophotometer.

Using plastic disposable cuvettes – these are adequate for work in the near-UV region, e.g. for enzyme studies using nicotinamide coenzymes, at 340 nm (p. 273), as well as the visible range.

Examples The molar absorptivity of NADH is $6.22 \times 10^3\,\text{l}\,\text{mol}^{-1}\,\text{cm}^{-1}$ at 340 nm. For a test solution giving an absorbance of 0.21 in a cuvette with a light path of 5 mm, using Eqn [41.3] this is equal to a concentration of:

$$0.21 = 6.22 \times 10^3 \times 0.5 \times [C]$$
$$[C] = 0.000\,067\,5\,\text{mol}\,\text{l}^{-1}$$
(or $67.5\,\mu\text{mol}\,\text{l}^{-1}$).

The specific absorptivity ($10\,\text{g}\,\text{l}^{-1}$) of double-stranded DNA is 200 at 260 nm, therefore a solution containing $1\,\text{g}\,\text{l}^{-1}$ will have an absorbance of $200/10 = 20$. For a DNA solution, giving an absorbance of 0.35 in a cuvette with a light path of 1.0 cm, using Eqn [41.3] this is equal to a concentration of:

$$0.35 = 20 \times 1.0\,[C]$$
$$[C] = 0.0175\,\text{g}\,\text{l}^{-1}$$
(equivalent to $17.5\,\mu\text{g}\,\text{ml}^{-1}$).

Chlorophylls a and b of vascular plants and green algae can be extracted in 90% v/v acetone/water, assayed by measuring the absorbance of the mixed solution at 2 wavelengths, according to the formulae:

Chlorophyll a $(\text{mg}\,\text{l}^{-1}) =$
$11.93\,A_{664} - 1.93\,A_{647}$

Chlorophyll b $(\text{mg}\,\text{l}^{-1}) =$
$20.36\,A_{647} - 5.5\,A_{664}$

Note: different equations are required for other solvents.

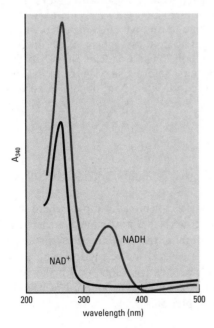

Fig. 41.2 Absorption spectra of nicotinamide adenine dinucleotide in oxidised (NAD$^+$) and reduced (NADH) form. Note the 340 nm absorption peak (A_{340}), used for quantitative work.

cuvettes, so remove any deposits using acetone on a cotton bud, or soak overnight in $1\,\text{mol}\,\text{l}^{-1}$ nitric acid. Corrosive and hazardous solutions must be used in cuvettes with tightly fitting lids, to prevent damage to the instrument and to reduce the risk of accidental spillage.

Basic instruments use photocells similar to those used in simple colorimeters or photodiode detectors. In many cases, a different photocell must be used at wavelengths above and below 550–600 nm, due to differences in the sensitivity of such detectors over the visible waveband. The detectors used in more sophisticated instruments give increased sensitivity and stability when compared to photocells.

Digital displays are increasingly used in preference to needle-type meters, as they are not prone to parallax errors and misreading of the absorbance scale. Some digital instruments can be calibrated to give a direct readout of the concentration of the test substance.

Types of UV/visible spectrophotometer

Basic instruments are single beam spectrophotometers in which there is only one light path. The instrument is set to zero absorbance using a blank solution, which is then replaced by the test solution, to obtain an absorbance reading. An alternative approach is used in double beam spectrophotometers, where the light beam from the monochromator is split into two separate beams, one beam passing through the test solution and the other through a reference blank. Absorbance is then measured by an electronic circuit which compares the output from the reference (blank) and sample cuvettes. Double beam spectrophotometry reduces measurement errors caused by fluctuations in output from the light source or changes in the sensitivity of the detection system, since reference and test solutions are measured at the same time (Box 41.1). Recording spectrophotometers are double beam instruments, designed for use with a chart recorder, either by recording the difference in absorbance between reference and test solutions across a predetermined waveband to give an absorption spectrum (Fig. 41.2), or by recording the change in absorbance at a particular wavelength as a function of time (e.g. in an enzyme assay, see Chapter 55).

Quantitative spectrophotometric analysis

A single (purified) substance in solution can be quantified using the Beer–Lambert relationship (Eqn [41.3]), provided its absorptivity is known at a particular wavelength (usually at the absorption maximum for the substance, since this will give the greatest sensitivity). The molar absorptivity is the absorbance given by a solution with a concentration of $1\,\text{mol}\,\text{l}^{-1}$ $(= 1\,\text{kmol}\,\text{m}^{-3})$ of the compound in a light path of 1 cm. The appropriate value may be available from tabulated spectral data (e.g. Anon., 1963), or it can be determined experimentally by measuring the absorbance of known concentrations of the substance (Box 41.1) and plotting a standard curve (see Chapter 37). This should confirm that the relationship is linear over the desired concentration range and the slope of the line will give the molar absorptivity.

The specific absorptivity is the absorbance given by a solution containing $10\,\text{g}\,\text{l}^{-1}$ (i.e. 1% w/v) of the compound in a light path of 1 cm. This is useful for substances of unknown molecular weight, e.g. proteins or nucleic acids, where the amount of substance in solution is expressed in terms of its mass, rather than as a molar concentration. For

Basic spectroscopy

1. **Switch on and select the correct lamp** for your measurements (e.g. deuterium for UV, tungsten for visible light).

2. **Allow up to 15 min for the lamp to warm up** and for the instrument to stabilise before use.

3. **Select the appropriate wavelength:** on older instruments a dial is used to adjust the monochromator, while newer machines have microprocessor-controlled wavelength selection.

4. **Select the appropriate detector:** some instruments choose the correct detector automatically (on the basis of the specified wavelength), while others have manual selection.

5. **Choose the correct slit width** (if available): this may be specified in the protocol you are following, or may be chosen on the manufacturer's recommendations.

6. **Insert appropriate reference blank(s):** single beam instruments use a single cuvette, while double beam instruments use two cuvettes (a matched pair for accurate work). The reference blanks should match the test solution in all respects apart from the substance under test, i.e. they should contain all reagents apart from this substance. *Make sure that the cuvettes are positioned correctly, with their polished (transparent) faces in the light path, and that they are accurately located in the cuvette holder(s).*

7. **Check/adjust the 0% transmittance:** most instruments have a control which allows you to zero the detector output in the absence of any light (termed 'dark current' correction). Some microprocessor-controlled instruments carry out this step automatically.

8. **Set the absorbance reading to zero:** usually *via* a dial, or digital readout.

9. **Analyse your samples:** replace the appropriate reference blank with a test sample, allow the absorbance reading to stabilise (5–10 s) and read the absorbance value from the meter/readout device. For absorbance readings greater than 1 (i.e. < 10% transmission), the signal-to-noise ratio is too low for accurate results. Your analysis may require a calibration curve or you may be able to use the Beer–Lambert relationship (Eqn [41.3]) to determine the concentration of test substance in your samples.

10. **Check the scale zero at regular intervals** using a reference blank, e.g. after every 10 samples.

11. **Check the reproducibility of the instrument:** measure the absorbance of a single solution several times during your analysis. It should give the same value.

Problems (and solutions): inaccurate/unstable readings are most often due to incorrect use of cuvettes, e.g. dirt, fingerprints or test solution on outside of cuvette (wipe the clear faces using a soft tissue before insertion into the cuvette holder and handle only by the opaque faces), condensation (if cold solutions aren't allowed to reach room temperature before use), air bubbles (which scatter light and increase the absorbance; tap gently to remove), insufficient solution (causing refraction of light at the meniscus), particulate material in the solution (check for 'cloudiness' in the solution and centrifuge before use, where necessary) or incorrect positioning in light path (locate in correct position).

Measuring absorbances in colorimetric analysis – if any final solution has an absorbance that is too high to be read with accuracy on your spectrophotometer (i.e. A > 2), it is bad practice to dilute the solution so that it can be measured. This dilutes both the sample molecules and the colour reagents to an equal extent. Instead, you should dilute the original sample and reassay.

use in Eqn [41.3], the specific absorptivity should be divided by 10 to give the solute concentration in $g\,l^{-1}$.

This simple approach cannot be used for mixed samples where several substances have a significant absorption at a particular wavelength. In such cases, it may be possible to estimate the amount of each substance by measuring the absorbance at several wavelengths, e.g. protein estimation in the presence of nucleic acids (pp. 366–7). Further details of spectrophotometric methods of determining the amount of protein in an aqueous sample are given in Chapter 50.

Fluorescence

With most molecules, after electrons are raised to a higher energy level by absorption of electromagnetic radiation, they soon fall back to the ground

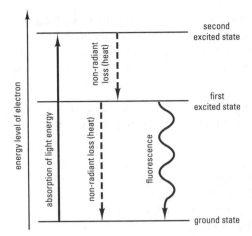

Fig. 41.3 Energy levels and energy transitions in fluorescence.

Fig. 41.4 Fluorescein – a widely used fluorescent label, showing (i) a planar conjugated system of fused rings; (ii) heteroatoms within the conjugated structures; (iii) an electron-donating group; and (iv) an electron-attracting group. In fluorogenic enzyme substrates (p. 379), linkage is usually *via* one of the two hydroxyl groups, while in fluoroscein-labelled proteins, linkage is *via* an isothiocyanate group (N═C═S) on the lowermost ring (*)

Table 41.1 Examples of compounds with intrinsic fluorescence

Drugs
Aspirin, morphine, barbiturates, propanalol, ampicillin, tetracyclines

Vitamins
Riboflavin, vitamins A, B6 and E, nicotinamide

Pollutants
Naphthalene, anthracene, benzopyrene

state by radiationless transfer of energy (heat) to the solvent. However, with some molecules, the events shown in Fig. 41.3 may occur, i.e. electrons may lose only part of their energy by non-radiant routes and the rest may be emitted as electromagnetic radiation, a phenomenon known as fluorescence. Since not all of the energy that was absorbed is emitted (due to non-radiant loss), the wavelength of the fluorescent light is longer than the absorbed light (longer wavelength = lower energy). Thus, a fluorescent molecule has both an absorption spectrum and an emission spectrum. The difference between the excitation wavelength (λ_{ex}) and the emission wavelength (λ_{em}), measured in nm, is known as the Stokes shift, and is fundamental to the sensitivity of fluorescence techniques. The existence of a Stokes shift means that emitted light can be detected against a low background, independently of the excitation wavelength.

Most fluorescent molecules have the following features:

- A highly conjugated system (alternating double and single bonds), involving aromatic or heterocyclic rings, usually containing O or N (as heteroatoms).
- A condensed system of fused rings, with one or more heteroatoms.
- Electron-donating groups such as $-OH$, $-OCH_3$, $-NH_2$ and $-NR_2$, together with electron-attracting groups elsewhere in the molecule, in conjugation with the electron-donating groups.
- A rigid, planar structure.

Figure 41.4 illustrates many of these features for fluorescein, used in a range of biological applications including nucleic acid detection, fluorescent antibody tests, etc.

Fluorescence spectrophotometry

The principal components of a fluorescence spectrophotometer (fluorimeter) are shown in Fig. 41.5. The instrument contains two monochromators, one to select the excitation wavelength and the other to monitor the light emitted, usually at 90° to the incident beam (though light is actually emitted in all directions). As an example, the wavelengths used to measure the highly fluorescent compound aminomethylcoumarin are 388 nm (excitation) and 440 nm (emission). Some examples of biomolecules with intrinsic fluorescence are given in Table 41.1 and the use of fluorogenic enzyme substrates is discussed further in Chapter 55, p. 379.

Compared with UV/visible spectrophotometry, fluorescence spectroscopy has certain advantages, including:

- Enhanced sensitivity (up to 1000-fold), since the emitted light is detected against a background of zero, in contrast to spectrophotometry where small changes in signal are measured against a large 'background' (see Eqn 41.3).
- Increased specificity, because not one, but two specific wavelengths are required for a particular compound.

However, there are also certain drawbacks:

- Not all compounds show intrinsic fluorescence, limiting its application. However, some non-fluorescent compounds may be coupled to fluorescent dyes, or fluorophores (e.g. proteins may be coupled to fluorescamine).

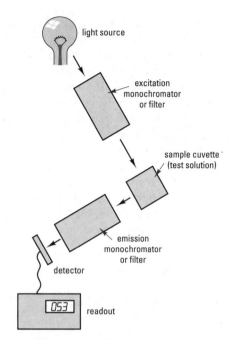

light source

excitation monochromator or filter

sample cuvette (test solution)

emission monochromator or filter

detector

053 readout

Fig. 41.5 Components of a fluorimeter (fluorescence spectrophotometer). Note that sample cuvettes for fluorimetry must have clear sides all round.

- The light emitted can be less than expected due to quenching, i.e. when substances in the sample (e.g. oxygen) either interfere with energy transfer, or absorb the emitted light (in some instances, the sample molecules may self-quench if they are present at high concentration).

The sensitivity of fluorescence has made it invaluable in techniques in which specific antibodies are linked to a fluorescent dye, including:

- fluorescence immunoassay (FIA);
- immunohistochemistry, which requires the use of a fluorescence microscope, e.g. using fluorescent antibodies, or fluorescent *in situ* hybridisation (FISH) for nucleic acid detection;
- flow cytometry – a fluorescence-activated cell sorter (FACS) uses cell surface protein-specific monoclonal antibodies labelled with fluorescent dyes to separate and enumerate cells such as lymphocytes.

Phosphorescence and luminescence

A phenomenon related to fluorescence is phosphorescence, which is the emission of light following inter-system crossing between electron orbitals (e.g. between excited singlet and triplet states). Light emission in phosphorescence usually continues after the exciting energy is no longer applied and, since more energy is lost in inter-system crossing, the emission wavelengths are generally longer than with fluorescence. Phosphorescence has limited applications in biomolecular sciences.

Luminescence (or chemiluminescence) is another phenomenon in which light is emitted, but here the energy for the initial excitation of electrons is provided by a chemical reaction rather than by electromagnetic radiation. An example is the action of the enzyme luciferase, extracted from fireflies, which catalyses the following reaction:

$$\text{luciferin} + \text{ATP} + O_2 \Rightarrow \text{oxyluciferin} + \text{AMP} + PP_i + CO_2 + \text{light}$$
[41.4]

The light produced is either yellow–green (560 nm) or red (620 nm). This system can be used in biomolecular analysis of ATP, either to determine ATP concentration in a biological sample, or to follow a coupled reaction (p. 379). Measurement can be performed using the photomultiplier tubes of a scintillation counter (p. 260) to detect the emitted light, with calibration of the output using a series of standards of known ATP content.

Atomic spectroscopy

Safe working in atomic spectroscopy – the use of high pressure gas cylinders can be particularly hazardous. Always consult a member of staff before using such apparatus.

Atoms of certain metals will absorb and emit radiation of specific wavelengths when heated in a flame, in direct proportion to the number of atoms present. Atomic spectrophotometric techniques measure the absorption or emission of particular wavelengths of UV and visible light, to identify and quantify such metals.

Flame atomic emission spectrophotometry (or flame photometry)

The principal components of a flame photometer are shown in Fig. 41.6. A liquid sample is converted into an aerosol in a nebuliser (atomiser) before being introduced into the flame, where a small proportion

Fig. 41.6 Components of a flame photometer.

(typically less than 1 in 10 000) of the atoms will be raised to a higher energy level, releasing this energy as light of a specific wavelength, which is passed through a filter to a photocell detector. Flame photometry is used to measure the alkali metal ions K^+, Na^+, and Ca^{++} in biological fluids.

When using a flame photometer:

- Allow time for the instrument to stabilise. Switch on the instrument, light the flame and wait at least 5 min before analysing your solutions.
- Check for impurities in your reagents. For example, if you are measuring K^+ in an acid digest of some biological material, check the K^+ content of a reagent blank, containing everything except the biological material, processed in exactly the same way as the samples. Subtract this value from your sample values to obtain the true K^+ content. If using acid digestion, always work within a fume hood and wear gloves and safety glasses at all times. Rinse any spillages with a large volume of water.
- Quantify your samples using a calibration curve (Chapter 37). Calibration standards should cover the expected concentration range for the test solutions – your calibration curve may be non-linear (especially at concentrations above $1\,mmol\,l^{-1}$, i.e. $1\,mol\,m^{-3}$ in SI units).
- Analyse all solutions in duplicate, so that reproducibility can be assessed.
- Check your calibration. Make repeated measurements of a standard solution of known concentration after every six or seven samples, to confirm that the instrument calibration is still valid.
- Consider the possibility of interference. Other metal atoms may emit light which is detected by the photocell, since the filters cover a wider waveband than the emission line of a particular element. This can be a serious problem if you are trying to measure low concentrations of a particular metal in the presence of high concentrations of other metals (e.g. Na^+ in sea water), or other substances which form complexes with the test metal, suppressing the signal (e.g. phosphate).

Atomic absorption spectrophotometry (or flame absorption spectrophotometry)

This technique is applicable to a broad range of metal ions, including those of Pb, Cu, Zn, etc. It relies on the absorption of light of a specific wavelength by atoms dispersed in a flame. The appropriate wavelength is provided by a cathode lamp, coated with the element to be analysed, focused through the flame and onto the detector. When the sample is introduced into the flame, it will decrease the light detected in direct proportion to the amount of metal present. Practical advantages over flame photometry include:

- improved sensitivity,
- increased precision,
- decreased interference.

Newer variants of this method include flameless atomic absorption spectrophotometry and atomic fluorescence spectrophotometry, both of which are more sensitive than the flame absorption technique.

Text reference

Anon. (1963) *Tables of Spectrophotometric Absorption Data for Compounds used for the Colorimetric Detection of Elements (International Union of Pure and Applied Chemistry)*. Butterworth-Heinemann, London.

Sources for further study

Anon. *World Nuclear Association Homepage*. Available: http://www.world-nuclear.org/info/info.htm
Last accessed 08/01/03
[Information on the use of radioisotopes in medicine and industry.]

Gore, M.G. (ed.) (2000) *Spectrophotometry and Spectrofluorimetry: A Practical Approach*, 2nd edn. Oxford University Press, Oxford.

Harris, D.A. (1996) *Light Spectroscopy*. Bios, Oxford.
[Gives practical guidance on techniques, applications and interpretation of results.]

Van Dyke, K., van Dyke, C. and Woodfork, K. (2002) *Luminescence Biotechnology: Instruments and Applications*. CRC Press, Boca Raton.

Wilson, K. and Walker, J. (eds.) (2000) *Principles and Techniques of Practical Biochemistry*, 5th edn. Cambridge University Press, Cambridge.
[Also covers a range of other topics, including chromatography and centrifugation.]

Study exercises

41.1 Write a protocol for using a spectrophotometer. After reading this chapter, prepare a detailed stepwise protocol explaining how to use one of the spectrophotometers in your Department. Ask another student or a tutor to evaluate your protocol and provide you with feedback.

41.2 Use the Beer–Lambert relationship in quantitative spectrophotometric analysis. Calculate the following (express your answer to 3 significant figures):

(a) The concentration of NADH ($\mu mol\,l^{-1}$) in a test solution giving an absorbance at 340 nm (A_{340}) of 0.53 in a cuvette with a path length of 1 cm, based on a molar absorptivity for NADH of $6220\,l\,mol^{-1}\,cm^{-1}$ at this wavelength.

(b) The amount of NADH (nmol) in 20 ml of a test solution where $A_{340} = 0.62$ in a cuvette with a path length of 5 cm, based on a molar absorptivity for NADH of $6220\,l\,mol^{-1}\,cm^{-1}$ at this wavelength.

(c) The mass concentration ($\mu g\,ml$) of double-stranded DNA in a test solution giving an absorbance at 260 nm (A_{260}) of 0.57 in a cuvette of path length 5 mm, based on an absorptivity of $20\,l\,g^{-1}\,cm^{-1}$.

(d) The amount (ng) of double stranded DNA in a $50\,\mu l$ sub-sample from a test solution where $A_{260} = 0.31$ in a cuvette of path length 1 cm, based on an absorptivity of $20\,l\,g^{-1}\,cm^{-1}$.

(e) The chlorophyll *a* content, in μg (g fresh weight)$^{-1}$, of a plant leaf of fresh weight 1.56 g extracted in 50 ml of 90% acetone, where $A_{664} = 0.182$ at 664 nm and $A_{647} = 0.035$, based on the following equation:

$$\text{Chlorophyll } a \text{ (mg l}^{-1}) = 11.93\, A_{664} - 1.93\, A_{647}$$

41.3 Determine the molar absorptivity of a substance in aqueous solution. A solution of *p*-nitrophenol containing $8.8\,\mu\text{g ml}^{-1}$ gave an absorbance of 0.535 at 404 nm in a cuvette of path length 1 cm. What is the molar absorptivity of *p*-nitrophenol at 404 nm, expressed to 3 significant figures? (Note: M_{r} of *p*-nitrophenol is 291.27.)

41.4 Determine the concentration of metal ions based on atomic spectroscopy of test and standard solutions. The following data represent a set of calibration standards for K^+ in aqueous solution, measured by flame photometry:

Absorbance of standard solutions containing K^+ at up to 0.5 mmol l^{-1}

K^+ concentration (mmol l^{-1})	Absorbance
0	0.000
0.1	0.155
0.2	0.279
0.3	0.391
0.4	0.537
0.5	0.683

Draw a calibration curve using the above data and use this to estimate the amount of K^+ in a test sample prepared by digestion of 0.482 g of tissue in a final volume of 25 ml of solution, giving an absorbance of 0.429 when measured at the same time as the standards shown above. Express your answer in $\mu\text{mol}\,K^+$ (g tissue)$^{-1}$, to 3 significant figures. See also study exercise 37.1 for a similar exercise, based on atomic absorption spectrophotometry of Zn.

41.5 Explain the basis of fluorescence. Why is the wavelength of the emitted light longer than that used to excite a fluorescent molecule?

41.6 Account for the difference in design between spectrophotometer and fluorimeter cuvettes. Why does a spectrophotometer cuvette have only two clear sides while a fluorimeter cuvette has four clear sides?

Advanced spectroscopy and spectrometry

Definitions

Spectroscopy – any technique involving the production and subsequent recording of a spectrum of electromagnetic radiation, usually in terms of wavelength or energy.

Spectrometry – any technique involving the measurement of a spectrum, e.g. of electromagnetic radiation, molecular masses.

Wavenumber – the reciprocal of the wavelength (expressed as cm^{-1}): a term used widely in IR spectroscopy, but rarely in other types of analysis.

Origins of spectra – *the IR spectrum is due to changes in charge displacement in bonds. The Raman spectrum is due to changes in polarisability in bonds.*

The following techniques are unlikely to be encountered in the early stages of your course, though they may be presented as a demonstration. Alternatively, you may be shown spectra for interpretation and analysis. The various types of spectroscopy, and their relationship with the electromagnetic spectrum, are shown in Table 42.1.

Infra-red (IR) and Raman spectroscopy

Both of these techniques involve the measurement of frequencies produced by the vibration of chemical bonds (bending and stretching). The IR/Raman region is generally considered to be from 800 to 2500 nm (for near-IR) and up to 16 000 nm (for mid-IR). Near-IR spectroscopy involves recording the spectrum in that region in a manner analogous to UV/visible spectroscopy, and quantitative analysis is possible. However, the most widely used technique is mid-IR spectroscopy, which allows identification of groups or atoms in a sample compound, but is inappropriate for quantitative measurement. A peak at a particular frequency can be identified by reference to libraries or computer databases of IR spectra, e.g. a peak at a wavenumber of 1730–$1750\,cm^{-1}$ corresponds to a carbonyl group – ($\sim$C$=$O), which is present in fatty acids and proteins. The 1400–$600\,cm^{-1}$ region is known as the 'fingerprint' region because no two compounds give identical spectra.

The value of IR spectroscopy is greatly enhanced by Fourier transformation (FT), named after the mathematician J.B. Fourier. FT is a procedure for interconverting frequency functions and time or distance functions. In FT-IR, information is obtained from an interferometer, which splits the incident beam so that it passes through both the sample and a reference. When the beam is recombined, interference patterns arise because the two path lengths are different. The interference pattern has the same relationship to a normal spectrum as a hologram has to a picture, and integral computers use FT to convert the pattern into a spectrum in under a minute. The overall result is a greatly enhanced signal : noise ratio.

Table 42.1 The electromagnetic spectrum and types of spectroscopy

Type of radiation	Origin	Wavelength	Type of spectroscopy
γ-rays	Atomic nuclei	<0.1 nm	γ-ray spectroscopy
X-rays	Inner shell electrons	0.1–1.0 nm	X-ray fluorescence (XRF)
Ultraviolet (UV)	Ionisation	10–200 nm	UV spectroscopy
UV/visible	Valency electrons	200–800 nm	UV/visible spectroscopy
Infra-red	Molecular vibrations	0.8–25 μm	Infrared spectroscopy (IR) and Raman
Microwaves	Electron spin alignment	400 μm–30 cm	Electron spin resonance (ESR)
Radiowaves	Nuclear spin resonance	>100 cm	Nuclear magnetic resonance (NMR)

IR spectra

A typical IR spectrum is shown in Fig. 42.1 and you should note the following points:

The use of wavenumber – this is a well-established convention, since high wave-number = high frequency = high energy = short wavelength. Expression of the IR range, 4000 cm^{-1} to 650 cm^{-1}, is in 'easy' numbers and the high energy is found on the left-hand side of the spectrum. Note that IR spectroscopists often refer to wavenumbers as 'frequencies', e.g. 'the peak of the C=O stretching 'frequency' is at 1720 cm^{-1}'.

- The x-axis, the wavelength of the radiation, is given in wavenumbers ($\bar{\nu}$) and expressed in reciprocal centimetres (cm^{-1}). You may still see some spectra from old instruments using microns (μ, equivalent to the SI unit 'micrometres', μm, at 1×10^{-6} m) for wavelength.
- The y-axis, expressing the amount of radiation absorbed by the molecule, is usually shown as % transmittance. When no radiation is absorbed (all is transmitted through the sample) there is 100% transmittance while 0% transmittance implies all radiation is absorbed at a particular wavenumber. Since the y-axis scale goes from 0 to 100% transmittance, the absorption peaks are displayed *down* from the 100% line; this is *opposite* to most other common spectra.
- The cells holding the sample usually display imperfections and are not completely transparent to IR radiation, even when empty. Therefore the base line of the spectrum is rarely set on 100% transmittance and quantitative applications of IR spectroscopy are more complex than for UV/visible spectrophotometry (p. 273).

Applications of IR and Raman spectroscopy

The principal use of IR and Raman spectroscopy is in the identification of drugs (e.g. penicillin), small peptides, pollutants and food contaminants. When an IR spectrometer is coupled to a gas–liquid chromatograph, it can be used for the analysis of drug metabolites.

Using IR – the rapid analysis possible with gaseous samples makes IR ideal for studying CO$_2$ metabolism in photosynthesis and respiration (p. 398).

One possible future use of IR is for the non-invasive analysis of organic compounds that are of diagnostic significance (e.g. glucose in diabetics). This involves illuminating a small area of skin with IR radiation and using the resultant IR spectrum to quantify a specific compound: an example of such a system is the Diasensor® blood glucose monitor (see: http://www.diasensor.com/operat.html).

Fig. 42.1 IR spectrum for ethanol.

(a)

(b)

Fig. 42.2 Effect of an applied magnetic field, B_0, on magnetic nuclei. (a) Nuclei in magnetic field have one of two orientations – either with the field or against the field (in the absence of an applied field, the nuclei would have random orientation). (b) Energy diagram for magnetic nuclei in applied magnetic field.

Nuclear magnetic resonance (NMR)

Electromagnetic radiation (at radiofrequencies of 1–500 MHz) is used to identify and monitor compounds. This is possible because of differences in the magnetic states of atomic nuclei, involving very small transitions in energy levels. The atomic nuclei of isotopes of many elements are magnetic because they are charged and have spin. Typical magnetic nuclei are ^{1}H, ^{13}C, ^{14}N, ^{15}N, ^{19}F and ^{31}P. When these nuclei interact with a uniform external magnetic field, they behave like tiny compass needles and align themselves in a direction either parallel or antiparallel to the field. The two orientations have different energies, with the parallel direction having a lower energy than the antiparallel (Fig. 42.2). The energy difference between the two levels (ΔE) corresponds to a precise electromagnetic frequency (ν), according to similar quantum principles to those for the excitation of electrons (p. 271). When a sample containing an isotope with a magnetic nucleus is placed in a magnetic field and exposed to an appropriate radiofrequency, transitions between the energy levels of magnetic nuclei will occur when the energy gap and the applied frequency are in *resonance* (i.e. when they are matched exactly). Differences in energy levels, and hence resonance frequencies (ν_0), depend on the magnitude of the applied magnetic field (B_0) and the magnetogyric ratio (λ), according to the equation:

$$\nu_0 = \lambda B_0 / 2\pi \qquad [42.1]$$

The magnetogyric ratio varies from one isotope to another, so NMR is performed at different frequencies for different nuclei at any given value of B_0. The principal components of an NMR spectrometer are shown in Fig. 42.3.

For magnetic nuclei in a given molecule, an NMR spectrum is generated because, in the presence of the applied field, different nuclei experience different local magnetic fields depending on the arrangement of electrons in their vicinity. The effective field (B) at the nucleus can be expressed as:

$$B = B_0(1 - \sigma) \qquad [42.2]$$

where σ (the shielding constant) expresses the contribution of the small secondary field generated by nearby electrons. The magnitude of σ is dependent on the electronic environment of a nucleus, so nuclei in different environments give rise to different resonance frequencies, according to the equation:

$$\nu_0 = \lambda B_0(1 - \sigma) / 2\pi \qquad [42.3]$$

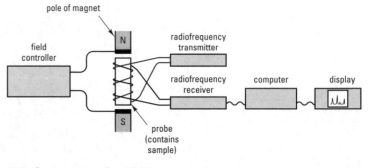

Fig. 42.3 Components of an NMR spectrometer.

The separation of resonance frequencies from a reference value is termed the *chemical shift*, and is expressed in dimensionless terms, as parts per million (ppm). By convention, the chemical shift is positive if the sample nucleus is less shielded than the reference and negative if it is more shielded.

Understanding NMR spectra of biomolecules

Figure 42.4 illustrates the principle underlying this technique – the different chemical environments of the hydrogen atoms in a simple biomolecule such as acetic acid result in two different ^{1}H resonances or 'signals', one corresponding to those of protons in $\sim CH_3$, and the other from that in $\sim COOH$. Furthermore, the relative intensities of the NMR signals, as measured by their areas, are proportional to the number of contributing nuclei, so the relative areas of the peaks due to the protons in $\sim CH_3$ and (undissociated) $\sim COOH$ would be $3:1$. Similarly, with ^{31}P NMR of a biologically important molecule such as ATP, there are signals corresponding to the α, β and γ phosphates, the P nuclei of which are in different chemical environments (Fig. 42.5). Thus every molecule that contains one or more magnetic nuclei has its own characteristic NMR fingerprint that may be used for identification and analysis. Spectra such as those shown in Figs 42.4 and 42.5 can be obtained using FT of a large number of individual responses to radiowave pulses. Other factors such as the spin-lattice relaxation time (Gadian, 1996) can affect signal intensities (peak sizes), and resonances may be split into several lines due to spin–spin coupling (interactions between neighbouring nuclei).

In terms of resolution, narrow signals are obtained only from molecules that are fairly mobile, so most high resolution studies are carried out using solutions. However, since many metabolites in biological samples (cells, tissues, etc.) are in aqueous solution and freely mobile, they can give rise to high resolution spectra, as shown in Fig. 42.5 for the ^{31}P-containing compounds, ATP, phosphocreatine and inorganic phosphate. On the other hand ^{31}P signals from immobile molecules such as DNA or phospholipids are very broad, and could be as wide as the whole scale shown in Fig. 42.5.

Fig. 42.4 ^{1}H NMR spectrum of acetic acid (CH$_3$COOH). The relative areas of the two signals are 1:3 and the frequencies (chemical shifts) are expressed in terms of ppm, relative to the reference signal (tetramethyl silane, TMS).

Fig. 42.5 Typical ^{31}P NMR spectrum from intact skeletal muscle (a) at rest and (b) after a fatiguing series of contractions. In (b) ATP levels are preserved at the expense of phosphocreatinine (PCr). Also, hydrolysis of ATP during contraction results in a large phosphate (P$_i$) peak which is shifted to the right compared to (a), reflecting the decrease in intracellular pH that accompanies glycolysis.

Using NMR – in contrast to most conventional metabolic studies, NMR is non-invasive and the time course of metabolic reactions can be followed using a single experimental subject or preparation, eliminating variation between samples.

Biomolecular applications of NMR

The sensitivity of NMR has improved dramatically with the development of more powerful magnets. Details of the major uses of various magnetic nuclei are given in Table 42.2. The principal applications include:

- studies on the structure and function of macromolecules and biological systems, such as membranes;
- metabolic investigations on living organisms, including humans, since NMR can be used to obtain a 'fingerprint' of a particular molecule and changes in the intensity of spectra can be used for kinetic studies (e.g. Fig. 42.5). This involves use of 'surface coils' as sources of radiation, or placing the organism within the core of an electromagnet;
- measurement of intracellular pH by determination of the chemical shift of the phosphate peak, as this changes with pH in a predictable manner;
- magnetic resonance imaging (MRI), which is a form of proton NMR that uses a field gradient (as opposed to a uniform field) to produce signals that are translated by computers into anatomical images (Gadian, 1996). Body tissues have different water contents (typically 60–90% w/w). Signals arising from protons in water in different tissues can be used to differentiate between tissues (e.g. 'grey' and 'white' matter in the brain), and between normal tissue and tumours. Fat deposits can be detected, due to the difference between the ^1H signal from fatty acids and that of the water in the surrounding tissue.

Electron spin resonance (ESR)

This technique is based on energy transitions of spinning electrons in a magnetic field. As with NMR, the low energy state occurs when the electromagnetic field generated by the spinning electron is parallel to the externally generated field, while the high energy state occurs when the electron-generated field is antiparallel. ESR is very useful for

Table 42.2 The relative merits and disadvantages of various magnetic nuclei in biomolecular studies

Nucleus	Relative sensitivity	Natural abundance	Comments
^1H	100	99.98%	Multiple, but specific, spectral lines are obtained for individual biomolecules. For mixtures, the ubiquitous occurrence of ^1H gives complex, overlapping signals that are often difficult to interpret. Gives a large solvent peak with aqueous samples (can be avoided by using D_2O as solvent). Mainly used for structural studies of pure macromolecules. Essential for MRI.
^{31}P	6.6	100%	Very useful for studies on living systems, with narrow resonance peaks and a wide range of chemical shifts for different molecules. Spectra are simpler and easier to interpret than for ^1H, but are not as distinctive: different compounds may give similar ^{31}P spectra. Several important P-containing compounds (including ATP, ADP and inorganic phosphate) can be detected in intact cells – useful in bioenergetic studies.
^{13}C	0.016	1.1%	Gives narrow signals and a wide range of chemical shifts. Resolution is better than for ^1H, and a wide range of organic biomolecules can be detected. Low natural abundance gives low sensitivity, extending the time required to accumulate spectra. However, low natural abundance also means that specific metabolites can be selected for ^{13}C isotope enrichment, allowing particular metabolic pathways to be investigated, e.g. carbon assimilation.

studying metalloproteins and can be used to monitor the activity of such proteins (e.g. cytochrome oxidase) in intact mitochondria or chloroplasts. It can also be used to detect free radicals, for example in irradiated foodstuffs.

Mass spectrometry (MS)

This technique involves the disintegration of organic compounds into fragment ions in a gas phase. These ions are accelerated to specific velocities using an electric field and then separated on the basis of their different masses. Each fragment of a particular mass is detected sequentially with time. The most widely used method in MS is electron impact ionisation (EI), where the electron source is a heated metal, such as a tungsten filament, subjected to an appropriate potential gradient. The stream of emitted electrons may then interact with biomolecules (M) in the sample by either:

1. electron removal – where an electron in a bond within the sample molecule is 'knocked out' by bombarding electrons, leaving the bond with only one unpaired electron and resulting in the production of a cationic free radical, i.e. $M + e^- \rightarrow M^{+\bullet} + 2e^-$;
2. electron capture – where addition of an extra electron results in the production of an anionic free radical, i.e. $M + e^- \rightarrow M^{-\bullet}$.

Where it is not known whether cations or anions are formed, the radical is given the symbol $^-$, i.e. as $M^{\bullet-}$. The first ions formed (parent ions) are unstable, and rapidly undergo further disintegration to give smaller fragments and daughter ions, subsequently separated in the mass spectrometer (Fig. 42.6), to give a mass spectrum such as that shown in Fig. 42.7.

For *in vivo* metabolic studies, the technique of isotope ratio mass spectroscopy (IRMS) is useful since it removes the need to use radioactive isotopes. This technique exploits the ability of MS to distinguish between isotopes such as ^{13}C and ^{12}C. For example, compounds containing ^{13}C have a greater mass than the same compound containing ^{12}C and can be differentiated in the mass spectrum. By selectively labelling a key metabolite with a non-radioactive isotope, the fate of this metabolite can be followed by MS analysis of sequential samples. Normally, the materials used are combusted in oxygen to give gases such as $^{13}CO_2$ and $^{15}NO_2$, followed by exposure of such gases to an EI source; useful metabolic data can be obtained by determining the isotope ratio, e.g. of $^{13}CO_2^{-\bullet}$ and $^{12}CO_2^{\bullet}$.

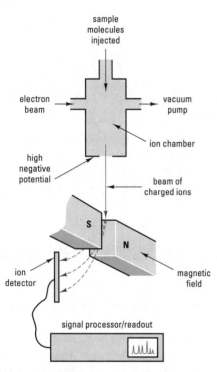

Fig. 42.6 Components of an electron-impact mass spectrometer.

Pyrolysis-mass spectrometry (PY-MS)

This is another variant of mass spectroscopy that is useful for biomolecular applications. The molecules in a sample are volatilised by heating to a precisely controlled high temperature for a specific time period. The volatile material is then removed by a vacuum, ionised by EI, and subjected to MS. Complex mixtures of pyrolysis products are produced, but interpretation is made easier by computer-based multivariate analysis. A useful application of PY-MS is in microbial identification, especially with small samples of organisms that are difficult to culture, e.g. mycobacteria.

Fig. 42.7 Mass spectrum for methanol. M/*z* = mass/charge ratio.

Fast atom bombardment–mass spectrometry (FAB-MS)

This is particularly useful for biomolecular applications because it can be used with aqueous solutions. The solution containing the analyte is mixed with glycerol and applied to a probe which is inserted into a vacuum chamber. The mixture is bombarded with a high velocity stream of atoms (usually argon or xenon) rather than electrons, which induces fragmentation of the biomolecules and allows production of the mass spectrum. One problem with FAB-MS is the suppression effect phenomenon – with a mixed sample, not all components may be equally accessible to the atomic bombardment depending on the way they are distributed in the sample–glycerol mixture. This can be overcome by coupling FAB-MS to techniques that can give high resolution separation of components, e.g. gas–liquid chromatography (GC, p. 298), high performance liquid chromatography (HPLC, p. 297), or capillary electrophoresis (p. 325). Johnstone and Rose (1996) give further information on biomolecular aspects of MS.

Text references

Gadian, D.G. (1996) *NMR and its Applications to Living Systems*, 2nd edn. Oxford University Press, Oxford.

Johnstone, R.A.W. and Rose, M.E. (1996) *Mass Spectrometry for Chemists and Biochemists*, 2nd edn. Cambridge University Press, Cambridge.

Sources for further study

Hildrum, K.I. (1999) *Near Infra Red Spectroscopy*. Ellis-Horwood, Chichester.

Hore, P.J., Jones, J.A. and Wimperis, S. (2000) *NMR: the Toolkit*. Oxford University Press, Oxford.
[A 'primer' text – succinct, and inlcudes relevant biological applications.]

Macomber, R.H. (2000) *A Complete Introduction to Modern NMR Spectrometry*. Wiley, New York.
[An accessible introductory text, with relevant biomedical information and examples.]

Nelson, J.H. (2002) *Nuclear Magnetic Resonance Spectroscopy*. Prentice Hall, Harlow.

Siudzak, G. (1996) *Mass Spectrometry for Biotechnology*. Academic Press, New York.
[Written for bioresearchers, it covers principles and applications without extensive use of maths.]

Study exercises

42.1 Interpret IR signals. The figure shows the IR spectra of acetic acid (ethanoic acid). Using the information provided below, identify the resonance corresponding to (a) the O–H and (b) C=O of the carboxylic acid group in the acetic acid spectrum.

Typical IR absorption ranges for different functional groups

Bond	Location	Wavenumber (cm^{-1})
C–O	esters, alcohols	1000–1300
C=O	ketones, aldehydes, carboxylic acids, esters, amides	1680–1750
O–H	carboxylic acids (H-bonded)	2500–3300
O–H	alcohols (H-bonded)	3230–3350
O–H	free	3580–3670
N–H	amines	3100–3500

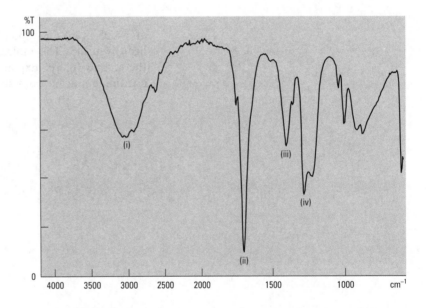

42.2 Investigate appropriate reference compounds for biological applications of NMR. Why are reference compounds important when measuring chemical shifts in NMR? Which compounds are suitable references for (a) ^{1}H, (b) ^{13}C and (c) ^{31}P NMR?

42.3 Test your understanding of the NMR terminology. Distinguish between the term ppm as used in NMR and as a concentration term (p. 140).

42.4 Interpret NMR signals from biomolecules in body fluids. A ^{1}H NMR spectrum (range 1–4.5 ppm) of a human urine sample obtained from a healthy adult is shown in the first figure (overleaf). The spectrum reveals a large number of components/ peaks. The two most intense of these peaks (at approximately 3.05

and 4.05 ppm) correspond to creatinine (C), which is abundant in healthy urine. The molecular structure of creatinine is shown in the second figure. Explain why the the 1H NMR 'fingerprint' of creatinine in urine consists of just two discrete peaks.

43 Centrifugation

Particles suspended in a liquid will move at a rate that depends on:

- the applied force – particles in a liquid within a gravitational field, e.g. a stationary test tube, will move in response to the earth's gravity;
- the density difference between the particles and the liquid – particles less dense than the liquid will float upwards while particles denser than the liquid will sink;
- the size and shape of the particles;
- the viscosity of the medium.

For most biological particles (cells, organelles or molecules) the rate of flotation or sedimentation in response to the earth's gravity is too slow to be of practical use in separation.

KEY POINT A centrifuge is an instrument designed to produce a centrifugal force far greater than the earth's gravity, by spinning the sample about a central axis (Fig. 43.1). Particles of different size, shape or density will thereby sediment at different rates, depending on the speed of rotation and their distance from the central axis.

Fig. 43.1 Principal components of a low-speed bench centrifuge. Diagram of Fisher Scientific Model MSE Centaur 2, low-speed bench centrifuge, reproduced by kind permission of Fisher Scientific UK Ltd.

Table 43.1 Relationship between speed (r.p.m.) and acceleration (relative centrifugal field, RCF) for a typical bench centrifuge with an average radius of rotation, $r_{av} = 115\,mm$

r.p.m.	RCF*
500	30
1000	130
1500	290
2000	510
2500	800
3000	1160
3500	1570
4000	2060
4500	2600
5000	3210
5500	3890
6000	4630

*RCF values rounded to nearest 10.

Centrifugation

$9.80\,\mathrm{m\,s^{-2}}$.

Examples Suppose you wanted to calculate the RCF of a bench centrifuge with a rotor of $r_{av} = 95$ mm running at a speed of 3000 r.p.m. Using Eqn [43.1] the RCF would be: $1.118 \times 95 \times (3)^2 = 956\,g$.

You might wish to calculate the speed (r.p.m.) required to produce a relative centrifugal field of 2000 g using a rotor of $r_{av} = 85$ mm. Using Eqn [43.2] the speed would be: $945.7\sqrt{(2000 \div 85)} = 4587$ r.p.m.

Fig. 43.2 Differential sedimentation. (a) Before centrifugation, the tube contains a mixed suspension of large, medium and small particles of similar density. (b) After low-speed centrifugation, the pellet is predominantly composed of the largest particles. (c) Further high-speed centrifugation of the supernatant will give a second pellet, predominantly composed of medium-sized particles. (d) A final ultracentrifugation step pellets the remaining small particles. Note that all of the pellets apart from the final one will have some degree of cross-contamination.

Fig. 43.3 Density gradients. (a) A continuous (linear) density gradient. (b) A discontinuous (stepwise) density gradient, formed by layering solutions of decreasing density on top of each other. (c) A single-step density barrier, designed to allow selective sedimentation of one type of particle.

How to calculate centrifugal acceleration

The acceleration of a centrifuge is usually expressed as a multiple of the acceleration due to gravity ($g = 9.80\,\mathrm{m\,s^{-2}}$), termed the relative centrifugal field (RCF, or 'g value'). The RCF depends on the speed of the rotor (n, in revolutions per minute, r.p.m.) and the radius of rotation (r, in mm) where:

$$\text{RCF} = 1.118\,r\left(\frac{n}{1000}\right)^2 \qquad [43.1]$$

This relationship can be rearranged, to calculate the speed (r.p.m.) for specific values of r and RCF:

$$n = 945.7\sqrt{\left(\frac{\text{RCF}}{r}\right)} \qquad [43.2]$$

However, you should note that RCF is not uniform within a centrifuge tube: it is highest near the outside of the rotor (r_{max}) and lowest near the central axis (r_{min}). In practice, it is customary to report the RCF calculated from the average radius of rotation (r_{av}), as shown in Fig. 43.5. It is also worth noting that RCF varies as a *squared* function of the speed: thus the RCF will be doubled by an increase in speed of approximately 41% (Table 43.1).

Centrifugal separation methods

Differential sedimentation (pelleting)

By centrifuging a mixed suspension of particles at a specific RCF for a particular time, the mixture will be separated into a pellet and a supernatant (Fig. 43.2). The successive pelleting of a suspension by spinning for a fixed time at increasing RCF is widely used to separate organelles from cell homogenates. The same principle applies when cells are harvested from a liquid medium.

Density gradient centrifugation

The following techniques use a density gradient, a solution which increases in density from the top to the bottom of a centrifuge tube (Fig. 43.3).

- Rate-zonal centrifugation. By layering a sample onto a shallow pre-formed density gradient, followed by centrifugation, the larger particles will move faster through the gradient than the smaller ones, forming several distinct zones (bands). This method is time-dependent, and centrifugation must be stopped before any band reaches the bottom of the tube (Fig. 43.4).
- Isopycnic centrifugation. This technique separates particles on the basis of their buoyant density. Several substances form density gradients during centrifugation (e.g. sucrose, CsCl, Ficoll®, Percoll®, Nycodenz®). The sample is mixed with the appropriate substance and then centrifuged – particles form bands where their density corresponds to that of the medium (Fig. 43.4). This method requires a steep gradient and sufficient time to allow gradient formation and particle redistribution, but is unaffected by further centrifugation.

Bands within a density gradient can be sampled using a fine Pasteur pipette, or a syringe with a long, fine needle. Alternatively, the tube may be punctured and the contents (fractions) collected dropwise in several tubes. For accurate work, an upward displacement technique can be used (see Ford and Graham, 1991, or Graham, 2001).

Fig. 43.4 Density gradient centrifugation. The central tube shows the position of the sample prior to centrifugation, as a layer on top of the density gradient medium. Note that particles sediment on the basis of size during rate-zonal centrifugation (a), but form bands in order of their densities during isopycnic centrifugation (b). ●, large particles, intermediate density; ▲, medium-sized particles, low density; ▬ small particles, high density.

Density barrier centrifugation

A single step density barrier (Fig. 43.3c) can be used to separate cells from their surrounding fluid, e.g. using a layer of silicone oil adjusted to the correct density using dinonyl phthalate. Blood cell types can be separated using a density barrier of e.g. Ficoll®.

Types of centrifuge and their uses

Low-speed centrifuges

These are bench-top instruments for routine use, with a maximum speed of 3000–6000 r.p.m. and RCF up to $6\,000\,g$ (Fig. 43.1). They are used to harvest cells, larger organelles (e.g. nuclei, chloroplasts) and coarse precipitates (e.g. antibody–antigen complexes, p. 251). Most modern machines also have a sensor that detects any imbalance when the rotor is spinning and cuts off the power supply (Fig. 43.1). However, some of the older models do not, and must be switched off as soon as any vibration is noticed, to prevent damage to the rotor or harm to the operator.

Microcentrifuges (microfuges)

These are bench-top machines, capable of rapid acceleration up to $12\,000$ r.p.m. and $10\,000\,g$. They are used to sediment small sample volumes (up to 1.5 ml) of larger particles (e.g. cells, precipitates) over short timescales (typically, 0.5–15 min). They are particularly useful for the rapid separation of cells from a liquid medium, e.g. silicone oil microcentrifugation. Box 43.1 gives details of operation for a low-speed centrifuge.

Continuous flow centrifuges

Useful for harvesting large volumes of cells from their growth medium. During centrifugation, the particles are sedimented as the liquid flows through the rotor.

High-speed centrifuges

These are usually larger, free-standing instruments with a maximum speed of up to $25\,000$ r.p.m. and RCF up to $60\,000\,g$. They are used for microbial cells, many organelles (e.g. mitochondria, lysosomes) and protein precipitates. They often have a refrigeration system to keep the rotor cool at high speed. You would normally use such instruments only under direct supervision.

Ultracentrifuges

These are the most powerful machines, having maximum speeds in excess of $30\,000$ r.p.m. and RCF up to $600\,000\,g$, with sophisticated refrigeration and vacuum systems. They are used for smaller organelles (e.g. ribosomes, membrane vesicles) and biological macromolecules. You would not normally use an ultracentrifuge, though your samples may be run by a member of staff.

Rotors

Many centrifuges can be used with tubes of different size and capacity, either by changing the rotor, or by using a single rotor with different buckets/adaptors.

- Swing-out rotors: sample tubes are placed in buckets which pivot as the rotor accelerates (Fig. 43.5a). Swing-out rotors are used on many

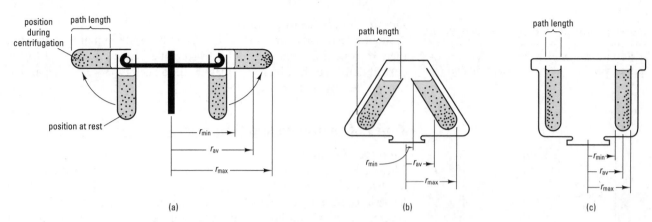

Fig. 43.5 Rotors: (a) swing-out rotor; (b) fixed angle rotor; (c) vertical tube rotor.

low-speed centrifuges: their major drawback is their extended path length and the resuspension of pellets due to currents created during deceleration.

- Fixed-angle rotors: used in many high-speed centrifuges and microcentrifuges (Fig. 43.5b). With their shorter path length, fixed rotors are more effective at pelleting particles than swing-out rotors.

Box 43.1 How to use a low-speed bench centrifuge

1. **Choose the appropriate tube size and material for your application**, with caps where necessary. Most low-speed machines have four-place or six-place rotors – use the correct number of samples to *fill* the rotor assembly whenever possible.

2. **Fill the containers to the appropriate level**: do not overfill, or the sample may spill during centrifugation.

3. **It is vital that the rotor is balanced during use**. Therefore, *identical* tubes must be prepared, to be placed opposite each other in the rotor assembly. This is particularly important for density gradient samples, or for samples containing materials of widely differing densities, e.g. soil samples, since the density profile of the tube will change during a run. However, for low speed work using small amounts of particulate matter in aqueous solution, it is sufficient to counterbalance a sample with a second tube filled with water, or a saline solution of similar density to the sample.

4. **Balance each pair of sample tubes** (plus the corresponding caps, where necessary) to within 0.1 g using a top-pan balance; add liquid dropwise to the lighter tube, until the desired weight is reached. Alternatively, use a set of scales. For small sample volumes (up to 10 ml) added to disposable, lightweight plastic tubes, accurate pipetting of your solution may be sufficient for low speed use.

5. **For centrifuges with swing-out rotors**, check that each holder/bucket is correctly positioned in its locating slots on the rotor and that it is able to swing freely. All buckets must be in position on a swing-out rotor, even if they do not contain sample tubes – buckets are an integral part of the rotor assembly.

6. **Load the sample tubes into the centrifuge**. Make sure that the outside of the centrifuge tubes, the sample holders and sample chambers are dry: any liquid present will cause an imbalance during centrifugation, in addition to the corrosive damage it may cause to the rotor. For sample holders where rubber cushions are provided, make sure that these are correctly located. Balanced tubes must be placed opposite each other – use a simple code if necessary, to prevent mix-ups.

7. **Bring the centrifuge up to operating speed** by gentle acceleration. Do not exceed the maximum speed for the rotor and tubes used.

8. **If the centrifuge vibrates at any time during use, switch off** and find the source of the problem.

9. **Once the rotor has stopped spinning, release the lid and remove all tubes**. If any sample has spilled, make sure you clean it up thoroughly using a non-corrosive disinfectant, e.g. Virkon®, so that it is ready for the next user.

10. **Close the lid (to prevent the entry of dust) and return all controls to zero**.

- Vertical tube rotors: used for isopycnic density gradient centrifugation in high-speed centrifuges and ultracentrifuges (Fig. 43.5c). They cannot be used to harvest particles in suspension as a pellet is not formed.

Centrifuge tubes

These are manufactured in a range of sizes (from 1.5 ml up to 1000 ml) and materials. The following aspects may influence your choice:

- Capacity. This is obviously governed by the volume of your sample. Note that centrifuge tubes must be completely full for certain applications, e.g. for high-speed work.
- Shape. Conical-bottomed centrifuge tubes retain pellets more effectively than round-bottomed tubes, while the latter may be more useful for density gradient work.
- Maximum centrifugal force. Detailed information is supplied by the manufacturers. Standard Pyrex® glass tubes can only be used at low centrifugal force (up to 2000 g).
- Solvent resistance. Glass tubes are inert, polycarbonate tubes are particularly sensitive to organic solvents (e.g. ethanol, acetone), while polypropylene tubes are more resistant. See manufacturer's guidelines for detailed information.
- Sterilisation. Disposable plastic centrifuge tubes are often supplied in sterile form. Glass and polypropylene tubes can be repeatedly sterilised. Cellulose ester tubes should *not* be autoclaved. Repeated autoclaving of polycarbonate tubes may lead to cracking/stress damage.
- Opacity. Glass and polycarbonate tubes are clear, while polypropylene tubes are more opaque.
- Ability to be pierced. If you intend to harvest your sample by puncturing the tube wall, cellulose acetate and polypropylene tubes are readily punctured using a syringe needle.
- Caps. Most fixed-angle and vertical tube rotors require tubes to be capped, to prevent leakage during use and to provide support to the tube during centrifugation. For low speed centrifugation, caps must be used for any hazardous samples. Make sure you use the correct caps for your tubes.

Safe working practice with centrifuge tubes – never be tempted to use a tube or bottle which was not designed to fit the machine you are using (e.g. a general-purpose glass test tube, or a screw-capped bottle), or you may damage the centrifuge and cause an accident.

Using microcentrifuge tubes – the integral push-on caps of microcentrifuge tubes must be correctly pushed home before use or they can come off during centrifugation.

Balancing tubes – never balance centrifuge tubes 'by eye' – use a balance. Note that a 35 ml tube full of liquid at an RCF of 3000 g has an effective weight greater than a large adult man.

Balancing the rotor

For the safe use of centrifuges, the rotor must be balanced during use, or the spindle and rotor assembly may be damaged permanently; in severe cases, the rotor may fail and cause a serious accident.

KEY POINT *It is vital that you balance your loaded centrifuge tubes before use.* As a general rule, *balance all sample tubes to within 1% or better,* using a top-pan balance or scales. Place balanced tubes opposite each other.

Safe practice

Given their speed of rotation and the extremely high forces generated, centrifuges have the potential to be extremely dangerous, if used incorrectly. For safety reasons, all centrifuges are manufactured with an armoured casing that should contain any fragments in cases of rotor failure. Machines usually have a safety lock to prevent the motor from being switched on unless the lid is closed and to stop the lid from being opened while the rotor is moving. Don't be tempted to use older machines without a safety lock, or centrifuges where the locking mechanism is damaged/inoperative. Be particularly careful to make sure that hair and clothing are kept well away from moving parts.

Text references

Ford, T.C. and Graham, J.M. (1991) *An Introduction to Centrifugation*. Bios, Oxford.

Graham, J. (2001) *Biological Centrifugation*. Bios, Oxford.

Sources for further study

Boyer, R. (2000) *Modern Experimental Biochemistry*, 3rd edn. Benjamin Cummings, San Francisco.
[Also covers other topics, including chromatography and spectroscopy.]

Rickwood, D., Ford, T. and Steensgard, J. (1994) *Centrifugation: Essential Data*. Wiley, New York.

Study exercises

43.1 Decide on the type of centrifuge required for a particular application. What centrifuge would you use for each of the following?
  (a) Separating mitochondria from a cell homogenate.
  (b) Separating yeast cells from their surrounding medium in an experiment to study the uptake of a radiolabelled amino acid as a function of time.
  (c) Harvesting cells from a bioreactor containing 25 litres of growth medium.

43.2 Determine centrifugal acceleration for a specific centrifuge. Calculate the centrifugal acceleration (RCF, i.e. the g value) of the following (express your answers to 3 significant figures):
  (a) A bench centrifuge with an average radius of rotation of 125 mm operating at 4000 r.p.m.
  (b) A bench-top microcentrifuge with an average radius of rotation of 60 mm, operating at 12 000 r.p.m.
  (c) An ultracentrifuge with an average radius of rotation of 186 mm, operating at 30 000 r.p.m.

43.3 Determine the speed required to give a particular centrifugal acceleration (g value). Calculate the speed required (r.p.m. value) for each of the following (express your answers to 3 significant figures):
  (a) RCF of 1500 g, using a bench centrifuge with an average radius of rotation of 95 mm.
  (b) RCF of 50 000 g, using a high-speed centrifuge with an average radius of rotation of 135 mm.
  (c) RCF of 13 000 g, using a bench-top microcentrifuge with an average radius of rotation of 5.5 cm.

43.4 Calculate the difference in centrifugal acceleration (*g* value) between the top, middle and bottom of a centrifuge tube. Assuming that the minimum, average and maximum radial distances of a centrifuge tube in a swing-out rotor of a bench centrifuge operating at 5000 r.p.m. are 45 mm, 70 mm and 95 mm respectively, what are the corresponding *g* values at the top, middle and bottom of the tube when the centrifuge is operating? (Express your answer to 3 significant figures.)

Chromatography – separation methods

Chromatography is used to separate the individual constituents within a sample on the basis of differences in their physical characteristics, e.g. molecular size, shape, charge, volatility, solubility and/or adsorptivity. The essential components of a chromatographic system are:

- A stationary phase, either a solid, a gel or an immobilised liquid, held by a support matrix.
- A chromatographic bed: the stationary phase may be packed into a glass or metal column, spread as a thin layer on a sheet of glass or plastic, or adsorbed on cellulose fibres (paper).
- A mobile phase, either a liquid or a gas which acts as a solvent, carrying the sample through the stationary phase and eluting from the chromatographic bed.
- A delivery system to pass the mobile phase through the chromatographic bed.
- A detection system to monitor the test substances (Chapter 45).

Individual substances interact with the stationary phase to different extents as they are carried through the system, enabling separation to be achieved.

KEY POINT In a chromatographic system, those substances which interact strongly with the stationary phase will be retarded to the greatest extent while those which show little interaction will pass through with minimal delay, leading to differences in distances travelled or elution times.

Types of chromatographic system

Chromatographic systems can be categorised according to the form of the chromatographic bed, the nature of the mobile and stationary phases and the method of separation.

Thin-layer chromatography (TLC) and paper chromatography

Here, you apply the sample as a single spot near one end of the sheet, by microsyringe or microcapillary. This sheet is allowed to dry fully, then it is transferred to a glass tank containing a shallow layer of solvent (Fig. 44.1). Remove the sheet when the solvent front has travelled across 80–90% of its length.

You can express movement of an individual substance in terms of its relative frontal mobility, or R_F value, where:

$$R_F = \frac{\text{distance moved by substance}}{\text{distance moved by solvent}}$$ [44.1]

Alternatively, you may express movement with respect to a standard of known mobility, as R_X, where:

$$R_X = \frac{\text{distance moved by test substance}}{\text{distance moved by standard}}$$ [44.2]

The R_F (or R_X) value is a constant for a particular substance and solvent system (under standard conditions) and closely reflects the partitioning of

glass tank with lid

solvent front

direction of travel of sample components

point of application of samples

solvent (mobile phase)

glass plate with silica gel layer

Fig. 44.1 Components of a TLC system.

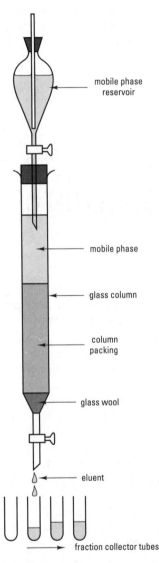

mobile phase reservoir

mobile phase

glass column

column packing

glass wool

eluent

fraction collector tubes

Fig. 44.2 Equipment for column chromatography (gravity feed system).

the substance between the stationary and mobile phases. Tabulated ... are available for a range of biological molecules and solvents (e.g. ... 1969, or Touchstone, 1980). However, you should analyse one or m... reference compounds on the same sheet as your unknown sample, ... check their R_F values.

Column chromatography

Here, you pack a glass column with the appropriate stationary phase and equilibrate the mobile phase by passage through the column, either by gravity (Fig. 44.2), or using a low pressure peristaltic pump. You can then introduce the sample to the top of the column, to form a discrete band of material. This is then flushed through the column by the mobile phase. If the individual substances have different rates of migration, they will separate within the column, eluting at different times as the mobile phase travels through the column.

You can detect eluted substances by collecting the mobile phase as it elutes from the column in a series of tubes (discontinuous monitoring), either manually or with an automatic fraction collector. Fractions of 2–5% of the bed volume are usually collected and analysed, e.g. by chemical assay. You can now construct an elution profile (or chromatogram) by plotting the amount of substance against either time, elution volume or fraction number, which should give a symmetrical peak for each substance (Fig. 44.3).

You can express the migration of a particular substance at a given flow rate in terms of its retention time (t), or elution volume (V_e). The separation efficiency of a column is measured by its ability to distinguish between two similar substances, assessed in terms of:

- selectivity (α), measured using the following equation, which takes into account the retention times of the two peaks (i.e. t_a and t_b), plus the column dead time (t_0):

$$\alpha = \frac{t_b - t_0}{t_a - t_0} \qquad [44.3]$$

The column dead time is the time it takes for an unretained compound to pass through the column without any interaction with the stationary phase.

- resolution (R), quantified in terms of the retention time and the base width (W) of each peak:

$$R = \frac{2(t_a - t_b)}{W_a + W_b} \qquad [44.4]$$

where the subscripts a and b refer to substances a and b respectively (Fig. 44.3). For most practical purposes, R values of 1 or more are satisfactory, corresponding to 98% peak separation for symmetrical peaks.

High performance liquid chromatography (HPLC)

Column chromatography originally used large 'soft' stationary phases that required low pressure flow of the mobile phase to avoid compression; separations were usually time-consuming and of low resolution ('low performance'). Subsequently, the production of small, incompressible, homogeneous particulate support materials and high pressure pumps with reliable, steady flow rates have enabled high performance systems to be developed. These systems operate at pressures up to 10 MPa, forcing the mobile phase through the column at a high flow rate to give rapid separation with reduced band broadening, due to smaller particle size.

HPLC columns are usually made of stainless steel, and all components, valves, etc., are manufactured from materials which can withstand the high pressures involved. The choice of solvent delivery system depends on the type of separation to be performed:

- Isocratic separation: a single solvent (or solvent mixture) is used throughout the analysis.
- Gradient elution separation: the composition of the mobile phase is altered using a microprocessor-controlled gradient programmer, which mixes appropriate amounts of two different substances to produce the required gradient.

Problems with peaks – *non-symmetrical peaks may result from column overloading, co-elution of solutes, poor packing of the stationary phase, or interactions between the substance and the support material.*

Fig. 44.3 Peak characteristics in a chromatographic separation, i.e. a chromatogram. For symbols, see Eqn [44.4].

Fig. 44.4 Components of an HPLC system.

Most HPLC systems are linked to a continuous monitoring detector of high sensitivity, e.g. proteins may be detected spectrophotometrically by monitoring the absorbance of the eluent at 280 nm as it passes through a flow cell (cuvette). Other detectors can be used to measure changes in fluorescence, current or potential (Chapter 45). Most detection systems are non-destructive, which means that you can collect eluent with an automatic fraction collector for further study (Fig. 44.4).

The speed, sensitivity and versatility of HPLC make this the method of choice for the separation of many small molecules of biological interest, normally using reverse phase partition chromatography (p. 299). Separation of macromolecules (especially proteins and nucleic acids) usually requires 'biocompatible' systems in which stainless steel components are replaced by titanium, glass or fluoroplastics, using lower pressures to avoid denaturation, e.g. the Pharmacia FPLC® system. Such separations are carried out using ion-exchange, gel permeation and/or hydrophobic interaction chromatography (pp. 301–2).

Gas chromatography (GC)

Modern GC uses capillary chromatography columns (internal diameter 0.1–0.5 mm) up to 50 m in length (Fig. 44.5). The stationary phase is generally a cross-linked silicone polymer, coated as a thin film on the inner wall of the capillary: at normal operating temperatures, this behaves in a similar manner to a liquid film, but is far more robust. The mobile phase ('carrier gas') is usually nitrogen or helium. Selective separation is achieved as a result of the differential partitioning of individual compounds between the carrier gas and silicone polymer phases. The

Fig. 44.5 Components of a GC system.

separation of most biomolecules is influenced by the temperature of the column, which may be constant during the analysis ('isothermal' – usually 50–250 °C) or, more commonly, may increase in a pre-programmed manner (e.g. from 50 °C to 250 °C at 10 °C per min). Samples are injected onto the 'top' of the column, through a sample injection port containing a gas-tight septum. The output from the column can be monitored by flame ionisation, electron capture or thermal conductivity (Chapter 45).

Spectrometric detection systems include mass spectrometry (GC-MS) and infra-red spectroscopy (GC-IR). GC can only be used with samples capable of volatilisation at the operating temperature of the column, e.g. short chain fatty acids. Other substances may need to be chemically modified to produce more volatile compounds, e.g. long chain saturated fatty acids (Chapter 51) are usually analysed as methyl esters while monosaccharides (Chapter 52) are converted to their trimethylsilyl derivatives.

Separation methods

Adsorption chromatography

This is a form of solid–liquid chromatography. The stationary phase is a porous, finely divided solid which adsorbs molecules of the test substance on its surface due to dipole–dipole interactions, hydrogen bonding and/or van der Waals interactions (Fig. 44.6). The range of adsorbents is limited, e.g. polystyrene-based resins (for non-polar molecules), silica, aluminium oxide and calcium phosphate (for polar molecules). Most adsorbents must be activated by heating to 110–120 °C before use, since their adsorptive capacity is significantly decreased in the presence of bound water. Adsorption chromatography can be carried out in column or thin-layer form, using a wide range of organic solvents.

Partition chromatography

This is based on the partitioning of a substance between two liquid phases, in this instance the stationary and mobile phases. Substances which are more soluble in the mobile phase will pass rapidly through the system while those which favour the stationary phase will be retarded (Fig. 44.7). In normal phase partition chromatography the stationary phase is a polar solvent, usually water, supported by a solid matrix (e.g. cellulose fibres in paper chromatography) and the mobile phase is an immiscible, non-polar organic solvent. For reverse-phase partition chromatography the stationary phase is a non-polar solvent (e.g. a C_{18} hydrocarbon, such as octadecylsilane) which is chemically bonded to a porous support matrix (e.g. silica), while the mobile phase can be chosen from a wide range of polar solvents, usually water or an aqueous buffered solution containing one or more organic solvents, e.g. acetonitrile. Solutes interact with the stationary phase through non-polar interactions and so the *least* polar solutes elute last from the column. Solute retention and separation are controlled by changing the composition of the mobile phase (e.g. % v/v acetonitrile). Reverse-phase high performance liquid chromatography (RP–HPLC) is used to separate a broad range of non-polar, polar and ionic biomolecules, including peptides, proteins, oligosaccharides and vitamins for ionic and ionisable solutes.

Ion-exchange chromatography

Here, separations are carried out using a column packed with a porous matrix which has a large number of ionised groups on its surfaces, i.e. the

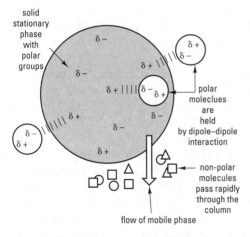

Fig. 44.6 Adsorption chromatography (polar stationary phase).

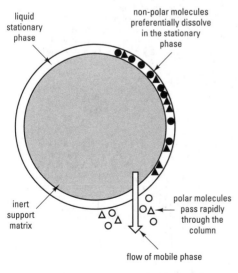

Fig. 44.7 Liquid–liquid partition chromatography, e.g. reverse-phase HPLC.

Chromatography – separation methods

Selecting a separation method – *it is often best to select a technique that involves direct interaction between the substance(s) and the stationary phase, (e.g. ion-exchange, affinity or hydrophobic interaction chromatography), due to their increased capacity and resolution compared to other methods, (e.g. partition or gel permeation chromatography).*

Maximising resolution in IEC (and HIC) – *keep your columns as short as possible. Once the sample components have been separated, they should be eluted as quickly as possible from the column in order to avoid band broadening resulting from diffusion of sample ions in the mobile phase.*

Using a gel permeation system – *keep your sample volume as small as possible, in order to minimise band broadening due to dilution of the sample during passage through the column.*

stationary phase is an ion-exchange resin. The groups may be cation or anion exchangers, depending upon their affinity for positive or negative ions. The net charge on a particular resin depends on the pK_a of the ionisable groups and the pH of the solution, in accordance with the Henderson–Hasselbalch equation (p. 150).

For most practical applications, you should select the ion-exchange resin and buffer pH so that the test substances are strongly bound by electrostatic attraction to the ion-exchange resin on passage through the system, while the other components of the sample are rapidly eluted (Fig. 44.8). You can then elute the bound components by raising the salt concentration of the mobile phase, either stepwise or as a continuous gradient, so that exchange of ions of the same charge occurs at oppositely charged sites on the stationary phase. Weakly bound sample molecules will elute first, while more strongly bound molecules will elute at a higher concentration. Computer-controlled gradient formers are available: if two or more components cannot be resolved using a linear salt gradient, an adapted gradient can be used in which the rate of change in salt concentration is decreased over the range where these components are expected to elute.

Ion-exchange chromatography can be used to separate mixtures of a wide range of ionic biomolecules, including amino acids, peptides, proteins and nucleotides. Electrophoresis (Chapters 46 and 47) is an alternative means of separating charged biomolecules.

Gel permeation chromatography (GPC) or gel filtration

Here, the stationary phase is in the form of beads of a cross-linked gel containing pores of a discrete size (Fig. 44.9). The size of the pores is controlled so that at the molecular level, the pores act as 'gates' that will exclude large molecules and admit smaller ones. However, this gating effect is not an all or nothing phenomenon: molecules of intermediate size partly enter the pores. A column packed with such beads will have within it two

Fig. 44.8 Ion-exchange chromatography (cation exchanger).

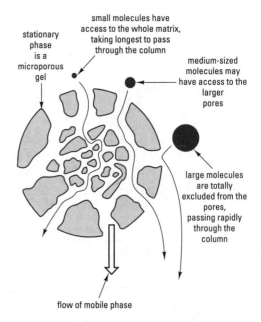

Fig. 44.9 Gel permeation chromatography.

Table 44.1 Fractionation ranges of selected gel permeation chromatography media

M_r	Medium
50–1000	Sephadex G15
	Biogel P-2
1000–5000	Sephadex G-25
1500–30 000	Sephadex G-50
	Biogel P-10
4000–150 000	Sephadex G-100
5000–250 000	Sephadex G-200
20 000–1 500 000	Sephacryl S 300
60 000–20 000 000	Sepharose 4B

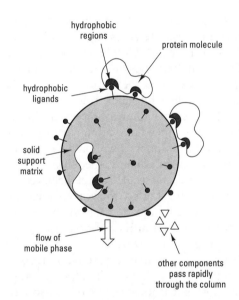

Fig. 44.10 Hydrophobic interaction chromatography. Hydrophobic interactions between ligands and hydrophobic amino acid residues release 'structured' water, making the interactions thermodynamically favourable.

Using HIC for purification – HIC can be used immediately after salt precipitation, when the salt concentration is high. If the desired biomolecule is then eluted using a gradient of reducing salt concentration, it may be possible to follow HIC directly by IEC (which requires an initial buffer of low ionic strength) without changing the buffer.

effective volumes that are potentially available to sample molecules in the mobile phase, i.e. V_i, the volume surrounding the beads, and V_{ii}, the volume within the pores. If a sample is placed at the top of such a column, the mobile phase will carry the sample components down the column, but at different rates according to their molecular size. A very large molecule will have access to all of V_i but to none of V_{ii}, and will therefore elute in the minimum possible volume (the 'void volume', or V_o, equivalent to V_i). A very small molecule will have access to all of V_i and all of V_{ii}, and therefore it has to pass through the total liquid volume of the column (V_t, equivalent to $V_i + V_{ii}$) before it emerges. Molecules of intermediate size have access to all of V_i but only part of V_{ii}, and will elute at a volume between V_o and V_t, in order of decreasing size depending on their access to V_{ii}.

Cross-linked dextrans (e.g. Sephadex®), agarose (e.g. Sepharose®) and polyacrylamide (e.g. Bio-gel®) can be used to separate mixtures of macromolecules, particularly enzymes, antibodies and other globular proteins (see Table 44.1 for details). Selectivity in GPC is solely dependent on the stationary phase, with the mobile phase being used solely to transport the sample components through the column. Thus, it is possible to estimate the molecular mass of a sample component by calibrating a given column using molecules of known molecular mass and similar shape. A plot of elution volume (V_e) against $\log_{10}$ molecular mass is approximately linear. A further application of GPC is the general separation of low molecular mass and high molecular mass components, e.g. 'desalting' a protein extract by passage through a Sephadex® G-25 column is faster and more efficient than dialysis.

Hydrophobic interaction chromatography (HIC)

This technique is used to separate proteins, and exploits the fact that many proteins have hydrophobic sites, with hydrophobic amino acid residues (e.g. leucine, isoleucine, valine, phenylalanine) on their surfaces. Proteins differ in the nature and extent of these hydrophobic regions. The underlying principle is similar to that of RP-HPLC in that it involves hydrophobic interactions between the sample components and a non-polar stationary phase. However, RP-HPLC is only useful for analytical separations of proteins where retention of biological activity is not required, and is unsuitable for separation of native proteins for several reasons:

- the stationary phase in RP-HPLC columns tends to be densely packed with hydrophobic groups, leading to tight protein binding, possibly through multi-site attachment;
- the use of polar organic solvents may lead to protein denaturation;
- the high pressures used to obtain rapid flow rates in HPLC may also denature proteins.

The groups used on HIC stationary phases are both less densely packed and less hydrophobic than those used in RP-HPLC, and this results in milder adsorption of proteins (octyl or phenyl groups are commonly used in HIC, rather than octadecyl groups). Furthermore, retention and elution can be achieved using aqueous solutions so that an individual protein can be isolated with its 3-D conformation intact.

Separations are based on interactions between the three components of the system, i.e. the hydrophobic stationary phase, the hydrophobic sample molecules, and the aqueous stationary phase. In an aqueous environment, hydrophobic groups tend to associate, and this results in certain proteins binding to the stationary phase, where the strength of binding is related to the degree of hydrophobicity of the protein (Fig. 44.10). This tendency is promoted by the presence of certain salts, most commonly ammonium sulphate, that produce 'salting out' effects. Elution of components can be achieved by a variety of means:

- reducing the ammonium sulphate concentration of the mobile phase, to decrease the 'salting out' effect;
- changing the salt in the mobile phase to one that does not promote salting out;
- including non-ionic detergents (e.g. Triton X-100) to reduce hydrophobic interactions;
- including aliphatic alcohols, reducing the polarity of the mobile phase;
- changing the pH;
- reducing the temperature.

Affinity chromatography (AC)

Affinity chromatography enables biomolecules to be purified on the basis of their biological specificity rather than by differences in physicochemical properties, and a high degree of purification (>1000-fold) can be expected. It is especially useful for isolating small quantities of material from large amounts of contaminating substances. The technique involves the immobilisation of a complementary binding substance (the ligand) onto a solid matrix in such a way that the specific binding affinity of the ligand is preserved. When a biological sample is applied to a column packed with this affinity support matrix, the molecule of interest will bind specifically to the ligand, while contaminating substances will be washed through with buffer (Fig. 44.11). Elution of the desired molecule can be achieved by changing the pH or ionic strength of the buffer, to weaken the non-covalent interactions between the molecule and the ligand, or by the addition of other substances that have greater affinity for the ligand.

In AC, the ligand must show specific, but reversible, interaction with the molecule to be purified. It must also contain a reactive functional group, independent of the biospecific site, that will allow covalent attachment to the matrix. The support matrix must be free of non-specific adsorption effects and have sufficient reactive functional groups for the attachment of ligands. Agarose is an ideal support matrix for use in AC. If the ligand is small and the molecule to be purified is large, binding may be restricted due to the proximity of the matrix surface. This problem may be overcome by the introduction of a 'spacer arm' (e.g. a hexane group) between the ligand and the matrix (Fig. 44.11).

A potential disadvantage of the specificity of AC is that a new ligand may have to be sought for each individual separation – a potentially time-consuming and expensive process. It may be more practical to use 'group-specific adsorbents' which contain ligands that have an affinity for a class of biochemically related substances. Examples of group-specific adsorbents include:

- Lectins, which are a group of proteins produced from moulds, plants and animals, that bind reversibly with specific sugar residues. They are very useful for the purification of sugar-containing macromolecules such as glycoproteins, serum lipoproteins, and membrane proteins such as receptors. Different lectins show different

Avoiding protein precipitation in HIC – certain protein components may precipitate in high ionic strength buffers. If this occurs, dilute your sample and inject larger volumes.

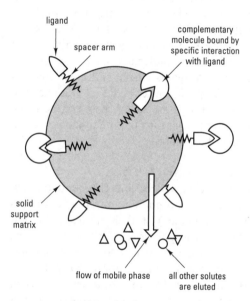

Fig. 44.11 Affinity chromatography.

Examples Biospecific molecules used in affinity chromatography include:

- enzymes and inhibitors/cofactors/ substrates;
- hormones and receptor proteins;
- antibodies and antigens;
- complementary base sequences in DNA and RNA (p. 365).

Elution of substances from an affinity system – make sure that your elution conditions do not affect the interaction between the ligand and the stationary phase, or you may elute the ligand from the column.

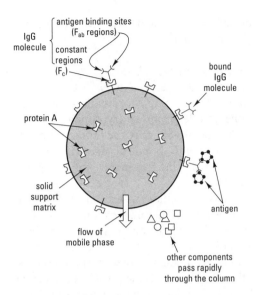

Fig. 44.12 Affinity chromatography using protein A as a ligand to bind IgG antibodies via the F_c region.

Fig. 44.13 Covalent chromatography. A protein with a free surface thiol group reduces the ligand disulphide, releasing the blocking group and forming a new disulphide.

specificities, e.g. concanavalin A and lentil lectin bind to sugars having –OH groups at C-3, C-4 and C-5 (i.e. mannose and glucose), while wheatgerm lectin binds to *N*-acetyl glucosamine residues. Once bound, substances can be resolved by eluting the column with a salt gradient, or by including free sugars to act as competitive binding agents. Lectins are sometimes called agglutinins because of their ability to agglutinate different types of erythrocyte (e.g. A, B and O) by binding to the specific receptors on their surfaces.

- Protein A, which is a commercially available surface protein from the bacterium *Staphylococcus aureus* that has a specific binding capacity for the constant (F_c) region of IgG-type antibodies from most mammalian species (Fig. 44.12). As well as being useful in the purification of IgG, protein A can also be used for the isolation of other molecules, as long as an antibody can be raised against them. This is possible because interaction of protein A with IgG occurs via the F_c segment of immunoglobulins of this class, irrespective of their F_{ab} components (see Fig. 38.1). Immobilisation of a specific IgG antibody onto a protein A-agarose column produces an affinity support that can be used to purify the desired antigen.

- Immobilised dyes, which can be used to purify a wide range of enzymes and proteins. One of the most widely used dyes is Cibacron Blue F3G-A, available as an affinity support as Blue Sepharose®. This dye has some structural similarities to nucleotide cofactors such as NAD^+ and $NADP^+$, and is useful for the purification of enzymes that require such cofactors. Chemical modification of such dyes increases their specificity, and it is likely that computer modelling will play a role in the future development of new dye-based affinity supports. Dyes are also used in the related non-chromatographic technique of affinity precipitation. This makes use of two dye molecules linked *via* a spacer molecule; when this 'bis-ligand' is added to a solution containing the molecule to be purified, the ligand specifically binds two desired molecules, forming an insoluble complex. Alternatively, a heterobifunctional ligand can be used – a combination of a specific ligand and a group that can be used to initiate precipitation once the desired molecule has bound to the ligand. Such interactions are equivalent to the precipitin reaction in immunology (p. 251).

- Poly(U)-agarose is an affinity support that can be used for the isolation of mRNA because of the biospecific hybridisation of poly(U) with the poly(A) 'tail' sequence characteristic of mRNAs. It can also be used to isolate proteins and enzymes that bind to RNA, such as reverse transcriptases.

Covalent chromatography

This is a variant of affinity chromatography which involves the formation of fairly strong, but reversible, covalent bonds between the affinity support and the molecule to be purified. One type of covalent chromatography is used for the purification of proteins containing thiol (–SH) groups (Fig. 44.13). If the sample is applied to a column containing matrix-attached disulphide 2′-pyridyl groups, thiol-containing proteins displace the 2′-pyridyl group on the support and become immobilised *via* disulphide bridges. Elution of bound components can be achieved by including thiol reagents such as cysteine, glutathione, 2-mercaptoethanol or dithiothreitol (DTT) in the mobile phase. Another form of covalent chromatography uses immobilised boronic acid, which binds certain carbohydrate groups (e.g. in glycoproteins).

Immobilised metal affinity chromatography (IMAC)

This exploits the ability of certain metal ions, especially Ni^{2+}, Cu^{2+}, Zn^{2+}, Hg^{2+} and Cd^{2+}, to bind to proteins by forming coordination complexes with imidazole groups of histidine, indole groups of tryptophan, or thiol groups of cysteine residues. The metal ion may be immobilised by chelation with iminodiacetic acid covalently bound to agarose. Proteins that bind to the metal ions can be eluted using free metal-binding ligands (e.g. amino acids) in the mobile phase.

A very useful application of IMAC is in the purification of 'histidine-tagged' recombinant proteins, e.g. using pET plasmid vectors (see p. 446). The technique exploits the affinity of histidine-containing proteins for a chelating gel, typically Ni^{2+} immobilised on agarose. The histidine tag present at the *N*- or *C*-terminus of a recombinant protein forms complexes with the transition metal and is therefore bound to the gel. The proteins can be desorbed (eluted) from the gel with increasing concentration of a substrate with an affinity for the chelated metal ion, e.g. imidazole, using either a gradient or a stepwise approach. Alternatively, chelating agents (e.g. EDTA) or low pH can be used for protein elution.

Optimising chromatographic separations

In any chromatographic technique, sample components leave the column at different elution volumes/different times, and are then monitored by a suitable detector (Chapter 45). The responses of the detector are recorded on a chart or a screen in the form of a *chromatogram*. Ideally the sample biomolecules will be completely separated and detection of components will result in a series of discrete individual peaks corresponding to each type of biomolecule (e.g. Fig. 44.3). However, to minimise the possibility of overlapping peaks, or of peaks composed of more than one component, it is important to maximise the separation efficiency of the technique, which depends on:

- the selectivity, as measured by the relative retention times of the two components, or by the volume of mobile phase between the peak maxima of the two components after they have passed through the column; this depends on the ability of the chromatographic method to separate two components with similar properties;
- the band-broadening properties of the chromatographic system, which influence the width of the peaks; these are mainly due to the effects of diffusion.

The separation efficiency, or resolution of two adjacent components, can be defined in terms of selectivity and peak broadening, using Eqn 44.4. In practical terms, good resolution is achieved when there is a large 'distance' (either time or volume) between peak maxima, and the peaks are as narrow as possible. The resolution of components is also affected by the relative amount of each substance: for systems showing low resolution, it can be difficult to resolve small amounts of a particular component in the presence of larger amounts of a second component. If you cannot obtain the desired results from a poorly resolved chromatogram, other chromatographic conditions, or even different methods, should be tried in

Assaying analytes – *remember that you cannot quantify a particular analyte without first identifying it: the presence of a single peak on a chromatogram does not prove that a single type of analyte is present.*

Separating small biomolecules – *these will diffuse faster than large molecules, so they should be separated using faster flow rates.*

an attempt to improve resolution. For liquid chromatography, changes in the following factors may improve resolution:

- Stationary phase particle size – the smaller the particle, the greater the area available for partitioning between the mobile phase and the stationary phase. This partly accounts for the high resolution observed with HPLC and FPLC compared with low pressure methods.
- The slope of the salt gradient in eluting IEC or HIC columns, e.g. using computer-controlled adapted gradients (p. 372).
- In low pressure liquid chromatography, the flow rate of the mobile phase must be optimised because this influences two band-broadening effects which are dependent on diffusion of sample molecules, i.e. (i) the flow rate must be slow enough to allow effective partitioning between the mobile phase and the stationary phase, and (ii) it must be fast enough to ensure that there is minimal diffusion along the column once the molecules have been separated. To allow for these opposing influences, a compromise flow rate must be used.
- If you prepare your own columns, they must be packed correctly, with no channels present that might result in uneven flow and eddy diffusion.

Learning from experience – if you are unable to separate your biomolecule using a particular method, do not regard this as a failure, but instead, think about what this tells you about either the substance(s) or the sample.

Text references

Stahl, E. (1969) *Thin Layer Chromatography – a Laboratory Handbook*, 2nd edn. Springer-Verlag, Berlin.

Touchstone, J.C. (1980) *Thin Layer Chromatography: Quantitative Environmental and Clinical Applications*. Wiley, New York.

Sources for further study

Boyer, R. (2000) *Modern Experimental Biochemistry*, 3rd edn. Benjamin Cummings, San Francisco.
[Also covers other topics, including centrifugation and spectroscopy.]

Braithwaite, A. and Smith, F.J. (1990) *Chromatographic Methods*, 4th edn. Chapman and Hall, London.

Gooding, K.M. and Regnier, F.E. (2002) *HPLC of Biological Macromolecules Revised and Expanded*. Marcel Dekker, New York.

Miller, P. (1999) *High Resolution Chromatography: A Practical Approach*. Oxford University Press, Oxford.

Wilson, K. and Walker, J. (eds) (2000) *Principles and Techniques of Practical Biochemistry*, 5th edn. Cambridge University Press, Cambridge.
[Also covers a range of other topics, including spectroscopy and centrifugation.]

Study exercises

44.1 Calculate R_F and R_X values from a chromatogram. The figure represents the separation of three pigments by thin-layer chromatography.
   (a) What is the R_F value of each pigment?

(b) What is the mobility of pigments B and C, relative to pigment A (R_A)?

Express both answers to 3 significant figures.

Thin-layer chromatographic separation of a mixture of three pigments (A, B and C).

44.2 Calculate the resolution and selectivity of two components from a chromatogram. Two compounds were separated by column chromatography, giving retention times of 4 min 30 s for A and 6 min 12 s for B, while a compound that was completely excluded from the stationary phase was eluted in 1 min 35 s. The base width of peak A was 40 s and the base width of peak B was 44 s. Calculate (a) the selectivity and (b) the resolution for these two compounds (express all answers to 3 significant figures).

44.3 Predict chromatographic behaviour on ion-exchange columns using protein titration curves. The variation of net charge with pH for two proteins, A and B, is shown in the figure.
(a) What is the isoelectric point (pI) of each protein?
(b) If a mixture of these proteins was passed down an anion exchange column (e.g. Q-Sepharose®) equilibrated with buffer at pH 7.0, how would each protein behave in terms of elution and retention?
(c) If the proteins were bound to a cation exchanger (e.g. S-Sepharose®) at pH 5.5, predict the order in which the proteins would elute using a salt gradient.

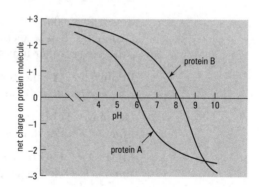

44.4 Test your understanding of the action of ammonium sulphate on proteins. Explain why mobile phases containing a concentration of ammonium sulphate promote the binding of many proteins to HIC columns.

Chromatography – detection and analysis

Once the individual components in a sample mixture have been separated by a given chromatographic technique (Chapter 44), a suitable detection system is required to monitor and record the elution of the components of the mixture as they pass through a 'flow cell'.

KEY POINT The most appropriate detector depends on the type of chromatography and the application: ideally, the detector should show high sensitivity, a low detection limit and minimal noise or drift. These terms are defined in Chapter 49.

Liquid chromatography detectors

UV/visible detectors

These are widely used and have the advantages of versatility, sensitivity and stability. Such detectors are of two types: fixed wavelength and variable wavelength. Fixed-wavelength detectors are simple to use, with low operating costs. They usually contain a mercury lamp as a light source, emitting at several wavelengths between 254 and 578 nm; a particular wavelength is selected using suitable cut-off filters. The most frequently used wavelengths for analysis of biomolecules are 254 nm (for nucleic acids) and 280 nm (for proteins). Variable-wavelength detectors use a deuterium lamp and a continuously adjustable monochromator for wavelengths of 190–600 nm. For both types of detector, sensitivity is in the absorbance range 0.001–1.0 (down to $\cong 1$ ng), with noise levels as low as 4×10^{-5}. Note that sensitivity is partly influenced by the path length of the flow cell (typically 10 mm). Monitoring at short wavelength UV (e.g. below 240 nm) may give increased sensitivity but decreased specificity, since many biological molecules absorb in this range. Additional problems with short wavelength UV detection include instrument instability, giving a variable baseline, and absorption by components of the eluting buffer (e.g. TRIS, which absorbs at 206 nm).

An important development in chromatographic monitoring is diode array detection (DAD). The incident light comprises the whole spectrum of light from the source, which is passed through a diffraction grating and the diffracted light detected by an array of photodiodes. A typical DAD can measure the absorbance of each sample component at 1–10 nm intervals over the range 190–600 nm. This gives an absorbance spectrum for each eluting substance which may be used to identify the compound and give some indication as to its purity. An example of a three-dimensional diode array spectrum is shown in Fig. 45.1.

Fluorescence detectors

Many biomolecules, including some vitamins, nucleotides and porphyrins show natural fluorescence (Table 41.1), or can be made to fluoresce by pre-column or post-column derivatisation with a fluorophore. Fluorescence detection is more sensitive than UV/visible detection (p. 275), and may allow analysis in the pg range. A fluorescence detector consists of a light source (e.g. a xenon lamp), a diffraction grating

UV detection of proteins – note that the absorbance at 280 nm is mostly due to tryptophan and tyrosine residues; if a protein contains low amounts of these amino acids, its absorbance at this wavelength will be low.

Fig. 45.1 Diode array detector absorption spectra of the eluent from an HPLC separation of a mixture of four steroids, taken every 15 seconds.

Overcoming interference with fluorescence detectors – use a dual flow cell to offset background fluorescence due to components of the mobile phase.

to supply light at the excitation wavelength, and a photomultiplier to monitor the emitted light (usually arranged to be at right angles to the excitation beam). The use of instruments with a laser light source can give an extremely narrow excitation waveband, and increased sensitivity and specificity.

Electrochemical detectors

These offer very high sensitivity and specificity, with the possibility of detection of fg amounts of electroactive compounds such as catecholamines, vitamins, thiols, purines, ascorbate and uric acid. The two main types of detector, amperometric and coulometric, operate on similar principles, i.e. by measuring the change in current or potential as sample components pass between two electrodes within the flow cell. One of these electrodes acts as a reference (or counter) electrode (e.g. calomel electrode), while the other – the working electrode – is held at a voltage that is high enough to cause either oxidation or reduction of sample molecules. In the oxidative mode, the working electrode is usually glassy carbon, while in reductive mode a mercury electrode is used. In either case, a current flow between the electrodes is induced and detected.

Gas chromatography detectors

The most commonly used detectors for GC analysis of biomolecules are:

Flame ionisation detector (FID)

This is a widely used detector, being particularly useful for the analysis of a broad range of organic biomolecules. It involves passing the exit gas stream from the column through a hydrogen flame that has a potential of >100 V applied across it (Fig. 45.2). Most organic compounds, on passage through this flame, produce ions and electrons that create a small current across the electrodes, and this is amplified for measurement purposes. The FID is very sensitive (down to ≈ 0.1 pg), with a linear response over a wide concentration range. One drawback is that the sample is destroyed during analysis.

Thermal conductivity detector (TCD)

This simple detector is based on changes in the thermal conductivity of the gas stream brought about by the presence of separated sample molecules. The detector elements are two electrically heated platinum wires, one in a chamber through which only the carrier gas flows (the reference detector cell), and the other in a chamber that takes the gas flow from the column (the sample detector cell). In the presence of a constant gas flow, the temperature of the wires (and therefore their electrical resistance) is dependent on the thermal conductivity of the gas. Analytes in the gas stream are detected by temperature-dependent changes in resistance dependent on the thermal conductivity of each separated molecule; the size of the signal is directly related to concentration of the analyte.

The advantages of TCD include its applicability to a wide range of organic and inorganic biomolecules and its non-destructive nature, since the sample can be collected for further study. Its major limitation is its low sensitivity (down to ≈ 10 ng), compared with other systems.

Fig. 45.2 Components of a flame ionisation detector (FID).

electrical output

collector electrode (anode)

radioactive foil (^{63}Ni)

cathode

ECD body

gas flow from column

Fig. 45.3 Components of an electron capture detector (ECD).

Electron capture detector (ECD)

This highly sensitive detector (Fig. 45.3) is useful for the detection of certain compounds with electronegative functional groups, e.g. halogens, peroxides and quinones. The gas stream from the column passes over a β-emitter (p. 258) such as ^{63}Ni, which provides electrons that cause ionisation of the carrier gas (e.g. nitrogen). When carrier gas alone is passing the β-emitter, its ionisation results in a constant current flowing between two electrodes placed in the gas flow. However, when electron-capturing sample molecules are present in the gas flow, a decrease in current is detected. An example of the application of the ECD is in detecting and quantifying chlorinated pesticides.

Interfacing GC or HPLC with mass spectrometry

Mass spectrometry (p. 285) used in conjunction with chromatographic methods can provide a powerful tool for identifying the components of complex mixtures, e.g. aqueous pollutants. The procedure requires computer control of instruments and data storage/analysis. One drawback is the limited capacity of the mass spectrometer – due to its vacuum requirements – compared with the volume of material leaving the chromatography column. For capillary GC, the relatively small output can be fed directly into the ionisation chamber of the mass spectrometer. For packed column GC, a 'jet separator' is used to remove most of the carrier gas from the molecules to be analysed before they enter the spectrometer. Similarly, in HPLC, devices have been developed for solving the problem of large solvent volumes, e.g. by splitting the eluent from the column so only a small fraction reaches the mass spectrometer.

The computer-generated outputs from the mass spectrometer are similar to chromatograms obtained from other methods, and show peaks corresponding to the elution of particular components. However, it is then possible to select an individual peak and obtain a mass spectrum for the component in that peak to aid in its identification (p. 285). This has helped to identify hundreds of components present in biological systems, including flavour molecules in food, drug metabolites and water pollutants.

Coupling capillary GC columns with FT-IR spectrometers (p. 280–1) provides another powerful means of separating and identifying compounds in complex biological mixtures.

Recording and interpreting chromatograms

Recording detector output

For analytical purposes, the detector output is usually connected to a computer-based data acquisition and analysis system. This consists of a personal computer (PC) with data acquisition hardware to convert the analogue detector signal to digital format, plus software to control the data acquisition process, store the signal information and display the resulting chromatogram. The software will also detect peaks and calculate their retention times and sizes (areas) for quantitative analysis. The software often incorporates functions to control the chromatographic equipment, enabling automatic operation. In sophisticated systems, the detector output may be compared with that from a 'library' of chromatograms for known compounds, to suggest possible identities of unknown sample peaks.

Interpreting chromatograms – never assume that a single peak is a guarantee of purity: there may be more than one compound with the same chromatographic characteristics.

In simpler chromatographic systems, you may need to use a chart recorder for detector output. Two important settings must be considered before using a chart recorder:

1. The baseline reading – this should be set only after a suitable quantity of mobile phase has passed through the column (prior to injection of the sample) and stability is established. The chart recorder is usually set a little above the edge of the chart paper grid, to allow for baseline drift.

2. The detector range – this must be set to ensure that the largest peaks do not go off the top of the chart. Adjustment may be based on the expected quantity of analyte, or by trial-and-error process. Use the maximum sensitivity that gives intact peaks. If peaks are still too large, you may need to reduce the amount of sample used, or prepare and analyse a diluted sample.

Interpretation of chromatograms

Make sure you know the direction of the horizontal axis (usually, either volume or time) – it may run from right to left or *vice versa*, and make a note of the detector sensitivity on the vertical axis.

Ideally, the baseline should be 'flat' between peaks, but it may drift up or down due to a number of factors including:

- changes in the composition of the mobile phase (e.g. in gradient elution, p. 300);
- tailing of material from previous peaks;
- carry-over of material from previous samples; this can be avoided by efficient cleaning of columns between runs – allow sufficient time for the previous sample to pass through the column before you introduce the next sample;
- loss of stationary phase from the column (column 'bleed'), caused by extreme elution conditions;
- air bubbles (in liquid chromatography); if the buffers used in the mobile phase are not effectively degassed, air bubbles may build up in the flow cell of the detector, leading to a gradual upward drift of the baseline, followed by a sharp fall when the accumulated air is released. Small air bubbles that do not become trapped may give spurious small peaks.

A peak close to the origin may be due to non-retained sample molecules, flowing at the same rate as the mobile phase, or to artefacts, e.g. air (GC) or solvent (HPLC) in the sample. Whatever its origin, this peak can be used to measure the column dead time void volume (p. 297). No peaks from genuine sample components should appear before this peak.

Peaks can be denoted on the basis of their elution volume (used mainly in liquid chromatography) or their retention times (mainly in GC). If the peaks are not narrow and symmetrical, they may contain more than one component. Where peaks are more curved on the trailing side compared with the leading side, this may indicate too great an association between the component and the stationary phase, or overloading of the column.

Quantitative analysis

Most detectors and chemical assay systems give a linear response with increasing amounts of the test substance over a given 'working range' of

Using a fraction collector – make sure you can relate individual fractions to the position of peaks on the chromatogram. Most fraction collectors send a signal to the recorder each time a fraction is changed.

Avoiding problems with air bubbles in liquid chromatography – always ensure that buffers are effectively degassed by vacuum treatment before use, and regularly clean the flow cell of the detector.

Quantifying biomolecules – note that quantitative analysis often requires assumptions about the identity of separated components (p. 343) and that further techniques may be required to provide information about the nature of the biomolecules present, e.g. mass spectrometry (see Chapter 42).

concentration. Alternative ways of converting the measured response to an amount of substance are:

- External standardisation: this is applicable where the sample volume is sufficiently precise to give reproducible results (e.g. HPLC, column chromatography). You measure the peak areas (or heights) of known amounts of the substance to give a calibration factor or calibration curve which can be used to calculate the amount of test substance in the sample.

- Internal standardisation: where you add a known amount of a reference substance (not originally present in the sample) to the sample, to give an additional peak in the elution profile. You determine the response of the detector to the test and reference substances by analysing a standard containing known amounts of both substances, to provide a response factor (r), where

$$r = \frac{\text{peak area (or height) of test substance}}{\text{peak area (or height) of reference substance}} \qquad [45.1]$$

Use this response factor to quantify the amount of test substance (Q_t) in a sample containing a known amount of the reference substance (Q_r), from the relationship:

Using an external standard – samples and standards should be analysed more than once, to confirm the reproducibility of the technique.

$$Q_t = \frac{\text{peak area (or height) of test substance}}{\text{peak area (or height) of reference substance}} \times (Q_r/r) \qquad [45.2]$$

Internal standardisation should be the method of choice wherever possible, since it is unaffected by small variations in sample volume (e.g. for GC microsyringe injection). The internal standard should be chemically similar to the test substance(s) and must give a peak that is distinct from all other substances in the sample. An additional advantage of an internal standard which is chemically related to the test substance is that it may show up problems due to changes in detector response, incomplete derivatisation, etc. A disadvantage is that it may be difficult to fit an internal standard peak into a complex chromatogram.

Using an internal standard – you should add the internal standard to the sample at the first stage in the extraction procedure, so that any loss or degradation of test substance during purification is accompanied by an equivalent change in the internal standard, as long as the extraction characteristics of the internal standard and the test substance are very similar.

Sources for further study

Braithwaite, A. and Smith, F.J. (1990) *Chromatographic Methods*, 4th edn. Chapman and Hall, London.

Gooding, K.M. and Regnier, F.E. (2002) *HPLC of Biological Macromolecules Revised and Expanded*. Marcel Dekker, New York.

Grob, R.L. (1995) *Modern Practice of Gas Chromatography*, 3rd edn. Wiley, New York.

Huber, L. and George, S.A. (1993) *Diode Array Detection in HPLC*. Marcel Dekker, New York.

McKay, P. *An Introduction to Chromatography*. Available: http://www.accessexcellence.org/TSN/SS/chromatography_background.html Last accessed 08/01/03.

Scott, R.P.W. (1996) *Chromatography Detectors: Design, Function and Operation*. Marcel Dekker, New York.

Chromatography – detection and analysis

Study exercises

45.1 Test your knowledge of detector terminology. Explain what the following acronyms stand for:
(a) FID;
(b) TCD;
(c) ECD;
(d) DAD.

45.2 Check your knowledge of liquid chromatography detectors. Make a list of the various major types of liquid chromatography detectors in order, from highest to lowest sensitivity. Which of these methods is most versatile and why?

45.3 Consider how fluorescence detection can be applied to non-fluorescent molecules. Fluoresence detection of natural molecules is limited to molecules such as porphyrins, nucleotides and some vitamins, e.g. riboflavin. What procedures can convert a non-fluorescent molecule into a form suitable for sensitive fluorescence detection? How does this increase the selectivity of the analysis?

45.4 Calculate the amount of substance in a chromatographic separation using an internal standard. The chromatogram shown in the figure represents the separation of three carbohydrates by gas chromatography. Peak A corresponds to mannitol, peak B to sucrose and peak C to the internal standard, trehalose, at 1.50 mg. The results shown in the table were obtained for the retention times and areas of the three peaks.

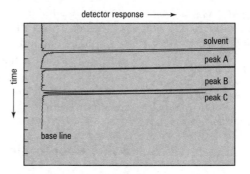

Gas-liquid chromatographic separation of three carbohydrates (A, B and C). Note that the plotter shows peaks A and B to be off-scale: however, the instrument still gives a valid area measurement for these two peaks (see table).

Retention times and peak areas for carbohydrates A, B and C

Peak	Retention time (min)	Area (relative)
A	3.92	2060
B	5.82	1898
C	6.03	604

Given a response factor (*r*) of 1.26 for mannitol and 0.92 for sucrose (relative to the internal standard), determine the amount of A and B in the sample (express your answer to 3 significant figures).

46 Principles and practice of electrophoresis

KEY POINT Electrophoresis is a separation technique based on the movement of charged molecules in an electric field. Dissimilar molecules move at different rates and the components of a mixture will be separated when an electric field is applied. It is a widely used technique, particularly for the analysis of complex mixtures or for the verification of purity (homogeneity) of isolated biomolecules.

While electrophoresis is mostly used for the separation of charged macromolecules, techniques are available for high resolution separations of small molecules such as amino acids (for example, by capillary electrophoresis, p. 325). This chapter deals mainly with the electrophoretic separation of proteins, which has many applications including clinical diagnosis. However, the principles apply equally to other molecules (separation of nucleic acids is considered in Chapter 60).

The electrophoretic mobility of a charged molecule depends on:

- Net charge – negatively charged molecules (anions) migrate towards the anode (+), while positively charged molecules (cations) migrate towards the cathode (−); highly charged molecules move faster towards the electrode of opposite charge than those with lesser charge.
- Size – frictional resistance exerted on molecules moving in a solution means that smaller molecules migrate faster than large molecules.
- Shape – the effect of friction also means that the shape of the molecule will affect mobility, e.g. globular proteins compared with fibrous proteins, linear DNA compared with circular DNA.
- Electrical field strength – mobility increases with increasing field strength (voltage), but there are practical limitations to using high voltages, especially due to heating effects.

The combined influence of net charge and size means that mobility (μ) is determined by the charge : density or the charge : mass ratio, according to the formula:

$$\mu = \frac{q\,E}{r} \qquad [46.1]$$

where q is the net charge on the molecule, r is the molecular radius and E is the field strength.

Electrophoresis and the separation of proteins

The net charge of a sample molecule determines its direction of movement and significantly affects its mobility. The net charge of a protein molecule is pH dependent, and is determined by the relative numbers of positively and negatively charged amino acid side chains at a given pH (Table 46.1). The degree of ionisation of each amino acid side chain is pH dependent, resulting in a variation of net charge on the protein at different pH values (Fig. 46.1). Since an individual protein will have a unique content of ionisable amino acids, each protein will have a characteristic 'titration curve' when net charge is plotted against pH. Thus, electrophoresis is always carried out at *constant* pH and a suitable buffer must be present along with the sample in order to maintain that pH (Chapter 25). If the

---

Definition

Electrophoretic mobility – the rate of migration of a particular type of molecule in response to an applied electrical field.

Understanding electrophoresis – this is, in essence, an incomplete form of electrolysis (p. 334), since the applied electrical field is switched off well before sample molecules reach the electrodes.

Table 46.1 pK_a values of ionisable groups in selected amino acid residues of proteins

Group/residue	pK_a^1
Terminal carboxyl	3.1
Aspartic acid	4.4
Glutamic acid	4.4
Histidine	6.5
Terminal amino	8.0
Cysteine	8.5
Tyrosine	10.0
Lysine	10.0
Arginine	12.0

[1]Note that these are typical values: the pK_a will change with temperature and ionic strength. Acidic residues will tend to be negatively charged at pH values above their pK_a, while basic residues will tend to be positively charged below their pK_a.

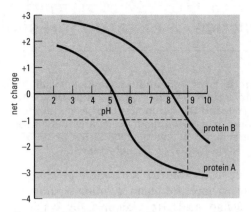

Fig. 46.1 Titration curves for two proteins, A and B containing different proportions of acidic and basic amino acid residues.

Fig. 46.2 Apparatus for vertical slab electrophoresis (components move downwards from wells, through the gel matrix).

Minimising diffusion – *make the sample zone as narrow as possible, and fix and stain the protein bands as soon as possible after the run.*

Definition

Ohm's law $V = IR$, where V = voltage, I = current and R = resistance.

Optimising electrophoresis – *attempting to minimise heat production using very low currents is not practical, since it leads to long separation times and therefore to increased diffusion.*

proteins shown in Fig. 46.1 were subjected to electrophoresis at pH 9.0, and if the proteins were of similar size and shape, then the rate at which protein A (net charge, -3) migrates towards the anode would be faster than that for protein B (net charge, -1). Separation of proteins is usually carried out at alkaline pH, where most proteins carry a net negative charge.

Basic apparatus

Most types of electrophoresis using supporting media (described below) are simple to carry out and the apparatus can be easily constructed, although inexpensive equipment is commercially available. High resolution techniques such as 2D-electrophoresis and capillary electrophoresis require more sophisticated equipment, both for separation and analysis (p. 325).

Simple electrophoretic separations can be performed either vertically (Fig. 46.2) or horizontally (Fig. 60.2). The electrodes are normally made of platinum wire, each in its own buffer compartment. In vertical electrophoresis, the buffer solution forms the electrical contact between the electrodes and the supporting medium in which the sample separation takes place. In horizontal electrophoresis electrical contact can be made by buffer-soaked paper 'wicks' dipping in the buffer reservoir and laid upon the supporting medium. The buffer reservoir normally contains a divider acting as a barrier to diffusion (but not to electrical current), so that localised pH changes which occur in the region of the electrodes (as a result of electrolysis, p. 334) are not transmitted to the supporting medium or the sample. Individual samples are spotted onto a solid supporting medium containing buffer or are applied to 'wells' formed in the supporting medium. The power pack used for most types of electrophoresis should be capable of delivering $\approx500\,V$ and $\approx100\,mA$.

Using a supporting medium

The effects of convection currents (resulting from the heating effect of the applied field) and the diffusion of molecules within the buffer solution can be minimised by carrying out the electrophoresis in a porous supporting medium. This contains buffer electrolytes and the sample is added in a discrete location or zone. When the electrical field is applied, individual sample molecules remain in sharp zones as they migrate at different rates. After separation, post-electrophoretic diffusion of selected biomolecules (e.g. proteins) can be avoided by 'fixing' them in position on the supporting medium, e.g. using trichloracetic acid (TCA).

The heat generated during electrophoresis is proportional to the square of the applied current and to the electrical resistance of the medium: even when a supporting medium is used, heat production will lead to zone broadening by increasing the rate of diffusion of sample components and buffer ions. Heat denaturation of sample proteins may also occur, resulting in loss of biological activity e.g. with enzymes (p. 382). Another problem is that heat will reduce buffer viscosity, leading to a decrease in resistance. If the electrophoresis is run at constant voltage, Ohm's law dictates that as resistance falls, the current will increase, leading to further heat production. This can be avoided by using a power pack that provides constant power. In practice, most electrophoresis equipment incorporates a cooling device;

even so, distortions of an electrophoretic zone from the ideal 'sharp, linear band' can often be explained by inefficient heat dissipation.

Types of supporting media

These can be subdivided into:

- Inert media – these provide physical support and minimise convection: separation is based on charge density only (e.g. cellulose acetate).
- Porous media – these introduce molecular sieving as an additional effect: their pore size is of the same order as the size of molecules being separated, restricting the movement of larger molecules relative to smaller ones. Thus, separation depends on both the charge density and the size of the molecule.

With some supporting media, e.g. cellulose acetate, a phenomenon called electro-endosmosis or electro-osmotic flow (EOF) occurs. This is due to the presence of negatively charged groups on the surface of the supporting medium, attracting cations in the electrophoresis buffer solution and creating an electrical double layer. The cations are hydrated (surrounded by water molecules) and when the electric field is applied, they are attracted towards the cathode, creating a flow of solvent that opposes the direction of migration of anionic biomolecules towards the anode. The EOF can be so great that weakly anionic biomolecules (e.g. antibodies) may be carried towards the cathode.

Where necessary, EOF can be avoided by using supporting media such as agarose or polyacrylamide (p. 316), but it is not always a hindrance to electrophoretic separation. Indeed, the phenomenon of EOF is used in the high resolution technique of capillary electrophoresis (p. 325).

Cellulose acetate

Acetylation of the hydroxyl groups of cellulose produces a less hydrophilic structure than cellulose in the form of paper: as a result it holds less water and diffusion is reduced, with a corresponding increase in resolution. Cellulose acetate is often used in the electrophoretic separation of plasma proteins in clinical diagnosis – it can be carried out quickly ($\approx$45 min) and its resolution is adequate to detect gross differences in various types of protein (e.g. paraproteins in myeloma). Cellulose acetate has a fairly uniform pore structure and the pores are large enough to allow unrestricted passage of all but the largest of molecules as they migrate through the medium.

Agarose

Agarose is the neutral, linear polysaccharide component of agar (from seaweed), consisting of repeating galactose and 3,6-anhydrogalactose subunits (Fig. 46.3). Powdered agarose is mixed with electrophoresis buffer at concentrations of 0.5–3.0% w/v, boiled until the mixture becomes clear, poured onto a glass plate, then allowed to cool until it forms a gel. Gelation is due to the formation of hydrogen bonds both between and within the agarose polymers, resulting in the formation of pores. The pore size depends on the agarose concentration. Low concentrations produce gels with large pores relative to the size of proteins, allowing them to migrate relatively unhindered through the gel,

Fig. 46.3 Structure of agarose. Additional sulphate and pyruvyl groups are attached at selected hydroxyls in the polymer.

as determined by their individual charge densities. Low concentrations of agarose gel are suitable for techniques such as immunoelectrophoresis (p. 252) and isoelectric focusing (p. 324), where charge is the main basis of separation. The smaller pores produced by higher concentrations of agarose may result in molecular sieving.

When agarose gels are used for the separation of DNA, the large fragment size means that molecular sieving is observed, even with low concentration gels. This is the basis of the electrophoretic separation of nucleic acids (see Chapter 60).

Polyacrylamide

Polyacrylamide gel electrophoresis (PAGE) has a major role in protein analysis, both for one-dimensional and two-dimensional separations. The gel is formed by polymerising acrylamide monomer into long chains and cross-linking these chains using N, N'-methylene bisacrylamide (often abbreviated to 'bis'). The process is shown in Fig. 46.4. In most protocols, polymerisation is initiated by free radicals produced by ammonium persulphate in the presence of N, N, N', N'-tetramethylethylenediamine (TEMED). The photodecomposition of riboflavin can also be used as a source of free radicals.

The formation of polyacrylamide from its acrylamide monomers is extremely reproducible under standard conditions, and electrophoretic separations are correspondingly precise. The pore size, and hence the extent of molecular sieving, depends on the total concentration of monomer (% T), i.e. acrylamide plus bisacrylamide in a fixed ratio. This means that pores in the gel can be 'tailored' to suit the size of biomolecule to be separated: gels containing 3% acrylamide have large pores and are used in methods where molecular sieving should be avoided (e.g. in isoelectric focusing, p. 324), while higher concentrations of acrylamide (5–30% T) introduce molecular sieving to various degrees depending on the size of the sample components, i.e. with 30% acrylamide gels, molecules as small as M_r 2000 may be subject to molecular sieving. Gels of <2.5% are necessary for molecular sieving of molecules of $M_r > 10^6$, but such gels are almost fluid and require 0.5% agarose to make them solid. Note that a gel of 3% will separate DNA by molecular sieving, due to the large size of the nucleic acid molecules (p. 429).

Before you embark on a particular PAGE protein separation, you will need to think about the general strategy for that separation and make certain choices, including whether to use:

- Rod or slab gels – flat slab gels are formed between glass plates, using plastic spacers 0.75–1.5 mm thick: rod gels are made in narrow bore tubes. For most separations using several samples, a slab gel saves time because up to 25 samples can be separated under identical conditions in a single gel, while rod gels can only be used for individual samples. Rectangular slab gels are also easier to read, by densitometry, and photograph. However, rod gels are useful in preliminary separations, for determining a suitable pH and gel concentration, and for applications where the gel is sliced in order to extract and assay proteins of interest. (In 2D-electrophoresis, a rod may be used for one dimension, and a slab for the second, p. 325.)
- Dissociating or non-dissociating conditions – the most widely used PAGE protein separation technique uses an ionic detergent, usually

Advantages of polyacrylamide gels – in addition to their versatility in terms of pore size, these gels are chemically inert, stable over a wide range of pH, ionic strength and temperature, and transparent.

Safe working and PAGE – both acrylamide and bisacrylamide are extremely potent neurotoxins, so you must wear plastic gloves when handling solutions containing these reagents. Although the polymerised gel is non-toxic, it is still advisable to wear gloves when handling the gel, because some monomer may still be present.

Preparing polyacrylamide gels – most solutions used for gel preparation can be made in advance, but the ammonium persulphate solution must be prepared immediately before use.

Fig. 46.4 Reactions involved in the formation of polyacrylamide gels.

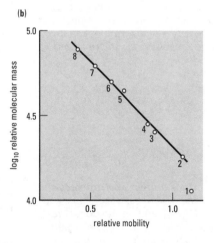

Fig. 46.5 Determination of relative molecular mass (M_r) of proteins by SDS-PAGE: (a) gel samples: 1, cytochrome c; 2, myoglobin; 3, γ-globulin; 4, carbonic anhydrase; 5, ovalbumin; 6, albumin; 7, transferrin; 8, mixture of samples 1–7 (photo courtesy of Pharmacia Biotech). (b) plot of log M_r against distance travelled through gel.

Table 46.2 Molecular masses of standard proteins used in electrophoresis

Protein	M_r	$\log_{10} M_r$
Cytochrome c	11 700	4.068
Myoglobin	17 200	4.236
γ-globulin (light chain)	23 500	4.371
Carbonic anhydrase	29 000	4.462
Ovalbumin	43 000	4.634
γ-globulin (heavy chain)	50 000	4.699
Human albumin	68 000	4.832
Transferrin	77 000	4.886
Myosin (heavy chain)	212 000	5.326

Following the progress of PAGE – add bromophenol blue solution (0.002% w/v) to the sample in the ratio 1:25 (dye : sample). This highly ionic, small M_r dye migrates with the electrophoretic front.

Choosing a buffer system – discontinuous systems are more time-consuming to prepare, but have the advantage over continuous systems in that relatively large volumes of dilute sample can be used and good resolution is still obtained.

Choosing a pH for protein electrophoresis – many proteins have isoelectric points in the range pH 4–7 and in response to electrophoresis with buffers in the region pH 8.0–9.5, most proteins will migrate towards the anode.

Separating protein mixtures – for high resolution, a combination of dissociating and discontinuous PAGE in slab gels is the system of choice.

sodium dodecyl sulphate (SDS), which dissociates proteins into their individual polypeptide subunits and gives a uniform net charge along each denatured polypeptide. This technique, known as SDS-PAGE, requires only μg amounts of sample and is quick and easy to carry out. On the other hand, if it is necessary to preserve the native protein conformation and biological activity, non-dissociating conditions are used, i.e. no SDS is added. In SDS-PAGE the sample protein is normally heated to 100 °C for 2 min, in buffer containing 1% (w/v) SDS and 1% (w/v) 2-mercaptoethanol, the latter to cleave any disulphide bonds. The resultant polypeptides bind to SDS in a constant weight ratio, with 1.4 g of SDS per g of protein. As a result, the intrinsic net charge of each polypeptide is 'swamped' by the negative charge imposed by SDS, and there is a uniform negative charge per unit length of polypeptide. Since the polypeptides now have identical charge densities, when they are subject to PAGE (with SDS present) using a gel of appropriate pore size, molecular sieving will occur and they will migrate strictly according to polypeptide size. This not only gives effective separation, but the molecular mass of a given polypeptide can be determined by comparing its mobility to polypeptides of known molecular mass run under the same conditions (Fig. 46.5). Several manufacturers (e.g. Pharmacia®, Sigma®) supply molecular mass standard kits which may include polypeptides of M_r 11 700 to 212 000 (Table 46.2), together with details of their preparation and use. Where necessary, the treated sample can be concentrated by ultrafiltration and the buffer composition can be altered by diafiltration (p. 376).

- Continuous or discontinuous buffer systems – a continuous system is where the same buffer ions are present in the sample, gel and buffer reservoirs, all at the same pH. The sample is loaded directly onto a gel (the 'separating gel' or 'resolving gel') that has pores small enough to introduce molecular sieving. In contrast, discontinuous systems have different buffers in the gel compared to the reservoirs, both in terms of buffer ions and pH. The sample is loaded onto a large-pore 'stacking gel', previously polymerised on top of a small-pore separating gel (Fig. 46.6). The individual proteins in the sample concentrate into very narrow zones during their migration through the large-pore gel and stack up according to their charge densities, prior to separation in the small-pore gel, giving enhanced results compared with continuous systems.

- pH and buffer for the separation – PAGE can be carried out between pH 3 and 10. The pH is not critical for continuous SDS-PAGE, since SDS-treated polypeptides are negatively charged over a wide pH range. However, when using non-dissociating systems, the pH can be critical, particularly if the biological activity of the molecules is to be retained.

- Gel concentration – at one extreme, a gel with a very high percentage T might totally exclude the sample components, while a gel with a very low percentage T might lead to all SDS-treated proteins migrating at the same rate, i.e. with the electrophoretic front. A sensible approach is to set up a series of rod gels in the range 5–15% T and observe the separation and resolution obtained. Alternatively, a gradient gel can be used, in which the percentage T increases, and hence pore size decreases, in the direction of protein migration. A

Table 46.3 Preparation of gels for PAGE and SDS-PAGE. The gel solutions are made by mixing the components in the proportions and in the order shown. Figures are ml of each solution required to give the stated 90 gel strength

Solution (added in order shown)	PAGE		SDS-PAGE	
	3.5% gel (T = 3.6%)	7.5% gel (T = 7.7%)	5% gel (T = 5.1%)	10% gel (T = 10.2%)
1. Distilled water	19.3	7.5	14.9	—
2. TRIS-glycine buffer, pH 8.9, 0.1 mol^{-1}	33.0	33.0	—	—
3. Imidazole buffer, pH 7.0, 0.1 mol l^{-1} plus 0.2% w/v SDS	—	—	33.0	33.0
4. Acrylamide solution 22.2% w/v and 0.6% w/v bis	10.4	22.2	14.8	29.7
5. Ammonium persulphate solution, 0.15% w/v	3.2	3.2	3.2	3.2
6. TEMED	0.1	0.1	0.1	0.1
Final volume (ml)	66.0	66.0	66.0	66.0

If your polyacrylamide gels fail to set – polymerisation is inhibited by oxygen, so solutions should be degassed, and the surfaces of the polymerisation mixture exposed to air should be overlayed with water; if your gels still do not polymerise, the most common cause is the use of 'old' ammonium persulphate stock solution. If low pH buffers are used, polymerisation may be delayed because TEMED is required in the free base form.

useful gradient for a preliminary experiment would be 5–20% T. Such gels are able to resolve protein mixtures with a wide range of molecular masses. Furthermore, as proteins migrate into regions of ever-decreasing pore size, the movement of the leading edge of a zone will become increasingly restricted. This allows the trailing edge to catch up, resulting in considerable zone sharpening. Gradient formers are fairly simple to make, and are commercially available.

Practical details of the preparation of PAGE and SDS-PAGE gels are given in Table 46.3 (see Westermeier and Barnes, 2001, or Gersten, 1996 for further details).

Fig. 46.6 Apparatus for discontinuous electrophoresis.

Post-electrophoretic procedures – handling of the supporting medium, staining and analysis

For protein electrophoresis, the following stages are appropriate: details for nucleic acids are given on pp. 429–30.

Handling

All types of supporting medium should be handled carefully: wearing gloves is advisable, for safety and to avoid transfer of proteins from the skin. Cellulose acetate strips should be immediately transferred to a fixing and staining solution. Agarose gels should be dried quickly before staining. Polyacrylamide gels in vertical slabs must be freed carefully from one of the glass plates in which they are formed, taking care to lever the glass at a point well away from the part of the gel containing the wells: once free, the gels should be immediately transferred to fixing or staining solution.

Rod gels are recovered by a process called 'rimming', a technique that takes a little practice to master. To remove the gel from the tube, hold the tube in one hand and, using a syringe with a long blunt needle, squirt water between the gel and the inner wall of the tube: while squirting, move the needle gently up and down and rotate the tube. If the gel does not become free, perform the same procedure at the other end of the tube, until the gel is released. If necessary, a Pasteur pipette bulb applied to one end can be used to push the gel out of the tube.

Fixing, staining and destaining

To prevent the separated proteins from diffusing, they are usually fixed in position. Proteins on cellulose acetate strips can be fixed and stained using Ponceau S (0.2% w/v in 3% v/v aqueous trichloracetic acid, TCA).

Fixing is also required for most types of gel electrophoresis: 3% v/v TCA is often used. The most widely used stain for protein separations in gels is Coomassie Blue R-250 (where R = reddish hue): the detection limit is $\approx 0.2\,\mu g$ and staining is quantitative up to $20\,\mu g$ for some proteins. It is normal for background staining of the gel to occur, and removal of background colour ('destaining') can be achieved either by diffusion or electrophoresis. To destain by diffusion, transfer the gel to isopropanol : acetic acid : water (12.5 : 10 : 77.5 v/v/v) and allow to stand for 48 h, or change the solution several times to speed up the staining process. Electrophoretic destaining can remove Coomassie Blue, which is anionic: stained gels are placed between porous plastic sheets with electrodes on each side, and the tank is filled with 7% acetic acid. Passing a current of up to 1.0 A destains the gel in $\approx 30\,\text{min}$.

If you need greater sensitivity (e.g. for ng to fg amounts), or when using high resolution techniques such as 2D-electrophoresis (p. 325), silver staining can be used. Depending on the protocol chosen and the proteins being stained, the silver technique can be 5 to 200-fold more sensitive than Coomassie Blue. The method involves a fixation step (e.g. with TCA), followed by exposure to silver nitrate solution and development of the stain. The silver ions are thought to react with basic and thiol groups in proteins, and subsequent reduction (e.g. by formaldehyde at alkaline pH, or by photodevelopment) leads to deposits of silver in the protein bands. Most proteins stain brown or black, but lipoproteins may stain blue, and some glycoproteins stain yellow or red. Some proteins lacking in amino acids with reducing groups (e.g. those lacking cysteine residues) may stain negatively, i.e. the bands are more transparent than the background staining of the gel. Although many protocols have been published, silver stain kits are commercially available, e.g. from Bio-Rad.

Although silver staining has clear advantages in terms of sensitivity, for routine work it is more laborious and expensive to carry out than the Coomassie Blue method. It also requires high purity water, otherwise significant background staining occurs. Another feature is that the staining can be non-specific, since DNA and polysaccharides may stain on the same gel as proteins.

Other methods for the detection of separated components include:

- autoradiography for proteins labelled with ^{32}P or ^{125}I (p. 262);
- fluorescence for proteins pre-labelled with fluorescent dyes (p. 349);
- periodic acid-Schiff (PAS) stain using dansyl hydrazine for glycoproteins.

Blotting

The term 'blotting' refers to the transfer of separated proteins from the gel matrix to a thin sheet such as nitrocellulose membrane

---

Handling gels – *avoid touching gels with paper as it sticks readily and is difficult to remove without tearing.*

Avoiding overloaded gels and band distortion – *determine the protein concentration of the sample beforehand. Around 100 µg of a complex mixture, or 1–10 µg of an individual component, will be sufficient, but bear in mind that underloading may result in bands being too faint to be detected.*

Optimising resolution – *keep the sample volume as small as possible; methods for concentrating protein solutions are considered on pp. 373–6. For vertical slab gels and for rod gels, include 10% w/v sucrose or glycerol to increase density and allow buffer solution to be overlaid on the sample without dilution.*

Origins of 'Western' blotting – *following the description of 'Southern' blotting of DNA by Dr. Ed Southern (p. 431), other points of the compass have been used to describe other forms of blotting, with 'Western' blotting for proteins.*

Example For detection of lactate dehydrogenase (LDH): when a solution containing lactate, NAD$^+$, phenazine methasulphate (PMS) and methyl thiazolyl tetrazolium (MTT) is added to a gel containing LDH, a series of redox reactions occurs in the enzyme-containing regions, starting with the oxidation of lactate to pyruvate, and proceeding via NAD$^+$, PMS and MTT to the eventual reduction of MTT to formazan dye. After incubation at 37 °C in the dark (since MTT is light-sensitive), LDH is detected by the appearance of blue–black bands on the gel.

Detecting enzymes in gels – *minimise zone spreading by incorporating substrates, etc. in a thin agarose indicator gel poured over the separating gel.*

Measuring peak areas – *a valid 'low-tech' alternative to computer-based systems is to cut out and weigh peaks from a recorder chart.*

(commercially available from e.g. Millipore, Amersham). The proteins bind to this membrane, and are immobilised. Blotting of proteins is usually achieved by electrophoretic transfer, and this process is normally referred to as Western blotting (see also Southern blotting and Northern blotting for DNA and RNA respectively, pp. 431–2). Its major advantage is that the immobilised proteins on the surface of the membrane are readily accessible to detection reagents, and staining and destaining can be achieved in less than 5 min. Use of labelled antibodies to detect specific proteins (immunoblotting) can take less than 6 h. In addition, it is easy to dry and store Western blots for long periods, for further analysis.

Detection of enzymes

If you need to detect enzyme activity you should use a non-denaturing gel. The gel matrix will hinder diffusion of the enzyme, but will allow access to the small molecular weight substrates, co-factors and dyes necessary to localise enzyme activity *in situ*. Most methods for detecting enzymes on gels are modifications of protocols originally developed by histochemists, e.g.:

- NAD$^+$-requiring oxidoreductases can be detected by incubating the gels with substrate, NAD$^+$ and a solution of a tetrazolium salt which, when reduced, forms an insoluble coloured formazan dye.
- Transferases and isomerases can be detected by coupling their reactions to an oxidoreductase-requiring reaction, visualised as described above.
- Hydrolases can be detected using appropriate chromogenic or fluorogenic substrates.
- Phosphatases can be detected by precipitating any phosphate released from the substrate with Ca^{2+}.

For more details, see Manchenko (1994).

Recording and quantification of results

A number of expensive, dedicated instruments are available for the analysis of gels, e.g. laser densitometers. Alternatively, gel scanning attachments can be purchased for standard spectrophotometers, allowing measurement and recording of the absorbance of the Coomassie Blue stained bands at 560–575 nm: for instruments connected to a computer, quantification of individual components can be achieved by integrating the areas under the peaks.

You can photograph gels using a conventional camera (fine grain film), digital camera, or using a photocopier. Alternatively, a dedicated image capture and analysis system may be used, e.g. GelDoc®. The gel should be placed on a white glass transilluminator. A red filter will increase contrast with bands stained with Coomassie Blue. If the gels themselves need to be retained, they can be preserved in 7% acetic acid. Alternatively, they can be dried using a commercially available gel dryer.

Text references

Gersten, D. (1996) *Gel Electrophoresis: Proteins* (Essential Techniques Series). Wiley, New York.

Manchenko, G.P. (1994) *Detection of Enzymes on Electrophoretic Gels: A Handbook*. CRC Press, Boca Raton.

Westermeier, R. and Barnes, N. (2001) *Electrophoresis in Practice: A Guide to Methods and Applications of DNA and Protein Separation*, 3rd edn. VCH, Berlin.

Sources for further study

Anon. *The Electrophoresis Society Homepage*. Available:
http://www.aesociety.org
Last accessed 08/01/03.
[Includes details on a variety of electrophoretic techniques.]

Anon. *British Electrophoresis Society Homepage*. Available:
http://www.proteinworks.com/bes
Last accessed 08/01/03.
[Includes links to databases and other relevant websites.]

Hames, B.D. and Rickwood, D. (1998) *Gel Electrophoresis of Proteins: A Practical Approach*, 3rd edn. Oxford University Press, Oxford.

Martin, R.M. (1996) *Gel Electrophoresis: Nucleic Acids* (Introduction to Biotechniques Series). Bios, Oxford.

Tietz, D. (1998) *Nucleic Acid Electrophoresis*. Springer-Verlag, Berlin.

Study exercises

46.1 Find out why the net charge on a protein molecule varies with pH. Identify the amino acids primarily responsible for determining the net charge on a protein molecule and draw simple diagrams to represent the ionisation of their side chains, indicating how you would expect these side chains to be charged at acid, neutral and alkaline pH values.

46.2 Explain the function of the various reagents used in SDS-PAGE analysis of proteins. What is the function of each of the following SDS-PAGE reagents? (a) acrylamide; (b) N,N'-methylene bisacrylamide; (c) ammonium persulphate; (d) N,N,N',N'-tetramethylethylenediamine; (e) sodium dodecyl sulphate; (f) 2-mercaptoethanol; (g) buffer; (h) Coomassie Blue R-250; (i) bromophenol blue.

46.3 Test your knowledge of 'blotting' terminology. What is Western blotting, and how does it differ from Northern and Southern blotting?

46.4 Determine the M_r of subunits of a protein by SDS-PAGE. A number of proteins of known molecular weight were analysed by SDS-PAGE and the results are shown in the table. In the same experiment, a sample of purified lactate dehydrogenase (LDH), was treated in identical fashion and run, producing a band with a relative mobility of 0.77. (a) What is the M_r of the polypeptide produced from the LDH sample?

Relative mobilities of molecular weight standards by SDS-PAGE

Protein	M_r	Relative mobility
Myoglobin	17 200	1.00
Carbonic anhydrase	29 000	0.84
Ovalbumin	43 000	0.67
Human albumin	68 000	0.51
Transferrin	77 000	0.46

(b) If the M_r of native LDH is 136 000, what do you conclude about the subunit structure of this enzyme?

46.5 Find out about 'troubleshooting' problems with gels. Investigate the pitfalls of working with and polymerising gels.

Advanced electrophoretic techniques

Although the resolution obtained using the basic electrophoretic techniques described in Chapter 46 is adequate for many biomolecular applications, a number of advanced techniques are available that give very high resolution and which can be used with very small amounts of sample material.

Isoelectric focusing (IEF)

In contrast to electrophoresis, which is carried out at constant pH, IEF is carried out using a pH gradient. The gradient is formed using small molecular mass ampholytes, which are analogues and homologues of polyamino-, polycarboxylic acids that collectively have a range of isoelectric points (pI values) between pH 3 and 10. The mixture of ampholytes (p. 146), either in a gel or in free solution, is placed between the anode in acid solution (e.g. H_3PO_4), and the cathode in alkaline solution (e.g. NaOH). When an electric field is applied, each ampholyte migrates to its own pI and forms a stable pH gradient which will persist for as long as the field is applied. When a protein sample is applied to this gradient separation is achieved, since individual proteins will migrate to their isoelectric points. The net charge on the protein when first applied will depend on the specific 'titration curve' for that protein (Fig. 47.1). As an example, consider two proteins, X and Y, having pI values of pH 5 and pH 8 respectively, which are placed together on the gradient at pH 6 (Fig. 47.2). At that pH, protein X will have a net negative charge, and will migrate towards the anode, progressively losing charge until it reaches its pI (pH 5) and stops migrating. Protein Y will have a net positive charge at pH 6, and so will migrate towards the cathode until it reaches its pI (pH 8).

Using a polyacrylamide gel as a supporting medium and a narrow pH gradient, proteins differing in pI by 0.01 units can be separated. Even greater resolution is possible in free solution (e.g. in capillary electrophoresis, p. 325). Such resolution is possible because protein molecules that diffuse away from the pI will acquire a net charge (negative at increased pH, positive at decreased pH) and immediately be focused back to their pI. This focusing effect will continue for as long as the electric field is applied.

A useful variant of IEF is in obtaining *titration curves* for proteins. A pH gradient is set up, and the sample applied in a line at a right angle to the gradient. The net charge on a given protein will vary according to its position on the gradient – when electrophoresis is carried out at right angles to the pH gradient, the protein will migrate at a velocity and direction governed by that charge. When stained, each protein will appear as a continuous curved line, corresponding to its titration curve (Fig. 47.3). This technique can be usefully performed during protein purification, prior to ion-exchange chromatography (p. 299): by obtaining the titration curve for a protein of interest and those of major contaminants, the mobile phase pH that gives optimal separation can be selected.

In IEF, it is important that electro-osmotic flow (EOF) is avoided, as this would affect the ability of the proteins to remain stationary at their pIs. For gel IEF, polyacrylamide minimises EOF, while capillary IEF uses narrow bore tubing with an internal polymer coating (p. 328).

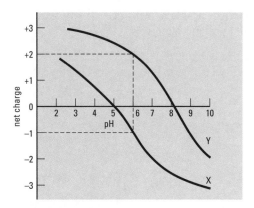

Fig. 47.1 Titration curves for two proteins, X and Y.

Fig. 47.2 The migration of two proteins, X and Y, in response to a pH gradient.

Fig. 47.3 Titration curves of bovine muscle proteins produced by electrofocusing-electrophoresis (photo courtesy of Pharmacia Biotech).

Two-dimensional electrophoresis

The most commonly used version of this high resolution technique involves separating proteins by charge in one dimension using IEF in polyacrylamide gel, followed by separation by molecular mass in the second dimension using denaturing SDS-PAGE (p. 318). The technique allows up to 1000 proteins to be separated from a single sample. Typically, the first dimension IEF run (pH 3–10) is carried out in rod gels, varying in diameter from 1 to 5 mm: with narrow rods a thin thread is sometimes polymerised within the gel to aid handling during transfer to the second-dimension gel. At 1 kV with 2 mA current, the pH gradient takes ≈30 min to reach equilibrium, and separation of the applied sample takes a further 60 min. After the IEF stage, the rods must be removed from the glass tubes in which they were formed. This can be done by 'rimming' (p. 319), or by freezing the gels at −20 °C and cracking the glass tubes in a vice. The gel must be allowed to warm up before it is run in the second dimension.

It is common for the second-dimension SDS-PAGE separation to be carried out on a discontinuous slab gel 0.5–1.5 mm thick, which includes a low percentage T stacking gel and a separating gel with an exponential gradient of 10–16% T. The separating gel can be prepared in advance, but the stacking gel must be formed shortly before addition of the rod gel from the 1D run.

After equilibration with the buffer used in SDS-PAGE, the 1D rod gel is loaded onto the 2D gel (still between the glass plates in which it was formed) and sealed in position using acrylamide or agarose. Before the sealing gel sets, a well should be formed in it at one end to allow addition of molecular mass markers. The second-dimension is run at 100–200 V until the dye front is ≈1 cm from the bottom edge of the slab. After running, the gel is processed for the detection of polypeptides, e.g. using Coomassie Blue or silver stain. Analysis of the complex patterns that result from 2D electrophoresis requires computer-aided gel scanners to acquire, store and process data from a gel, such as that shown in Fig. 47.4. These systems can compare, adjust and match up patterns from several gels, allowing both accurate identification of spots and quantification of individual proteins. Allowance is made for the slight variations in patterns found in different runs, using internal references ('landmarks'), which are either added standard proteins or particular spots known to be present in all samples.

Capillary electrophoresis

The technique of capillary electrophoresis (CE) combines the high resolving power of electrophoresis with the speed and versatility of HPLC (p. 297). The technique largely overcomes the major problem of carrying out electrophoresis without a supporting medium, i.e. poor resolution due to convection currents and diffusion. A capillary tube has a high surface area : volume ratio, and consequently the heat generated as a result of the applied electric current is rapidly dissipated. A further advantage is that very small samples (5–10 nl) can be analysed. The versatility of CE is demonstrated by its use in the separation of a range of biomolecules, e.g. amino acids, proteins, nucleic acids, drugs, vitamins, organic acids and inorganic ions; CE can even separate neutral species, e.g. steroids, aromatic hydrocarbons (see Weinberger, 2000).

low pH ← IEF → high pH

SDS – PAGE

Fig. 47.4 Two-dimensional separation of proteins from 100× concentrated urine (2.5 μg total protein; silver stain. Courtesy of T. Marshall and K.M. Williams).

high voltage supply

capillary coil

detector

⊖

⊕

outlet vial

inlet vial

data acquisition and analysis

Fig. 47.5 Components of a capillary electrophoresis system.

The components of a typical CE apparatus are shown in Fig. 47.5. The capillary is made of fused silica and externally coated with a polymer for mechanical strength. The internal diameter is usually 25–50 μm, a compromise between efficient heat dissipation and the need for a light path that is not too short for detection using UV/visible spectrophotometry. A gap in the polymer coating provides a window for detection purposes. Samples are injected into the capillary by a variety of means, e.g. electrophoretic loading or displacement. In the former, the inlet end of the capillary is immersed in the sample and a pulse of high voltage is applied. The displacement method involves forcing the sample into the capillary, either by applying pressure in the sample vial using an inert gas, or by introducing a vacuum at the outlet. The detectors used in CE are similar to those used in chromatography (p. 307), e.g. UV/visible spectrophotometric systems. Fluorescence detection is more sensitive, but this may require sample derivitisation. Electrochemical and conductivity detection is also used in some applications, e.g. conductivity detection of inorganic cations such as Na^+ and K^+.

Electro-osmotic flow (EOF), described on p. 315, is essential to the most commonly used types of CE. The existence of EOF in the capillary is the result of the net negative charge on the fused silica surface at pH values over 3.0. The resulting solvent flow towards the cathode is greater than the attraction of anions towards the anode, so they will flow towards the cathode (note that the detector is situated at the cathodic end of the capillary). The greater the net negative charge on an anion, the greater is its resistance to the EOF and the lower its mobility. Separated components migrate towards the cathode in the order: (1) cations, (2) neutral species, (3) anions.

Capillary zone electrophoresis (CZE)

This is the most widely used form of CE, and is based on electrophoresis in free solution and EOF, as discussed above. Separations are due to the charge : mass ratio of the sample components, and the technique can be used for almost any type of charged molecule, and is especially useful for peptide separation and confirmation of purity.

Micellar electrokinetic chromatography (MEKC)

This technique involves the principles of both electrophoresis and chromatography. Its main strength is that it can be used for the separation of neutral molecules as well as charged ones. This is achieved by including surfactants (e.g. SDS, Triton X-100) in the electrophoresis buffer at concentrations that promote the formation of spherical micelles, with a hydrophobic interior and a charged, hydrophilic surface. When an electric field is applied, these micelles will tend to migrate with or against the EOF depending on their surface charge. Anionic surfactants like SDS are attracted by the anode, but if the pH of the buffer is high enough to ensure that the EOF is faster than the migration velocity of the micelles, the net migration is in the direction of the EOF, i.e. towards the cathode. During this migration, sample components partition between the buffer and the micelles (acting as a pseudo-stationary phase); this may involve both hydrophobic and electrostatic interactions. For neutral species it is only the partitioning effect that is involved in separation; the more hydrophobic a sample molecule, the more it will interact with the micelle, and the longer will be its migration time, since the micelle resists the EOF. The versatility of MEKC enables it to be used for separations of biomolecules as diverse as amino acids and polycyclic hydrocarbons. MEKC is also known as micellar electrokinetic capillary chromatography (MECC).

Chiral capillary electrophoresis (CCE)

Resolution of a pair of chiral enantiomers (optical isomers) represents one of the biggest challenges for separation science, because each member of the pair will have identical physicochemical properties. CE offers an effective method of separating enantiomers by inducing a 'chiral selector' in the electrophoresis medium. The most commonly used chiral selectors are cyclodextrins such as the highly sulphated cyclodextrins (HSCDs) (Fig. 47.6). As the enantiomers migrate along the capillary, one will tend to interact more strongly than the other and its mobility will be reduced relative to the other. Figure 47.7 shows separation of the R and S forms of amphetamine using 5% HSCD in the electrophoresis buffer. The R-form has greater affinity for the HSCD used, so its retention time on the capillary is longer than that of the S-form.

Note that HSDCs can also be used in HPLC, but CCE is more effective, with shorter development times and lower reagent costs.

Capillary gel electrophoresis (CGE)

The underlying principle of this technique is directly comparable with that of conventional PAGE, i.e. the capillary contains a polymer that acts as a molecular sieve. As charged sample molecules migrate through the polymer network, larger molecules are hindered to a greater extent than smaller ones and will tend to move more slowly. CGE differs from CZE

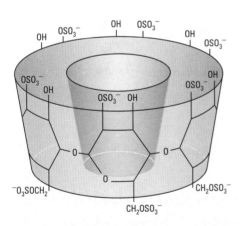

Fig. 47.6 General structure of highly sulphated cyclodextrins (HSCDs). The central cavity of the cyclodextrin (shaded blue) can interact differently with the R and S isomers of a biomolecule, enabling separation in CE. Copyright © 1999–2002 Beckman Coulter, Inc. http://www.beckmancoutler.com/products/splashpage/chiral38/default.asp/

Fig. 47.7 CE separation of R and S enantiomers of amphetamine using Beckman Coulter highly sulphated gamma cyclodextrin. Copyright © 1999–2002 Beckman Coulter, Inc. http://www.beckmancoulter.com/products/splashpage/chiral38/default.asp/

and MEKC in that the inner surface of the capillary is polymer-coated in order to prevent EOF; this means that for most applications (e.g. polypeptide or oligonucleotide separations) sample components will migrate towards the anode at a rate determined by their size. The technique also differs from conventional PAGE in that a 'polymer network' is used rather than a gel: the polymer network may be polyacrylamide or agarose.

CGE offers the following advantages over conventional electrophoresis:

- efficient heat dissipation means that a high electrical field can be applied, giving shorter separation times;
- detection of the separated components as they move towards the anodic end of the capillary (e.g. using a UV/visible detector) means that staining is unnecessary;
- automation is feasible.

Capillary isoelectric focusing (CIEF)

This is used mainly for protein separation. Here, the principles of IEF are valid as long as EOF is prevented by using capillaries that are polymer-coated on their inner surface. Sample components migrate to their isoelectric points and become stationary. Once separated (<10 min), the components must be mobilised so that they flow past the detector. This is achieved by changing the NaOH solution in the cathodic reservoir with an NaOH/NaCl solution. When the electric field is reapplied, Cl^- enters the capillary, causing a decrease in pH at the cathodic end and the subsequent migration of sample components.

Choosing a detector for capillary electrophoresis – most types of HPLC detector are suitable for CE and related applications (see Chapter 45).

Text reference

Weinberger, R. (2000) *Practical Capillary Electrophoresis*. Academic Press, New York.

Sources for further study

Anon. *The Electrophoresis Society Homepage*. Available:
http://www.aesociety.org
Last accessed 08/01/03.
[Includes details on electrophoretic techniques including IEF and CE.]

Anon. *Cyclodextrin Resource*. Available: http://www.cyclodex.com
Last accessed 08/01/03.
[Information on cyclodextrin structure, applications, etc.]

Cunico, R.L., Gooding, K.M. and Wehr, T. (1998) *Basic HPLC and CE of Biomolecules*. Bay Bioanalytical, Hercules.

Khaledi, M.G. (1998) *High Performance Capillary Electrophoresis: Theory, Techniques and Applications*. Wiley, New York.
[Detailed manual of CE techniques and procedures.]

Link, A.J. (1998) *2-D Proteome Analysis Protocols*. Humana Press, Totowa.

Palfrey, S.M. (1999) *Clinical Applications of Capillary Electrophoresis*. Humana Press, New Jersey.

Westermeier, R. (2001) *Electrophoresis in Practice*, 3rd edn. VCH, Berlin.
[Covers the principles underlying IEF.]

Weston, A. and Brown, P.R. (1997) *HPLC and CE: Principles and Practice*. Academic Press, New York.
[Covers practical aspects including applications, optimisation and troubleshooting.]

Study exercises

47.1 Consider the requirements for sample application in PAGE and IEF. Explain why in PAGE the sample is applied in a discrete narrow band, usually at the cathodic end of the gel, while in IEF the sample can be applied at any point along the length of the gel without concern about location or narrowness of the sample zone.

47.2 Choose a suitable CE technique for a range of applications. Which variant of CE would you consider most suitable for the following applications? (a) Separation of small peptides of similar size; (b) separation of oligonucleotides of different lengths; (c) separation of proteins with different isoelectric points; and (d) a sample of urine tested for several anabolic steroids.

47.3 Check the similarities and differences between electrophoresis and isoelectric focusing. Complete the following table, indicating (i) whether each of the factors listed is relevant to each technique and (ii) briefly explain why, in each case.

Potential factors influencing electrophoresis and isoelectric focusing

Factor	Electrophoresis	Isoelectric focusing
Dependence upon ionisable groups in proteins		
Requirement for the application of an electric field		
Dependence upon differences in net charge between sample molecules		
Dependence upon differences in pI values between sample molecules		
Requirement for buffer at constant pH		
Requirement for a pH gradient		
Requirement for ampholytes to be included in solution		
Use of a supporting medium with molecular sieving properties		
Treatment of samples with SDS is possible		
Diffusion of separated proteins is significant		

47.4 Identify proteins by 2D electrophoresis. The figure represents the separation of a mixture of 10 proteins by 2D electrophoresis. Using the information in the table, identify the individual proteins A–J.

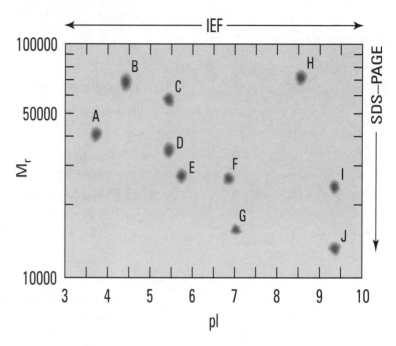

M_r and pI values of selected protein subunits

Protein	Subunit M_r	Subunit pI
Nerve growth factor	13 300	9.3
Ribonuclease	13 700	7.8
Haemoglobin	16 000	7.0
β-lactoglobulin	17 500	5.2
Ceramide trihexosidase	22 000	3.0
Trypsinogen	24 500	9.3
Triose phosphate isomerase	27 000	5.7
Galactokinase	27 000	5.7
Arginase	30 000	9.2
Glycerol-3-phosphate dehydrogenase	34 000	6.4
Alcohol dehydrogenase	35 000	5.4
Deoxyribonuclease II	38 000	10.2
Aldolase	40 000	5.2
Pepsinogen	41 000	3.7
Hexokinase	51 000	5.3
Lipoxidase	54 000	5.7
Catalase	57 500	5.4
Alkaline phosphatase	69 000	4.4
Acetylcholine esterase	70 000	4.5
Glyceraldehyde-3-phosphate dehydrogenase	72 000	8.5

Electroanalytical techniques

Electrochemical methods are used to quantify a broad range of different biomolecules, including ions, gases, metabolites, drugs and hormones.

KEY POINT The basis of all electrochemical analysis is the transfer of electrons from one atom or molecule to another atom or molecule in an obligately coupled oxidation–reduction reaction (a redox reaction).

It is convenient to separate such redox reactions into two half-reactions and, by convention, each is written as:

$$\text{oxidised form} + \text{electron(s)} \ (n\text{e}^-) \underset{oxidation}{\overset{reduction}{\rightleftharpoons}} \text{reduced form} \qquad [48.1]$$

You should note that the half-reaction is reversible: by applying suitable conditions, reduction *or* oxidation can take place. As an example, a simple redox reaction occurs when metallic zinc (Zn) is placed in a solution containing copper ions (Cu^{2+}), as follows:

$$Cu^{2+} + Zn \rightarrow Cu + Zn^{2+} \qquad [48.2]$$

The half-reactions are (i) $Cu^{2+} + 2e^- \rightarrow Cu$ and (ii) $Zn^{2+} + 2e^- \rightarrow Zn$. The oxidising power of (i) is greater than that of (ii), so in a coupled system, the latter half-reaction proceeds in the opposite direction to that shown above, i.e. as $Zn - 2e^- \rightarrow Zn^{2+}$. When Zn and Cu electrodes are placed in separate solutions containing their ions, and connected electrically (Fig. 48.1), electrons will flow from the Zn electrode to Cu^{2+} via the Cu electrode due to the difference in oxidising power of the two half-reactions.

By convention, the electrode potential of any half-reaction is expressed relative to that of a standard hydrogen electrode (half-reaction $2H^+ + 2e^- \rightarrow H_2$) and is called the standard electrode potential, E^o. Table 48.1 shows the values of E^o for selected half-reactions. With any pair of half-reactions from this series, electrons will flow from that having the lowest electrode potential to that of the highest. E^o is determined at pH = 0. It is often more appropriate to express standard electrode potentials at pH 7 for biological systems, and the symbol $E^{o\prime}$ is used: in all circumstances, it is important that the pH is clearly stated.

The arrangement shown in Fig. 48.1 represents a simple galvanic cell where two electrodes serve as the interfaces between a chemical system and an electrical system. For analytical purposes, the magnitude of the potential (voltage) or the current produced by an electrochemical cell is related to the concentration (strictly the activity, *a*, p. 140) of a particular chemical species. Electrochemical methods offer the following advantages:

- excellent detection limits, and wide operating range (10^{-1}–10^{-8} mol l^{-1});
- measurements may be made on very small volumes (μl) allowing small amounts (pmol) of sample to be measured in some cases;
- miniature electrochemical sensors can be used for certain *in vivo* measurements, e.g. pH, glucose, oxygen content.

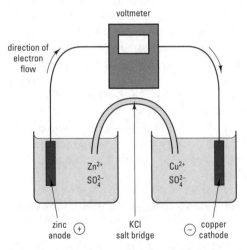

Fig. 48.1 A simple galvanic electrochemical cell. The KCl salt bridge allows migration of ions between the two compartments but prevents mixing of the two solutions.

Definition

Galvanic cell – an electrochemical cell in which reactions occur spontaneously at the electrodes when they are connected externally by a conductor, producing electrical energy.

Electroanalytical techniques

Table 48.1 Standard electrode potentials* (E^0) for selected half-reactions

Half-reaction	E^0 at 25 °C (V)
$Cl_2 + 2e^- \rightleftharpoons 2Cl^-$	+1.36
$O_2 + 4H^+ + 4e^- \rightleftharpoons 2H_2O$	+1.23
$Br_2 + 2e^- \rightleftharpoons 2Br^-$	+1.09
$Ag^+ + e^- \rightleftharpoons Ag$	+0.80
$Fe^{3+} + e^- \rightleftharpoons Fe^{2+}$	+0.77
$I_3^- + 2e^- \rightleftharpoons 3I^-$	+0.54
$Cu^{2+} + 2e^- \rightleftharpoons Cu$	+0.34
$Hg_2Cl_2 + 2e^- \rightleftharpoons 2Hg + 2Cl^-$	+0.27
$AgCl + e^- \rightleftharpoons Ag + Cl^-$	+0.22
$Ag(S_2O_3)_2^{3-} + e^- \rightleftharpoons Ag + 2S_2O_3^{2-}$	+0.01
$2H^+ + 2e^- \rightleftharpoons H_2$	+0.00
$AgI + e^- \rightleftharpoons Ag + I$	−0.15
$PbSO_4 + 2e^- \rightleftharpoons Pb + SO_4^{2-}$	−0.35
$Cd^{2+} + 2e^- \rightleftharpoons Cd$	−0.40
$Zn^{2+} + 2e^- \rightleftharpoons Zn$	−0.76

*From Milazzo *et al.* (1978).

Using a calomel electrode – *always ensure that the KCl solution is saturated by checking that KCl crystals are present.*

Fig. 48.2 Components of a potentiometric cell.

Potentiometry and ion-selective electrodes

Operating principles

These systems involve galvanic cells (p. 331) and are based on measurement of the potential (voltage) difference between two electrodes in solution when no net current flows between them: no net electrochemical reaction occurs and measurements are made under equilibrium conditions. These systems include methods for measuring pH, ions and gases such as CO_2 and NH_3. A typical potentiometric cell is shown in Fig. 48.2. It contains two electrodes:

1. a 'sensing' electrode, the half-cell potential of which responds to changes in the activity (concentration) of the substance to be measured; the most common type of indicator electrodes are ion-selective electrodes (ISE);
2. a 'reference' electrode, the potential of which does not change, forming the second half of the cell.

To assay a particular analyte, the potential difference between these electrodes is measured by an mV meter (e.g. a standard pH meter).

Reference electrodes for potentiometry are of three main types:

1. The standard hydrogen electrode, which is the reference half-cell electrode, defined as 0.0 V at all temperatures, against which values of E^o are expressed. H_2 gas at 1 atmosphere pressure is bubbled over a platinum electrode immersed in an acid solution with an activity of unity. This electrode is rarely used for analytical work, since it is unstable and other reference electrodes are easier to construct and use.
2. The calomel electrode (Fig. 48.3), which consists of a paste of mercury covered by a coat of calomel (Hg_2Cl_2), immersed in a saturated solution of KCl. The half-reaction: $Hg_2Cl_2 + 2e^- \rightarrow 2Hg + 2Cl^-$ gives a stable standard electrode potential of +0.24 V.
3. The silver/silver chloride electrode. This is a silver wire coated with AgCl and immersed in a solution of constant chloride concentration. The half-reaction: $AgCl + e^- \rightarrow Ag + Cl^-$ gives a stable, standard electrode potential of +0.20 V.

KEY POINT Ion-selective electrodes (ISEs) are based on measurement of a potential across a membrane which is selective for a particular analyte.

An ISE consists of a membrane, an internal reference electrode, and an internal reference electrolyte of fixed activity. The ISE is immersed in a sample solution that contains the analyte of interest, along with a reference electrode. The membrane is chosen to have a specific affinity for a particular ion, and if activity of this ion in the sample differs from that in the reference electrolyte, a potential develops across the membrane that is dependent on the ratio of these activities. Since the potentials of the two reference electrodes (internal and external) are fixed, and the internal electrolyte is of constant activity, the measured potential, E, is dependent on the membrane potential and is given by the Nernst equation (Robinson and Stokes, 2000) as:

$$E = K + 2.303 \frac{RT}{zF} \log [a] \qquad [48.3]$$

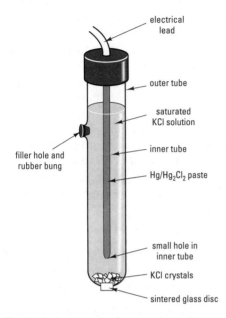

Fig. 48.3 A calomel reference electrode.

Fig. 48.4 Underlying principles of a gas-sensing electrode.

where K represents a constant potential which is dependent on the reference electrode, z represents the net charge on the analyte, $[a]$ represents the activity of analyte in the sample and all other symbols and constants have their usual meaning (p. 178). For a series of standards of known activity, a plot of E against $\log [a]$ should be linear over the working range of the electrode, with a slope of $2.303\,RT/zF$ (0.059 V at 25 °C). Although ISEs strictly measure *activity*, the potential differences can be approximated to concentration as long as (i) the analyte is in dilute solution (p. 22), (ii) the ionic strength of the calibration standards matches that of the sample, e.g. by adding appropriate amounts of a high ionic strength solution to the standards, and (iii) the effect of binding to sample macromolecules (e.g. proteins, nucleic acids) is minimal. Potentiometric measurements on undiluted biological fluids, e.g. K^+ and Na^+ levels in plasma, tissue fluids or urine, are likely to give lower values than flame emission spectrophotometry, since the latter procedure measures total ion levels, rather than just those in aqueous solution.

All of the various types of membrane used in ISEs operate by incorporating the ion to be analysed into the membrane, with the accompanying establishment of a membrane potential. The scope of electrochemical analysis has been extended to measuring gases and non-ionic compounds by combining ISEs with gas-permeable membranes, enzymes, and even immobilised bacteria or tissues.

Glass membrane electrodes

The most widely used ISE is the glass membrane electrode for pH measurement (p. 148). The membrane is thin glass (50 μm wall thickness) made of silica which contains some Na^+. When the membrane is soaked in water, a thin hydrated layer is formed on the surface in which negative oxide groups ($Si\text{-}O^-$) in the glass act as ion exchange sites. If the electrode is placed in an acid solution, H^+ exchanges with Na^+ in the hydrated layer, producing an external surface potential: in alkaline solution, H^+ moves out of the membrane in exchange for Na^+. Since the inner surface potential is kept constant by exposure to a fixed activity of H^+, a consistent, accurate potentiometric response is observed over a wide pH range. Glass electrodes for other cations (e.g. Na^+, NH_4^+) have been developed by changing the composition of the glass, so that it is predominantly sensitive to the particular analyte, though the specificity of such electrodes is not absolute. The operating principles and maintenance of such electrodes are broadly similar to those for pH electrodes (p. 148).

Gas-sensing glass electrodes

Here, an ISE in contact with a thin external layer of aqueous electrolyte (the 'filling solution') is kept close to the glass membrane by an additional, outer membrane that is selectively permeable to the gas of interest. The arrangement for a CO_2 electrode is shown in Fig. 28.4: in this case the outer membrane is made of CO_2-permeable silicone rubber. When CO_2 gas in the sample selectively diffuses across the membrane and dissolves in the filling solution (in this case an aqueous $NaHCO_3/NaCl$ mixture), a change in pH occurs due to the shift in the equilibrium:

$$CO_2 + H_2O \rightleftharpoons H_2CO_3 \rightleftharpoons H^+ + HCO_3^- \qquad [48.4]$$

The pH change is 'sensed' by the internal ion-selective pH electrode, and its response is proportional to the partial pressure of CO_2 of the solution

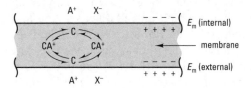

internal solution

external (sample) solution

Fig. 48.5 Underlying principles of a liquid membrane ion-selective electrode. A^+ = analyte; C = neutral carrier ionophore; E_m = surface potential; membrane potential = E_m(internal) – E_m(external).

(PCO_2). A similar principle operates in the NH_3 electrode, where a Teflon® membrane is used, and the filling solution is NH_4Cl.

Liquid and polymer membrane electrodes

In this type of ISE, the liquid is a water-insoluble viscous solvent containing a soluble ionophore, i.e. an organic ion-exchanger, or a neutral carrier molecule, that is specific for the analyte of interest. When this liquid is soaked into a thin membrane such as cellulose acetate, it becomes effectively immobilised. The arrangement of analyte (A^+) and ionophore in relation to this membrane is shown in Fig. 48.5. The potential on the inner surface of the membrane is kept constant by maintaining a constant activity of A^+ in the internal solution, so the potential change measured is that which results from A^+ in the sample interacting with the ionophore in the outer surface of the membrane.

A relevant example of a suitable ionophore is the antibiotic valinomycin (p. 393), which specifically binds K^+. Other ionophores have been developed for measurement of e.g. NH_4^+, Ca^{2+}, Cl^-. In addition, electrodes have been developed for organic species by using specific ion-pairing reagents in the membrane that interact with ionic forms of the organic compound, e.g. with drugs such as 5,5-diphenylhydantoin.

Solid-state membrane electrodes

These contain membranes made from single crystals or pressed pellets of salts of the analyte. The membrane material must show some permeability to ions and must be virtually insoluble in water. Examples include:

- the fluoride electrode, which uses LaF_3 impregnated with Eu^{2+} (the latter to increase permeability to F^-). A membrane potential is set up when F^- in the sample solution enters spaces in the crystal lattice;
- the chloride electrode, which uses a pressed pellet membrane of Ag_2S and $AgCl$.

Voltammetric methods

Voltammetric methods are based on measurements made using an electrochemical cell in which electrolysis is occurring. Voltammetry, sometimes also called amperometry, involves the use of a potential applied between two electrodes (the working electrode and the reference electrode) to cause oxidation or reduction of an electroactive analyte. The loss or gain of electrons at an electrode surface causes current to flow, and the size of the current (usually measured in mA or μA) is directly proportional to the concentration of the electroactive analyte. The materials used for the working electrode must be good conductors and electrochemically inert, so that they simply transfer electrons to and from species in solution. Suitable materials include Pt, Au, Hg and glassy carbon.

Two widely used devices that operate on the voltammetric principle are the oxygen electrode and the glucose electrode. These are sometimes referred to as amperometric sensors.

Oxygen electrodes

The Clark (Rank) oxygen electrode

These instruments measure oxygen in solution using the polarographic principle, i.e. by monitoring the current flowing between two electrodes when a voltage is applied. The most widespread electrode is the Clark type (Fig. 48.6), manufactured by Rank Bros, Cambridge, UK, which is suitable for measuring O_2 concentrations in cell, organelle and enzyme suspensions. Pt and Au electrodes are in contact with a solution of electrolyte (normally saturated KCl). The electrodes are separated from the medium by a Teflon® membrane, permeable to O_2. When a potential is applied across the electrodes, this generates a current proportional to the O_2 concentration. The reactions can be summed up as:

$$4Ag \rightarrow 4Ag^+ + 4e^-$$ (at silver anode)

$$O_2 + 2e^- + 2H^+ \rightleftharpoons H_2O_2$$ (in electrolyte solution; O_2 replenished by diffusion from test solution)

$$H_2O_2 + 2e^- + 2H^+ \rightleftharpoons 2H_2O$$ (at platinum cathode)

Setting up and using a Clark (Rank) oxygen electrode

Box 48.1 describes the steps involved: if you are setting up from scratch, perform steps 1–13; if a satisfactory membrane is already in place, start at step 7.

The temperature of the incubation vessel can be controlled by passing water (e.g. from a water bath) through the outer chamber. Cells or organelles may be present in the solution added to the incubation chamber or can be added via the hole in the stopper using a syringe, as can chemicals such as metabolic substrates or inhibitors. Take care not to introduce air bubbles and remove any that appear by gently raising and lowering the stopper. The electrode can be used repeatedly, providing the membrane is satisfactory: remove solutions carefully (e.g. using a pipette, or vacuum line and trap). Keep water in the chamber when not in use. Replace the membrane if:

- the reading becomes noisy;
- the electrode will not zero after adding sodium dithionite;

Working out the amount of O_2 (mol) present at saturation – *multiply the appropriate saturation concentration (Table 48.2) in mol m^{-3} by the volume of solution in the chamber, in m^3.*

Fig. 48.6 Transverse section through a Clark (Rank) oxygen electrode.

- the response becomes too slow (check by switching off stirrer – oxygen concentration should drop rapidly as the available oxygen is consumed).

KEY POINT **If the Teflon® membrane becomes contaminated or dirty, it should be changed. While replacing the Teflon® membrane, make sure that the electrodes are clean: use a mild abrasive cleaning paste.**

Oxygen probes

Clark-type oxygen electrodes are also available in probe form for immersion in the test solution (Fig. 48.7), e.g. for field studies, allowing direct measurement of oxygen status *in situ*, in contrast to chemical assays. The main point to note is that the solution must be stirred during measurement, to replenish the oxygen consumed by the electrode ('boundary layer' effect).

Converting chart traces to rates of O_2 consumption or evolution

1. Calibrate the chart recorder using the zero and fully saturated values as reference points. The concentration of O_2 in saturated aqueous solution changes as a function of temperature and salt concentration (see Table 48.2), so multiply the appropriate value by the volume of the solution in the incubation chamber (in m^3) to obtain the number of moles of O_2 present. Divide by the number of chart divisions to find the number of moles per chart division.
2. Convert the gradient of the trace into a rate of oxygen consumption or evolution. Only use portions of the trace showing a stable rate for

Examples At 37 °C, air-saturated distilled water contains O_2 at $0.211\,mol\,m^{-3}$ (Table 48.2), so in $5 \times 10^{-6}\,m^3$ (5 ml) of medium, there will be $1.06\,\mu mol\,O_2$. If the deflection between zero and fully saturated solution is 67 divisions, each division will correspond to $1.06 \div 67$ $= 0.0158\,\mu mol\,O_2$ ($15.8\,nmol$ per division).

For the above calibration, for a trace with a gradient of -14 units over 2 cm of chart paper at a speed of $0.2\,cm\,min^{-1}$ (10 min), the O_2 consumption rate would be $14 \div 10 \times 15.8 = 22.1\,nmol\,min^{-1}$.

If there were 1.2×10^9 cells in the electrode, the O_2 consumption rate on a cellular basis would be $22.1 \times 10^{-9} \div 1.2 \times 10^9 = 18.4\,amol\,O_2\,min^{-1}\,cell^{-1}$.

Fig. 48.7 A Clark-type oxygen probe.

leads to battery and recorder

filler (plus plug)

saturated KCl

silver anode

glass electrode body

rubber 'O' ring

Teflon membrane

platinum cathode

Box 48.1 How to set up a Clark (Rank) oxygen electrode

1. **Detach the base of the incubation vessel** (see Fig. 48.6) by unscrewing the locking ring.

2. **Add enough saturated KCl to cover the electrodes**.

3. **Cut a 1 mm square hole in the centre of a 10 × 10 mm square of lens tissue** and place this on the KCl solution so that the hole is over the central platinum cathode.

4. **Cut a 10 × 10 mm square of Teflon® membrane and place over the lens tissue**; seal by gently lowering the incubation vessel and tightening the locking ring, making sure that the rubber O-ring is correctly positioned over the membrane.
   (a) Do not overtighten the locking ring.
   (b) Take care not to trap air bubbles beneath the membrane.
   (c) Make sure that the membrane does not become twisted.

5. **Clamp the electrode over the magnetic stirrer base using the clamping screw**.

6. **Connect the electrode leads to the polarising unit/recording device** (silver anode to positive, platinum cathode to negative). In most cases, the output will be passed to a chart recorder, to give a readout of oxygen status as a function of time.

7. **Add air-saturated experimental solution and a small Teflon®-coated magnetic stirrer bar to the** chamber. The volume of the incubation chamber can be adjusted by moving the locking nut on the stopper. To adjust, add the appropriate amount of liquid to the chamber using a pipette, insert the stopper and screw the locking nut until the solution just fills the incubation chamber.

8. **Gently push the stopper (volume adjuster) into position**, making sure that no air bubbles are trapped in the chamber, and switch on the stirrer.

9. **Adjust the sensitivity control of the recorder** to give a suitable reading and allow to stabilise – this may take 5–10 min. This is the air-saturated reading.

10. **Add a few crystals of sodium dithionite to absorb all of the O_2 in solution;** this gives a zero reading (an alternative is to bubble N_2 through the solution for several minutes).

11. **Rinse the incubation chamber thoroughly and add fresh experimental solution.** Make sure that all traces of sodium dithionite are removed.

12. **Carry out your experiment.**

13. **Remove the solution and check the calibration** (steps 7 to 10). If the recorder deflections are different, the electrode's sensitivity or the temperature may have changed and you may need to repeat the measurement.

Table 48.2 Oxygen saturation values for distilled water and sea water at standard atmospheric pressure and a range of temperatures (derived from Green and Carritt, 1967)

Temperature (°C)	Distilled water			Sea water		
	$mol\,m^{-3}$	$mg\,l^{-1}$	$ml\,l^{-1}$	$mol\,m^{-3}$	$mg\,l^{-1}$	$ml\,l^{-1}$
0	0.460	14.7	10.3	0.359	11.5	8.04
2	0.435	13.9	9.75	0.342	10.9	7.65
4	0.413	13.2	9.24	0.326	10.4	7.30
6	0.392	12.5	8.78	0.311	9.95	6.97
8	0.373	11.9	8.35	0.298	9.54	6.66
10	0.355	11.4	7.95	0.285	9.12	6.37
12	0.339	10.8	7.59	0.273	8.74	6.11
14	0.324	10.4	7.25	0.261	8.35	5.85
16	0.310	9.92	6.94	0.251	8.03	5.62
18	0.297	9.50	6.65	0.241	7.71	5.40
20	0.285	9.12	6.38	0.232	7.42	5.19
22	0.274	8.77	6.12	0.224	7.17	5.00
24	0.263	8.42	5.89	0.215	6.88	4.82
26	0.253	8.1	5.67	0.208	6.66	4.64
28	0.244	7.81	5.46	0.200	6.40	4.48
30	0.235	7.52	5.27	0.193	6.18	4.32
37	0.211	6.75	4.71	0.174	5.57	3.88

Notes: $mol\,m^{-3} \equiv mmol\,l^{-1} \equiv \mu mol\,ml^{-1}$. Tabulated values assume atmospheric pressure = 101.3 kPa ($\approx$760 mm Hg); for more accurate work, a correction for any deviation can be made by multiplying the appropriate figures from the table by the ratio of the real pressure to the assumed pressure.

Fig. 48.8 Underlying principles of a glucose electrode.

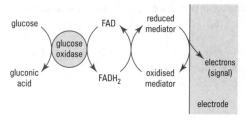

Fig. 48.9 Operating principles of a glucose biosensor. In the ExacTech® system, the mediator is a ferrocene derivative.

at least 5 min. Work out the gradient as divisions per unit time, taking account of the speed of the chart recorder. Use the calibration to convert this to a rate of O_2 consumption or evolution.

3. Express the rate on a cellular, chlorophyll or protein basis. Find the number of cells in the suspension (e.g. by using a haemocytometer, p. 229) and divide the figure obtained in (2) by this. Alternatively, find the chlorophyll or protein concentration (pp. 273 and 348 respectively) and divide by this value.

Glucose electrodes

These are simple types of biosensor; a simple design is shown in Fig. 48.8. It consists of a Pt electrode, overlaid by two membranes. Sandwiched between these membranes is a layer of the immobilised enzyme glucose oxidase. The outer membrane is glucose-permeable and allows glucose in the sample to diffuse through to the glucose oxidase layer, where it is converted to gluconic acid and H_2O_2. The inner membrane is selectively permeable to H_2O_2, which is oxidised to O_2 at the surface of the Pt electrode. The current arising from this release of electrons is proportional to the glucose concentration in the sample within the range 10^{-7}–10^{-3} mol l^{-1}. The efficiency of a biosensor can be increased by including an electrode surface that is capable of capturing electrons directly. This is the basis of recently developed blood glucose meters for diabetics such as the ExacTech® meter (Medisense-Abbott Laboratories). Here a pinprick blood sample is applied to a test strip containing glucose oxidase: if glucose is present a series of reactions occurs as shown in Fig. 48.9.

The electrons produced are donated to the electrode surface, producing an initial current that is proportional to the initial rate at which glucose is oxidised which, in turn, is proportional to the glucose concentration in the blood sample. The future design of biosensors is likely to involve microchip technology in which the biocatalyst and the transducer are even more intimately linked (for more details, see Eggins, 2002).

Electrochemical detectors used in chromatography operate by voltammetric principles and currents are produced as the mobile phase flows over electrodes set at a fixed potential: to achieve maximum sensitivity, this potential must be set at a level that allows electrochemical reactions to occur in all analytes of interest.

Coulometric methods

Here, the charge required to completely electrolyse a sample is measured: the time required to titrate an analyte is measured at constant current and related to the amount of analyte using Faraday's law. There are few biological applications of this technique, though it is sometimes used for determination of Cl^- in serum and body fluids.

Text references

Eggins, B.R. (2002) *Chemical Sensors and Biosensors*. Wiley, New York.

Green, E.J. and Carritt, D.E. (1967) New Tables for Oxygen Saturation of Seawater, *Journal of Marine Research*, **25**, 140–7.

Milazzo, G., Caroli, S. and Sharma, V.K. (1978) *Tables of Standard Electrode Potentials*. Wiley, London.

Robinson, R.A. and Stokes, R.H. (2000) *Electroylte Solutions*. Dover Publications, New York.

Sources for further study

Anon. *Rank Dissolved Oxygen Electrode*. Available: http://www.rankbrothers.co.uk/prod1.htm
Last accessed 08/01/03.
[Homepage of the manufacturing company – contains technical details and contact information.]

Anon. *Dissolved Oxygen Measurement*. Available: http://www.dep.state.pa.us/dep/deputate/waterops/Redesign/ NPDES%20Lab/Chapter%204.doc
Last accessed 08/01/03.
[Details of sampling and measurement, oxygen probes and chemical assay (Winkler method), plus self-test quizzes.]

Fisher, A.C. (1996) *Electrode Dynamics*. Oxford University Press, Oxford.

Golterman, H.L., Clymo, R.S. and Ohnstad, M.A.M. (1978) *Methods for Physical and Chemical Analysis of Fresh Waters*. Blackwell Scientific Publications, Oxford.

Hitchman, M.L. (1988) *Measurement of Dissolved Oxygen*. Krieger, Melbourne.

Linek, V. (1988) *Measurement of Oxygen by Membrane-covered Probes*. Ellis-Horwood, Chichester.

Sanders, G.H.W., Compton, R.G. and Compton, S. (1996) *Electrode Potentials*. Oxford University Press, Oxford.
[Covers the underlying theory, plus applications relating to ion-selective electrodes.]

Raluca-Ioana, S. and van Staden, J.F. (2001) *Electrochemical Sensors in Bioanalysis*. Marcel Dekker, New York.

Wilson, K. and Walker, J. (eds) (2000) *Principles and Techniques of Practical Biochemistry*, 5th edn. Cambridge University Press, Cambridge.
[Also covers a range of other topics, including chromatography, spectroscopy and centrifugation.]

Study exercises

48.1 Test your understanding of the circumstances under which ion-selective electrodes can be used. List the three main assumptions underlying the measurement of ion concentration using an ion-selective electrode.

48.2 Test your knowledge of biosensor design. List the two main functional components of biosensor such as the glucose electrode. Research a specific application – note that it should be different from the ones used in this chapter (e.g. using the Web).

48.3 Calculate the oxygen content of specified volumes of water at defined temperatures. Using the information in Table 48.2 and assuming air equilibration at 101.3 kPa, what is the amount of oxygen in each of the following (give all answers to 3 significant figures):

(a) 4 ml of distilled water at 20 °C (express your answer in μmol);
(b) 20 ml of sea water at 12 °C (express your answer in μmol);
(c) 10 ml of distilled water at 15 °C (express your answer in μmol);
(d) 250 ml of distilled water at 37 °C (express your answer in mg);
(e) 200 ml of sea water at 25 °C (express your answer in ml).

48.4 Calculate respiration using data from an oxygen electrode readout. An oxygen electrode was set up to contain 5.0 ml of air-equilibrated distilled water at 30 °C, giving a full-scale reading on a chart recorder (200 divisions on the chart recorder paper), while a zero reading gave no deflection (0 divisions on the chart recorder paper). A yeast cell suspension (containing 4.1×10^9 cells in total) was added to the same electrode system along with a suitable growth medium, giving an approximately linear trace on the chart recorder with a slope of -25 units per cm, at a chart speed of $0.5 \, \text{cm min}^{-1}$. What is the respiratory oxygen consumption in $\text{nmol min}^{-1} \, (10^9 \, \text{cells})^{-1}$? (Give your answer to 3 significant figures.)

48.5 Determine net photosynthetic rate from oxygen electrode readings. The table below represents oxygen electrode readings taken every minute for an illuminated suspension of a cyanobacterium in a 5.0 ml chamber of an oxygen electrode at 20 °C. The system was first calibrated to read 100.0 for air-equilibrated distilled water and 0.0 for anaerobic water, in effect making the scale read in terms of percentage oxygen saturation. The chlorophyll a content of an equivalent amount of cyanobacterial suspension to that used in the electrode chamber was measured at $2.13 \, \mu\text{g ml}^{-1}$. What is the net photosynthetic rate of the cyanobacterial suspension, in $\mu\text{mol min}^{-1} \, (\text{mg chlorophyll } a)^{-1}$? (Express your answer to 3 significant figures.)

Output from an illuminated oxygen electrode containing a cyanobacterial suspension

Time (min)	Readout (%)
0	70.4
1	73.6
2	75.3
3	78.5
4	83.6
5	85.9
6	88.2
7	91.4
8	94.1

Assaying biomolecules and studying metabolism

49 Analysis of biomolecules: fundamental principles

Table 49.1 Some examples of colorimetric assays

Analyte	Reagent/wavelength
Amino acids	ninhydrin/540 nm (p. 347)
Proteins	biuret/520 nm (p. 348)
	Folin–Ciocalteau/600 nm (p. 349)
Carbohydrates	anthrone/625 nm (p. 360)
Reducing sugars	dinitrosalicylate/540 nm (p. 361)
DNA	diphenylamine/600 nm (p. 367)
RNA	orcinol/660 nm (p. 368)

Biochemical analysis involves the characterisation of biological components within a sample using appropriate laboratory techniques. Most analytical methods rely on one or more chemical or physical properties of the test substance (the analyte) for detection and/or measurement. There are two principal approaches:

1. Qualitative analysis – where a sample is assayed to determine whether a biomolecule is present or absent. As an example, a blood sample might be analysed for a particular drug or a specific antibody (p. 250), or a bacterial cell might be probed for a nucleic acid sequence (p. 432).
2. Quantitative analysis – where the quantity of a particular biomolecule in a sample is determined, either as an amount (e.g. as g, or mol) or in terms of its concentration in the sample (e.g. as $g\,l^{-1}$, or $mol\,m^{-3}$). For example, a blood sample might be analysed to determine its pH ($-\log_{10} [H^+]$), alcohol concentration in $mg\,ml^{-1}$, or glucose concentration in $mmol\,l^{-1}$. Skoog and Leary (1997) give details of methods.

Your choice of approach will be determined by the purpose of the investigation and by the level of accuracy and precision required (p. 171). Many of the basic quantitative methods described in Chapters 50–53 rely on chemical reactions of the analyte and involve assumptions about the nature of the test substance and the lack of interfering compounds in the sample: such assumptions are unlikely to be wholly valid at all times. If you need to make more exacting measurements of a particular analyte, it may be necessary to separate it from the other components in the sample, e.g. using chromatography (Chapter 44), ultracentrifugation (Chapter 43), or electrophoresis (Chapter 46), and then identify the separated components, e.g. using spectroscopic methods (Chapter 41). However, each stage in the separation and purification procedure may introduce further errors and/or loss of sample, as described in detail for protein purification in Chapter 54.

KEY POINT In general, you should aim to use the simplest procedure that satisfies the purpose of your investigation – there is little value in using a complex, time-consuming or costly analytical procedure to answer a simple problem where a high degree of accuracy is not required.

Most of the routine methods based on chemical analysis are destructive, since the analyte is usually converted to another substance which is then assayed, e.g. in colorimetric assays of the major types of biomolecules (Table 49.1). In contrast, many of the analytical methods based on physical properties are non-destructive (e.g. the intrinsic absorption and emission of electromagnetic radiation in spectrophotometry, p. 271, or nuclear magnetic resonance techniques, p. 282). Non-destructive methods are often preferred, as they allow the further characterisation of a particular sample. Most biological methods are destructive: bioassays are often sensitive to interference and require validation (p. 231).

Validity and quantitative analysis

Before using a particular procedure, you should consider its possible limitations in terms of:

- measurement errors, and their likely magnitude: these might include processing errors (e.g. in preparing solutions and making dilutions), instrumental errors (e.g. a pH electrode that has not been set up correctly), calibration errors (e.g. converting a digital readout analyte concentration) and errors due to the presence of interfering substances;
- sampling errors: these may occur if the material used for analysis is not representative, e.g. due to biological differences between the individual organisms used in the sampling procedure (p. 475).

Replication will allow you to make quantitative estimates of several potential sources of error: for example, repeated measurements of the same sample can provide information on the precision of the analytical method, e.g. by calculating the coefficient of variation (p. 480), while measurements of several different samples can provide information on biological and sample variability, e.g. by calculating the standard deviation (Chapter 66). Analyses of different sets of samples at different times (e.g. on different days) can provide information on 'between batch' variability, as opposed to 'within batch' variability (based on a single set of analytical data).

The reliability of a particular method can be assessed by measuring 'standards' (sometimes termed 'controls'). These are often prepared in the laboratory by adding a known amount of analyte to a real sample (this is often termed 'spiking' a sample), or by preparing an artificial sample containing a known amount of analyte along with other relevant components (e.g. the major sample constituents and possible interfering substances). In many instances, several standards (including a 'blank' or 'zero') are assayed to construct a 'standard curve', which is then used to convert sample measurements to amounts of analyte (see Chapter 37 for details). Such standard curves form the basis of many routine laboratory assays: while hand-drawn linear calibration curves are sufficient for basic assays, more complex curves are often fitted to a particular mathematical function using a computer program (e.g. bioassays, p. 231). Standards can also be used to check the calibration of a particular method: a mean value based on repeated measurements of an individual 'standard' can be compared with the true value using a modified t test (p. 491, Eqn 67.1), in which there is only one standard error term, i.e. that associated with the measured values.

Validation of a particular method can be important in certain circumstances, e.g. in a forensic science laboratory, or in a clinical biochemistry laboratory, where particular results can have important implications. Such laboratories operate strict validation procedures, which include: (i) adherence to standard operating procedures for each analytical method; (ii) calibration of assays using certified reference materials containing known amount of analyte and traceable to a national reference laboratory; (iii) effective quality assurance and quality control systems; (iv) detailed record-keeping, covering all aspects of the analysis and recording of results. Although such rigour is not required for routine analysis, the general principles of standardisation, calibration, assessment of performance and record-keeping are equally valid for all analytical work.

Evaluating a new method – results from a novel technique can be compared with an established 'standardised' technique by measuring the same set of samples by each method and analysing the results by correlation (p. 493).

Interpreting results from 'spiked' samples – remember that such procedures tell you nothing about the extraction efficiency of biomolecules from a particular sample, e.g. during homogenisation (Chapter 36).

Criteria for the selection of a particular analytical method:

- the required level of accuracy and precision;
- the number of samples to be analysed;
- the amount of each sample available for analysis;
- the physical form of the samples;
- the expected concentration range of the analyte in the samples;
- the sensitivity and detection limit of the technique;
- the likelihood of interfering substances;
- the speed of analysis;
- the ease and convenience of the procedure;
- the skill required by the operator;
- the cost and availability of the equipment.

Text reference

Skoog, D.A. and Leary, J.J. (1997) *Principles of Instrumental Analysis*, 5th edn. Brooks-Cole, Pacific Grove.

Sources for further study

Anon. *Guidance on Analytical Methods Validation*. Available:
http://www.fda.gov/cber/gdlns/methval.htm
Last accessed 08/01/03.
[US FDA guidance/details of reference standards, procedures for method validation, etc.]

Anon. *International Union of Biochemistry and Molecular Biology*. Available:
http://www.chem.qmw.ac.uk/iubmb/
Last accessed 08/01/03.

Anon. *Valid Analytical Measurement Homepage*. Available:
http://www.vam.org.uk
Last accessed 08/01/03.

Venn, R.F. (2000) *Principles and Practice of Bioanalysis*. Taylor and Francis, London.

Wilson, K. and Walker, J. (eds) (2000) *Principles and Techniques of Practical Biochemistry*, 5th edn. Cambridge University Press, Cambridge.

Study exercises

49.1 Check your understanding of the fundamental principles of biomolecular analysis. Distinguish between each of the following pairs of terms:
(a) qualitative analysis and quantitative analysis;
(b) sensitivity and selectivity;
(c) accuracy and precision;
(d) validation and replication;
(e) noise and drift.

49.2 Research sources of calibration standards and reference materials. Using the Web, find a supplier of a validated reference standard for the following:
(a) cortisol in serum;
(b) cotinine in urine.

49.3 Compare equipment specifications. The table (overleaf) gives operational details for two glucose meters, A and B. Which meter has:
(a) the lower detection limit?
(b) the wider linear dynamic range?
(c) the greater accuracy?
(d) the better level of precision?
(e) the smaller sample volume?

Performance of two glucose meters

Aspect	Meter A	Meter B
Units of measurement	mmol 1^{-1}	mg dl^{-1}
Detection limit	0.10	1.00
Linearity	to 20.0	to 250.0
Accuracy	±0.050	±1.50
Relative standard deviation (%)	3.5	2.5
Sample volume	40 μl	0.05 ml

50 Assaying amino acids and proteins

Proteins are linear polymers, formed by the linkage of α-amino acids (Fig. 50.1) via peptide bonds to create polypeptide chains. The 20 amino acids most commonly incorporated into proteins are listed in Table 50.1. Others may be found when a protein is hydrolysed, due to post-translational modification (e.g. hydroxyproline).

Fig. 50.1 Structure of α-amino acids. R = side chain (see Table 50.1 for examples).

Table 50.1 The 20 amino acids incorporated into protein, grouped according to their side chains

Name	Three letter code	Capital letter code
Aliphatic side chains		
Glycine	gly	G
Alanine	ala	A
Valine	val	V
Leucine	leu	L
Isoleucine	ile	I
Aromatic side chains		
Phenylalanine	phe	F
Tyrosine	tyr	Y
Tryptophan	trp	W
S-containing side chains		
Cysteine	cys	C
Methionine	met	M
Side chains with –OH groups[1]		
Serine	ser	S
Threonine	thr	T
Basic side chains		
Histidine	his	H
Lysine	lys	K
Arginine	arg	R
Acidic side chains		
Aspartate	asp	D
Glutamate	glu	E
Amide side chains		
Asparagine	asn	N
Glutamine	gln	Q
Cyclic structure (imino acid)		
Proline	pro	P

[1]tyr also has an OH group.

Definitions

Simple protein – a protein composed entirely of amino acid residues.

Conjugated protein – a protein containing a non-amino acid component (the prosthetic group), in addition to a polypeptide component (the apoprotein).

Peptide – a short polymer, containing up to 50 amino acid residues.

KEY POINT In all amino acids apart from glycine, the α-carbon atom is asymmetrical, resulting in stereoisomers. Most life scientists use the D- and L- nomenclature (Fischer convention) when referring to stereo-isomers of amino acids, although the R- and S- convention (p. 327) can be a useful alternative when considering enzymatic reaction mechanisms.

While most of the chemical properties of stereoisomers are identical, enzymes (including those involved in protein synthesis) can distinguish between them and, with the exception of a few bacterial components, only the L-isomers of amino acids are normally used in protein synthesis.

Amino acids and their properties

There is no agreed formal classification of amino acids but, in terms of protein structure and function, the side chains of amino acid residues can be grouped into:

- those that carry a charge (e.g. asp, glu, lys, arg, his) – they may participate in electrostatic interactions and charge–dipole (hydrophilic) interactions;
- those that contain O, N or S (e.g. ser, met, thr, asn, gln, cys, tyr) – they can participate in hydrogen bonding and hydrophilic interactions;
- those that are hydrocarbon in nature (e.g. ala, leu, val, ile, phe, trp) – they may participate in hydrophobic interactions;
- cysteine – this amino acid can form intra- and inter-polypeptide disulphide bridges.

Detection and quantification of amino acids

The primary amino group of amino acids will react with ninhydrin to give a purple-coloured product – this reaction can be used for qualitative assay, e.g. to detect individual amino acids in chromatography (p. 296), or for quantitative colorimetric assay by measuring the absorbance at 570 nm using a spectrophotometer (p. 274). Note that different amino acids give different amounts of coloured product on reaction with ninhydrin, so careful standardisation is needed. The secondary amino groups of the cyclic imino acids hydroxyproline and proline give yellow products with ninhydrin and are assayed at 440 nm.

Proteins and their properties

The diversity of protein structure must be taken into account when considering a suitable analytical method. Globular proteins (e.g. albumin, antibodies) are relatively soluble in dilute salt solutions while fibrous proteins (e.g. collagens, keratin) are typically insoluble, unless hydrolysed (e.g. using $6\,mol\,l^{-1}$ HCl). Conjugated proteins (e.g. metalloproteins, glycoproteins, nucleoproteins) also include non-amino acid components, which may influence the choice of analytical method.

Chemical properties of proteins

The features most commonly exploited for quantitative analysis are:

- the peptide bond, which forms a violet-coloured complex with Cu^{2+} in the biuret reaction (Box 50.1);
- the phenolic group of tyr and the indole group of trp, which react with the oxidising agents phosphotungstic and phosphomolybdic acids in the Folin–Ciocalteau reagent to produce a blue colour. This is combined with the biuret reaction in the Lowry method (Box 50.1);
- dye binding to hydrophobic regions, e.g. in the Bradford assay (Box 50.1);
- the primary amino groups of lys residues, the guanidino group of arg residues and the N-terminal amino acid residue will react with ninhydrin, allowing colorimetric assay similar to that described above for isolated amino acids. However, a more sensitive method uses the reaction of

---

Box 50.1 Methods of determining the amount of protein in an aqueous solution

For all of the following methods, the amounts are appropriate for semi-micro cuvettes (1.5 ml volume, path length 1 cm). Appropriate controls (blanks) must be analysed, to assess possible interference (e.g. due to buffers, etc.).

Biuret method

This is based on the specific reaction between cupric ions (Cu^{++}) in alkaline solution and two adjacent peptide bonds, as found in proteins. As such, it is not significantly affected by differences in amino acid composition between proteins.

1. **Prepare protein standards over an appropriate range** (typically, between 1 and 10 mg ml^{-1}).

2. **Add 1 ml of each standard solution to separate test tubes. Prepare a reagent blank, using 1 ml of distilled water, or an appropriate solution.**

3. **Add 1 ml of each unknown solution to separate test tubes.**

4. **Add 1 ml of biuret reagent (1.5 g $CuSO_4 \cdot 5H_2O$, 6.0 g sodium potassium tartrate in 300 ml of 10 w/v NaOH) to all standard and unknown tubes and to the reagent blank.**

5. **Incubate at 37 °C for 15 min.**

6. **Read the absorbance of each solution at 520 nm against the reagent blank.** The colour is stable for several hours.

The main limitation of the biuret method is its lack of sensitivity – it is unsuitable for solutions with a protein content of less than 1 mg ml^{-1}.

Direct measurement of UV absorbance (Warburg–Christian method)

Proteins absorb EMR maximally at 280 nm (due to the presence of aromatic amino acids) and this forms the basis of the method. The principal advantages of this approach are its simplicity and the fact that the assay is non-destructive. The most common interfering substances are nucleic acids, which can be assessed by measuring the absorbance at 260 nm: a pure solution of protein will have a ratio of absorption (A_{280}/A_{260}) of approximately 1.8, decreasing with increasing nucleic acid contamination. Note also that any free aromatic amino acids in your solution will absorb at 280 nm, leading to an overestimation of protein content. The simplest procedure, which includes a correction for small amounts of nucleic acid, is as follows (use quartz cuvettes throughout):

1. **Measure the absorbance of your solution at 280 nm (A_{280}):** if A_{280} is greater than 1, dilute by an appropriate amount and remeasure (see p. 274).

2. **Repeat at 260 nm (A_{260}).**

3. **Estimate the approximate protein content using the following relationship:**

$$[\text{protein}]\,\text{mg ml}^{-1} = 1.45\,A_{280} - 0.74\,A_{260} \qquad [50.1]$$

This equation is based on the work of Warburg and Christian (1942), for enolase. For other proteins, it should not be used for quantitative work, since it gives only a rough approximation of the amount present, due to variations in aromatic amino acid composition.

Box 50.1 – continued

Lowry (Folin–Ciocalteau) method

This is a colorimetric assay, based on a combination of the biuret method, described above, and the oxidation of tyrosine and tryptophan residues with Folin and Ciocalteau's reagent to give a blue–purple colour. The method is extremely sensitive (down to a protein content of $20 \mu g \, ml^{-1}$), but is subject to interference from a wide range of non-protein substances, including many organic buffers (e.g. TRIS, HEPES), EDTA, urea and certain sugars. Choice of an appropriate standard is important, as the intensity of colour produced for a particular protein is dependent on the amount of aromatic amino acids present.

1. **Prepare protein standards within an appropriate range for your samples** (the method can be used from 0.02 to 1.00 mg ml^{-1}).

2. **Add 1 ml of each standard solution to separate test tubes. Prepare a reagent blank, using 1 ml of distilled water, or an appropriate solution.**

3. **Add 1 ml of each of your unknown solutions to separate test tubes.**

4. **Then, add 5 ml of 'alkaline solution' (prepared by mixing 2% w/v Na_2CO_3 in $0.1 \, mol \, l^{-1}$ NaOH, 1% w/v aqueous $CuSO_4$ and 2% w/v aqueous Na K tartrate in the ratio 100 : 1 : 1. Mix thoroughly and allow to stand for at least 10 min.**

5. **Add 0.5 ml of Folin–Ciocalteau reagent (commercial reagent, diluted 1 : 1 with distilled water on the day of use). Mix rapidly and thoroughly and then allow to stand for 30 min.**

6. **Read the absorbance of each sample at 600 nm.**

Dye-binding (Bradford) method

Coomassie brilliant blue combines with proteins to give a dye–protein complex with an absorption maximum of 595 nm. This provides a simple and sensitive means of measuring protein content, with few interferences. However, the formation of dye–protein complex is affected by the number of basic amino acids within a protein, so the choice of an appropriate standard is important. The method is sensitive down to a protein content of approximately $5 \mu g \, ml^{-1}$ but the relationship between absorbance and concentration is often non-linear, particularly at high protein content.

1. **Prepare protein standards over an appropriate range (between 5 and 100 $\mu g \, ml^{-1}$).**

2. **Add 100 μl of each standard solution to separate test tubes. Prepare a reagent blank, using 100 μl of distilled water, or an appropriate solution** (note that these small volumes must be accurately dispensed, e.g. using a calibrated pipettor, p. 123).

3. **Add 100 μl of your unknown solutions to separate test tubes.**

4. **Add 5.0 ml of Coomassie brilliant blue G250 solution (0.1 g l^{-1}).**

5. **Mix and incubate for at least 5 min: read the absorbance of each solution at 595 nm.**

Other methods are less widely used. They include determination of the total amount of nitrogen in solution (e.g. using the Kjeldahl technique) and calculating the protein content, assuming a nitrogen content of 16%. An alternative approach is to precipitate the protein (e.g. using trichloracetic acid, tannic acid or salicylic acid) and then measure the turbidity of the resulting precipitate (using a nephelometer, or a spectrophotometer, p. 274).

Exploiting the biological properties of proteins – relevant analytical methods include immunoassay (p. 250), enzymatic analysis (p. 378) and affinity chromatography (p. 302), based on specific biological interactions.

these groups with fluorescamine to give an intensely fluorescent product, which you can measure by spectrofluorimetry (p. 275).

Most assays for protein content do not give an absolute value, but require standard solutions, containing appropriate concentrations of a particular protein, to be analysed at the same time, so that a standard curve can be constructed. Bovine serum albumin (BSA) is commonly used as a protein standard. However, you may need an alternative standard if the protein you are assaying has an amino acid composition which is markedly different from that of BSA, depending on your chosen method.

Physical properties of proteins

The characteristics that can be used for separation and analysis include:

- absorbance of aromatic amino acid residues (phe, tyr and trp) at 280 nm (Warburg–Christian method, Box 50.1);

- prosthetic groups of conjugated proteins – these often have characteristic absorption maxima, e.g. the haem group of haemoglobin absorbs strongly at 415 nm, allowing quantitative assay;
- density – most proteins have a density of $1.33 \, kg \, l^{-1}$, but lipoproteins have a lower density. This can be used to separate lipoproteins from other classes of protein, or to subdivide the various classes of lipoproteins;
- net charge – proteins differ in the types and number of amino acids with ionisable groups in their side chains. The ionisation of these side chains is pH dependent, resulting in variation of net charge with pH (p. 313). This property is exploited in the techniques of electrophoresis (Chapter 46), isoelectric focusing (Chapter 47) and ion-exchange chromatography (Chapter 44);
- water solubility and surface hydrophobicity – these are exploited in salt fractionation (p. 373) and hydrophobic interaction chromatography (p. 301).

Determining the primary structure of a protein

The term 'primary structure' refers to the linear sequence of amino acid residues along the polypeptide: ultimately this determines the 3D shape of the molecule and hence its biological properties.

Amino acid analysis

Once a particular protein has been purified (Chapter 54), the first step in determining its primary structure is to hydrolyse the polypeptide (e.g. by treating with $6 \, mol \, l^{-1}$ HCl at $110 \, °C$ for 24–72 h) and then determine the constituent amino acids. This can be achieved by several techniques, including thin layer chromatography and high performance liquid chromatography (Chapter 44). Often a dedicated amino acid analyser is used for quantitative assays: a polystyrene resin-based cation exchange column is used to separate the amino acids on the basis of ion-exchange and hydrophobic interactions.

Sequence analysis

Having obtained the amino acid composition of the protein, the next step is to determine the order of the amino acid residues along the polypeptide chain. This may be achieved by:

1. Cleavage of the polypeptide at specific peptide bonds resulting in smaller fragments (peptides); e.g. using cyanogen bromide (CnBr), which cleaves peptide bonds formed by the carboxyl group of met, or by proteolytic enzymes, e.g. trypsin (cleaving after lys and arg residues) and chymotrypsin (cleaving after phe, tyr and trp).
2. Separation of the peptides, e.g. by column chromatography.
3. Determination of the sequence of each peptide by a process called Edman degradation. This involves the selective removal of the N-terminal amino acid by treating the fragments with phenyl isothiocyanate ($C_6H_5N{=}C{=}S$) followed by acid hydrolysis; the substituted phenylthiohydantoin formed can then be identified by chromatography. The process can be repeated as many as 50 times, releasing the N-terminal residue on each occasion, and allowing the sequence of each fragment to be established.

Purifying a protein – the practical procedures involved in the purification of a particular protein from a biological sample are considered in detail in Chapter 54.

Investigating the secondary and tertiary structure of a protein – computer-based molecular modelling programs can be used to predict the 3D conformation of a protein from information based on the primary structure (Chapter 11).

4. Matching of the sequenced, overlapping peptide fragments, to determine the overall sequence of amino acid residues in the original protein.

Text reference

Warburg, O and Christian, W. (1942) Isolierung und Kristallisation des Garungferments Enolase. *Biochemische Zeitschrift*, **310**, pp. 384–421.

Sources for further study

Dey, P.M., Harbourne, J.B. and Rogers, L.E. (1997) *Methods in Plant Biochemistry: Amino Acids, Proteins and Nucleic Acids*. Academic Press, New York.

Milo, F.R. and Loffredo, W.M. (1995) *Qualitative Tests for Amino Acids and Proteins*. Chemical Education Resources, Thomson, Cincinnati.

White, J.S. and White, D.C. (2002) *Proteins, Peptides and Amino Acids Sourcebook*. Humana Press, Totowa.

Study exercises

50.1 Test your knowledge of the basis of protein assays. Match up each of the following methods with the corresponding underlying reaction:
Method:
(a) Warburg–Christian;
(b) Bradford;
(c) Lowry (Folin–Ciocalteau);
(d) Biuret.
Reaction:
  (i) Coomassie Blue binding;
  (ii) Cupric ion–peptide bond interaction;
  (iii) Absorption of UV radiation by aromatic amino acids;
  (iv) A combination of the cupric ion–peptide bond reaction and the oxidation of tyrosine and tryptophan residues.

50.2 Determine the amount of amino acid in samples, using a 'standard curve' (see also study exercise 37.2 for an equivalent exercise for protein assay). The following data are for a set of calibration standards, measured using the ninhydrin method, which is non-linear at high amino acid concentrations.

Absorbance measurements for a series of amino acid standards (total assay volume 5 ml)

Amino acid concentration in assay tube ($\mu g\,ml^{-1}$)	Absorbance of standard (A_{570})
0.0	0.000
2.0	0.151
4.0	0.305
6.0	0.481
8.0	0.623
10.0	0.751
12.0	0.866
14.0	0.935
16.0	0.977
18.0	1.012
20.0	1.028

(a) Draw a calibration curve by hand using graph paper and estimate the concentration of amino acid in three different test samples giving the following A_{570} values:
(i)   0.341
(ii) 0.686
(iii) 0.969

(b) Assuming that these A_{570} values were obtained using the following dilutions and sample volumes in a total assay volume of 5 ml for all samples and standards alike, calculate the amino acid concentration of each of the three original samples, consisting of:
(i) $100\,\mu l$ of undiluted sample;
(ii) $50\,\mu l$ of a 10-fold dilution of sample;
(iii) $80\,\mu l$ of a 25-fold dilution of sample.
Give all answers in $mg\,ml^{-1}$, to 1 decimal place.

50.3 Determine the amino acid sequence of a polypeptide from cleavage fragment data. The following data represent the results for a polypeptide of unknown amino acid sequence, when a subsample of the polypeptide was digested to completion with trypsin while another subsample was cleaved with cyanogen bromide (CNBr). In both cases, four peptide fragments were produced. These peptide fragments produced were then subjected to Edman degradation and the following results were obtained for each peptide, in order of successive rounds of Edman degradation:

Tryptic digestion products:
fragment (i): val asn lys
fragment (ii): ala gly met ser arg
fragment (iii): trp phe met ala ala
fragment (iv): his gly met ala glu lys

CNBr cleavage products:
fragment (i): ala ala
fragment (ii): his gly met
fragment (iii): ser arg trp phe met
fragment (iv): ala glu lys val asn lys ala gly met

What is the sequence of the intact polypeptide?

51 Assaying lipids

Table 51.1 Some examples of fatty acids

No. of carbon atoms	Systematic name	Trivial name
Saturated fatty acids (no C=C bonds)		
12	*n*-Dodecanoic	Lauric
14	*n*-Tetradecanoic	Mystiric
16	*n*-Hexadecanoic	Palmitic
18	*n*-Octadecanoic	Stearic
20	*n*-Eicosanoic	Arachidic
22	*n*-Docosanoic	Behenic
Mono-unsaturated fatty acids (one C=C bond)		
12	*cis*-9-Dodecenoic	Lauroleic
14	*cis*-9-Tetradecenoic	Myristoleic
16	*cis*-9-Hexadecenoic	Palmitoleic
18	*cis*-9-Octadecenoic	Oleic
20	*cis*-9-Eicosenoic	Gadoleic
22	*cis*-9-Docosenoic	Erucic

Note: palmitic, stearic, palmitoleic and oleic acids are quantitatively the most common fatty acids in the majority of organisms. Major polyunsaturated fatty acids include linoleic acid (C_{18}, 2 double bonds), linolenic acid (C_{18}, three double bonds) and arachidonic acid (C_{20}, four double bonds).

Fig. 51.1 Example of a neutral lipid: the structure of a triacylglycerol. R = remainder of fatty acid.

The term 'lipid' is used to describe a broad group of compounds with a wide variety of chemical structures, physical properties and biological functions. Lipids in biological systems are often combined with either proteins (e.g. in lipoproteins) or polysaccharides (e.g. in lipopolysaccharides). This chapter can provide only a brief outline of the techniques used in lipid analysis (for further details, see Gunstone *et al.*, 1994).

KEY POINT The defining feature of lipids is their relative insolubility in water: consequently, they are extracted from biological material using organic solvents, e.g. acetone, ether and chloroform. Because of their diversity and complexity, they are often referred to by more than one name, and the various types of non-systematic names can be confusing.

Biological lipids are often subdivided into two main types, each of which contains fatty acids as a major structural component:

Simple or neutral lipids

These are esters of fatty acids and an alcohol (e.g. Fig. 51.1). Fatty acids are straight-chain carboxylic acids, typically with an even number of carbon atoms and chain lengths of C_{12}–C_{22}, which may be saturated or unsaturated (Table 51.1). The greater the chain length and the fewer the number of double bonds, the higher the melting point, making most long chain saturated fatty acids solids at room temperature. Glycerol is the most common alcohol found in simple lipids, though higher M_r alcohols occur in waxes and cyclic alcohols (sterols, e.g. cholesterol) occur in bile acids, steroid hormones and vitamins (e.g. vitamin K). While glycerol is a liquid at room temperature, cholesterol remains solid up to 150 °C.

Neutral fats (triglycerides or triacylglycerol) are esters of fatty acids and glycerol, as shown in Fig. 51.1. Many animal triglycerides ('fats') contain mainly saturated fatty acids and are solids at room temperature, while plant triglycerides ('oils') often have shorter chain lengths and a greater degree of unsaturation and are liquids at room temperature. Waxes are esters of fatty acids with alcohols of higher M_r than glycerol. The major biological functions of simple lipids include (i) energy storage, e.g. oils in plant seeds, (ii) insulation, e.g. subcutaneous fat deposits in whales, and (iii) waterproofing, e.g. waxes in the cuticles of plant leaves.

Complex, compound or conjugated lipids

These are acyl esters of glycerol, or the amino alcohol sphingosine, that also include a hydrophilic group (e.g. a phosphoryl or carbohydrate group). They are often described in terms of this hydrophilic group, e.g. phospholipids contain a phosphoryl group while glycolipids contain a carbohydrate group.

KEY POINT An important feature of complex lipids is their amphipathic nature, i.e. each molecule has a polar (hydrophilic) and a nonpolar (hydrophobic) region.

The two major types of complex lipid are:

1. Phospholipids – the most common types (phosphoglycerides) are based on phosphatidic acid, with two fatty acids esterified to glycerol. Most phospholipids also contain an amino alcohol or a similar group, attached to the phosphoryl group. The principal phospholipid classes are: (i) phosphatidyl cholines (or lecithins), which form stable emulsions with water and dissolve completely on addition of bile salts. These are insoluble in acetone, a feature that enables lecithins to be separated from most other lipids; (ii) phosphatidyl ethanolamines (or cephalins) – unlike lecithins, they are insoluble in ethanol and methanol; (iii) phosphatidyl serine; (iv) phosphatidyl inositol; and (v) plasmalogens.

2. Sphingolipids – these incorporate the amino dialcohol, sphingosine, rather than glycerol. Fatty acids are linked to sphingosine via an amide bond to form ceramides, which include: (i) cerebrosides (glyco-sphingolipids); (ii) sulphatides (sulphated cerebrosides); (iii) gangliosides (glycosphingolipids containing sialic acid residues); and (iv) phospho-sphingolipids, including sphingomyelins, which are esters of a ceramide and phosphoryl choline.

Complex lipids have important roles in biological membranes: phospholipids are major structural components while sphingolipids are involved in cell–cell recognition and similar membrane features, e.g. glycosphingolipids are determinants of human ABO blood groups.

Extraction and analysis of lipids

Solvent extraction

Lipid extraction is carried out in a suitable organic solvent, using a homogeniser to disrupt cell and tissue structure (Chapter 36). There are two possible approaches:

1. Total extraction of all lipids, followed by separation of the different lipid classes. A commonly used solvent mixture is methanol : chloroform : water (2 : 1 : 0.5, v/v/v). Adding an equal volume of aqueous 1% w/v NaCl solution to the extract results in the formation of two layers: the lipids are present in the lower layer, while the upper aqueous layer contains other biomolecules (e.g. proteins). Hexane : isopropanol (3 : 2, v/v) can be used instead of chloroform : methanol, since it is less toxic and it dissolves very little non-lipid material.

2. Selective lipid extraction. Neutral lipids, e.g. within storage tissue, can be extracted by relatively non-polar solvents including hexane, diethyl ether and chloroform. Extraction of membrane lipids (e.g. phospholipids) requires disruption of the membrane using more polar solvents (e.g. methanol or ethanol), with selective precipitation by adding cold, dry acetone. Glycolipids can be extracted using acetone.

The principal disadvantages of solvent extraction methods include: (i) the requirement for large volumes of potentially hazardous solvents; and (ii) the possible formation of an emulsion, with incomplete extraction of component lipids.

Adsorption chromatography

Silica gel, octadecylsilane-bonded silica or ion-exchange resins can be used to bind solvent-extracted lipids by a combination of polar, ionic and van der Waals forces. In practice, a glass column is packed with a slurry of

Safe working with solvents – *chloroform and benzene must be used with care, due to their high toxicity: they are often replaced by dichloromethane and toluene respectively. All mixing and pouring steps should be carried out in a spark-free fume cupboard. Note that ethers may form explosive peroxides on prolonged storage. Lipid extracts extracted in flammable solvents must be stored in a spark-proof refrigerator, not in routine lab fridges.*

Definition

Emulsion – a colloidal mixture where one liquid is dispersed (but not dissolved) in another liquid, e.g. lipids often aggregate to form micelles in aqueous solutions.

adsorbent in an appropriate organic solvent, and the lipid extract (dissolved in the same solvent) is applied to the top of the column. Lipids can then be selectively eluted; a mixture can be broadly separated into neutral lipids, glycolipids and phospholipids using solvents of increasing polarity, e.g. chloroform → acetone → methanol. It is possible to further separate the lipid subfractions on silica gel columns, as follows:

- Neutral lipids can be separated and eluted using hexane containing increasing proportions of diethyl ether (0 → 100% v/v) in the order: hydrocarbons, cholesterol esters, triacylglycerols, free fatty acids, cholesterol, diacylglycerols, then monoacylglycerols.
- Glycolipids and sulpholipids can be separated by first eluting the glycolipids with chloroform : acetone (1 : 1 v/v), then using acetone to elute the sulpholipids.
- Phospholipids can be eluted using chloroform containing increasing proportions of methanol (5% → 50% v/v) in the order: phosphatidic acid, phosphatidyl ethanolamine, phosphatidyl serine, phosphatidyl choline, phosphatidyl inositol, sphingomyelin.

Thin layer chromatography (TLC) of lipids

This can be used to separate lipid mixtures into their constituents, or to quantify particular lipids, as part of an analytical procedure. The principle of the technique is described in Chapter 44.

Silica gel G60 is the most frequently used stationary phase, acting as a polar absorbent. When the separation is carried out with a non-polar mobile phase, non-polar lipids will migrate more rapidly (i.e. they will have high R_F values, p. 296), while polar lipids will migrate more slowly. By increasing the polarity of the solvent, the R_F values of the polar lipids can be increased. Your choice of solvent will depend on the lipids in the extract:

- For a broad range of neutral lipids, a typical solvent system is hexane : diethyl ether : glacial acetic acid at 80 : 20 : 2 (v/v/v), separating in the following order of decreasing R_F: steryl esters, wax esters, fatty acids, methyl esters, triacylglycerols, fatty acids, fatty alcohols, sterols, 1,2-diacylglycerols, monoacylglycerols.
- For polar lipids, silica gel H is preferred, as silica gel G prevents the separation of acidic phospholipids. Most solvent systems for polar lipids are based on chloroform : methanol : water, e.g. at 65 : 25 : 4 (v/v/v). In this system, the relative order of migration is: monogalactosyldiacylglycerol, cerebrosides, phosphatidic acid, cardiolipin, lysophosphatidyl ethanol-amine, phosphatidyl ethanolamine and digalactosyldiacylglycerol, sulphatides, phosphatidyl choline, phosphatidyl inositol, sphingomyelin and phosphatidyl serine.

KEY POINT No single solvent system will completely separate all lipid components in a single TLC procedure. However, 2D TLC may separate up to 200 individual constituents from a sample.

Lipids can also be separated by reversed-phase TLC (RP-TLC), where the silica gel is made non-polar (e.g. by silanisation), and highly polar solvents are used as the mobile phase: here, the polar lipids will have the highest R_F values and the non-polar lipids the lowest R_F values. Lipids separated by TLC can be located by staining. Several stains are non-specific, enabling almost all types of lipid to be visualised, while others will locate particular lipid classes. Staining can be carried out by immersion of the TLC plate in the stain, or by spraying. Non-specific staining methods include:

- Spraying with iodine solution (e.g. 1–3% w/v in chloroform) – most lipids appear as brown spots on a yellow background, though glycolipids stain weakly by this method.
- Treatment with a strong oxidising agent followed by charring (e.g. spray with 5% v/v sulphuric acid in ethanol, followed by heating in an oven at 180 °C for 30–60 min) – lipids appear as black deposits; the detection limit is 1–2 μg. Scanning densitometry (Chapter 45) can provide quantitative information.
- Fluorescent stains (e.g. the widely used 2',7'-dichlorofluorescein, DCF, at 0.1–0.2% w/v in ethanol). Under UV, lipids appear as bright yellow spots on a yellow–green background; the limit of detection is 5 μg. Other fluorescent stains such as 1-anilo-8-naphthalene sulphonate (ANS, 0.1% w/v in water) can detect ng quantities of lipid.

Quantitative assay of lipids and their components

While TLC can be used to quantify particular lipids, it is more common to assay the compounds released on hydrolysis of simple or complex lipids, namely the alcohols, fatty acids or other components, rather than the native lipid. Alkali hydrolysis of lipids containing fatty acids results in the formation of a soap (i.e. saponification): the incubation of tripalmitin with KOH yields potassium palmitate and glycerol. Acid hydrolysis of triacylglycerols releases 'free' fatty acids and glycerol.

Basic information about the relative size of the fatty acid component of oils and fats is given by the saponification value, determined by titration against 0.8 mol l^{-1} KOH; the lower the saponification value, the higher the M_r of the fatty acids. The degree of unsaturation of the fatty acids is given by the iodine number; the higher the iodine number, the greater the content of unsaturated fatty acids.

To obtain the iodine number for a particular fat, the free iodine remaining after reaction is titrated against 0.1 mol l^{-1} sodium thiosulphate ($Na_2S_2O_3$) using a trace amount of starch as an indicator, giving a titration volume for the test solution, V_t. A blank containing no fat is also titrated, to establish the volume of sodium thiosulphate required to titrate the initial free iodine, V_o. This allows the amount of iodine that reacts with the fat to be calculated according to the formula:

$$\text{iodine number (in g)} = \frac{1.27(V_0 - V_t)}{m} \qquad [51.1]$$

where m is the mass of test fat (in g), and V_o and V_t are expressed in ml.

Measurement of glycerol content

Glycerolipids can be quantified by measuring the glycerol released on hydrolysis. A widely used method involves a coupled enzyme assay

---

Definitions

Saponification value – the amount of KOH (in mg) required to completely saponify 1 g of fat. Typically within the range 150–300.

Iodine number – the amount of iodine (g) absorbed by 100 g of fat, due to the reaction of iodine with C=C bonds within the fat. Typically within the range 30–200.

(p. 379), with the following reactions:

$$\text{triacylglycerol} \xrightarrow{\textit{lipase}} \text{glycerol} + \text{fatty acids} \qquad [51.2]$$

$$\text{glycerol} + \text{ATP} \underset{\textit{glycerol kinase, Mg}^{2+}}{\rightleftharpoons} \text{glycerol-3-phosphate} + \text{ADP} \qquad [51.3]$$

$$\text{ADP} + \text{phosphoenolpyruvate} \underset{\textit{pyruvate kinase}}{\rightleftharpoons} \text{ATP} + \text{pyruvate} \qquad [51.4]$$

$$\text{pyruvate} + \text{NADH} + \text{H}^+ \underset{\textit{lactate dehydrogenase}}{\rightleftharpoons} \text{lactate} + \text{NAD}^+ \qquad [51.5]$$

The glycerol concentration is determined by measuring the decrease in absorbance of NADH at 340 nm, compared to that of a blank with no added lipase. Details of the conversion of A_{340} to [NADH] are given on p. 273.

Measurement of cholesterol content

Cholesterol in cholesterol esters can be estimated after hydrolysis to free cholesterol using cholesterol esterase. The subsequent assay is as follows:

$$\text{cholesterol} + \text{O}_2 \xrightarrow{\textit{cholesterol oxidase}} \text{cholest-4-en-3-one} + \text{H}_2\text{O}_2 \qquad [51.6]$$

The hydrogen peroxide produced as a result of the action of cholesterol oxidase can be measured amperometrically (p. 158) or colorimetrically, via the peroxidase-catalysed reaction:

$$2\text{H}_2\text{O}_2 + \text{phenol} + \text{4-aminoantipyrene} \xrightarrow{\textit{peroxidase}} \text{quinoneimine} + 4\text{H}_2\text{O} \quad [51.7]$$

This is the basis of many commercially available cholesterol testing kits. An alternative approach is to measure the cholest-4-en-3-one directly, via its absorbance maximum at 240 nm.

Gas chromatography (GC) of lipids and lipid components

This technique is used for the quantitative and qualitative analysis of a broad range of lipids. Volatile lipids may be analysed without modification, while non-volatile lipids must first be converted to a more volatile form, either by degradation (e.g. phospholipids), or derivatisation (p. 299). The most effective GC columns are support-coated open tubular (SCOT) capillary columns, with a thin film (0.1–10 μm) of the stationary phase coated onto the internal wall (p. 298). The choice of stationary phase depends on the components to be separated, e.g. some non-polar stationary phases cannot resolve methyl esters of saturated and monounsaturated fatty acids. Many stationary phases are based on silicone greases or polysiloxane, ranging from the non-polar dimethyl polysiloxanes (e.g. OV-101) to the polar trifluoropropyl methyl polysiloxanes (e.g. OV-210). Other polar stationary phases are based on polyethylene glycol (e.g. Carbowax 20M).

Text reference

Gunstone, F.D., Harwood, J.L. and Padley, F.B. (1994) *The Lipid Handbook*. CRC Press, Boca Raton.

Example Fatty acids are derivatised to their methyl esters by boiling for 2–3 min with boron tetrafluoride (BF$_3$) solution (14% w/v in methanol), prior to GC analysis, to increase their volatility and stability in the gas phase. The separated components are normally detected by flame ionisation (p. 308).

Sources for further study

Anon. *Cyberlipid Center Homepage*. Available: http://www.cyberlipid.org
Last accessed 08/01/03.

Gunstone, F.D. and Padley, F.B. (1997) *Lipid Technologies and Applications*. Marcel Dekker, New York.

Gurr, M.I., Harwood, J.L. and Frayn, K.N. (2002) *Lipid Biochemistry*. Blackwell, Oxford.

Hemming, F.W., Hawthorne, J.N. and White, D.A. (1996) *Lipid Analysis*. Bios, Cambridge.

Study exercises

51.1 Consider how to avoid oxidative rancidity. What practical steps could you take to avoid lipid oxidation during extraction and analysis?

51.2 Use the Web to discover more about lipid structure and analysis. Visit the Cyberlipid Center website (at http://www.cyberlipid.org/index.htm), a resource giving details of a wide range of lipid structures, including triglycerides, phospholipids and glycolipids: (a) identify the main lipid components of beeswax and (b) suggest which separation methods might be appropriate for the analysis of these components.

51.3 Derive the equation for calculation of the iodine number of a lipid. Given that the following reactions (i)–(iii) are involved in the volumetric analysis for calculating the iodine number of a lipid, show how Eqn 51.1 is derived:
(i) $-CH=CH- + ICl \rightarrow -(I)CH-CH(Cl)-$
(ii) $ICl + KI \rightarrow HCl + I_2$
(iii) $I_2 + 2Na_2S_2O_3 \rightarrow 2NaI + Na_2S_4O_6$

51.4 Interpret a GC chromatogram for a lipid mixture. The chromatogram shown in the figure represents a GC analysis of triacylglycerols in butter fat. There are 15 peaks, corresponding to lipids with even numbers of acyl carbon atoms between 26 and 54. How would you expect the lipids of different hydrocarbon lengths to be associated with the retention times of the different peaks? (Give a brief explanation of the reasoning underlying your expectation.)

52 Assaying carbohydrates

These are compounds with a formula based on $C_x(H_2O)_x$. They play a key role in energy metabolism, and are essential constituents of cell walls and membranes. They may exist individually, or as heteropolymers, e.g. linked to protein in glycoproteins (where carbohydrates form the minor component), or proteoglycans (where they form the major component).

Fig. 52.1 Ring and straight chain forms of glucose. Note that β-D-glucose has H and OH groups reversed at C-1 in the pyranose form.

> **KEY POINT** The identification and quantitative analysis of carbohydrates in biological samples can be difficult, due to structural and physicochemical similarities between related compounds. Several routine analytical methods cannot distinguish between isomeric forms of a particular carbohydrate.

Monosaccharides

The simplest carbohydrates are the monosaccharide sugars, which are polyhydroxy aldehydes and polyhydroxy ketones (so-called aldoses and ketoses), typically with three to seven carbon atoms per molecule. The common names end with the suffix '-ose', e.g. glucose (Fig. 52.1), which contains six carbon atoms and is a hexose. The simplest aldose is the three-carbon compound (triose) glyceraldehyde (Fig. 52.2a), and the other aldoses can be considered to be derived from glyceraldehyde by the addition of successive secondary alcohol groups (H–C–OH). In a similar manner, all ketoses can be considered to be structurally related to the triose dihydroxyacetone (Fig. 52.2b).

Fig. 52.2 Structure of (a) glyceraldehyde and (b) dihydroxyacetone.

Monosaccharides are assigned as D or L isomers according to a convention based on D-glyceraldehyde as the reference compound, with the carbon atoms numbered from the end of the chain containing the reactive group. Most of the carbohydrates found in biological systems are D isomers. While trioses and tetroses exist in linear form, pentoses and larger monosaccharides can be represented either as a linear structure (Fischer form) or as a ring structure (Haworth form), as in Fig. 52.1. The cyclic structure results from the reaction of the carbonyl group (aldehyde or ketone) at one end of the molecule with a hydroxyl group at the other end of the chain, forming a hemiacetal or hemiketal, as shown for glucose (Fig. 52.1) and fructose (Fig. 52.3).

The formation of a hemiacetal or hemiketal creates another asymmetric carbon atom, so that two ring forms exist – one with the –OH group on this asymmetric carbon positioned below the plane of the ring (α) and another with the –OH group above the plane of the ring (β). These different isomeric forms are called anomers and are particularly difficult to separate by chromatographic methods. The six-membered ring structure shown for glucose has a structure similar to that of pyran and is termed glucopyranose. A few monosaccharides have a five-membered ring structure similar to that of furan, e.g. fructofuranose.

While the open chain form is present in very small amounts in aqueous solution it has a very reactive carbonyl group which is responsible for the reducing properties of sugars: several analytical methods are based on this feature (see p. 360).

Fig. 52.3 Ring and straight chain forms of fructose. Note that β-D-fructose has OH and CH$_2$OH groups reversed at C-2 in the furanose form.

Fig. 52.4 Formation of a glycosidic link (α 1, 4) in the disaccharide maltose.

Fig. 52.5 The repeating structure of cellulose ($\beta 1 \rightarrow 4$ glycosidic links) $n \approx 5000$.

Glycosides

These are formed when a covalent bond, or glycosidic link, is created between the hemiacetal or hemiketal group of a carbohydrate (e.g. a monosaccharide) and the hydroxyl group of a second compound (e.g. a polyhydroxy alcohol, or another monosaccharide). If the sugars are not joined *via* their reactive groups, they will still show reducing properties, as in the disaccharide maltose (Fig. 52.4). In contrast, sucrose is a non-reducing disaccharide, since the hemiacetal and hemiketal groups of glucose and fructose are involved in the formation of the glycosidic link.

Polymeric carbohydrates have important biological roles – oligosaccharides contain up to 10 sugars, while polysaccharides are larger polymers with M_r of up to several million, e.g. glycogen, amylopectin, cellulose. The structure of polysaccharides is not fully defined, in contrast to proteins (Chapter 50) and nucleic acids (Chapter 53). Polysaccharide structure is the result of the separate actions of a number of biosynthetic enzymes, producing a range of molecules that may vary in the number of monosaccharide residues and the types of glycosidic bond. The terminology used to describe the glycosidic links in such compounds denotes the anomer involved (α or β) and the C atoms involved in the link, e.g. $\alpha 1 \rightarrow 4$ in maltose (Fig. 52.4), $\beta 1 \rightarrow 4$ in cellulose (Fig. 52.5).

Extraction and analysis of carbohydrates

While most low M_r carbohydrates are soluble in water, ethanol : water (80% v/v) is more often used, since polysaccharides and other biological macromolecules are insoluble in aqueous ethanol. In contrast, poly-saccharides are more diverse, and the isolation procedures vary greatly, e.g. boiling water, mild acid or mild alkali can be used to solubilise storage polysaccharides, e.g. starch, while more vigorous treatment is required for structural polysaccharides, e.g. 24% w/v KOH for cellulose. Among the techniques used to purify extracted polysaccharides are gel permeation chromatography (p. 300) and ultracentrifugation (p. 291).

Identification and quantification of carbohydrates

This can be achieved by a variety of procedures, including:

Chemical methods   Several monosaccharide assay methods are based on the reductive capacity of the aldehyde or ketone groups (Table 52.1). A widely used method for quantitative analysis is that based on reduction of 3,5-dinitrosalicylate. This method is also suitable for glycosides, provided the reducing carbonyl groups are not involved in the glycosidic links. Certain polysaccharides react with iodine in acid solution to form coloured complexes: starch gives a blue colour, while glycogen gives a red–brown colour. The anthrone method (typically using $0.1\,\mathrm{g\,l^{-1}}$ anthrone in H_2SO_4, at $100\,°C$ for $10\,\mathrm{min}$, then assayed at $630\,\mathrm{nm}$) is an alternative assay for estimating total carbohydrate content. Careful choice of calibration standards is required for quantitative work – try to use a standard that matches the likely composition of the samples. While such chemical methods can give a general indication of the relative amount of carbohydrate in a sample, they can provide little useful information on the types of carbohydrate present.

Enzymatic methods   These offer a higher degree of specificity in monosaccharide assay, and may allow differentiation between the

Table 52.1 Methods for carbohydrate analysis

Method	Principle	Comments
Chemical assay		
Benedict's test (and Fehling's test)	Reduction of Cu^{2+} to Cu^+ in presence of reducing sugar; alkaline solution plus heat results in formation of Cu_2O; solution turns from blue, through yellow, to red.	Usually presence/absence test; quantitative assay involves measurement of Cu_2O formed.
Dinitrosalicylate (DNS)	Reduction of DNS (yellow) to orange-red derivative; alkaline solution plus heat ($100\,°C$, $10\,min$).	Quantitative: read at $540\,nm$.
Enzymatic assay		
Glucose oxidase (coupled reaction)	$$\beta\text{-D-glucose} + O_2 \xrightarrow{\quad glucose\ oxidase \quad} \text{gluconic acid} + H_2O_2$$ $$H_2O_2 + \text{reduced dye} \xrightarrow{\quad peroxidase \quad} H_2O + \text{oxidised dye}$$	Mutarotation allows reaction to reach completion; hydrogen peroxide formed may be measured using peroxidase; ABTS[1] is a suitable dye. Assay at $437\,nm$.

[1]ABTS = 2,2'-azino-di-[3-ethylbenzthiazoline]-6-sulphonate.

various stereoisomeric and anomeric forms. The glucose-specific method based on glucose oxidase shown in Table 52.1 also forms the basis of the glucose electrode (see Chapter 48). Hydrogen peroxide may be assayed using peroxidase and a suitable chromogenic substrate, as shown, or by electrochemical methods, e.g. using an amperometric sensor. Alternatively, the consumption of oxygen in the initial reaction can be measured using an oxygen electrode (p. 334). Glycosidases can be used to hydrolyse specific disaccharides or polysaccharides into their constituent monosaccharides, which can then be identified and quantified, e.g. α-glucosidase, which hydrolyses the $\alpha(1 \rightarrow 4)$ linkage between the glucose residues in maltose (Fig. 52.4). However, you should note that it is rare for such enzymes to show absolute specificity for a particular substrate, so you should be alert to the possibility of interference due to related compounds in the sample, or to impurities in the enzyme preparation.

Measuring carbohydrate migration in TLC systems – the distance migrated by glucose is taken as a reference ($R_F = 100$), and the migration of other carbohydrates is given as the R_G value, where R_G is:

$$\frac{distance\ moved\ by\ carbohydrate}{distance\ moved\ by\ glucose} \times 100$$

Chromatographic methods Traditional methods include paper and thin layer chromatographic procedures. Suitable supports for TLC include microcrystalline cellulose (in which the sugars partition between the mobile phase and the cellulose-bound water complex) and silica gel. A wide range of traditional solvent systems can be used (Stahl, 1965, gives details) and your choice of mobile phase will depend upon the expected composition of the mixture, e.g. cellulose with ethyl acetate : pyridine : water ($100 : 35 : 25$ v/v/v) gives a good separation of pentoses and hexoses, and will resolve glucose and galactose, as well as some disaccharides. Staining methods usually exploit the reducing properties of carbohydrates. Of the high resolution techniques, HPLC (p. 297) is the preferred method for the analysis of simple monosaccharide mixtures, and for oligosaccharide analysis and purification. Ion-exchange columns are often used for these purposes, with refractive index, or electrochemical, detection of separated components (Chapter 44). GC is more suitable for complex monosaccharide mixtures, and can analyse subnanomolar amounts of carbohydrates and their derivatives, e.g. polyols, including glycerol (p. 353). However, a preliminary step is necessary to produce volatile derivatives of the carbohydrates in the mixture, e.g. methylation or, more often, trimethylsilation (adding hexamethyldisilazane and trimethylchlorosilane at 2 : 1 v/v at room temperature rapidly produces trimethylsilyl ethers – TMS derivatives). Efficient separations can be obtained with a non-polar stationary phase, e.g. methylpolysiloxy gum (OV-1): the use of SCOT columns (p. 357) can enable over 30 components to be resolved. A disadvantage of GC methods is that the carbohydrates are first converted to a derivative form, then quantified by destructive means, preventing further analysis.

Capillary electrophoresis (Chapter 47) is a powerful technique for the separation of carbohydrates, though it is usual to modify uncharged carbohydrates by reductive amination to form primary amines to allow their separation within the capillary.

Characterisation of polysaccharides

Polysaccharides are characterised according to the relative proportions of the constituent sugar residues, the various types of glycosidic links and the M_r. To investigate a given type of polysaccharide, its glycosidic links must be hydrolysed (e.g. by heating with concentrated HCl at 60 °C for 30 min), followed by separation, identification and quantification of the individual components. The position of glycosidic linkages can be determined by methylation of all free hydroxyl groups of the polysaccharide followed by complete hydrolysis to give a mixture of partially methylated monosaccharides. These are then reduced to alditols, and acetylated. The partially methylated alditol acetates can be identified by GC-mass spectrometry (p. 286), allowing the types of glycosidic links to be deduced from the positions of the acetylated groups. The α and β configuration of the glycosidic linkages can be determined by enzymic assay or by NMR spectroscopy (p. 282).

Lignins are a specialised class of structural polymer, found in some plant tissues and composed mainly of residues of the amino acids phenylalanine and tyrosine (p. 347) together with some carbohydrate constituents. In contrast to polysaccharides, lignins are difficult to characterise as they are extremely resistant to hydrolysis.

Text reference and sources for further study

Anon. *GenomeWeb Carbohydrate Analysis Homepage*. Available: http://www.cbi.pku.edu.cn/mirror/GenomeWeb/carbohydrate-anal.html Last accessed 08/01/03.
[Focused towards carbohydrates in glycoproteins.]

Chaplin, M.F. and Kennedy, J.F. (1994) *Carbohydrate Analysis: A Practical Approach*. Oxford University Press, Oxford.

Davis, B.G. and Fairbanks, A.J. (2002) *Carbohydrate Chemistry*. Oxford University Press, Oxford.
[A primer on carbohydrate chemistry.]

Lindhorst, T.K. (2000) *Essentials of Carbohydrate Chemistry and Biochemistry*. VCH, Berlin.

Robyt, J.F. (1998) *Essentials of Carbohydrate Chemistry*. Springer-Verlag, Berlin.

Stahl, E. (1965) *Thin Layer Chromatography – a Laboratory Handbook*. Springer, Berlin.

Study exercises

52.1 Check your understanding of the terminology of carbohydrate structure. For each of the following terms (i) provide a definition and (ii) give an example of a representative compound:
(a) aldose;
(b) pentose;
(c) hemiacetal;
(d) pyranoside;
(e) β anomer.

52.2 Identify sugars by thin layer chromatography (TLC). A typical TLC separation of sugars on silica gel is shown in the figure below.
(a) Identify the sugars present in the hydrolysed raffinose sample. Check the structure of raffinose, to see whether your findings are consistent with the monosaccharide constituents.
(b) If the relative frontal mobility of unhydrolysed raffinose relative to glucose (R_G, Chapter 44) is known to be 0.34, and the distance migrated by glucose is 35 mm, how far (in mm) would you expect the raffinose to have migrated?

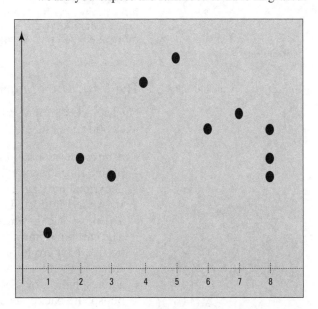

Fig. SE52.1 Thin-layer chromatographic separation of sugars: lane 1, lactose; lane 2, glucose; lane 3, galactose; lane 4, xylose; lane 5, ribose; lane 6, fructose; lane 7, arabinose; lane 8, hydrolyzed raffinose (dotted line indicates origin and arrow indicates direction of solvent flow).

52.3 Consider the operating principles underlying chemical methods for quantitative assay of carbohydrates. Why is the dinitrosalicylate (DNS) method unsuitable for the assay of the disaccharide sucrose, yet it is suitable for measuring its constituent monosaccharides, i.e. glucose and fructose? Is DNS unsuitable for all disaccharides?

Fig. 53.1   Nitrogenous bases in nucleic acids.

Nucleic acids are nitrogen-containing compounds of high M_r, often found within nucleic acid–protein (nucleoprotein) complexes in cells. The two main groups of nucleic acids are:

1. Deoxyribonucleic acid (DNA) – found in chromosomes and the principal molecule responsible for the storage and transfer of genetic information (Chapter 58).
2. Ribonucleic acid (RNA) – involved with the DNA-directed synthesis of proteins in cells. Three principal types of RNA exist: messenger RNA (mRNA), ribosomal RNA (rRNA) and transfer RNA (tRNA). In some viruses, RNA acts as the genetic material. In eukaryotes, mRNA molecules initially synthesised in the nucleus from genomic DNA (nascent mRNA) will contain several sequences – called introns – that are not transcribed into protein. These are successively excised in the nucleus, leaving only coding sequences (exons) in the mRNA that migrates to the cytoplasm, to be translated at the ribosome.

> **KEY POINT**   Nucleic acids are important in the transmission of information within cells, and one of the most important aspects of nucleic acid analysis is to 'decipher' the coded information within these molecules (see also Chapters 11 and 60).

The structure of nucleic acids

Nucleic acids are polymers of nucleotides (polynucleotides), where each nucleotide consists of:

- a nitrogenous base, of which there are five main types. Two have a purine ring structure, i.e. adenine (A) and guanine (G), and three have a pyrimidine ring, i.e. thymine (T), uracil (U) and cytosine (C), as shown in Fig. 53.1. Their carbon atoms are numbered C-1, C-2, etc;
- a pentose sugar, which is ribose in RNA and deoxyribose in DNA. The carbon atoms are denoted as C-1', C-2', etc. and deoxyribose has no hydroxyl group on C-2' (Fig. 53.2). The C-1' of the sugar is linked either to the N-9 of a purine or the N-1 of a pyrimidine;
- a phosphate group, which links with the sugars to form the sugar–phosphate backbone of the polynucleotide chain.

A compound with sugar and base only is called a nucleoside (Fig. 53.2) and the specific names given to the various nucleosides and nucleotides are listed in Table 53.1. The individual nucleotides within nucleic acids are linked by phosphodiester bonds between the 3' and 5' positions of the sugars (Fig. 53.3).

> **KEY POINT**   RNA and DNA differ both in the nature of the pentose sugar residue, and in their base composition: both types contain adenine, guanine and cytosine, but RNA contains uracil while DNA contains thymine.

Fig. 53.2   A nucleoside triphosphate – deoxyadenosine 5' triphosphate (dATP).

Table 53.1 Nomenclature of nucleosides and nucleotides

Base	Nucleoside	Nucleotide
Adenine	Adenosine	Adenylic acid
Guanine	Guanosine	Guanylic acid
Uracil[1]	Uridine	Uridylic acid
Cytosine	Cytidine	Cytidylic acid
Thymine[2]	Thymidine	Thymidylic acid

[1] In DNA.
[2] In RNA.

Minimising damage to chromosomes – chromosomes vary in size from 0.3 to 200 megabase pairs (Mb), so some breaks in DNA inevitably occur during manipulation. Shear effects can be minimised by using wide-mouthed pipettes, gentle mixing, by avoiding rotamixing, and by precipitating DNA with ethanol at $-20\,^\circ$C.

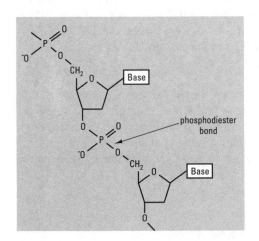

Fig. 53.3 Linkage of nucleotides in nucleic acids.

Working with precipitated DNA – this can be spooled from solution by winding it around a glass rod.

Differences also exist in the conformation of the two types of nucleic acid. DNA typically exists as two interwoven helical polynucleotide chains, with their structure stabilised by hydrogen bonds between matching base pairs on the adjacent strands: A always pairs with T (two hydrogen bonds), and G with C (three hydrogen bonds). This complementarity is important since it stabilises the DNA duplex (double helix) and provides the basis for replication and transcription (Chapter 60). While most double stranded (ds) DNA molecules are in this form, i.e. as a double helix, some viral DNA is single stranded (ss). Intact DNA molecules are very large indeed, with high M_r values (e.g. 10^9). In the main, RNA is single stranded and in the form of a gentle right-handed helix stabilised by base-stacking interactions, although some sections of RNA (i.e. tRNA) have regions of self-complementarity, leading to base pairing. Typical values for M_r of RNA range from 10^4 for tRNA to 10^6 for other types.

Extraction and purification of nucleic acids

The types of nucleic acid most commonly isolated are chromosomal DNA, plasmid DNA and mRNA. Irrespective of the source, extraction and purification involve the following stages, in sequence:

- disruption of cells to release their contents;
- removal of non-nucleic acid components (e.g. protein), leaving DNA and/or RNA;
- concentration of the remaining nucleic acids.

DNA isolation procedures

Specific details for the preparation of plasmid DNA from bacterial cells are given in Chapter 62. For other sources of DNA, such as mammalian tissue or plant material, the following steps are required:

1. Homogenisation – tissues can be disrupted by the methods described in detail in Chapter 36, e.g. by lysis in a buffered solution containing the detergent sodium dodecyl sulphate (SDS) or Triton X-100.
2. Enzymic removal of protein and RNA – using proteinase (e.g. proteinase K at $0.1\,\mathrm{mg\,ml^{-1}}$) and ribonuclease (typically at $0.1\,\mu\mathrm{g\,ml^{-1}}$) for 1–2 h.
3. Phenol–chloroform extraction – to remove any remaining traces of contaminating protein.
4. Precipitation of nucleic acids – usually by adding twice the volume of ethanol.
5. Solubilisation in an appropriate volume of buffer (pH 7.5) – ribonuclease is often added to remove any traces of contaminating RNA.

Density gradient centrifugation (p. 291) is an alternative approach to the separation of DNA from contaminating RNA, as described below.

RNA isolation procedures

Each mammalian cell contains about 10 pg of RNA, made up of rRNA (80–85%), tRNA (10–15%) and mRNA (1–5%). While rRNA and tRNA components are of discrete sizes, mRNA is heterogeneous and varies in length from several hundred to several thousand nucleotides.

Avoiding RNase degradation of RNA – endogenous RNases can be inhibited by including diethyl pyrocarbonate (DEP) (at 0.1% v/v g ml^{-1}) in solutions used for RNA extraction.

KEY POINT RNA is more difficult to purify than DNA, partly because of degradation during the extraction process due to the action of contaminating ribonucleases, and partly because the rigorous treatment required to dissociate the RNA from protein in ribosomes may fragment the polyribonucleotide strands.

RNA can be prepared either from the cytoplasm of cells (to give mainly rRNA, tRNA and fully processed mRNA), or from whole cells, in which case nascent mRNA from the nucleus will also be present (p. 364):

- Preparation of cytoplasmic RNA involves lysis of cells or protoplasts with a hypotonic buffer, leaving the nuclei intact. Cell debris and nuclei are then removed by centrifugation (Chapter 43), and sodium dodecyl sulphate (SDS) is added to the supernatant (the cytoplasmic fraction) to inhibit ribonuclease. Proteinase K can be added to release rRNA from ribosomes. Phenol–chloroform extraction removes contaminating proteins, as for DNA preparation (p. 443), and the RNA present in the aqueous phase can then be precipitated by addition of twice the volume of ethanol.

- Preparation of whole-cell RNA requires more vigorous cell lysis, e.g. with a solution containing $6 \, \text{mol} \, l^{-1}$ guanidinium chloride and 2-mercaptoethanol: this effectively denatures any ribonuclease present. Caesium chloride is added to the extract to give a final concentration of $2.4 \, \text{mol} \, l^{-1}$, and the solution is processed by density gradient centrifugation (Chapter 43) at $100\,000\,g$ for $18 \, \text{h}$, using a cushion of $5.7 \, \text{mol} \, l^{-1}$ CsCl. DNA and protein remain in the upper layers of CsCl, while RNA forms a pellet at the base of the tube. The RNA pellet is redissolved in buffer, and precipitated in cold ethanol. After resuspension of the cellular RNA, mRNA can be purified by affinity chromatography using poly (U)-Sepharose® (p. 302).

Avoiding contamination of glassware by RNases – autoclave all glassware before use, to denature RNases. These enzymes are present in skin secretions: use gloves at all times and use plasticware wherever possible.

Separating nucleic acids

Electrophoresis is the principal method used for separating nucleic acids. At alkaline pH values, linear DNA and RNA molecules have a uniform net negative charge per unit length due to the charge on the phosphoryl group of the backbone. Electrophoresis using a supporting medium that acts as a molecular sieve (e.g. agarose or polyacrylamide, p. 315) enables DNA fragments or RNA molecules to be separated on the basis of their relative sizes (see Chapter 46 for further details).

Quantitative analysis of nucleic acids

Measuring nucleic acid content

The concentration of reasonably pure samples of DNA or RNA can be measured by spectrophotometry (p. 273). In contrast, measurement of the nucleic acid content of whole cell or tissue homogenates requires chemical methods, since the homogenates will contain many substances that would interfere with the spectroscopic methods. The principles involved in each technique are as follows:

Measuring nucleic acids by spectrophotometry – ideally, the nucleic acid extracts should be prepared to give A$_{260}$ values of between 0.10 and 0.50, for maximum accuracy and precision.

- Spectrophotometry – DNA and RNA both show absorption maxima at $\approx 260 \, \text{nm}$, due to the conjugated double bonds present in their constituent bases. At 260 nm, an A_{260} value of 1.0 is given by a $50 \, \mu g \, ml^{-1}$ solution of dsDNA, or a $40 \, \mu g \, ml^{-1}$ solution of ssRNA. If the absorbance at 260 nm is also measured, protein contamination

Fig. 53.4 Ethidium bromide (EtBr), a fluorescent molecule used for the detection and assay of DNA.

Safe working with ethidium bromide – this compound is highly toxic and mutagenic. Avoid skin contact (wear gloves) and avoid ingestion. Use a safe method of disposal (e.g. adsorb from solution using an appropriate adsorbant).

Fig. 53.5 The diphenylamine reaction for assay of DNA.

can be quantified. Pure nucleic acids give A_{260}/A_{280} ratios of 1.8–2.0, and a value below 1.6 indicates significant protein contamination. Further purification steps are required for contaminated samples, e.g. by repeating the phenol–chloroform extraction step. RNA contamination of a DNA preparation is indicated if A_{260} decreases when the sample is treated with 2.5 μl of RNase at 20 μg μl^{-1}. DNA contamination of an RNA preparation might be suspected if the sample is very viscous, and this can be confirmed by electrophoresis.

- Spectrofluorimetry – this is the best approach for samples where the DNA concentration is too low to allow direct assay by the spectrophotometric method described above. The method uses the fluorescent dye ethidium bromide (Fig. 53.4), which binds to dsDNA by insertion between stacked base pairs, a phenomenon termed 'intercalation'. The fluorescence of ethidium bromide is enhanced 25-fold when it interacts with dsDNA. Since ssDNA gives no significant enhancement of fluorescence, dsDNA can be quantified in the presence of denatured DNA. The concentration of dsDNA in solution $[\text{dsDNA}]_x$ can be calculated by comparing its fluorescence (excitation wavelength, 525 nm; emission wavelength, 590 nm) with that of a standard dsDNA solution of known concentration $[\text{dsDNA}]_{std}$ using the following relationship:

$$[\text{dsDNA}]_x = \frac{[\text{dsDNA}]_{std} \times \text{fluorescence of unknown}}{\text{fluorescence of standard}} \quad [53.1]$$

- Chemical methods – these are mostly based on colorimetric reactions with the pentose groups of nucleic acids. The total DNA concentration can be measured by the diphenylamine reaction (Fig. 53.5), which is specific for 2-deoxypentoses. The diphenylamine reaction involves heating 2 ml of DNA solution with 4 ml of freshly prepared diphenylamine reagent (diphenylamine, at 10 g l^{-1} in glacial acetic acid, plus 25 ml concentrated sulphuric acid) for 10 min in a boiling water bath. The acids cleave some of the phosphodiester bonds, and hydrolyse the glycosidic links between the deoxyribose and purines. Deoxyribose residues are converted to ω-hydroxylaevulinyl aldehyde (Fig. 53.5), which reacts with the diphenyl-amine to produce a blue pigment, assayed at 600 nm. By constructing a DNA standard curve ranging from 0 to 400 μg ml^{-1}, the DNA concentration of the unknown can be determined.

RNA concentration can be measured by the orcinol reaction, which is a general assay for pentoses. The orcinol reaction involves heating 2 ml of RNA solution with 3 ml of orcinol reagent (prepared by dissolving 1 g of FeCl$_3$·6H$_2$O in 1 litre of concentrated HCl, and adding 35 ml of 6% w/v orcinol in ethanol) in a boiling water bath for 20 min. The acid cleaves some phosphodiester bonds and hydrolyses the glycosidic links between the ribose and purines. The hot acid also converts the ribose to furfural (Fig. 53.6), which reacts with orcinol in the presence of ferric ions to produce green-coloured compounds, assayed at 660 nm. A standard curve for RNA ranging from 0 to 400 μg ml^{-1} is used to determine the RNA concentration of the unknown. The orcinol reaction is less specific than the diphenylamine reaction, as deoxyribose reacts to some extent and DNA gives about 10% of the colour given by the same concentration of RNA. If the DNA concentration of the extract is known (e.g. from a diphenylamine

RNA

↓ acid

ribose

↓ acid

furfural

↓

reaction with orcinol to form green-coloured compounds

Fig. 53.6 The orcinol reaction for assay of RNA.

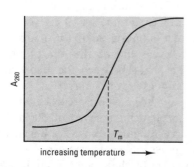

Fig. 53.7 Effect of temperature on the absorbance (A_{260}) of DNA in solution. T_m is the temperature for the mid-point of the absorbance change.

assay), the contribution of DNA to A_{660} can be measured for a standard prepared to have the same DNA concentration as the sample: the A_{660} due to DNA can then be subtracted from the result of the orcinol reaction, and the remaining A_{660} value is then used to determine RNA concentration from the RNA standard curve.

Assaying the relative proportions of base pairs in DNA

Double stranded DNA has a lower molar absorptivity at 260 nm than single stranded DNA, due to electron interactions between the stacked base pairs and hydrogen bonding between the complementary bases of dsDNA. When a dsDNA solution is heated slowly, there is little change in absorbance until a temperature is reached where the hydrogen bonds are broken and the DNA strands separate. At this so-called 'melting temperature' (T_m), the A_{260} value increases sharply (Fig. 53.7). This temperature-dependent increase in absorbance is often referred to as the 'hyperchromic effect'. The actual value of the T_m (and hence the stability of dsDNA) is dependent on the base-pair composition of the DNA being studied: GC base pairs have three double bonds while AT base pairs have two, and the higher the % GC content, the higher the value of the T_m. The length of the molecule also affects the T_m, since short dsDNA molecules do not show a hyperchromic effect. Studies on a number of DNA samples have shown the following relationship, for GC contents between 30 and 70%:

$$\% \text{ GC} = 2.44(T_m - 69.3) \qquad [53.2]$$

The relative proportion of AT base pairs can then be calculated by subtracting the % GC value from 100, giving % AT.

Sources for further study
(See also Chapter 11 for nucleic acid databases and related information.)

Blackburn, G.M. and Gait, M.G. (1996) *Nucleic Acids in Chemistry and Biology*. IRL Press, Oxford.

Dey, P.M., Harbourne, J.B. and Rogers, L.E. (1997) *Methods in Plant Biochemistry: Amino Acids, Proteins and Nucleic Acids*. Academic Press, New York.

Martin, R.M. (1996) *Gel Electrophoresis: Nucleic Acids*. Bios, Oxford.

Neidle, S. (1999) *Oxford Handbook of Nucleic Acid Structure*. Oxford University Press, Oxford.

Study exercises

53.1 Calculate the concentration of DNA in a sample using a fluorescence assay (see also exercises 41.2c and 41.2d, p. 278, for equivalent exercises using UV spectrophotometry). A volume of 10 μl of a DNA standard solution (of concentration 50 μg ml^{-1}) was added to 3 ml of an ethidium bromide solution (containing 0.5 mg l^{-1} ethidium bromide, buffered at pH 7.5) in a fluorimeter cuvette, mixed, then read in a spectrofluorimeter using an excitation wavelength of 525 nm and an emission wavelength of 590 nm, giving a relative fluorescence intensity (RFI) of 58. This was repeated using 10 μl of a DNA solution of unknown concentration instead of the DNA standard solution, giving an RFI of 32. What is the DNA concentration of the unknown? (Express your answer to 3 significant figures.)

53.2 Investigate the binding properties of ethidium bromide. Find out (i) why ethidium bromide fluorescence is enhanced by DNA, and (ii) under what circumstances ethidium bromide can also bind to RNA.

53.3 Consider how to avoid problems in DNA spectrofluorometric analysis caused by the presence of RNA in a sample. What steps could you take to ensure that all the fluorescence obtained from a cell extract was due to the reaction of ethidium bromide with DNA rather than from DNA plus contaminating RNA?

54 Protein purification

Much of the current knowledge about metabolic and physiological events has been gained from *in vitro* studies of purified proteins. Such studies range from investigations into the kinetics and regulation of enzymes (Chapter 55) to the determination of the structure of a protein and its relationship to function. In addition, certain purified proteins have a role as therapeutic agents, e.g. Factor VIII in the treatment of haemophilia.

> **KEY POINT** The purification of most proteins involves a series of procedures, based on differential solubility and/or chromatography, that selectively separate the protein of interest from contaminating proteins and other material. It is rare for purification to be a one-step process.

Deciding on your objectives

Purity, yield and cost are the major considerations, and the relative importance of these factors will depend on the purpose of the purification. For studies on the biological activity of a protein (e.g. an enzyme), only μg amounts may be required and, as long as there are no interfering substances present, 100% purity may not be necessary. For structural studies, mg amounts may be needed and the protein must be pure. A protein produced for industrial applications (e.g. an enzyme for use in starch degradation) needs to be produced in large amounts (g or kg), but purity usually is not essential. In contrast, commercially produced proteins for therapeutic use need to be free of any significant contamination.

The cost of the purification will depend on the nature of the source material, the number of purification steps required, and the price of materials for the separation techniques employed. Inevitably, some protein will be lost at each stage of the purification procedure.

> **KEY POINT** You should aim to use the smallest number of purification steps that will give you the yield and purity required for your application.

Preliminary considerations

Finding out about the protein

Rather than approaching every purification step on a 'trial and error' basis, try to find out as much as you can about the physical and biological properties of the desired protein before you begin your practical work. Even if the protein to be purified is novel, it is likely that similar proteins will be described in the literature. Information on the isoelectric point (pI) and M_r, of both the protein and of the likely major contaminants, is particularly useful for ion-exchange and gel permeation chromatography (p. 300). Knowledge of other factors such as metal ion and co-enzyme requirements, presence of thiol groups, and known inhibitors can indicate useful chromatographic steps, and may allow you to take steps to preserve the tertiary structure and biological activity of the desired protein during the purification process.

Preventing loss of protein during purification – silicone-coated glass containers prevent the adsorption of proteins to the surface of a glass vessel.

Definition

Isoelectric point (pI) – the pH value at which a protein has a net charge of zero, i.e. where positive and negative charges on amino acid side chains are balanced.

Choosing the source material

If you have a choice of starting material, use a convenient source in which the protein of interest is abundant. This can vary from animal tissues (e.g. heart, kidney or liver) obtained from an abattoir or from laboratory animals, to plant material, or to microbial cells from a laboratory culture.

Homogenisation and solubilisation

Unless the protein is extracellular, the cells in the source material need to be disrupted and homogenised by one of the methods described in Chapter 36. Following homogenisation, proteins from the cytosol or extracellular fluid will normally be present in a soluble form, but membrane-bound proteins and those within organelles will require further treatment. Isolation of organelles by differential centrifugation (p. 290) will provide a degree of purification, while membrane-bound proteins will need organic solvents or detergents to render them soluble. Once the protein of interest is in a soluble form, any particulate material in the extract should be removed, e.g. by centrifugation or filtration.

Preserving enzyme activity during purification

Once an enzyme has been released from its intracellular environment, it will encounter potentially adverse conditions that may result in denaturation and permanent inactivation, e.g. a lower pH, an oxidising environment, or exposure to lysosomal proteases. During homogenisation, and in some or all of the purification steps, buffers should contain reagents that can counteract these potentially damaging effects (see Chapter 36). Fewer precautions may be needed with extracellular enzymes. For most proteins, the initial procedures should be carried out at 4°C, to minimise the risk of proteolysis.

Devising a strategy for protein purification

Any successful protein purification scheme will exploit the unique properties of the desired protein in terms of its size, net charge, hydrophobic nature, biological activity, etc. The chromatographic techniques that separate on the basis of these properties are detailed in Chapter 44. However, the *order* in which the various purification steps are carried out needs some thought, and each stage needs to be considered in relation to the following factors:

- Capacity – the amount of material (volume or concentration) that the technique can handle. High capacity techniques such as ammonium sulphate precipitation (see later) and ion-exchange chromatography (p. 299) should be used at an early stage, to reduce the sample volume.
- Resolution – the efficiency of separating one component from another. At later stages of the purification, the sample volume will be considerably reduced, but any contaminating proteins may well have very similar properties to those of the protein of interest. Therefore, a high resolution (but low capacity) technique will be required, such as covalent chromatography or immobilised metal affinity chromatography (IMAC).
- Yield – the amount of protein recovered at each step, expressed as a percentage of the initial amount. For example, yields of >80% can be obtained with ammonium sulphate precipitation. With certain types of

Table 54.1 Principal causes of decreased yield in protein purification

Cause	Possible solution
Denaturation	Include EDTA or reducing agents in buffers; avoid extreme temperatures
Inhibition	Check buffer composition for possible inhibitors
Proteolysis	Include protease inhibitors in buffers
Non-elution	Alter salt concentration or pH of the eluting buffer
Co-factor loss	Recombine fractions on a trial-and-error basis

Calculating total protein content – multiply the protein concentration by the total volume, making sure that the units are consistent, e.g. mg ml^{-1} × ml. A similar procedure is required to determine the total amount of enzyme.

Using immunoassays – note that the inactive or denatured forms of the protein may be detected along with the biologically active form.

affinity chromatography, where harsh elution conditions need to be employed, yields may be quite low (e.g. <20%). Some of the other possible reasons for a decreased yield are considered in Table 54.1.

An ideal purification procedure will have the following features:

1. an initial step that has a high capacity, but not necessarily a high resolution;
2. a series of chromatographic steps, each of which exploits a different property of the protein to increase purity;
3. a minimum number of manipulations and changes in conditions (e.g. in buffer composition) between steps.

The following series of steps would meet the above conditions:

Step 1   Ammonium sulphate precipitation – a high capacity, low resolution technique that yields a protein solution with a greatly reduced volume and a high concentration of ammonium sulphate.

Step 2   Hydrophobic interaction chromatography (HIC) – an absorption technique (p. 301) using a starting buffer with a high ammonium sulphate concentration. During development of the column, the ionic strength of the mobile phase is reduced in a gradient elution.

Step 3   Ion-exchange chromatography (IEC) – another absorption technique (p. 299). Here the starting buffer has a low ionic strength, and a gradient of increasing ionic strength is used to separate components.

Step 4   Gel permeation chromatography (GPC) – a low capacity method (p. 300) where separation is independent of the composition of the mobile phase.

The sample from step 1 may be able to be applied directly to the HIC column, and that from step 2 may be used for IEC without changing the buffer. A concentration step (pp. 373–6) would be required before step 4. The above scheme is very much an idealised approach: in practice, buffers may need to be changed by dialysis or ultrafiltration, as described later. However, the principle of using the minimum number of manipulations to obtain the desired purification remains valid.

Monitoring purification

At each step, the separated material is usually collected as a series of 'fractions'. Each fraction must be assayed for the protein of interest, and fractions containing that protein are pooled prior to the next step. The assay performed will depend on the properties of the protein of interest but specific enzyme assays or immunoassays are most commonly used. The protein concentration (p. 348) and the volume of the pooled fraction must be determined, and these values, together with those obtained for the amount of the protein of interest, are used to determine the purity and yield after each step. For enzymes, the biological activity is measured and used to calculate the specific activity (the enzyme activity per unit mass of protein) as described on p. 378. By determining the specific activity of the enzyme at each step, the degree of purification, or purification factor (*n*-fold purification), can be obtained from the following relationship:

$$\text{Purification factor} = \frac{\text{specific activity after a particular step}}{\text{specific activity of initial sample}} \quad [54.1]$$

Table 54.2 Example of a record of purification for an enzyme

Step	Procedure	Total protein (mg)	Total enzyme (IU)	Specific activity	Purification factor	Enzyme yield (%)
Initial sample	—	210	1984	9.43	—	100.0
Step 1	'Salting out'	112	1740	15.53	1.6	87.7
Step 2	HIC	30	1701	56.70	6.0	85.7
Step 3	IEC	6	1604	267.33	28.4	80.8
Step 4	GPC	3	1550	516.66	54.8	78.1

Increased purification usually represents a decrease in total protein relative to the biological activity of the protein of interest, though in some instances it may reflect the loss of an inhibitor during a purification step.

Calculation of the yield of enzyme at each step is straightforward, since:

$$\text{Yield} = \frac{\text{total enzyme activity after a particular step}}{\text{total enzyme activity in initial sample}} \times 100 \ (\%) \quad [54.2]$$

Note that the yield equation uses the total amount of enzyme and is therefore unaffected by the volume of the solutions involved. You should make a record of the progress of your purification procedure at each step, as in Table 54.2.

Monitoring progress using electrophoresis

Polyacrylamide gel electrophoresis (PAGE) of subsamples from each step will give an indication of the number of proteins still present: ideally, a pure protein will give only one band after silver staining (p. 326); however, this stain is so sensitive that even trace impurities can be detected in what you expect to be a pure sample, so don't be dismayed by the appearance of the gel after staining.

Carrying out SDS-PAGE and isoelectric focusing (or, ideally, 2D-PAGE, p. 325) on subsamples also gives information on the M_r and pI of any remaining contaminants, and this can be taken into account when planning the next chromatographic step.

Differential solubility separation techniques

Often the volume and protein concentration of the initial soluble extract will be quite high. Application of a differential solubility technique at this stage results in the precipitation of selected proteins. These can be recovered by filtration or centrifugation, washed, and then resuspended in an appropriate buffer. This will reduce the sample volume and may give a small degree of purification, making the sample more suitable for subsequent chromatographic steps.

Ammonium sulphate precipitation ('salting out')

This is the most widely used differential solubility technique, having the advantage that most precipitated enzymes are not permanently denatured, and can be redissolved with restoration of activity. Precipitation depends on the existence of hydrophobic 'patches' on the surface of proteins, inducing a reorganisation of water molecules in their vicinity. When ammonium sulphate is added to the extract, it dissolves to give ions that become hydrated, leaving fewer water molecules in association with the

Assaying enzymes – if possible, use a preliminary screening technique to detect active fractions prior to quantitative assay, e.g. by using tetrazolium dyes in microtitre plates to detect oxidoreductases (p. 321).

Measuring the mass of proteins – this is sometimes expressed in daltons (Da), or kilodaltons (kDa), where 1 dalton = 1 atomic mass unit. M_r is an alternative, numerically equivalent expression (p. 139).

Table 54.3 Amount of $(NH_4)_2SO_4$ (g l^{-1}) required for a particular percentage saturation

Final concentration (%) →	20	30	40	50	60	70	80	90	100
Initial concentration (%) ↓	Ammonium sulphate added (g l^{-1})								
0	107	166	229	295	366	442	523	611	707
10	54	111	171	236	305	379	458	545	636
20	—	56	115	177	244	316	392	476	565
30		—	57	119	184	253	328	408	495
40			—	59	122	190	262	340	424
50				—	61	127	197	272	353
60					—	63	131	204	283
70						—	66	136	212
80							—	68	141
90								—	71

protein. As a result, the hydrophobic patches become 'exposed', and hydrophobic interactions between different protein molecules lead to their aggregation and precipitation. The basis of fractionation in this method is that, as the salt concentration of the extract is increased, proteins with larger or more abundant hydrophobic patches will precipitate before those with smaller or fewer patches. Although the phenomenon of salting out is seen with several salts, $(NH_4)_2SO_4$ is the most widely used because it is highly soluble (saturating at $\approx 4\,mol\,l^{-1}$), inexpensive, and can be obtained in very pure form.

Unless you can obtain information from the literature about the $(NH_4)_2SO_4$ concentration that will precipitate your target protein, fractionation is done on a trial-and-error basis. The $(NH_4)_2SO_4$ concentration is expressed in terms of the percentage saturation value: Table 54.3 shows the amount of $(NH_4)_2SO_4$ required to give 20–100% saturation. For each percentage saturation chosen, the $(NH_4)_2SO_4$ salt should be added slowly while stirring, and the mixture left at $4\,°C$ for 1 h before centrifuging at $3000\,g$ for 40 min. For an effective separation, start with the maximum percentage saturation that does not precipitate the protein of interest, then increase the percentage saturation by the minimum amount that will then precipitate it. The proteins precipitated between any two values of percentage saturation (say between 30 and 50%) are referred to as a 'cut'. An alternative approach is to add saturated $(NH_4)_2SO_4$ solution – the volume (V_a) to be added to an initial volume of solution (V_i) with an initial saturation S_i, to give a final saturation S_f, is given by the equation:

$$V_a = \frac{V_i(S_f - S_i)}{1 - S_f} \qquad [54.3]$$

where S_i and S_f are expressed as fractional saturation, e.g. $S_f = 0.5 \equiv 50\%$ saturation, and both volumes are expressed in the same terms, e.g. ml.

Precipitation by changing pH

Proteins are least soluble at their isoelectric points because, at that pH, there is no longer the repulsion that occurs between positively or negatively charged protein molecules at physiological pH values. If the precipitated proteins are required for further purification, it is essential

Example To prepare a solution of 40% $(NH_4)_2SO_4$ saturation ($S_f = 0.4$) from 100 ml (V_i) containing no added $(NH_4)_2SO_4$ using Eqn 54.3:
$V_a = 100(0.4 - 0) \div (1 - 0.4) = 67$ ml of saturated $(NH_4)_2SO_4$ solution, giving a volume of 167 ml.
For a 40–60% 'cut' of this sample ($V_i = 167$ ml), using Eqn 54.3:
$V_a = 167(0.6 - 0.4) \div (1 - 0.6) = 83.5$ ml of saturated $(NH_4)_2SO_4$ solution, to give a final volume of 250.5 ml.

Purifying bacterial proteins – adjusting the extract to pH 5 can be useful, since many bacterial proteins have pI values in this region.

that the protein of interest is not irreversibly denatured. The method is probably best employed by precipitating contaminating proteins, leaving the desired protein in solution. Use citric acid for <pH 3, acetic acid for <pH 4, and sodium carbonate or ethanolamine for >pH 8.

Heat denaturation

Exposure of most proteins to high temperatures disrupts their conformation through effects on non-covalent interactions such as hydrogen bonds and van der Waals forces. However, different proteins are denatured, and hence precipitated, at different temperatures, and this can provide a basis for the separation of some heat-stable proteins. By incubating small aliquots ($\approx$1 ml) of extract for 1 min at a range of temperatures between 45 and 65 °C, it is possible to determine the temperature that gives maximum precipitation of contaminating protein with minimal inactivation of the desired protein.

Solvent and polymer precipitation methods

Organic solvents (e.g. acetone, ethanol) cause precipitation of proteins by lowering the dielectric constant of the solution. Performing the precipitation at 0 °C minimises permanent denaturation. Stepwise concentration (% v/v) increments are used, giving 'cuts' of precipitated proteins, as with ammonium sulphate precipitation.

Organic polymers, particularly polyethylene glycol (PEG), also lower the dielectric constant, but at lower concentrations than with acetone or ethanol. The most commonly used PEG preparations have M_r values of 6000 or 20 000, and these can be removed from the sample by ultrafiltration. PEG precipitation does not involve salts, so it may be a useful preliminary step prior to ion-exchange chromatography which starts with low salt buffer. Also, since the techniques of PEG and ammonium sulphate precipitation involve different principles, they can be used sequentially.

Concentration by ultrafiltration

This involves forcing water and small molecules through a semi-permeable membrane using high pressure or centrifugation. A range of membranes with 'nominal' molecular weight cut-offs between 500 and 300 000 are commercially available (e.g. Amicon®, Millipore®), with pore sizes of 0.1–10 μm. Concentration of small samples (<5 ml) can be achieved using either a membrane backed by an absorbent pad (e.g. Minicon®, Fig. 54.1, available with M_r cut-off from 5000 to 30 000), or by using a centrifugal concentrator (e.g. Centricon®). Larger volumes (up to 400 ml) can be concentrated using a stirred ultrafiltration chamber (an ultrafiltration 'cell') where the liquid is forced through the membrane using nitrogen or an inert gas.

Ultrafiltration not only concentrates the sample, but also may give a degree of purification. It can also be used to change the buffer composition by diafiltration (see below). Note that molecular weight cut-off values are quoted for globular proteins – fibrous proteins of higher M_r may pass through the ultrafiltration membrane.

Removing salts and changing the buffer

Although you should aim to use the minimum number of manipulations to obtain the desired purification, it may be necessary to remove salts or to

(a)

sample in well

absorbent pad

membrane

impermeable seal

wall of vessel

(b)

absorbent pad now contains water from sample

membrane

concentrated sample in well

impermeable seal

Fig. 54.1 Minicon® ultrafiltration system (a) with sample added, (b) after ultrafiltration.

change the buffer before the next step will work effectively (e.g. when carrying out IEC, the ionic strength or the pH of the sample may need to be changed before the target protein will bind to the column). Several methods are available, including:

- Dialysis: the sample is placed in a bag consisting of semi-permeable membrane (e.g. Visking® tubing) and placed in at least 20 volumes of the required buffer. The membrane allows molecules of $M_r < 20\,000$ to pass freely, while retaining larger molecules (note that dialysis is not suitable for small proteins). The small molecules diffuse through the membrane until the osmotic pressure between the sample and the dialysis buffer is equalised. Several changes of dialysis buffer may be required to obtain the desired buffer conditions within the sample. Normally dialysis is carried out overnight at 4 °C. Efficient stirring is required – use a magnetic stirrer and stirrer bar.

- Diafiltration: quicker than dialysis and more suitable for larger volumes. It involves addition of the desired buffer to the sample solution, followed by ultrafiltration. Several buffer addition and ultrafiltration steps may be necessary to obtain the desired sample conditions.

- Gel permeation chromatography (gel filtration): a gel filtration medium of small pore size (e.g. Sephadex® G-25) is used to prepare a column of ≈5 times the volume of the sample. When the sample passes through the column, the large protein molecules will elute with the void volume, while salt ions are retained. This method is only suitable for small volumes, and it results in dilution of the sample.

Using Visking® tubing – this must be boiled before use to ensure a uniform pore size and to remove heavy metal contaminants.

Avoiding protein precipitation during dialysis or gel filtration – make sure your buffer pH is either above or below the pI of the proteins.

Fig. 54.2 The hanging drop technique for protein crystallisation.

Fig. 54.3 Image of protein crystals produced by the hanging drop method (image courtesy of S. Charnock).

Protein crystallisation

Much of the information on protein structure that is now available on protein sequence databases (see Table 11.1, p. 62) has been obtained by X-ray crystallographic studies on protein crystals. To obtain protein crystals, the protein should be purified to at least 90–95% and its concentration in solution should be 10–20 µg. The method most widely used for crystallisation is the hanging drop vapour diffusion technique (Fig. 54.2). Here, a small droplet of the protein sample (usually about 1–2 µl) is mixed with a crystallisation reagent on a siliconised glass coverslip and inverted over a microtitre plate well containing 0.5–1.0 ml of the same crystallisation reagent. The presence of protein in the droplet means that the initial concentration of crystallisation reagent in the droplet is less than that in the well. As a result, water will diffuse from the droplet into the vapour phase until an equilibrium is achieved between the droplet, the vapour phase and the solution in the well. During this equilibration, the protein is concentrated within the droplet, enhancing the formation of protein crystals. The essential components of a crystallisation reagent are a (i) protein precipitant and (ii) buffer. The specific reagents differ, depending on the type of protein to be crystallised. Commercially available reagents include the PEG/Ion Screen® reagents (Hampton Research, USA) and the Clear Strategy Screen® reagents (Molecular Dimensions, UK). An image of protein crystals produced by this method is shown in Fig. 54.3.

Sources for further study

Deutscher, M.P., Simon, M.I. and Abelson, J.N. (1997) *Guide to Protein Purification: Methods in Enzymology.* Academic Press, New York.

Howard, G.C. and Brown, W.E. (2002) *Modern Protein Chemistry: Practical Aspects.* CRC Press, Boca Raton.

Roe, S. (2001) *Protein Purification Applications: A Practical Approach,* 2nd edn. Oxford University Press, Oxford.

Rosenberg, I.M. (1996) *Protein Analysis and Purification: Benchtop Techniques.* Springer-Verlag, Berlin.

Scopes, R.K. (1994) *Protein Purification: Principles and Practice.* Springer-Verlag, Berlin.

Study exercises

54.1 Practise ammonium sulphate fractionation calculations. For a mixture of three proteins, A, B and C, in 100 ml of aqueous solution, you are provided with the information that protein A precipitates at a $(NH_4)_2SO_4$ concentration of 40%, and that protein B precipitates in the 40–60% 'cut' while protein C is not precipitated by 60% $(NH_4)_2SO_4$. Determine how much solid $(NH_4)_2SO_4$ (in grams) would be needed to achieve 40% saturation, and once protein A is removed, how much $(NH_4)_2SO_4$ will then need to be added to the solution to reach 60% saturation. What will be the fate of protein C in this procedure?

54.2 Select a chromatographic technique for use with a particular protein. Using the information given in Chapter 44, which affinity techniques would be most suitable for the following proteins: (a) an enzyme that uses $NAD^+/NADH$ as a cofactor, (b) a genetically engineered protein with a polyhistidine tag at its N-terminal end, and (c) a glycoprotein?

54.3 Calculate yield and relative purification of an enzyme. The table below shows representative data for an enzyme purification involving five stages. Calculate the yield and *n*-fold purification (relative to the initial values) at each stage. Give all answers to 3 significant figures.

Volume, protein concentration and enzyme activity at several stages during a protein purification procedure

Stage	Total volume of extract (ml)	Enzyme activity ($U\,ml^{-1}$)	Protein concentration ($mg\,ml^{-1}$)
1	78	1.2	4.8
2	70	1.2	1.7
3	10	6.4	2.5
4	5	10.8	1.4
5	0.6	65.7	3.4

Enzyme studies

Enzymes are globular proteins that increase the rate of specific biochemical reactions. Each enzyme operates on a limited number of substrates of similar structure to generate products under well-defined conditions of concentration, pH, temperature, etc. In metabolism, groups of enzymes work together in sequential pathways to carry out complex molecular transformations, e.g. the multi-reaction conversion of glucose to lactate (glycolysis).

Example Enzyme EC 1.1.1.1 is usually known by its trivial name, alcohol dehydrogenase.

KEY POINT Enzymes are categorised according to the chemical reactions they catalyse, leading to a four-figure Enzyme Commission code number and a systematic name for each enzyme. Most enzymes also have a recommended trivial name, often denoted by the suffix 'ase'.

Measuring enzyme reactions

Activity

This is measured in terms of the rate of enzyme reaction. Activity may be expressed directly as amount of substrate utilised per unit time (e.g. nmol min^{-1}, etc.), or in terms of the non-SI international unit (U, or sometimes IU), defined as the amount of enzyme which will convert $1\,\mu$mol of substrate to product(s) in 1 min under specified conditions. However, the recommended (SI) unit of enzyme activity is the katal (kat), which is the amount of enzyme which will convert 1 mol of substrate to product(s) in 1 s under optimal conditions, determined from the following equation:

$$\text{enzyme activity (kat)} = \frac{\text{substrate converted (mol)}}{\text{time (s)}} \qquad [55.1]$$

This unit is relatively large ($1\,\text{kat} = 6 \times 10^7\,\text{U}$) so SI prefixes are often used, e.g. nkat or pkat (p. 176). Note that the units are amount of substrate (mol), not concentration ($mol\,l^{-1}$ or $mol\,m^{-3}$).

Example The hydrolysis of one molecule of maltose to give two glucose molecules by α-glucosidase means that enzyme activity specified in terms of substrate consumption (nmol maltose) would be half the value expressed with respect to product formation (nmol glucose).

For enzymes with macromolecular substrates of unknown molecular weight (e.g. deoxyribonuclease, amylase), activity can be expressed as the mass of substrate consumed (e.g. ng DNA min^{-1}), or amount of product formed (e.g. nmol glucose min^{-1}). You must ensure that your units clearly specify the substrate or product used, especially when the enzyme transformations involve different numbers of substrate or product molecules. Specific activity, expressed in terms of the amount or mass of substrate or product, is useful for comparing the purity of different enzyme preparations (e.g. p. 372).

The turnover number of an enzyme is the amount of substrate (mol) converted to product in 1 s by 1 mol of enzyme operating under optimum conditions. In practice, this requires information on the molecular weight of the enzyme, the amount of enzyme present and its maximum activity.

Definition

Specific activity – enzyme activity (e.g. kat, U, ng min^{-1}) expressed per unit mass of protein present (e.g. mg, μg).

Types of assay

The rate of substrate utilisation or product formation must be measured under controlled conditions, using some characteristic which changes in direct proportion to the concentration of the test substance.

Spectrophotometric assays

Many substrates and products absorb visible or UV light and the change in absorbance at a particular wavelength provides a convenient assay method (p. 273). In other cases, a product may be measured by a colorimetric chemical reaction.

Several assays are based on interconversion of the nicotinamide adenine dinucleotide coenzymes NAD^+ or $NADP^+$ which are reversibly reduced in many enzymic reactions. The reduced form (either NADH or NADPH) can be detected at 340 nm, where the oxidised form has negligible absorbance (p. 273). An alternative approach is to use a coupled enzyme assay, where a product of the test enzyme is used as a substrate for a second enzyme reaction which involves oxidation/reduction of nucleotide coenzymes. Such assays are particularly useful for continuous monitoring of enzyme activity and for reactions where the product from the test substance is too low to detect by other methods, since coupled assays are more sensitive. Note that the reaction of interest (test enzyme) must be the rate-limiting process, not the indicator reaction (second enzyme).

Radioisotopic assays

These are useful where the substrate and product can be easily separated, e.g. in decarboxylase assays using a ^{14}C-labelled substrate, where gaseous $^{14}CO_2$ is produced.

Electrochemical assays

Enzyme reactions involving acids and bases can be monitored using a pH electrode (p. 148), though the change in pH will affect the activity of the test enzyme. An alternative approach is to measure the amount of acid or alkali required to maintain a constant preselected pH in a pH-stat.

An oxygen electrode can be used if O_2 is a substrate or a product (p. 334). Other ion-specific electrodes can monitor ammonia, nitrate, etc.

Chromogenic and fluorogenic enyzme substrates

Artificial substrates that generate either (i) a coloured product (i.e. they are chromogens) or (ii) a fluorescent product (fluorogens) are used widely for the detection and quantification of enzymes, especially when no suitable spectrophotometric assay is available for the natural product or the natural substrate. In most cases, these artificial substrates are analogues of the natural substrates, composed of a 'core molecule' that is either fluorescent (p. 275) or coloured, coupled to another group by a covalent bond. The addition of this group to the core molecule usually causes a decrease in fluorescence and a shift in the excitation and emission signal to longer wavelengths, or converts the coloured compound to a non-coloured form. The covalent bond between core molecule and added group is recognised and cleaved by the target enzyme to liberate the core molecule, thereby generating either a fluorescent or a coloured product that can be measured fluorimetrically (p. 275) or spectrophotometrically (p. 272). The principle is best illustrated using a specific example of each type of substrate (see Fig. 55.1).

Such substrates serve as a sensitive and specific means of detecting individual enzymes in the presence of a range of other biomolecules. Applications include:

- biochemical identification of bacteria, on the basis of enzyme profiles (p. 213, *see also* Fig. 55.1);

Example Phosphoenolpyruvate carboxylase (PEP carboxylase) can be assayed by coupling to malate dehydrogenase (MDH): the PEP carboxylase reaction converts phosphoenolpyruvate to oxaloacetate, which is then oxidised to malate by MDH (present in excess), with a stoichiometric reduction of NAD^+. The coupled assay is monitored spectophotometrically as an increase in A_{340} against time (p. 273).

Working with radioisotopes – this is covered in Chapter 39, p. 258.

Understanding fluorescence – the basis of fluorescence is explaind on pp. 274–5.

- enzyme-linked immunoassays, e.g. ELISA (p. 254);
- nucleic acid hybridisation and blotting (p. 431);
- detection of specific enzymes in living cells, e.g. enzymes that inactivate antibiotics – an example would be the use of a fluorescent chloramphenicol derivative to detect chloramphenicol acetyl transferase enzymes in resistant bacteria;
- quantitative assay for enzyme activity – e.g. fluorogenic substrates for HIV protease.

Note that care is required for quantitative fluorimetric assay, since impurities in the enzyme preparation can lead to background fluoresence or to quenching (reduction) of the signal: appropriate controls must be run at the same time as test samples. A wide range of chromogenic core molecules (chromophores) are used in artificial substrates, including: nitrophenols (e.g. ONP, Fig. 55.1); nitroanilines (e.g. Z-arginine-*para*-nitroanilide derivatives for assaying trypsin activity); indoxyl substrates (e.g. 5-bromo-4-chloro-3-indolyl-β-D-galactoside, also known as X-GAL, which is used widely to detect the activity of the *lacZ* gene in molecular biology, p. 445), along with derivatives of alizarin and 3,3′,5,5′-tetramethylbenzidine. Similarly, several different fluorophores are commercially available, including coumarin derivatives (e.g. 4-methylumbelliferone, MU, Fig. 55.1, and 7-amino-4-methylcoumarin, AMC, which fluoresce blue), fluorescein (Fig. 41.4, p. 275, which gives green fluorescent products) and resorufin (red fluorescence). For further details, see James (1994).

Fig. 55.1 (a) The chromogenic substrate *ortho*-nitrophenyl-β-D-galactoside (ONP-β-GAL); (b) the fluorogenic substrate 4-methylumbelliferyl-β-D-glucuronide (MU-β-GUR). Both substrates show minimal colour and/or fluorescence due to the coupling of the core molecule to a carbohydrate group. ONP-β-GAL is cleaved by the enzyme β-galactosidase to liberate ONP, which is yellow (usually assayed spectrophotometrically at 420 nm). In contrast, the cleavage of MU-β-GUR by the enzyme β-glucuronidase liberates MU, which is strongly fluorescent under UV light (e.g. excitation wavelength 360 nm, emisson wavelength 440 nm). These two substrates are used to detect and differentiate between coliform bacteria (which contain β-galactosidase) and *Escherichia coli* (which contains both β-galactosidase and β-glucuronidase), e.g. in the IDEXX Colilert® system for water analysis (see: http://www.idexx.com/Water/Products/Prod.cfm?ID=2).

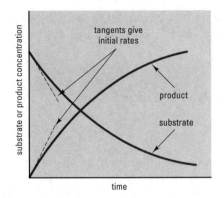

Fig. 55.2 Enzyme reaction progress curve: substrate utilisation/product formation as a function of time.

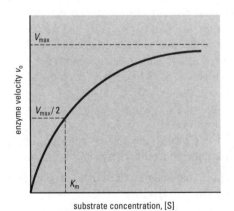

Fig. 55.3 Effect of substrate concentration on enzyme activity.

Methods of monitoring substrate utilisation/product formation

Continuous assays (kinetic assays)

The change in substrate or product is monitored as a function of time, to provide a progress curve for the reaction (Fig. 55.2). These curves start off in a near-linear manner, decreasing in slope as the reaction proceeds and substrate is used up. The initial velocity of the reaction (v_0) is obtained by drawing a tangent to the curve at zero time and measuring its slope. Continuous monitoring can be used when the test substance can be assayed rapidly (and non-destructively), e.g. using a chromogenic substrate. Reaction rate analysers allow simultaneous addition of reactant(s) or enzyme, mixing and measurement of absorbance: this enables the initial rate to be determined accurately.

Discontinuous assays (fixed time assays)

It is sometimes necessary to measure the amount of substrate consumed or product formed after a fixed time period, e.g. where the test substance is assayed by a (destructive) colorimetric chemical method. It is vital that the time period is kept as short as possible, with the change in substrate concentration limited to around 10%, so that the assay is within the linear part of the progress curve (Fig. 55.2). A continuous assay may be carried out as a preliminary step, in order to determine whether the reaction is approximately linear over the time period to be used in the fixed time assay.

Enzyme kinetics

For most enzymes, when the initial reaction rate (v_0) using a fixed amount of an enzyme is plotted as a function of the concentration of a single substrate [S] with all other substrates present in excess, a rectangular hyperbola is obtained (Fig. 55.3). At low substrate concentrations v_0 is directly proportional to [S], with a decreasing response as substrate concentration is increased until saturation is achieved. The shape of this plot can be described by a mathematical relationship, known as the Michaelis–Menten equation:

$$v_0 = \frac{V_{max}[S]}{K_m + [S]} \qquad [55.2]$$

This equation makes use of two kinetic constants:

- V_{max}, the maximum velocity of the reaction (at infinite substrate concentration).
- K_m, the Michaelis constant, is the substrate concentration where $v_0 = \frac{1}{2}V_{max}$.

V_{max} is a function of the amount of enzyme and is the appropriate rate to use when determining the specific activity of a purified enzyme. The Michaelis constant is expressed in terms of substrate concentration ($mol\,l^{-1}$) and is independent of enzyme concentration. K_m is derived from the individual rate constants of the reaction – for example, with a single substrate (S) and single product (P) enzymic reaction, the process can be described as follows:

$$E + S \underset{k_2}{\overset{k_1}{\rightleftharpoons}} ES \xrightarrow{k_3} E + P \qquad [55.3]$$

Enzyme studies

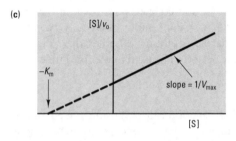

Fig. 55.4 Graphical transformations for determining the kinetic constants of an enzyme. (a) Lineweaver–Burk plot. (b) Eadie–Hofstee plot. (c) Hanes–Woolf plot.

where E = enzyme, ES = enzyme–substrate complex, and k_1, k_2 and k_3 are rate constants. The Michaelis constant can be expressed as:

$$K_m = \frac{k_2 + k_3}{k_1} \qquad [55.4]$$

For many enzymes, $k_3 \ll k_2$, and Eqn [55.4] simplifies to:

$$K_m = \frac{k_2}{k_1} = \frac{[E]\,[S]}{[ES]} \qquad [55.5]$$

When this applies, K_m provides a measure of the affinity of an enzyme for the substrate, and this is an important characteristic of each particular enzyme. Values for mammalian enzymes usually fall within the range 10^{-2}–$10^{-5}\,\text{mol}\,l^{-1}$. Thus an enzyme with a large K_m usually has a low affinity for its substrate, while an enzyme with a small K_m usually has a high affinity. K_m values can be used to select a substrate concentration that will give maximum reaction velocity (p. 383) or to compare the affinities of different substrates for a given enzyme, or the same substrate with different enzymes.

Your first step in determining the kinetic constants for a particular enzyme is to measure the rate of reaction at several substrate concentrations, as in Fig. 55.3. There are various ways to obtain K_m and V_{max} from such data, mostly involving drawing a graph representing a linear transformation of Eqn [55.2]:

- The Lineweaver–Burk plot: a graph of the reciprocal of the reaction rate ($1/v_0$) against the reciprocal of the substrate concentration ($1/[S]$) gives $-1/K_m$ as the intercept of the x-axis and $1/V_{max}$ as the intercept of the y-axis (Fig. 55.4a). The slope of the plot is most affected by the least accurate values, i.e. those measured at low substrate concentration.
- The Eadie–Hofstee plot: v_0 against $v_0/[S]$, where the intercept on the y-axis gives V_{max} and the slope equals $-K_m$ (Fig. 55.4b).
- The Hanes–Woolf plot: $[S]/v_0$ against $[S]$, giving $-K_m$ as the intercept of the x-axis and $1/V_{max}$ from the slope (Fig. 55.4c).
- The direct linear plot (Isenbhal and Cornish) is another option that may give more accurate estimates of kinetic constants than the other plots.

There are several computer packages that will plot the above relationships and calculate the kinetic constants from a given set of data using linear regression analysis (p. 494). While the Eadie–Hofstee and Hanes–Woolf plots distribute the data points more evenly than the Lineweaver–Burk plot, the best approach to such data is to use non-linear regression on untransformed data. This is usually outside the scope of the simpler computer programs, though tailor-made commercial packages can carry out such analyses. Note also that some enzymes, particularly those involved in the control of metabolism, do not show Michaelis–Menten kinetics.

Factors affecting enzyme activity

If you want to measure the maximum rate of a particular enzyme reaction, you will need to optimise the following:

Temperature
Enzyme activity increases with temperature, until an optimum is reached. Above this point, activity decreases as a result of protein denaturation

Removing a bottle of freeze dried enzyme from a freezer or fridge – do not open it until it has been warmed to room temperature or water may condense on the contents – this will make weighing inaccurate and may lead to loss of enzyme activity.

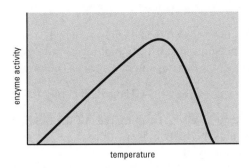

Fig. 55.5 Effect of temperature on enzyme activity.

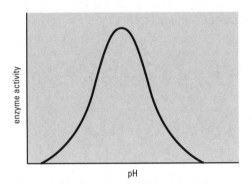

Fig. 55.6 Effect of pH on enzyme activity.

(Fig. 55.5). Note that the optimum temperature for enzyme *activity* may not be the same as that for maximum *stability* (enzymes are usually stored at temperatures near to or below 0 °C, to maximise stability).

pH

Enzymes work best at a particular pH, due to changes in ionisation of the substrates or of the amino acid residues within the enzyme (Fig. 55.6). Most enzyme assays are performed in buffer solutions (p. 150), to prevent changes in pH during the assay. Note that some enzymes have different pH optima for different substrates.

Cofactors

Many enzymes require appropriate concentrations of specific cofactors for maximum activity. These are subdivided into coenzymes (soluble, low molecular weight organic compounds which are actively involved in catalysis by accepting or donating specific chemical groups, i.e. they are co-substrates of the enzyme); examples include NAD^+ and ADP); and activators (inorganic metal ions, required for maximal activity, e.g. Mg^{2+}, K^+).

Substrate concentration

A substrate must be present in excess to ensure maximum reaction velocity. The K_m of an enzyme can be used to predict the substrate concentration required for the enzyme to operate at or near its maximum rate – this occurs when all active sites of the enzyme are filled. Using the Michaelis–Menten equation, the fraction of active sites filled (f_{ES}) for a given reaction velocity, v_o, is given by:

$$f_{ES} = \frac{v_o}{V_{max}} = \frac{[S_o]}{[S_o] + K_m} \qquad [55.6]$$

When $[S_o] = K_m$, 50% of active sites are filled, and the reaction proceeds at $\frac{1}{2} V_{max}$. When $[S_o]$ is 10-fold greater than K_m, 91% of active sites are filled. When $[S_o]$ is 100-fold greater than K_m, 99% of active sites are filled and the reaction proceeds at 99% of V_{max}.

KEY POINT Note that temperature and pH optima are dependent upon reaction conditions, including cofactor and substrate concentrations – you should therefore specify the experimental conditions under which such optima are determined.

Enzyme inhibition

It is important to investigate the inhibition of enzyme activity by specific molecules and ions because:

- enzyme inhibition is an important control mechanism in biological systems (e.g. negative feedback by a product);
- many drugs act by inhibiting enzymes;
- the action of many toxins can be explained by enzyme inhibition.

In terms of their interaction with enzymes, inhibitors can be involved in either reversible or irreversible reactions, and the inhibition can be competitive, non-competitive or uncompetitive, depending on whether inhibition can be reduced by an increase in the concentration of the natural substrate.

Irreversible inhibitors

These are substances, usually not of biological origin, which react covalently with an enzyme (E), preventing substrate binding or catalysis, e.g. iodoacetamide, which binds to thiol groups in enzymes as follows:

$$E—CH_2—SH + ICH_2CONH_2 \longrightarrow E—CH_2—S—CH_2CONH_2 + HI \quad [55.7]$$

The thiol group may be within the active site, forming part of the binding and/or the catalytic sites, or it may be further from the active site and affect the 3D conformation of the enzyme.

The toxicity of heavy metal ions (e.g. Hg^{2+}) is largely due to their irreversible effects on enzyme activity. Other examples include the inhibition of acetylcholinesterase by organophosphate pesticides and nerve agents. In such cases, it is often an active site serine residue that is affected, e.g. with diisopropylfluorophosphate (DFP):

$$E—CH_2OH + F—\overset{\overset{R}{|}}{\underset{\underset{R}{|}}{P}}{=}O \rightarrow E—CH_2O—\overset{\overset{R}{|}}{\underset{\underset{R}{|}}{P}}{=}O + HF \quad [55.8]$$

where R = isopropyl residue.

Reversible inhibitors

These inhibitors do not react covalently with an enzyme, but show rapid reversible binding and dissociation. The velocity of the enzyme-catalysed reaction is reduced by the formation of enzyme–inhibitor (EI) or enzyme–substrate–inhibitor (ESI) complexes. Reversible inhibitors are subdivided according to their effects on K_m and V_{max}:

- Competitive inhibitors bind reversibly to groups in the active site. Often the inhibitor resembles the substrate, and the occupation of the active site by an inhibitor molecule prevents a substrate molecule from binding to the same active site (Fig. 55.7a). The enzyme (E) can bind to the substrate (S), to form an ES complex, or to the inhibitor (I), to form EI, but cannot bind to both (ESI). A competitive inhibitor lowers the rate of catalysis by reducing the proportion of enzyme molecules bound to the substrate. It is possible to reverse competitive inhibition by increasing the substrate concentration; V_{max} is unaffected, but K_m increases (see p. 385). An example of competitive inhibition is the inhibition of succinate dehydrogenase by malonate, an analogue of the natural substrate, succinate.
- Non-competitive reversible inhibition occurs when an inhibitor binds to an enzyme whether or not the active site is occupied by the substrate. This type of inhibition often involves natural inhibitors of enzymes, and is important in the control of metabolism. The inhibitor binds to a site other than the active site (Fig. 55.7b). K_m is unchanged because the affinity of substrate molecules that bind to any uninhibited enzyme is unaffected, but V_{max} decreases due to the concentration of active enzyme molecules being effectively reduced by the presence of inhibitor.
- Uncompetitive inhibition, where the inhibitor binds only after the substrate has bound to the enzyme (Fig. 55.7c). It is most common in reactions involving more than one substrate.

> **Determining the effects of an inhibitor on enzyme kinetics** – measure enzyme activity at $\geqslant 6$ substrate concentrations, both in the presence and absence of inhibitor.

Fig. 55.7 Representation of (a) competitive inhibition, where the inhibitor (I) binds to the same site on the enzyme (E) as the substrate (S); (b) simple linear non-competitive inhibition; (c) uncompetitive inhibition (P = products).

(a)

(b)

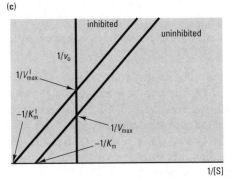

(c)

Fig. 55.8 Lineweaver–Burk plots showing the effect of (a) competitive inhibition, (b) simple linear non-competitive inhibition, (c) un-competitive inhibition.

Using enzyme inhibition kinetics to identify the type of inhibitor

Enzyme kinetics can be used to distinguish between the different forms of inhibition and to provide quantitative information on the effectiveness of various inhibitors, by allowing the dissociation constant of the enzyme–inhibitor complex, K_i, to be determined. K_i is an expression that relates to the strength of binding of the inhibitor to the enzyme.

Competitive inhibition

With inhibitor present, the enzyme can react with the substrate (Eqn [55.3]), but can also react reversibly with the inhibitor (I), to give an inactive enzyme–inhibitor complex (EI), as follows:

$$E + I \underset{k_2'}{\overset{k_1'}{\rightleftharpoons}} EI \qquad [55.9]$$

As a result, the presence of I decreases the amount of free enzyme [E] available for interaction with S, i.e. $[E] = [E_T] - [ES] - [EI]$, where E_T is the total amount of enzyme present. The concentration of the EI complex depends on the concentration of free inhibitor and on the dissociation constant, K_i, where:

$$K_i = \frac{[E][I]}{[EI]} = \frac{k_2'}{k_1'} \qquad [55.10]$$

The Michaelis–Menten equation (Eqn [55.2]) must be modified to account for the presence of inhibitor and for a competitive inhibitor, and results in the Lineweaver–Burk plot shown in Fig. 55.8. The lines in the presence and absence of inhibitor intersect on the ordinate (y-axis), indicating that with competitive inhibition, the inhibitory effect disappears at high substrate concentration (when $1/[S] = 0$, $[S] = \infty$). The value of K_i can be calculated either from knowledge of the K_m values obtained in the presence and absence of inhibitor (intercepts on the abscissa or x-axis), since the following relationship applies:

$$\text{slope}_{\text{inhibited}} = \text{slope}_{\text{uninhibited}} \frac{(1 + [I])}{(K_i)} \qquad [55.11]$$

Non-competitive inhibition

In this case, not only can I bind E, but I can also bind to the ES complex to give an inactive ESI complex, i.e. $E + I \rightleftharpoons EI$ and $ES + I \rightleftharpoons ESI$. In the simplest case, the binding of S has no effect on the binding of I, and *vice versa*, so the dissociation constant of ESI is the same as that of ES, i.e. the K_m. A typical Lineweaver–Burk plot for a non-competitive inhibitor is shown in Fig. 55.8b. This indicates that this type of inhibitor decreases V_{max} but does not affect K_m. Effectively, this means that the inhibitor removes a certain fraction of active enzyme from operation, no matter what the concentration of substrate. The V_{max} changes by a factor of $(1 + [I])/K_i$ and K_i can be obtained by comparison of the slopes obtained with the uninhibited enzyme and the inhibited enzyme, as described above for a competitive inhibitor.

Uncompetitive inhibition

An uncompetitive inhibitor leads to a Lineweaver–Burk plot as shown in Fig. 55.8c. Parallel lines are obtained, and both K_m and V_{max} are affected. Here K_i pertains to the dissociation of I from ESI. Uncompetitive inhibitors are fairly rare.

Regulatory enzymes

In cell metabolism, groups of enzymes work together in sequential pathways to carry out a given metabolic process. In such enzyme systems, the reaction product of the first enzyme becomes the substrate for the next. Most of the enzymes in each system obey Michaelis–Menten kinetics. However in each system, there is at least one enzyme – often the first in the sequence – that sets the rate of the overall sequence (the flux through the pathway) because it catalyses the slowest or rate-limiting step. These regulatory enzymes exhibit increased or decreased catalytic activity in response to certain signals. By the action of such regulatory enzymes, the rate of each metabolic sequence is constantly adjusted to meet changes in the cell's demands for energy and biosynthesis.

The activities of regulatory enzymes are altered by non-covalent binding of various types of signal molecules, which are generally small metabolites or cofactors termed 'modulators'. Such enzymes are generally described as 'allosteric'.

Properties of allosteric enzymes

The following general characteristics enable allosteric enzymes to be identified:

- Feedback inhibition: in some multi-enzyme systems the regulatory enzyme is specifically inhibited by the end-product of the pathway whenever the end-product increases in excess of the cell's needs. The end-product does not bind to the active site but binds to another, specific, site termed the regulatory site. This binding is non-covalent and readily reversible. Thus if the concentration of the end-product decreases, the rate of enzyme activity increases.
- Modulators for allosteric enzymes may be either inhibitory or stimulatory. An activator is often the substrate itself, and regulatory enzymes for which substrate and modulator are identical are called homotropic. When a modulator is a molecule other than the substrate the enzyme is heterotropic. Some enzymes have two or more modulators.
- Each enzyme molecule has one or more regulatory or allosteric sites for binding the modulator. Just as the enzyme's active site is specific for its substrate, the allosteric site is specific for its modulator. Enzymes with several modulators generally have different specific binding sites for each. In homotropic enzymes the active site and regulatory site are the same.
- These enzymes are generally larger and more complex than simple enzymes and normally consist of two or more subunits, e.g. aspartate transcarbamoylase, the principal regulatory enzyme in the synthetic pathway for CTP, has six catalytic subunits and six regulatory subunits. A useful technique for preliminary determination of subunit structure is SDS-PAGE (Chapter 46).

Definition

Allosteric enzyme – an enzyme having more than one shape or conformation induced by the binding of modulators (Greek allos, 'other'; stereos, 'solid' or 'shape').

Example *In the multi-stage conversion of* L-*threonine into* L-*isoleucine in bacteria, the first enzyme in the sequence (threonine dehydratase) is inhibited by isoleucine, the final product.*

- Michaelis–Menten kinetics are not followed. When v_o is plotted against [S] a sigmoid saturation curve normally results (Fig. 55.9), rather than the hyperbolic curve shown by non-regulatory enzymes (Fig. 55.3). With sigmoidal kinetics, although a value of [S] can be determined at which v_o is half maximal, this value is not equivalent to K_m. Instead the symbol $[S]_{0.5}$, or $K_{0.5}$, is often used to represent the substrate concentration giving half maximum velocity of the reaction catalysed by an allosteric enzyme. Sigmoid kinetic behaviour generally reflects cooperative interactions between multiple protein subunits, i.e. changes in the structure of one subunit result in structural changes in adjacent subunits that affect substrate binding. In general, allosteric activators cause the curve to become more nearly hyperbolic (Fig. 55.9), with a decrease in $K_{0.5}$, but no change in V_{max}, and therefore v_o is higher for any value of substrate concentration. However, some allosteric enzymes respond to an activator by an increase in V_{max} with little change in $K_{0.5}$. In contrast, an allosteric inhibitor may produce a more sigmoidal curve with an increase in $K_{0.5}$ (Fig. 55.9).

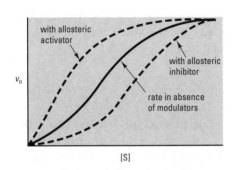

Fig. 55.9 Allosteric effects in enzyme kinetics. The graph shows the rate of enzyme reaction (v_o) against substrate concentration [S].

Example The binding of adrenaline to receptors in skeletal muscle triggers a series of reactions that culminates in the phosphorylation of a particular serine residue in the enzyme glycogen phosphorylase: this activates the enzyme, resulting in increased glycogen breakdown.

Covalently modified regulatory enzymes

Some enzymes are regulated by covalent modification, e.g. by phosphorylation of the hydroxyl groups of specific serine, threonine or tyrosine residues. Depending on the enzyme, this may result in activation or inactivation: in most cases, the non-phosphorylated form of the enzyme is relatively inactive. Often these modifications are under hormonal control. Some regulatory enzymes are influenced both by covalent modification and by allosteric effects.

Text reference

James, A.L. (1994) Enzymes in Taxonomy and Diagnostic Bacteriology. In M. Goodfellow and A.G. McDonnell (eds) *Chemical Methods in Bacterial Systematics*, pp. 471–92. Wiley, London.

Sources for further study

Anon. *International Union of Biochemistry and Molecular Biology*. Available:
http://www.chem.qmw.ac.uk/iubmb/
Last accessed 08/01/03.
[Links to enzyme nomenclature database and other relevant websites.]

Copeland, R.A. (2000) *Enzymes: A Practical Introduction to Structure, Mechanism, and Data Analysis*. Wiley, New York.
[Covers basic principles, kinetics and experimental systems.]

Cornish-Bowden, A. (1995) *Analysis of Enzyme Kinetic Data*. Oxford University Press, Oxford.

Eisethal, R. and Danson, M. (2002) *Enzyme Assays: A Practical Approach*, 2nd edn. Oxford University Press, Oxford.

Passonneau, J.V. and Lowry, O.H. (1993) *Enzymatic Analysis: A Practical Guide*. Humana Press, New Jersey.

Purich, D.L. and Allison, R.D. (2000) *Handbook of Biochemical Kinetics*. Academic Press, New York.

Segel, I.H. (1993) *Enzyme Kinetics: Behavior and Analysis of Rapid Equilibrium and Steady-State Enzyme Systems*. Wiley, New York.
[In-depth coverage of theoretical and practical aspects.]

Study exercises

55.1 Determine enzyme activity and purity (specific activity). An extract of α-glucosidase containing 2.5 mg of protein was incubated with *p*-nitrophenol-α-D-glucose at $1.0\,mmol\,l^{-1}$ and assayed by following the liberation of *p*-nitrophenol at 404 nm. This gave a progress curve with an initial velocity equal to an absorbance change of $0.25\,min^{-1}$. Given that the conversion of 10 nmol of substrate to product results in an absorbance change of 0.122:
(a) Determine the amount of product formed in $nmol\,min^{-1}$;
(b) Calculate the enzyme activity in kat;
(c) Determine the specific activity, in terms of (i) $nmol\,min^{-1}$ (mg protein)$^{-1}$ and (ii) kat (mg protein)$^{-1}$.
(Quote all answers to 3 significant figures.)

55.2 Estimate K_m and V_{max} for an enzyme. The table below shows repre-sentative data for enzyme activity as a function of substrate concentration. Use a suitable graphical method to determine the kinetic constants K_m and V_{max} of the enzyme (give your answers to 3 significant figures).

Enzyme activity at various substrate concentrations

Substrate concentration ($\mu mol\,l^{-1}$)	Enzyme activity (U)
0	0
5	16.2
7	20.5
10	28.1
15	32.7
25	39.2
50	56.7
100	68.2

55.3 Identify the type of enzyme inhibition shown by therapeutic drugs. In the treatment of acquired immunodeficiency syndrome (AIDS), a possible mode of therapy is to inhibit the reverse transcriptase (RT) of the human immunodeficiency virus (HIV), which is required for the retrovirus to be propagated by RNA-directed DNA synthesis. In the figure, one of the substrates for RT is thymidine (a); two drugs, AZT (b) and HBY097 (c) are known to inhibit HIV RT.

Look at the structures and predict the type of inhibition (i.e. competitive or non-competitive) likely to be shown by each drug. Outline an experiment that would enable you to confirm the type of inhibition by investigating enzyme kinetics and explain how you would interpret the results.

Membrane transport processes

(a)

(b)

Fig. 56.1 Time course of (a) tracer influx and (b) tracer efflux (A_t). A_α = tracer activity at equilibrium.

Example Suppose 5 ml of a red cell suspension containing 2 mg protein ml^{-1} accumulated 1050 Bq of radiolabelled solute of specific activity 210 Bq nmol^{-1} in 8 min. The net rate of solute accumulation over this time period, expressed in nmol mg protein^{-1} min^{-1}, would be
1050 ÷ 210 ÷ 10 ÷ 8 = 0.0625
(≡ 62.5 pmol mg protein^{-1} min^{-1}).

All cells operate a variety of processes whereby solutes move across membranes, including those processes involved in the uptake of nutrients and the loss of metabolic waste products at the plasma membrane, or the intracellular transport of substances across internal membranes, e.g. mitochondria. Membrane transport processes serve to regulate the intracellular environment, creating suitable conditions for internal metabolism. In microbes, the plasma membrane plays the principal role in the selective movement of biomolecules into, or out of, the cell. In multicellular animals and plants, membrane transport processes in the outermost epithelial layers are especially important in determining the solute composition of tissues and organs. Individual organs often have specialised transport functions, e.g. in animals, nutrient absorption by intestinal epithelial cells and urea excretion *via* the proximal tubular epithelial cells of the kidney or, in plants, the uptake of nutrients by root hair cells.

Measuring solute transport

Usually, the rate of movement of a solute in a particular biological system is determined using a radioisotope-labelled (p. 258) or a stable isotope-labelled solute (p. 285) as a 'tracer'. Typically, in solute uptake (influx), the labelled solute is added to the external medium and its accumulation is then monitored by assaying samples of cells or tissue after known time intervals, enabling you to plot the accumulation of tracer as a function of time. Loss of solute (efflux) is studied using cells or tissues pre-loaded with labelled solute and then transferred to a tracer-free incubation medium: samples of the medium can be assayed after known time intervals, allowing the time course to be followed without destruction of the biological material. For microbial cell suspensions, filtration or silicone oil microcentrifugation (p. 291) may be used to separate the cells from their incubation medium.

KEY POINT Determination of the relationship between the amount of tracer and the amount of solute (the 'specific activity', p. 261) enables the uptake or loss of solute to be expressed in terms of the net amount of solute transported per unit biomass (e.g. per mg protein, or per cell) per unit time. If the relationship between biomass and membrane area is known, the net uptake or loss of solute can be expressed per m^2 surface area per unit time.

Short-term tracer studies will give approximate values for the unidirectional flux rate from the labelled side of the membrane: longer-term studies may show more complex kinetics, due to two-way tracer movement or to secondary transport within the cells.

For non-metabolised solutes that are accumulated to particular levels within individual cells, e.g. inorganic ions such as K$^+$, Na$^+$, Cl$^-$, the time course for tracer accumulation or loss will often show exponential kinetics, as the transport process allows the tracer to equilibrate across the cell membrane (Fig. 56.1). Such exponential plots can be transformed to give linear plots using the relationship ln$(1 - A_t/A_\alpha)$ for influx, where A_α is the activity at equilibrium and A_t is the activity after time $= t$, while a plot of $\ln A_t/A_\alpha$ should be linear when the cell behaves as a single compartment with respect to tracer exchange. The slope of such a plot gives a rate constant for exchange (k) that can be used to quantify the unidirectional solute movement, either influx or efflux (ϕ) from the following equation:

$$\phi = \frac{k[C_i]}{M_a} \qquad [56.1]$$

where $[C_i]$ is the internal solute content, determined either from tracer equilibration or by chemical assay (p. 343), and M_a is the membrane surface area. For some cells and tissues, an initial, short-term component is observed, due to tracer exchange between the extracellular space and the bulk medium – this can be subtracted from the longer-term component, allowing correction for extracellular tracer content.

Metabolised solutes pose additional problems, since they do not simply equilibrate across membranes – for example, glucose may be used as a source of carbon or energy after being transported into a cell. Transport studies of metabolised solutes may need to account for such processes, e.g. by separating and assaying the various labelled metabolites. A simpler alternative is to use a non-metabolised analogue of the solute, enabling transmembrane movement to be studied in the absence of metabolism and simplifying the interpretation of tracer studies.

Identifying the transport mechanism for a particular solute

Many studies are carried out to provide information on the nature of the transport process. Solute movement is often subdivided into a number of categories:

Simple diffusion – passive transport

In accordance with Fick's first law of diffusion, an uncharged molecule can move through the lipid bilayer of a membrane with a net flux, J, determined by its lipid solubility and by the difference in concentration (strictly, the difference in activity) across the membrane, according to the relationship:

$$J = P([C_o] - [C_i]) \qquad [56.2]$$

where P is the permeability coefficient for the substance while $[C_o]$ and $[C_i]$ are external and internal solute concentrations respectively. The permeability coefficients of various solutes correlate with their partition coefficients between non-polar organic solvents and water, reflecting their relative solubility in the lipid phase. At a practical level, the flux rate calculated from Eqn [56.2] will apply only to the initial state, since diffusion will reduce the concentration gradient and hence the flux rate.

At a practical level, a number of characteristics can be used to recognise simple diffusion, including:

- The measured rates of transport are consistent with the lipid permeabilities of artificial lipid bilayers (e.g. values in Stein, 1997).
- The rate of transport is directly proportional to the concentration gradient (Eqn [56.2]), giving a straight line relationship with no evidence of saturation, in contrast to *all* other transport systems.
- Movement is insensitive to inhibitors, including structural analogues of the solute, metabolic inhibitors and chemical inactivators.

Example 3-O-methyl glucose and 2-deoxyglucose are non-metabolised analogues of glucose, while methyl-β-D-thiogalactoside is a non-metabolised analogue of lactose.

Definition

Fick's first law of diffusion – each solute diffuses in a direction that eliminates its concentration gradient and at a rate proportional to the size of the gradient.

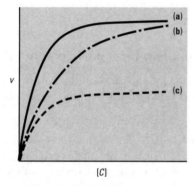

Fig. 56.2 Relationship between the rate of transport (*v*) and solute concentration [*C*] for (a) uninhibited 'control', (b) with a competitive inhibitor, (c) with a non-competitive inhibitor.

Determining kinetic parameters in transport studies – since Eqn [56.3] is equivalent to the Michaelis–Menten equation, the same approaches can be used to determine V_{max} and K_s (see p. 381).

- Passive diffusion lacks specificity – chemically similar solutes with comparable lipid solubilities will show similar rates of transmembrane movement.

Simple diffusion can account for the movement of only a limited number of low M_r, uncharged substances, including O_2, CO_2, NH_3 and non-polar hydrocarbons. There is negligible transbilayer diffusion of all other polar and ionic solutes, due to their hydrophilic, lipophobic nature and to the presence of a surrounding shell of water molecules, preventing movement through the hydrophobic interior of the membrane.

KEY POINT All solutes not transported across membranes by simple diffusion are moved by protein-mediated transporters, often termed 'permeases', 'porters' or 'translocators'.

Facilitated diffusion – passive transport

Here, the transmembrane movement is the result of specific membrane proteins (often termed 'uniporters'). While net movement is energetically 'downhill', as in simple diffusion, the rate of movement is more rapid than would be predicted from Eqn [56.2], since the individual uniporter molecules act as solute-specific channels across the membrane. Examples include glucose transport across the erythrocyte membrane, maltodextrin transport across the outer membrane of Gram-negative bacteria and the stretch activated ion channels in stomatal membranes. The diagnostic features of facilitated diffusion include:

- The measured rates of transport are far greater than can be accounted for by simple diffusion and Fick's first law: for example, the erythrocyte glucose system operates at more than 10 000 times the rate predicted from permeability coefficients of synthetic lipid bilayers.
- The system exhibits specificity, transporting the solute but not chemically related compounds with a different 3D shape.
- The rate of transport should show saturation kinetics similar to those observed for enzymes (Fig. 56.2), with a hyperbolic relationship between the rate of transport (*v*) and solute concentration [*C*] according to the relationship:

$$v = \frac{V_{max}[C]}{K_s + [C]}$$ [56.3]

where V_{max} is the maximum rate of transport and K_s, the half saturation constant, is a measure of the affinity of the transport system for the solute – a low K_s generally indicates a high-affinity transport system while a high K_s shows that the transport system has a low affinity for the solute.

- Movement is sensitive to competitive inhibitors – the presence of structurally similar compounds will reduce the rate of solute transport. Competitive inhibitors decrease the affinity of the permease (increased K_s), but V_{max} is not affected (Fig. 56.2).
- Facilitated diffusion systems are susceptible to inactivation by non-competitive inhibitors that act as protein denaturants, e.g. heavy metal salts. Such irreversible inactivation confirms that the transport process is mediated by a protein. At low concentrations of inhibitor, only some of the permease molecules will be inactivated, giving a decreased V_{max} but unchanged K_s (Fig. 56.2).

If facilitated diffusion of an uncharged solute occurs, then net solute movement will occur down the transmembrane concentration gradient. However, for charged solutes (ions), net movement will depend on the transmembrane electrical potential (the membrane potential), as well as the concentration gradient. The transmembrane equilibrium potential for a particular ion, E_n, can be calculated from the Nernst equation, as:

$$E_n = 2.303 \frac{RT}{zF} \log \frac{[C_o]}{[C_i]}$$

[56.4]

Example A membrane potential of $-100\,mV$ (interior negative) can account for a 50-fold passive accumulation of a monovalent cation and a 50-fold passive exclusion of a monovalent anion.

where all symbols have their usual meanings (p. 178, see also Chapter 48). A comparison of the equilibrium potential and the membrane potential will show whether the ion is in electrochemical equilibrium across the membrane, or whether it has been transported against the electrochemical potential gradient.

KEY POINT The transmembrane electrical potential, responsible for the facilitated diffusion of ions, is usually established as a direct result of the action of one or more ion-pumping, active transport systems, e.g. H^+-ATPases.

Measuring membrane potentials – depending on the cell type, this can be carried out using microelectrodes, lipophilic cations or fluorescent dyes (see p. 405).

Ionophores (Table 56.1) can be viewed as simple models of facilitated diffusion systems: they can be used to study the effects of an increase in the permeability of membranes to a single solute or group of solutes, to create transmembrane movements of ions, or to monitor specific ions in solution.

Table 56.1 Ionophores and inhibitors of transmembrane solute movement[1]

Ionophores	Effect
valinomycin	electrogenic carrier: increased permeability to K^+ and Rb^+
gramicidin A	electrogenic channel: uniport of monovalent ions, particularly H^+
monensin	electroneutral carrier: exchange of Na^+ or Li^+ for H^+
nigericin	electroneutral carrier: exchange of K^+ or Rb^+ for H^+
A-23187	electroneutral carrier: exchange of divalent cations (e.g. Ca^{++}, Mg^{++}) for $2H^+$
2,4-dinitrophenol (DNP)	electrogenic carrier: increased H^+ permeability (protonophore)
carbonylcyanide *m*-chlorophenyl-hydrazone (CCCP)	electrogenic carrier: increased H^+ permeability (protonophore)
carbonylcyanide *p*-trifluoromethoxy-phenylhydrazone (FCCP)	electrogenic carrier: increased H^+ permeability (protonophore)
nonactin	increased permeability of monovalent cations
amphotericin B	anion channel (weak selectivity)
nystatin	anion channel (weak selectivity)
Transport inhibitors[2]	**Effect**
oligomycin	inhibition of F_0F_1-type H^+-ATPases (mitochondria, bacteria, chloroplasts)
ouabain	inhibition of Na^+-K^+-ATPases (mammalian cell plasma membrane)
digitoxigenin	inhibition of Na^+-K^+-ATPases (mammalian cell plasma membrane)
vanadate	inhibition of E_1E_2-type ATPases (plant plasma membrane)
N,N-dicyclohexylcarbodiimide (DCCD)	inhibition of F_0F_1 and V-type ATPases (mitochondria and plant tonoplast)
N-ethylmaleimide (NEM)	inhibition of plant tonoplast V-type ATPases
phlorizin	inhibition of Na^+-glucose symporters (intestinal epithelial cells)
furosemide	inhibition of cotransporters (mammalian cell membrane)
cytochalasin B	inhibition of glucose transporters (mammalian cell membrane)
amiloride	inhibition of Na^+/H^+ antiporters (mammalian and plant cells)
4,4′-diisothiocyano-2,2′-stilbene-disulphonate (DIDS)	inhibition of mammalian anion antiporters

[1]*Safety note:* all of these inhibitors are highly toxic and must be handled carefully, observing the appropriate safety precautions.
[2]Details of electron transport inhibitors are given in Chapter 57.

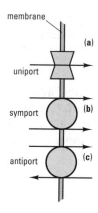

membrane

(a)

uniport

symport (b)

antiport (c)

Fig. 56.3 Diagrammatic representation of various membrane transport systems, indicating the direction of movement of transported solute molecules.

Interpreting inhibitor experiments – while short-term effects may be unique to a particular inhibitor, in the longer term more general, non-specific effects are likely. For example, inhibitors of primary active transport will eventually affect secondary transport systems, due to their effects on ion gradients and membrane potentials.

Active transport

The principal criterion to establish active transport is that movement of the solute occurs against its electrochemical potential gradient. The energy for such 'uphill' transport can be provided by one of two mechanisms:

1. Primary active transport. The movement of solute molecules is coupled to the hydrolysis of ATP, via a membrane-bound solute-specific ATPase, or to a redox chain. For example, the Na^+-K^+ ATPase of mammalian cells is a primary active transporter, moving $3 Na^+$ ions outwards and $2 K^+$ ions inwards for every molecule of ATP hydrolysed, i.e. it is *electrogenic*, with a net charge separation across the membrane. Some of the most important primary active transport processes are those which create a transmembrane H^+ gradient, or proton-motive force (Δp), either via a H^+-translocating ATPase or an electron transport chain (p. 405). In many membranes, Δp provides the major driving force for the movement of other solutes (see Nicholls and Ferguson, 1997, for details). Some Gram-negative bacteria use a variation of phosphoryl-driven active transport to accumulate certain sugars – this is known as 'group translocation' since it involves the simultaneous phosphorylation of each sugar molecule as it is transported. Because the cell membrane is impermeable to sugar phosphates, the bacterial 'phosphotransferase' system can concentrate these solutes within cells.

2. Secondary active transport, or secondary transport. Here, the movement of solute is coupled to the 'downhill' movement of another solute, either via a 'symporter' (co-transporter) that simultaneously transports the two solutes in the same direction, or an 'antiporter' (counter-transporter) that simultaneously moves the two solutes in opposite directions across the membrane (Fig. 56.3). These systems are 'active' only in the sense that the 'downhill' movement of the other solute can only occur after primary active transport has established a transmembrane solute gradient (e.g. for H^+ or Na^+). Thus, lactose uptake in bacterial cells is coupled to the transmembrane proton gradient, via the lactose–H^+ symporter, while Na^+ efflux from plant cells is mediated by an Na^+–H^+ antiporter. In both instances, the H^+ gradient is created by a primary active transport system that pumps protons out of the cell, generating a proton-motive force that can be utilised by secondary transport systems. Similarly, the Na^+–K^+ primary active transport system creates an Na^+ gradient that can be utilised for nutrient uptake in mammalian cells, e.g. via the Na^+– glucose symporter (a secondary transporter). Primary and secondary transport systems can be envisaged as operating as a 'circuit' for the movement of ions across membranes (Fig. 56.3).

In addition to the characteristics of specificity, saturation and inhibition shared by facilitated diffusion, active transport systems can be identified by the following features:

- The transmembrane distribution of the solute is not consistent with Eqn [56.2] (where $J = 0$ at equilibrium, i.e. $[C_o] = [C_i]$) for an uncharged solute, or Eqn [56.4] for an ion.
- The active component will be sensitive to metabolic inhibitors, e.g. ATPase inhibitors, for primary active transport, or specific inhibitors of secondary transporters (see Table 56.1).

For secondary transport systems, dissipation of the primary ion gradient using a suitable ionophore will inhibit transport of the solute. Conversely, artificially generated ion gradients can be used to drive solute movement, either in whole cells or in membrane vesicle preparations.

Studying membrane transport using patch-clamp techniques

In this technique, part of a membrane (a 'patch') is sealed to the end of a heat-polished micropipette of diameter $\approx 1\,\mu m$ and the flow of current across the membrane patch is then measured for different bathing solutions and/or transmembrane voltages, set at particular values ('clamped') by a feedback amplifier. The size and orientation of the membrane patch can be controlled, as shown in Fig. 56.4. Since the membrane patch can be relatively small, the operation of ion-transporting proteins can be seen as changes in current flow, due to the opening or closing of individual membrane 'channels' (voltage-sensitive transporters). While the physiological factors controlling the *in vivo* operation of such channels remain unclear, patch clamping provides a powerful means of studying channel-mediated ion movements *in vitro*, enabling investigation of:

- the voltage required to produce 'channel' opening;
- the membrane conductance under conditions where the ion concentrations on both sides of the membrane are known;
- temporal effects, including opening and closing times, frequency of opening, etc.;
- the ion selectivity of particular 'channels';
- the effects of inhibitors, ionophores, etc.

When whole cells are used, the flow of ions through primary active ion transport systems (ion 'pumps') can be studied, since changes in current flow represent the sum of many transporters, acting together. Patch-clamp systems have provided a considerable amount of information on the transport properties of individual membranes, e.g. the plasma membrane and tonoplast of plant cells (see Flowers and Yeo, 1992, for details).

Fig. 56.4 Patch-clamp techniques: (a) whole plant cell, (b) inside-out membrane patch, (c) outside-out membrane patch.

Text references and sources for further study

Baldwin, S.A. (2000) *Membrane Transport: A Practical Approach*. Oxford University Press, Oxford.

Flowers, T.J. and Yeo, A.R. (1992) *Solute Transport in Plants*. Blackie, London.

Nicholls, D.G. and Ferguson, S.J. (1997) *Bioenergetics*, 2nd edn. Academic Press, London.

Stein, W.D. (1997) *Channels, Carriers and Pumps: An Introduction to Membrane Transport*. Academic Press, New York.

Study exercises

56.1 Calculate flux rates of various solutes based on data from tracer studies. Using the following data for rate constant (k), internal concentration ($[C_i]$) and membrane surface area (M_a), calculate the unidirectional flux of each solute (express your answers to 3 significant figures, in all of the study exercises in this chapter):

(a) Solute uptake for a cell where $k = 0.0001\,s^{-1}$, $[C_i] = 150\,mol\,m^{-3}$ and $M_a = 50\,000\,m^2\,m^{-3}$.

(b) K^+ efflux from a protozoan, where $k = -1.65 \times 10^{-4}\,s^{-1}$, $[C_i] = 106\,mol\,m^{-3}$ and $M_a = 8.25 \times 10^4\,m^2\,m^{-3}$.

(c) Na^+ uptake into a bacterial cell, where $k = 4.75 \times 10^{-5}\,s^{-1}$, $[C_i] = 10.5\,mmol\,dm^{-3}$ and $M_a = 1.66 \times 10^{-9}\,m^2\,dm^{-3}$.

56.2 Determine passive transmembrane fluxes of uncharged solutes. What is the direction and magnitude of the net passive transmembrane flux for each of the following cases, all involving uncharged solutes:

(a) Movement of glycerol in a halotolerant bacterial cell with an internal concentration of $10\,mol\,m^{-3}$, an external concentration of $1.5\,mol\,m^{-3}$ and a permeability coefficient of $2 \times 10^{-7}\,m\,s^{-1}$.

(b) Glucose movement in an animal cell with an internal concentration of $8.65\,mol\,m^{-3}$, an external concentration of $0.03\,mol\,m^{-3}$ and a permeability coefficient of $1.6 \times 10^{-9}\,m\,s^{-1}$.

(c) Methanol flow in a fungal cell with an internal concentration of $0.25\,mmol\,dm^{-3}$, an external concentration of $3.45\,mmol\,dm^{-3}$ and a permeability coefficient of $2.6 \times 10^{-3}\,cm\,s^{-1}$.

56.3 Interpret kinetic parameters of transport systems. Details of the kinetic parameters for the transport of an amino acid into cells of three different types are given in the table.

Kinetic parameters for amino acid uptake into three different cell types

Cell type	V_{max}	K_s
A	$15.2\,pmol\,dm^{-3}\,s^{-1}$	$1.24 \times 10^{-6}\,pmol\,dm^{-3}$
B	$9.6\,nmol\,m^{-3}\,s^{-1}$	$6.54 \times 10^5\,nmol\,m^{-3}$
C	$84 \times 10^{-11}\,mol\,m^{-3}\,s^{-1}$	$2.54 \times 10^{-4}\,mol\,m^{-3}$

(a) Which cell type has the highest maximum rate of transport?

(b) Which cell type has the highest affinity for the amino acid?

(c) Which cell type gives the fastest rate of uptake at an amino acid concentration of $1 \times 10^{-4}\,mol\,m^{-3}$?

56.4 Compare calculated transmembrane equilibrium potentials with the membrane potential to decide whether an ion has been actively transported. At $25\,°C$, a marine algal cell has a measured plasma membrane potential of $-56\,mV$ and the following internal (cytoplasmic) and external ion concentrations:

Internal and external ion concentrations for a marine alga

Ion	Internal concentration (mol m^{-3})	External concentration (mol m^{-3})
K^+	197	10
Na^+	8.4	225
Cl^-	27.3	235

(a) What is the transmembrane equilibrium potential for each of these ions?

(b) Which ions appear to be in electrochemical equilibrium and which appear to be actively transported (and in what direction)?

57 Photosynthesis and respiration

Techniques for investigating photosynthesis and respiration are considered together, since:

- Gas exchange processes in these two processes may be studied using similar techniques, and interpreted in similar stoichiometric terms, e.g. by relating changes in O_2 or CO_2 to those of other reactants or products.
- Membrane-bound electron transport systems are involved in the production of a transmembrane H^+ gradient that drives ATP synthesis via an ATPase embedded in the same membrane. Measurement of electron transport in photosynthesis and respiration often makes use of redox dyes as artificial electron donors or acceptors, with spectrophotometric analysis of the reactions.
- Some electron transport inhibitors can affect both photosynthesis and respiration, while others are specific to one or the other process.

KEY POINT Photosynthesis and respiration are complex, multistage metabolic pathways involving a large number of cellular components: they may be studied as a whole, or as isolated components and individual metabolic reactions, to gain a deeper insight into the underlying processes.

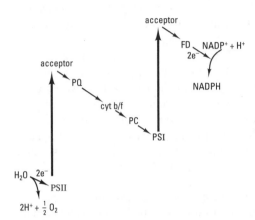

Fig. 57.1 Non-cyclic electron transport from H_2O to $NADP^+$ in plant photosynthesis (Z scheme) showing the principal components: PS II, photosystem II; PQ, plastoquinone; cyt, cytochrome; PC, plastocyanin; PS I, photosystem I; FD, ferredoxin; $NADP^+$, nicotinamide adenine dinucleotide phosphate.

Measuring photosynthetic pigments – equations for spectrophotometric analysis of chlorophylls are given on p. 273.

Definitions

C_3 **plants** – those in which phosphoglyceric acid is the first stable product.

C_4 **plants** – those in which malate or aspartate are the principal products, via oxaloacetic acid, in a reaction catalysed by phosphoenolpyruvate (PEP) carboxylase.

CAM plants – those in which malic acid is produced, via oxaloacetic acid, by PEP carboxylase activity at night, with little or no net assimilation of CO_2 during the day (crassulacean acid metabolism).

Photosynthesis

This is the conversion of light energy to chemical energy by photoautotrophic plants and bacteria. The overall process is often summarised in terms of the synthesis of carbohydrate, $(CH_2O)_n$, driven by the energy within photons of light (hv), as:

$$nCO_2 + 2nH_2O^* + 4nhv \rightarrow (CH_2O)_n + nO_2^* + nH_2O \quad [57.1]$$

where the asterisks show that all of the O_2 is derived from the photolysis of water. Carbohydrate synthesis occurs as a result of two distinct processes, namely (i) light reactions and (ii) dark reactions. In the former, light energy is absorbed by pigments within membrane-bound reaction centres (photosystems). The water-splitting light reactions generate electrons, protons and molecular oxygen. Electron and proton movement via a series of membrane-bound redox carriers leads to the reduction of $NADP^+$ and the generation of ATP (photophosphorylation), driven by a transmembrane H^+ gradient, or proton-motive force (p. 405). The light reactions of plant-type photosynthesis are often represented by the 'Z scheme' (Fig. 57.1).

The dark reactions use the products of the light reactions to 'fix' CO_2, via a series of soluble enzymes known as the Calvin cycle, or reductive pentose phosphate cycle. The primary carboxylating enzyme in temperate green plants (C_3 plants) and cyanobacteria is ribulose bisphosphate carboxylase ('Rubisco'). This enzyme catalyses the addition of CO_2 to ribulose bisphosphate (C_5), producing two molecules of phosphoglyceric acid (C_3) which are then reduced to triose phosphate (C_3) by enzymes that utilise the NADPH and ATP generated by the light reactions. Thus both light and dark reactions operate in a coupled manner when photosynthetically active cells are illuminated with visible light.

Correcting for photorespiration and respiration – measuring the rate of O_2 consumption or CO_2 production in the first few minutes after the plant material has been transferred from the light to darkness will give you the best estimate of photorespiratory and respiratory gas exchange. Use this rate to convert net photosynthesis to gross photosynthesis.

Preventing oxygen supersaturation in oxygen electrode studies – lower the O_2 content of your experimental solutions by bubbling them with N_2 before use, so that the O_2 evolved during the experiment remains in solution.

Measuring photosynthetic activity

Eqn [57.1] shows that the rate of photosynthesis can be measured in terms of the amount of O_2 evolved or CO_2 fixed. However, several other metabolic processes may lead to concurrent changes in O_2 and/or CO_2 status, particularly:

- Photorespiration – light-dependent O_2 uptake, due to the oxygenase activity of Rubisco, leading to the production of glycollic acid (C_2) and the subsequent release of CO_2 due to the operation of a 'scavenging' pathway where two molecules of glycollate are converted to one of phosphoglyceric acid (C_3). The relative rates of photosynthesis and photorespiration depend upon the concentration of O_2 and CO_2 at the active site of Rubisco – in C_3 plants, photorespiration is highest under conditions of high temperature, high light and low water availability, while C_4 plants show low levels of photorespiration.

- Respiration – generation of ATP *via* carbohydrate oxidation, as in non-photosynthetic cells (p. 403). In most photoautotrophs, respiratory activity is likely to be lower during the day than at night. However, plant tissues often respond to wounding or environmental stress by *increasing* their rate of respiration – this may be significant if you are measuring photosynthetic activity in tissue fragments, isolated cells or protoplasts. If you wish to calculate gross rates of photosynthesis, you must make appropriate allowances for both respiration and photorespiration.

Measurement of oxygen production This is most often used with aquatic systems, including algae and photosynthetic bacteria, higher plant cells, protoplasts, chloroplast suspensions (p. 237) or isolated thylakoids. Oxygen in solution can be determined by end-point chemical analysis (e.g. the Winkler method, often used in ecological and field studies) or, more conveniently, by continuous monitoring using an oxygen electrode and chart recorder, to give the rate of net O_2 production (Chapter 48) under various conditions, e.g. light, temperature, etc. For photosynthesis–irradiance (*P–I*) curves using an O_2 electrode, you should note that the electrode assembly can act as a lens, so the light within the chamber can be higher than that measured at the outside surface. The rate of gross photosynthesis is obtained by correcting for O_2 uptake when the electrode assembly is transferred to darkness (e.g. using a thick black cloth).

Measurement of carbon dioxide uptake For higher plant studies, this is most easily achieved using an infra-red gas analyser, or IRGA. Most modern instruments are portable and generally incorporate: (i) a cuvette, with a transparent window that attaches to a whole leaf or a known area of leaf providing a gas-tight seal, and within which the air is stirred by a fan; (ii) a gas supply system that allows control over input gases; (iii) miniaturised infra-red analysers (p. 280) to detect differences in CO_2 and H_2O content of input and output gas streams; (iv) systems for measuring (and possibly controlling) other environmental variables, e.g. light and temperature; (v) an on-board microprocessor for calculating results as rates of photosynthesis and transpiration and estimating the leaf's internal pCO_2 (C_i) and for exporting these and other data (e.g. time, leaf temperature, photosynthetic photon flux density, etc.) to PCs. Portable IRGAs are particularly useful for the rapid construction of photosynthesis–irradiance (*P–I*) and photosynthesis–pCO_2 (*P–C$_i$*) curves used to estimate photosynthetic efficiency, photosynthetic capacity and compensation points.

Definitions

Photosynthetic efficiency – the rate of photosynthesis when limited either by (i) supply of photons or (ii) by supply of CO_2, determined from the initial gradient of a P–I or P–C_i curve respectively.

Photosynthetic capacity – the rate of photosynthesis under saturating photon flux density (PFD) or CO_2 supply, determined from the upper asymptote of a P–I or P–C_i curve respectively.

Compensation point – PFD or pCO_2 at which net photosynthesis = 0, i.e. where gross photosynthesis, respiration and photorespiration are balanced: from the intercept of a P–I or P–C_i curve (x-axis).

Interpreting ^{14}C fixation data – short-term studies of a few minutes may estimate gross photosynthesis, while longer-term studies will give a rate closer to net photosynthesis, since some of the fixed ^{14}C will be respired.

Studying the release of photoassimilated ^{14}C in aquatic photoautotrophs – the loss of glycollate and other metabolites can be quantified by acidifying a known amount of medium, to drive off unfixed ^{14}C, then counting directly, or after an appropriate separation procedure.

Measurement of radiocarbon (^{14}C) fixation The tracer may be supplied as $^{14}CO_2$ for gas exchange studies or, more readily, as $H^{14}CO_3^-$ for studies in aqueous systems, since there will be an interconversion of soluble CO_2, HCO_3^- and $H_2CO_3^{2-}$ in accordance with Eqn [48.4]. In aqueous systems, the plant material is incubated in medium containing ^{14}C-labelled bicarbonate for a known time period, then removed and prepared for liquid scintillation counting (p. 260). Microalgal cells and photosynthetic bacteria can be separated from the experimental medium by filtration, or silicone oil microcentrifugation (p. 291) – mild acid treatment (e.g. $50 \, mmol \, l^{-1}$ HCl) will ensure that any unfixed ^{14}C is released as $^{14}CO_2$. To express the results in terms of the amount of C assimilated, you will need to calculate (i) the total inorganic C content of the medium, i.e. $CO_2 + HCO_3^- + H_2CO_3^{2-}$, obtained from pH and alkalinity measurements or by IR spectroscopy of the CO_2 produced when a known amount of the medium is acidified and (ii) the relationship between the total inorganic C content and the amount of ^{14}C tracer added (i.e. the specific activity of the experimental solution, p. 261).

One of the advantages of studying the photoassimilation of ^{14}C is that the radiotracer can be used to follow the fate of fixed carbon, by separating and fractionating the various cellular components prior to counting, e.g. by sequential solvent extraction of the plant material in 80% ethanol (low molecular weight solutes) then boiling water (polysaccharides), leaving a residual fraction (structural polysaccharides, proteins and nucleic acids). More sophisticated separation techniques must be used to quantify the amount of radioactivity within individual biomolecules, e.g. using column chromatography (p. 297) and autoradiography (p. 262), or 2-D thin layer chromatography (p. 296) and autoradiography. High specific activity $H^{14}CO_3^-$ and short incubation times of a few seconds are required to study the early stages in carbon photoassimilation.

Using stable carbon isotopes Measurements of stable carbon isotopes in organic material and in the air passing over photosynthetically active plant material can be used as a probe of photosynthetic physiology. 'Light' and 'heavy' isotopes of carbon (^{12}C and ^{13}C respectively) have different diffusion rates within the leaf and Rubisco also discriminates against ^{13}C, leading to changes in the isotope composition of photoassimilated carbon compared to that of air. By measuring this discrimination, the physiological processes associated with carbon fixation and metabolism can be investigated in a time-integrated manner. Analysis of stable isotope composition makes use of mass spectrometric measurements of the ratio of heavy to light isotopes in the sample under investigation and in a predefined standard.

The mass spectrometer (p. 285) compares the mass-to-charge ratio (m/z) of the 44 and 45 masses of $^{12}CO_2$ and $^{13}CO_2$ respectively, to give the isotopic composition of (i) a sample and (ii) a standard, in terms of the ^{13}C molar abundance ratio (R), where:

$$R = \frac{^{13}CO_2}{^{12}CO_2} \qquad [57.2]$$

These values are then used to calculate the isotopic composition of the sample relative to the standard as a $\delta^{13}C$ value, usually expressed in parts per thousand (‰, see p. 140 – note that this is a proportion, and *not* a unit – spoken as 'per mil'). The original standard was CO_2 derived from a fossil

Belemnite from the Pee Dee deposits in South Carolina (PDB standard: $R = 0.011\,24$). The $\delta^{13}C$ value of a sample in parts per thousand is then calculated as:

$$\delta^{13}C = \frac{R_{sample} - R_{standard}}{R_{standard}} \times 1000 \qquad [57.3]$$

Isotopic composition values may also be used to calculate discrimination (Δ), which takes into account the isotopic composition of the standard, source and sample, according to the following equation:

$$\Delta = \frac{\delta_a - \delta_p}{1 + \delta_p} \qquad [57.4]$$

where δ_a and δ_p are the carbon isotope discrimination values for air (source) and plant (sample) respectively, expressed in fractional terms (see worked examples in margin). In contrast to $\delta^{13}C$ values which are negative when PDB is used as the standard, values for Δ are positive for plant material, since ^{12}C is favoured over ^{13}C. The advantage in using Δ notation is that it is more straightforward to make comparisons, avoiding the possible confusion involved in discussing more and less negative $\delta^{13}C$ values. Like $\delta^{13}C$ values, Δ values are usually expressed in parts per thousand (‰). Values for Δ values in C_3 plants, where Rubisco is the main carboxylating enxyme, usually fall within the range 16–25‰, since Rubisco shows substantial discrimination against ^{13}C. In contrast, Δ values for C_4 plants, where PEP is the main carboxylating enzyme, are lower – typically in the range 3–7‰ – since PEP carboxylase shows minimal discrimination against ^{13}C.

Advances in the study of hydrogen, oxygen and nitrogen isotope ratios have further extended the range of tools available to physiologists to investigate areas including plant water relations and nitrogen economy at the individual plant and ecosystem levels. Since the stable carbon isotope ratio of a plant is a broad measure of the overall balance between carbon uptake (photosynthesis) and water loss (transpiration), Δ is found to vary with changes in transpiration rate, with a lower value corresponding to a higher water use efficiency. It has been proposed that concurrent analysis of $^{18}O/^{16}O$ ratios can enable researchers to interpret variations in Δ in terms of water use efficiency: this can be useful in plant breeding studies, where improved water use efficiency results in closely coupled ^{13}C and ^{18}O signals.

Chlorophyll fluorescence This can be used to provide a non-destructive indication of photosynthetic function. When light energy is absorbed by the light-harvesting apparatus of green plants, several reactions compete for the deactivation of excited chlorophyll molecules. Principally, there are three possible outcomes: (i) the light energy may be trapped and used to reduce photosystem II (PS II) and drive photochemical reactions (Fig. 57.1); (ii) the energy may be lost as heat; or (iii) the energy may be re-emitted as fluorescence, measured at wavelengths around 685 nm using a purpose-built chlorophyll fluorometer. Since these three processes are mutually exclusive, measurements of chlorophyll fluorescence can provide information about changes in photochemistry and heat dissipation, since the maximum potential fluorescence yield is 'quenched' (reduced) by (i) photochemical and (ii) non-photochemical processes. Most measurements are made using pulse-amplified modulated (PAM) fluorometers, where the light source used to generate the chlorophyll fluorescence can be

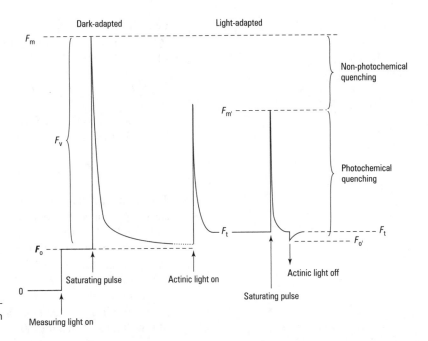

Fig. 57.2 Representation of chlorophyll fluorescence measurement using the saturation pulse method (for details, see text).

turned on and off at high frequency (pulse modulated), enabling the chlorophyll fluorescence signal to be separated from all other light, and therefore allowing measurements to be made in light-adapted leaves under 'natural' conditions.

To interpret fluorescence changes, the relative contribution of the two quenching processes must be established. The starting point is to consider what happens when a strong light is shone on in a dark-adapted leaf: there is a rapid rise in chlorophyll fluorescence to a maximum value, as photosynthetic electron transport is rapidly saturated and no further electrons can be accepted by PS II. If the light remains on, the chlorophyll fluorescence falls progressively, due to photochemical processes (e.g. activation of carbon-fixing enzymes) and non-photochemical processes (dissipation of chlorophyll energy as heat). By measuring changes in chlorophyll fluorescence, the relative contributions of these two processes can be quantified. At a practical level, this is achieved by first shining a single flash of high-intensity light (the saturating pulse) onto a leaf in the dark-adapted state and the resulting maximum fluorescence signal, F_m (see Fig. 57.2 for detail) is then used to determine the potential maximum quantum yield of PS II as:

$$\text{Maximum quantum yield PS II} = (F_m - F_0) \div F_m \qquad [57.5]$$

The leaf is then allowed to adapt to ambient light, and the saturation pulse is then reapplied: the reduction in maximum fluorescence (to $F_{m'}$) is the result of non-photochemical quenching (NPQ), i.e. dissipation of energy as heat (Fig. 57.2). This can be determined from the relationship:

$$\text{NPQ} = (F_m - F_{m'}) \div F_{m'} \qquad [57.6]$$

Non-photochemical quenching processes protect the protein components of the photosynthetic apparatus from oxidative damage due to excess light. The remaining fraction is equivalent to photochemical quenching (qP), a measure of the proportion of PS II centres that are 'open', calculated from the relationship:

$$qP = (F_{m'} - F_t) \div (F_{m'} - F_{0'})$$ [57.7]

The quantum yield of PS II ($\Phi_{PS\,II}$), which is a measure of the efficiency of PS II photochemistry, can be determined as:

$$\Phi_{PS\,II} = (F_{m'} - F_t) \div F_{m'}$$ [57.8]

The light and dark reactions of photosynthesis are coordinated, since electron transport generates the ATP and NADPH required for CO_2 fixation. For example, a reduction in the rate of CO_2 assimilation due to a metabolic inhibitor will be mirrored by a decrease in $\Phi_{PS\,II}$ and, in many cases, by an increase in NPQ as the light intensity is increased to levels in excess of those required for photosynthesis. Fluorescence measurements can give insights into the stress responses of plants, e.g. the extent of photoinhibition under field conditions – further details are provided by Maxwell and Johnson (2000).

Studying photosynthetic electron transport

Robert Hill first showed that isolated chloroplasts can evolve O_2 in the absence of CO_2 fixation, as long as they are provided with an artificial electron acceptor that intercepts electrons from the photosynthetic electron transport chain. The net result of this 'Hill reaction' is the photolysis of water and the reduction of the Hill acceptor (A), as follows:

$$2nH_2O + 4nA \rightarrow 4nAH + nO_2$$ [57.9]

The practical significance of the Hill reaction is that it allows the photochemical reactions of the electron transport system to be studied independently of the dark reactions of photosynthesis. Many of the Hill acceptors are redox dyes that show changes in absorbance as they are reduced, e.g. ferricyanide ($Fe(CN)_6^{3-}$), which accepts electrons from the PS I complex, or 2,6-dichlorophenolindophenol (DCPIP), which intercepts electrons from the electron transport chain between PS II and PS I (Fig. 57.1). The reduction of these artificial electron acceptors can be followed spectrophotometrically, allowing the Hill reaction to be quantified. Alternatively, an O_2 electrode can be used to follow O_2 evolution from PS II in the presence of various artificial electron acceptors. Redox mediators can be used to investigate the following aspects of photosynthetic electron flow:

- the activity of PS II and PS I operating in series can be studied in whole chloroplasts using a suitable terminal acceptor, e.g. ferricyanide;
- the activity of PS II can be studied in whole chloroplasts using DCPIP (membrane-permeable), or in fragmented chloroplasts using ferricyanide;
- the activity of PS I can be measured if PS II is blocked by the herbicide diuron (DCMU) and if electron flow is maintained by the addition of an artificial electron donor, e.g. ascorbate plus DCPIP.

Measuring photosynthetic quotients – in studies where both O_2 and CO_2 are measured, the photosynthetic quotient (PQ) can be determined from the relationship: $PQ = O_2$ evolved $\div CO_2$ consumed. In the simplest case, where fixed carbon accumulates as carbohydrate, a value of 1 should be obtained. However, the PQ may vary, depending on the amount of carbon incorporated into fats, proteins, etc. and the utilisation of photosynthetic energy for other metabolic processes and growth, e.g. NO_3^- assimilation, carbon storage.

Measuring the Hill reaction using DCPIP – since the dye will revert to its oxidised (blue) form as soon as the chloroplasts are removed from the light, you must measure the absorbance as quickly as possible.

Table 57.1 Some inhibitors of photosynthetic electron transport[1]

Inhibitor	Target site
Hydroxylamine (NH$_2$OH)	photolysis of H$_2$O
DCMU (3(3,4-dichlorophenyl)-1,1-dimethylurea)	electron transport from PS II to plastoquinone
DBMIB (2,5-dibromo-3-methyl-6-isopropyl-*p*-benzoquinone)	electron flow from plastoquinone to cytochrome f
Methyl viologen (Paraquat)	electron flow from PS I to NADP$^+$
Atrazine (2-chloro-4-(2-propylamino)-6-ethylamine-5-triazine)	electron flow to plastoquinone
HOQNO (2-heptyl-4-hydroxyquinoline-N-oxide)	electron flow between quinones and cytochromes
DSPD (disalicylidinepropanediamine)	electron flow *via* ferredoxin

[1]See also Table 56.1 for uncouplers and ATPase inhibitors.

Safety note – make sure you treat all inhibitors with respect, observing appropriate safety precautions, and that you know the procedure to be followed in case of accident or spillage.

Note that this cannot be measured by O$_2$ evolution, since PS II is inoperative – methyl viologen can be used as an electron acceptor from PS I and is rapidly reoxidised, consuming O$_2$ in a reaction which can be measured using an O$_2$ electrode (as O$_2$ *uptake*, rather than O$_2$ production);

- the sites of action of inhibitors (Table 57.1) can be determined by measuring their effects on the various components of the electron transport system, measured using redox dyes or the methyl viologen/O$_2$ electrode system.

Respiration

At the cellular level, respiration can be considered as the oxidation of organic compounds coupled to the production of so-called high-energy intermediates, such as ATP. The overall process is often represented in terms of the oxidation of glucose, as:

$$C_6H_{12}O_6 + 12O_2{}^* + 6H_2O + n\text{ADP} + n\text{P}_i \rightarrow$$
$$6CO_2 + 12H_2O^* + n\text{ATP} + n\text{H}_2O \qquad [57.10]$$

the asterisks showing that O$_2$ is converted to water, and where n has a *maximum* value of 38. The process can be divided into three principal stages, namely (i) glycolysis, (ii) the tricarboxylic acid (TCA) cycle and (iii) oxidative phosphorylation. The glycolytic pathway operates in the cytosol and results in the partial breakdown of glucose (C$_6$) to two molecules of pyruvate (C$_3$) plus two molecules of NADH and two molecules of ATP. The mitochondrial TCA cycle involves the sequential dismantling of pyruvate to CO$_2$ (*via* an intermediate step involving decarboxylation to acetyl-coA), producing one molecule of FADH$_2$, four molecules of NADH and one of GTP for each pyruvate. The final stage occurs at the inner mitochondrial membrane – the movement of electrons and protons along the respiratory transport chain from reductant to O$_2$ as the terminal electron acceptor creates a transmembrane H$^+$ gradient that leads to the net synthesis of ATP, as summarised in Fig. 57.3. Thus, as in photosynthesis, respiration involves enzyme-catalysed interconversion of organic compounds plus membrane-bound electron transport reactions that are coupled to ATP synthesis.

The enzymic reactions of glycolysis and the TCA cycle can be studied using ^{14}C-labelled intermediates and pulse-chase experiments, using techniques similar to those used to investigate the dark reactions of photosynthesis (p. 397), or by purification and characterisation of the

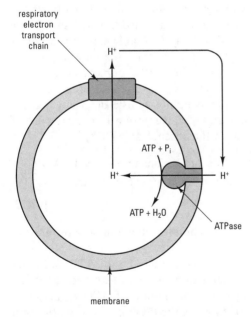

Fig. 57.3 Proton flow in mitochondrial oxidative phosphorylation: the creation of a transmembrane H$^+$ gradient due to the respiratory electron transport chain drives ATP synthesis via a membrane-bound ATPase.

Fig. 57.4 Representative data for O_2 uptake by a suspension of mitochondria in response to additions of substrate and ADP.

Interpreting respiratory quotients – the complete oxidation of carbohydrates should give values close to 1.0, in agreement with Eqn [57.11], while the oxidation of fats will give values close to 0.7 and protein oxidation will produce values of about 0.8.

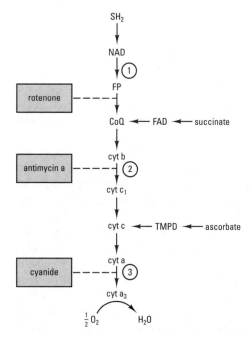

Fig. 57.5 The mitochondrial electron transport system, showing the sites of action of various inhibitors (dotted lines) and the three sites of ATP synthesis (numbered 1–3). S, substrate; FP, flavoprotein; CoQ, coenzyme Q; cyt, cytochrome; TMPD, tetramethylphenylene-diamine.

individual enzymes (p. 378). Oxidative phosphorylation can be studied using techniques appropriate for electron transport reactions.

Measuring the respiratory activity of cells and tissues

The overall rate of cellular respiration is usually measured in terms of the amount of O_2 consumed by a known amount of material in a given time, e.g. as μmol O_2 mg protein^{-1} min^{-1}.

The principal techniques include:

- Manometry – this traditional approach involves measuring either the pressure change (Warburg manometer) or volume change (Gilson manometer) as gases are produced or consumed during respiration. Manometry is relatively insensitive and may be subject to large measurement errors: the principal application is in studying the relationship between the amounts of O_2 consumed and CO_2 evolved in terms of the respiratory quotient (RQ) for a particular substrate, from the relationship:

$$RQ = \frac{CO_2 \text{ evolved}}{O_2 \text{ consumed}} \qquad [57.11]$$

The calculations involved in determining CO_2 production or O_2 consumption are complex and are specific to individual instruments – manufacturer's guidelines should be followed carefully.

- Oxygen electrode studies – this has largely replaced manometry, as the apparatus is more versatile and less complex to set up and interpret, giving a continuous readout of O_2 status via a chart recorder (p. 337). Net O_2 evolution can be measured using whole cells, mitochondrial suspensions (p. 237) or sub-mitochondrial preparations.

Using an oxygen electrode to study respiratory electron transport

Intact mitochondria suspended in an isotonic medium will show little respiratory activity unless supplied with (i) a suitable electron donor or substrate (e.g. NADH), (ii) ADP and (iii) P_i: this is termed respiratory control and the mitochondria are said to be tightly coupled, since there is a close link between electron transport, O_2 consumption and phosphorylation. The extent of this coupling can be determined using an O_2 electrode (p. 334) to measure O_2 consumption in the presence of substrate, P_i and ADP, with that in the absence of ADP (Fig. 57.4), as:

$$\text{respiratory control ratio} = \frac{\text{rate of } O_2 \text{ consumption with ADP}}{\text{rate of } O_2 \text{ consumption without ADP}}$$

$$[57.12]$$

Freshly prepared, tightly coupled mitochondria should have a respiratory control ratio of $\geqslant 4$.

To investigate the relationship between the number of ATP molecules produced per substrate molecule, substrate and P_i are supplied in excess and the O_2 uptake produced by a known amount of ADP is measured using an O_2 electrode (Fig. 57.5), allowing the P/O ($\equiv$ADP/O) ratio for a particular substrate to be calculated as:

$$\text{P/O ratio} = \frac{\mu\text{mol ADP added}}{2 \times \mu\text{mol } O_2 \text{ consumed}} \qquad [57.13]$$

Fig. 57.6 Representative data for O_2 uptake by mitochondria in response to the addition of (a) electron transport inhibitors and substrates, or (b) inhibitors of ATP synthesis and uncouplers. Steeper slopes indicate faster rates of O_2 uptake.

Note that the amount of O_2 is multiplied by 2, since O_2 is a diatomic molecule. The P/O ratio is determined by the site at which electrons are transferred to the respiratory chain (Fig. 57.6). Thus NADH should give a P/O ratio of 3, while succinate and $FADH_2$ should have values of 2. Artificial electron donors to cytochrome c have P/O ratios of 1, e.g. ascorbate/tetramethylphenylenediamine (TPMD). However, measured P/O ratios are always less than these values, due to partial uncoupling and the action of ATPases.

The effects of inhibitors of respiratory electron transport on the rate of oxygen consumption of mitochondria can be used to determine their site of action (Fig. 57.5). Thus, an inhibitor of electron flow will prevent O_2 uptake while an artificial substrate that donates electrons at a location beyond the site of inhibition will restore O_2 uptake, as shown in Fig. 57.6.

'Uncouplers' act by increasing the permeability of membranes to protons, causing the dissipation of the transmembrane H^+ gradient. Addition of an uncoupler increases electron flow along the respiratory chain in the absence of phosphorylation, i.e. there is loss of respiratory control. Uncouplers can reverse the effects of inhibitors such as oligomycin, whose target is the mitochondrial ATPase (Table 56.1, p. 393). Oligomycin prevents the return of H^+ to the interior of the mitochondrion, thereby inhibiting respiratory electron transport and O_2 uptake – the addition of an uncoupler (e.g. CCCP) reverses this inhibition.

Measuring the components of the proton-motive force in chloroplasts and mitochondria

According to chemiosmotic principles, the transmembrane electrochemical potential gradient of protons drives ATP synthesis in photophosphorylation and oxidative phosphorylation via a membrane-bound ATPase (Fig. 57.3). This gradient is often expressed as the proton-motive force, or pmf (Δp), expressed in mV as:

$$\Delta p = E_m - 59(pH_i - pH_o) \qquad [57.14]$$

at 25 °C, where E_m is the transmembrane electrical potential (mV) and pH_i and pH_o are internal and external pH values. The individual components of the proton-motive force can be determined by a variety of methods:

- Transmembrane electrical potential, by the distribution of a suitable radiolabelled lipophilic cation, e.g. tetraphenylphosphonium (TPP^+), in accordance with the Nernst equation (see p. 393); by the measurement of K^+ or Rb^+ in the presence of the ionophore valinomycin (p. 393); or by the quenching of a fluorescent dye (e.g. cyanine or oxanol dyes).
- Transmembrane pH gradient from the equilibrium distribution of a radiolabelled weak permeant acid, e.g. 5,5-dimethyl-2,4-oxazolidinedione (DMO); by quenching of a fluorescent pH probe, e.g. 9-aminoacridine; or by ^{31}P-NMR (p. 283).

For radiolabelled probes, organelles or membrane vesicles can be separated from the bathing medium by silicone oil microcentrifugation (p. 291), with suitable correction for carry-over of external medium, e.g. using a membrane-impermeant solute, labelled with a second radioisotope. Care is required in such double-labelled experiments, as carry-over can represent a significant component, leading to substantial measurement errors if uncorrected.

Typical measurements for Δp across energy-transducing membranes are 180–200 mV (inside-negative): in mitochondria, E_m is the principal component while ΔpH represents the largest component of Δp in thylakoid membranes.

Text reference

Maxwell, K. and Johnson, G.N. (2000) Chlorophyll fluorescence – a practical guide. *Journal of Experimental Botany*, **51**, pp. 659–68.

Sources for further study

James, D.C. and Matthews, G.S. (1991) *Understanding the Biochemistry of Respiration*. Cambridge University Press, Cambridge.

Ridge, I. (ed.) (2002) *Plants*. Oxford University Press, Oxford.
[Chapter 2 is a good general introduction to the physiology of photosynthesis.]

San Pietro, A. (1997) *Methods in Enzymology: Photosynthesis and Nitrogen Fixation*. Academic Press, New York.

Taiz, L. and Zeiger, E. (2002) *Plant Physiology*. Sinauer, Sunderland, USA.
[Provides a detailed treatment of photosynthesis.]

Wilson, K. and Walker, J. (eds) (2000) *Principles and Techniques of Practical Biochemistry*, 5th edn. Cambridge University Press, Cambridge.
[Also covers other topics, including spectroscopy and centrifugation.]

Study exercises

(See also exercises 48.4 and 48.5, p. 340, for calculations of respiratory oxygen consumption and photosynthetic oxygen evolution based on oxygen electrode measurements.)

57.1 Check your understanding of photosynthesis and respiration. Having read through this chapter, distinguish between each of the following pairs of terms:
(a) net photosynthesis and gross photosynthesis;
(b) C_3 photosynthesis and C_4 photosynthesis;
(c) the oxygenase and carboxylase functions of Rubisco;
(d) coupling and uncoupling;
(e) respiratory quotient and respiratory control ratio.

57.2 Calculate rates of photosynthetic carbon fixation from ^{14}C data. A sample of the photosynthetic cyanobacterium *Spirulina platensis* containing 0.29 mg chlorophyll *a* (chl a) was incubated in the light for 3 min in 10 ml of an aqueous solution containing inorganic carbon (HCO_3^-) at a concentration of 12 mmol l^{-1} and at a specific activity of 12 Bq pmol^{-1} ($\equiv 0.72$ d.p.m. nmol^{-1}) At the end of this period, the cyanobacterial cells were separated from the medium and assayed by liquid scintillation counting, giving a quench-corrected value of 2808 d.p.m. What is the photosynthetic rate, expressed in terms of μmol C fixed per mg chl a per minute? (Express your answer to 3 significant figures.)

57.3 Interpret results from an experiment using DCPIP to study photosynthetic electron transport. The table below shows data for the change in A_{600} of a chloroplast suspension incubated with the Hill acceptor DCPIP, plus different levels of the herbicide simazine.

A_{600} measurements for a chloroplast suspension incubated with DCPIP and various levels of simazine

Time (s)	Control (no simazine)	Simazine at:		
		1.0 nmol l^{-1}	10.0 nmol l^{-1}	100.0 nmol l^{-1}
0	0.462	0.461	0.464	0.462
30	0.372	0.394	0.41	0.436
60	0.320	0.345	0.371	0.413
90	0.284	0.315	0.343	0.397
120	0.253	0.284	0.317	0.385

(a) What is the reason for the rapid decrease in A_{600} in the control sample, with no added simazine?

(b) How do you account for the fact that increasing amounts of simazine lead to a reduction in the extent of change in A_{600} with time?

(c) Plot a graph of A_{600} against time to show the composite data from the table. Use this to determine the initial rate of change in A_{600}. Then, calculate the percentage inhibition at each simazine concentration. Finally, plot percentage inhibition against simazine concentration, to determine the concentration causing 50% inhibition (I_{50}); give your answer to 3 significant figures.

57.4 Check your understanding of respiratory quotients. Which of the following values would you expect for the respiratory quotient of aerobic bacteria growing on the following substrates as their principal source of carbon and energy: (a) glucose; (b) triglycerides; (c) casein:

(i) 0.7

(ii) 0.8

(iii) 1.0

Give brief explanations for your choices.

57.5 Calculate the P/O ratio for a respiring mitochondrial suspension. An oxygen electrode chamber containing a mitochondrial suspension (0.5 ml), NADH (0.5 ml) and buffer (4 ml) showed a fall in oxygen concentration from 218 to 174 micromol l^{-1} on addition of 0.05 ml of a 25 mmol l^{-1} ADP solution. What was the P/O ratio over this period?

57.6 Calculate mitochondrial proton-motive force. A suspension of mitochondria in buffer at an external pH of 7.2 had a measured internal (matrix) pH of 8.6 and a measured transmembrane potential (inner membrane) of −85.6 mV. Calculate the proton-motive force across the inner membrane (express your answer to 3 significant figures). What is your interpretation of the calculated value?

Genetics

58 Mendelian genetics

Gregor Mendel, an Austrian monk, made pioneering studies of the genetics of eukaryotic organisms in the middle of the nineteenth century. He made crosses between different forms of flowering plants. Through careful examination and numerical analysis of the observable characteristics, or phenotype, of the parents and their progeny, Mendel was able to deduce much about their genetic characteristics, or genotype. The principles derived from these experiments explain the basis of heredity, and hence underpin our understanding of sexual reproduction, biodiversity and evolution. Mendelian genetics is concerned primarily with the transmission of genetic information, as opposed to molecular genetics which deals with the molecular details of the genome and techniques for altering genes (see Chapters 60–62) and genome analysis (genomics) in Chapter 11.

> **KEY POINT** A common initial stumbling block in genetics is terminology. In many cases the definitions are interdependent, so your success in this subject depends on your grasp of all of the definitions and underlying ideas explained below.

Important terms and concepts

Each character in the phenotype is controlled by the organism's genes, the basic units of inheritance. Each gene includes the 'genetic blueprint' (DNA) which usually defines the amino acid sequence for a specific polypeptide or protein – often an enzyme or a structural protein. The protein gives rise to the phenotype through its activity in metabolism or its contribution to the organism's structure. The full complement of genes in an individual is known as its genome. Individual genes can exist in different forms, each of which generally leads to a different form of the protein it codes for. These different gene forms are known as alleles.

In eukaryotes, the genes are located in a particular sequence on chromosomes within the nucleus. The number of chromosomes per cell is characteristic for each organism (its chromosome number, n). For example, the chromosome number for man is 23. In cells of most 'higher' organisms, there are two of each of the chromosomes (2n). This is known as the diploid state. As a result of the process of meiosis which precedes reproduction, special haploid cells are formed (gametes) which contain only one of each chromosome (1n). In sexual reproduction, haploid gametes from two individuals fuse to form a zygote, a diploid cell with a new genome, which gives rise to a new individual through the process of mitosis. Cell numbers are increased by this process, producing genetically identical cells.

Organisms vary in the span of the diploid and haploid phases. In some 'lower' organisms, the haploid phase is the longer lasting form; in most 'higher' organisms, the diploid phase is dominant. Since each diploid individual carries two of each chromosome, it has two copies of each gene

Definitions

Phenotype – the observable characteristics of an individual organism; the consequence of the underlying genotype and its interaction with the environment.

Genotype – an individual's genetic make-up, i.e. the organism's genes.

Essential vocabulary for Mendelian genetics – *make sure you know what the following terms and symbols mean:*
- *chromosome, sex chromosome, autosome;*
- *gene, allele;*
- *dominant, recessive, lethal;*
- *haploid, diploid, gamete, zygote;*
- *heterozygous, homozygous;*
- *P, F1, F2, ♀, ♂.*

Genomes and chromosome numbers – *remember that mitochondria and chloroplasts contain DNA molecules, but these are not included when calculating the chromosome number.*

Definitions

Meiosis – division of a diploid cell which results in haploid daughter cells carrying half the original number of chromosomes. Occurs during gamete (sperm and egg) formation.

Mitosis – division of a cell into two new cells, each with the same chromosome number. Occurs in somatic cells, e.g. during growth, development, repair, replacement.

Mendelian genetics

Fig. 58.1 Flowchart for tackling problems in Mendelian genetics.

in every cell. The number of alleles of each character present depends on whether the relevant genes are the same – the homozygous state – or whether they are different – the heterozygous state. Hence, while there may be many alleles for any given gene, an individual could have two at most, and might only have one if it were homozygous. This will depend on the alleles present in the parental gametes that fused when the zygote was formed. Offspring that inherit a different combination of alleles at the two loci compared with their parents are known as recombinants.

The basis of Mendel's experiments and of many exercises in genetics are crosses, where individuals showing particular phenotypes are mated and the phenotypes of the offspring, or F₁ generation, are studied (see Box 58.1). If homozygous individuals carrying alternative alleles for a character are crossed, one of the alleles may be dominant, and all the F₁ generation will show that character in their phenotype. The character not evident is said to be recessive.

In describing crosses, geneticists denote each character with a letter of the alphabet, a capital letter being used for the dominant allele and lower case for the recessive. Taking, for example, a gene with dominant and recessive forms A and a respectively, there are three possibilities for each individual: it can be (a) homozygous recessive aa; (b) homozygous dominant AA; or (c) heterozygous Aa.

The reasons for dominance might relate to the activity of an enzyme coded by the relevant gene; for example, Mendel's yellow pea allele is dominant because the gene involved codes for the breakdown of chlorophyll. In the homozygous recessive case, none of the functional enzyme will be present, chlorophyll breakdown cannot occur and the seeds remain green. Not all alleles exhibit dominance in this form. In some cases, the heterozygous state results in a third phenotype (incomplete or partial dominance); in others, the heterozygous individual expresses both genotypes (codominance). Another possible situation is epistasis, in which one gene affects the expression of another gene that is independently inherited. Note also that many genes, such as those coding for human blood groups, have multiple alleles.

KEY POINT Genetics problems may well involve one of the 'standard' crosses shown in Box 58.1. Before tackling the problem, try to analyse the information provided to see if it fits one of these types of cross. Figure 58.1 is a flowchart detailing the steps you should take in answering genetics problems.

Unless otherwise stated or obvious from the evidence, you should assume that the genes being considered in any given case are on separate chromosomes. This is important because it means that they will assort independently during meiosis. Thus, the fact that an allele of gene A is present in any individual will not influence the possibility of an allele of gene B being present. This allows you to apply simple probability in predicting the genetic make-up of the offspring of any cross (see p. 415).

Where genes are present on the same chromosome, they are said to be linked genes, and thus it would appear that they would not be able to assort independently during metaphase 1 of meiosis, when homologous chromosomes are independently orientated. However, although physically attached to each other, they may become separated when

Pedigree notation:

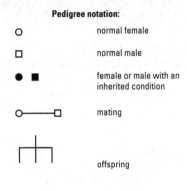

○   normal female

□   normal male

● ■   female or male with an inherited condition

○—□   mating

    offspring

Example of simple family pedigree:

This diagram shows the offspring of a normal male and female. The two daughters are normal, but the son has the inherited condition.

Fig. 58.2 Pedigree notation and family trees.

crossing over occurs between the homologous chromosomes at an early stage of meiosis. Exchange of genetic information between homologous chromosomes is called recombination. Linkage can be detected from a cross between individuals heterozygous and homozygous recessive for the relevant genes, e.g. AaBb × aabb. If the genes A and B are on different chromosomes, we expect the ratio of AaBb, aabb, Aabb and aaBb to be 1 : 1 : 1 : 1 in the F_1. However, if the dominant alleles of both genes occur on the same chromosome, the last two combinations will occur, but rarely. Just how rarely depends on how far apart they lie on the relevant chromosome – the further apart, the more likely it is that crossing over will occur. This is the basis of chromosome mapping (see Box 58.1).

Another complication you will come across is sex-linked genes. These occur on one of the X or Y chromosomes that control sex. Because one or other of the sexes – depending on the organism – is determined as XX and the other as XY (see Box 58.1), this means that rare recessive genes carried on the X chromosome may be expressed in XY individuals. Sex-linked genes are sometimes obvious from differences in the frequencies of phenotypes in male and female offspring. Pedigree charts (Fig. 58.2) are codified family trees that are often used to show the inheritance and expression of sex-linked characteristics through various generations.

Analysis of crosses

There are two basic ways of working out the results of crosses from known or assumed genotypes:

- The Punnett square method provides a good visual indication of potential combinations of gametes for a given cross. Lay out your Punnett squares consistently as shown in Fig. 58.3. Then group together the like genotypes to work out the genotype ratio and proceed to work out the corresponding phenotype ratio if required.

Denoting linked genes – *these are often shown diagrammatically, with a double line indicating the chromosome pair. For example, the two possible linkages for the genotype AaBb would be shown as:*

$$\frac{A \quad b}{a \quad B} \quad or \quad \frac{A \quad B}{a \quad b}$$

Fig. 58.3 Layout for a simple Punnett square for the cross Aa × Aa. The genotypic ratios for this cross are 1 : 2 : 1 for AA : Aa : aa, and the phenotypic ratio would be 3 : 1 for characteristic A to characteristic a. In this simple Punnett square, the allele frequencies are treated as equal ($f = 0.5$); if different from this, the probability of genotypes in each combination will be the relevant frequencies multiplied together (see p. 331).

Box 58.1 Types of cross and what you can (and can't) learn from them

Monohybrid cross – the simplest form of cross, considering two alleles of a single gene.

Example: AA × aa

If only the parental *phenotypes* are known, you can't always deduce the parental genotypes from the phenotype ratio in the F_1. An individual of dominant phenotype in the F_1 could arise from a homozygous dominant or heterozygous genotype. However, crossing the F_1 generation with themselves to give an F_2 generation may provide useful information from the phenotype ratios that are found.

Dihybrid cross – a cross involving two genes, each with two alleles.

Example: AaBB × AaBb

As with a monohybrid cross, you can't always deduce the parental genotype from the phenotype ratio in the F_1 generation alone.

Test cross – a cross of an unknown genotype with a homozygous recessive.

Example: AABb × aabb

A test cross is one between an individual dominant for A and B with one recessive for both genes. The progeny will all be dominant for A, revealing the homozygous nature of the parent for this gene, but the progeny phenotypes will be split approximately 1:1 dominant to recessive for gene B, revealing the heterozygous nature of the parent for this gene. This type of cross reveals the unknown parental genotype in the proportions of phenotypes in the F_1.

Sex-linked cross – a cross involving a gene carried on the X chromosome; this can be designated as dominant or recessive using appropriate superscripts (e.g. X^A and X^a).

Example: $X^A X^a × X^A Y$

In sex-linked crosses you need to know the basis of sex determination in the species concerned – which of XX or XY is male (for example, the former in birds,

butterflies and moths, the latter in mammals and *Drosophila*). The expected ratios of phenotypes in the offspring will depend on this. Note that the recessive genotype a will be expressed in the $X^a Y$ case.

Crosses with linked genes – genes are linked if they are on the same chromosome. This is revealed from a cross between individuals heterozygous and homozygous recessive for the relevant genes.

Example 1 (genes on separate chromosomes): expected offspring frequency from the cross AaBb × aabb is AaBb, aabb, Aabb and aaBb in the ratio 1:1:1:1.

Example 2 (linked genes): the frequencies of the last two combinations in example 1 might be skewed according to the direction of parental linkage.

Chromosome mapping uses the frequency of crossing-over of linked genes to estimate their distance apart on the chromosome on the basis that crossing over is more likely, the further apart are the genes. So-called 'map units' are calculated on the following basis:

$$\frac{\text{No. of recombinant progeny}}{\text{Total no. of progeny}} \times 100 = \% \text{ crossing over}$$

[58.1]

By convention, 1% crossing over = 1 map unit (centimorgan, cM). The order of a number of genes can be worked out from their relative distances from each other. Thus, if genes A and B are 12 map units apart, while A and B are respectively 5 and 7 map units from C, the assumed order on the chromosome is ACB (Fig. 58.4).

Fig. 58.4 Genetic map showing relative positions of genes A, B and C.

Using probability calculations – this can be simpler and faster than Punnett squares when two or more genes are considered.

- Probability calculations are based on the fact that the chance of a number of independent events occurring is equal to the probabilities of each event occurring, multiplied together. Thus if the probability P of a child being a boy is 0.5 and the probability of the child of particular parents being blue-eyed is 0.5, then the probability of that couple having a blue-eyed son is $0.5 \times 0.5 = 0.25$, and that of having two blue-eyed boys is:

$$P = (0.5 \times 0.5) \times (0.5 \times 0.5) = 0.0625$$

How do you decide whether the results of an experimental cross fit your expectation from theory as calculated above? This isn't easy, because of the element of chance in gene crossing-over during meiosis. Thus, while you might expect to see a 3 : 1 phenotype ratio of progeny for a given cross, in 500 offspring you might actually observe a ratio of 379 : 121, which is a ratio of just over 3.13 : 1. Can you conclude that this is significantly different from 3 : 1 in the context of random error? The answer to this problem comes from statistics. However, the answer isn't certain, and your conclusion will be based on a balance of probabilities (see Box 58.2 and Table 58.1).

Limitation of the chi^2 test – the formula cited in Box 58.2 is valid only if expected numbers are greater than 5.

Box 58.2   Example of a chi^2 (χ^2) test

This test allows you to assess the difference between observed (O) and expected (E) values and is extremely useful in biology. It is particularly valuable in determining whether progeny phenotype ratios fit your assumptions about their genotypes. The operation of the test is best illustrated by the use of an example. Assume that your null hypothesis (see p. 485) is that the phenotypic ratio is 3 : 1 and you observe that in 500 offspring the phenotype ratio is 379 : 121 whereas the expected ratio is 375 : 125.

Start the test by calculating the test statistic χ^2. The general formula for calculating χ^2 is:

$$\chi^2 = \sum \frac{(O - E)^2}{E} \qquad \text{[58.2]}$$

In this example, this works out as:

$$\chi^2 = \frac{(379 - 375)^2}{375} + \frac{(121 - 125)^2}{125} = \frac{16}{375} + \frac{16}{125} = 0.171$$

The probability associated with this value can be obtained from χ^2 tables for $(n - 1)$ degrees of freedom (d.f.), where $n =$ the number of categories = number of phenotypes considered. Here the d.f. value is $2 - 1 = 1$. Since the χ^2 value of 0.171 is lower than the tabulated value for 1 d.f. (3.84, Table 58.1), we therefore accept the null hypothesis and conclude that the difference between observed and expected results is not significant (since $P > 0.05$). Had χ^2 been >3.84, then $P < 0.05$ and we would have rejected the null hypothesis and concluded that the difference was significant, i.e. that the progeny phenotype did not fit the expected ratio.

Table 58.1 Values of chi^2 (χ^2) for which $P = 0.05$. The value for $(n - 1)$ degrees of freedom (d.f.) should be used, where $n =$ the number of categories ($=$ phenotypes) considered (normally fewer than 4 in genetics problems). If χ^2 is less than this value, accept the null hypothesis that the observed values arose by chance; if χ^2 is greater than this value, reject the null hypothesis and conclude that the difference between the observed and expected values is statistically significant

Degrees of freedom	χ^2 value for which $P = 0.05$
1	3.84
2	5.99
3	7.82
4	9.49

Population genetics

Population genetics is largely concerned with the frequencies of alleles in a population and how these may change in time. The Hardy–Weinberg Principle states that the frequency of alleles f remains the same between generations, unless influenced by some outside factor(s).

To understand why this is the case, consider alleles H and h for a particular gene, which exist in the breeding population at frequencies p and q respectively. If the individuals carrying these alleles interbreed randomly, then the expected phenotype and allele ratios in the F_1 generation can be calculated simply as:

$$f(HH) = p^2;$$
$$f(Hh) = 2pq; \quad \text{and}$$
$$f(hh) = q^2$$

If you wish to confirm this, lay out a Punnett square with appropriate frequencies for each allele. Now, by summation, the frequency of H in the $F_1 = p^2 + pq$ (a similar calculation can be made for allele h); and since in this example there are only two alleles, $p + q = 1$ and so $q = (1 - p)$. Substituting $(1 - p)$ for q, the frequency of H in the F_1 is thus:

$$p^2 + p(1 - p) = p^2 + p - -p^2 = p$$

i.e. the frequency of the allele is unchanged between generations. A similar relationship exists for the other alleles.

The Hardy–Weinberg Principle was named after its first, independent, protagonists. It holds so long as the following criteria are satisfied:

1. random mating – so that no factors influence each individual's choice of a mate;
2. large population size – so that the laws of probability will apply;
3. no mutation – so that no new alleles are formed;
4. no emigration, immigration or isolation – so that there is no interchange of genes with other populations nor isolation of genes within the population;
5. no natural selection – so that no alleles have a reproductive advantage over others.

Population geneticists use the Hardy–Weinberg Principle to gain an idea of the rate of evolution and the influences on evolution. By ensuring that criteria 1–4 hold, if there are any changes in allele frequency between generations, then the rate of change of allele frequencies indicates the rate of evolutionary change (natural selection).

Example Cystic fibrosis occurs in 0.04% of Caucasian babies. If this condition results from a double recessive allele *aa*, then following the Hardy–Weinberg Principle, $q^2 = 0.0004$ (0.04% expressed as a fraction of 1) and so $q = \sqrt{0.0004} = 0.02$, or 2%. Since $p = (1 - q)$, $p = 0.98$, or 98%. The frequency of carriers of cystic fibrosis in the Caucasian population (people having the alleles Aa) is given by $2pq$. From the above, $2pq = 2(0.02 \times 0.98) = 0.0392$. Hence 3.92% of the Caucasian population are carriers (roughly one in 25).

Sources for further study

Anon. *Online Mendelian Inheritance in Man*. Available: http://www.ncbi.nlm.nih.gov/omim/ Last accessed 08/01/03.

Blumberg, R.B. *MendelWeb*. Available: http://www.mendelweb.org/ Last accessed 08/01/03.
[A resource for students interested in the origins of classical genetics.]

Falconer, D.S. and MacKay, T.F.C. (1996) *Introduction to Quantitative Genetics*, 4th edn. Addison-Wesley, New York.

Klug, W.S. and Cummings, M.R. (2002) *Essentials of Genetics*, 4th edn. Prentice Hall, Upper Saddle River.

Winter, P.C., Hickey, G.I. and Fletcher, H.L. (1998) *Instant Notes in Genetics*. Bios, Oxford.

Study exercises

58.1 Use a Punnett square to predict the outcome of a cross. Lay out a Punnett square for a cross between genotypes RrOO × RrOo, where R is a semi-dominant gene for flower colour such that RR = red, Rr = pink and rr = white; and O is a dominant gene for corolla shape such that OO = closed corolla, Oo = closed corolla and oo = open corolla. From the Punnett square, derive both the genotypic and phenotypic ratios for the cross.

58.2 Use probability to predict the outcome of a cross. Two hazel-eyed parents are heterozygous for the eye-colour gene B. When expressed as bb, the individual is blue-eyed. Mum's hair is (genuine) blonde but Dad's is mousy-brown. In this case she is double recessive (mm) for the hair-colour gene M and he is heterozygous (Mm). What is the probability that they will have a blue-eyed, blonde daughter?

58.3 Work out a likely genetic scenario for a given set of results. Five tail-less female mice were crossed with normal males (with tails). There were 31 normal mice and 28 tail-less mice in the F_1 progeny. When pairs of tail-less mice from the F_1 generation were crossed, their (F_2) progeny were as follows: normal, 27; tail-less, 55; dead on birth, but tail-less, 30. In each case the ratio of males to females was roughly 50 : 50. Provide a logical explanation for these results.

58.4 Predict parental genotypes from the results of crosses involving sex-linked genes. A red-eye gene is known to be sex-linked in *Drosophila*; that is, the alleles R (red-eyed) or r (white-eyed) are carried on the X chromosome, while the Y chromosome does not carry these eye-colour alleles. In the fruit fly, XX = female and XY = male. Predict the possible parental genotypes from the following F_1 progeny ratios:
(a) 35 red-eyed female, 17 red-eyed male, 19 white-eyed male;
(b) 27 red-eyed male, 29 red-eyed female;
(c) 19 red-eyed female, 18 white-eyed female, 22 red-eyed male, 21 white-eyed male.

58.5 Carry out a χ^2 (chi^2) test. A geneticist expects the results of a test cross to be in the phenotype ratio 1 : 2 : 1. He observes 548 progeny from his cross in the ratio 125 : 303 : 120. What should he conclude?

59 Bacterial and phage genetics

Using and interpreting standard nomenclature in bacterial genetics – different forms of three letter abbreviations are used for:

- **phenotypic features** – *non-italic text, with superscripts where appropriate, e.g.* Lac⁺;
- **genotypic features** – *lower case italic text, with individual letters to denote individual genes, e.g.* lacZ;
- **gene products** *(polypeptides and proteins) – the non-italicised equivalent of the abbreviation for the gene and with a capitalised first letter, e.g. the* LacZ *protein, which is a β-galactosidase and is the product of the* lacZ *gene in* Lac⁺ *cells.*
- **transposon** – *inactivated genes show the transposon after the individual gene, separated by two colons, e.g.* lacZ::Tn6.

Several abbreviations may be combined, e.g. a single strain might have the phenotype Ampʳ Lac⁺ Trp⁻.

In eukaryotic organisms, genetic reassortment usually involves the fusion of two haploid gametes to form a zygote and a new generation (p. 411).

KEY POINT **Bacterial genetics is very different from eukaryotic genetics (Chapter 58), due to the nature of the bacterial genome, which typically consists of a single chromosome plus none, one or several types of plasmid and/or phage, depending on the particular strain of bacterium.**

In most bacteria, the chromosome is usually a covalently closed circular DNA molecule, carrying genes for essential metabolic functions and structural components. As a consequence, bacteria can be regarded as haploid organisms. Plasmids are additional 'mini-chromosomes', typically coding for non-essential features, e.g. antibiotic resistance, heavy metal tolerance. They are often present at a higher copy number than the chromosome and may carry genes within mobile transposable elements (transposons). A single bacterium may contain more than one type of plasmid (though not if they are closely related plasmids, i.e. from the same incompatibility group). Plasmids can be introduced into a bacterial cell by conjugation (p. 422), or by transformation (p. 447). Bacteria can be 'cured' of their plasmids by chemical treatment, e.g. using acridine dyes that interfere with replication, or by growth under particular conditions, e.g. at high temperatures, where plasmid replication is unable to keep up with cell division.

A phage may replicate inside a bacterial cell or, in selected instances (temperate phages, p. 202), may exist within the cell in a non-replicating (latent) state, termed a prophage. As such, phages represent additional genetic elements that may be present within a bacterial cell, forming an important component of several aspects of bacterial genetics at the practical level.

The principal characteristics of experimental bacterial genetics ('crosses') are:

- the processes are completely distinct from sexual reproduction in eukaryotes;
- the processes are directional, from a donor cell (exogenote) to a recipient cell (endogenote);
- usually, only part of the donor cell's genome is transferred;
- in several instances, the recipient cell becomes a merozygote, with more than one copy of a gene, or genes. The merozygote may be a transient or a stable state, depending on circumstances;
- recombination (synapsis and 'crossing over') may or may not be involved, depending on the process and strains involved.

KEY POINT **Bacterial crosses are best described as gene *transfer* rather than gene exchange, since the latter term suggests reciprocal DNA movement.**

Minimal medium – a chemically defined medium, containing only sufficient nutrients to meet the requirements of wild-type cells, i.e. inorganic salts plus a particular carbon source.

Auxotrophs – mutants requiring an additional organic compound (e.g. an amino acid or growth factor) in order to grow in minimal medium.

Prototrophs – wild types (from which auxotrophs are derived) and all other strains capable of growth in minimal medium.

Differential medium – usually a complex medium with additional compounds that distinguish between two types of bacteria, e.g. wild-type and mutant strains, often using pH indicator dyes (p. 147) or chromogenic/ fluorogenic substrates (p. 379).

Take care when distinguishing between carbon source and nutritional mutants – note that a Lac⁻ mutant is unable to grow if provided with lactose as the sole carbon source, while a Trp⁻ mutant is unable to grow unless it is provided with tryptophan.

Working with bacterial mutants

To study bacterial genetics, it is necessary to use mutant strains, which have phenotypic characteristics that allow them to be distinguished from wild-type strains. The principal types of bacterial mutant include:

- Morphological mutants, with different structural characteristics from the wild type, e.g. so-called 'rough' mutants of selected bacteria, such as *Streptococcus* and *Klebsiella*, are defective in their synthesis of capsular polysaccharides, giving small, dull colonies on agar-based media. This is in contrast to 'smooth' wild-type strains, where colonies are large and glistening due to the hydrophilic polysaccharide capsule. At a practical level, it is relatively straightforward to work with such mutants, since wild-type and mutant bacteria will grow on the same medium, the mutants having a feature that visibly distinguishes them from wild types. However, there are few examples in general use.

- Resistant mutants, which grow in the presence of an inhibitory substance such as an antibiotic, a toxic compound or a particular phage. The isolation of an ampicillin-resistant mutant (Amp^r phenotype) is made possible by including ampicillin in the growth medium, since the growth of sensitive wild-type cells (Amp^s phenotype) will be inhibited.

- Carbon source mutants, which are unable to use a particular substance as a source of carbon or energy, e.g. *E. coli* mutants unable to use lactose (Lac⁻ phenotype), in contrast to Lac⁺ wild types. A Lac⁻ mutant would be unable to grow on a minimal medium containing lactose as the principal carbon source. In order to identify and characterise such mutants, a differential medium must be used, e.g. MacConkey agar (a complex medium containing lactose as a *supplementary* carbon source, plus a pH indicator dye – colonies of Lac⁺ and Lac⁻ strains are distinguished on the basis of size and pigmentation, p. 208).

- Nutritional mutants, which have an additional requirement for a particular nutrient, compared to the wild type. For example, a strain auxotrophic for the amino acid tryptophan (Trp⁻) would grow only if the medium contained tryptophan (e.g. in a minimal medium plus tryptophan). Since it is not possible to devise a single medium which will allow an auxotroph to be distinguished from the corresponding prototrophic wild type, the selection and identification of such mutants require a different approach, involving replica plating from (a) nutrient-rich medium onto (b) minimal medium and (c) minimal medium supplemented with the particular nutrient (Fig. 59.1).

- Mutants created by transposon mutagenesis, where a gene has been inactivated by the insertion of a transposon, e.g. *lacZ* inactivated by Tn10 (p. 418).

- Strains with different forms of a particular gene on the chromosome and also on a plasmid (partial diploids): the genes carried on the plasmid can be shown as follows: *lacZ*::Tn10/F′*lacZ*⁺ with the slash separating the transposon-inactivated chromosomal gene from the F′ plasmid with its functional *lacZ* gene.

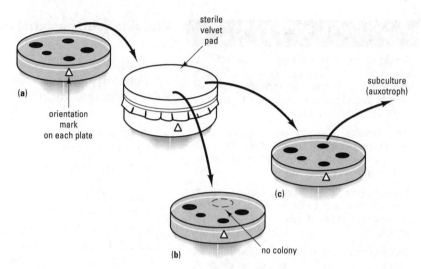

Fig. 59.1 Identification of auxotrophs using replica plating: a mixed suspension of wild-type and mutant cells is first cultured on the surface of a master plate containing nutrient-rich medium (a), then transferred to a sterile pad which is then used to inoculate minimal medium (b) and minimal medium plus a particular nutrient (c). Failure to grow on (b), coupled with growth on (c), infers auxotrophy for that particular nutrient and allows the auxotroph to be further subcultured and studied.

● Conditional lethal mutants, which have a defect that causes death under a specific set of circumstances (the 'restrictive condition'), e.g. in *E. coli* temperature-sensitive mutants that grow at 30 °C, but not 40 °C, often as a result of the temperature-dependent inactivation of mutant enzymes.

DNA transfer in bacteria

KEY POINT The traditional approach to genetic analysis in prokaryotes involves mapping the position of individual genes using information provided from 'crosses', based on gene transfer. Typically, the recipient cell will be a mutant and the donor DNA will carry wild-type genes, enabling the transfer of wild-type characteristics to be studied in the laboratory.

The principal bacterial gene transfer processes are:

Natural transformation

In contrast to genetic engineering techniques, where DNA uptake is induced under specific laboratory conditions (p. 447), natural transformation involves the release of DNA to the external medium (e.g. death and lysis of the donor cell) and its subsequent uptake and incorporation into the genome of the recipient cell. Natural transformation is restricted to a limited number of bacterial groups and only occurs if the recipient cells are in the correct physiological state, termed *competence*, often in the early exponential (log) growth phase (p. 226). Transformation is a relatively rare event, occurring at frequencies of ≤1 transformant per 10^3 cells. In a competent cell, DNA will be taken up and, if homologous (i.e. from another strain of the same species), may then be incorporated into the genome of the recipient cell by homologous recombination via a double 'crossover' (two recombination events, as shown in Fig. 59.2).

Fig. 59.2 Homologous recombination between donor DNA (from transformation, transduction or conjugation) and the recipient genome *via* a double crossover.

Performing co-transformation tests using auxotrophic recipients – controls must be set up without added donor DNA to determine the number of revertants (spontaneous mutants), giving the actual rate of transformation by subtraction.

The principal application of transformation has been in mapping the position of genes in those bacteria showing natural competence (e.g. *Bacillus subtilis*). The experiments are often easiest to perform with auxotrophic recipients and prototrophic (wild-type) donor DNA, since transformants can be selectively grown on media lacking one or more individual nutrients. The frequency of co-transformation of two genes is a measure of how close together they are likely to be on the donor DNA strand – a high co-transformation frequency implies that they are close together on the chromosome, reaching a recipient cell on the same fragment of DNA.

KEY POINT While co-transformation frequencies are inversely related to map distances, they are not directly equivalent to the recombination frequencies used in mapping eukaryotic genomes (p. 414), because they are also influenced by the size distribution of the fragments of donor DNA and by the likelihood of homologous recombination.

Transformation mapping has several limitations, since it requires a fairly large number of complex replica plating experiments to produce a chromosomal map, and the relative position of genes that are very far apart cannot be determined directly – the 'jigsaw' requires a large number of available pieces, before the underlying structure can be seen. It is also insensitive for small map distances – two genes that are adjacent, or very close together, will give similar high co-transformation values.

Transduction

Here, the DNA exchange is mediated by a phage (p. 202), in one of two processes:

Performing generalised transduction in **E. coli** – *P1 phage is often used, since it gives a high proportion of transducing particles (≈0.3% of the total), with a large fragment size (≈2.5% of the E. coli genome), making it easier to locate individual transductants.*

1. Generalised transduction: occasionally, a fragment of chromosomal or plasmid DNA within an infected bacterial cell may be packaged within the protein coat of a phage, in place of the phage genome. This fragment might be derived from any part of the host cell genome (exogenote). After release, on lysis of the donor cell, the transducing particle may introduce the DNA fragment into a new recipient cell. The introduced DNA may then be incorporated into the host genome by a double crossover, in a homologous recombination event similar to that shown in Fig. 59.2 for transformation. Generalised transduction can be used to establish gene order and for mapping purposes, using broadly similar principles to transformation, as only closely spaced genes will show co-transduction, with a co-transduction frequency that is inversely related to the distance between the two genes. Since a generalised transducing particle can carry a fairly small amount of DNA, the relative frequency of co-transduction can be used to provide finer detail of gene order over shorter distances than for transformation.

2. Specialised transduction: this is mediated only by a temperate phage, e.g. λ phage, which integrates at a specific site on the chromosome by a single crossover event. It involves a restricted number of genes – typically, a pair of genes on either side of the integration site for a particular temperate phage (Fig. 59.3). Specialised transduction will only occur if, on entry into the lytic cycle (phage replication, p. 202), there is an incorrect (abnormal) excision of the prophage and a part of

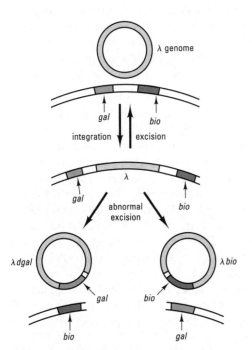

Fig. 59.3 Integration, excision and abnormal excision of λ phage, creating a modified phage genome (either λ*dgal* or λ*bio*), prior to specialised transduction.

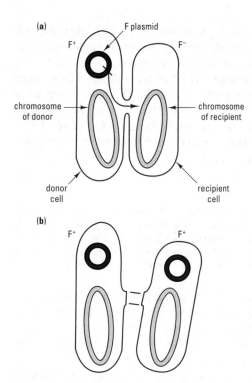

(a)

F plasmid

F⁺   F⁻

chromosome of donor   chromosome of recipient

donor cell   recipient cell

(b)

F⁺   F⁺

Fig. 59.4 Conjugation between F⁺ donor and F⁻ recipient. A single strand of F plasmid DNA is cut and transferred in linear form to the recipient (a), followed by recircularisation and complementary strand synthesis, converting the recipient to F⁺ (b).

Example The *E. coli* strain HfrH has the F proplasmid integrated at a site close to genes for the synthesis of threonine, so these genes would be transferred early during HfrH × F⁻ conjugation.

Example F′*lac* is an F′ plasmid that incorporates wild-type chromosomal DNA coding for lactose utilisation.

the bacterial genome is incorporated, giving a specialised transducing particle (a modified phage, carrying a bacterial gene). In the case of λ phage (Fig. 59.3), the transducing particle may carry either the biotin gene (λ*bio*), or the galactose gene (λ*gal*, also termed λ*dgal*, since the modified phage is defective due to the loss of an essential part of the phage genome, and therefore is incapable of replicating without the aid of a co-infecting, non-defective 'helper' phage). On entry into the recipient cell, the modified phage may become latent, creating a partial diploid. The practical applications of specialised transduction are limited to those genes flanking the integration sites of temperate phages. The most common investigations are of complementation in merozygotes containing two copies of a particular gene. Where donor and recipients of the same mutant phenotype have mutations in different genes, the creation of a partial diploid can produce a wild-type phenotype.

Conjugation

Here, the transfer occurs as a result of cell-to-cell contact, with direct transmission of DNA from donor to recipient cell. In *E. coli*, the donor cell carries specific surface pili (protein microtubules), allowing a donor cell to attach to receptors on the surface of a recipient cell and bringing the paired cells into close contact (Fig. 59.4). In the simplest instance, the donor cell carries an additional plasmid, the F plasmid (originally termed 'F factor'), that encodes the genes responsible for conjugation, including those for the protein subunits of the specialised pili. In conventional notation, the donor is termed F⁺ and the recipient F⁻. During conjugation between F⁺ donor and F⁻ recipient, a single strand of the circular F plasmid is cut and transferred (in linear form) to the recipient cell, which becomes F⁺ once the entire plasmid has been transferred and a complementary strand has been synthesised – this process takes a few minutes. At a practical level, crosses involving F⁺ donors give little useful information, apart from mapping the position of genes on the F plasmid. However, two other types of donor are more useful:

1. Hfr strains, where the F plasmid DNA has become integrated into the chromosome, as a proplasmid, in an analogous manner to a temperate phage such as λ (Fig. 59.3). Such strains show a *high frequency of recombination* (hence Hfr), since chromosomal genes are transferred to the recipient cell at a far greater frequency than in crosses using F⁺ donors. The Hfr × F⁻ cross is illustrated in Fig. 59.5: a part of the F proplasmid is first to be transferred, followed by chromosomal DNA and, finally, the remaining fragment of the F proplasmid. After transfer, donor chromosomal DNA can be integrated into the recipient's genome by homologous recombination (Fig. 59.2). The conjugating pair usually breaks apart before the process is complete and the recipient cell remains F⁻, since only the leading fragment of the F plasmid reaches the recipient cell. A number of different Hfr strains of *E. coli* are available, with the F proplasmid inserted at different chromosomal locations.

2. F′ ('F prime') donors, with a modified F plasmid incorporating one or more chromosomal genes, formed as a result of defective excision of the F proplasmid from the chromosome in a similar manner to λ*bio* (Fig. 59.3). The F′ plasmid will transfer its chromosomal genes at very

(a)

(b)

Fig. 59.5 Conjugation between Hfr donor and F⁻ recipient. The F proplasmid is cut and leads the chromosome (in single stranded form) from the donor (a), followed by homologous recombination in the recipient (b).

high frequency to a recipient, which will also become F′ once transfer of the F′ plasmid DNA is complete. This process is sometimes referred to as F-duction (or, less appropriately, as 'sexduction').

Mapping with Hfr donors using interrupted conjugation

Mating an antibiotic-sensitive wild-type Hfr donor with an antibiotic-resistant mutant F⁻ recipient provides a simple means of detecting recombinants, since the donor cells will be unable to grow on a medium containing the antibiotic while unmodified recipient cells will have a different phenotype from the recombinant recipient cells. The method is even simpler for the most common crosses, using nutritional mutants, where a prototrophic Hfr donor is crossed with an auxotrophic F⁻ recipient and only the recombinants are able to grow on minimal medium with added antibiotic; this approach can be extended to multiple genes, using a multiple auxotroph F⁻ recipient. By carrying out a series of experiments where the conjugation process is terminated at different times (e.g. using vigorous mixing in a vortex mixer, p. 133), the time required to transfer a particular characteristic can be determined as the earliest time at which this interruption no longer prevents recombinants from appearing. Typical results from a cross involving several genetic markers are shown in Fig. 59.6a: by plotting the result graphically and extrapolating the curves to their intersect with the x-axis, the *time of entry* of a particular marker can be determined accurately.

The different times of entry of each characteristic reflect their relative positions on the chromosome, with genes near to the origin of transfer of the F proplasmid having short times of entry and those further along the chromosome having later times of entry. The times of entry can be used to locate the genes on a chromosome map (Fig. 59.6b), representing map distances relative to the origin of transfer. This map differs from those produced from transformation and transduction analysis, since it is a transfer order map, rather than a linkage map. However, as transfer of the entire chromosome requires ≈100 minutes, it is difficult to map genes far from the origin of transfer, due to the decreasing number of recombinants with increasing time (Fig. 59.6a): this is overcome by combining mapping

Fig. 59.6 Recombinants obtained from interrupted conjugation for a number of characters (a to e), plotted to show the time of entry of each character (a): the same data have been used to map the position of each character on the bacterial chromosome (b).

Bacterial and phage genetics

Genome mapping using interrupted conjugation – while this technique works well for widely spaced markers, it is less useful than transformation and transduction for closely linked genes.

Definitions

Trans (Latin 'across') – on separate DNA molecules.

Cis (Latin 'here') – on the same DNA molecule.

data from several Hfr strains, each with the F plasmid integrated at a different position. In fact, this approach was originally used to demonstrate the circularity of the *E. coli* chromosome and, subsequently, to determine the location of over 1500 individual genes in this organism.

Genetic analysis using F′ plasmids

Since cells containing an F′ plasmid are stable merozygotes, their principal use is in studying the behaviour of genes under diploid conditions, for example:

- to determine whether a particular mutation (on the F′ plasmid) is dominant or recessive over another (on the chromosome);
- to test whether a particular gene complements another: if two mutations are in different genes, then they can complement each other in a stable merozygote, while two mutations in the same gene cannot complement each other in a stable merozygote;
- to examine whether a particular regulatory gene located on an F′ plasmid influences the expression of one or more chromosomal genes, i.e. whether it can operate in the *trans* position. The alternative test is to construct a merozygote with two genes in a chromosomal location (i.e. the *cis* position), for example, using specialised transduction (p. 421). This type of analysis has been used to investigate the molecular basis of gene expression and the function of regulatory regions of the chromosome.

KEY POINT Note that, while many of the above procedures have proved to be useful in the early stages of bacterial genome analysis, the techniques and methods of molecular biology (Chapters 60–62) can be used to provide more detailed genetic information, without the need to obtain certain types of mutant, or carry out specific crosses between particular donors and recipients.

Phage crosses

In practical classes, you may carry out experiments using phages, often using T-even phages of *E. coli* (e.g. T4 coliphage). The methods used to map the phage genome superficially resemble those used for eukaryotic organisms (Chapter 58) since the 'progeny' of two 'parental' phages with contrasting genotypes are analysed for recombinants and the frequency of recombination is used to measure the distance between linked genes.

KEY POINT A phage cross (sometimes termed a 'mating') does not involve meiosis, gamete production or zygote formation, but is a result of a *mixed infection*, where a single bacterial cell is infected with phages of the two original genotypes.

Performing phage crosses – large numbers of both types of phage must be used to ensure that every bacterial cell is infected with at least one of each type, i.e. there is a high multiplicity of infection.

Following a single round of replication, the 'progeny' from this mixed infection are screened for the various possible genotypes, as plaques on a 'lawn' of a susceptible strain of *E. coli*, using conventional phage culture techniques (p. 202).

Phage mutants

The phage genes most widely used in crosses are those affecting:

- plaque morphology – for example, mutants may form large plaques as opposed to small plaques, or plaques with a different margin, e.g. a light turbid halo as opposed to a dark halo;
- host range – e.g. T-even mutants may infect different strains of *E. coli* from the parental types;
- conditional lethality, especially T4 phage mutants of the *rII* locus, unable to grow on *E. coli* K12(λ) in contrast to wild-type T4.

Phage mapping

By crossing a mutant for plaque morphology with a mutant for host range, the relative frequency of recombinants (i.e. progeny with double mutant and wild-type phenotypes) can be expressed in terms of the proportion of the total number of plaques, as a recombination frequency (R), where:

$$R = \frac{\text{number of double mutants and wild-type plaques}}{\text{total number of plaques}} \quad [59.1]$$

This value is sometimes multiplied by 100 and expressed as a percentage, or as map units, equivalent to 'centimorgans' (1 cM = 1% crossing over) in conventional Mendelian crosses (p. 414).

The pioneering work of Seymour Benzer established that the *rII* region of the T4 genome consisted of two distinct genes (*rIIA* and *rIIB*), each of which can give rise to the same mutant phenotype. T4 *rII* mutants are most often used for demonstrating *trans* complementation between these two genes and for demonstrating the principles of fine structure mapping of this region of the genome, since the conditional lethality of the rII phenotype simplifies the search for rare recombinant wild-type phages, as only these recombinants are able to form plaques on *E. coli* K12(λ).

Learning from Benzer's work – detailed fine structure mapping of the rII region of T4 coliphage established that recombination can occur within a single gene, and even between adjacent nucleotides. Before these experiments, a gene was regarded as an indivisible unit – nowadays we appreciate that the smallest unit in genetics is the base pair.

Sources for further study

Anon. *Information about bacteriophage lambda.* Available: http://www.asmusa.org/division/m/fax/LamFax.html
Last accessed 08/01/03.
[Provides an overview of phage λ.]

Dale, J.W. (1998) *Molecular Genetics of Bacteria*, 3rd edn. Wiley, London.

Eynard, N., and Teisse, J. (2000) *Electrotransformation of Bacteria.* Springer-Verlag, Berlin.

Hartl, D.L. and Jones, E. W. *GeNETics on the Web.* Available: http://www.jbpub.com/genetics/chapters.cfm
Last accessed 08/01/03.

Snyder, L. and Champness, W. (1997) *Molecular Genetics of Bacteria.* American Society for Microbiology, Washington, DC.

Study exercises

59.1 Test your understanding of bacterial and phage genetics. Distinguish between each of the following pairs of terms:

(a) zygote and merozygote;

(b) transformation and transposition;

(c) generalised and specialised transduction;

(d) prototroph and auxotroph;

(e) HFr and F′ strains.

59.2 Interpret the codes commonly used to describe bacterial mutant strains. Describe the *E. coli* phenotypes represented by the following:

(a) Ampr Lac$^+$ Trp$^-$

(b) His$^-$ Lac$^-$

(c) *glnA*::Tn10

(d) *trpA*::Tn 6/F′*trpA*$^+$

(e) a Gal$^+$ strain lysogenised with *λdgal*

59.3 Interpret results from an HFr mapping experiment. Three different HFr strains were used to map the genome of a bacterium in a series of interrupted conjugation experiments. The strains transferred genes to the F′ recipient cell in the following orders:

Strain (a): X W C Z A

Strain (b): Y D F X W

Strain (c): Z A E B Y

Assuming that all of these genes are present only once on a single circular chromosome, what is their order?

59.4 Construct a chromosomal map. The table below represents data for an interrupted conjugation study using an HFr donor strain containing four 'marker' genes. These were distinguished by plating onto four different media, with the following major components:

Medium A: glucose, histidine (trace amount), tryptophan (trace amount), ampicillin.

Medium B: glucose, histidine (trace amount).

Medium C: glucose, tryptophan (trace amount).

Medium D: lactose, histidine (trace amount), tryptophan (trace amount).

(a) What is tested for by each of these four different media?

(b) Based on the composition of these media and the data below, what is the phenotype of (i) the HFr donor and (ii) the F$^-$ recipient?

(c) Given a chromosome map size of 60 min, where would each of these genes be located on the bacterial chromosome?

Colony numbers following interrupted mating, with plating on medium A, B, C or D

Time (min)	Medium A	Medium B	Medium C	Medium D
0	0	0	0	0
10	0	32	0	0
20	0	287	38	0
30	34	339	182	0
40	156	341	226	28
50	179	338	229	89
60	180	340	227	95

60 Molecular genetics I – fundamental principles

Deoxyribonucleic acid (DNA) is the genetic material of all cellular organisms. Its structure is outlined in Chapter 53.

KEY POINT The sequence of the bases A, G, T and C carries the genetic information of the organism. A section of DNA that encodes the information for a single polypeptide or protein is referred to as a gene, while the entire genetic information of an organism is called the genome.

Definitions

Units of nucleic acid size (length) –
Kilobase pair (kbp) = 10^3 base pairs
Megabase pair (Mbp) = 10^6 base pairs

Table 60.1 The Genetic Code – combinations of nucleotide bases coding for individual amino acids

1st Base	\multicolumn{4}{c}{2nd Base}				3rd Base
	U	C	A	G	
U	F	S	Y	C	U
	F	S	Y	C	C
	L	S	*	*	A
	L	S	*	W	G
C	L	P	H	R	U
	L	P	H	R	C
	L	P	Q	R	A
	L	P	Q	R	G
A	I	T	N	S	U
	I	T	N	S	C
	I	T	K	R	A
	M	T	K	R	G
G	V	A	D	G	U
	V	A	D	G	C
	V	A	E	G	A
	V	A	E	G	G

* = termination codons.
Standard abbreviations for the above amino acids are as given in Table 50.1.
Note that AUG (=M) is the initiation codon. The above codons are given for mRNA – the coding strand of DNA would have T in place of U, while the template strand would have complementary bases to those given above.

The amount of DNA in the genome is usually expressed in terms of base pairs (bp), rather than M_r, and its size depends on the complexity of the organism: for example, the human papilloma virus has a genome of 8×10^3 base pairs (8 kbp), that of *Escherichia coli* is 4×10^6 base pairs (4 Mbp), while the human haploid genome is very large, comprising 3×10^9 base pairs (3000 Mbp). The human genome contains about 23 000 genes (distributed on 23 pairs of chromosomes), which represent only about 1 per cent of the total amount of genomic DNA (i.e. 99 per cent of human DNA is non-coding). Organisms with smaller genomes have smaller amounts of non-coding DNA: some viral genomes have 'overlapping' genes, where the same base sequences carry information for more than one protein.

The size of each individual gene varies considerably: the largest ones may exceed 10 Mbp. Chromosomes represent the largest organisational units of DNA: in eukaryotes, they are usually linear molecules, complexed with protein and RNA, varying in length from tens to hundreds of Mbp. The unit used to denote physical distance between genes (base pairs) differs from that used to describe genetic distance (centimorgan, cM), which is based on recombination frequency (p. 414). In humans, $1 \text{cM} \approx 1 \text{Mbp}$, though this relationship varies widely, depending on recombination frequency within particular regions of a chromosome.

Each template for the synthesis of RNA (transcription) begins at a promoter site upstream of the coding sequence and terminates at a specific site at the end of the gene. The base sequence of this RNA is complementary to the 'template strand' and equivalent to the 'coding strand' of the DNA. In eukaryotic cells, transcription occurs in the nucleus, where the newly synthesised RNA, or primary transcript, is also subject to processing, or 'splicing', in which non-coding regions within the gene (introns) are excised, joining the coding regions (exons) together into a continuous sequence. Further processing results in the addition of a polyadenyl 'tail' at the 3′ end and a 7-methylguanosine 'cap' at the 5′ end of what is now mature eukaryotic messenger RNA (mRNA). The mRNA then migrates from the nucleus to the cytoplasm, where it acts as a template for protein synthesis (translation) at the ribosome: the translated portion of mRNA is read in coding units, termed codons, consisting of three bases.

Each codon corresponds to a specific amino acid, including a codon for the initiation of protein synthesis (Table 60.1). Individual amino acids are brought to the ribosome by specific transfer RNA (tRNA) molecules that recognise particular codons. The amino acids are incorporated into the growing polypeptide chain in the order dictated by the sequence of codons until a termination codon is recognised, after which the protein is released from the ribosome.

The techniques described in this and subsequent chapters are used widely in many aspects of molecular biology, including the identification and characterisation of genes, gene cloning and genetic engineering, medical genetics and genetic fingerprinting.

KEY POINT An important characteristic of nucleic acids is their ability to hybridise: two single strands with complementary base pairs will hydrogen bond (anneal) to produce a duplex, as in conventional double stranded (ds)DNA. This duplex can be converted to single stranded (ss)DNA (i.e. 'melted') by conditions that disrupt hydrogen bonding, e.g. raising the temperature or addition of salt, and then reannealed by lowering the temperature or by removal of salt.

DNA can be easily purified and assayed (Chapter 53), and it is relatively stable in its pure form. Most of the problems of working with such a large biomolecule have been overcome by the following:

- using restriction enzymes (see below) to cut DNA precisely and reproducibly: mammalian DNA may yield millions of fragments, with sizes ranging from a few hundred base pairs to tens of kbp, while small viral genomes may give only a few fragments;
- electrophoretic methods for the separation of DNA fragments on the basis of their sizes (p. 429);
- segments of DNA can be detected by 'probes' that specifically hybridise with the DNA of interest (p. 431);
- once separated, specific segments of DNA can be obtained in almost unlimited quantities by insertion into vectors and multiplication within suitable host cells (DNA cloning, Chapter 62);
- methods are now available for rapidly determining the base sequence of DNA segments (p. 434), together with strategies for combining information from several adjacent segments to give contiguous sequences representing entire genomes in well-studied organisms (Chapter 11);
- specific target sequences of DNA within a genome can be amplified by more than a billion-fold by the polymerase chain reaction (PCR, see Chapter 61).

Producing DNA fragments

Fragments of DNA can be produced by mechanical shearing or ultrasonication (p. 239), producing a random array of fragment sizes. Reproducible cleavage can be achieved using type II restriction endonucleases (commonly called restriction enzymes) which recognise and cleave at a specific palindromic sequence of double stranded DNA (usually four or six base pairs), known as the restriction site. Each enzyme is given a code name derived from the name of the organism from which it is isolated, e.g. *Hin* dIII was the third restriction enzyme to be obtained from *Haemophilus influenzae* strain Rd (Fig. 60.1). Most restriction enzymes will cut each DNA strand at a slightly different position within the restriction

Fig. 60.1 Recognition base sequence and cleavage site for the restriction enzyme *Hin* dIII. This is the conventional representation of double-stranded DNA, showing the individual bases, where A is adenine, C cytosine, G guanine and T thymine. The cleavage site on each strand is shown by an arrow.

site to produce short, single stranded regions known as cohesive ends, or 'sticky ends', as shown in Fig. 60.1. A few restriction enzymes cleave DNA to give blunt-ended fragments (e.g. *Hin* dII or *Sma* I).

Separation of nucleic acids using gel electrophoresis

Separation of DNA by agarose and polyacrylamide gel electrophoresis
Electrophoresis is the term used to describe the movement of ions in an applied electrical field. DNA molecules are negatively charged, migrating through an agarose gel towards the anode at a rate which is dependent upon molecular size – smaller, compact DNA molecules can pass through the sieve-like agarose matrix more easily than large, extended fragments. Electrophoresis of plasmid DNA is usually carried out using a submerged agarose gel (Fig. 60.2). The amount of agarose is adjusted, depending on the size of the DNA molecules to be separated, e.g. 0.3% w/v agarose is used for large fragments (>20 000 bp) while 0.8% is used for smaller fragments. Very small fragments are best separated using a poly-acrylamide gel (Table 60.2). Note the following:

- Individual samples are added to pre-formed wells using a pipettor. The volume of sample added to each well is usually less than 25 μl so a steady hand and careful dispensing are needed to pipette each sample.
- The density of the samples is usually increased by adding a small amount of glycerol or sucrose, so that each sample is retained within the appropriate well.

Maximising recovery of DNA – these large molecules are easily damaged by mechanical forces, e.g. vigorous shaking or stirring during extraction. In addition, all glassware must be scrupulously cleaned and gloves must be worn, to prevent deoxyribonuclease contamination of solutions.

Working with small values in molecular biology – use a pipettor of appropriate size (e.g. P2 or P20 Gilson Pipetman®) with a fine tip. For very small volumes, and pre-wet the top before delivering the required volume.

Fig. 60.2 Agarose gel electrophoresis of DNA.

Using molecular weight standards – for accurate molecular weight determination your standards must have the same conformation as the DNA in your sample, i.e. linear DNA standards for linear (restriction) fragments and closed circular standards for plasmid DNA.

Safe handling of ethidium bromide – ethidium bromide is carcinogenic so always use gloves when handling stained gels and make sure you do not spill any staining solution.

Table 60.2 Gel concentrations for the separation of DNA of various sizes

Type of gel	% (w/v)	Range of resolution of DNA (bp)
Polyacrylamide	20.0	5–100
	15.0	20–150
	5.0	75–500
	3.5	100–1000
Agarose	2.0	100–5000
	1.2	200–8000
	0.8	400–20 000
	0.3	1000–70 000

Assaying nucleic acids in solution – double stranded DNA at $50\,\mu g\,ml^{-1}$ has an A_{260} of 1, and the same absorbance is obtained for single stranded DNA at $33\,\mu g\,ml^{-1}$ and (single stranded) RNA at $40\,\mu g\,ml^{-1}$. These values can be used to convert the absorbance of a test solution to a concentration of nucleic acid.

Definition

Chromosome walking – *a method for analysing areas of interest in DNA, in which the end of a segment of DNA is used as a probe to locate other segments that overlap the first segment: long stretches of DNA can be analysed by subsequent use of probes made from the ends of successive overlapping segments.*

- A water-soluble anionic tracking dye (e.g. bromophenol blue) is also added to each sample, so that migration can be followed visually.
- Molecular weight standards are added to one or more wells. After electrophoresis, the relative positions of bands of known molecular weight can be used to prepare a calibration curve (usually by plotting log_{10} of the molecular weight of each band against the distance travelled).
- The gel should be run until the tracking dye has migrated across 80% of the gel (see manufacturer's instructions for appropriate voltages/times). Note that the tank cover must be in position during electrophoresis, to prevent evaporation and to reduce the possibility of electric shock.
- After electrophoresis, the bands of DNA can be visualised by soaking the gel for around 5 min in $0.1–0.5\,mg\,l^{-1}$ ethidium bromide (Fig. 53.4), which binds to DNA by intercalation between the paired nucleotides of the double helix.
- Under UV light, bands of DNA are visible due to the intense fluorescence of the ethidium bromide. The limit of detection using this method is around 10 ng DNA per band. Suitable plastic safety glasses or goggles will protect your eyes from the UV light. The migration of each band from the well can be measured using a ruler. Alternatively, a photograph can be taken, using a digital camera and adaptor, or a dedicated system, e.g. GelDoc®.
- If a particular band is required for further study (e.g. a plasmid), the piece of gel containing that band is cut from the gel using a clean scalpel. The DNA can be separated from the agarose by solubilising the gel slice and then binding it to an anion exchange resin, followed by elution in water or buffer (e.g. TE buffer, containing $10\,mmol\,l^{-1}$ TRIS/HCl at pH 8.0 plus $1\,mmol\,l^{-1}$ EDTA). Various commercial kits based on this approach are also available.

Electrophoretic separation of RNA

Total cellular RNA or purified mRNA can be separated on the basis of size by electrophoretic separations similar to those used for DNA fragments. However, under the conditions used to separate dsDNA, RNA molecules tend to develop a secondary structure, and this leads to anomalous mobilities. To eliminate RNA secondary structure, samples are pretreated by heating in dilute formamide or glyoxal, and electrophoresis is carried out in 'denaturing gels' which include buffers containing formaldehyde.

Pulsed field gel electrophoresis (PFGE)

If structural information is to be gained about large stretches of genomic DNA, then the order of the relatively short DNA segments (generated by the restriction enzymes described above) needs to be established. This is technically possible by techniques such as 'chromosome walking', but is time-consuming and potentially difficult, especially when dealing with large chromosomes such as those from yeast (a few Mbp) and humans (50–100 Mb), in contrast to the smaller genomes of bacteria and viruses. The technique of PFGE allows separation of DNA fragments of up to ≈12 Mb.

Very large DNA fragments (>100 kbp) can be generated from chromosomal DNA by the use of certain restriction enzymes that

(a)

Fig. 60.3 The configuration of electrodes for conventional PFGE (a) and CHEF/PACE (b).

recognise base sequences that are present at relatively low frequency, e.g. the enzyme *Not* I, which recognises a sequence of 8 bp rather than 4–6 bp. These enzymes are sometimes called 'rare cutters'. Genomic DNA prepared in the normal way is not suitable for digestion by these enzymes, as shearing during extraction fragments the DNA. Therefore, genomic DNA for analysis by PFGE is prepared as follows:

- cells are embedded in an agarose block;
- the block is incubated in solutions containing detergent, RNase and proteinase K, lysing the cells and hydrolysing RNA and proteins. The products of RNase and proteinase digestion diffuse away, leaving behind genomic DNA molecules exceeding several thousand kbp;
- the block is incubated *in situ* in a buffered solution containing an appropriate 'rare cutter': restriction fragments are produced, of up to ≈800 kbp.

PFGE differs from conventional electrophoresis in that it uses two or more alternating electric fields. An explanation for the effectivess of the technique is that large DNA fragments will be distorted by the voltage gradient, tending to elongate in the direction of the electric field and 'snaking' through pores in the gel. If the original electric field (Fig. 60.3a), is removed, and a second is applied at an angle to the first (Fig. 60.3b), the DNA must reorientate before it can migrate in the new direction. Larger (longer) DNA molecules will take more time to reorientate than smaller molecules, resulting in size-dependent separations.

The original configuration of electrodes used in PFGE is shown in Fig. 60.3a; this tends to produce 'bent' lanes that make lane-to-lane comparisons difficult. This can be overcome by using one of the many variants of the technique, one of which employs contour clamped homogeneous electric fields (CHEF). Here, multiple electrodes are arranged in a hexagonal array around the gel (Fig. 60.3b) and these are used to generate homogeneous electric fields with reorientation angles of up to 120°. A further development of CHEF involves programmable, autonomously controlled electrodes (PACE), which allows virtually unlimited variation of field and pulsing configurations, and can fractionate DNA molecules from 100 bp to 6 Mbp.

Identification of specific nucleic acid molecules using blotting and hybridisation techniques

Southern blotting

After separation by conventional agarose gel electrophoresis (p. 429), the fragments of DNA can be denatured and immobilised on a filter membrane using a technique named after its inventor, E.M. Southern. The main features of the conventional apparatus for Southern blotting are shown in Fig. 60.4. The principal stages in the procedure are:

1. To ensure efficient transfer, the gel is first soaked in HCl, leading to random cleavage of the DNA into smaller fragments.
2. The gel is subsequently soaked in alkali to denature the dsDNA to ssDNA, then neutralised: this is necessary to allow hybridisation with probe DNA after blotting.
3. A nitrocellulose or nylon membrane is then placed directly on the gel, followed by several layers of absorbent paper. The DNA is 'blotted' onto the filter as the buffer solution soaks into the paper by capillary action.

glass plate

weight

absorbent material (e.g. paper towels)

filter paper sheets

nitrocellulose membrane

filter paper wick

agarose gel

support

buffer solution

glass plate

cling film

Fig. 60.4 Components of Southern blotting apparatus.

4. The filter is baked in a vacuum oven at 80 °C for 3–5 h or exposed to UV light, in order to 'fix' the DNA.
5. Specific DNA fragments are identified by incubation (6–24 h) with complementary labelled probes of ssDNA, which will hybridise with a particular sequence, followed by visualisation, often using an enzyme-based system. If radiolabelled probes are used (see below), the desired fragments are located by autoradiography (p. 262).

Modifications of the method use either a vacuum apparatus, an electric field ('electroblotting') or positive pressure to transfer the DNA fragments from the gel to the membrane. These modifications reduce the time for transfer by around 10-fold.

Northern blotting

This process is virtually identical to Southern blotting, but RNA is the molecule that is separated and probed.

Dot blotting or slot blotting

Here, samples containing denatured DNA or RNA samples are applied directly to the nitrocellulose membrane (*via* small individual round or slot-like templated holes) without prior digestion with restriction enzymes or electrophoretic separation. The 'blot' is then probed in a similar manner to that described for Southern blotting. This allows detection of a particular nucleic acid sequence in a sample – clinical applications include the detection of specific pathogenic microbes and the detection of particular genes.

Types of probe

The probes used in blotting and DNA hybridisation can be obtained from a variety of sources including:

- cDNA (complementary or copy DNA) which is produced from isolated mRNA using reverse transcriptase. This retroviral enzyme catalyses RNA-directed DNA synthesis (rather than the normal transcription of DNA to RNA). After the mRNA has been reverse transcribed, it is degraded by the addition of alkali or ribonuclease, leaving the ssDNA copy. This is then used as a template for a DNA polymerase, which directs the synthesis of the second complementary DNA strand to form dsDNA. This is denatured to ssDNA before use.
- Oligonucleotide probes (15–30 nucleotides) can be produced if the amino acid sequence of the gene product is known. Since the genetic code is degenerate, i.e. some amino acids are coded for by more than one codon (see Table 60.1) it may be necessary to synthesise a mixture of oligonucleotides to detect a particular DNA sequence: this mixture of oligonucleotides is termed a 'degenerate probe'.
- Specific genomic DNA sequences, where the gene has been characterised.
- PCR-generated fragments (Chapter 61).
- Heterologous probes, i.e. sequences for the same gene, or its equivalent, in another organism.

Example For a simple tripeptide containing methionine, aspartate and phenylalanine, the synthetic oligonucleotide probes would include combinations of the following codons:
1st codon (met): ATG
2nd codon (asp): GAT, GAC
3rd codon (phe): TTT, TTC

Labelling of probes

Detection of very low concentrations of target DNA sequences requires probes that can be detected with high sensitivity. This is achieved by radiolabelling, e.g. using ^{33}P, or by using enzyme-linked methods, which are often available in kit form:

- Radiolabelled probes can be made by several methods, including the nick-translation technique. This uses DNA polymerase I from *E. coli*, which has (i) an exonuclease activity that 'nicks' dsDNA and removes a nucleotide, and (ii) a polymerase activity that can replace this with a labelled deoxyribonucleotide. After several cycles of nick-translation, the labelled DNA is denatured to ssDNA for use as probes. Newer approaches include random priming of single stranded template DNA, followed by the synthesis of radiolabelled DNA fragments complementary to the template using a DNA polymerase and a radiolabelled deoxynucleoside triphosphate (dNTP). Probe hybridisation to a target sequence is detected by autoradiography. Oligonucleotide probes cannot be labelled using the above methods and require 'end labelling', where a kinase is used to replace the $5'$ terminal phosphate group with a radiolabelled group.

- Enzyme-linked methods involve incorporating a modified nucleotide precursor, such as biotinylated dTTP, into the DNA by nick-translation or random priming. When the probe hybridises with the target sequence, it can be detected by addition of an enzyme (e.g. horse radish peroxidase) coupled to streptavidin. The streptavidin binds specifically to the biotin attached to the probe and the addition of a suitable fluorogenic or chromogenic substrate for the enzyme allows the probe to be located. An analogous chemiluminescent system is also available, based on dioxygenin-labelled nucleotides.

Hybridisation of probes

The stability of the duplex formed between the probe and its target is directly proportional to the number and type of complementary base pairs that can be formed between them: stability increases with the amount of G + C, since these bases form three hydrogen bonds per base pair, rather than two (p. 365). Duplex stability is also influenced by temperature, ionic strength and pH of the hybridisation buffer, and these can be varied to suit the stringency of hybridisation required:

- In 'low stringency' hybridisation, duplex formation with less than perfect complementarity is promoted, either by lowering the temperature, or increasing ionic strength. This might be useful when using a heterologous probe, i.e. from another species.

- 'Stringent' hybridisation conditions usually involve high temperatures, or decreased ionic strength, and will sustain only perfectly matched duplexes. An example of the use of these conditions would be for detecting a single base change in a mutant gene using a dot-blot hybridisation with a specific oligonucleotide probe.

DNA sequencing

By fragmenting target DNA with several restriction enzymes and then sequencing the overlapping fragments, it is possible to determine the nucleotide sequences of very large stretches of DNA, including entire genomes. Sequencing methods rely on polyacrylamide gel electrophoresis

Using commercial kits – do not blindly follow the protocol given by the manufacturer without making sure you understand the principles of the method and the reasons for the procedure. This will help you to recognise when things go wrong and what you might be able to do about it.

Molecular genetics I – fundamental principles

Fig. 60.5 A 2′,3′-dideoxynucleoside triphosphate.

(p. 316). The Sanger, or chain termination, method is the most widely used in DNA sequencing. This makes use of dideoxynucleotides (Fig. 60.5), which have no –OH group at either the C-2 or C-3 of ribose. A dideoxynucleoside triphosphate (ddNTP) can be added to a growing DNA chain, but since it lacks an –OH group at the C-3 position it cannot form a phosphodiester bond with the incoming dNTP of the growing chain. Therefore a dideoxynucleotide acts as a terminator at the site it occupies. Details of the Sanger sequencing method are given in Box 60.1 and Fig. 60.6.

Box 60.1 DNA sequencing using the chain termination (Sanger) method

The DNA to be sequenced must first be obtained as single-stranded fragments, typically around 200 bp, e.g. using a denatured plasmid. Sequencing is often performed using a commercial kit and the principal stages are as follows:

1. **Set up the strand synthesis reaction:** four separate tubes are required, each containing a small amount of one of the dideoxynucleoside triphosphates. Each tube contains all of the other components required for DNA synthesis, i.e. (i) the DNA selected for analysis (template DNA), e.g. denatured plasmid, (ii) a DNA polymerase (e.g. thermostable *Taq* polymerase), (iii) a [^{35}S] oligonucleotide primer of known sequence, to allow synthesis of the complementary DNA strand, (iv) dGTP, dATP, dCTP, dTTP (in excess) together with (v) one type of ddNTP (i.e. ddGTP, ddATP, ddCTP or ddTTP) in limited concentration. New DNA strands are synthesised by addition of dNTPs to the primer, guided by the template DNA until a ddNTP is added. As an example of the principle of the method, consider the ddTTP tube. When T is required to pair with A on the template DNA strand, the dTTP will be competing with the ddTTP, but because the dTTP is in excess this will normally be added to the chain at the appropriate position. However on occasions a ddTTP will be inserted at a given site and this will terminate DNA synthesis on the template strand. Thus, synthesis will be halted at all possible sites where ddT has substituted for dT and several strands of different length will be formed in the reaction mixture, each ending with ddT.

2. **Terminate the strand synthesis reaction:** after 5–10 min at 37 °C add a 'stop' solution containing formamide to disrupt hydrogen bonding between complementary bases and incubate at 80 °C for 15 min, to produce ssDNA.

3. **Separate the fragments using polyacrylamide gel electrophoresis:** 4–6% (w/v) denaturing acrylamide gels are used, containing urea (46% w/v) as the denaturing agent. Thin gels (0.35 mm thickness) are used, typically 20 cm wide by 50 cm long. The products in each of the four tubes are placed in four lanes side by side on the same gel and are separated by electrophoresis at 35–40 W (up to 32 mA, 1.5 kV) for 2.5 h. The high voltage raises the gel temperature to ≈50 °C, helping denaturation. A single gel can separate DNA fragments that differ in length by a single nucleotide.

4. **Locate the positions of individual bands by autoradiography:** the gel is fixed for 15 min with 10% (v/v) acetic acid, covered with Whatman 3MM paper and Saran wrap, then vacuum-dried, to avoid quenching the radicisotope signal (p. 261) and to prevent it from sticking to the X-ray film. The gel is unwrapped and placed next to an X-ray film for 24 h.

5. **Read the gel:** the nucleotide sequence can be read directly from the band positions that represent the newly made DNA segments of varying lengths (Fig. 60.6). The smallest segment is represented by the band at the bottom, since it travels furthest in the gel. The nucleotide sequence of the template strand can be deduced directly from that of the new strand, since the base on the template strand will be represented by an incomplete chain that terminates with the complementary dd nucleotide, i.e. template A with ddT, G with ddC, T with ddA, and C with ddG (Fig. 60.6).

Troubleshooting and other points to note: streaking can be due to damage to wells, air bubbles in wells/gel, or contamination by dirt/dust; faint and fuzzy gels may be due to insufficient template DNA, primer and/or dNTPs, due to poor annealing of primer and template, or to errors in preparing or running the gel; bands in more than one lane can indicate contamination of the template DNA, more than one primer site on the template, or secondary structure of DNA, giving 'ghost' banding.

Fig. 60.6 Sanger sequencing gel, showing how the banding pattern is converted into a sequence of nucleotide bases.

Using PCR (p. 437) for sequencing – *with the four ddNTPs tagged using different fluorophores, the products can be run in the same lane and detected by laser excitation at the end of the gel, with the sequence of fluorophores giving the base sequence.*

The alternative approach to sequencing is based on chemical degradation (the Maxam and Gilbert method), using different reagents to break the target DNA sequence into fragments which are then separated by polyacrylamide gel electrophoresis. The Maxam and Gilbert method is more involved than the Sanger technique, and is reserved for specialised applications, e.g. for studying the interaction between DNA and proteins.

Automated DNA sequencing

The development of automated DNA sequencing machines (so-called 'DNA sequenators') has enabled sequencing to be performed several orders of magnitude faster than with manual methods. Base-specificity is achieved by using primers labelled with fluorophores with different fluorescence characteristics in each of the four reaction tubes (Box 60.1). After the reactions are separately completed, the four sets of products can be pooled and fractionated by electrophoresis in a single lane. The fluorophore-labelled fragments are detected as they pass a scanning laser detector and the DNA sequence is determined by using both the specific wavelength emitted by the fragment (indicating the base) and by the migration time (indicating the fragment size, which corresponds to the base location in the DNA sequence). Nowadays, automated DNA sequencing tends to be performed by capillary electrophoresis (p. 325) rather than polyacrylamide gel electrophoresis.

Sources for further study

Brown, T.A. (2000) *Essential Molecular Biology: A Practical Approach*, Vols 1 and 2, 2nd edn. IRL Press, Oxford.

Hames, B.D. and Higgins, S.J. (1995) *Gene Probes: A Practical Approach*. IRL Press, Oxford.

Juo, P.S. (2002) *Concise Dictionary of Biomedicine and Molecular Biology*, 2nd edn. CRC Press, Boca Raton.

Monaco, A.P. (1995) *Pulsed Field Gel Electrophoresis: A Practical Approach*. IRL Press, Oxford.

Sambrook, J. and Russell, D.W. (2001) *Molecular Cloning: A Laboratory Manual*, 3rd edn. Cold Spring Harbor Lab, Cold Spring Harbor.

Schwarzacher, T. and Heslop-Harrison, P. (1999) *Practical in situ Hybridization*. Springer-Verlag, Berlin.

Study exercises

60.1 Practise the calculations involved in working with nucleic acids. Imagine that you have been supplied with a freeze-dried sample of a single stranded DNA probe 24 bases in length, which you reconstitute in 1 ml of buffer (reconstituted probe). You take $5\,\mu$l, add it to $495\,\mu$l of water and determine the A_{260} as 0.14.

(a) What is the mass concentration of the probe in this solution, in μg ml^{-1}?

(b) Assuming the average M_r of a nucleotide is 325, what is the concentration of the probe in the solution, expressed in micromolar terms (i.e. as $\mu mol\,l^{-1}$)?

(c) The concentration of probe required in a blotting procedure is $10\,pmol\,ml^{-1}$ and a total of 10 ml of this solution is required. You have been asked to prepare 5 ml of a stock solution of the DNA probe at $100\times$ the concentration required in the blotting procedure, so that 0.100 ml can be diluted to 10 ml for the final blotting procedure, while the rest will be stored at $-20\,°C$, for subsequent experiments. How would you prepare the $100\times$ stock solution?
Express all answers to 3 significant figures.

60.2 **Select an electrophoretic technique for separating DNA fragments of different sizes**. Which technique would you use to separate DNA fragments in the following ranges: (a) 1–70 kbp; (b) 75–500 bp; (c) 100–6 Mbp.

60.3 **Test your understanding of the term 'stringency' in relation to nucleic acid probes**. What does the term 'stringency' mean in the context of molecular biology? What factors cause increased stability between a nucleic acid probe and its target sequence? Give examples of when you might use 'low stringency' and 'high stringency' hybridisation.

60.4 **Interpret the results of a Sanger sequencing gel**. The figure represents a typical gel from a dideoxynucleotide sequencing procedure. Determine the sequence of the original DNA strand.

Molecular genetics II – PCR and related applications

The polymerase chain reaction (PCR) is a rapid, inexpensive and simple means of producing μg amounts of DNA from minute quantities of template.

Applications of PCR – *these include:*

- *diagnosis and screening of genetic diseases and cancer;*
- *rapid detection of slowly growing microorganisms (e.g. mycobacteria) and viruses (e.g. HIV);*
- *HLA typing in transplantation;*
- *analysis of DNA in archival material;*
- *DNA fingerprinting in forensic science;*
- *preparation of nucleic acid probes;*
- *clone screening, mapping and subcloning (p. 443).*

KEY POINT PCR offers an alternative approach to gene cloning (Chapter 62) for the production of many copies of an identical sequence of DNA. The starting material may be genomic DNA (e.g. from a single cell), RNA, DNA from archival specimens, cloned DNA or forensic samples.

The technique uses *in vitro* enzyme-catalysed DNA synthesis to create millions of identical copies of DNA. If the base sequence of the adjacent regions of the DNA to be amplified is known, this enables synthetic oligonucleotide primers to be constructed that are complementary to these so-called 'flanking regions'. Initiation of the PCR occurs when these primers are allowed to hybridise (anneal) to the component single strands of the target DNA, followed by enzymatic extension of the primers (from their 3′ ends) using a thermostable DNA polymerase. A single PCR cycle consists of three distinct steps, carried out at different temperatures (Fig. 61.1), as follows:

1. Denaturation of dsDNA by heating to 94–98 °C separating the individual strands of the target DNA.
2. Annealing of the primers, which occurs when the temperature is reduced to 37–65 °C.
3. Extension of the primers by a thermostable DNA polymerase (e.g. *Taq* polymerase, isolated from <u>*Thermus aquaticus*</u>) at 72 °C; this step should last long enough to generate the PCR product: approximately 1 min of reaction time is required per kbp of sequence.

In the first cycle, the product from one primer is extended beyond the region of complementarity of the other primer, so each newly synthesised strand can be used as a template for the primers in the second cycle (Fig. 61.1). Successive cycles will thus generate an exponentially increasing number of DNA fragments, the termini of which are bounded by the 5′ ends of the primers (length of each fragment = length of primers + length of target sequence). Since the amount of DNA produced doubles in each cycle, the amount of DNA produced = 2^n, where n is the number of cycles. Up to 1 μg of amplified target DNA can be produced in 25–30 cycles from a single-copy sequence within 50 ng of genomic DNA, assuming close to 100% efficiency during the cycling process. After electrophoresis, the PCR product is normally present in sufficient quantity to be visualised directly with ethidium bromide (p. 367).

The temperature changes in PCR are normally achieved using a thermal cycler, which is simply a purpose-built incubator block that can be programmed to vary temperatures, incubation times and cycle numbers.

KEY POINT PCR is so sensitive that one of the main problems associated with the technique is contamination with 'foreign' DNA. Great care is required to avoid sample contamination during *in vitro* amplification (Box 61.1).

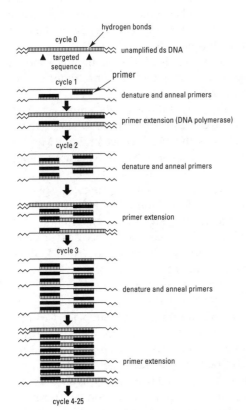

Fig. 61.1 The polymerase chain reaction (PCR).

Storing primers for PCR – *primers are best stored in ammonia solution, which remains liquid at −20°C, avoiding the need for repeated freezing and thawing when dispensed. Before use, aliquots of stock solution should be heated in a fume cupboard, to drive off the ammonia.*

Using dNTP solutions – *make up stock solutions, pool in small volumes (50–100 μl of each dNTP) and store separately at −20°C.*

Understanding codes for primers and probes – *oligomeric nucleotides are often referred to by the number of bases, e.g. a 20-mer primer will contain 20 nucleotide bases.*

PCR components and conditions

These are readily available in kit form from commercial suppliers; they include a thermostable DNA polymerase, such as *Taq* polymerase, dNTPs, buffer, a detergent (e.g. Triton), KCl, $MgCl_2$ or $MgSO_4$, and primers. Protocols for PCR vary considerably for particular applications – a typical procedure is given in Box 61.1. However, if you are trying to develop your own PCR procedure, the following information may be useful:

- Primers need to be at least 18 nucleotides long (primers longer than 18 nucleotides should be unique, even in a large eukaryotic genome); both primers should have similar annealing temperatures, T_m, p. 368), with a minimal degree of self-complementarity (to avoid formation of secondary structures), and no complementarity to each other (so that primer dimers are not formed).

- For most applications, the final concentration of each primer should be $0.1–0.5\,\mu mol\,l^{-1}$, which gives an excess of primers of about 10^7 with respect to the template, e.g. target genomic DNA at a concentration of 50 ng per 10 μl reaction mixture.

- Annealing temperatures are based around T_m, the temperature at which 50% of the primers are annealed to their target sequence (Fig. 53.7). For primers of <20 bases, T_m can be roughly calculated in °C from the equation:

$$T_m = 4(G+C) + 2(A+T) \qquad [61.1]$$

where G, C, A and T are the number of bases in the primer. Using this as a starting point, the optimum annealing temperature can be determined by trial and error. The T_m values of the two primers should be within 5 °C of each other (and, therefore, be ideally identical in G + C content). The annealing temperature is then set 5 °C below the lowest T_m of the primer pair.

- The last two bases at the 3′ end (where elongation is initiated) should be either G or C (3 hydrogen bonds, giving strong annealing), rather than either A or T (only 2 hydrogen bonds).

- dNTPs should be used at equal concentrations of $200\,\mu mol\,l^{-1}$, which should provide the initial excess required for incorporation into DNA.

- One of the key variables in PCR is the Mg^{2+} concentration; Mg^{2+} is required as a cofactor for the thermostable DNA polymerase (Anon., 2002). Excess Mg^{2+} stabilises dsDNA and may prevent complete denaturation of product at each cycle; it also promotes spurious annealing of primers, leading to the formation of undesired products. However, very low Mg^{2+} concentration impairs polymerisation. The Mg^{2+} concentration that gives optimal yield and specificity can be determined by trial and error. The purpose of gelatin and Triton X-100 is to stabilise the DNA polymerase during thermal cycling.

- The most frequently used thermostable DNA polymerase is *Taq* polymerase, which extends primers at a rate of 2–4 kbp per min at 72 °C. It should be used at a concentration of $\geq 1\,nmol\,l^{-1}$ ($\geq 0.1\,U$ per 5 μl reaction mixture). A disadvantage of *Taq* polymerase is that it has a relatively high rate of misincorporation of bases (one aberrant nucleotide per 100 000 nucleotides per cycle). Other polymerases are available (e.g. *Pfu* polymerase from *Pyrococcus* sp., VENT polymerase from *T. litoralis* or genetically modified forms of *Taq* polymerase), which have lower misincorporation rates.

Box 61.1 How to carry out the polymerase chain reaction (PCR)

The protocol given below is typical for a standard PCR. Note that temperatures, incubation times and the number of cycles will vary with the particular application, as discussed in the text.

1. **Make sure you have the required apparatus and reagents to hand**, including: (i) a thermal cycler; (ii) template thermostable DNA ($\geqslant 50$ ng/μl); (iii) stock solution of all dNTPs (5 mmol l^{-1} for each dNTP); (iv) a DNA polymerase (at 5 U/μl); (v) primers at e.g. 30 μmol l^{-1}; (vi) stock buffer solution, e.g. containing 100 mmol l^{-1} TRIS (pH 8.4), 500 mmol l^{-1} KCl, 15 mmol l^{-1} MgCl$_2$, 1% (w/v) gelatin, 1% (v/v) Triton X-100 (this stock is often termed '10x PCR buffer stock').

2. **Prepare a reaction mixture**: for example, a mixture containing: 1.0 μl genomic DNA; 2.5 μl stock buffer solution; 1.0 μl primer 1; 1.0 μl primer 2; 1.0 μl of each of the stock solutions of dNTPs, 0.1 μl *Taq* polymerase; 15.4 μl distilled deionised water, to give a total volume of 25.0 μl.

3. **Use appropriate positive and negative controls**: a positive control is a PCR template that is known to work under the conditions used in the laboratory, e.g. a plasmid, with appropriate primers, known to amplify at the annealing temperature to be used. A commonly used negative control is the PCR mixture minus the template DNA, though negative controls can be set up lacking any one of the reaction components.

4. **Cycle in the thermal cycler**: for example, an initial period of 5 min at 94 °C, followed by 30 cycles of 94 °C for 1 min (denaturation), then 60 °C for 1 min (primer annealing), then 72 °C for 1 min (chain extension).

5. **Assess the effectiveness of the PCR**: for example, by gel electrophoresis and ethidium bromide staining.

Troubleshooting

- If no PCR product is detected, repeat the procedure, checking carefully that all components are added to the reaction mixture. If there is still no product, check that the annealing temperature is not too high, or the denaturing temperature is not too low.

- If too many bands are present, this may indicate that either (i) the primers may not be specific, (ii) the annealing temperature is too low, (iii) too many cycles have been used, or (iv) there is an excess of Mg^{2+}, dNTPs, primers or enzyme.

- Bands corresponding to primer-dimers indicate that either (i) the 3′ ends of the primers show partial complementarity, (ii) the annealing temperature is not high enough, or (iii) the concentration of primers is too high.

Avoiding contamination in diagnostic PCR

The sensitivity of PCR is also the major drawback, since the technique is susceptible to contamination, particularly from DNA from the skin and hair of the operator, from previous PCR products, from airborne microbes and from positive control plasmids. A number of routine precautions can be taken to avoid such contamination:

- use a laminar flow cabinet (p. 199) dedicated to PCR use and located in a separate lab from that used to store PCR products or prepare clones;

- keep separate supplies of pipettors, tips, microfuge tubes and reagents – these should be exclusive to the PCR, with separate sets for sample preparation, reagents and product analysis;

- autoclave all buffers, distilled deionised water, pipette tips and tubes;

- wear disposable gloves at all times and change them frequently: protective coverings for the face and hair are also advisable;

- avoid contamination due to carry-over by including dUTP in the PCR mixture instead of dTTP. Thus copies will contain U rather than T. Before the template denaturing step, treat the mixture with uracil-N-glycosylase (UNG, available commercially as AmpEase®): this will destroy any strands containing U, i.e. any strands carried over from a previous reaction, or any contaminating material from another PCR. The target DNA will contain T, rather than U and will not be degraded by UNG. At the first heating step, the UNG will be denatured, so any newly synthesised U-containing copies will remain intact.

- for very sensitive work, use a strong UVC light (p. 267) inside the PCR workstation for 20–30 minutes before starting your work, to degrade any contaminating DNA. Note that you must not expose your skin or eyes to such a UVC source.

restriction site   DNA of known sequence   restriction site

unknown sequence   restrict DNA   unknown sequence

circularise and ligate DNA

restriction site 2

restrict with second enzyme

use primers that anneal to regions within known sequence for PCR

Fig. 61.2 Inverse PCR – basic principles.

Example Random amplification of polymorphic DNA (RAPD-PCR) can be used as a form of 'molecular typing' (p. 214), to identify a particular strain of an organism, e.g. in tracing the route of transmission of a pathogenic microbe.

PCR variations

Nested PCR

This can be used when the target sequence is known, but the number of DNA copies is very small (e.g. a single DNA molecule from a microbial genome), or if the sample is degraded (e.g. a forensic sample). The process involves two consecutive 'rounds' of PCR. The first PCR uses so-called 'external' primers, and the second PCR uses two 'internal' (or 'nested') primers that anneal to sequences within the product of the first PCR. This increases the likelihood of amplification of the target sequences by selecting for it using different primers during each round. Thus, nested PCR also increases the specificity of the reaction, since a single set of primers used in isolation may give a reasonable yield but several bands, while the use of a second set of primers ensures that a unique sequence is amplified, e.g. in microbial diagnostics.

Inverse PCR

This is a useful technique for amplifying a DNA sequence flanking a region of known base sequence (Fig. 61.2), e.g. to provide material for characterising an unknown region of DNA. The DNA is cut with a restriction enzyme so that both the region of known sequence and the flanking regions are included. This restriction fragment is then circularised and cut with a second restriction enzyme with specificity for a region in the known sequence. The now linear DNA will have part of the known sequence at each terminus, and by using primers that anneal to these parts of the known sequence, the unknown region can be amplified by conventional PCR. The product can then be sequenced and characterised (Chapter 60).

Reverse transcriptase-PCR (RT-PCR)

This technique is useful for detecting cell-specific gene expression (as evident by the presence of specific mRNA) when the amount of biological material is limited. Using either an oligo-dT primer to anneal to the 3' polyadenyl 'tail' of the mRNA, or random hexamer primers, together with reverse transcriptase, cDNA is produced which is then amplified by PCR. RT-PCR is often a useful method of generating a probe, the identity of which can be confirmed by sequencing (p. 434).

Amplification fragment length polymorphism (AFLP)

This term refers to several closely related techniques in which a single oligonucleotide primer of arbitrary sequence is used in a PCR reaction under conditions of low stringency, so that the primer is able to anneal to a large number of different sites within the target DNA. Some of the multiple amplification products will be polymorphic (e.g. the presence or absence of a particular annealing site will result in presence or absence of a particular band on the gel, after PCR and electrophoresis). Such polymorphisms can be used to detect differences between dissimilar DNA sequences.

PCR and DNA fingerprinting techniques

Genetic mapping and sequencing studies have led to the discovery of highly variable regions in the non-coding regions of DNA between

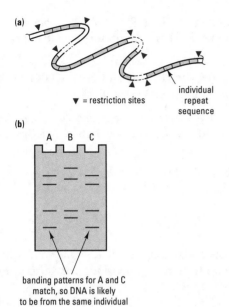

▼ = restriction sites

individual repeat sequence

(b)

banding patterns for A and C match, so DNA is likely to be from the same individual

Fig. 61.3 Simplified representation of DNA fingerprinting: (a) tandem repeat sequences within DNA are cut using a restriction enzyme to yield fragments of different size; (b) these fragments are then separated by agarose gel electrophoresis on the basis of their size (M_r), giving a banding pattern that is a characteristic of the DNA used.

different individuals. These hypervariable regions, often termed 'minisatellite DNA', are found at many sites throughout the genome. Each minisatellite contains a defined sequence of nucleotides which is repeated a number of times in a tandem fashion (Fig. 61.3); the greater the number of repeats, the longer the minisatellite. The number of tandem repeats in any particular minisatellite varies from one person to another (i.e. they have a variable number of tandem repeats or VNTRs). This is exploited in identifying individuals on the basis of their DNA profile, by carrying out the following steps:

1. Extraction of DNA from cells of the individual (e.g. leukocytes, buccal cells, spermatozoa).
2. Digestion of the DNA with a restriction enzyme that cuts at sites other than those within the minisatellite, to produce a series of fragments of different M_r.
3. Electrophoresis and Southern blotting of the restriction fragments using probes that are specific to the particular minisatellite.

The size of the fragments identified will depend on the number of minisatellites that each fragment contains, and the pattern obtained in the Southern blot is characteristic of the individual being profiled (Fig. 61.3).

PCR is widely used in DNA profiling in circumstances where there is a limited amount of starting material. By selecting suitable primers, highly variable regions can be amplified from very small amounts of DNA, and the information from several such regions is used to decide, with a very low chance of error, whether any two samples of DNA are from the same individual or not, e.g. in forensic science (see Kirby, 1997).

KEY POINT You should note that the PCR technique is continually being updated, with subtle new variations being produced on a regular basis – novel approaches and novel acronyms are very likely to be reported within the lifetime of this book.

Text references

Anon. *PCR Optimization*. Available:
http://www.promega.com/guides/pcr_guide/default.htm
Last accessed 08/01/03.
[Details of how to optimise Mg^{2+} and polymerase concentration, etc.]

Kirby, L.T. (1997) *DNA Fingerprinting: An Introduction. Breakthroughs in Molecular Biology*. Oxford University Press, Oxford.

Sources for further study

Anon. *Electronic PCR*. Available:
http://ludwig-sun2.unil.ch/˜ylinayip/Module5_Perl/electronic_pcr.htm
Last accessed 08/01/03.
[Try out primers against a particular sequence, to see how it works *in silico*.]

Burden, D.W. and Whitney, D. (1995) *Biotechnology: Proteins to PCR: A Course in Strategies and Lab Techniques*. Springer-Verlag, Berlin.

Dieffenback, C.W. and Dveksler, G.S. (1995). *PCR Primer: A Laboratory Manual*. Cold Spring Harbor Laboratory, Cold Spring Harbor.

McPherson, M.J., Moller, S.G., Benyon, R. and Howe, C. (2000) *PCR Basics: From Background to Bench*. Springer-Verlag, Berlin.

Sambrook, J. and Russell, D.W. (2001) *Molecular Cloning: A Laboratory Manual*, 3rd edn. Cold Spring Harbor Lab, Cold Spring Harbor.

Siebert, P. and Larrick, J.W. (eds) (2002) *Gene Cloning and Analysis by RT-PCR*. Eaton, Westborough.

Study exercises

61.1 Investigate the role of magnesium ions in PCR. Find out why optimising the Mg^{2+} concentration is important for successful amplification of target DNA in PCR.

61.2 Check your knowledge of primer design. List the principal factors that should be taken into account when designing primers for PCR.

61.3 Carry out a T_m calculation for a primer. For the following primer, what would be the temperature at which 50% of the molecules are annealed to their target sequence (i.e. T_m)?

5′-TGCATGGCTGGATTAGCG-3′

61.4 Consider how the risk of contamination can be reduced in PCR. List the most important practical steps that can be taken to reduce the possibility of contamination.

61.5 Select appropriate primers for a specific PCR amplification. The following sequence represents a region of DNA that is to be amplified by PCR:

5′-TCGCTGAAGGACATGTCGATGCTAGCTACGGTCGAGACGTAAGGACATGTCGGCTAGATCGC-3′
3′-AGCGACTTCCTGTACAGCTACGATCGATGCCAGCTCTGCATTCCTGTACAGCGGATCTAGCG-5′

Which of the following three pairs of primers is most suited to amplify a PCR product from the above sequence?
(a) 5′-TCGCTGAAGGACATGTCG-3′ and
5′-CGATCTAGGCGACATGTCG-3′
(b) 5′-TCGCTGAAGGACATGTCG-3′ and
5′-TCCTTAGGTCTCGACCGTA-3′
(c) 5′-TCGCTGAAGGACATGTCG-3′ and
5′-GACATGTCCTTACGTCTCG-3′

61.6 Find out what types of DNA analysis might be suitable for forensic examination of degraded DNA samples. In 1918 Tsar Nicholas of Russia, his wife Tsarina Alexandra, and their five children were executed and buried in a shallow grave in Yekaterinberg, Russia. Samples from the bones of the family were analysed by the UK Forensic Science Service (FSS). What types of DNA-based tests would you expect to have been carried out to confirm that a family group was present in the grave?

62 Molecular genetics III – genetic engineering techniques

Advances in the procedures used to manipulate nucleic acids *in vitro* have increased our understanding of the structure and function of genes at the molecular level. Additionally, these techniques can be used to alter the genome of an organism (genetic engineering), e.g. to create a bacterium capable of synthesising a foreign protein such as a potentially useful hormone or vaccine component, or an unusual variant of a normal protein. The procedures are often termed 'recombinant DNA technology', since they involve the creation of novel combinations of DNA (i.e. recombinant DNA) under controlled laboratory conditions.

In the UK, the **Genetically Modified Organisms (Contained Use) Regulations (2000)** *provide the regulatory framework for all research procedures involving the genetic modification of organisms.*

KEY POINT While genetic engineering must be carried out under strict containment, in accordance with appropriate legislation, the procedures involved in the isolation, recombination and cloning of DNA are often used at undergraduate level, to illustrate the general features of the techniques.

Basic principles

Genetic engineering involves several steps:

1. Isolation of the DNA sequence (gene) of interest from the genome of an organism, or from a gene library. This usually involves DNA purification followed by enzymic digestion or mechanical fragmentation, to liberate the target DNA sequence, or PCR amplification (p. 437) of the target DNA sequence.
2. Creation of an artificial recombinant DNA molecule (rDNA), by inserting the target sequence into a DNA molecule capable of replicating in a host cell, i.e. a 'cloning vector'. Suitable cloning vectors for bacterial cells include plasmids (p. 445) and bacteriophages (p. 446).
3. Introduction of the recombinant DNA molecule into a suitable host, e.g. *E. coli*. The process is termed transformation when a plasmid is used or transfection for a virus vector.
4. Selection and growth of the transformed (or transfected) cell, using the techniques of cell culture (p. 197). Since a single transformed host cell can be grown to give a clone of genetically identical cells, each carrying the target DNA of interest, the technique is often referred to as 'gene cloning', or molecular cloning.

Extraction and purification of plasmid DNA

Specific details of the steps involved in the isolation of DNA vary, depending upon the source material. However, the following protocol shows the principal stages in the purification of plasmid DNA from bacterial cells:

1. Cell wall digestion: incubation of bacteria in a lysozyme solution will hydrolyse the peptidoglycan cell wall. This is often carried out under isotonic conditions, to stop the cells from bursting open and releasing chromosomal DNA. Note that Gram-negative bacteria are relatively insensitive to lysozyme, requiring additional treatment to allow the

Preparing glassware – all glassware for DNA purification must be siliconised, to prevent adsorption of DNA. All glass and plastic items must be sterilised before use.

enzyme to reach the peptidoglycan layer (p. 237), e.g. osmotic shock, or incubation with a chelating agent, e.g. ethylenediaminetetra-acetate (EDTA). The latter treatment will also inactivate any bacterial deoxyribonucleases (DNases) in the solution, preventing enzymic degradation of plasmid DNA during extraction.

2. Lysis using strong alkali (NaOH) and a detergent, e.g. sodium dodecyl sulphate, to solubilise the cellular membranes and partially denature the proteins. Neutralisation of this solution (e.g. using potassium acetate) causes the chromosomal DNA to aggregate as an insoluble mass, leaving the plasmid DNA in solution.

3. Removal of other macromolecules, particularly RNA and proteins by, for example, enzymic digestion using ribonuclease and proteinase. Additional steps give further increases in purity: most laboratories now use small-scale chromatographic columns containing an anion exchange resin for routine extraction of nucleic acids. These are available in kit form, e.g. Wizard® miniprep columns. This approach gives more reliable purification than traditional methods, such as phenol/chloroform extraction.

4. Precipitation of DNA by adding two volumes of absolute ethanol to one volume of aqueous extract, followed by centrifugation, to recover the DNA as a pellet. Further washing with 70% v/v ethanol will remove any residual salt from the previous stages. After removal of residual ethanol by evaporation, the purified DNA is dissolved in buffer and can be stored for months at $-20\,°C$.

The simplest approach to quantifying the amount of nucleic acid in an aqueous solution is to measure the absorbance of the solution at 260 nm (A_{260}) using a spectrophotometer, as detailed on p. 274. Any contaminating protein would also contribute to A_{260}; protein can be detected by measuring the absorbance of the solution at 280 nm. Purified nucleic acids have a value for A_{260}/A_{280} of 1.8–2.0 and contaminating protein will give a lower ratio. If your solution gives a ratio substantially lower than this, you should carry out further purification steps.

Enzymatic manipulation of DNA

Restriction enzymes

Type II restriction endonucleases can be used to produce linear fragments of DNA with either single stranded 'sticky' ends or 'blunt' ends (Fig. 60.1): most commercial preparations of restriction enzymes will completely cleave a sample of DNA, producing a 'restriction digest', within 1 h at $37\,°C$. The position of individual restriction sites can be used to create a diagnostic restriction map for a particular molecule, e.g. a plasmid cloning vector (Fig. 62.1). An important additional feature is that, under appropriate conditions, the sticky ends of any two restriction fragments cut with the same enzyme (Fig. 62.2) can anneal (base pair), due to the formation of hydrogen bonds between individual bases within this region, allowing them to be joined together (ligated), irrespective of the sources of the two restriction fragments.

DNA ligase

To construct a recombinant DNA molecule, a suitable vector must be ligated to the DNA fragment to be cloned: this is performed using another

---

Safe working practices – note that phenol is toxic and corrosive while chloroform is potentially carcinogenic (p. 128). Take appropriate safety precautions (e.g. wear gloves, extinguish all naked flames, use a fume hood, where available).

Extracting DNA from organisms other than bacteria – different homogenisation techniques will be required (see Chapter 36). DNA can be extracted from the resulting homogenate by (i) complexation with the detergent cetrymethylammonium bromide (CTAB), e.g. for plant DNA, or (ii) anion-exchange column chromatography (p. 299).

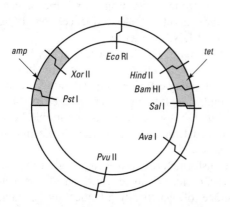

Fig. 62.1 Restriction map of the plasmid pBR 322. The position of individual restriction sites is shown together with the genes for ampicillin resistance (*amp*) and tetracycline resistance (*tet*).

Definition

Type II restriction endonucleases – intracellular enzymes, produced by certain strains of bacteria: their function is to restrict the growth of phages within the cell by cutting phage DNA at particular sites (host DNA is protected by methylation at these sites).

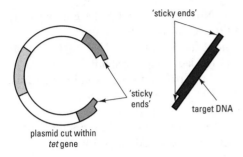

Fig. 62.2 Restriction of plasmid and foreign DNA with *Hin* dIII.

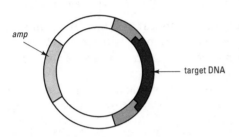

Fig. 62.3 Annealing and ligation of plasmid and target DNA to give a recombinant plasmid which confers resistance to ampicillin only. As target DNA has been inserted within the *tet* gene, the gene is now discontinuous and inactive.

Understanding the nomenclature for plasmid vectors – pBR322 is named according to standard rules: 'p' indicates the vector is a plasmid, 'BR' identifies the researchers Bolivar and Rodriguez and '322' is the specific code given to this plasmid, to distinguish it from others developed by the same workers.

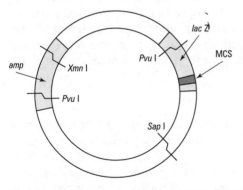

Fig. 62.4 Restriction map of the plasmid pUC19. The position of some individual restriction sites is shown together with the genes for ampicillin resistance (*amp*) and β-galactosidase (*lacZ*). MCS = multiple cloning site for 40 restriction enzymes within the *lacZ* gene.

microbial enzyme, DNA ligase (usually obtained from T4-infected *E. coli*). This ATP-dependent enzyme is capable of forming covalent phosphodiester bonds between annealed DNA molecules, thereby creating recombinant DNA (Fig. 62.3). When the two molecules involved are the cloning vector and the target DNA, the size of the recombinant molecule can be predicted (e.g. a plasmid of 4.5 kbp, plus a target DNA fragment of 2.5 kbp will give a recombinant molecule of 7 kbp), allowing separation and recovery by agarose gel electrophoresis (p. 429). Ligation is usually carried out at lower temperatures (to encourage annealing), over an extended time period of several hours (to allow the enzyme to operate), e.g. an overnight incubation at ≃16 °C. The volume of the ligation mixture is kept as low as possible (typically, <10 μl), with approximately a 2:1 ratio of target DNA to vector DNA, to encourage annealing between the two different types of DNA molecule and to reduce the chance of circularisation of vector or target DNA fragments.

Choosing a suitable vector

The features to be considered when selecting a suitable vector are:

- the ease of purification – e.g. reliable procedures have been developed to allow plasmid DNA to be extracted and purified from bacterial cells;
- the efficiency of insertion of the recombinant vector into a new host cell;
- the presence of single copies of suitable restriction sites;
- the presence of selectable markers (e.g. 'reporter genes', p. 447);
- the size of the DNA insert to be cloned;
- the copy number of the vector in the host cell.

Plasmids

The simplest bacterial cloning vectors are those based on small plasmids – circular DNA molecules, capable of autonomous replication within a bacterial cell. The general characteristics of plasmids are described in Chapter 59. One of the first cloning vectors to be developed for *E. coli* was pBR322, a genetically engineered plasmid of 4.4 kbp containing an origin of replication, two antibiotic resistance genes and single sites for a range of restriction enzymes (Fig. 62.1). Subsequently, other plasmid vectors have been developed, with additional features: for example, plasmids of the pUC series (Fig. 62.4) are now widely used for transformation of *E. coli*, having the following advantages over earlier types:

- high copy number: several hundred identical copies of the plasmid may be present in each bacterial cell, giving improved yield of plasmid DNA;
- single-step selection of recombinants using the *lacZ'* gene (p. 448);
- clustering of restriction sites within a short region of the *lacZ'* gene – restriction using two enzymes (a 'double digest') cuts a small fragment from this 'multiple cloning site' or 'polylinker', producing a cleaved plasmid with two different 'sticky ends' (e.g. *Eco* RI at one end and *Hin* dIII at the other), allowing complementary fragments of target DNA to be ligated in a particular orientation ('directional cloning').

Fig. 62.5 Map of a pET plasmid vector (Novagen®) showing the location of the genes for ampicillin resistance (*amp*) and lactose repressor protein (*lacI*) which controls expression of the T7 promoter *via* the lac operator (binding of the Lac repressor protein is countered by addition of isothiopropylgalactoside, IPTG). Expression of a gene cloned into the multiple cloning site (MCS) can thus be controlled, since DNA transcription only occurs when IPTG is added to the growth medium.

Fig. 62.6 Bacteriophage λ.

The pET series of plasmid vectors (Novagen®; Fig. 62.5) are now widely used, since they offer several additional advantages, including:

- high levels of protein expression, as the cloned DNA is under the control of the T7 promoter and the lac operon system;
- specialised vectors and hosts for the production of soluble proteins, disulphide bond formation, protein export, etc;
- the attachment of a short histidine 'tag' on the end of an expressed protein, to enable the protein to be purified by immobilised metal affinity chromatography (IMAC), as described on p. 304.

Phages

Bacteriophage vectors can offer several advantages over plasmid vectors:

- some phages have been engineered to carry larger fragments of foreign DNA – plasmid vectors work best with relatively short inserts of 1–2 kbp, while some phage vectors can accept 10 kbp or more of foreign DNA;
- a recombinant phage has a ready-made mechanism for transferring rDNA to a new host cell: the process is broadly similar to phage transduction, described on p. 421.

A number of vectors have been developed from *E. coli* phage λ (genome = 49 kbp of dsDNA in linear form, Fig. 62.6). For example, λZAPII, an insertion vector capable of accepting up to 10 kbp of additional (foreign) DNA and with the *lacZ'* gene and multiple cloning site for selection, or λEMBL4, a replacement vector, where part of the vector DNA is removed and replaced by foreign DNA (up to 23 kbp) during the cloning procedure.

Most vectors based on λ are virulent phages, released by lysis of the infected cell at the end of the replication phase: such vectors are cloned using standard techniques for phages, e.g. as plaques of lysis on a 'lawn' of bacteria growing on an agar-based medium (p. 202). Note that suitable strains of *E. coli* must be used for each of the various cloning vectors, e.g. vectors containing *lacZ'* can only be used with those *E. coli* strains that are deficient in this part of their genome (*lacZ'* codes for the α-component of the enzyme β-galactosidase, present in wild-type *E. coli*). In some instances, a second phage (a 'helper phage') must be used along with the vector, to carry out some of the functions removed from the vector genome, e.g. phage packaging and assembly functions. In some instances, more specialised phage vectors may be required, e.g. M13mp19, a single stranded phage vector, sometimes used for sequencing studies.

Cosmids and other vectors

Cosmid vectors contain the single stranded cohesive terminal sequences from λ phage (so-called 'cos' sites) inserted into a plasmid cloning vector. They can be used to clone up to 40 kbp of foreign DNA, using the 'cos' sites to allow *in vitro* packaging into the λ phage coat: such large fragments are required for the production of gene libraries, as described below. Other hybrid vectors have been produced by the fusion of a phage and a plasmid vector – they can be manipulated in the laboratory as plasmids for ease of DNA uptake, or converted to phage-like particulate form for ease of storage.

Screening clones – *a particular gene can be detected using Southern blotting (p. 431), or the expressed gene product (protein) may be detected by a suitable method, e.g. an immunoassay (p. 251). While it is relatively simple to describe the screening process, finding a specific gene (= clone) in a clone library is likely to be a time-consuming process.*

Using cloned cDNA – *information from the sequence of a particular cDNA clone may be useful in designing a suitable oligonucleotide probe to locate a particular gene in a genomic library.*

Recognising transformants – *after plating bacteria onto medium containing ampicillin, you may notice a few small 'satellite' colonies surrounding a single larger (transformant) colony. These satellite colonies are derived from non-transformed cells which survive due to the breakdown of antibiotic in the medium around the transformant colony, and should not be selected for subculture.*

Creating a gene library

For viruses with small genomes, an individual gene may be identified by hybridisation of a single fragment with a suitable probe, following digestion with a particular restriction enzyme (Chapter 60). However, for most genomes, such a digest would contain a very complex mixture of fragments and a 'clone library' must be created. The isolation and identification of a particular gene are then carried out by screening individual clones from this library. Two types of clone library can be used:

1. A genomic library – prepared from the entire genome of the organism under study. The genome is fragmented to give overlapping fragments, e.g. by partial restriction (incomplete digestion, e.g. at low temperature), or by mechanical shearing. Individual fragments are then incorporated into a suitable vector, e.g. a cosmid, to create a vector library (e.g. a cosmid library). Each recombinant vector is then transferred to a separate host cell, which is cultured, giving a collection of transformants that represents the clone library. This approach is sometimes termed 'shotgun cloning'.

2. A cDNA library (cDNA = complementary, or copy DNA) – prepared by converting mRNA into DNA using the retroviral enzyme reverse transcriptase. Such a library consists only of genes expressed in those cells used to create the library, making individual genes easier to locate and identify, since the number of clones represented is usually smaller than for a genomic library. Another feature of cDNA is that it is complementary to the processed transcript (mRNA), so it contains no information on non-coding regions (introns) or transcriptional sequences (promoter regions, etc.).

Transferring rDNA to a suitable host cell

- Once a recombinant vector has been produced *in vitro*, it must be introduced into a suitable host cell. Packaged phage vectors have a built-in transfer mechanism, while naked phage DNA and plasmids must be introduced by treatments that cause a temporary increase in membrane permeability resulting in transformation. These treatments include:

- physicochemical shock treatment – Box 62.1 gives details of a typical procedure using $CaCl_2$ and heat shock treatment to transform *E. coli* with the plasmid pUC19;

- electroporation – cells or protoplasts are subjected to electric shock treatment (typically, $>10\,kV\,cm^{-1}$) for very short periods ($<10\,ms$);

- a range of techniques can be used for animal and plant cells, e.g. electroporation of protoplasts, or various microinjection treatments, either using a microsyringe, DNA-coated microprojectiles ('biolistics') or cationic lipids, such as lipofectamine, which form lipid–DNA complexes that fuse with cell membranes and allow DNA entry. *Agrobacterium* can be used for rDNA transfer in certain plants.

Selection and detection of transformants

As the efficiency of transformation is very low, many of the plasmid vectors used in genetic engineering carry genes coding for antibiotic resistance, e.g. pBR322 carries separate genes for ampicillin resistance,

Molecular genetics III – genetic engineering techniques

Table 62.1 Examples of genes used to detect transformants

Gene	Product/assay
lacZ / lacZ'	β-galactosidase/chromogenic substrate (e.g. X-GAL) or fluorogenic substrate (e.g. MU-GAL)
uidA	β-glucuronidase/chromogenic substrate (e.g. X-GLUC) or fluorogenic substrate (e.g. MU-GLAC, p. 380)
lux	luciferase/bioluminescence in the presence of luciferin (p. 276)
amp	β-lactamase/resistance to ampicillin
cat	chloramphenicol acetyltransferase/resistance to chloramphenicol
gfp	green fluorescent protein from *Aequorea victoria*, visualised under UV light

amp, and tetracycline resistance, *tet* (Fig. 62.1). These genes act as 'markers' for the vector. One gene (e.g. *amp*) can be used to select for transformants, which would form colonies on an agar-based medium containing the antibiotic, while non-transformed (ampicillin-sensitive) cells would be killed. The other gene (e.g. *tet*) can be used as a marker for the recombinant plasmid vector, since ligation of the target sequence into this gene causes insertional inactivation (Fig. 62.3). Thus, cells transformed with the recombinant plasmid will be resistant to ampicillin only, while cells transformed with the recircularised ('native') plasmid will be resistant to both antibiotics. These two types of transformant can be distinguished using replica plating (see p. 420). For those genes where the product is an enzyme, the presence or absence of the functional gene can be assessed using a suitable substrate. For example, the insertional inactivation of *lacZ'* can be detected by including a suitable inducer of β-galactosidase (e.g. isopropylthiogalactoside, IPTG) and the chromogenic substrate 5-bromo-4-chloro-3-indolyl-β-D-galactoside (X-GAL) within the agar medium: a transformant colony derived from the native plasmid will be blue while a transformant containing the recombinant molecule (inactive *lacZ'*) will grow to produce a white colony. A number of other relevant examples are given in Table 62.1.

Box 62.1 Transformation of *E. coli* and selection of transformants

The following procedure illustrates the principal stages of the process: the efficiency of transformation will depend on the choice of *E. coli* strain and plasmid, and on the handling procedures prior to and during the process – for example, some strains do not require all of the stages listed below (for further details, see Hanahan *et al.*, 1995). Sterile equipment and appropriate technique (Chapter 32) are required at all times:

1. **Grow the cells under appropriate conditions:** the best results are often obtained using actively growing mid-log phase cells, rather than cells that have been grown to stationary phase (p. 226). Actively growing cells can be stored under appropriate conditions, e.g. as a 'frozen stock' – in suspension in concentrated glycerol at −85 °C.

2. **Induce cell competence by transfer to a suitable sterile transformation buffer:** this would normally contain divalent and monovalent salts, e.g. a salt solution containing $CaCl_2$ at 50–100 mmol l^{-1}, plus KCl and MnCl at 10–20 mmol l^{-1}. Cells are usually kept on ice in this solution for 10–15 min, to encourage the binding of plasmid DNA, added at a later stage.

3. **Add reagents to increase the permeability of cellular membranes:** typically dimethyl sulphoxide (DMSO, at up to 7% v/v) and dithiothreitol (DTT at up to 0.2 mmol l^{-1}), incubated on ice for a few minutes. DMSO is readily oxidised, reducing the effectiveness of the transformation procedure, and should be stored at −80 °C when not in use, to minimise oxidation.

4. **Add plasmid DNA:** typically at 10–1000 ng per transformation. Maintain on ice for at least 10 min in a minimal volume of solution, to allow the plasmid to become associated with the cell surface.

5. **Heat shock the cells:** briefly raise the temperature to 42–45 °C for 60–120 s, then return to ice for a few minutes. It is important that this treatment gives a *rapid* change in temperature – use a small, thin-walled (disposable) sterile plastic tube containing the minimum volume of solution to maximise the rate of temperature change.

6. **Allow the cells to recover from heat shock and to express any new genes** (e.g. to synthesise enzymes conferring antibiotic resistance in transformed cells): add sterile nutrient broth (e.g. 1 ml) and then incubate at 37 °C for up to 60 min.

7. **Plate onto an appropriate medium, to allow selection and detection of transformants:** for example, using pUC19, surface spread (p. 200) the suspension onto a medium containing ampicillin (at 25 mg l^{-1}), plus IPTG (at 15 mg l^{-1}) and X-GAL (at 25 mg l^{-1}), to detect the *lacZ'* gene product, as described in the text.

Text reference

Hanahan, D., Jessee, J. and Bloom, F.R. (1995) 'Techniques for transformation of *E. coli*' in Glover, D.M. and Hames, B.D. *DNA Cloning I*, Practical Approach Series. IRL Press, Oxford.

Sources for further study

Brown, T.A. (2001) *Gene Cloning and DNA Analysis:An Introduction*, 4th edn. Blackwell, Oxford.

Brown, T.A. (2000). *Essential Molecular Biology: A Practical Approach*, Vols 1 and 2, 2nd edn. IRL Press, Oxford.
[A practical manual on the basic principles involved in gene cloning and recombinant DNA technology.]

Hardy, K.G. (1987). *Plasmids: A Practical Approach*. IRL Press, Oxford.

Howe, C. (1995) *Gene Cloning and Manipulation*. Cambridge University Press, Cambridge.

Jones, P. (1997) *Vectors: Expression Systems: Essential Techniques*. Wiley, New York.

Study exercises

62.1 Explain the terminology of restriction enzymes. Why were *Hin* dIII and *Eco* RI given these names?

62.2 Explain the purpose of the various stages involved in the extraction and purification of DNA. Having read through this chapter, briefly describe the main purpose of each of the following reagents within a DNA extraction protocol, and rearrange them into their order of use within the procedure:
(a) anion exchange resin column chromatography;
(b) incubation in 70% v/v ethanol : water;
(c) ribonuclease and proteinase digestion;
(d) incubation with lysozyme/EDTA;
(e) sodium dodecyl sulphate incubation;
(f) NaOH treatment, followed by neutralisation with potassium acetate.

62.3 Construct a restriction map. The margin figure represents an electrophoretic separation of plasmid pRD, digested with different restriction enzymes, both individually and in combination. All of the enzymes cut the plasmid only once. Use this information to construct a simple restriction map of the plasmid.

62.4 Calculate transformation efficiency. A volume of 100 μl of *E. coli* cells was transformed using 20 μl of plasmid DNA (prepared at 0.1 ng μl^{-1})and then made up to a final volume of 500 μl in buffer. A 10-fold dilution of this suspension was prepared and 200 μl of this dilution was surface spread (p. 200) onto a suitable medium containing an antibiotic to select for transformants, giving 180 colonies on the spread plate after overnight incubation. What is the transformation efficiency, expressed as the number of transformants (colony-forming units, CFU) per μg DNA? (Give your answer in exponential notation, to 3 significant figures.)

Analysis and presentation of data

Using graphs

Fig. 63.1 Effect of antibiotic on yield of two bacterial isolates: ○, sensitive isolate; □, resistant isolate. Vertical bars show standard errors ($n = 6$).

Graphs can be used to show detailed results in an abbreviated form, displaying the maximum amount of information in the minimum space. Graphs and tables present findings in different ways. A graph (figure) gives a visual impression of the content and meaning of your results, while a table provides an accurate numerical record of data values. You must decide whether a graph should be used, e.g. to illustrate a pronounced trend or relationship, or whether a table (Chapter 64) is more appropriate.

A well-constructed graph will combine simplicity, accuracy and clarity. Planning of graphs is needed at the earliest stage in any write-up as your accompanying text will need to be structured so that each graph delivers the appropriate message. Therefore, it is best to decide on the final form for each of your graphs before you write your text. The text, diagrams, graphs and tables in a laboratory write-up or project report should be complementary, each contributing to the overall message. In a formal scientific communication it is rarely necessary to repeat the same data in more than one place (e.g. as a table and as a graph). However, graphical representation of data collected earlier in tabular format may be applicable in laboratory practical reports.

Practical aspects of graph drawing

The following comments apply to graphs drawn for laboratory reports. Figures for publication, or similar formal presentation are usually prepared according to specific guidelines, provided by the publisher/organiser.

KEY POINT Graphs should be self-contained – they should include all material necessary to convey the appropriate message without reference to the text. Every graph must have a concise explanatory title to establish the content. If several graphs are used, they should be numbered, so they can be quoted in the text.

Selecting a title – it is a common fault to use titles that are grammatically incorrect: a widely applicable format is to state the relationship between the dependent and independent variables within the title, e.g. 'The relationship between enzyme activity and external pH'.

Remembering which axis is which – a way of remembering the orientation of the x-axis is that x is a 'cross', and it runs 'across' the page (horizontal axis).

- Consider the layout and scale of the axes carefully. Most graphs are used to illustrate the relationship between two variables (x and y) and have two axes at right angles (e.g. Fig. 63.1). The horizontal axis is known as the abscissa (x-axis) and the vertical axis as the ordinate (y-axis).
- The axis assigned to each variable must be chosen carefully. Usually the x-axis is used for the independent variable (e.g. treatment) while the dependent variable (e.g. biological response) is plotted on the y-axis (p. 183). When neither variable is determined by the other, or where the variables are interdependent, the axes may be plotted either way round.
- Each axis must have a descriptive label showing what is represented, together with the appropriate units of measurement, separated from the descriptive label by a solidus or 'slash' (/), as in Fig. 63.1, or by brackets, as in Fig. 63.2.
- Each axis must have a scale with reference marks ('tics') on the axis to show clearly the location of all numbers used.
- A figure legend should be used to provide explanatory detail, including a key to the symbols used for each data set.

Using graphs

Fig. 63.2 Frequency distribution of masses for a sample of animals (sample size 24 085); the size class interval is 2 g.

Example For a data set where the smallest number on the log axis is 12 and the largest number is 9000, three-cycle log-linear paper would be used, covering the range 10–10 000.

Choosing between a histogram and a bar chart – use a histogram for continuous quantitative *variables* and a bar chart for discrete *variables* (see Chapter 28 for details of these types of measurement scale).

Fig. 63.3 Bar chart, showing the number of students belonging to each ABO blood group ($n = 29$).

Handling very large or very small numbers

To simplify presentation when your experimental data consist of either very large or very small numbers, the plotted values may be the measured numbers multiplied by a power of 10: this multiplying power should be written immediately before the descriptive label on the appropriate axis (as in Fig. 63.2). However, it is often better to modify the primary unit with an appropriate prefix (p. 176) to avoid any confusion regarding negative powers of 10.

Size

Remember that the purpose of your graph is to communicate information. It must not be too small, so use at least half an A4 page and design your axes and labels to fill the available space without overcrowding any adjacent text. If using graph paper, remember that the white space around the grid is usually too small for effective labelling. The shape of a graph is determined by your choice of scale for the *x* and *y*-axes which, in turn, is governed by your experimental data. It may be inappropriate to start the axes at zero (e.g. Fig. 63.1). In such instances, it is particularly important to show the scale clearly, with scale breaks where necessary, so the graph does not mislead. Note that Fig. 63.1 is drawn with 'floating axes' (i.e. the *x* and *y*-axes do not meet in the lower left-hand corner), while Fig. 63.2 has clear scale breaks on both *x* and *y* axes.

Graph paper

In addition to conventional linear (squared) graph paper, you may need the following:

- Probability graph paper. This is useful when one axis is a probability scale (e.g. p. 489).
- Log-linear graph paper. This is appropriate when one of the scales shows a logarithmic progression, e.g. the exponential (log) growth of cells in liquid culture (p. 226). Log-linear paper is defined by the number of logarithmic divisions covered (usually termed 'cycles') so make sure you use a paper with the appropriate number of cycles for your data. An alternative approach is to plot the log-transformed values on 'normal' graph paper.
- Log-log graph paper. This is appropriate when both scales show a logarithmic progression.

Types of graph

Different graphical forms may be used for different purposes, including:

- Plotted curves – used for data where the relationship between two variables can be represented as a continuum (e.g. Fig. 63.1).
- Scatter diagrams – used to visualise the relationship between individual data values for two interdependent variables (e.g. Fig. 67.7) often as a preliminary part of a correlation analysis (p. 493).
- Three-dimensional graphs show the inter-relationships of three variables, often one dependent and two independent (e.g. Fig. 45.1). A contour diagram is an alternative method of representing such data.
- Histograms represent frequency distributions of continuous variables (e.g. Fig. 63.2).

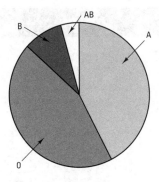

Fig. 63.4 Pie chart: relative abundance of blood groups in man.

Choosing graphical symbols – plotted curves are usually drawn using a standard set of symbols: ●, ○, ■, □, ▲, △, ◆, ◇. By convention, paired symbols ('closed' and 'open') are often used to represent 'plus' (treatment) and 'minus' (control) treatments.

- Frequency polygons emphasise the form of a frequency distribution by joining the coordinates with straight lines, in contrast to a histogram. This is particularly useful when plotting two or more frequency distributions on the same graph.
- Bar charts represent frequency distributions of a discrete qualitative or quantitative variable (e.g. Fig. 63.3). An alternative representation is the line chart (p. 66.3).
- Pie charts illustrate portions of a whole (e.g. Fig. 63.4).

The plotted curve

This is the commonest form of graphical representation used in biology. The key features are outlined below and given in checklist form in Box 63.1.

Data points

Each data point must be shown accurately, so that any reader can determine the exact values of x and y. In addition, the results of each treatment must be readily identifiable. A useful technique is to use a dot for each data point, surrounded by a hollow symbol for each treatment (see Fig. 63.1). An alternative is to use symbols only (Fig. 59.6, p. 423), though the coordinates of each point are defined less accurately. Use the same symbol for the same entity if it occurs in several graphs and provide a key to all symbols.

Statistical measures

If you are plotting average values for several replicates and if you have the necessary statistical knowledge, you can calculate the standard error (p. 480), or the 95% confidence limits (p. 493) for each mean value and show these on your graph as a series of vertical bars (see Fig. 63.1). Make it clear in the legend whether the bars refer to standard errors or 95% confidence limits and quote the value of n (the number of replicates per

---

Box 63.1   Checklist for the stages in drawing a graph

The following sequence can be used whenever you need to construct a plotted curve: it will need to be modified for other types of graph.

1. **Collect all of the data values and statistical values** (in tabular form, where appropriate).
2. **Decide on the most suitable form of presentation**: this may include transformation to convert data to linear form.
3. **Choose a concise descriptive title**, together with a reference (figure) number and date, where necessary.
4. **Determine which variable is to be plotted on the x-axis and which on the y-axis.**
5. **Select appropriate scales for both axes** and make sure that the numbers and their location (scale marks) are clearly shown, together with any scale breaks.
6. **Decide on appropriate descriptive labels for both axes**, with SI units of measurement, where appropriate.
7. **Choose the symbols for each set of data points** and decide on the best means of representation for statistical values.
8. **Plot the points** to show the coordinates of each value with appropriate symbols.
9. **Draw a trend line for each set of points.** Use a see-through ruler, so you can draw the line to have an equal number of points on either side of it.
10. **Write a figure legend**, to include a key which identifies all symbols and statistical values and any descriptive footnotes.

Box 63.2 How graphs can misrepresent and mislead

1. **The 'volume' or 'area' deception** – this is mainly found in histogram or bar chart presentations where the size of a symbol is used to represent the measured variable. For example, the amount of hazardous waste produced in different years might be represented on a chart by different sizes of a chemical drum, with the *y*-axis (height of drum) representing the amount of waste. However, if the symbol retains its *shape* for all heights as in Fig. 63.5a, its *volume* will increase as a cubic function of the height, rather than in direct proportion. To the casual observer, a twofold increase may look like an eightfold one, and so on. Strictly, the *height* of the symbol should be the measure used to represent the variable, with no change in symbol width, as in Fig. 63.5b.

2. **Effects of a non-zero axis** – A non-zero axis acts to emphasise the differences between measures by reducing the range of values covered by the axis. For example, in Fig. 63.6a, it looks as if there are large differences in mass between males and females; however, if the scale is adjusted to run from zero, then it can be seen that the differences are not large as a proportion of the overall mass. Always scrutinise the scale values carefully when interpreting any graph.

3. **Use of a relative rather than absolute scale** – this is similar to the above, in that data compared using relative scales (e.g. percentage or ratio) can give the wrong impression if the denominator is not the same in all cases. In Fig. 63.7a, two treatments are shown as equal in *relative* effect, both resulting in 50% relative response compared (say) to the respective controls. However, if treatment A is 50% of a control value of 200 and treatment B is 50% of a control value of 500, then the actual difference in *absolute* response would have been masked, as shown by Fig. 63.7b.

4. **Effects of a non-linear scale** – when interpreting graphs with non-linear (e.g. logarithmic) scales, you may interpret any changes on an imagined linear scale. For example, the pH scale is logarithmic, and linear changes on this scale mean less in terms of absolute H^+ concentration at high (alkaline) pH than they do at low (acidic) pH. In Fig. 63.8a, the cell density in two media is compared on a logarithmic scale, while in Fig. 63.8b, the same data are graphed on a linear scale. Note, also, that the log *y*-axis scale in Fig. 63.8a cannot be shown to zero, because there is no logarithm for 0.

Fig. 63.5 Increase in pesticide use over a 30 year period.

Fig. 63.6 Average mass of males and females in test group.

Fig. 63.7 Responses to treatments A and B.

Fig. 63.8 Effect of different media on cell density.

Box 63.2 Continued

5. **Unwarranted extrapolation** – a graph may be extrapolated to indicate what would happen if a trend continued, as in Fig. 63.9a. However, this can only be done under certain assumptions (e.g. that certain factors will remain constant or that relationships will hold under new conditions). There may be no guarantee that this will actually be the case. Figure 63.9b illustrates other possible outcomes if the experiment were to be repeated with higher values for the *x*-axis.

6. **Failure to account for data point error** – this misrepresentation involves curves that are overly complex in relation to the scatter in the underlying data. When interpreting graphs with complex curves, consider the errors involved in the data values. It is probably unlikely that the curve would pass through all the data points unless the errors were very small. Figure 63.10a illustrates a curve that appears to assume zero error and is thus overly complex, while Fig. 63.10b shows a curve that takes possible errors of the points into account.

7. **Failure to reject outlying points** – this is a special case of the previous example. There may be many reasons for outlying data, from genuine mistakes to statistical 'freaks'. If a curve is drawn through such points on a graph, it indicates that the point carries equal weight with the other points, when in fact, it should probably be ignored. To assess this, consider the accuracy of the measurement, the number and position of adjacent points, and any special factors that might be involved on a one-off basis. Figure 63.11a shows a curve where an outlier (arrowed) has perhaps been given undue weight when showing the presumed relationship. If there is good reason to think that the point should be ignored, then the curve shown in Fig. 63.11b would probably be more valid.

8. **Inappropriate fitted line** – here, the mathematical function chosen to represent a trend in the data might be inappropriate. A straight line might be fitted to the data, when a curve would be more correct, or *vice versa*. These cases can be difficult to assess. You need to consider the theoretical validity of the model used to generate the curve (this is not always stated clearly). For example, if a straight line is fitted to the points, the implicit underlying model states that one factor varies in direct relation to another, when the true situation may be more complex. In Fig. 63.12a, the relationship has been shown as a linear relationship, whereas an exponential relationship, as shown in Fig. 63.12b, could be more correct.

Fig. 63.9 Extrapolation of data under different assumptions.

Fig. 63.10 Fitted curves under different assumptions of data error.

Fig. 63.11 Curves with and without outlier taken into account.

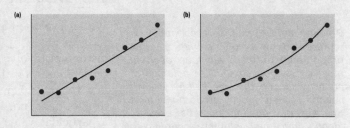

Fig. 63.12 Different mathematical model used to represent trends in data.

data point). Another approach is to add a least significant difference bar (p. 490) to the graph.

Interpolation

Once you have plotted each point, you must decide whether to link them by straight lines or a smoothed curve. Each of these techniques conveys a different message to your reader. Joining the points by straight lines may seem the simplest option, but may give the impression that errors are very low or non-existent and that the relationship between the variables is complex. Joining points by straight lines is appropriate in certain graphs involving time sequences (e.g. the number of animals at a particular site each year), or for repeat measurements where measurement error can be assumed to be minimal (e.g. recording a patient's temperature in a hospital, to emphasise any variation from one time point to the next). However, in most plotted curves the best straight line or curved line should be drawn (according to appropriate mathematical or statistical models, or by eye), to highlight the relationship between the variables – after all, your choice of a plotted curve implies that such a relationship exists. Don't worry if some of your points do not lie on the line: this is caused by errors of measurement and by biological variation. Most curves drawn by eye should have an equal number of points lying on either side of the line. You may be guided by 95% confidence limits, in which case your curve should pass within these limits wherever possible.

Curved lines can be drawn using a flexible curve, a set of French curves, or freehand. In the latter case, turn your paper so that you can draw the curve in a single, sweeping stroke by a pivoting movement at the elbow (for larger curves) or wrist (for smaller ones). Do not try to force your hand to make complex, unnatural movements, as the resulting line will not be smooth.

Conveying the correct message – the golden rule is: 'always draw the simplest line that fits the data reasonably well and is biologically reasonable'.

Extrapolation

Be wary of extrapolation beyond the upper or lower limit of your measured values. This is rarely justifiable and may lead to serious errors. Whenever extrapolation is used, a dotted line ensures that the reader is aware of the uncertainty involved. Any assumptions behind an extrapolated curve should also be stated clearly in your text.

Extrapolating plotted curves – try to avoid the need to extrapolate by better experimental design.

The histogram

While a plotted curve assumes a continuous relationship between the variables by interpolating between individual data points, a histogram involves no such assumptions and is the most appropriate representation if the number of data points is too few to allow a trend line to be drawn. Histograms are also used to represent frequency distributions (pp. 454, 475), where the y-axis shows the number of times a particular value of x-was obtained (e.g. Fig. 63.2). As in a plotted curve, the x axis represents a continuous variable which can take any value within a given range (e.g. plant height), so the scale must be broken down into discrete classes and the scale marks on the x-axis should show either the mid-points (mid-values) of each class, or the boundaries between the classes.

Drawing a histogram – each datum is represented by a column with an area proportional to the magnitude of y: in most cases, you should use columns of equal width, so that the height of each column is then directly proportional to y. Shading or stippling may be used to identify individual columns, according to your needs.

The columns are adjacent to each other in a histogram, in contrast to a bar chart, where the columns are separate because the x-axis of a bar chart represents discrete values.

Using computers to produce graphs – never allow a computer program to dictate size, shape and other aspects of a graph: find out how to alter scales, labels, axes, etc. and make appropriate selections. Draw curves freehand if the program only has the capacity to join the individual points by straight lines.

Interpreting proportions and percentages – you will need to establish how the values have been calculated (see pp. 469–70).

Interpreting graphs

The process of analysing a graph can be split into five phases:

1. Consider the context. Look at the graph in relation to the aims of the study in which it was reported. Why were the observations made? What hypothesis was the experiment set up to test? This information can usually be found in the Introduction or Results section of a report. Also relevant are the general methods used to obtain the results. This might be obvious from the figure title and legend, or from the Materials and Methods section.
2. Recognise the graph form and examine the axes. First, what kind of graph is presented (e.g. histogram, plotted curve)? You should be able to recognise the main types summarised on pp. 454–5 and their uses. Next, what do the axes measure? You should check what quantity has been measured in each case and what units are used.
3. Look closely at the scale of each axis. What is the starting point and what is the highest value measured? For the x-axis, this will let you know the scope of the treatments or observations (e.g. whether they lasted for 5 min or 20 years; whether a concentration span was two-fold or 50-fold). For each axis, it is especially important to note whether the values start at zero; if not, then the differences between any treatments shown may be magnified by the scale chosen (see Box 63.2).
4. Examine the symbols and curves. Information will be provided in the key or legend to allow you to determine what these refer to. If you have made your own photocopy of the figure, it may be appropriate to note this directly on it. You can now assess what appears to have happened. If, say, two conditions have been observed while a variable is altered, when exactly do they differ from each other; by how much; and for how long?
5. Evaluate errors and statistics. It is important to take account of variability in the data. For example, if mean values are presented, the underlying errors may be large, meaning that any difference between two treatments or observations at a given x-value could simply have arisen by chance. Thinking about the descriptive statistics used (Chapter 66) will allow you to determine whether apparent differences could be significant in both statistical and biological senses.

Sometimes graphs are used to mislead. This may be unwitting, as in an unconscious favouring of a 'pet' hypothesis of the author. Graphs may be used to 'sell' a product in the field of advertising or to favouring of a viewpoint as, perhaps, in politics. Experience in drawing and interpreting graphs will help you spot these flawed presentations, and understanding how graphs can be erroneously presented (Box 63.2) will help you avoid the same pitfalls.

Sources for further study

Anon. (2000a) *Working with Charts, Graphs and Tables*. Open University, Milton Keynes.

Anon. (2000b) *More Charts, Graphs and Tables*. Open University, Milton Keynes.

Anon. (2000c) *Biological Nomenclature: Recommendations on Terms, Units and Symbols*. Institute of Biology, London.
[Includes a section on presentation of data.]

Briscoe, M.H. (1996) *Preparing Scientific Illustrations: A Guide to Better Posters, Presentations and Publications*. Springer-Verlag, New York.

Carter, M., Wiebe, E.N. and Ferzli, M. *Graphing with Excel®*. Available: http://www.ncsu.edu/labwrite/res/gt/gt-menu.html
Last accessed 08/01/03.
[Online-tutorial from the LabWrite 2000 Project, sponsored by the US-NSF.]

Simmonds, D. and Reynolds, L. (1994) *Data Presentation and Visual Literacy in Medicine and Science*. Butterworth-Heinemann, London.

Study exercises

63.1 Select appropriate graphical presentations (see also exercise 37.3, p. 249). Choose an appropriate graphical form for each of the following examples:
   (a) Interaction between pH and cation concentration on enzyme activity.
   (b) Proportion of different eye colours in a survey of undergraduates attending your University.
   (c) Relationship between pulse rate and age in humans.
   (d) Number of bacteria per field of view for several different samples.
   (e) Effect of copper concentration on the activity of an enzyme.

63.2 Create a pie chart. Display the following information in the form of a hand-drawn pie chart. Do *not* use a spreadsheet for this exercise.

Number of bacterial strains isolated from a water sample

Bacterium	Number of strains isolated
Escherichia coli	37
Aeromonas hydrophila	8
Klebsiella spp.	13
Salmonella enterica	2
Enterococcus spp.	25

63.3 Create a frequency distribution histogram. The table below gives data for the haemoglobin levels of 100 people. Plot a histogram showing the frequency distribution of the data. Write a brief description of the important features of the distribution.

Haemoglobin content (g l^{-1}) in blood

11.1	14.2	13.5	9.8	12.0	13.9	14.1	14.6	11.0	12.3
13.4	12.9	12.9	10.0	13.1	11.8	12.6	10.7	8.1	11.2
13.8	12.4	12.9	11.3	12.7	12.4	14.6	15.1	11.2	9.7
11.3	14.7	10.8	13.3	11.9	11.4	12.5	13.0	11.6	13.1
9.3	13.5	14.6	11.2	11.7	10.9	12.4	12.0	12.1	12.6
10.9	12.1	13.4	9.5	12.5	11.6	12.2	8.8	10.7	11.1
10.2	11.7	10.4	14.0	14.9	11.5	12.0	13.2	12.1	13.3
12.4	9.4	13.2	12.5	10.8	11.7	12.7	14.1	10.4	10.5
13.3	10.6	10.5	13.7	11.8	14.1	10.3	13.6	10.4	13.9
11.7	12.8	10.4	11.9	11.4	10.6	12.7	11.4	12.9	12.1

63.4 Find examples of misleading graphs. Create a portfolio of examples of misleading graphs taken from newspapers. For each graph, state what aspect is misleading (see Box 63.2) and, where possible, attempt to show the data correctly in a new graph.

Presenting data in tables

A table is often the most appropriate way to present numerical data in a concise, accurate and structured form. Assignments and project reports should contain tables which have been designed to condense and display results in a meaningful way and to aid numerical comparison. The preparation of tables for recording primary data is discussed on p. 172.

Decide whether you need a table, or whether a graph is more appropriate. Histograms and plotted curves can be used to give a visual impression of the relationships within your data (p. 453). On the other hand, a table gives you the opportunity to make detailed numerical comparisons.

> **KEY POINT** Always remember that the primary purpose of your table is to communicate information and allow appropriate comparison, not simply to put down the results on paper.

Preparation of tables

Title

Constructing titles – take care over titles as it is a common mistake in student practical reports to present tables without titles, or to misconstruct the title.

Every table must have a brief descriptive title. If several tables are used, number them consecutively so they can be quoted in your text. The titles within a report should be compared with one another, making sure they are logical and consistent and that they describe accurately the numerical data contained within them.

Structure

Saving space in tables – you may be able to omit a column of control data if your results can be expressed as percentages of the corresponding control values.

Display the components of each table in a way that will help the reader understand your data and grasp the significance of your results. Organise the columns so that each category of like numbers or attributes is listed vertically, while each horizontal row shows a different experimental treatment, organism, sampling site, etc. (as in Table 64.1). Where appropriate, put control values near the beginning of the table. Columns that need to be compared should be set out alongside each other. Use rulings to subdivide your table appropriately, but avoid cluttering it up with too many lines.

Table 64.1 Characteristics of selected photoautotrophic microbes

Division	Species	Optimum [NaCl]* $(mol\,m^{-3})$	Intracellular carbohydrate	
			Identity	Quantity[†] $(nmol\,(g\,dry\,wt)^{-1})$
Chlorophyta	*Scenedesmus quadruplicatum*	340	Sucrose	49.7
	Chlorella emersonii	780	Sucrose	102.3
	Dunaliella salina	4700	Glycerol	910.7
Cyanobacteria	*Microcystis aeruginosa*	<20[‡]	None	0.0
	Anabaena variabilis	320	Sucrose	64.2
	Rivularia atra	380	Trehalose	ND

* Determined after 28-day incubation in modified Von Stosch medium.
[†] Individual samples, analysed by gas-liquid chromatography.
[‡] Poor growth in all media with added NaCl (minimum NaCl concentration $5\,mol\,m^{-3}$).
ND Sample lost: no quantitative data.

Headings and subheadings

These should identify each set of data and show the units of measurement, where necessary. Make sure that each column is wide enough for the headings and for the longest data value.

Numerical data

Within the table, do not quote values to more significant figures than necessary, as this will imply spurious accuracy (pp. 171, 467). By careful choice of appropriate units for each column you should aim to present numerical data within the range 0 to 1000. As with graphs, it is less ambiguous to use derived SI units, with the appropriate prefixes, in the headings of columns and rows, rather than quoting multiplying factors as powers of 10. Alternatively, include exponents in the main body of the table (see Table 25.1), to avoid any possible confusion regarding the use of negative powers of 10.

Other notations

Avoid using dashes in numerical tables, as their meaning is unclear; enter a zero reading as '0' and use 'NT' not tested or 'ND' if no data value was obtained, with a footnote to explain each abbreviation. Other footnotes, identified by asterisks, superscripts or other symbols in the table, may be used to provide relevant experimental detail (if not given in the text) and an explanation of column headings and individual results, where appropriate. Footnotes should be as condensed as possible. Table 64.1 provides examples.

Statistics

In tables where the dispersion of each data set is shown by an appropriate statistical parameter, you must state whether this is the (sample) standard deviation, the standard error (of the mean) or the 95% confidence limits and you must give the value of n (the number of replicates). Other descriptive statistics should be quoted with similar detail, and hypothesis-testing statistics should be quoted along with the value of P (the probability). Details of any test used should be given in the legend, or in a footnote.

Text

Sometimes a table can be a useful way of presenting textual information in a condensed form (see examples on pp. 259 and 284).

When you have finished compiling your tabulated data, carefully double-check each numerical entry against the original information, to ensure that the final version of your table is free from transcriptional errors. Box 64.1 gives a checklist for the major elements of constructing a table.

Examples If you measured the width of a fungal hypha to the nearest one-tenth of a micrometre, quote the value in the form '52.6 μm'.

Quote the width of a fungal hypha as 52.6 μm, rather than 0.000 052 6 m or 52.6 10^{-6} m.

Saving further space in tables – in some instances a footnote can be used to replace a whole column of repetitive data.

Using microcomputers and word processing packages – these can be used to prepare high quality versions of tables for project work (p. 74).

Box 64.1 Checklist for preparing a table

Every table should have the following components:
1. **A title**, plus a reference number and date where necessary.
2. **Headings for each column and row**, with appropriate units of measurement.
3. **Data values**, quoted to the nearest significant figure and with statistical parameters, according to your requirements.
4. **Footnotes** to explain abbreviations, modifications and individual details.
5. **Rulings to emphasise groupings** and distinguish items from each other.

Sources for further study

Kirkup, L. (1995) *Experimental Methods: An Introduction to the Analysis and Presentation of Data*. Wiley, New York.

Simmonds, D. and Reynolds, L. (1994) *Data Presentation and Visual Literacy in Medicine and Science*. Butterworth-Heinemann, London.

Study exercises

64.1 Redesign a table of data. Using the following example, redraft the table to improve layout and correct inconsistencies.

Concentrations of low molecular weight solutes in bacteria

Bacterium	Constituent	Concentration
Escherichia coli	Proline	21.0 mmol l^{-1}
Escherichia coli	Trehalose	1.547×10^2 kmol m^{-3}
Bacillus subtilis	Proline	39.7 mmol l^{-1}
Bacillus subtilis	Glutamate	0.0521 mmol cm^{-3}
*Staphylococcus aureus**	Glutamate	15 260 mmol m^{-3}
Escherichia coli	Glutamate	0.50% w/v
Bacillus subtilis	Trehalose	<0.001% w/v

* Proline and trehalose were not measured.

64.2 Devise a text-based table. After reading through this chapter and working from memory, draw up a table listing the principal components of a typical table in the first column, and brief comments on the major features of each component in the second column.

64.3 Interpret data from a table. The table below shows representative data for energy, protein and niacin (vitamin B3) as a function of age for human males and females. The typical average mass ('weight') of each class is also shown.

(a) In what age class does the mass of females exceed that of males?

(b) In what age class is the energy requirement of males greatest in proportion to the energy requirement of females?

(c) Over what age range do males and females have the same protein requirement?

(d) In what age class do males have their highest niacin requirement, and how does this compare with females?

Selected age-related characteristics of human males and females

Age (years)	Average mass (kg)		Energy requirement (MJ)		Protein requirement (g)		Niacin requirement (mg)	
	Male	Female	Male	Female	Male	Female	Male	Female
<1	8	8	3.4	3.2	14	14	6	6
1–3	13	13	5.2	4.9	16	16	9	9
4–6	20	20	7.2	6.5	24	24	12	12
7–10	28	28	8.2	7.3	28	28	13	13
11–14	45	46	9.3	7.7	45	46	17	15
15–18	66	55	11.5	8.8	59	44	20	15
19–50	79	63	10.6	8.1	63	50	19	15
>50	77	65	9.5	7.7	63	50	15	13

Hints for solving numerical problems

Biology often requires a numerical or statistical approach. Not only is mathematical modelling an important aid to understanding, but computations are often needed to turn raw data into meaningful information or to compare them with other data sets. Moreover, calculations are part of laboratory routine, perhaps required for making up solutions of known concentration (see p. 130 and below) or for the calibration of a microscope (see p. 162). In research, 'trial' calculations can reveal what input data are required and where errors in their measurement might be amplified in the final result (see p. 182).

KEY POINT If you find numerical work difficult, practice at problem-solving is especially important.

Practising at problem-solving:

- demystifies the procedures involved, which are normally just the elementary mathematical operations of addition, subtraction, multiplication and division (Table 65.1);
- allows you to gain confidence so that you don't become confused when confronted with an unfamiliar or apparently complex form of problem;
- helps you recognise the various forms a problem can take as, for instance, in crossing experiments in classical genetics (Chapter 58).

Table 65.1 Sets of numbers and operations

Sets of numbers

Whole numbers:	0, 1, 2, 3, ...
Natural numbers:	1, 2, 3, ...
Integers:	... −3, −2, −1, 0, 1, 2, 3, ...
Real numbers:	integers and anything between (e.g. −5, 4.376, 3/16, π, $\sqrt{5}$)
Prime numbers:	subset of natural numbers divisible by 1 and themselves only (i.e. 2, 3, 5, 7, 11, 13, ...)
Rational numbers:	p/q where p (integer) and q (natural) have no common factor (e.g. 3/4)
Fractions:	p/q where p is an integer and q is natural (e.g. −6/8)
Irrational numbers:	real numbers with no exact value (e.g. π)
Infinity:	(symbol ∞) is larger than any number (technically not a number as it does not obey the laws of algebra)

Operations and symbols

Basic operators:	+, −, × and ÷ will not need explanation; however, / may substitute for ÷, * may substitute for × or this operator may be omitted
Powers:	a^n, i.e. 'a to the power n', means a multiplied by itself n times (e.g. $a^2 = a \times a =$ 'a squared', $a^3 = a \times a \times a =$ 'a cubed'). n is said to be the index or exponent. Note $a^0 = 1$ and $a^1 = a$
Logarithms:	the common logarithm (log) of any number x is the power to which 10 would have to be raised to give x (i.e. the log of 100 is 2; $10^2 = 100$); the antilog of x is 10^x. Note that there is no log for 0, so take this into account when drawing log axes by breaking the axis. Natural or Napierian logarithms (ln) use the base e ($= 2.71828 ...$) instead of 10
Reciprocals:	the reciprocal of a real number a is $1/a$ ($a \neq 0$)
Relational operators:	$a > b$ means 'a is greater (more positive) than b', $<$ means less than, $\leqslant$ means less-than-or-equal-to and $\geqslant$ means greater-than-or-equal-to
Proportionality:	$a \propto b$ means 'a is proportional to b' (i.e. $a = kb$, where k is a constant). If $a \propto 1/b$, a is inversely proportional to b ($a = k/b$)
Sums:	Σx_i is shorthand for the sum of all x values from $i = 0$ to $i = n$ (more correctly the range of the sum is specified under the symbol)
Moduli:	$|x|$ signifies modulus of x, i.e. its absolute value (e.g. $|4| = |{-4}| = 4$)
Factorials:	$x!$ signifies factorial x, the product of all integers from 1 to x (e.g. 3! = 6). Note 0! = 1! = 1

Steps in tackling a numerical problem

The step-by-step approach outlined below may not be the fastest method of arriving at an answer, but most mistakes occur where steps are missing, combined or not made obvious, so a logical approach is often better. Error tracing is distinctly easier when all stages in a calculation are laid out.

Have the right tools ready

Scientific calculators (p. 114) greatly simplify the numerical part of problem-solving. However, the seeming infallibility of the calculator may lead you to accept an absurd result which could have arisen because of faulty key-pressing or faulty logic. Make sure you know how to use all the features on your calculator, especially how the memory works; how to introduce a constant multiplier or divider; and how to obtain an exponent (note that the 'exp' button on most calculators gives you 10^x, not 1^x or y^x; so 1×10^6 would be entered as $\boxed{1}\ \boxed{\text{exp}}\ \boxed{6}$, *not* $\boxed{10}\ \boxed{\text{exp}}\ \boxed{6}$).

Approach the problem thoughtfully

If the individual steps have been laid out on a worksheet, the 'tactics' will already have been decided. It is more difficult when you have to adopt a strategy on your own, especially if the problem is presented as a story and it isn't obvious which equations or rules need to be applied.

- Read the problem carefully as the text may give clues as to how it should be tackled. Be certain of what is required as an answer before starting.
- Analyse what kind of problem it is, which effectively means deciding which equation(s) or approach will be applicable. If this is not obvious, consider the dimensions/units of the information available and think how they could be fitted to a relevant formula. In examinations, a favourite ploy of examiners is to present a problem such that the familiar form of an equation must be rearranged (see Table 65.2 and Box 65.1). Another is to make you use two or more equations in series (see Box 65.2). If you are unsure whether a recalled formula is correct, a dimensional analysis can help: write in all the units for the variables and make sure that they cancel out to give the expected answer.
- Check that you have, or can derive, all of the information required to use your chosen equation(s). It is unusual but not unknown for examiners to supply redundant information. So, if you decide not to use some of the information given, be sure why you do not require it.
- Decide on what format and units the answer should be presented in. This is sometimes suggested to you. If the problem requires many changes in the prefixes to units, it is a good idea to convert all data to base SI units (multiplied by a power of 10) at the outset.
- If a problem appears complex, break it down into component parts.

Present your answer clearly

The way you present your answer obviously needs to fit the individual problem. The example shown in Box 65.2 has been chosen to illustrate several important points, but this format would not fit all situations. Guidelines for presenting an answer include:

(a) Make your assumptions explicit. Most mathematical models of biological phenomena require that certain criteria are met before they can be legitimately

---

Using a computer spreadsheet – this may be very useful in repetitive work or for 'what if?' case studies (see Chapter 12).

Table 65.2 Simple algebra – rules for manipulating

If $a = b + c$, then $b = a - c$ and $c = a - b$
If $a = b \times c$, then $b = a \div c$ and $c = a \div b$
If $a = b^c$, then $b = a^{1/c}$ and $c = \log a \div \log b$
$a^{1/n} = \sqrt[n]{a}$
$a^{-n} = 1 \div a^n$
$a^b \times a^c = a^{(b+c)}$ and $a^b \div a^c = a^{(b-c)}$
$(a^b)^c = a^{(b \times c)}$
$a \times b = \text{antilog}(\log a + \log b)$

Show the steps in your calculations – most markers will only penalise a mistake once and part marks will be given if the remaining operations are performed correctly. This can only be done if those operations are visible!

Box 65.1   Example of using the algebraic rules of Table 65.2

Problem: if $a = (b - c) \div (d + e^n)$**, find** e**.**

1. Multiply both sides by $(d + e^n)$; formula becomes:

    $$a(d + e^n) = (b - c)$$

2. Divide both sides by a; formula becomes: $d + e^n = \dfrac{b - c}{a}$

3. Subtract d from both sides; formula becomes: $e^n = \dfrac{b - c}{a} - d$

4. Raise each side to the power $1/n$; formula becomes:

    $$e = \left\{\dfrac{b - c}{a} - d\right\}^{1/n}$$

---

applied (e.g. 'assuming the tissue is homogeneous …'), while some approaches involve approximations which should be clearly stated (e.g. 'to estimate the mouse's skin area, its body was approximated to a cylinder with radius x and height y …').

(b) Explain your strategy for answering, perhaps giving the applicable formula or definitions which suit the approach to be taken. Give details of what the symbols mean (and their units) at this point.

(c) Rearrange the formula to the required form with the desired unknown on the left-hand side (see Table 65.2).

(d) Substitute the relevant values into the right-hand side of the formula, using the units and prefixes as given (it may be convenient to convert values to SI beforehand). Convert prefixes to appropriate powers of 10 as soon as possible.

(e) Convert to the desired units step by step, i.e. taking each variable in turn.

(f) When you have the answer in the desired units, rewrite the left-hand side and underline the answer. Make sure that the result is presented with an appropriate number of significant figures (see below).

Check your answer

Having written out your answer, you should check it methodically, answering the following questions:

-   Is the answer of a realistic magnitude? You should be alerted to an error if an answer is absurdly large or small. In repeated calculations, a result standing out from others in the same series should be double-checked.
-   Do the units make sense and match up with the answer required? Don't, for example, present a volume in units of m^2.
-   Do you get the same answer if you recalculate in a different way? If you have time, recalculate the answer using a different 'route', entering the numbers into your calculator in a different form and/or carrying out the operations in a different order.

Rounding: decimal places and significant figures

In many instances, the answer you produce as a result of a calculation will include more figures than is justified by the accuracy and precision of the original data. Sometimes you will be asked to produce an answer to a

Units – *never write any answer without its unit(s) unless it is truly dimensionless.*

Rounding off – *do not round off numbers until you arrive at the final answer or you will introduce 'rounding' errors.*

Box 65.2 Model answer to a mathematical problem

Problem

Estimate the total length and surface area of the fibrous roots on a maize seedling from measurements of their total fresh weight and mean diameter. Give your answers in m and cm² respectively to four significant figures.

Measurements

Fresh weight[a] = 5.00 g, mean diameter[b] = 0.5 mm.

Answer

Assumptions: (1) the roots are cylinders with constant radius[c] and the 'ends' have negligible area; (2) the root system has a density of $1000 \, kg \, m^{-3}$ (i.e. that of water[d]).

Strategy: from assumption (1), the applicable equations are those concerned with the volume and surface area of a cylinder, namely:

$$V = \pi r^2 h \qquad\qquad [65.1]$$
$$A = 2\pi rh \text{ (ignoring ends)} \qquad [65.2]$$

where V is volume (m^3), A is surface area (m^2), $\pi \approx 3.14159$, h is height (m) and r is radius (m). The total length of the root system is given by h and its surface area by A. We can find h by rearranging Eqn [65.1] and then substitute its value in Eqn [65.2] to get A.

To calculate total root length: rearranging Eqn [65.1], we have $h = V/\pi r^2$. From measurements[e], $r = 0.25 \, mm = 0.25 \times 10^{-3} \, m$.

From density = weight/volume,

$$\begin{aligned} V &= \text{fresh weight/density} \\ &= 5\,g/1000\,kg\,m^{-3} \\ &= 0.005\,kg/1000\,kg\,m^{-3} \\ &= 5 \times 10^{-6}\,m^3 \end{aligned}$$

Total root length,

$$h = V/\pi r^2$$
$$5 \times 10^{-6}\,m^3/3.14159 \times (0.25 \times 10^{-3}\,m)^2$$

Total root length = 25.46 m

To calculate surface area of roots: substituting value for h obtained above into Eqn [65.2], we have:

Root surface area

$$\begin{aligned} &= 2 \times 3.14159 \times 0.25 \times 10^{-3}\,m \times 25.46\,m \\ &= 0.04\,m^2 \\ &= 0.04 \times 10^4\,cm^2 \\ &\quad \text{(there being } 100 \times 100 = 10^4\,cm^2\,per\,m^2) \end{aligned}$$

Root surface area = 400.0 cm²

Notes

(a) The fresh weight of roots would normally be obtained by washing the roots free of soil, blotting them dry and weighing.

(b) In a real answer you might show the replicate measurements giving rise to the mean diameter.

(c) In reality, the roots will differ considerably in diameter and each root will not have a constant diameter throughout its length.

(d) This will not be wildly inaccurate as about 95% of the fresh weight will be water, but the volume could also be estimated from water displacement measurements.

(e) Note conversion of measurements into base SI units at this stage and on line 3 of the root volume calculation. Forgetting to halve diameter measurements where radii are required is a common error.

specified number of decimal places or significant figures and other times you will be expected to decide for yourself what would be appropriate.

KEY POINT Do not simply accept the numerical answer from a calculator or spreadsheet, without considering whether you need to modify this to give an appropriate number of significant figures or decimal places.

Rounding to n *decimal places*

This is relatively easy to do.

1. Look at the number to the right of the nth decimal place.
2. If this is less than five, simply 'cut off' all numbers to the right of the nth decimal place to produce the answer (i.e. round down).
3. If the number is greater than five, 'cut off' all numbers to the right of the nth decimal place and add one to the nth decimal place to produce the answer (i.e. round up).

Examples
The number 4.123 correct to 2 decimal places is 4.12
The number 4.126 correct to 2 decimal places is 4.13
The number 4.1251 correct to 2 decimal places is 4.13
The number 4.1250 correct to 2 decimal places is 4.12
The number 4.1350 correct to 2 decimal places is 4.14
The number 99.99 correct to one decimal place is 100.0

Examples
The number of significant figures in 194 is 3
The number of significant figures in 2305 is 4
The number of significant figures in 0.003 482 is 4
The number of significant figures in 210×10^8 is 3 (21×10^9 would be 2)

Examples
The number of significant figures in 3051.93 is 6
To 5 significant figures, this number is 3051.9
To 4 significant figures, this number is 3052
To 3 significant figures, this number is 3050
To 2 significant figures, this number is 3100
To 1 significant figure, this number is 3000
3051.93 to the nearest 10 is 3050
3051.93 to the nearest 100 is 3100
Note that in this last case you must include the zeros before the decimal point to indicate the scale of the number (even if the decimal point is not shown). For a number less than 1, the same would apply to the zeros before the decimal point. For example, 0.003 051 93 to 3 significant figures is 0.003 05.
Alternatively, use scientific notation (in this case, 3.05×10^{-3}).

4. If the number is 5, then look at further numbers to the right to determine whether to round up or not.
5. If the number is *exactly* 5 (i.e. there are no further numbers to the right), then round to the nearest *even* nth decimal number (round to the nearest even number). *Note:* When considering a large number of calculations, this procedure will not affect the overall mean value. Some rounding systems do the opposite to this (i.e. round to the nearest odd number), while others always round up where the number is exactly 5 (which *will* affect the mean). Take advice from your tutor and stick to one system throughout a series of calculations.

When you see numbers quoted, you should assume that the last digit has been rounded. For example, in the number 22.4, the '.4' is assumed to be rounded and the calculated value may have been between 22.35 and 22.45.

Quoting to n *significant figures*

The number of significant figures indicates the degree of approximation in the number. For most cases, it is given by counting all the figures except zeros that occur at the beginning or end of the number. Zeros *within* the number are always counted as significant. The number of significant figures in a number like 200 is ambiguous and could be one, two or three; if you wish to specify clearly, then quote as e.g. 2×10^2 (one significant figure), 2.0×10^2 (two significant figures), etc. When quoting a number to a specified number of significant figures, use the same rules as for rounding to a specified number of decimal places, but do not forget to keep zeros before or after the decimal point. The same principle is used if you are asked to quote a number to the 'nearest 10', 'nearest 100', etc.

When deciding for yourself how many significant figures to use, adopt the following rules of thumb:

- Always round *after* you have done a calculation. Use all significant figures available in the measured data during a calculation.
- If adding or subtracting with measured data, then quote the answer to the number of decimal places in the data value with the least number of decimal places (e.g. $32.1 - 45.67 + 35.6201 = 22.1$, because 32.1 has one decimal place).
- If multiplying or dividing with measured data, keep as many significant figures as are in the number with the least number of significant places (e.g. $34\,901 \div 3445 \times 1.341\,034\,4 = 13.59$, because 3445 has 4 significant figures).
- For the purposes of significant figures, assume 'constants' (e.g. number of mm in a m) have an infinite number of significant figures.

Some reminders of basic mathematics

Errors in calculations sometimes appear because of faults in mathematics rather than computational errors. For reference purposes, Tables 65.1 and 65.2 give some basic mathematical principles that may be useful. Eason *et al.* (1992) should be consulted for more advanced needs.

Percentages and proportions

A percentage is just a fraction expressed in terms of hundredths, indicated by putting the percentage sign (%) after the number of hundredths. So

Examples
1/8 as a percentage is $1 \div 8 \times 100 = 100 \div 8 = 12.5\%$
0.602 as a percentage is $0.602 \times 100 = 60.2\%$

Examples
190% as a decimal fraction is
$190 \div 100 = 1.9$
5/2 as a percentage is $5 \div 2 \times 100 = 250\%$

Example A population falls from 4 million to 3.85 million. What is the percentage change? The decrease in numbers is $4 - 3.85 = -0.15$ million. The fractional decrease is $-0.15 \div 4 = -0.0375$ and we multiply by 100 to get the percentage change = minus 3.75%.

Example $2^3 = 2 \times 2 \times 2 = 8$

Example Avogadro's number, $\approx 602\,352\,000\,000\,000\,000\,000\,000$, is more conveniently expressed as $6.023\,52 \times 10^{23}$

35% simply means 35 hundredths. To convert a fraction to a percentage, just multiply the fraction by 100. When the fraction is in decimal form, multiplying by 100 to obtain a percentage is easily achieved just by moving the decimal point two places to the right.

To convert a percentage to a fraction, just remember that, since a percentage is a fraction multiplied by 100, the fraction is the percentage divided by 100. For example: $42\% = 42/100 = 0.42$. In this example, since we are dealing with a decimal fraction, the division by 100 is just a matter of moving the decimal point two places to the left (42% could be written as 42.0%). Percentages greater than 100% represent fractions greater than 1. Percentages less than 1 may cause confusion. For example, 0.5% means half of one per cent (0.005) and must not be confused with 50% (which is the decimal fraction 0.5).

To find a percentage of a given number, just express the percentage as a decimal fraction and multiply the given number. For example: 35% of 500 is given by $0.35 \times 500 = 175$. To find the percentage change in a quantity, work out the difference (= value 'after' − value 'before'), and divide this difference by the original value to give the fractional change, then multiply by 100.

Exponents

Exponential notation is an alternative way of expressing numbers in the form a^n ('a to the power n'), where a is multiplied by itself n times. The number a is called the base and the number n the exponent (or power or index). The exponent need not be a whole number, and it can be negative if the number being expressed is less than 1. See Table 65.2 for other mathematical relationships involving exponents.

Scientific notation

In scientific notation, also known as 'standard form', the base is 10 and the exponent a whole number. To express numbers that are not whole powers of 10, the form $c \times 10^n$ is used, where the coefficient c is normally between 1 and 10. Scientific notation is valuable when you are using very large numbers and wish to avoid suggesting spurious accuracy. Thus if you write 123 000, this may suggest that you know the number to ±0.5, whereas 1.23×10^5 might give a truer indication of measurement accuracy (i.e. implied to be ±500 in this case). Engineering notation is similar, but treats numbers as powers of 10 in groups of 3, i.e. $c \times 10^0$, 10^3, 10^6, 10^9, etc. This corresponds to the SI system of prefixes (p. 156).

A useful property of powers when expressed to the same base is that when multiplying two numbers together, you simply add the powers, while if dividing, you subtract the powers. Thus, suppose you counted 8 bacteria in a 10^{-7} dilution (see p. 126), there would be 8×10^7 in the same volume of undiluted solution; if you now dilute this 500-fold (5×10^2), then the number present in the same volume would be $8/5 \times 10^{(7-2)} = 1.6 \times 10^5 = 160\,000$.

Logarithms

When a number is expressed as a logarithm, this refers to the power n that the base number a must be raised to give that number, e.g. $\log_{10}(1000) = 3$, since $10^3 = 1000$. Any base could be used, but the two most common are 10, when the power is referred to as $\log_{10}$ or simply log, and the constant e (2.718 282), used for mathematical convenience in certain situations, when the power is referred to as $\log_e$ or ln. Note that (a) logs need not be whole numbers; (b) there is no log value for the number zero; and (c) that $\log_{10} = 0$ for the number 1.

To obtain logs, you will need to use the log key on your calculator, or special log tables (now largely redundant). To convert back ('antilog') use

- the $\boxed{10^x}$ key, with $x = $ log value;
- the $\boxed{\text{inverse}}$ then the $\boxed{\text{log}}$ key; or
- the $\boxed{y^x}$ key, with $y = 10$ and $x = $ log value.

If you used log tables, you will find complementary antilogarithm tables to do this.

There are many uses of logarithms in biology, including pH ($= -\log[H^+]$), where $[H^+]$ is expressed in $mol\,l^{-1}$ (see p. 146); the exponential growth of micro-organisms, where if log(cell number) is plotted against time, a straight-line relationship is obtained (see p. 226); and allometric studies of growth and development, where if data are plotted on log axes, a series of straight-line relationships may be found.

Linear functions and straight lines

One of the most straightforward and widely used relationships between two variables x and y is that represented by a straight-line graph, where the corresponding mathematical function is known as the equation of a straight line, where:

$$y = a + bx \qquad [65.3]$$

In this relationship, a represents the intercept of the line on the y (vertical) axis, i.e. where $x = 0$, and therefore $bx = 0$, while b is equivalent to the slope (gradient) of the line, i.e. the change in y for a change in x of 1. The constants a and b are sometimes given alternative symbols, but the mathematics remains unchanged, e.g. in the equivalent expression for the slope of a straight line, $y = mx + c$. Figure 65.1 shows what happens when these two constants are changed, in terms of the resultant straight lines.

The two main applications of the straight-line relationship are:

1. Function fitting. Here, you determine the mathematical form of the function, i.e. you estimate the constants a and b from a data set for x and y, either by drawing a straight line by eye (p. 456) and then working out the slope and y intercept, or by using linear regression (p. 493) to obtain the most probable values for both constants. When putting a straight line of best fit by eye on a hand-drawn graph, note the following:

   - Always use a transparent ruler, so you can see data points on either side of the line.
   - For a data series where the points do not fit a perfect straight line, try to have an equal number of points on either side of the line, as in Fig. 65.2a, and try to minimise the average distance of these points from the line.
   - Once you have drawn the line of best fit use this line, rather than your data values, in all subsequent procedures (e.g. in a calibration curve, Chapter 37).

(a)

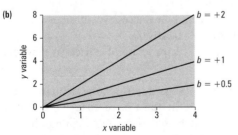

(b)

Fig. 65.1 Straight-line relationships ($y = a + bx$), showing the effects of (a) changing the intercept at constant slope, and (b) changing the slope at constant intercept.

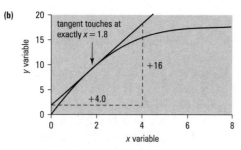

Fig. 65.2 Drawing straight lines. (a) Simple linear relationship, giving a straight line with an intercept of 2.3 and a slope of −1.6 ÷ 4.0 = 0.4. (b) Tangent drawn to a curve at $x = 1.8$, giving a slope of 16 ÷ 4 = 4.

Example   Using Eqn [65.4], the predicted value for x for a linear function where $a = 1.5$ and $b = 2.5$, where $y = −8.5$ is: $x = (−8.5 − 1.5) ÷ 2.5 = −4$.
Using Eqn [65.4] the predicted x intercept for a linear function where $a = 0.8$ and $b = 3.2$ is: $x = (0 − 0.8) ÷ 3.2 = −0.25$.

Example   A lab schedule states that 5 g of a compound with a relative molecular mass of 220 are dissolved in 400 ml of solvent. For writing up your Materials and Methods, you wish to express this as $mol\,l^{-1}$.
1. If there are 5 g in 400 ml, then there are $5 ÷ 400$ g in 1 ml.
2. Hence, 1000 ml will contain $5 ÷ 400 × 1000$ g = 12.5 g.
3. 12.5 g = $12.5 ÷ 220$ mol = 0.0568 mol, so [solution] = $56.8\,mmol\,l^{-1}$ $(= 56.8\,mol\,m^{-3})$.

- Tangents drawn to a curve give the slope (gradient) at a particular point, e.g. in an enzyme reaction progress curve, Fig. 55.2. These are best drawn by bringing your ruler up to the curve at the exact point where you wish to estimate the slope and then trying to make the two angles immediately on either side of this point approximately the same, by eye (Fig. 65.2b).
- Once you have drawn the straight line or tangent, choose two points reasonably far apart at either end of your line and then draw construction lines to represent the change in y and the change in x between these two points: make sure that your construction lines are perpendicular to each other. Determine the slope as the change in y divided by the change in x (Fig. 65.2b).

2. Prediction. Where a and b are known, or have been estimated, you can use Eqn [65.3] to predict any value of y for a specified value of x, e.g. during exponential growth of a cell culture (p. 226), where log_{10} cell number (y) increases as a linear function of time (x): note that in this example the dependent variable has been transformed to give a linear relationship. You will need to rearrange Eqn [65.3] in cases where a prediction of x is required for a particular value of y (e.g. in calibration curves, p. 246, or bioassays, p. 231), as follows:

$$x = (y − a) ÷ b \qquad [65.4]$$

This equation can also be used to determine the intercept on the x (horizontal) axis, i.e. where $y = 0$.

Hints for some typical problems

Calculations involving proportions or ratios

The 'unitary method' is a useful way of approaching calculations involving proportions or ratios, such as those required when making up solutions from stocks (see also Chapter 24) or as a subsidiary part of longer calculations.

1. If given a value for a multiple, work out the corresponding value for a single item or unit.
2. Use this 'unitary value' to calculate the required new value.

Calculations involving series

Series (used in e.g. dilutions, see also p. 131) can be of three main forms:

1. Arithmetic, where the *difference* between two successive numbers in the series is a constant, e.g. 2, 4, 6, 8, 10, . . .
2. Geometric, where the *ratio* between two successive numbers in the series is a constant, e.g. 1, 10, 100, 1000, 10 000, . . .
3. Harmonic, where the values are reciprocals of successive whole numbers, e.g. $1, \frac{1}{2}, \frac{1}{3}, \frac{1}{4}, \ldots$

Note that the logs of the numbers in a geometric series will form an arithmetic series (e.g. 0, 1, 2, 3, 4, . . . in the above case). Thus, if a quantity y varies with a quantity x such that the rate of change in y is proportional to the value of y (i.e. it varies in an exponential manner), a semi-log plot of such data will form a straight line. This form of relationship is relevant for exponentially growing cell cultures (p. 226) and radioactive decay (p. 259).

Statistical calculations

The need for long, complex calculations in statistics has largely been removed because of the widespread use of spreadsheets with statistical functions (Chapter 12) and specialised programs such as Minitab®. It is, however, important to understand the principles behind what you are trying to do (see Chapters 66 and 67) and interpret the program's output correctly, either using the 'help' function or a reference manual.

Problems in Mendelian genetics

These cause difficulties for many students. The key is to recognise the different types of problem and to practise so you are familiar with the techniques for solving them. Chapter 58 deals with the different types of cross you will come across and methods of analysing them, including the use of the χ^2 (chi^2) test.

Text reference

Eason, G., Coles, C.W. and Gettinby, G. (1992) *Mathematics and Statistics for the Bio-Sciences*. Ellis Horwood, Chichester.

Sources for further study

Anon. *S.O.S. Mathematics*. Available: http://www.sosmath.com
Last accessed 08/01/03.
[A basic Web-based guide with very wide coverage.]

Batschelet, E. (1992) *Introduction to Mathematics for Life Scientists*, 3rd edn. Springer-Verlag, New York.

Causton, D.R. (1987) *A Biologist's Advanced Mathematics*. Unwin Hyman, London.

Causton, D.R. (1992) *A Biologist's Basic Mathematics*. Cambridge University Press, Cambridge.

Koehler, K.R. *College Physics for Students of Biology and Chemistry*. Available: http://www.rwc.uc.edu/koehler/biophys/text.html
Last accessed 08/01/03.
[A 'hypertextbook' written for first-year undergraduates. Assumes that you have a working knowledge of algebra.]

Study exercises

65.1 Rearrange a simple formula. The Beer–Lambert relationship, Eqn [41.3] (p. 271), is written in the form $A = \varepsilon l \,[\text{C}]$. Rearrange, in the form:
(a) $[\text{C}] =$
(b) $\varepsilon =$

65.2 Rearrange the following formulae:
(a) If $y = ax + b$, find b
(b) If $y = ax + b$, find x
(c) If $x = y^3$, find y
(d) If $x = 3^y$, find y
(e) If $x = (1 - y)(z^p + 3)$, find z
(f) If $x = (y - z)^{1/n}/pq$, find n

65.3 Work with decimal places or significant figures. Give the following numbers to the accuracy indicated:
(a) 214.51 to 3 significant figures
(b) 107 029 to 3 significant figures
(c) 0.0450 to 1 significant figure
(d) 99.817 to 2 decimal places
(e) 99.897 to 2 decimal places
(f) 99.997 to 2 decimal places
(g) 6255 to the nearest 10
(h) 134 903 to the nearest ten thousand
State the following:
(i) the number of significant figures in 3400
(j) the number of significant figures in 3400.3
(k) the number of significant figures in 0.001 67
(l) the number of significant figures in 1.001 67
(m) the number of decimal places in 34.46
(n) the number of decimal places in 0.001 67

65.4 Carry out calculations involving percentages. Answer the following questions, giving your answers to two decimal places:
(a) What is 6/35ths expressed as a percentage?
(b) What is 0.0755 expressed as a percentage?
(c) What is 4.35% of 322?
(d) A rat's weight increased from 55.23 to 75.02 g. What is the % increase in its weight?

65.5 Practise using exponents and logarithms.
(a) Write out (i) the charge on an electron and (ii) the speed of light *in vacuo* in longhand (i.e. without using powers of 10). See Table 29.4 (p. 178) for values given in scientific notation.
(b) Compute the following values: $10^{3.624}$; $\log(6.37)$; $e^{-2.32}$; $\ln(1123)$; $6^{3.2}$. A calculator should be used, but round the output to give 5 significant figures.

65.6 Practise working with linear functions (note also that Chapter 37 includes study exercises based on linear functions and plotting straight lines). Assuming a linear relationship between x and y, calculate the following (give your answers to 3 significant figures):
(a) x, where $y = 7.0$, $a = 4.5$ and $b = 0.02$;
(b) x, where $y = 15.2$, $a = -2.6$ and $b = -4.46$;
(c) y, where $x = 10.5$, $a = 0.2$ and $b = -0.63$;
(d) y, where $x = 4.5$, $a = -1.8$ and $b = 4.1$.

The purpose of most practical work is to observe and measure a particular characteristic of a biomolecule or biological system. However, it would be extremely rare if the same value was obtained every time the characteristic was measured, or with every experimental subject. More commonly, such measurements will show variability, due to measurement error, sampling variation and/or biological variability (p. 171). Such variability can be displayed as a frequency distribution (e.g. Fig. 63.2), where the *y*-axis shows the number of times (frequency, *f*) each particular value of the measured (dependent) variable (*Y*) has been obtained. Descriptive (or summary) statistics quantify aspects of the frequency distribution of a sample. You can use them to condense a large data set, for presentation in figures or tables. An additional application of descriptive statistics is to provide estimates of the true values of the underlying frequency distribution of the population being sampled, allowing the significance and precision of the observations to be assessed (pp. 480, 486).

KEY POINT The appropriate descriptive statistics to choose will depend on both the type of data, i.e. whether quantitative, ranked or qualitative (see p. 169) and the nature of the underlying frequency distribution.

In many instances, the normal (Gaussian) distribution (Chapter 67) best describes the observed pattern, giving a symmetrical, bell-shaped frequency distribution (p. 488), for example, measurements of a quantitative continuous variable in a number of individuals (e.g. blood plasma pH of several adult males), or replicate measurements of a particular characteristic (e.g. repeated measurements of the blood plasma pH of an individual adult male). If you have no clear theoretical grounds for assuming what the underlying frequency distribution is like, graph one or more sample frequency distributions, ideally with a sample size >100.

Three important features of a frequency distribution that can be summarised by descriptive statistics are:

- the sample's location, i.e. its position along a given dimension representing the dependent (measured) variable (Fig. 66.1);
- the dispersion of the data, i.e. how spread out the values are (Fig. 66.2);
- the shape of the distribution, i.e. whether symmetrical, skewed, U-shaped (Fig. 66.3).

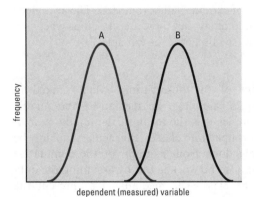

Fig. 66.1 Two distributions with different locations but the same dispersion. The data set labelled B could have been obtained by adding a constant to each datum in the data set labelled A.

Measuring location

Here, the objective is to pinpoint the 'centre' of the frequency distribution, i.e. the value about which most of the data are grouped. The chief measures of location are the mean, median and mode. Figure 66.4 shows how to choose among these for a given data set.

Mean

The mean (denoted $\bar{Y}$ and also referred to as the arithmetic mean) is the average value of the data. It is obtained from the sum of all the data values divided by the number of observations (in symbolic terms, $\Sigma Y/n$). The mean

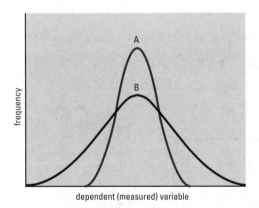

Fig. 66.2 Two distributions with different dispersions but the same location. The data set labelled A covers a relatively narrow range of values of the dependent (measured) variable while that labelled B covers a wider range.

Descriptive statistics

Example Box 66.1 shows a set of data and the calculated values of the measures of location, dispersion and shape for which methods of calculation are outlined here. Check your understanding by calculating the statistics yourself and confirming that you arrive at the same answers.

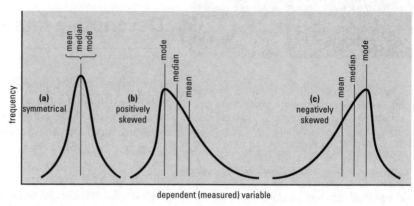

Fig. 66.3 Symmetrical and skewed frequency distributions, showing relative positions of mean, median and mode.

is a good measure of the centre of symmetrical frequency distributions. It uses all of the numerical values of the sample and therefore incorporates all of the information content of the data. However, the value of a mean is greatly affected by the presence of extreme values (outliers). The arithmetic mean is a widely used statistic in biology, but there are situations when you should be careful about using it (see Box 66.2 for examples).

Median

The median is the mid-point of the observations when ranked in increasing order. For odd-sized samples, the median is the middle observation; for even-sized samples it is the mean of the middle pair of observations. Where data are grouped into classes, the median can only be estimated. This is most simply done from a graph of the cumulative frequency distribution, but can also be worked out by assuming the data to be evenly spread within the class. The median may represent the

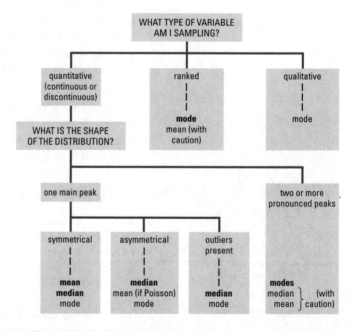

Fig. 66.4 Choosing a statistic for characterising a distribution's location. Statistics written in bold are the preferred option(s).

Box 66.1 Descriptive statistics for a sample of data – an example

Value (Y)	Frequency (f)	Cumulative frequency	fY	fY²
1	0	0	0	0
2	1	1	2	4
3	2	3	6	18
4	3	6	12	48
5	8	14	40	200
6	5	19	30	180
7	2	21	14	98
8	0	21	0	0
Totals	$21 = \Sigma f\ (=n)$		$104 = \Sigma fY$	$548 = \Sigma fY^2$

In this example, for simplicity and ease of calculation, integer values of Y are used. In many practical exercises, where continuous variables are measured to several significant figures and where the number of data values is small, giving frequencies of 1 for most of the values of Y, it may be simpler to omit the column dealing with frequency and list all the individual values of Y and Y^2 in the appropriate columns. To gauge the underlying frequency distribution of such data sets, you would need to group individual data into broader classes (e.g. all values between 1.0 and 1.9, all values between 2.0 and 2.9, etc.) and then draw a histogram (p. 456). Calculation of certain statistics for data sets that have been grouped in this way (e.g. median, quartiles, extremes) can be tricky and a statistical text should be consulted.

Statistic	Value*	How calculated
Mean	4.95	$\Sigma fY/n$, i.e. 104/21
Mode	5	The most common value (Y value with highest frequency)
Median	5	Value of the $(n+1)/2$ variate, i.e. the value ranked $(21+1)/2 = 11$th (obtained from the cumulative frequency column)
Upper quartile	6	The upper quartile is between the 16th and 17th values, i.e. the value exceeded by 25% of the data values
Lower quartile	4	The lower quartile is between the 5th and 6th values, i.e. the value exceeded by 75% of the data values
Semi-interquartile range	1.0	Half the difference between the upper and lower quartiles, i.e. $(6-4)/2$
Upper extreme	7	Highest Y value in data set
Lower extreme	2	Lowest Y value in data set
Range	5	Difference between upper and lower extremes
Variance (s^2)	1.65	$s^2 = \dfrac{\Sigma fY^2 - (\Sigma fY)^2/n}{n-1}$ $= \dfrac{548 - (104)^2/21}{20}$
Standard deviation (s)	1.28	$\sqrt{s^2}$
Standard error (SE)	0.280	$s/\sqrt{n}$
95% confidence limits	4.36 – 5.54	$\bar{Y} \mp t_{0.05}[20] \times \text{SE}$, (where $t_{0.05}[20] = 2.09$, Table 67.2)
Coefficient of variation (cov)	25.9%	$100s/\bar{Y}$

*Rounded to three significant figures (see p. 469), except when it is an exact number.

Definition
An outlier – any datum that has a value much smaller or bigger than most of the data.

location of the main body of data better than the mean when the distribution is asymmetric or when there are outliers in the sample.

Mode

The mode is the most common value in the sample. The mode is easily found from a tabulated frequency distribution as the most frequent value. If data have been grouped into classes then the term modal class is used for the class containing most values. The mode provides a rapidly and easily found estimate of sample location and is unaffected by outliers. However, the mode is affected by chance variation in the shape of a sample's distribution and it may lie distant from the obvious centre of the distribution. Note that the mode is the only statistic to make sense of qualitative data, e.g. 'the modal (most frequent) eye colour was blue'.

The mean, median and mode have the same units as the variable under discussion. However, whether these statistics of location have the same or similar values for a given frequency distribution depends on the symmetry and shape of the distribution. If it is near-symmetrical with a single peak, all three will be very similar; if it is skewed or has more than one peak, their values will differ to a greater degree (see Fig. 66.3).

Measuring dispersion

Here, the objective is to quantify the spread of the data about the centre of the distribution. Figure 66.5 indicates how to decide which measure of dispersion to use.

Range

The range is the difference between the largest and smallest data values in the sample (the extremes) and has the same units as the measured variable.

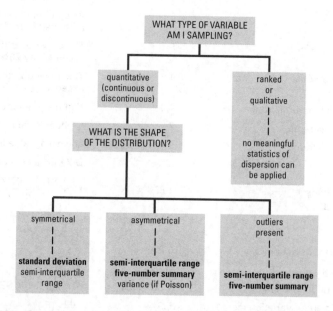

Fig. 66.5 Choosing a statistic for characterising a distribution's dispersion. Statistics written in bold are the preferred option(s). Note that you should match statistics describing dispersion with those you have used to describe location, i.e. standard deviation with mean, semi-interquartile range with median.

Fig. 66.6 Illustration of median, quartiles, range and semi-interquartile range.

The range is easy to determine, but is greatly affected by outliers. Its value may also depend on sample size: in general, the larger this is, the greater will be the range. These features make the range a poor measure of dispersion for many practical purposes.

Semi-interquartile range

The semi-interquartile range is an appropriate measure of dispersion when a median is the appropriate statistic to describe location. For this, you need to determine the first and third quartiles, i.e. the medians for those data values ranked below and above the median of the whole data set (see Fig. 66.6). To calculate a semi-interquartile range for a data set:

1. Rank the observations in ascending order.
2. Find the values of the first and third quartiles.
3. Subtract the value of the first quartile from the value of the third.
4. Halve this number.

For data grouped in classes, the semi-interquartile range can only be estimated. Another disadvantage is that it takes no account of the shape of the distribution at its edges. This objection can be countered by using the so-called 'five number summary' of a data set, which consists of the three quartiles and the two extreme values; this can be presented on graphs as a box and whisker plot (see Fig. 66.7) and is particularly useful for summarising skewed frequency distributions. The corresponding 'six number summary' includes the sample's size.

Variance and standard deviation

For symmetrical frequency distributions, an ideal measure of dispersion would take into account each value's deviation from the mean and provide a measure of the average deviation from the mean. Two such statistics are the sample variance, which is the sum of squares ($\Sigma(Y - \bar{Y})^2$) divided by

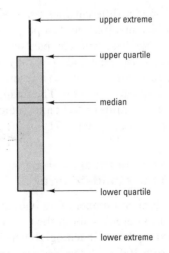

Fig. 66.7 A box and whisker plot, showing the 'five number summary' of a sample as it might be used on a graph.

$n - 1$ (where n is the sample size), and the sample standard deviation, which is the positive square root of the sample variance.

The variance (s^2) has units which are the square of the original units, while the standard deviation (s, or SD) is expressed in the original units, one reason s is often preferred as a measure of dispersion. Calculating s or s^2 longhand is a tedious job and is best done with the help of a calculator or computer. If you don't have a calculator that calculates s for you, an alternative formula that simplifies calculations is:

$$s = +\sqrt{\frac{\Sigma Y^2 - (\Sigma Y)^2/n}{n-1}} \qquad [66.1]$$

To calculate s using a calculator:

1. Obtain ΣY, square it, divide by n and store in memory.
2. Square Y values, obtain ΣY^2, subtract memory value from this.
3. Divide this answer by $n - 1$.
4. Take the positive square root of this value.

Take care to retain significant figures, or errors in the final value of s will result. If continuous data have been grouped into classes, the class mid-values or their squares must be multiplied by the appropriate frequencies before summation (see example in Box 66.1). When data values are large, longhand calculations can be simplified by coding the data, e.g. by subtracting a constant from each datum, and decoding when the simplified calculations are complete (see Sokal and Rohlf, 1994).

Coefficient of variation

The coefficient of variation (CoV) is a dimensionless measure of variability relative to location which expresses the sample standard deviation, usually as a percentage of the sample mean, i.e.

$$\text{CoV} = 100s/\bar{Y} (\%) \qquad [66.2]$$

This statistic is useful when comparing the relative dispersion of data sets with widely differing means or where different units have been used for the same or similar quantities.

A useful application of the CoV is to compare different analytical methods or procedures, so that you can decide which involves the least proportional error – create a standard stock solution, then base your comparison on the results from several subsamples analysed by each method. You may find it useful to use the CoV to compare the precision of your own results with those of a manufacturer, e.g. for an autopippettor (p. 123). The smaller the CoV, the more precise (repeatable) is the apparatus or technique (note: this does not mean that it is necessarily more *accurate*, see p. 171).

Measuring the precision of the sample mean as an estimate of the true value using the standard error

Most practical exercises are based on a limited number of individual data values (a sample) which are used to make inferences about the population from which they were drawn. For example, the haemoglobin content might be measured in blood samples from 100 adult females and used as an estimate of the adult female haemoglobin content, with the sample mean ($\bar{Y}$) and sample standard deviation (s) providing estimates of the

Using a calculator for statistics – *make sure you understand how to enter individual data values and which keys will give the sample mean (usually shown as $\bar{X}$ or $\bar{x}$) and sample standard deviation (often shown as σ_{n-1}). In general, you should not use the population standard deviation (usually shown as σ_n).*

Example Consider two methods of bioassay for a toxin in fresh water. For a given standard, Method A gives a mean result of $= 50$ 'response units' with $s = 8$, while Method B gives a mean result of $= 160$ 'response units' with $s = 18$. Which bioassay gives the more reproducible results? The answer can be found by calculating the CoV values, which are 16 and 11.25% respectively. Hence, Method B is the more precise ($\equiv$reproducible), even though the absolute value of s is larger.

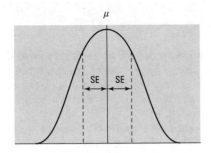

Fig. 66.8 Frequency distribution of sample means around the population mean (μ). Note that SE is equivalent to the standard deviation of the sample means, for sample size = n.

true values of the underlying population mean (μ) and the population standard deviation (σ). The reliability of the sample mean as an estimate of the true (population) mean can be assessed by calculating a statistic termed the standard error of the sample mean (often abbreviated to standard error or SE), from:

$$SE = s/\sqrt{n} \qquad\qquad [66.3]$$

Strictly, the standard error is an estimate of the dispersion of repeated sample means around the true (population) value: if several samples were taken, each with the same number of data values (n), then their means would cluster around the population mean (μ) with a standard deviation equal to SE, as shown in Fig. 66.8. Therefore, the *smaller* the SE, the more reliable the sample mean is likely to be as an estimate of the true value, since the underlying frequency distribution would be more tightly clustered around μ. At a practical level, Eqn [66.3] shows that SE is directly affected by the dispersion of individual data values within the sample, as represented by the sample standard deviation (s). Perhaps more importantly, SE is inversely related to the *square root* of the number of data values (n). Therefore, if you wanted to increase the precision of a sample mean by a factor of 2 (i.e. to reduce SE by half), you would have to increase n by a factor of 2^2 (i.e. fourfold).

Summary descriptive statistics for the sample mean are often quoted as $\bar{Y} \pm SE\,(n)$, with the SE being given to one significant figure more than the mean. For example, summary statistics for the sample mean and standard error for the data shown in Box 66.1 would be quoted as 4.95 ± 0.280 ($n = 21$). You can use such information to carry out a *t*-test between two sample means (Box 67.1); the SE is also useful because it allows calculation of confidence limits for the sample mean (p. 493).

Describing the 'shape' of frequency distributions

Frequency distributions may differ in the following characteristics:

- number of peaks;
- skewness or asymmetry;
- kurtosis or pointedness.

The shape of a frequency distribution of a small sample is affected by chance variation and may not be a fair reflection of the underlying population frequency distribution: check this by comparing repeated samples from the same population or by increasing the sample size. If the original shape were due to random events, it should not appear consistently in repeated samples and should become less obvious as sample size increases.

Genuinely bimodal or polymodal distributions may result from the combination of two or more unimodal distributions, indicating that more than one underlying population is being sampled (Fig. 66.9). An example of a bimodal distribution is the height of adult humans (females and males combined).

A distribution is skewed if it is not symmetrical, a symptom being that the mean, median and mode are not equal (Fig. 66.3). Positive skewness is where the longer 'tail' of the distribution occurs for higher values of the measured variable; negative skewness where the longer tail occurs for lower values. Some biological examples of characteristics distributed in a

Box 66.2 Three examples where simple arithmetic means are inappropriate

Mean	n
6	4
7	7
8	1

1. **If means of samples are themselves meaned, an error can arise if the samples are of different size.** For example, the arithmetic mean of the means in the table shown left is 7, but this does not take account of the different 'reliabilities' of each mean due to their sample sizes. The correct weighted mean is obtained by multiplying each mean by its sample size (n) (a 'weight') and dividing the sum of these values by the total number of observations, i.e. in the case shown, $(24 + 49 + 8)/12 = 6.75$.

2. **When making a mean of ratios (e.g. percentages) for several groups of different sizes, the ratio for the combined total of all the groups is not the mean of the proportions for the individual groups.** For example, if 20 rats from a batch of 50 are male, this implies 40% are male. If 60 rats from a batch of 120 are male, this implies 50% are male. The mean percentage of males $(50 + 40)/2 = 45\%$ is *not* the percentage of males in the two groups combined, because there are $20 + 60 = 80$ males in a total of 170 rats $= 47.1\%$ approx.

pH value	$[H^+]$ (mol l^{-1})
6	1×10^{-6}
7	1×10^{-7}
8	1×10^{-8}
mean	3.7×10^{-7}
$-\log_{10}$ mean	6.43

3. **If the measurement scale is not linear, arithmetic means may give a false value.** For example, if three media had pH values 6, 7 and 8, the appropriate mean pH is not 7 because the pH scale is logarithmic. The definition of pH is $-\log_{10}[H^+]$, where $[H^+]$ is expressed in mol l^{-1} ('molar'); therefore, to obtain the true mean, convert data into $[H^+]$ values (i.e. put them on a linear scale) by calculating $10^{(-pH\,value)}$ as shown. Now calculate the mean of these values and convert the answer back into pH units. Thus, the appropriate answer is pH 6.43 rather than 7. Note that a similar procedure is necessary when calculating statistics of dispersion in such cases, so you will find these almost certainly asymmetric about the mean.

Mean values of log-transformed data are often termed geometric means – they are sometimes used in microbiology and in cell culture studies, where log-transformed values for cell density counts are averaged and plotted (p. 226), rather than using the raw data values. The use of geometric means in such circumstances serves to reduce the effects of outliers on the mean.

skewed fashion are volumes of plant protoplasts, insulin levels in human plasma and bacterial colony counts.

Kurtosis is the name given to the 'pointedness' of a frequency distribution. A platykurtic frequency distribution is one with a flattened peak, while a leptokurtic frequency distribution is one with a pointed

Fig. 66.9 Frequency distributions with different numbers of peaks. A unimodal distribution (a) may be symmetrical or asymmetrical. The dotted lines in (b) indicate how a bimodal distribution could arise from a combination of two underlying unimodal distributions. Note here how the term 'bimodal' is applied to any distribution with two major peaks – their frequencies do not have to be exactly the same.

Fig. 66.10 Examples of the two types of kurtosis.

peak (Fig. 66.10). While descriptive terms can be used, based on visual observation of the shape and direction of skew, the degree of skewness and kurtosis can be quantified and statistical tests exist to test the 'significance' of observed values (see Sokal and Rohlf, 1994), but the calculations required are complex and best done with the aid of a computer.

Text references and sources for further study

Dytham, C. (2003) *Choosing and Using Statistics: A Biologists' Guide*, 2nd edn. Blackwell, Oxford.

Heath, D. (1995) *An Introduction to Experimental Design and Statistics for Biology*. UCL Press Ltd, London.

Maber, J. (1999) *Data Analysis for Biomolecular Sciences*. Longman, Harlow.

Sokal, R.R. and Rohlf, F.J. (1994) *Biometry*, 3rd edn. W.H. Freeman and Co., San Francisco.

Wardlaw, A.C. (2000) *Practical Statistics for Experimental Biologists*, 2nd edn. Wiley, New York.

Study exercises

66.1 Determine descriptive statistics and make appropriate conclusions from them. Determine the mean, median and mode of the following data set. Using these descriptive statistics only, and referring to Fig. 66.3, state whether you think the underlying population distribution is symmetrical, positively skewed or negatively skewed.

Set of data

4	4	3	3	5	4	3	7	7	3	5	3
6	2	9	7	3	4	5	6	6	9	4	8
5	3	2	5	4	5	7	2	8	3	6	3
11	3	5	2	4	3	7	8	4	4	4	3
3	6	8	5	6	4	3	4	3	6	10	5

66.2 Practise calculating descriptive statistics. Using the data set given in the table in Study exercise 66.1, calculate the following statistics:
(a) range
(b) variance
(c) standard deviation
(d) coefficient of variation
(e) standard error.
Answers (b) to (e) should be given to 4 significant figures.

66.3 Calculate and interpret standard errors. Two samples, A and B, gave the following descriptive statistics (measured in the same units): Sample A, mean = 16.2, standard deviation = 12.7, number of data values = 12; Sample B, mean = 13.2, standard deviation

14.4, number of data values $= 20$. Which has the lower standard error in absolute terms and in proportion to the sample mean? (Express answers to 3 significant figures.)

66.4 Compute a mean value correctly. A researcher finds that the mean size of larvae in three replicate samples designated A, B and C is 3.0, 2.5 and 2.0 mm respectively. He computes the mean larval size as 2.5 mm, but forgets that the sample sizes were 24, 37 and 6 respectively. What is the true mean size of the larvae? (Answer to 3 significant figures.)

67 # Choosing and using statistical tests

This chapter outlines the philosophy of hypothesis-testing statistics, indicates the steps to be taken when choosing a test, and discusses features and assumptions of some important tests. For details of the mechanics of tests, consult appropriate texts (e.g. Sokal and Rohlf, 1994; Heath, 1995; Wardlaw, 2000). Most tests are now available in statistical packages for computers (see p. 78) and many in spreadsheets (Chapter 12).

To carry out a statistical test:

1. Decide what it is you wish to test (create a null hypothesis and its alternative).
2. Determine whether your data fit a standard distribution pattern.
3. Select a test and apply it to your data.

Setting up a null hypothesis

Hypothesis-testing statistics are used to compare the properties of samples either with other samples or with some theory about them. For instance, you may be interested in whether two samples can be regarded as having different means, whether the counts of an organism in different quadrats can be regarded as randomly distributed, or whether property A of an organism is linearly related to property B.

> **KEY POINT** You can't use statistics to *prove* any hypothesis, but they can be used to assess *how likely* it is to be wrong.

Statistical testing operates in what at first seems a rather perverse manner. Suppose you think a treatment has an effect. The theory you actually test is that it has no effect; the test tells you how improbable your data would be if this theory were true. This 'no effect' theory is the null hypothesis (NH). If your data are very improbable under the NH, then you may suppose it to be wrong, and this would support your original idea (the 'alternative hypothesis'). The concept can be illustrated by an example. Suppose two groups of subjects were treated in different ways, and you observed a difference in the mean value of the measured variable for the two groups. Can this be regarded as a 'true' difference? As Fig. 67.1 shows, it could have arisen in two ways:

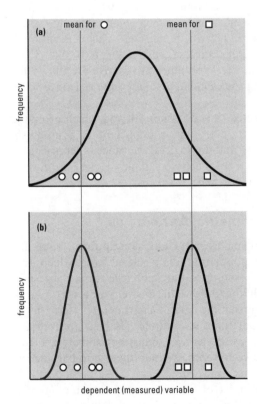

Fig. 67.1 Two explanations for the difference between two means. In case (a) the two samples happen by chance to have come from opposite ends of the same frequency distribution, i.e. there is no true difference between the samples. In case (b) the two samples come from different frequency distributions, i.e. there is a true difference between the samples. In both cases, the means of the two samples are the same.

- Because of the way the subjects were allocated to treatments, i.e. all the subjects liable to have high values might, by chance, have been assigned to one group and those with low values to the other (Fig. 67.1a).
- Because of a genuine effect of the treatments, i.e. each group came from a distinct frequency distribution (Fig. 67.1b).

A statistical test will indicate the probabilities of these options. The NH states that the two groups come from the same population (i.e. the treatment effects are negligible in the context of random variation). To test this, you calculate a test statistic from the data, and compare it with tabulated critical values giving the probability of obtaining the observed or a more extreme result by chance (see Boxes 67.1 and 67.2). This probability is sometimes called the significance of the test.

Note that you must take into account the degrees of freedom (d.f.) when looking up critical values of most test statistics. The d.f. is related to the size(s) of the samples studied; formulae for calculating it depend on the test being used. Biologists normally use two-tailed tests, i.e. we have no expectation beforehand that the treatment will have a positive or negative effect compared to the control (in a one-tailed test we expect one particular treatment to be bigger than the other). Be sure to use critical values for the correct type of test.

By convention, the critical probability for rejecting the NH is 5% (i.e. $P = 0.05$). This means we reject the NH if the observed result would have come up less than one time in 20 by chance. If the modulus of the test statistic is less than the tabulated critical value for $P = 0.05$, then we accept the NH and the result is said to be 'not significant' (NS for short). If the modulus of the test statistic is greater than the tabulated value for $P = 0.05$, then we reject the NH in favour of the alternative hypothesis that the treatments had different effects and the result is 'statistically significant'.

Two types of error are possible when making a conclusion on the basis of a statistical test. The first occurs if you reject the NH when it is true and the second if you accept the NH when it is false. To limit the chance of the first type of error, choose a lower probability, e.g. $P = 0.01$, but note that the critical value of the test statistic increases when you do this and results in the probability of the second error increasing. The conventional significance levels given in statistical tables (usually 0.05, 0.01, 0.001) are arbitrary. Increasing use of statistical computer programs now allows the actual probability of obtaining the calculated value of the test statistic to be quoted (e.g. $P = 0.037$).

Note that if the NH is rejected, this does not tell you which of many alternative explanations are true. Also, it is important to distinguish between statistical significance and biological relevance: identifying a statistically significant difference between two samples doesn't mean that this will carry any biological importance.

Comparing data with parametric distributions

A parametric test is one that makes particular assumptions about the mathematical nature of the population distribution from which the samples were taken. If these assumptions are not true, then the test is obviously invalid, even though it might give the answer we expect. A non-parametric test does not assume that the data fit a particular pattern, but it may assume some things about the distributions. Used in appropriate circumstances, parametric tests are better able to distinguish between true but marginal differences between samples than their non-parametric equivalents (i.e. they have greater 'power').

The distribution pattern of a set of data values may be biologically relevant, but it is also of practical importance because it defines the type of statistical tests that can be used. The properties of the main distribution types found in biology are given below with both rules-of-thumb and more rigorous tests for deciding whether data fit these distributions.

Binomial distributions

These apply to samples of any size from populations when data values occur independently in only two mutually exclusive classes (e.g. type A or type B). They describe the probability of finding the different possible

---

Definition

Modulus – the absolute value of a number, e.g. modulus −3.385 = 3.385.

Quoting significance – the convention for quoting significance levels in text, tables and figures is as follows:
P > 0.05 = 'not significant' (or NS)
*P = 0.05 = 'significant' (or *)*
*P = 0.01 = 'highly significant' (or **)*
*P = 0.001 = 'very highly significant' (or ***)*
Thus, you might refer to a difference in means as being 'highly significant (P < 0.01)'. For this reason, the word 'significant' in its everyday meaning of 'important' or 'notable' should be used with care in scientific writing.

Choosing between parametric and non-parametric tests – always plot your data graphically when determining whether they are suitable for parametric tests as this may save a lot of unnecessary effort later.

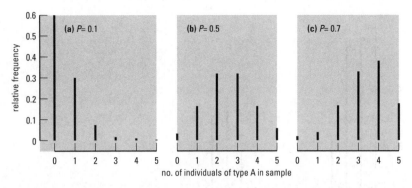

Fig. 67.2 Examples of binomial frequency distributions with different probabilities. The distributions show the expected frequency of obtaining *n* individuals of type A in a sample of 5. Here *P* is the probability of an individual being type A rather than type B.

combinations of the attribute for a specified sample size k (e.g. out of 10 specimens, what is the chance of 8 being type A). If p is the probability of the attribute being of type A and q the probability of it being type B, then the expected mean sample number of type A is kp and the standard deviation is $\sqrt{kpq}$. Expected frequencies can be calculated using mathematical expressions (see Sokal and Rohlf, 1994). Examples of the shapes of some binomial distributions are shown in Fig. 67.2. Note that they are symmetrical in shape for the special case $p = q = 0.5$ and the greater the disparity between p and q, the more skewed the distribution.

Some biological examples of data likely to be distributed in binomial fashion are: possession of two alleles for seed coat morphology (e.g. smooth and wrinkly); whether an organism is infected with a microbe or not; whether an animal is male or female. Binomial distributions are particularly useful for predicting gene segregation in Mendelian genetics and can be used for testing whether combinations of events have occurred more frequently than predicted (e.g. more siblings being of the same sex than expected). To establish whether a set of data is distributed in binomial fashion: calculate expected frequencies from probability values obtained from theory or observation, then test against observed frequencies using a χ^2-test (p. 415) or a G-test (see Wardlaw, 2000).

Poisson distributions

These apply to discrete characteristics which can assume low whole number values, such as counts of events occurring in area, volume or time. The events should be 'rare' in that the mean number observed should be a small proportion of the total that could possibly be found. Also, finding one count should not influence the probability of finding another. The shape of Poisson distributions is described by only one parameter, the mean number of events observed, and has the special characteristic that the variance is equal to the mean. The shape has a pronounced positive skewness at low mean counts, but becomes more and more symmetrical as the mean number of counts increases (Fig. 67.3).

Some examples of characteristics distributed in a Poisson fashion are: number of plants in a quadrat; number of microbes per unit volume of medium; number of animals parasitised per unit time; number of radioactive disintegrations per unit time. One of the main uses for the Poisson distribution is to quantify errors in count data such as estimates of

Tendency towards the normal distribution – *under certain conditions, binomial and Poisson distributions can be treated as normally distributed:*

- *where samples from a binomial distribution are large (i.e. > 15) and p and q are close to 0.5;*
- *for Poisson distributions, if the number of counts recorded in each outcome is greater than about 15.*

Fig. 67.3 Examples of Poisson frequency distributions differing in mean. The distributions are shown as line charts because the independent variable (events per sample) is discrete.

cell densities in dilute suspensions (see p. 228). To decide whether data are Poisson distributed:

- Use the rule of thumb that if the coefficient of dispersion ≈ 1, the distribution is likely to be Poisson.
- Calculate 'expected' frequencies from the equation for the Poisson distribution and compare with actual values using a χ^2-test or a G-test.

It is sometimes of interest to show that data are *not* distributed in a Poisson fashion, e.g. the distribution of parasite larvae in hosts. If $s^2/\bar{Y} > 1$, the data are 'clumped' and occur together more than would be expected by chance; if $s^2/\bar{Y} < 1$, the data are 'repulsed' and occur together less frequently than would be expected by chance.

Definition

Coefficient of dispersion $= s^2/\bar{Y}$. This is an alternative measure of dispersion to the coefficient of variation (p. 480).

Normal distributions (Gaussian distributions)
These occur when random events act to produce variability in a continuous characteristic (quantitative variable). This situation occurs

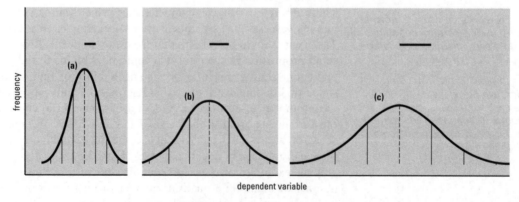

Fig. 67.4 Examples of normal frequency distributions differing in mean and standard deviation. The horizontal bars represent population standard deviations for the curves, increasing from (a) to (c). Vertical dashed lines are population means, while vertical solid lines show positions of values ± 1, 2 and 3 standard deviations from the means.

Fig. 67.5 Example of a normal probability plot. The plotted points are from a small data set where the mean $\bar{Y} = 6.93$ and the standard deviation $s = 1.895$. Note that values corresponding to 0% and 100% cumulative frequency cannot be used. The straight line is that predicted for a normal distribution with $\bar{Y} = 6.93$ and $s = 1.895$. This is plotted by calculating the expected positions of points for $\bar{Y} \pm s$. Since 68.3% of the distribution falls within these bounds, the relevant points on the cumulative frequency scale are $50 \pm 34.15\%$; thus this line was drawn using the points (4.495, 15.85) and (8.285, 84.15) as indicated on the plot.

frequently in biology, so normal distributions are very useful and much used. The bell-like shape of normal distributions is specified by the population mean and standard deviation (Fig. 67.4): it is symmetrical and configured such that 68.27% of the data will lie within ± 1 standard deviation of the mean, 95.45% within ± 2 standard deviations of the mean, and 99.73% within ± 3 standard deviations of the mean.

Some biological examples of data likely to be distributed in a normal fashion are: fresh weight of plants of the same age; linear dimensions of bacterial cells; height of either adult female or male humans. To check whether data come from a normal distribution, you can:

- Use the rule of thumb that the distribution should be symmetrical and that nearly all the data should fall within $\pm 3s$ of the mean and about two-thirds within $\pm 1s$ of the mean.
- Plot the distribution on normal probability graph paper. If the distribution is normal, the data will tend to follow a straight line (see Fig. 67.5). Deviations from linearity reveal skewness and/or kurtosis (see p. 420), the significance of which can be tested statistically (see Sokal and Rohlf, 1994).
- Use a suitable statistical computer program to generate predicted normal curves from the $\bar{Y}$ and s values of your sample(s). These can be compared visually with the actual distribution of data and can be used to give 'expected' values for a χ^2-test or a G-test.

The wide availability of tests based on the normal distribution and their relative simplicity means you may wish to transform your data to make them more like a normal distribution. Table 67.1 provides transformations that can be applied. The transformed data should be tested for normality as described above before proceeding – don't forget that you may need to check that transformed variances are homogeneous for certain tests (see below).

A very important theorem in statistics, the Central Limit Theorem, states that as sample size increases, the distribution of a series of means from any frequency distribution will become normally distributed. This fact can be used to devise an experimental or sampling strategy that ensures that data are normally distributed, i.e. using means of samples as if they were primary data.

Table 67.1 Suggested transformations altering different types of frequency distribution to the normal type. To use, modify data by the formula shown; then examine effects with the tests described on pp. 486–9.

Type of data; distribution suspected	Suggested transformation(s)
Proportions (including percentages); binomial	arcsine $\sqrt{x}$ (also called the angular transformation)
Scores; Poisson	$\sqrt{x}$ or $\sqrt{(x + 1/2)}$ if zero values present
Measurements; negatively skewed	x^2, x^3, x^4, etc. (in order of increasing strength)
Measurements; positively skewed	$1/\sqrt{x}$, $\sqrt{x}$, $\ln x$, $1/x$ (in order of increasing strength)

Checking the assumptions of a test – always acquaint yourself with the assumptions of a test. If necessary, test them before using the test.

Choosing a suitable statistical test

Comparing location (e.g. means)

If you can assume that your data are normally distributed, the main test for comparing two means from independent samples is Student's t-test (see Boxes 67.1 and 67.2, and Table 67.2). This assumes that the variances of the data sets are homogeneous. Tests based on the t-distribution are also available for comparing means of paired data or for comparing a sample mean with a chosen value.

When comparing means of two or more samples, analysis of variance (ANOVA) is a very useful technique. This method also assumes data are normally distributed and that the variances of the samples are homogeneous. The samples must also be independent (e.g. not subsamples). The nested types of ANOVA are useful for letting you know the relative importance of different sources of variability in your data. Two-way and multi-way ANOVAs are useful for studying interactions between treatments.

For data satisfying the ANOVA requirements, the least significant difference (LSD) is useful for making planned comparisons among several means (see Sokal and Rohlf, 1994). Any two means that differ by more than the LSD will be significantly different. The LSD is useful for showing on graphs.

The chief non-parametric tests for comparing the locations of two samples are the Mann–Whitney U-test and the Kolmogorov–Smirnov test. The former assumes that the frequency distributions of the samples are similar, whereas the latter makes no such assumption. In both cases the sample's size must be $\geqslant 4$ and for the Kolmogorov–Smirnov test the samples must have equal sizes. In the Kolmogorov–Smirnov test, significant differences found with the test could be due to differences in location or shape of the distribution, or both.

Table 67.2 Critical values of Student's t statistic (for two-tailed tests). Reject the null hypothesis at probability P if your calculated t value exceeds the value shown for the appropriate degrees of freedom $= (n_1 - 1) + (n_2 - 1)$

Degrees of freedom	Critical values for $P = 0.05$	Critical values for $P = 0.01$	Critical values for $P = 0.001$
1	12.71	63.66	636.62
2	4.30	9.92	31.60
3	3.18	5.84	12.94
4	2.78	4.60	8.61
5	2.57	4.03	6.86
6	2.45	3.71	5.96
7	2.36	3.50	5.40
8	2.31	3.36	5.04
9	2.26	3.25	4.78
10	2.23	3.17	4.59
12	2.18	3.06	4.32
14	2.14	2.98	4.14
16	2.12	2.92	4.02
20	2.09	2.85	3.85
25	2.06	2.79	3.72
30	2.04	2.75	3.65
40	2.02	2.70	3.55
60	2.00	2.66	3.46
120	1.98	2.62	3.37
∞	1.96	2.58	3.29

Box 67.1   How to carry out a *t*-test

The *t*-test was devised by a statistician who used the pen-name 'Student', so you may see it referred to as Student's *t*-test. It is used when you wish to decide whether two samples come from the same population or from different ones (Fig. 67.1). The samples might have been obtained by observation, or by applying two different treatments to an originally homogeneous population (Chapter 30).

The null hypothesis (NH) is that the two groups can be represented as samples from the same overlying population (Fig. 67.1a). If, as a result of the test, you accept this hypothesis, you can say that there is no significant difference between the group means.

The alternative hypothesis is that the two groups come from different populations (Fig. 67.1b). By rejecting the NH as a result of the test, you can accept the alternative hypothesis and say that there is a significant difference between the sample means, or, if an experiment were carried out, that the two treatments affected the samples differently.

How can you decide between these two hypotheses? On the basis of certain assumptions (see below), and some relatively simple calculations, you can work out the probability that the samples came from the same population. If this probability is very low, then you can reasonably reject the NH in favour of the alternative hypothesis, and if it is high, you will accept the NH.

To find out the probability that the observed difference between sample means arose by chance, you must first calculate a '*t* value' for the two samples in question. Some computer programs (e.g. Minitab®) provide this probability as part of the output, otherwise you can look up statistical tables (e.g. Table 67.2). These tables show 'critical values' – the borders between probability levels. If your value of *t* exceeds the critical value for probability *P*, you can reject the NH at this probability ('level of significance').

Note that:

- for a given difference in the means of the two samples, the value of *t* will get larger the smaller the scatter within each data set; and
- for a given scatter of the data, the value of *t* will get larger, the greater the difference between the means.

So, at what probability should you reject the NH? Normally, the threshold is arbitrarily set at 5% – you quite often see descriptions like 'the sample means were significantly different ($P < 0.05$)'. At this 'significance level' there is still up to a 5% chance of the *t* value arising by chance, so about 1 in 20 times, on average, the conclusion will be wrong. If *P* turns out to be lower, then this kind of error is much less likely.

Tabulated probability levels are generally given for 5%, 1% and 0.1% significance levels (see Table 67.2). Note that this table is designed for 'two-tailed' tests, i.e. where the treatment or sampling strategy could have resulted in either an increase or a decrease in the measured values. These are the most likely situations you will deal with in biology.

Examine Table 67.2 and note the following:

- The larger the size of the samples (i.e. the greater the 'degrees of freedom'), the smaller *t* needs to be to exceed the critical value at a given significance level.
- The lower the probability, the greater *t* needs to be to exceed the critical value.

The mechanics of the test

A calculator that can work out means and standard deviations is helpful.

1. **Work out the sample means $\bar{Y}_1$ and $\bar{Y}_2$ and calculate the difference between them.**

2. **Work out the sample standard deviations s_1 and s_2.** (NB if your calculator offers a choice, choose the '$n - 1$' option for calculating s – see p. 480).

3. **Work out the sample standard errors $SE_1 = s_1/\sqrt{n_1}$ and $SE_2 = s_2/\sqrt{n_2}$; now square each, add the squares together, then take the positive square root of this** (n_1 and n_2 are the respective sample sizes, which may, or may not, not be equal).

4. **Calculate *t* from the formula:**

$$t = \frac{\bar{Y}_1 - \bar{Y}_2}{\sqrt{((SE_1)^2) + ((SE_2)^2)}} \qquad [67.1]$$

The value of *t* can be negative or positive, depending on the values of the means; this does not matter and you should compare the modulus (absolute value) of *t* with the values in tables.

5. **Work out the degrees of freedom $= (n_1 - 1) + (n_2 - 1)$.**

6. **Compare the *t* value with the appropriate critical value (see e.g. Table 67.2).**

Box 67.2 provides a worked example – use this to check that you understand the above procedures.

Assumptions that must be met before using the test

The most important assumptions are:

- The two samples are independent and randomly drawn (or if not, drawn in a way that does not create bias). The test assumes that the samples are quite large.
- The underlying distribution of each sample is normal. This can be tested with a special statistical test, but a rule of thumb is that a frequency distribution of the data should be (a) symmetrical about the mean and (b) nearly all of the data should be within 3 standard deviations of the mean and about two-thirds within 1 standard deviation of the mean (see p. 489).
- The two samples should have uniform variances. This again can be tested (by an *F*-test), but may be obvious from inspection of the two standard deviations.

Box 67.2 Worked example of a *t*-test

Suppose the following data were obtained in an experiment (the units are not relevant):

Control: 6.6, 5.5, 6.8, 5.8, 6.1, 5.9
Treatment: 6.3, 7.2, 6.5, 7.1, 7.5, 7.3

Using the steps outlined in Box 67.1, the following values are obtained (denoting control with subscript 1, treatment with subscript 2):

1. $\bar{Y}_1 = 6.1167$; $\bar{Y}_2 = 6.9833$: difference between means $= \bar{Y}_1 - \bar{Y}_2 = -0.8666$

2. $s_1 = 0.495\,65$; $s_2 = 0.475\,04$

3. $SE_1 = 0.495\,65/2.449\,49 = 0.202\,348$
   $SE_2 = 0.475\,04/2.449\,49 = 0.193\,934$

4. $t = \dfrac{-0.8666}{\sqrt{(0.202\,348^2 + 0.193\,934^2)}} = \dfrac{-0.8666}{0.280\,277} = -3.09$

5. d.f. $= (5 + 5) = 10$

6. Looking at Table 67.2, we see that the modulus of this *t* value exceeds the tabulated value for $P = 0.05$ at 10 degrees of freedom ($= 2.23$). We therefore reject the NH, and conclude that the means are different at the 5% level of significance. If the modulus of *t* had been < 2.23, we would have accepted the NH. If modulus of *t* had been > 3.17, we could have concluded that the means are different at the 1% level of significance.

Suitable non-parametric comparisons of location for paired data (sample size $\geqslant 6$) include Wilcoxon's signed rank test, which is used for quantitative data and assumes that the distributions have similar shape. Dixon and Mood's sign test can be used for paired data scores where one variable is recorded as 'greater than' or 'better than' the other.

Non-parametric comparisons of location for three or more samples include the Kruskal–Wallis *H*-test. Here, the number of samples is without limit and they can be unequal in size, but again the underlying distributions are assumed to be similar. The Friedman *S*-test operates with a maximum of five samples and data must conform to a randomised block design. The underlying distributions of the samples are assumed to be similar.

Comparing dispersions (e.g. variances)

If you wish to compare the variances of two sets of data that are normally distributed, use the *F*-test. For comparing more than two samples, it may be sufficient to use the F_{max}-test, on the highest and lowest variances. The Scheffé–Box (log-ANOVA) test is recommended for testing the significance of differences between several variances. Non-parametric tests exist but are not widely available: you may need to transform the data and use a test based on the normal distribution.

Determining whether frequency observations fit theoretical expectation

The χ^2-test (Box 58.2) is useful for tests of 'goodness of fit', e.g. comparing expected and observed progeny frequencies in genetical experiments or comparing observed frequency distributions with some theoretical function. One limitation is that simple formulae for calculating χ^2 assume that no expected number is less than 5. The *G*-test (*2I* test) is used in similar circumstances.

Comparing proportion data

When comparing proportions between two small groups (e.g. whether 3/10 is significantly different from 5/10), you can use probability tables such as those of Finney *et al.* (1963) or calculate probabilities from formulae; however, this can be tedious for large sample sizes. Certain proportions can be transformed so that their distribution becomes normal.

Fig. 67.6 Graphical representation of confidence limits as 'error bars' for (a) a sample mean in a plotted curve, where both upper and lower limits are shown; and (b) a sample mean in a histogram, where, by convention, only the upper value is shown. For data that are assumed to be symmetrically distributed, such representations are often used in preference to the 'box and whisker' plot shown on p. 479. Note that SE is an alternative way of representing sample imprecision/error (e.g. Fig. 63.1).

Confidence limits for statistics other than the mean – consult an advanced statistical text (e.g. Sokal and Rohlf, 1994) if you wish to indicate the reliability of estimates of e.g. population variances.

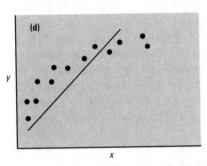

Fig. 67.7 Examples of correlation. The linear regression line is shown. In (a) and (b), the correlation between *x* and *y* is good: for (a) there is a positive correlation and the correlation coefficient, *r*, would be close to 1; for (b) there is a negative correlation and the correlation coefficient would be close to −1. In (c) there is a weak positive correlation and *r* would be close to 0. In (d) the correlation coefficient may be quite large, but the choice of linear regression is clearly inappropriate.

Placing confidence limits on an estimate of a population parameter

On many occasions, a sample statistic is used to provide an estimate of a population parameter, and it is often useful to indicate the reliability of such an estimate. This can be done by putting confidence limits on the sample statistic, i.e. by specifying an interval around the statistic within which you are confident that the true value (the population parameter) is likely to fall, at a specified level of probability. The most common application is to place confidence limits on the mean of a sample taken from a population of normally distributed data values. In practice, you determine a confidence factor for a particular level of probability which is added to and subtracted from the sample mean ($\bar{Y}$) to give the upper confidence limit and lower confidence limit respectively. These are calculated as:

$$\bar{Y} + (t_{P[n-1]} \times \text{SE}) \text{ for the upper limit and}$$
$$\bar{Y} - (t_{P[n-1]} \times \text{SE}) \text{ for the lower limit} \qquad [67.2]$$

where $t_{P[n-1]}$ is the tabulated critical value of Student's *t*-statistic for a two-tailed test with $n - 1$ degrees of freedom at a specified probability level (P) and SE is the standard error of the sample mean (p. 480). The 95% confidence limits (i.e. $P = 0.05$) tells you that on average, 95 times out of 100, the interval between the upper and lower limits will contain the true (population) value. Confidence limits are often shown as 'error bars' for individual sample means plotted in graphical form. Figure 67.6 illustrates how this is applied to plotted curves and histograms (note that this can be carried out for data series within a Microsoft Excel® graph (chart) using the *Format data series* and *Y error bars* commands).

Correlation and regression

These methods are used when testing the relationship between data values for two variables. Correlation is used to measure the extent to which changes in the two sets of data values occur together in a linear manner. If one variable can be assumed to be dependent upon the other (i.e. a change in *X* causes a particular change in *Y*), then regression techniques can be used to provide a mathematical description of the underlying relationship between the variables, e.g. to find a line of best fit for a data series. If there is no *a priori* reason to assume dependency, then correlation methods alone are appropriate.

A correlation coefficient measures the strength of the linear relationship between two variables, but does not describe the relationship. The coefficient is expressed as a number between −1 and +1: a positive coefficient indicates a direct relationship, where the two variables change in the same direction, while a negative coefficient indicates an inverse relationship, where one variable decreases as the other increases (Fig. 67.7). The nearer the coefficient is to −1 or +1, the stronger the linear relationship between the variables, i.e. the less 'scatter' there would be about a straight line of best fit (note that this does *not* imply that one variable is dependent upon the other). A coefficient of 0 implies that the two variables show no linear association and therefore the closer the correlation coefficient is to zero, the weaker the linear relationship. The importance of graphing data is shown by the case illustrated in Fig. 67.7d.

Pearson's product moment correlation coefficient (*r*) is the most commonly used statistic for testing correlations. The test is valid only if both variables are normally distributed. Statistical tests can be used to decide whether the correlation is significant (e.g. using a one-sample t-test to see whether r is significantly different from zero, based on the equation $t = r \div \sqrt{[(1 - r^2) \div (n - 2)]}$ at $n - 2$ degrees of freedom). If one or both variables are not normally distributed, then you should calculate an alternative non-parametric coeffcient, e.g. Spearman's coefficient of rank correlation (r_S) or Kendall's coefficient of rank correlation (τ). These require the two sets of data to be ranked separately, and the calculation can be complex if there are tied (equal) ranks. Spearman's coefficient is said to be better if there is any uncertainty about the reliability of closely ranked data values.

If underlying theory or empirical graphical analysis indicates a linear relationship between a dependent and an independent variable, then linear regression can be used to estimate the mathematical equation that links the two variables. Model I linear regression is the standard approach, and is available within general-purpose software programs such as Excel®, and on some scientific calculators. It is suitable for experiments where a dependent variable Y varies with an *error-free* independent variable X in accordance with the relationship $Y = a + bX + e_Y$, where e_Y represents the residual (error) variability in the Y variable. For example, this relationship might apply in a laboratory procedure where you have carefully controlled the independent variable and the X values can be assumed to have zero error (e.g. in a calibration curve, see Chapter 37, or in a time course experiment where measurements are made at exact time points). The regression analysis gives estimates for a and b (equivalent to the slope and intercept of the line of best fit, p. 471): computer-based programs usually provide additional features, e.g. residual values for Y (e_Y), estimated errors for a and b, predicted values of Y along with graphical plots of the line of best fit (the trend line) and the residual values. In order for the model to be valid, the residual (error) values should be normally distributed around the trend line and their variance should be uniform (homogeneous), i.e. there should be a similar scatter of data points around the trend line along the x-axis (independent variable).

If the relationship is not linear, try a transformation. For example, this is commonly done in analysis of enzyme kinetics (see Fig. 55.4). However, you should be aware that the transformation of data to give a straight line can lead to errors when carrying out linear regression analysis: take care to ensure that (a) the assumptions listed in the previous paragraph are valid for the transformed data set and (b) the data points are evenly distributed throughout the range of the independent variable. If these criteria cannot be met, non-linear regression may be a better approach, but for this you will require a suitable computer program, e.g. GraphPad Prism®.

The strength of the relationship between Y and X in model I linear regression is best estimated by the coefficient of determination (r^2 or R^2), which is equivalent to the square of the Pearson correlation coefficient. The coefficient of determination varies between 0 and $+1$ and provides a measure of the goodness of fit of the Y data to the regression line: the closer the value is to 1, the better the fit. In effect, r^2 represents the fraction of the variance in Y that can be accounted for by the regression equation. Conversely, if you subtract this value from 1, you will obtain the residual (error) component, i.e. the fraction of the variance in Y that cannot be

---

Using more advanced types of regression – these include:

- *Model II linear regression, which applies to situations where a dependent variable Y varies with an independent variable X, and where both variables may have error terms associated with them.*
- *Multiple regression, which applies when there is a relationship between a dependent variable and two or more independent variables.*
- *Non-linear regression, which extends the principles of linear regression to a wide range of functions. Technically, this method is more appropriate than transforming data to allow linear regression.*

Advanced statistics books should be consulted for details of these methods, which also may be offered by some statistical computer programs.

Example If a regression analysis gives a value for r^2 of 0.75 (i.e. $r = 0.84$), then 75% of the variance in Y can be explained by the trend line, with $1 - r^2 = 0.25$ (25%) remaining as unexplained (residual) variation.

explained by the line of best fit. Multiplying the values by 100 allows you to express these fractions in percentage terms.

Text references and sources for further study

Dytham, C. (2003) *Choosing and Using Statistics: A Biologists' Guide*, 2nd edn. Blackwell, Oxford.

Finney, D.J., Latscha, R., Bennett, B.M. and Hsu, P. (1963) *Tables for Testing Significance in a 2 × 2 Table*. Cambridge University Press, Cambridge.

Heath, D. (1995) *An Introduction to Experimental Design and Statistics for Biology*. UCL Press Ltd, London.

Maber, J. (1999) *Data Analysis for Biomolecular Sciences*. Longman, Harlow.

Sokal, R.R. and Rohlf, F.J. (1994) *Biometry*, 3rd edn. W.H. Freeman and Co., San Francisco.

Wardlaw, A.C. (2000) *Practical Statistics for Experimental Biologists*, 2nd edn. Wiley, New York.

Study exercises

67.1 Calculate 95% confidence limits. What are the 95% confidence limits of a sample with a mean = 24.7, standard deviation = 6.8 and number of data values = 16? (Express your answer to 3 significant figures.)

67.2 Use the Poisson distribution. In a sample of 15 snails, a researcher finds the following number of parasite larvae per snail: 0, 0, 0, 0, 1, 1, 1, 3, 4, 5, 5, 7, 7, 9, 9. Using the rules of thumb on p. 426, decide whether the parasites are 'clumped' or 'repulsed' in distribution on their host. What might this mean in biological terms?

67.3 Practise using a *t*-test. A biology student examined the effect of adding a plant hormone to pea plants. She dissolved an appropriate amount of the compound in ethanol and applied $25\mu l$ of this to the topmost parts of the treated plants. With the controls, she applied the same amount of pure ethanol. After 3 days, she measured the distance between the second and third internodes of the plants and obtained the results shown below. Carry out a *t*-test on the data and draw appropriate conclusions.

Internode distance in cm

Control	7.5	8.1	7.6	6.2	7.5	7.8	8.9
Treatment	5.6	7.5	8.2	6.7	3.5	6.5	5.9

67.4 Interpret the output from Excel® linear regression analysis. The following output represents a regression analysis for an experiment measuring the uptake of an amino acid by a cell suspension (in $pmol\,cell^{-1}$) against time (in minutes). Based on this output, what is the form and strength of the underlying linear relationship? (Express the coefficients to 3 significant figures.)

Output from Excel® spreadsheet linear regression analysis

Summary output

Regression statistics	
Multiple R	0.985335951
R square	0.970886937
Adjusted R square	0.963608672
Standard error	2.133876419
Observations	6

ANOVA

	df	SS	MS	F	Significance F
Regression	1	607.4062857	607.4063	133.3954	0.000320975
Residual	4	18.21371429	4.553429		
Total	5	625.62			

	Coefficients	Standard error	t Stat	P-value	Lower 95%	Upper 95%	Lower 95.0%	Upper 95.0%
Intercept	1.171428571	1.544386367	0.758507	0.490383	−3.11648428	5.459341423	−3.11648428	5.459341423
X variable 1	2.945714286	0.255047014	11.54969	0.000321	2.237588784	3.653839787	2.237588784	3.653839787

Answers to study exercises

We have attempted to provide an 'answer' to all of the study exercises. Where the question is open-ended and no 'correct' answer can be given, we have provided a *Tip* or *Tips*, which should either help with your general approach, indicate which resources are worth consulting, or provide a pointer to relevant material within the book. Where a non-numerical question has a 'correct' answer, we have provided a model text-based answer. If a calculation is involved, we have shown the steps involved and have indicated the **correct answer underlined in bold**.

1 The importance of transferable skills

1.1 *Tips:* Where you feel confident about skills you have learned at school, take care to consider whether they might need to be upgraded for university/college use. When thinking about opportunities for developing skills, remember that these may occur outside university, perhaps in work or social contexts.

1.2 *Tip:* Possible keywords/phrases for a Web search include: biology skills, C&IT skills, numeracy skills, study skills, time management.

1.3 *Tip:* You could create a grid to record your thoughts, with column headings 'University'; 'Work' and 'Social' and rows for 'Short term'; 'Medium term' and 'Long term'. Short term and medium term could refer to your time at university, while long term could refer to after graduation.

2 Managing your time

2.1 *Tips:* Model your spreadsheet on Fig. 2.1. It isn't too difficult to fill in details at the end of each day either directly into the spreadsheet or on a printed version. You will need to collect information for at least a week and possibly longer before you see patterns emerging.

2.2 *Tips:* It is important to include both social and study-related activities on your lists. Short-term lists deal with issues of the day or week; medium-term for the term or semester and longer-term for one year onwards. Relate each of these lists to appropriate goals you may have over these timescales.

2.3 *Tips:* This task could be related to (a) your self-analysis of transferable skills (Chapter 1), or (b) to some large task such as carrying out a final-year project. In the latter case, for example, there are small jobs that can be done as you proceed with the larger task, such as writing parts of the Introduction or compiling a list of references, and these will reduce time pressure towards the end of the task.

3 Working with others

3.1 *Tips:* Think about your contributions to past group activities while doing this exercise, and, if necessary, get feedback from friends and colleagues. You may feel that you fit into more than one 'natural' role: this is quite often the case.

3.2 *Tip:* This exercise might best be associated with a specific teamwork activity, but this need not be restricted to study – group contributions with clubs, societies or in employment are equally valid. Strategies for improvement will depend on your identified weaknesses. For example, if you felt too shy to contribute effectively, you might want to practise public speaking (see Chapter 15) or attend an assertiveness workshop.

3.3 *Tip:* Columns 4 and 5 of Table 3.1 are relevant, particularly if you are able to identify a 'natural' role or roles for yourself in group situations (as in exercise 3.1). Can you relate your strengths and weaknesses to specific events that have occurred during teamwork, and might you handle the situation differently in future?

4 Taking notes

4.1 *Tips:* If you are used to using a particular note-taking method that seems to work well, you may feel reluctant to experiment. Try out the new method by taking notes at a seminar, tutorial or meeting where it will not matter so much if the technique does not work well at the first attempt.

4.2 *Tip:* Make a list of any missing notes or handouts and ask a colleague if you can work from their notes to fill in these gaps.

4.3 *Tip:* To compare methods, test your recall some time afterwards. Take a blank sheet of paper and see what you can write about each topic.

5 Revising

5.1 *Tips:* When constructing your revision timetable, remember the following important points:
- Break large topics into 'bite-sized' units.
- Mix up hard or less interesting topics with those you enjoy revising (don't ignore them).
- Keep an appropriate balance between work and relaxation.
- Offer yourself rewards if work targets are completed.

5.2 *Tips:* You may wish to keep one of the past papers (preferably a recent one) aside to use in a mock exam. Remember that learning objectives can be just as important as exam papers in helping you to revise.

5.3 *Tips:* Read through the list of active revision tips on pp. 22–4 and decide which might work best for you. Carry out a trial of the method with one of your topics where the material has seemed difficult to learn. Experiment until you arrive at a solution that works, remembering (a) that different techniques might work best in different subjects and (b) a little variety might make the revision process more interesting.

Answers to study exercises

6 Assessments and exams

6.1 *Tip:* Some questions to ask yourself about past exam performances... Did you prepare well enough? Did you run out of time during the exam? Did you spend too long on a particular question or section, and have to rush another? Were your answers direct and at the appropriate depth? Did you misinterpret any questions, or miss out part of any answers? Were your writing skills, including planning, up to the standard required?

6.2 *Tip:* When revising, try to find a topic you find hard to understand and see whether your colleague has approached it in the same way as you. If not, you may be able to learn from this.

6.3 *Tip:* Discuss your tactics with a colleague sitting the same exam. What topics do you agree are likely to come up?

7 Preparing your curriculum vitae

7.1 *Tip:* This exercise might be attempted with a friend you can trust to give you a frank opinion. Remember that your personal qualities can be developed in both curricular and extra-curricular activities.

7.2 *Tip:* Working with a friend or group from your class, compare notes on how you have organised your CVs and then modify your own CV, taking on board good ideas from your peers. Create a physical file for your revised CV and add handwritten notes, updating it as and when required.

7.3 *Tip:* Use the 'Prospects' website noted in the sources for further study to gain ideas before your appointment with the careers service. The library or careers resource centre may have useful information, often accessible *via* the Web.

8 Finding and citing published information

8.1
(a) The Dewey Decimal Classification system; the US Library of Congress system; or other, as appropriate.
(b) *Nature*: Dewey: 505.0942; Library of Congress: Q1.N3; (or other, as appropriate). Note: the 'Per' or 'per' that may precede these numbers refers to the fact that this is a periodical, rather than a book.
(c) *Tip:* Answer as appropriate – this will depend on the layout of your particular library.
(d) (i) 'A structure for deoxyribose nucleic acid'; (ii) 'Analysis of the genome sequence of the flowering plant *Arabidopsis thaliana*'.

8.2 *Tips:* The main point here is that methods of writing down references are diverse. You should also find that the details recorded are the same, although they may be in a different order or font style. You must pay attention to the *precise* instructions given for your course, to ensure that you get this right when writing up a project report or dissertation.

8.3 *Tips:* Three possible sites are:
(a) SI units: http://www.ex.ac.uk/cimt/dictunit/dictunit.htm (last accessed 08/01/03)
(b) l'Institut Pasteur: http://www.pasteur.fr/externe (last accessed 08/01/03) is your starting point.

Reaching the culture collection is a little tricky – try via '*Scientific Research*', '*Biological Resources*', '*Bacteria Strain Search*'.
(c) Blood cells: http://www.ultranet.com/~jkimball/BiologyPages/B/Blood.html (last accessed 08/01/03).

8.4 *Tips:* When writing a handwritten essay, the variant of the Vancouver method in which references are listed in the order cited might be the most convenient to use, because you could write down all the references cited on a separate sheet as you wrote out the essay. However, if you felt that it was important for the reader to see the author(s) and publication dates of the papers, then the Harvard method might be more appropriate – however, you would need to wait until the essay was fully written before organising the literature cited section in author and date order. In a word processed review, you might prefer the Vancouver method as this might allow the text to flow more smoothly without being interrupted by lists of author names and dates. On the other hand, the Harvard system is easier to use as you write with a word processor, because you can simply 'slot' each new reference into the correct place in the list. In an academic journal, it might be assumed that the readership would want to know the authors and dates of the references cited, so the Harvard system would probably be the most appropriate. In contrast, the journal *Nature* uses the Vancouver system in order to present important new scientific advances to a wide audience. *Nature* readers want to be able to assimilate each paper's findings rapidly without getting distracted by citation details.

9 Evaluating information

9.1 (a) P; (b) P; (c) S; (d) S; (e) P; (f) S; (g) P; (h) P; (i) S; (j) S; (where P = primary, S = secondary). Where journals contain both original papers and reviews, we have classed them as primary.

9.2

Some potential debating points on whether '*Genetic modification of crops is a good thing*'

For	Against
Large increases in yield could be engineered, helping to alleviate hunger in developing countries	Transfer of new genes to other crops might occur, with unknown and unpredictable effects
The range of possible modifications to crops is much greater than in conventional breeding – entirely new forms of crops are possible	'Super weeds' derived from genetically modified plants might spread uncontrollably and disrupt the ecological balance
It is possible to modify crops much faster than with conventional breeding	The long-term effects of e.g. modified proteins on human health are untested

(continued)

Table continued

For	Against
Very specific changes are possible, e.g. adding a particular vitamin or specific amino acid to a crop, effectively improving nutrition rather than calorific intake	Our effort (and money) would be better applied to birth control, basic medicine and better implementation of cropping practice
Genetic modification can be used to deter pests, reducing pesticide use and thereby benefiting the environment	The public are so concerned about the safety of foods derived from genetically modified crops that they will fail economically anyway, since consumers will avoid food labelled as containing genetically modified material

9.3 *Tip:* Use Box 63.2 as a source to indicate ways in which graphs may be used to misrepresent information. You may find this exercise easier to accomplish with printed graphs. Those on television may not be shown for long enough to allow you to carry out a detailed analysis. Nevertheless, they represent a rich source of material to criticise!

10 Using the Internet and World Wide Web

10.1

(a) Barbara McClintock is famous for her work on the discovery of mobile genetic elements (transposons): she won the 1983 Nobel Prize in Medicine. See: http://www.nobel.se/medicine/laureates/1983/

(b) *Arabidopsis thaliana* is also known as mouse-ear cress. See: http://plants.usda.gov/cgi_bin/plant_profile.cgi?symbol=ARTH

(c) The postal address of the UK Biochemical Society is The Biochemical Society, 59 Portland Place, London, W1B 1QW, United Kingdom. See: http://www.biochemistry.org/feedback.htm

10.2 *Tips:* Note the number of hits found for each search engine. Make a note or printout of the top 10 sites located by each search engine. Compare these site listings to reveal the quality of data obtained. Repeat this exercise for meta-search engines. Make lists of the component search engines used by the main meta-search engines to help you devise a strategy for the best coverage of the Internet.

10.3 *Tips:* Within the bookmark editor for your browser, create folders for each of your study courses and then create sub-folders for each module that you are doing. Now use some searches to put relevant bookmarks in each folder. Don't forget to include a folder for transferable skills sites; there are a lot of supportive sites available that are worth visiting.

11 Bioinformatics – Internet resources

11.1

(a) The Entrez nucleotides database of GenBank®, available at: http://www.ncbi.nlm.nih.gov/entrez/query.fcgi?db=Nucleotide contained **20 197 497 568 (over 20 billion) bases on 5 July 2002** (note that this is likely to show a substantial increase over the life of this textbook).

(b) Hinxton Hall is the location of the UK campus of the European Bioinformatics Institute, located at Hinxton, Cambridge (see: http://www.ebi.ac.uk/Information/Travel/travel.html).

(c) Monterotondo, in the Lazio region of Italy, north of Rome (see: http://www.embl-monterotondo.it/ and: http://www.emma.rm.cnr.it/images/map1.html).

(d) PDB held **19 691 structures on 7 Jan 2003** (see: http://www.rcsb.org/pdb/holdings.html#holdings). Note that this number will increase over the life of this textbook.

(e) National Center for Biotechnology Information, National Library of Medicine, Building 38A, Bethesda, MD 20894, USA (see: http://www.ncbi.nlm.nih.gov/About/glance/contact_info.html).

11.2 The sequence gives a single 'hit' for part of the *Homo sapiens* chromosome 15 clone RP11-46M12 map 15q15 (accession code: AC012652), with a total of 17 consecutive identical bases (shown in blue): actgactcatagagtacccaccgtggtgct.

11.3

(a) The amino acid sequence gives a number of 'hits' for the alpha chain of haemoglobin.

(b) The haemoglobin alpha-3 chain from chimpanzee (accession code: HAG03C) gives **100% identity** (all 19 amino acids match).

(c) The highest score for a human sequence is for the alpha-1 globin chain of haemoglobin (AF349571), which gives 18 identical residues out of 19 (≈**95% identity**).

11.4 The results of the six-frame translation are: 5′ to 3′ frame 1: SERTHH; frame 2: QREPT; frame 3: RENPP; 3′ to 5′ frame 1: MetVGSLStop; frame 2: WWVLS; frame 3: GGFSL, so, **3′ to 5′ frame 1 contains a start (methionine) and a stop codon**. The predicted amino acid sequence for this frame is **MVGSL ≡ met-val-gly-ser-leu.** (Note that this sequence is far shorter than in a functional protein.)

11.5 *Tip:* Select *Summary of PDB structure* for key information on structure. The ID number of this enzyme in PDB is 1GOW.

(a) The enzyme is a **homotetramer**.

(b) There are two types of chain in the crystal structure: A and B, each containing **489 residues** with an identical amino acid sequence.

(c) There are **23 helices** in each chain. The structure is mainly parallel β-sheets (β-α-β units). Note that the crystal structure is a dimer whereas the functional enzyme is a tetramer (comprising 2 dimers).

(d) *Tips:* To save an image from a Web page, use the menu provided by clicking the right-hand mouse button ('*Save Pictue As*' function in Internet

Answers to study exercises

Explorer); to insert an image into a Word® document, use the '*Insert*' menu, then the '*Picture*' and '*From File*' options.

12 Using spreadsheets

12.1 See the figure below. ***Tips:*** Depending on the precise method you use, you may need to provide the *Name*, *Values* and *Category Labels* for the *Chart Wizard* or adjust those assumed. When creating the graph, select the 'as new sheet' option when prompted for a *Chart Location*. For printing in black and white, select black and white hatching/shading options after click-selecting chart segments. Ensure the segments of the chart are labelled (i.e. not the default legend option) using the *Chart/Chart Options* menu.

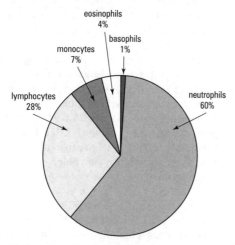

Relative abundance of the major types of leukocytes in adult blood.

12.2 See the figure below. ***Tips:*** When setting up the spreadsheet, create appropriate formulae in new columns for the transformed data; graph using the '*XY (Scatter)*' option in the Microsoft Excel® *Chart Wizard* to make sure the data are correctly spaced on the *x*-axis. Plot time on the *x*-axis and the transformed cell count data on the *y*-axis. You will need to create a separate graph to examine the effects of each transformation, because the *y*-axis

Log-linear graph of data of the table in study exercise 12.2.

scales will be different. Select the *Line None* option for the relevant (log transformed) series on the *Data Series* Menu, then use the *Add Trendline* option (linear model) within the *Chart* menu to add a linear regression line (note: this can also be done using the *Regression* command in the *Data Analysis* option on the *Tools* menu, but the procedures required are much more complex). Adjust the chart output to suit, e.g. by changing gridlines, background and legends, before copying and pasting to the MS Word® document.

12.3 ***Tips:*** Take care when entering the date data in the spreadsheet. You may need to specify the format of the cells for the date column (*Format* menu, *Cells* option). Highlight all parts of the spreadsheet table including column headers, then use the *Data* menu, *AZ↓ Sort* option to rearrange data. You do not need to fill in all the response boxes and can select 'none' if a box contains criteria from a previous sort.

13 Word processors, databases and other packages

13.1 ***Tips:***
(a) Ensure list components are in separate paragraphs; highlight list; from the *Table* menu select *AZ↓ Sort* function; ensure options are set to *paragraphs*, *text*, *ascending*.
(b) From the *Edit* menu, select *Replace* option, then fill in the relevant boxes.
(c) From *Edit* menu, select *Replace* option, then fill in the relevant boxes; select *More* ▾ then *Format*, *Font*, *Italic*.
(d) From the *View* menu, select *Header and Footer* and use the small on-screen menu to add text and numbering as desired. Formatting commands (e.g. centre) will work in the header and footer boxes. As an alternative for adding page numbers, this can be done from the *Insert* menu, *Page Numbers . . .* option.
(e) Margins can be adjusted from *File* menu, *Page Setup*, *Margins* option.
(f) Select paragraphed text, then use the *Format* menu, *Bullets and Numbering* option, using *Customise* if the option you desire is not displayed within the panel.
(g) Type 'alternative' within a Word page. Ensure cursor is within word (or highlight word); from *Tools* menu select *Language*, *Thesaurus* options. Perhaps 'option' might be a useful synonym?
(h) From *Tools* menu, select *Spelling and Grammar* to start a spell check. Take care if the checker queries UK spellings (it may be set to accept US spellings). Note: this is *not* a substitute for reading your document – the spell checker will miss typing errors like 'form' instead of 'from'.
(i) For whole document, triple click in left margin to select all, then use *Tools* menu, *Word Count* option. For selected text, highlight (select) the part you wish to count, then carry out same instructions.
(j) While in first document, use *File* menu, *Open* option to open another. You can switch between them using

the *Window* menu, where you will see all open documents listed. Note: remember to save changes to all documents when closing down your editing session.

13.2 *Tips:* Although there are several ways to modify tables, you may find it useful to try the following commands (think carefully about their order).

- *Table, Insert Table*
- *Table, Merge Cells*
- *Table, Distribute Columns Evenly*
- *Tables and borders*, modify borders commands (various)

Use the *Help* feature if you run into problems.

13.3 *Tips:* You might start your search on the networked 'desktop' and icons visible to you when you log on. Use 'help' menus and 'wizards' to investigate how to use the programs, or consult any manuals available in the computer suite.

14 Organising a poster display

14.1 *Tip:* use Figure 14.1 and the sub-headings of Chapter 14 as a starting point for assessing the pros and cons of your designs.

14.2 Ten-point checklist – what makes a good poster presentation?

- ☐ *Title* – is this concise, specific and interesting?
- ☐ *Author(s)* – does the poster show details of the names and addresses of all contributors?
- ☐ *Structure* – is the overall structure clear to the observer, with good use of sub-headings?
- ☐ *Flow* – is the layout of the poster clear, in terms of how the audience is expected to 'read' each section?
- ☐ *Content* – does the presentation have a clear introduction, main message and conclusion?
- ☐ *Text* – does the poster contain an appropriate amount of written material in a 'readable' font?
- ☐ *Graphics* – does the poster make good use of diagrams, figures and images?
- ☐ *Size and scale* – does the poster make effective use of the space available?
- ☐ *Colour* – does the presentation use colour effectively?
- ☐ *Conclusion* – is the 'take-home message' clear to the observer?

14.3 *Tip:* you might use the 10-point checklist given above, or your own version from exercise 14.2 to assess selected posters by giving a mark out of 10 for each item in the list. In a group exercise, you can see how your 'scores' compare with those of other students, and discuss items where scores are different.

15 Giving a spoken presentation

15.1 Ten-point checklist – what makes a good spoken presentation?

- ☐ *Introduction* – does the speaker explain the structure and rationale of the topic at the outset?
- ☐ *Audience* – is the material presented at an appropriate level?
- ☐ *Content* – does the presentation cover the topic effectively?
- ☐ *Speed and structure* – are the main elements of the presentation presented clearly, and at an appropriate pace?
- ☐ *Voice* – is the presentation delivered in an engaging, active vocal style?
- ☐ *Audio-visual aids* – does the speaker make good use of visual images (e.g. graphs, photographs, etc.)?
- ☐ *Image* – does the presenter make good use of body language?
- ☐ *Notes* – does the speaker use notes to structure the talk, rather than reading from a written text?
- ☐ *Conclusion* – is a clear 'take-home message' delivered in the final stages of the presentation?
- ☐ *Questions* – does the presenter deal with questions effectively?

15.2 *Tips:* You could try marking speakers out of 10 for each of the points listed in exercise 15.1 (either using the checklist provided above or your own version), or you could simply prepare a list of the good and bad points of the presentations you have evaluated.

15.3 *Tips:* When evaluating your own performance: (i) remember that most of us are overcritical when viewing ourselves on video, tending to focus on relatively minor points, e.g. facial expression, rather than broader aspects, e.g. clarity of delivery and content; (ii) when giving a talk to a group of fellow students you might ask them to use all or part of the checklist from exercise 15.1 as a way of providing feedback.

16 General aspects of scientific writing

16.1 *Tips:* When brainstorming, think of all aspects of the topic that could be relevant (even if you could not give precise details at this stage). When you meet together, discuss which of your combined ideas would be most important in crafting an answer and what order you might place them in.

16.2 *Tip:* Try to apply what you have learned in the next assignment you write – ask a tutor for specific feedback if you are unsure about whether your technique has improved.

16.3 *Tips:* Use the spelling list to help you when writing and make a conscious effort to memorise the spelling each time you use it. The act of writing the vocabulary list will assist you to memorise new words and their meanings. If you have trouble learning definitions, e.g. terms in molecular biology, you could extend these ideas to create a personal glossary of terms and acronyms.

17 Writing essays

17.1 *Tip:* Can you determine what lies behind each question? Some question titles are quite direct, but others ask for information in a more subtle way. Use your imagination to think beyond the immediate question, linking to learning objectives or to other relevant material covered in lectures.

17.2 *Tips:* Compare your ideas with those of a partner, or ask tutors or lecturers what they think of your efforts. A useful adjunct to this exercise is to write the first sentence of your answer to avoid writer's block (p. 95).

17.3 *Tips:* Note that each of the stages requires a separate 'review' – it is difficult, if not impossible to make a good job of all aspects in a single 'pass' through the text. Ideally, you would reprint the essay between reviews, having made corrections.

18 Reporting practical and project work

18.1 *Tips:* To assimilate the required style for Materials and Methods, you may find it appropriate to read some research papers from the journal section of your library. Note particularly that the Materials and Methods are a description of 'what was done', not a set of instructions.

18.2 *Tips:* Again, you may find it appropriate to read some research papers from the journal section of your library to assimilate the normal style for describing research results.

18.3 *Tips:* Abstracts are difficult to write: try to include a synopsis of all the main sections of the paper, including its aims, methods, key results and conclusions. Ignore the word length restriction until you have noted the main points, then try to reduce (or, less likely, expand) your effort to match the requirement.

19 Writing literature surveys and reviews

19.1 Five differences between reviews and papers are:
1. Reviews deal with material in general terms, taking an overview, whereas papers tend to look at a focused, single aspect of a topic.
2. The subdivisions are generally not the same – papers usually follow the IMRaD format (p. 103), while reviews are structured according to the major components of the topic.
3. There is little or no reference to original data in reviews.
4. There is little *detail* of methods in reviews.
5. They tend to use different reference citation systems, with Harvard (p. 43) most commonly used in papers and Vancouver (p. 44) used in reviews.

19.2 *Tip:* It should be possible to do the second part of study exercise 19.2 on-line at your library – you may need to enlist the help of library staff if unsure of how to do this.

19.3 *Tip:* Obviously, the Abstract and Conclusions sections will provide information about the key points addressed. It might be helpful to use a highlighter on a photocopied version of the review to note important statements within the main body of the review.

20 Your approach to practical work

20.1 Possible reasons why practical work might be of value in a University course include:
- practicals reinforce lecture material, in agreement with the adage: 'I hear and I forget, I see and I remember, I do and I understand';
- practical procedures provide students with an opportunity to develop their manual skills and laboratory competences;

- investigative procedures and problem-solving practical exercises enable students to improve their skills in experimental design and the application of the scientific method;
- practicals enable students to develop their abilities to observe and measure biological systems, and to record the outcome;
- students are able to analyse and interpret the data from practical exercises and to consider the validity of their results, including sources of error, etc.;
- the results of practical procedures give students an opportunity to develop skills in reporting and presenting 'experiments' in written format.

20.2 *Tip:* Possible items for a snail dissection: scalpel; blunt seekers; coarse and fine scissors; wax dish and pins; pointed seeker; dissection microscope; paper tissues; water; Pasteur pipette; first aid kit near by – in case of accident.

20.3

(a) $\underline{\mathbf{40}}$
(b) 44.266 66°, expressed to 4 significant figures = $\underline{\mathbf{44.27}}$
(c) 0.019 531 25, expressed to 3 significant figures = $\underline{\mathbf{0.0195}}$
(d) $\underline{\mathbf{1.6 \times 10^5}}$
(e) 0.0313, expressed to 3 decimal places = $\underline{\mathbf{0.031}}$

21 Health and safety

21.1

(a) p. 117.
(b) Fig. 21.1 (p. 117).
(c) Fig. 21.2 (p. 118).
(d) Fig. 32.1 (p. 197).
(e) Fig. 39.4 (p. 265).

21.2 *Tip:* The locations of each item will vary, according to the layout of your chosen laboratory. You should ask someone in charge (e.g. demonstrator, lecturer, technician or laboratory manager) if you are unable to find any of the items listed.

21.3

(a) *Tip:* The answer will vary, according to your University, but is likely to cover the main points listed on p. 118.
(b) In the UK, water-filled fire extinguishers are red – use for wood, paper and textiles; CO_2 extinguishers are black, or have a black panel – use for flammable liquids and electrical fires; dry powder extinguishers are blue, or have a blue panel – use for all types of fires (wood, paper, textiles, gaseous fires, flammable liquids and electrical fires); foam extinguishers are beige, or have a beige panel – use for flammable liquids (note that other colour conventions may apply outside the UK).
(c) *Tip:* This will vary, depending upon your Department's procedure. However, it is likely to include a specific written record book for accidents.
(d) *Tip:* There will often be separate codes of practice for work involving non-pathogenic microbes (e.g. general microbiology classes) and pathogenic

microbes (e.g. in medical microbiology courses). The latter requires a higher level of safe working practice, and may include the use of disposable aprons, etc.

21.4 *Tip:* Use either your Department's chemical hazard information system or a Web database (e.g. the National Institute for Occupational Safety & Health Databases at: http://www.cdc.gov/niosh/database.html; or the Agency for Toxic Substances and Disease Registry ToxFAQs database at: http://www.atsdr.cdc.gov/toxfaq.html. Alternatively, you could use a 'portal' site such as Biochem Links at: http://biochemlinks.com/; or the material safety data sheet (MSDS) site at http://www.ilpi.com/msds/index.html).

(a) Formaldehyde is toxic and potentially carcinogenic (and also highly flammable in pure form): protective gloves and eye/face protection should be used during preparation of stock solutions. Formaldehyde can also cause allergic skin reactions and breathing the vapour should be avoided – working solutions should be used in a well-ventilated place or fume hood.

(b) Acetone is highly flammable and can form explosive peroxides on contact with strong oxidants. It should be used in a well-ventilated room, away from naked flames or spark-prone electrical equipment. Disposable gloves can be used to prevent skin contact.

(c) Sodium hydroxide is highly corrosive and an irritant. Protective gloves and safety glasses should be worn when preparing stock solutions using solid NaOH. Contact with moisture generates considerable heat, so it should always be added in small amounts to a large volume of water.

22 Working with liquids

22.1

(a) Use measuring cylinders (e.g. measure out 700 ml of ethanol using a 1000 ml measuring cylinder and measure out 300 ml of water using a 500 ml measuring cylinder: mix together in a large conical flask (e.g. 1000 ml capacity) or beaker.

(b) Use a pipettor (e.g. P20 Gilson Pipetman®) set to deliver 10.0 μl and sterile RNAse-free tips, manufactured for molecular biology (note also that some disposable tips are designed to have extended, fine tips, to aid gel loading).

(c) Weigh out 20.0 mg (0.0200 g) of DNA standard using a four-place balance, add this to a 100 ml volumetric flask and make up to 100 ml with distilled, deionised water.

(d) Use a burette (e.g. 50 ml burette) and beaker or flask (e.g. 250 ml capacity), plus a magnetic stirrer and 'flea' (p. 132) for mixing.

22.2 *Tip:* Box 22.1 gives stepwise details of how to use a pipettor.

22.3 *Tip:* You may find this type of calculation easier using a spreadsheet, rather than a calculator (Chapter 12 gives further details). The model A pipettor gave a mean delivery of 0.9795 ml, with a standard deviation of 0.010 40 ml (to 5

decimal places). The model B pipettor delivered, on average 1.0107 ml, with a standard deviation of 0.001 25 ml. The model C pipettor gave an average delivery of 1.0009 ml, with a standard deviation of 0.058 82 ml. Therefore, model C was the most accurate pipettor (with a mean value closest to the true value of 1.0000 ml) and model B was most precise (giving the most reproducible results, as shown by the lowest standard deviation). The model A pipettor was the least accurate (mean value furthest from the true value) while model C was the least precise (having the highest standard deviation).

23 Basic laboratory procedures

23.1 *Tip:* Box 23.1 and Box 24.1 give advice on preparing solutions.

(a) $50 \div 1000$ (number of moles required for 1 litre) $\times 0.1$ (volume required, expressed in litres) $\times 58.44$ (relative molecular mass of NaCl) $= 0.2922 = \mathbf{0.292\,g}$

(b) 0.1 (number of moles required for 1 litre) $\times 0.25$ (volume required, expressed in litres) $\times 182.17$ (relative molecular mass of mannitol) $= 4.554\,25 = \mathbf{4.55\,g}$

(c) 800 (number of μg in 1 ml) $\times 200$ (volume, in ml) $= 160\,000\,μg = \mathbf{160\,mg}$

(d) $22.5 \div 1000$ (number of moles required for 1 litre) $\times 0.5$ (volume required, in litres) $\times 203.30$ (relative molecular mass of $MgCl_2.6H_2O$) $= 2.287\,125 = \mathbf{2.29\,g}$

(e) 20 (number of ng in 1 μl) $\times 1000$ (number of μl in 1 ml) $\times 400$ (volume required, in ml) $= 8\,000\,000\,ng = \mathbf{8.00\,mg}$

23.2 *Tip:* All of these can be calculated using the relationship $[C_1]V_1 = [C_2]V_2$ (Eqn [24.2]). Do not forget to include the volumes of *both* solutions when calculating the final volume – e.g. in example (a) below, the final volume is 10 ml (1 + 9) and *not* 9 ml.

(a) $1 \times 0.4 = [C_2] \times 10$, therefore $[C_2] = (1 \times 0.4) \div 10 = 0.04\,mol\,l^{-1}$ and therefore $0.04 \times 1000 = \mathbf{40.0\,mmol\,l^{-1}}$.

(b) $10 \times 25 = [C_2] \times 500$, therefore $[C_2] = (10 \times 25) \div 500 = 0.5\,μg\,ml$ and therefore $0.5 \times 1000 = \mathbf{500\,ng\,ml^{-1}}$.

(c) $200 \times 0.01 = [C_2] \times 250$ (note that both volumes are expressed in ml), therefore $[C_2] = (200 \times 0.01) \div 250 = 0.008\,mmol\,l^{-1}$ and therefore $0.008 \times 1\,000\,000 = 8000\,nmol\,l^{-1}$ and therefore $8000 \div 1000 = \mathbf{8.00\,nmol\,ml^{-1}}$

(d) $0.2 \times V_1 = 0.02 \times 250$ (note that both concentrations are expressed in $mol\,l^{-1}$), therefore $V_1 = (0.02 \times 250) \div 0.2 = \mathbf{25.0\,ml}$ of KCl solution, made up to a final volume of 250 ml with water.

(e) First express the concentration of the glucose solution in $mol\,m^{-3}$, by dividing by M_r, therefore $20 \div 180.16 = 0.111\,012\,4\,mol\,m^{-3}$. Then use the relationship $[C_1]V_1 = [C_2]V_2$. Thus $0.111\,012\,4 \times V_1 = 50 \times 10^{-6} \times 1 \times 10^{-3}$, therefore $V_1 = (50 \times 10^{-6} \times 1 \times 10^{-3}) \div 0.111\,012\,4 = 4.504 \times 10^{-7}\,m^3 = \mathbf{450\,μl}$. Make up 450 μl of glucose solution to $1 \times 10^{-3}\,m^3$ (1000 ml) with water.

23.3 *Tip:* Either use the relationship $[C_1]V_1 = [C_2]V_2$ (Eqn [24.2]) to calculate the volumes required, or calculate the

Answers to study exercises

dilution factor from the ratio of the concentration in the stock solution to that required in the final solution.

(a) The dilution factor for KCl is 20-fold. To prepare the solution, use **0.050 ml (≡50.0 μl) of KCl stock solution, plus 0.950 ml (≡950 μl) of water**.

(b) The dilution factor is 40-fold for NaCl and 10-fold for glucose. To prepare the solution, use **1.25 ml of NaCl stock solution, 5.00 ml of glucose stock solution and 43.75 ml of water**.

(c) The dilution factor for NaCl is 20-fold, for KCl is 80-fold, for $CaCl_2$ is 4-fold and for glucose is 20-fold. To prepare the solution, use **5.00 ml of NaCl stock solution, 1.25 ml of KCl stock solution, 25.00 ml of $CaCl_2$ stock solution, 5.00 ml of glucose stock solution and 63.75 ml of water**.

(d) First, convert the required concentrations to the same units as those of the stock solutions. In this case, $\mu mol\,ml^{-1}$ and $mmol\,l^{-1}$ are directly equivalent (divide by 10^3 to convert from μmol to mmol, then multiply by 10^3 to convert from ml to l) so the numerical values remain the same. The dilution factor for NaCl is 5-fold, for $CaCl_2$ is 8-fold and for KCl is 10-fold. To prepare the solution, use **2.00 ml of NaCl stock solution, 1.25 ml of $CaCl_2$ stock solution, 1.00 ml of KCl stock solution and 5.75 ml of water**.

(e) First, convert the glucose concentration from $nmol\,ml^{-1}$ to $mmol\,l^{-1}$ (divide by 10^6 to convert nmol to mmol and multiply by 10^3 to convert ml to l), giving glucose at $0.2\,mmol\,l^{-1}$ (all other concentrations are in the same units as those of the stock solutions). The dilution factor for $CaCl_2$ is 20-fold, for KCl is 4-fold and for glucose is 25-fold. To prepare the solution, use **1.25 ml of $CaCl_2$ stock solution, 6.25 ml of KCl stock solution, 1.00 ml of glucose stock solution and 16.50 ml of water**.

24 Principles of solution chemistry

24.1 *Tip:* Box 23.1 and Box 24.1 give useful procedures and example calculations for molar concentrations.

(a) 1 molar $= 1\,mol\,l^{-1} = 58.44\,g$ in 1 litre of solution $=$ **58.440 g**.

(b) $110.99 \times 100 \div 1000$ (number of g required for $100\,mmol\,l^{-1}$) $\times 250 \div 1000$ (number of g in 250 ml) $= 2.774\,75 = $ **2.775 g**.

(c) $10\,nmol\,\mu l^{-1}$ is equivalent to $10\,mmol\,l^{-1} \div 1000$ (convert to $mol\,l^{-1}$) $\times 182.17$ (number of $g\,l^{-1}$) $\times 2.5$ (number of g in 2.5 l) $= 4.554\,25 = $ **4.554 g**.

(d) 5% w/v is equivalent to 5 g in 100 ml $\times 4$ (number of g in 400 ml) $= $ **20.000 g**.

(e) 2.50×180.16 (convert from $mol\,m^{-3}$ to $g\,m^{-3}$) $\times 250$ $\div 1\,000\,000$ (number of g in 250 ml) $= 0.1126 = $ **0.113 g**.

24.2 *Tip:* Make stepwise changes and always show your working out in any written report or assessment including calculations involving the interconversion of concentrations.

(a) $5 \div 342.3$ (convert $g\,l^{-1}$ to $mol\,l^{-1}$) $= 0.014\,607\,1 = $ **0.0146 mol l⁻¹**. Note that this can also be expressed as $14.6\,mmol\,l^{-1}$.

(b) 1×58.44 (convert $mol\,m^{-3}$ to $g\,m^{-3}$) $\div 1000$ (convert $g\,m^{-3}$ to $g\,l^{-1}$) $= 0.058\,44 = $ **0.0584 g l⁻¹**. Note that this could also be expressed as $58.4\,mg\,l^{-1}$.

(c) 5×0.789 (convert % v/v to % w/v) $\times 10$ (convert % w/v to $g\,l^{-1}$) $\div 46.06$ (convert $g\,l^{-1}$ to $mol\,l^{-1}$) $= 0.856\,491\,5 = $ **0.856 mol l⁻¹**. Note that this could also be expressed as $856\,mmol\,l^{-1}$.

(d) $150 \div 1000$ (convert from $mmol\,l^{-1}$ to $mol\,l^{-1}$) $\times 180.16$ (convert from $mol\,l^{-1}$ to $g\,l^{-1}$) $\div 10$ (convert from $g\,l^{-1}$ to % w/v) $= $ **2.70% w/v**.

(e) 1×74.55 (convert from $mol\,kg^{-1}$ to $g\,kg^{-1}$) $\div 10$ (convert from $g\,kg^{-1}$ to g per 100 g, i.e. % w/w) $= 7.455 = $ **7.46% w/w**.

24.3

(a) *Tip:* Use Eqn [24.6] and set $\phi = 1$ (ideal behaviour) to calculate the osmolality of individual solutes in each solution. (i) NaCl $= 50 \times 2 = $ **100 mosmol kg⁻¹**; (ii) KCl $= 200 \times 2 = 400\,mosmol\,kg^{-1}$; $CaCl_2 = 40 \times 3 = 120\,mosmol\,kg^{-1}$, giving a total osmolality of $400 + 120 = $ **520 mosmol kg⁻¹**. (iii) NaCl $= 100 \times 2 = 200\,mosmol\,kg^{-1}$; KCl $= 60 \times 2 = 120\,mosmol\,kg^{-1}$; $CaCl_2 = 75 \times 3 = 225\,mosmol\,kg^{-1}$, giving a total osmolality of $200 + 120 + 225 = $ **545 mosmol kg⁻¹**.

(b) *Tip:* To calculate osmotic pressure, use the relationship $1\,osmol\,kg^{-1} = 2.479\,MPa$ at $25\,°C$ (p. 143), as follows: $100 \div 1000$ (convert $mosmol\,kg^{-1}$ to $osmol\,kg^{-1}$) $\times 2.479 = 0.2479 = $ **0.248 MPa**. (i) $520 \div 1000$ (convert $mosmol\,kg^{-1}$ to $osmol\,kg^{-1}$) $\times 2.479 = 1.289\,08 = $ **1.29 MPa**. (ii) $545 \div 1000$ (convert $mosmol$ kg^{-1} to $osmol\,kg^{-1}$) $\times 2.479 = 1.351\,055 = $ **1.35 MPa**.
Tip: To calculate osmotic potential you can use Eqn [24.8] to calculate the value for each solution. In each case, the numerical value stays the same as that for osmotic pressure, as shown above, but there is a negative sign for osmotic potential, compared to osmotic pressure: (i) **−0.248 MPa**. (ii) **−1.29 MPa**. (iii) **−1.35 MPa**.

25 pH and buffer solutions

25.1 *Tip:* Use Eqn [25.5] to interconvert between pH and $[H^+]$.

(a) $7.4 = -\log_{10}[H^+]$, therefore $[H^+] = $ **3.98 × 10⁻⁸ mol l⁻¹**.

(b) $4.1 = -\log_{10}[H^+]$, therefore $[H^+] = 7.94 \times 10^{-5}\,mol\,l^{-1}$ and therefore **7.94 × 10⁻² mol m⁻³**.

(c) pH $= -\log_{10}[2 \times 10^{-5}]$, therefore pH $= $ **4.70**.

(d) pH $= -\log_{10}[10^{-12.5}]$, therefore pH $= $ **12.5**.

(e) First convert $[H^+]$ from $mol\,m^{-3}$ to $mol\,l^{-1}$. $[H^+] = 2.8 \times 10^{-8}\,mol\,l^{-1}$. Then use Eqn [25.5] pH $= -\log_{10}[2.8 \times 10^{-8}]$, therefore pH $= $ **7.55**.

25.2

(a) Since the assay does not involve whole cells or organelles (where toxicity would be a factor to consider), TRIS buffer would be suitable. It has a pK_a of 8.3 (Table 25.3), which is close to the required pH. If the enzymic reaction involves no major production of acids or bases a buffer concentration of $50\,mmol\,l^{-1}$ would be sufficient, otherwise a higher concentration (e.g. of $200\,mmol\,l^{-1}$) might be more appropriate.

(b) Here, you could use one of the zwitterionic 'Good buffers' such as MES, which has a pK_a of 6.1 (Table 25.3), and this is in the direction of any expected pH change during the experiment (*E. coli* cells normally show a decrease in pH during growth, as substrates are metabolised to acidic end-products). A reasonably high concentration of buffer would be appropriate (e.g. $200\,\mathrm{mmol\,l^{-1}}$) if the experiment is to run for any length of time.

(c) TRIS buffer would *not* be suitable, as it shows a large change in pH with temperature (p. 150) and can also inhibit photosynthetic activity – either MOPS, HEPES or PIPES (Table 25.3) would be suitable alternatives, based on their pK_a values.

(d) Zwitterionic 'Good buffers' would *not* be suitable, as they interfere with some protein assays (e.g. Lowry method, p. 349) – citrate or acetate buffer would be suitable alternatives.

25.3 *Tip:* Rearrange Eqn [25.7] to give $\log_{10}[A^-]/[HA] = pH - pK_a$.

(a) $\log_{10}[A^-]/[HA] = 3.8 - 4.8 = -1$, so $\underline{\mathbf{[A^-]/[HA] = 0.1}}$ (1 to 10);

(b) $\log_{10}[A^-]/[HA] = 9.5 - 9.2 = 0.3$ so $\underline{\mathbf{[A^-]/[HA] = 1.995}}$ (approximately 2 to 1);

(c) $\log_{10}[A^-]/[HA] = 8.1 - 7.5 = 0.6$ so $\underline{\mathbf{[A^-]/[HA] = 3.98}}$ (approximately 4 to 1).

26 Introduction to microscopy

26.1 (a) T; (b) F; (c) F; (d) T; (e) T; (f) T; (g) T; (h) F; (i) F; (j) T.

26.2 Missing words are: diffracted; near-transparent; resolution; interference; contrast; 3D; focus; optical sectioning; polarised; laser.

26.3

(a) Embed; stain
(b) Air dry; stain
(c) Dehydrate.

27 Setting up and using a light microscope

27.1 *Tip:* To memorise the parts, it may help to imagine yourself setting up a microscope.

27.2

(a) Provides optimal resolution by ensuring light source is focused on slide
(b) Provides magnified image to the eyepiece lenses
(c) Enhances image contrast by cutting down on stray light reaching the objective lens
(d) Sets up the microscope for the distance between your pupils, so you can use both eyepieces
(e) Allows you to return to same place on a slide

27.3 Answer (c) is correct (see pp. 159–61).

27.4 One eyepiece micrometer unit $= 100\,\mu m/11 = 9.09\,\mu m$; 25 eyepiece units $= 25 \times 9.09\,\mu m = \underline{\mathbf{227\,\mu m}}$

27.5

(a) Chlorazol black
(b) Phloroglucinol/HCL or toluidine blue
(c) Lactophenol cotton blue
(d) Neutral red

(e) Mallory
(f) Gram

28 Making and recording measurements

28.1

(a) quantitative, discontinuous, ratio
(b) quantitative, continuous, ratio
(c) qualitative, discontinuous, nominal
(d) quantitative, discontinuous, ratio
(e) qualitative, discontinuous, nominal
(f) qualitative, discontinuous, ordinal

28.2 The results indicate that balance A has a bias of $+0.05\,g$ across the weighing range, while balance B has a consistent bias of about $+0.04\%$. Both balances are precise, but not accurate.

28.3 *Tip:* Use a spreadsheet to lay out the table once you have decided what it needs to contain and what statistics you might wish to calculate. You can use spreadsheet functions to help you calculate some of the statistics.

29 SI units and their use

29.1

(a) **0.997 atmospheres**
(b) **836 000 mm^2**
(c) **568 ml**
(d) **310 K**
(e) **72.6 kg**

29.2

(a) **10 m**
(b) **15 μl**
(c) **5 gJ**
(d) **65 km s^{-1}**
(e) **100 pg**

29.3 *Tip:* The units can be put in place of the symbols and cancelled out as follows:

$$\frac{m^2 \times Pa}{Pa\,s \times m} = \frac{m^2}{m\,s} = m\,s^{-1}$$

30 Scientific method and design of experiments

30.1 A possible answer (one of many) is given in the figure:

A possible layout of treatments in the glasshouse experiment.

The Latin square design ensures that treatments appear with equal probability in each row and column; hence, if there are gradients of potentially confounding variables, such as temperature and light in this case, their effects are spread evenly among treatments.

30.2 *Tip:* For Microsoft Excel®, try the formula =INT(5*(RAND())+1).

30.3 *Tip:* It might be easier to lay out your answer like the table below:

Interactions between treatments in the cell proliferation experiment

Treatment	Mean result	Observed effect of treatment(s)	Expected effect of treatments	Classification
Control (baseline)	5.0	0.0	–	–
A	7.0	2.0	–	–
B	8.0	3.0	–	–
C	10.0	5.0	–	–
A + B	7.0	2.0	2 + 3 = 5	Antagonism
A + C	12.0	7.0	2 + 5 = 7	No interaction
B + C	17.0	12.0	3 + 5 = 8	Synergism
A + B + C	13.0	8.0	2 + 3 + 5 = 10	Antagonism

Notes:
- The observed effect is the mean result minus the control.
- The expected result is the additive effect of individual treatments.
- The classification is based on the difference between the observed and expected effects, shown in columns 3 and 4 above.

31 Project work

31.1 *Tips:*
- Divide the time available for your project into relevant parts concerned with different aspects of your work (note some of these could run in parallel, such as experimental work and research for your Introduction).
- A Gantt chart might be an appropriate method of presenting this (see e.g. http://associate.com/gantt).
- Set yourself realistic target dates for completion of each section.
- Identify important potential 'sticking points' (e.g. time taken for delivery of reagents and other supplies) and work around these (e.g. by doing library work).
- Make sure you allow some flexibility (say 5%) to allow for slippage or unforeseen problems.

31.2 *Tip:* Even if you prefer to write up your work on paper first, create appropriate computer files soon afterwards. Devise a simple and logical system for naming the files.

31.3 *Tip:* Remember that a word processor or a spreadsheet may have sufficient functions for your database needs for storing reference details (see p. 68).

32 Sterile technique and microbial culture

32.1
- Use a permanent marker;
- Write only on the *base* of the plate;
- Record information around the outermost region of the base;
- Record (i) date, (ii) medium, (iii) your name/initials, (iv) details of organism/treatment, etc.

32.2 *Tip:* Consider the suitability of the various types of sterilisation procedures listed in Chapter 32, and whether they might be applicable for each item.
(a) Tips for pipettors are often sterilised by irradiation during the manufacturing process and may be supplied in sterile form. Autoclaving (p. 198) the easiest approach to routine laboratory sterilisation of these items.
(b) Blood is collected and handled using sterile technique, to avoid contamination, and therefore it does not require sterilisation – it is added to sterilised agar medium after sterilisation, once the medium has cooled to below 50 °C.
(c) Autoclave, e.g. at 121 °C for 15 min.
(d) Either dry heat sterilisation in a metal pipette can within a hot air oven at 160 °C for ⩾2 h, or autoclaving at 121 °C for 15 min in the same type of pipette can.
(e) Red heat sterilisation in a Bunsen flame (Fig. 32.2).
(f) Filter sterilisation through a pre-sterilised filter unit, typically with a pore size of 0.45 or 0.2 μm. The filter-sterilised antibiotic solution is mixed thoroughly with the molten agar medium at 50 °C, then poured immediately. The filter unit may be purchased ready sterilised, or prepared by autoclaving.

32.3 *Tip:* You will need to consult UK ACDP guidelines and categorisation (for details, see sources for further study in Chapter 32, p. 203) – some information on categorisation and safe working with specific pathogens is available on the Web (note that other countries may use a slightly different categorisation, e.g. biosafety levels, BSL 1–4 in the USA):
(a) Category 2
(b) Category 2 (gloves should also be worn)
(c) Category 3
(d) Category 1
(e) Category 3
(f) Category 3
(g) Category 2 (a microbiological safety cabinet should be used)
(h) Category 3
(i) Category 1
(j) Category 4

32.4 The following list covers six important points, and is based on material in Chapter 32. However, you and your fellow students may think of other valid points:
- Spread plates show the typical colonial form of the microbe, whereas most of the colonies in a pour

plate are contained within the agar and typical colony morphology cannot be observed.

- Pour plates are more suitable for counting higher numbers of microbes, since the colonies are smaller and are contained within the agar medium, in contrast to spread plates.

- Heat-sensitive microbial cells may be damaged by the temperature of the molten agar used in pour plating (45–50 °C) and may not grow on subsequent incubation.

- Some liquid will adhere to the spreader, and this may give a lowered count compared to a pour plate. Similarly, when the sample and molten agar are pre-mixed before pouring (see Fig. 32.5), some of the cells may not reach the pour plate, leading to a reduced count (note that this is one reason why some workers carry out the mixing of sample and molten agar within the Petri plate, rather than in the bottle, though this needs to be done thoroughly to ensure an even distribution of sample within the molten medium).

- Each type of plating procedure requires different apparatus – spread plating requires a sterile spreader and pre-poured plates, while pour plating requires molten agar at 50 °C (usually kept in a water bath until needed).

- There is a fire risk associated with using ethanol to flame-sterilise a glass spreader. This risk is absent in pour plates, and can be removed in spread plates by using a disposable plastic spreader.

33 Isolating and identifying microbes

33.1

(a) A range of approaches is possible, including taking swabs, which are then surface spread onto an agar-based medium (e.g. a general-purpose medium such as nutrient agar, or blood agar), or direct 'imprints' from the skin surface onto agar-based 'contact' plates.

(b) Important factors to consider here are, firstly, limiting the exposure of the sample to oxygen – for example, but taking a core through the mud and putting the core into an anaerobic jar (p. 207) immediately after sampling and, secondly, keeping the sample cool, since the organisms are psychrotrophs – for example, by putting the anaerobic jar into an ice bucket during transportation to the laboratory.

(c) You will need to consider (i) where to sample; (ii) how much water to collect (typically, faecal bacteria are often counted in volumes of up to 100 ml of sea water); and (iii) how many samples to collect (typically, at least three separate volumes of 100 ml). The samples should not be exposed to sunlight, as this may inactivate the bacteria, should be kept at 1–4 °C during transit to the laboratory and processed within 6 h of collection.

(d) One approach is to take 'contact' plates by pressing the selected surface of the leaf onto a suitable agar-based medium (e.g. a non-selective medium such as place count agar for heterotrophic bacteria). This should be done as soon as possible after collecting the leaves, and is feasible under field conditions. Incubation at different temperatures would give counts for psychrophiles, mesophiles and thermophiles.

33.2

(a) Use positive phototaxis towards a unidirectional light source. 'Sloppy' agar (e.g. 0.5% w/v agar) can help reduce contamination due to other micro-organisms.

(b) Rinse free of other microbes using sterile water, then use sonication to disrupt the biofilm and create a suspension for further investigation (e.g. culture). Alternatively, you might try an enzyme mixture formulated to hydrolyse the biofilm polymers, if their composition is known.

(c) Use membrane filtration (e.g. pore size 0.45 μm) to 'concentrate' the enterococci, then transfer the membrane (face up) to a suitable selective medium (e.g. glucose azide medium) for enumeration after incubation at an appropriate temperature, e.g. at 44 °C.

(d) Use a micromanipulator to separate the target bacterium from the other microbes. Alternatively, you might try dilution to extinction (p. 206), but you would be likely to look through a large number of cultures before finding the distinctively shaped bacterium.

33.3

(a) NaCl at 7.5% is selective for halotolerant bacteria, while mannitol is present as a specific carbohydrate nutrient source for *S. aureus*. Phenol red in the medium turns yellow when mannitol is metabolised to acidic end-products. *S. aureus* grows as larger colonies with a yellow 'halo' in an otherwise red medium, due to mannitol breakdown. Other *Staphylococcus* spp. grow as smaller colonies, with no yellow 'halo'.

(b) The surfactant sodium lauryl sulphate is selective for coliform bacteria. Lactose is present as a specific carbohydrate nutrient source, plus phenol red as a pH indicator. Coliforms, including *E. coli*, grow in the presence of sodium lauryl sulphate and metabolise lactose to acidic end-products, giving large yellow colonies. A selective temperature of 44 °C can be used to grow thermotolerant (faecal) coliforms, most of which are *E. coli*.

(c) Sodium azide is the selective ingredient, inhibiting the growth of most obligate aerobes and facultative anaerobes but leaving *Enterococcus* spp. unaffected, as they are aerotolerant anaerobes (see Fig. 33.1). The medium also contains a tetrazolium salt as a general indicator of metabolic activity, used to help visualise the small blue–purple colonies.

Answers to study exercises

(d) Polymyxin is present as a selective agent for *Bacillus* spp. Mannitol and pyruvate are present as specific carbohydrate nutrient sources. *B. cereus*, in contrast to most other species of *Bacillus*, can utilise pyruvate but not mannitol, causing the pH to rise (most other *Bacillus* spp. use both mannitol and pyruvate, causing the pH to drop or remain stable). Bromophenol blue changes from green (neutral) to peacock blue (alkaline) for *B. cereus*. The egg yolk lecithin is broken down by a lecithinase produced by this bacterium, giving an opaque 'halo' of precipitated degradation products around the colonies.

33.4 Colony appearance is typically as follows (note that the growth medium can modify the appearance from that noted below):

(a) Shiny, off-white, mucoid, slightly raised circular colonies with an entire (smooth) margin, 2–3 mm in diameter.

(b) Mucoid, flat spreading colonies with an undulate margin, often with green pigmentation, 4–5 mm in diameter.

(c) Circular 'pinpoint' colonies, convex and often with yellow or orange pigmentation, 1–2 mm in diameter.

(d) Circular off-white colonies, with a depressed centre ('draughtsman' colonies), α-haemolytic on blood agar, 1–3 mm diameter.

(e) Flat irregular off-white colonies with a matt surface texture and lobed margin, 2–4 mm diameter.

(f) Raised circular white colonies with an entire (smooth) margin, 3–4 mm in diameter.

33.5

(a) N'-N'-N'-N'-tetramethyl-*p*-phenylenediamine acts as an electron donor to cytochrome oxidase and is converted from the colourless, reduced form to the oxidised form, which has a strong purple–blue colour (a positive result).

(b) Indole, produced as a result of the breakdown of tryptophan, can be detected by a variety of methods including Kovac's reagent (*para*-dimethylamino-benzaldehyde in alcohol).

(c) β-galactosidase can be detected using a suitable chromogenic substrate (a synthetic substrate that liberates a coloured product when cleaved by the target enzyme), such as *o*-nitrophenyl-β-D-galactoside (ONP-GAL), or a fluorogenic substrate (a synthetic substrate that liberates a fluorescent product when cleaved by the target enzyme), such as 4-methylumbelliferyl-β-D-galactoside (MU-GAL).

(d) Hydrolysis of urea to ammonia and CO_2 is most easily demonstrated by including a pH indicator such as phenol red, to visualise the alkalinisation that accompanies this reaction. In this instance, the medium turns from yellow to red as the pH rises.

(e) The decarboxylation of lysine under anaerobic conditions can be detected by an alkalinisation of the medium, usually visualised using bromophenol purple, which changes from yellow to purple as the pH rises due to the action of lysine decarboxylase.

(f) H_2S production from S-containing amino acids is most easily demonstrated by incorporating an iron-containing salt in the medium (e.g. ferrous ammonium sulphate). The H_2S produced by the growing bacteria combines with the ferrous ions to form a black deposit of iron sulphide. In tube tests, a filter paper strip containing lead acetate turns black on exposure to H_2S.

33.6

(a) *Proteus mirabilis*.
(b) *Escherichia coli*.
(c) *Salmonella* spp.
(d) *Morganella morganii*.
(e) *Escherichia coli*.

34 Working with animal and plant tissues and cells

34.1 *Tip:* See Chapter 24 for details of osmolarity. Assuming that each solute behaves in an ideal manner, then the osmolarity of each constituent will be equivalent to the amount in grams per litre divided by the relative molecular mass and multiplied by the number of osmotically active particles produced from each solute molecule when it dissolves in water. Thus $NaCl = 6 \div 58.44 \times 2 = 0.205\,338\,8$ osmol l^{-1}; $KCl = 0.075 \div 74.55 \times 2 = 0.002\,012\,1$ osmol l^{-1}; $CaCl_2 = 0.1 \div 110.99 \times 3 = 0.002\,702\,9$ osmol l^{-1}; $NaHCO_3 = 0.1 \div 84.01 \times 2$ (note that $NaHCO_3$ gives only 2 osmotically active entities in water) $= 0.002\,380\,7$ osmol l^{-1}. Added together, this gives an osmolarity of $0.212\,434\,5$ osmol l$^{-1} = \mathbf{212.4\,mosmol\,l^{-1}}$. Note that you should use the full numerical values until the last step, to avoid introducing 'rounding' errors.

34.2 *Tip:* The UK national culture collection website at http://www.ukncc.co.uk provides coordinated information for a number of individual UK collections. The UK National Collection of Type Cultures (NCTC) can be accessed at http://www.phls.co.uk/services/nctc and the American Collection of Type Cultures (ATCC) is at http://www.atcc.org while the World Federation of Culture Collections has a website at http://wdcm.nig.ac.jp/wfcc/index.xml. Box 10.3 gives further details on the evaluation of Web-based resources.

34.3

(a) HeLa cells are named after their source, Ms Henrietta Lacks, of Baltimore, USA.

(b) Vero cells are derived from the kidney of an African green monkey (*Cercopithecus aethiops*), known as the vervet monkey, hence 'vero'.

(c) BHK stands for 'baby hamster kidney', the original source of this cell line.

(d) CHO stands for 'Chinese hamster ovary', the original source of this cell line.

(e) TBY-2 stands for tobacco bright yellow strain 2, a plant cell line.

35 Culture systems and growth measurement

35.1 *Tip:* Use Eqns [35.1] and [35.2] for these calculations.

(a) Substituting the appropriate values into Eqn [35.1], $\mu = [2.303 (6.531\,478\,9 - 4.716\,003\,3)] \div 9 = 0.464\,56 = \mathbf{0.465\,h^{-1}}$. Similarly, using Eqn [35.2], $g = (0.301 \times 9) \div (6.531\,478\,9 - 4.716\,003\,3) = 1.492\,171 = \mathbf{1.49\,h}$ (approximately 1 h 29 min).

(b) Substituting the appropriate values into Eqn [36.1], $\mu = [2.303 (7.826\,074\,8 - 4.477\,121\,3) \div 200 = 0.038\,563\,2 = \mathbf{0.0386\,min^{-1}}$. Similarly, using Eqn [35.2], $g = (0.301 \times 200) \div (7.826\,074\,8 - 4.477\,121\,3) = 17.975\,765 = \mathbf{18.0\,min}$.

(c) Substituting the appropriate values into Eqn [35.1], $\mu = [2.303 (2.397\,94 - 1.505\,15)] \div 2.5 = 0.822\,438\,2 = \mathbf{0.822\,h^{-1}}$. Similarly, using Eqn [35.2], $g = (0.301 \times 2.5) \div (2.397\,94 - 1.505\,15) = 0.842\,863\,4 = \mathbf{0.843\,h}$ (approximately 51 min). Note that the time difference in this example is two and a half hours, not 2.3 hours!

35.2 *Tip:* Use Eqn [35.6] (Box 35.1) to carry out these calculations.

(a) $6.42 \div 1 \div (2.5 \times 10^{-7}) \times 1 = 2.568 \times 10^{-7} = \mathbf{2.57 \times 10^7\,ml^{-1}}$.

(b) Total cell count $= 698$, so $698 \div 20 \div (8 \times 10^{-7}) \times 1 = 4.3625 \times 10^7 = \mathbf{4.36 \times 10^7\,ml^{-1}}$.

(c) $78 \div 25 \div (2.5 \times 10^{-7}) \times 10^2 = 1.248 \times 10^9 = \mathbf{1.25 \times 10^9\,ml^{-1}}$ (note the correction factor of 10^2, to account for the dilution factor of 10^{-2}).

(d) $6.8 \div 1 \div (2 \times 10^{-5}) \times 0.1 = \mathbf{3.40 \times 10^4\,ml^{-1}}$ (note the correction factor of 0.1, because the suspension was concentrated by a factor of 10-fold).

35.3 *Tip:* Use Eqn [35.7] (Box 35.2) to carry out the calculations.

(a) $(54.4 \div 0.1) \times 10^5 = \mathbf{5.44 \times 10^7\,CFU\,ml^{-1}}$.

(b) The mean count per spread plate is $(34 + 40 + 37) \div 3 = 37.0$ CFU. So $(37.0 \div 0.2) \times 10^3 = \mathbf{1.85 \times 10^5\,CFU\,ml^{-1}}$.

(c) The mean count per pour plate is $(211 + 186 + 194 + 202) \div 4 = 198.25$ CFU. So $(198.25 \div 0.5) \times 20 = \mathbf{7.93 \times 10^3\,CFU\,ml^{-1}}$.

(d) The mean count per plate is $(35 + 41 + 32) \div 3 = 36$ CFU. So $(36 \div 1) \times 50 = 1800$ per g and therefore $1800 \times 100 = \mathbf{1.80 \times 10^5\,CFU\,per\,100\,g}$. Note that the multiplication factor to correct for dilution was 50 in this case, since the seafood had been diluted to 2% w/v.

(e) This example does not require Eqn [35.7] in full. The mean count for 250 ml was $(45 + 32) \div 2 = 38.5$ CFU. Therefore, the count per 100 ml is $38.5 \div 250 \times 100 = \mathbf{15.4\,CFU\,per\,100\,ml}$.

(f) The mean count per plate is $(28 + 32 + 39) \div 3 = 33.0$, so using Eqn [35.7], $(33.0 \div 0.5) \times 10^1 = \mathbf{660\,CFU\,ml^{-1}}$. This value is higher than the EU regulations (maximum 100 CFU ml^{-1}), so this water sample does not meet the specification required of mineral water.

35.4 *Tip:* You need to graph heart rate against log concentration values; this should give a sigmoidal curve (see below). Having obtained log concentration estimates graphically from the heart rate values for the two loch samples, convert back to mmol l^{-1} concentration by raising 10 to the power of the estimated log concentration (see p. 470–1).

(a) The estimate for (i) is approximately $\mathbf{1.58 \times 10^{-5}\,mol\,m^{-3}}$; and for (ii) **approximately $\mathbf{6.31 \times 10^{-5}\,mol\,m^{-3}}$**.

(b) Estimate (ii) is the least reliable owing to the shallowness of the log concentration versus heart rate curve at this point: a small error in heart rate will lead to a large difference in estimated concentration.

(c) If sample (ii) were diluted by about fivefold or so, then tested again, this would shift the 'expected' heart rate downwards to the most sensitive part of the graph. The dilution factor would need to be accounted for when estimating the true concentration.

(d) There is no guarantee that the only substance affecting the *Daphnia* sp. heart rate in the loch samples is the toxin tested. Other substances present might increase or decrease heart rate.

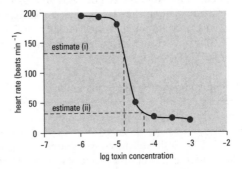

Responses of *Daphnia* to toxin.

35.5 *Tip:* You will first need to convert the nisin concentrations of the standard solutions to $\log_{10}$ values, before plotting zone diameter against $\log_{10}$ nisin concentration (see figure). Based on the calibration curve, solution 5 contains antilog$_{10}$ $1.24 = \mathbf{17.4\,\mu g\,ml^{-1}}$ (to 1 decimal place).

Effect of nisin on inhibitory zone diameter for *B. subtilis* colonies.

Answers to study exercises

36 Homogenisation and fractionation of cells and tissues

36.1 *Tip:* Table 36.1 provides a summary of techniques.

(a) Gram-negative bacteria have strong, multi-layered cell envelope (Fig. 36.1), best disrupted by EDTA treatment (to destabilise the outer membrane) and lysozyme (to digest the peptidoglycan that provides most of the structural strength of the cell wall). The procedure should be carried out in a dilute medium, to encourage the cells to burst. Mechanical techniques such as ultrasonication and the French pressure cell (Table 36.1) can be used, but are often less effective.

(b) Skeletal muscle is difficult to disrupt because of its high content of fibrous contractile proteins and connective tissue components such as collagen: vigorous mechanical methods are best, e.g. a rotor-stator.

(c) Plant tissue is usually quite resilient, due to major structural components in the cell wall such as cellulose, lignins and waxes. Incubation in a lytic enzyme mixture, followed by mechanical disruption (e.g. using a blender) is often the best approach.

36.2 Vigorous methods such as use of a Waring blender or a rotor-stator (Fig. 36.2) would be suitable for isolating a soluble protein, as it is not necessary to maintain the structure of organelles. However, less vigorous disruption, e.g. using a ground-glass or Teflon® homogeniser (Fig. 36.3), would ensure least disruption when isolating intact organelles.

36.3

Selection of components, with explanation

Selection	Explanation
(i): component (d)	A detergent such as Triton X-100 is required to disrupt the membrane, by interacting with the lipid component, and thereby allowing solubilisation of the membrane protein component (which will normally have extensive hydrophobic regions).
(ii): component (a)	When preparing mitochondria, sucrose is used at a concentration suitable to maintain the osmolarity of the medium at a level that will not result in osmotic lysis of the organelle. (Osmotic properties of solutions are further discussed in Chapter 24.)
(iii): component (c)	Dithiothreitol is a strong reducing agent that can prevent oxidation of thiol groups in proteins (p. 238) and thereby maintains biological activity of oxygen-sensitive enzymes and other proteins.
(iv): component (b)	Low ionic strength buffer is used because the contractile proteins actin and myosin are solubilised with increased salt concentration, leading to a highly viscous solution that is difficult to process further when high ionic strength buffers are used.

37 Calibration and its application to quantitative analysis

37.1 See the figure below – note that this calibration line is approximately linear up to $\approx 4.0\,\mu g\,ml^{-1}$ but it becomes increasingly curved above this point. Water sample (a) contains Zn at **$1.70\,\mu g\,ml^{-1}$**; water sample (b) contains Zn at $3.5 \times 20 = \underline{\mathbf{70.0\,\mu g\,ml^{-1}}}$; water sample (c) contains $8.3 \times 5 = \underline{\mathbf{41.5\,\mu g\,ml^{-1}}}$ (note that the graph curves at higher concentrations, making the estimate for water sample (c) less reliable than the other two – a better approach might have been to dilute this sample further and reassay).

Calibration curve for a series of solutions containing zinc, based on data in the table in study exercise 37.1.

37.2 Note that this data set is a very good fit to a straight line – linear regression analysis (p. 493) carried out using Excel® gives a value for r^2 of 0.996 829 051, with an intercept of 0.001 714 286 and a slope of 7.424 285 714. The protein content of each solution could be determined directly from a print-out of the graph (e.g. the figure below). However, the calculations below show how you can substitute values into the equation for a straight line, $Y = a + bX$ (p. 471), to give the required answers.

(a) $0.225 = 0.001\,714\,286 + 7.424\,285\,714X$, so $X = (0.225 - 0.001\,714\,286) \div 7.424\,285\,714 = 0.030\,375\,043 = \underline{\mathbf{0.0301}}$ **mg protein**.

(b) $0.465 = 0.001\,714\,286 + 7.424\,285\,714X$, so $X = (0.465 - 0.001\,714\,286) \div 7.424\,285\,714 = 0.062\,401\,385 = \underline{\mathbf{0.0624}}$ **mg protein**.

(c) $0.682 = 0.001\,714\,286 + 7.424\,285\,714X$, so $X = (0.682 - 0.001\,714\,286) \div 7.424\,285\,714 = 0.091\,629\,786 = \underline{\mathbf{0.0916}}$ **mg protein**.

Calibration curve for a series of protein standards, based on data in the table in study exercise 37.2.

37.3 *Tip:* Check that you understand the general requirements for good graph drawing, detailed in Chapter 63.

(a) The title of the figure in study exercise 37.3 ('calibration graph') does not give sufficient information to enable the reader to understand the content.

(b) No details are given as to the nature of each set of data values – are these curves for two separate substances?

(c) The *x*-axis has a poor choice of units – it would be better to use μg, then all of the values would be 1000 times smaller.

(d) The *x*-axis runs beyond the highest value (8 μg), wasting around 20% of the horizontal space.

(e) The scale marks (tic marks) on the *x*-axis are missing.

(f) The *x*-axis has no zero shown.

(g) The *y*-axis has too many numbers, and too many minor scale marks – it is probably better to have a tic mark every 0.1 absorbance units. (Note that absorbance (A) is a dimensionless term, so no units are required – this is *not* an error.)

(h) The data values represented by the square symbols show a reasonable fit to the lower linear trend line, but the data values represented by the round symbols do not – the latter set of data shows a clear curvilinear relationship and therefore a linear trend line is not appropriate.

(i) Lines should not run through the symbols, as is the case for several of the square symbols.

38 Immunological methods

38.1 *Tip:* Take care to make sure that your construction lines are carefully drawn by hand – they must be *parallel* to the appropriate axis. The test sample contains 7.5 μg of antigen.

38.2 *Tip:* Remember that you need to plot the *square* of the ring diameter versus the amount of antigen in each standard. The test sample has a squared ring diameter of 42.25 mm^2 and contains 11 μg of antigen (see the figure below).

Calibration curve for a series of standards assayed by single radial immunodiffusion, based on data in the table in study exercise 38.2.

38.3

(a) Wells 1 and 2 in the figure in study exercise 38.3 show the 'prozone' phenomenon, with a negative

haemagglutination test result (a small 'button' of cells), due to an excess of antibody. Wells 4 to 10 show strong positive haemagglutination, with an even 'carpet' of red blood cells rather than a 'button'. Wells 11 and 12 show a negative reaction, due to the further dilution of the test serum.

(b) The lowest dilution giving a positive result is well 10, which is nine doubling dilutions of the original 10-fold dilution, i.e. $10 \times 2^9 = 5120$-fold. Therefore the titre is 1 in 5120.

(c) The test serum is positive, since the titre is greater than 1 in 5000.

39 Radioactive isotopes and their uses

39.1 Assume a ^{14}C half-life of 5715 years (Table 39.2). Using Eqn [39.1], $e^x = 0.5725$, and so $x = \ln(0.5725) = -0.5578$. If $-0.5578 = -0.693(t/5715)$, then $t = (-0.5578/-0.693) \times 5715 = 4600$. **The rat visited about 4600 years ago**.

39.2

(a) **1200 Bq**.
(b) **4.44 × 10^7 d.p.m.**
(c) **1.20 μCi**.
(d) **30.0 Bq g^{-1}**.
(e) **28.0 pmol**.

39.3

(a) The solution contains $250 \times 10^{-6} \times 5$ mol $= 1.25 \times 10^{-3}$ mol. The specific activity is therefore $55 \times 10^6/1.25 \times 10^{-3}$ Bq mol$^{-1} = $ **4.4 × 10^{10} Bq mol^{-1}**.
(b) $79.2 \times 10^5/4.4 \times 10^{10} = 1.8 \times 10^{-4}$ mol per 2 h per 10^7 cells is equivalent to **2.5 fmol s^{-1}cell^{-1}**.

40 Light measurement

40.1 First convert PFFD to photosynthetic irradiance (PI) using Table 40.2: $1610 \div 4.6 = 350$ W m^{-2} ($\equiv$ J m^{-2} s^{-1}). Then, calculate the PI for the leaf area of 45 cm^2 ($\equiv 0.0045$ m^2): $350 \times 0.0045 = 1.575$ J s^{-1}. Finally, calculate the total energy supplied over the 30 min (1800 s) period: $1.575 \times 1800 = 2835$ J $= $ **2840 J**.

40.2 *Tip:* Convert values to PPFD expressed in μmol photons m^{-2} s^{-1} using the conversion factors given in Table 40.1, where necessary.

(a) 300×4.6 (to convert to PPFD) $= $ **1380 μmol photons m^{-2} s^{-1}**;
(b) $6.5 \div 1000$ (to convert to μmol) $\times 10\,000$ (to convert to m^{-2}) $= $ **65.0 μmol photons m^{-2} s^{-1}**;
(c) this value is already expressed in the appropriate units, **275 μmol photons m^{-2} s^{-1}**;
(d) 35.2×4.6 (to convert to PPFD) $= 161.92 = $ **162 μmol photons m^{-2}s^{-1}**;
(e) $1.15 \div 1000$ (to convert to W) $\times 10\,000$ (to convert to m^{-2}) $\times 5.0$ (to convert to PPFD) $= $ **57.5 μmol photons m^{-1} s^{-1}**;

The locations ranked in order of decreasing PPFD are therefore as follows: (a); (c); (d); (b); (e).

40.3 *Tip:* If you simply use the term 'light meter' in a general-purpose search engine (e.g. Google®), you will find out

Answers to study exercises

mostly about photographic light meters, and these are not suitable for scientific purposes – you'll need to add other terms, such as photosynthesis, quantum, irradiance, photon flux density, etc. Relevant features might include: measuring scale(s); range(s); detector/receiver type; cost; portability/weight; power supply; the type of sensor (e.g. 3D, flat or rod-shaped); whether the sensor can be used in water; whether the meter can be used with a data logger.

41 Basic spectroscopy

41.1 *Tip:* Box 41.1 gives stepwise instructions on using a spectrophotometer – check that you have covered all of the major points. However, the exact details will vary from instrument to instrument.

41.2 *Tip:* Substitute values into Eqn [41.3] and solve for $[C]$ (margin examples are given on p. 273).

(a) Using Eqn [41.3]: $0.53 = 6220 \times 1 \times [C]$, therefore $[C] = 0.000\,085\,209\,\text{mol}\,l^{-1} = \underline{\textbf{85.2}\,\mu\textbf{mol}\,l^{-1}}$.

(b) First calculate the concentration, using Eqn [41.3]: $0.62 = 6220 \times 5 \times [C] = 0.000\,019\,935\,7\,\text{mol}\,l^{-1} = 19.9357\,\mu\text{mol}\,l^{-1}$. Next, calculate the amount in 20 ml: $19.9357 \div 1000$ (amount in 1 ml) $\times 20$ (amount in 20 ml) $= 0.398\,714\,\mu\text{mol} = \underline{\textbf{398 nmol}}$.

(c) Using Eqn [41.3] (note that you must convert the path length from mm to cm beforehand): $0.57 = 20 \times 0.5 \times [C] = 0.057\,g\,l^{-1} = \underline{\textbf{57.0}\,\mu\textbf{g}\,\textbf{ml}^{-1}}$.

(d) First calculate the concentration, using Eqn [41.3]: $0.31 = 20 \times 1 \times [C] = 0.0155\,g\,l^{-1}$. Next, express the concentration in the required units: 0.0155×10^9 (convert to ng) $\div 10^6$ (convert to μl) $= 15.5\,\text{ng}\,\mu l^{-1}$. Then, calculate the amount in 50 μl: $15.5 \times 50 = \underline{\textbf{775 ng}}$.

(e) Substitute the values into the equation given: $(11.93 \times 0.182) - (1.93 \times 0.035) = 2.103\,71\,\text{mg}\,l^{-1}$. Next, calculate the amount in 50 ml: $2.103\,71 \div 1000$ (amount in 1 ml) $\times 50$ (amount in 50 ml) $= 0.105\,185\,5\,\text{mg}$. Since this is the amount of chlorophyll in 1.56 g fresh weight of leaf, divide by the fresh weight to give the content: $0.105\,185\,5 \div 1.56 = 0.067\,426\,6\,\text{mg}\,\text{g fresh weight}^{-1}$. Finally, convert to the specified units: $0.067\,426\,6 \times 1000$ (convert from mg to μg) $= 67.4266 = \underline{\textbf{67.4}\,\mu\textbf{g}\,\textbf{(g fresh weight)}^{-1}}$.

41.3 First determine the concentration of *p*-nitrophenol, in mol l^{-1}. Thus $8.8\,\mu g\,\text{ml}^{-1} \div 10^6$ (convert to $g\,\text{ml}^{-1}$) $\times 10^3$ (convert to $g\,l^{-1}$) $\div 291.27$ (convert to $\text{mol}\,l^{-1}$) $= 0.000\,030\,212\,5\,\text{mol}\,l^{-1}$. Next, substitute values into Eqn [41.3] and solve for ε: $0.535 = \varepsilon \times 1 \times 0.000\,030\,212\,5$, so $\varepsilon = 17\,707.902\,36 = \underline{\textbf{17 700}\,l\,\text{mol}^{-1}\,\text{cm}^{-1}}$. Note that you should use the full numerical value until the final stage, to avoid introducing 'rounding' errors.

41.4 The calibration graph is shown in the figure. The test solution has a K^+ concentration of $0.32\,\text{mmol}\,l^{-1}$. This is equivalent to $0.32 \div 1000 \times 25 = 0.008\,\text{mmol}$ in 25 ml (the test sample volume). Next, divide by the weight of tissue used in grams: $0.008 \div 0.482 = 0.016\,598\,\text{mmol}\,(\text{g tissue})^{-1} = \underline{\textbf{16.6}\,\mu\textbf{mol}\,\textbf{(g tissue)}^{-1}}$.

Calibration curve for a series of standards, assayed for K^+ and based on the data in the table in study exercise 41.4.

41.5 *Tip:* Fig. 44.3 shows the principles involved. Some of the excitation light energy absorbed by the molecule is dissipated as heat during the short time the molecule is in the excited state (typically $\approx 10^{-9}$ seconds), resulting in a decrease in energy from the second excited state to the first. Thus less energy is available for emission. Since the wavelength of light increases with decreasing energy (see Eqns [41.1] and [41.2]), the emitted light has a longer wavelength than the light used to excite the molecule. The difference between the emission wavelength (λ_m) and the excitation wavelength (λ_{ex}) is known as the Stokes shift.

41.6 *Tip:* A comparison of the light paths in Figs 41.1 and 41.5 should give you some clues to the answer. The spectrophotometer cuvette has two clear sides to allow transmitted light to pass directly through the solution from the source to the photocell detector. The opaque sides are for handling the cuvette (you should never handle spectrophotometer cuvettes by their clear faces). In contrast, a fluorimeter cuvette has four clear sides, since emitted light is detected at right angles to the excitation beam, resulting in low background readings and high sensitivity. In practical terms, this means that you must handle fluorimeter cuvettes close to the top, to avoid contaminating these surfaces (the excitation and emission beams are usually measured close to the centre of the cuvette).

42 Advanced spectroscopy and spectrometry

42.1

(a) Peak (i).

(b) Peak (ii).

42.2 *Tip:* the term 'chemical shift' refers to the position in a spectrum of a signal from an absorbing magnetic nucleus relative to the signal from a reference compound. Ideally, the reference compound will give a single, unambiguous, sharp resonance at a frequency relatively far from the resonances of the compounds under analysis.

(a) Tetramethylsilane (TMS) $[(CH_3)_4Si]$ is a suitable reference for ^1H as it contains 12 protons in identical environments, giving a single peak well-separated from those of the protons of most other molecules.

(b) TMS is also suitable as a reference compound for ^{13}C NMR in most biological applications.

(c) Phosphocreatine is a useful reference compound for metabolic studies using ^{31}P, as it is often present in the tissue or extract being studied, and therefore does not need to be added (for more detail, see Macomber, 2000, or Nelson, 2002, p. 286).

42.3 In both instances, ppm is an abbreviation for 'parts per million', and the units must be established from the context in which the expression is used. In NMR, ppm refers to the small frequency changes that occur relative to the reference standard, expressed in proportional terms. Thus 1 ppm in NMR means a frequency difference of 1 Hz per MHz, e.g. 270 Hz in a 270 mHz spectrum. When used as a concentration term, ppm is equivalent to the expression of a concentration in parts per million, e.g. as $\mu g\,ml^{-1}$ ($10^{-6}\,g\,ml^{-1}$) in w/v terms, or $\mu g\,g^{-1}$ ($10^{-6}\,g\,g^{-1}$) in w/w terms.

42.4 *Tip:* to explain the ^{1}H NMR spectrum, you need to consider the presence of exchangeable, ionisable or dissociable hydrogen atoms in the molecule's structure. The dissociable hydrogens in a molecule will readily exchange with any others in the sample, particularly with those of water, and therefore do not yield a discrete ^{1}H NMR signal. The molecular structure of creatinine contains hydrogen atoms in four distinct environments (see the second figure in study exercise 42.4). Of these, two are attached to nitrogen atoms and are likely to be easily dissociated in aqueous systems: the majority of hydrogens bonded to atoms other than carbon tend to be readily dissociated, especially oxygen-bonded and nitrogen-bonded hydrogens. Those hydrogens bonded to the carbon skeleton are not readily exchanged and therefore give the observed signal (two distinct peaks) in the first figure in study exercise 42.4.

43 Centrifugation

43.1

(a) Use a high speed centrifuge and differential centrifugation.

(b) Use silicone oil microcentrifugation (e.g. using an Eppendorf®-type microfuge).

(c) Use continuous flow centrifugation.

43.2 *Tip:* Substitute values into Eqn [43.1].

(a) $RCF = 1.118 \times 125\,(4000 \div 1000)^2 = \mathbf{2240\,g}$;

(b) $RCF = 1.118 \times 60\,(12\,000 \div 1000)^2 = \mathbf{9660\,g}$;

(c) $RCF = 1.118 \times 186\,(30\,000 \div 1000)^2 = \mathbf{187\,000\,g}$.

43.3 *Tip:* Substitute values into Eqn [43.2].

(a) $945.7\,\sqrt{(1500 \div 95)} = \mathbf{3760\,r.p.m.}$

(b) $945.7\,\sqrt{(50\,000 \div 135)} = \mathbf{18\,200\,r.p.m.}$

(c) First convert the radius of rotation from cm to mm before substituting into Eqn [43.2]:
$945.7\,\sqrt{(13\,000 \div 55)} = \mathbf{14\,500\,r.p.m.}$

43.4 *Tip:* Use Eqn [43.1] with each of the values in turn:
For $r_{min} = 45\,mm$, $1.118 \times 45\,(5)^2 = \mathbf{1260\,g}$.
For $r_{av} = 70\,mm$, $1.118 \times 70\,(5)^2 = \mathbf{1960\,g}$.
For $r_{max} = 95\,mm$, $1.118 \times 95\,(5)^2 = \mathbf{2660\,g}$.
This calculation illustrates the range of g values possible within a single centrifuge tube, with the maximum value being double the minimum value in this instance.

44 Chromatography

44.1 *Tip:* use Eqn [44.1] to determine R_F values and Eqn [44.2] for R_A values, based on the measured distances travelled by each component, relative to the solvent front.

(a) Using Eqn [44.1], the corresponding R_F values are:
pigment A $= 63 \div 114 = \mathbf{0.553}$;
pigment B $= 76 \div 114 = \mathbf{0.667}$;
pigment C $= 86 \div 114 = \mathbf{0.754}$.

(b) Using Eqn [44.2], the corresponding R_A values are:
pigment B $= 76 \div 63 = 1.206\,349\,2 = \mathbf{1.21}$.
pigment C $= 86 \div 63 = 1.365\,079\,4 = \mathbf{1.37}$.

44.2

(a) *Tip:* Calculate the selectivity using Eqn [44.3], using the elution time for the compound excluded from the stationary phase as the column dead time (t_0), with all times converted to seconds. Thus $\alpha = (372 - 95) \div (270 - 95) = 1.582\,857\,1 = \mathbf{1.58}$.

(b) *Tip:* Calculate the resolution using Eqn [44.4]. Thus $R = 2(372 - 270) \div (40 + 44) = 2.428\,571\,4 = \mathbf{2.43}$.
This is a good level of resolution for quantitative work, giving clear separation of the two peaks.

44.3

(a) *Tip:* The isoelectric point (pI) is the intercept on the x-axis. Protein A has a pI of $\mathbf{6.0}$. Protein B has a pI of $\mathbf{8.2}$.

(b) *Tip:* Use the pI values to predict the net charge of each protein at the pH used. Protein A has a pI of 6.0 so at pH 7.0 it will have a net negative charge and bind to the anion exchanger; at pH 7.0, protein B (pI $= 8.2$) will have a net positive charge and will not be bound to the positively charged matrix and will be rapidly eluted.

(c) At pH 5.5, both proteins will have a net positive charge and will bind to the negatively charged cation exchanger. However, the net charge on protein A will be less than that on protein B and the order of elution on a salt gradient will be A, followed by B.

44.4 *Tip:* Chapter 54 discusses the interaction of ammonium sulphate and proteins. Ammonium sulphate ions are hydrated and limit the water required to keep many proteins solvated. In interactions similar to 'salting out' (p. 373), proteins with hydrophobic regions on their surface interact more strongly with hydrophobic ligands on the stationary phase in the presence of high concentrations of ammonium sulphate.

45 Chromatography – detection and analysis

45.1

(a) Flame ionisation detector;

(b) Thermal conductivity detector;

(c) Electron capture detector;

(d) Diode array detector.

45.2 Electrochemical detectors, then fluorescence detectors, then UV/visible detectors. Many biomolecules, either intrinsically or after reaction with a colour reagent, can be detected by UV/visible spectroscopy. However, fewer biomolecules show native fluorescence or the electrical properties necessary for electrochemical detection, making UV/visible detection the most versatile approach.

45.3 Some biomolecules that do not fluoresce can be detected by carrying out either pre-column or post-column derivatisation with a suitable fluorophore, e.g. dansyl chloride is used to detect very small amounts of protein by means of the intense fluorescence of the sulphonamide formed when it reacts with the terminal amino group of proteins or peptides. Other molecules that can be used as fluorescent labels are detailed on p. 275. The selectivity of the analysis is increased since only certain molecules in the sample will be capable of the chemical reaction required.

45.4 *Tip:* Substitute relative area values for each peak in Eqn [45.2], as follows:

For mannitol (peak A): $Q_A = [2060 \div 604] \times [1.50 \div 1.26] = 4.060\,233\,4 = \underline{\textbf{4.06 mg}}$.

For sucrose (peak B): $Q_B = [1898 \div 604] \times [1.50 \div 0.92] = 5.123\,452\,3 = \underline{\textbf{5.12 mg}}$.

46 Principles and practice of electrophoresis

46.1 *Tip:* Table 50.1 shows the ionisable side chains of amino acids in proteins. The dissociation of two important amino acids is shown below:

Glutamate	R-COOH	$\Leftrightarrow$	R-COO$^-$ + H$^+$
	low pH		*neutral/high pH*

Lysine	R-NH$_3^+$	$\Leftrightarrow$	R-NH$_2$ + H$^+$
	low/neutral pH		*high pH*

Note that the charge on a given amino acid side chain at a given pH will depend on the dissociation constant (pK_a, see p. 150) of the ionisable group.

46.2 *Tip:* the basic principles are explained in Chapter 46 – for further details, consult Hames and Rickwood (1998) – see p. 322. (a) Acrylamide is the monomer which is polymerised to give long chains of polyacrylamide within the gel; (b) N,N'-methylene bisacrylamide is used to form cross-links between the polyacrylamide strands within the gel; (c) ammonium persulphate produces the free radicals required for the polymerisation mechanism *via* a base-catalysed mechanism: (d) N,N,N',N'-tetramethylethylene-diamine is the base used to catalyse the production of free radicals by ammonium persulphate; (e) sodium dodecyl sulphate is a detergent that binds to proteins, dissociating them into subunits and imparting a uniform net negative charge per unit length of the polypeptide; (f) 2-mercaptoethanol reduces disulphide bonds in proteins, causing dissociation of subunits and disruption of tertiary structure; (g) buffer is required to maintain a constant pH during electrophoresis and determines the net charge on each protein molecule; (h) Coomassie Blue R-250 is a useful stain for proteins; (i) bromophenol blue is a small, highly ionic dye that can be used to follow the progress of electrophoresis because it migrates with the electrophoretic front.

46.3 *Tip:* The different forms of blotting are listed on pp. 431–2. Transfer of proteins onto gels is termed Western blotting, while DNA transfer is known as Southern blotting and RNA transfer as Northern blotting (p. 321 explains the origins of the terms).

46.4 *Tip:* First convert M_r data to log format, then plot a graph of log M_r against relative mobility for the proteins of known M_r (see figure) and then use this to establish the M_r of the unknown protein (LDH).

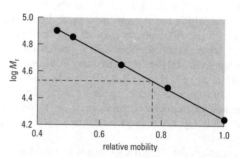

Log$_{10}$ M_r versus relative mobility for SDS-PAGE separation of a series of molecular weight standards (based on data in exercise 46.4), and showing the relative mobility of LDH (dotted line).

(a) From the figure, the log M_r of the polypeptide derived from SDS-treated LDH (relative mobility 0.77) is approximately 4.53, giving an antilog value (p. 471) of $33\,884.416 = \underline{\textbf{34\,900}}$ (to 2 significant figures).

(b) Since the M_r of native LDH is 136 000, and only a single band of $M_r \approx 34\,000$ is produced on SDS-PAGE, native LDH must contain $136\,000 \div 34\,000 = 4$ subunits of identical M_r.

46.5 The gel may not polymerise, or may polymerise unevenly: this is often due to the use of old ammonium persulphate (a fresh solution must be prepared daily, p. 316). Alternatively, the problem may be caused by a high level of dissolved oxygen in the gel (solutions can be degassed before use, if necessary, and the gel solution should be gently poured down the sides of the apparatus to avoid introducing air), or by the use of low pH buffers that slow down the polymerisation reaction (p. 319). Alternatively, the gel may polymerise too quickly, due to either (i) too much ammonium persulphate or TEMED (reduce the amounts used), or (ii) a high laboratory temperature (the gel mixture can be cooled before adding catalysts). For further details, consult Hames and Rickwood (1998) or Westermeier and Barnes (2001), see p. 322.

47 Advanced electrophoretic techniques

47.1 In PAGE any diffusion of sample proteins that occurs reduces resolution, so it is best to start with as narrow a sample zone as possible. For most protein separations the buffer pH is chosen so that the proteins are negatively charged and will migrate from the cathodic end to the anodic end of the gel. In IEF, the separation is carried out on a pH gradient: because proteins will all migrate to their pI values irrespective of the starting point, the position of sample application is not important. The only exception would be if any of the proteins to be separated were unstable at extreme pH values, in which case it would be best to avoid application at either end of the pH gradient (e.g. pH 3.0 and pH 10.0). Once a given protein has reached the position corresponding to its pI, it will remain in a narrow band because any diffusion away from the pI will result in the protein acquiring a net charge and being focused back to its pI.

47.2

(a) CE in free solution would be appropriate, which would separate the peptides on the basis of differences in net charge at the pH chosen for the analysis. CGE would be inappropriate because the peptides are of similar size.

(b) CGE would be appropriate here because the oligonucleotides will have a uniform net negative charge per unit length, and using a gel in the capillary will introduce a molecular sieving effect.

(c) CIEF will successfully separate proteins that differ in pI.

(d) MEKC, which separates molecules partly on the basis of the principles of CE (electrophoresis and electro-osmotic flow) and partly on partitioning of neutral molecules between micelles formed by detergents included in the electrophoresis medium, would be an appropriate technique for hydrophobic compounds such as steroids.

47.3

Potential factors influencing electrophoresis and isoelectric focusing

Factor	Electrophoresis	Isoelectric focusing
Dependence upon ionisable groups in proteins	Yes – this determines the net charge of each protein at a given pH	Yes – the number and types will determine the pI
Requirement for the application of an electric field	Yes – charged molecules migrate to the electrode of opposite charge	Yes – a pH gradient will be set up and proteins will migrate to their pI
Dependence upon differences in net charge between sample molecules	Yes – movement is dependent upon size, shape and net charge of molecules	No
Dependence upon differences in pI values between sample molecules	Only in that pI is related to the net charge at a given pH	Yes – molecules move to a position where pH = pI
Requirement for buffer at constant pH	Yes – proteins will have different net charges at a particular pH and will migrate towards the electrode of opposite charge	No
Requirement for a pH gradient	No	Yes – proteins will migrate to their pI and remain in place for as long as the electric field is applied
Requirement for ampholytes to be included in solution	No	Yes – these form the pH gradient (p. 324)
Use of a supporting medium with molecular sieving properties	Yes – this is one aspect of the separation process	No – it is important that proteins can migrate freely to their pI
Treatment of samples with SDS is possible	Yes – this gives protein subunits a uniform net charge per unit length and allows separation by molecular sieving, on the basis of M_r	No – SDS treatment eliminates differences in pI between native proteins
Diffusion of separated proteins is significant	Yes – though this is reduced by the presence of a supporting medium	No – proteins that move away from their pI acquire a net charge and are attracted back to their pI

47.4 *Tip:* Use a ruler across the scale marks, to help you to locate each component – but remember that the SDS-PAGE separation (*y*-axis) is based on log M_r.
A = pepsinogen. B = alkaline phosphatase; C = catalase;

D = alcohol dehydrogenase; E = galactokinase; F = triose phosphate isomerase; G = haemoglobin; H = glyceraldehyde-3-phosphate dehydrogenase; I = trypsinogen; J = nerve growth factor.

Answers to study exercises

48 Electroanalytical techniques

48.1 These assumptions are given on p. 333. The electrical potential measured at an ISE can be approximate to ion concentration assuming (i) the ion is in dilute solution (since the relationship is based on activity, Eqn [48.3]); (ii) the ionic strength of the calibration standards matches that of the test sample and (iii) there is no substantial binding of the ion to sample components (e.g. to proteins or nucleic acids).

48.2 The two functional components of a biosensor are (i) an immobilised enzyme (the biocatalyst) and (ii) a transducer, to convert the biochemical signal into the electrical signal that can be measured. A representative example (there are many others) would be the Biotrace luminescence-based system for monitoring microbial ATP in food, using luciferase (see: http://www.biotrace.com).

48.3

(a) $0.285 \div 1000 \times 4$ (to calculate mmol in 4 ml) $\times 1000$ (to convert from mmol to μmol) = **1.14 μmol**.

(b) $0.273 \div 1000 \times 20$ (to calculate mmol in 20 ml) $\times 1000$ (to convert from mmol to μmol) = **5.46 μmol**.

(c) 0.317 (estimated as the mid-point between the values at 14 and 16 °C) $\div 1000 \times 10$ (to calculate mmol in 10 ml) $\times 1000$ (to convert from mmol to μmol) = **3.17 μmol**.

(d) $6.75 \div 1000 \times 250$ (to calculate mg in 250 ml) = $1.6875 = $ **1.69 mg**.

(e) 4.73 (estimated as the mid-point between the values at 24 and 26 °C) $\div 1000 \times 200$ (to calculate ml in 200 ml) = 0.946 ml.

48.4 First, calculate the oxygen content of the electrode chamber as $0.235 \div 1000 \times 5 = 0.001\,175$ mmol ($\equiv 1.175\,\mu$mol). This is equal to 200 divisions on the chart recorder paper, so therefore each division will correspond to $1.175 \div 200 = 0.005\,875\,\mu$mol ($\equiv 5.875$ nmol). The rate of oxygen consumption was -25 units (-146.875 nmol) per 2 min, equivalent to $-146.875 \div 2 = -73.44$ nmol min^{-1}. Since this was the rate for 4.1×10^9 cells, the rate per 10^9 cells is $-73.44 \div 4.1 = $ **-17.9 nmol min^{-1} (10^9 cells)$^{-1}$**.

48.5 *Tip:* Use an Excel® spreadsheet (i) to convert the data to μmol and (ii) to plot the converted data and (iii) to estimate the slope of the line. The calculations are as follows: first calculate the amount of oxygen in the chamber, as 0.285 (value in mmol l^{-1} from Table 48.2) $\div 1000$ (amount in 1 ml) $\times 5$ (amount in 5 ml) $\times 1000$ (convert from mmol to μmol) = 1.425 μmol. Next, convert the data from the table in study exercise 48.5 from percentage to μmol by dividing by 100 and multiplying by 1.425, to give the values shown in the table below.

These values are then plotted as a graph (see figure), with the slope giving the rate of net photosynthesis: in this instance, the slope (rate of net oxygen production) is 0.043 083 μmol min^{-1} (based on linear regression analysis, in Excel®). Next, calculate the amount of chlorophyll *a* in the electrode chamber, as 2.13 (μg ml^{-1}) $\times 5$ (volume of chamber, in ml) = 10.65 μg.

Oxygen content of illuminated electrode chamber containing a cyanobacterial suspension, based on data in the table in study exercise 48.5

Time	Oxygen content of chamber (μmol)
0	1.003 2
1	1.048 8
2	1.073 025
3	1.118 625
4	1.191 3
5	1.224 075
6	1.256 85
7	1.302 45
8	1.340 925

Oxygen content of an illuminated electrode chamber containing a cyanobacterial suspension, based on data in Table 48.1.

Therefore the rate of net photosynthesis is 0.043 083 $\div 10.65 = 0.004\,045\,352$ 1 mol min^{-1} (μg chlorophyll *a*)$^{-1}$ and therefore **4.05 μmol min^{-1} (mg chlorophyll *a*)$^{-1}$**.

49 Analysis of biomolecules: fundamental principles

49.1 *Tip:* Most of these terms are defined on p. 343.

(a) qualitative analysis involves determining whether a biomolecule is present or absent in a sample, while quantitative analysis involves measuring either the amount or concentration of a biomolecule in a sample;

(b) sensitivity refers to the ability to discriminate between small differences in analyte concentration whereas selectivity is the extent to which a method is free from interference due to other substances;

(c) accuracy is the closeness of a measurement to the true value while precision is a measure of the reproducibility of repeated measurements (see also Chapter 28);

(d) validation is the process of checking an analytical method against specific standards whereas replication refers to the use of several samples or subsamples (the replicates) whose measurement can give information on sample/subsample variation;

(e) noise refers to random fluctuations in a continuously monitored signal, while drift refers to baseline movement, usually in a particular direction, e.g. a shift in zero as an instrument warms up to operating temperature.

49.2 Most validated reference standards are supplied by national or international organisations involved in chemical/biochemical analysis. Examples are given below:

(a) The International Federation of Clinical Chemistry and Laboratory Medicine (at: http://www.ifcc.org/products/default.htm) supplies serum-based cortisol standards.

(b) The laboratory of the Government Chemist (at: http://www.lgc.co.uk/ref.asp) supplies urine based standards for various pharmacologically-active substances, including cotinine.

49.3 *Tip:* Note that Chapter 28 discusses accuracy and precision in more detail, while Chapter 66 covers statistical aspects, e.g. relative standard deviation. Begin by expressing both sets of data in the same units, for ease of comparison. For example, convert meter B data to $mmol \, l^{-1}$, since M_r glucose is 180.2 ($\div 180.2$ to convert from mg to mmol $\times 10$ to convert from dl to l): detection limit $= 0.0554 \, mmol \, l^{-1}$; linearity to $13.9 \, mmol \, l^{-1}$; accuracy to $\pm 0.0832 \, mmol \, l^{-1}$ (all values expressed to 3 significant figures); sample volume for meter B $= 50 \, \mu l$ (note that relative standard deviation is already expressed in percentage terms for both meters).

(a) Meter B has the lower detection limit (0.0554 compared with $0.1 \, mmol \, l^{-1}$).

(b) Meter A has the wider range ($20.0 - 0.1 = 19.9$, compared with $13.9 - 0.0554 = 13.8446 \, mmol \, l^{-1}$).

(c) Meter A has the greater accuracy (± 0.05, compared with $\pm 0.0832 \, mmol \, l^{-1}$).

(d) Meter B has the better level of precision, with the lowest percentage relative standard deviation.

(e) Meter A has the lower sample volume ($40 \, \mu l$ compared with $50 \, \mu l$).

50   Assaying amino acids and proteins

50.1 *Tip:* Box 50.1 gives full details for each method.

(a) (iii)

(b) (i)

(c) (iv)

(d) (ii)

50.2 The figure shows the standard curve for the data in the table in study exercise 50.2.

(a) From the standard curve, the amino acid concentration of each assayed sample is: (i) $4.4 \, \mu g \, ml^{-1}$; (ii) $9.0 \, \mu g \, ml^{-1}$; (iii) $15.7 \, \mu g \, ml^{-1}$ (note that the value for sample (iii) is not so reliable, due to the high absorbance values and to the curvature of the calibration curve – it would be better to repeat the assay using either a smaller amount or a greater dilution of this sample).

(b) The calibration curve is expressed in terms of the *final concentration* of amino acid in the assay tube,

Calibration curve for a series of amino acid standards.

so first calculate the *amount* of amino acid in each sample tube (multiply the concentration, in $\mu g \, ml^{-1}$, by the assay volume, i.e. 5 ml). Since this is the total amount of amino acid (in μg) in the specified volume/dilution of sample used in the assay, you should then correct for volume and dilution factor. The answers for each sample are: (i) 4.4×5 (assay volume) $\div 0.1$ (sample volume, expressed in ml) $= 220 \, \mu g \, ml^{-1} = \underline{\textbf{0.220 mg ml}^{-1}}$; (ii) $9.0 \times 5 \div 0.05 \times 10$ (dilution factor) $= 9000 \, \mu g \, ml^{-1} = \underline{\textbf{9.00 mg ml}^{-1}}$; (iii) $15.7 \times 5 \div 0.080 \times 25 = 24531.25 \, \mu g \, ml^{-1} = \underline{\textbf{24.5 mg ml}^{-1}}$.

50.3 The first step in the elucidation of the sequence is to identify the C-terminal sequence. From p. 350 note that that CNBr cleaves after methionine residues and trypsin after lysine or arginine and that Edman degradation removes the N-terminal amino acid of each peptide sequentially. From the results of the Edman degradation it can be seen that the only sequences that do not end with *met* in the CNBr-treated sample, and *lys* or *arg* in the trypsin digest are *ala ala* (CNBr) and *trp phe met ala ala* (trypsin), so these represent the C-terminal sequence. The longest of these two sequences comes from the trypsin digest, so now look at the CNBr results for an overlapping sequence – this is *ser arg trp phe met* – giving the sequence so far as *ser arg trp phe met ala ala*. Continue to look for overlapping sequences between the two sets of results until the structure is complete. Hence, the complete amino acid sequence of the polypeptide (from N-terminal to C-terminal) is:

his gly met ala glu lys val asn lys ala gly met ser arg trp phe met ala ala

51   Assaying lipids

51.1 Oxidative rancidity is primarily due to photo-oxidation of lipids: practical steps include (i) keeping samples in darkness, or in a light-proof bottle to prevent exposure to light; (ii) bubbling samples with an oxygen-free gas, e.g. nitrogen or argon, to create anoxia; and (iii) adding an antioxidant (e.g. butlyated hydroxytoluene) to 'mop up' oxygen free radicals during long-term storage.

51.2

(a) The main components of beeswax are palmitate, palmitoleate, hydroxypalmitoleate and oleate esters of long-chain alcohols (C30–C32), making up around 70–80% of the total mass. Hydrocarbons (10–18% heptacosane and nonacosane), sterols (up to 2% as cholesterol, lanesterol and β-sitosterol), pheromones (geraniol, farnesol) and terpenoids are found in the remaining fraction.

(b) Appropriate separation methods include GC and HPLC. Some components will need to be derivatised before analysis (see p. 357).

51.3 The difference volume $(V_o - V_t)$ of $0.1\,\mathrm{mol\,l^{-1}}$ sodium thiosulphate used to titrate the free iodine before and after reaction with the fat is the starting point for calculating the amount of iodine used. From reaction (iii), 2 litres of $1\,\mathrm{mol\,l^{-1}}$ $Na_2S_2O_3$ is equivalent to 1 mol of I_2, therefore $(V_o - V_t)$ ml of $0.1\,\mathrm{mol\,l^{-1}}$ sodium thiosulphate $\equiv [(V_o - V_t) \times 0.1] \div [2 \times 1000]\,\mathrm{mol}$ I_2. The atomic weight of $I = 127$, therefore M_r of $I_2 = 2 \times 127$ and so the amount of I_2 used (in g) $= [(V_o - V_t) \times 0.1 \times 2 \times 127] \div 2 \times 1000$, which simplifies to $(V_o - V_t) \times 0.0127$. The mass of fat (in g) used in the experiment $= m$ and the iodine number is the amount of I_2 (in g) absorbed by $100\,\mathrm{g}$ fat (p. 356), therefore an appropriate equation is: $[(V_o - V_t) \times 0.0127 \times 100] \div m$, which simplifies to $[(V_o - V_t) \times 1.27] \div m$ (Eqn [51.1]).

51.4 Retention time in GC depends on the volatility of the sample molecules (Chapter 44): those lipids with shorter hydrocarbon chains will be more volatile at the high temperature used and will therefore elute first. There will be an approximately linear relationship between log retention time and the number of carbon atoms in the lipid molecule.

52   Assaying carbohydrates

52.1 *Tip:* The figures in Chapter 52 illustrate examples of most of these terms.

(a) An aldose is a sugar (-'ose') containing an aldehyde group, e.g. glyceraldehyde (Fig. 52.2);

(b) A pentose is a sugar containing five carbon atoms, e.g. ribose (53.6);

(c) A hemiacetal sugar has a cyclic structure, caused by the reaction of the aldehyde group with a hydroxyl, e.g. in fructose (Fig. 52.3 – ring form);

(d) A pyranoside is a sugar with a six-membered ring structure, e.g. glucopyranose (Fig. 52.1);

(e) The β anomer refers to the position of the hydroxyl group at the C atom involved in forming the ring structure: the β configuration refers to an OH group on the same side of the ring to the CH_2OH group at the chiral centre that designates the D or L configuration, perhaps more easily grasped as an upwardly pointing – OH group in the conventional Haworth representation, e.g. β-glucopyranose in cellulose (Fig. 52.5).

(Note: if you wanted to extend this exercise, you could try thinking of alternative structures to each of the terms given in (a)–(e), with a representative examples of each alternative).

52.2

(a) The figure in study exercise 52.2 shows that raffinose contains the monosaccharides galactose, glucose and fructose, since these are present in the hydrolysed

sample. Raffinose is a naturally occurring trisaccharide found in a wide range of plant families, with the composition: O-β-galactopyranosyl-$(1-6)$-α-D-glucopyranosyl-$(1-2)$-β-D-fructofuranoside (see: http://www.plantbiology.com/documents/R/raffinose.asp).

(b) *Tip:* Use Eqn [44.2] (p. 296) to calculate the migration distance for raffinose in this experiment, as follows: $0.34 = $ (distance moved by raffinose) $\div 35 = \underline{\mathbf{11.9\,mm}}$.

52.3 DNS is a yellow compound that can be reduced to an orange-red derivative, assayed at $540\,\mathrm{nm}$ (Table 52.1), by sugars that have free reducing groups in their structure, e.g. the aldehyde group in the straight chain form of glucose (Fig. 52.1) and the ketone group of fructose (Fig. 52.3). In sucrose, the glycosidic bond between the constituent glucose and fructose molecules is formed using the anomeric carbon atoms, i.e. those of the aldehyde and ketone groups of the respective monosaccharides, and it is therefore a 'non-reducing sugar' unable reduce DNS to its orange-red form. In other disaccharides such as maltose (Fig. 52.4), which consists of two glucose units, the glycosidic bond involves only the anomeric carbon atom of one glucose molecule, while the aldehyde group on the other glucose unit remains free to show reducing properties, thereby reacting with DNS to give a colour change.

53   Assaying nucleic acids and nucleotides

53.1 *Tip:* Substitute values into Eqn [53.1] to calculate the DNA concentration of the unknown, as: $(50 \times 32) \div 58 = 27.586\,206 = \underline{\mathbf{27.6\,\mu g\,ml^{-1}}}$ (note that the units for the concentration of the unknown are the same as those used for the standard).

53.2

(i) In aqueous solution, individual ethidium bromide molecules have a low fluorescence, due to the stacking of the planar molecules (Fig. 53.4). When ethidium bromide intercalates between two strands of DNA, this leads to a substantial enhancement in fluorescence – intercalation prevents the molecular collisions that would otherwise decrease fluorescence.

(ii) Ethidium bromide can also intercalate within double stranded regions of RNA, e.g. hairpin loops.

53.3 Measure the relative fluorescence intensity (RFI) of the sample (extract plus ethidium bromide), then add ribonuclease (RNase) to the cuvette and incubate in a water bath for $20\,\mathrm{min}$. Remeasure the RFI and compare this to the original RFI. If the RFI is lower after RNase treatment, the original preparation must have been contaminated with RNA. Note that the RNA must have some double stranded regions for ethidium bromide to intercalate.

54   Protein purification

54.1 *Tip:* Use Table 54.3 to determine the amount of $(NH_4)_2SO_4$ required, by taking into account the sample volume. To raise the $(NH_4)_2SO_4$ concentration of $100\,\mathrm{ml}$

(0.1 l) of solution from 0% (initial concentration) to 40% (final concentration) requires 22.9 g. This will precipitate protein A, which is then separated by centrifugation. A further 12.2 g of $(NH_4)_2SO_4$ needs to be added to the supernatant from the centrifugation step to increase the concentration from 40% (the new 'initial concentration') to 60% (final concentration). Remember that addition of solid $(NH_4)_2SO_4$ will increase the volume of solution, and the values shown in Table 54.3 already take this into account. After removal of protein B by a second centrifugation step, protein C will remain in solution.

54.2

(a) Cibacron Blue (Blue Sepharose®), which has structural similarities to $NAD^+/NADH$, is a suitable medium.

(b) A column with immobilised Ni^{2+} has particular affinity with histidine residues with which it chelates. This technique is often used for purification of expressed proteins produced by cloning (see p. 304).

(c) Lectins have affinity for the carbohydrate groups of glycoproteins (note that many different lectins are available, each with a particular affinity for a specific type of carbohydrate).

54.3 *Tip:* Prepare a table, with columns for each of the additional steps required, i.e. (i) total enzyme activity (activity per ml × total volume of extract), (ii) total protein content (protein concentration per ml × total volume of extract) and (iii) specific activity (total enzyme activity ÷ total protein content). Then, use Eqns [54.2] and [54.1] to calculate yield and n-fold purification respectively, and add these to two further columns. The table shows how this can be applied in this case (note that the values are not rounded off until the final stage).

Calculation of the yield and purification of an enzyme using data from the table in study exercise 54.3

Stage	Total enzyme activity (U)	Total protein content (mg)	Specific activity (U mg^{-1})	Percentage yield (to 3 significant figures)	n-fold purification (to 3 significant figures)
1	93.6	374.4	0.25	100	1.00
2	84.0	119.0	0.705 882 352	89.7	2.82
3	64.0	25.0	2.56	68.4	10.3
4	54.0	7.0	7.714 285 714	57.7	30.9
5	39.42	2.04	19.323 529 41	42.1	77.3

55 Enzyme studies

55.1

(a) *Tip:* Tackle this one by converting the absorbance change per minute to amount of product formed, in nmol: $0.25 \div 0.122 \times 10 = 20.491\,803$ nmol min^{-1} = **20.5 nmol min^{-1}**.

(b) *Tip:* express the activity in the appropriate units (mol s^{-1}) to give the number of katals. From part (a), enzyme activity = $20.491\,803$ nmol min^{-1} ÷ 60 = $0.341\,530\,1$ nmol s^{-1} = $0.341\,530\,1 \times 10^{-9}$ mol s^{-1} = $0.341\,530\,1 \times 10^{-9}$ kat = **0.342×10^{-9} kat** (or 0.342 nkat). Note that you should use the full numerical values in these calculations and not the answers expressed to 3 significant figures, to avoid introducing 'rounding' errors.

(c) *Tip:* Divide the enzyme activity by the amount of protein present in the assay to give the specific activity. Thus, in terms of nmol: $20.491\,803$ nmol min^{-1} ÷ 2.5 = $8.196\,721\,2$ = **8.20 nmol min^{-1} (mg protein)$^{-1}$**. In terms of kat: $0.341\,530\,1 \times 10^{-9} \div 2.5 = 0.136\,612 \times 10^{-9}$ = **0.137×10^{-9} kat (mg protein)$^{-1}$**.

55.2 *Tip:* If you do not have specialised software for determining kinetic constants, you can use Excel® to prepare a suitable plot, e.g. a Lineweaver–Burk plot. Enter the data from the table in study exercise 55.2 into two columns, then prepare a further two columns to contain the reciprocals of each value (note that you cannot plot the zero values, since there is no reciprocal). Then use the chart 'wizard' to prepare a double reciprocal plot: note that Excel® will only draw a trend line between the points – you will need either to extend this line by hand, as shown in the figure, or use linear regression analysis (p. 493) to give the Y intercept and slope (if you divide the Y intercept by the slope, this will give the X intercept, but without the negative sign). In the example shown below, the Y intercept ($1/V_{max}$) is $0.134\,437\,07$, so $V_{max} = 74.384\,247\,31$ = **74.4 U**. Similarly, the X intercept ($-1/K_m$) is $-0.055\,498\,669$, so $K_m = 18.018\,45$ = **18.0 μmol l^{-1}**.

Lineweaver–Burk double reciprocal plot of the data in the table in study exercise 55.2.

Answers to study exercises

55.3 *Tip:* Fig. 55.8 illustrates the principles involved. Competitive inhibitors are often structural analogues. In this example AZT (azidothymidine) is a structural analogue of thymidine, and is likely to be a competitive inhibitor. HBY (a quinoxaline derivative manufactured by Hoechst-Bayer®) is not an analogue of thymidine and it is more likely to be a non-competitive inhibitor. A simple kinetic experiment to show the type of inhibition would involve measuring enzyme activity (in this case, reverse transcriptase) over a range of pharmacologically relevant substrate concentrations (i) without inhibitor present, and (ii) in the presence of a fixed concentration of inhibitor. When the results are used to produce Lineweaver–Burk plots (p. 382), a competitive inhibitor will give the result shown in Fig. 55.8a, which shows that the V_{max} remains unchanged, but the K_m is increased (remember that a decrease in $-1/K_m$ is due to an increase in K_m, and a reduced affinity of the enzyme for the substrate). A non-competitive inhibitor will result in Lineweaver–Burk plots like those shown in Fig. 55.8b, where the K_m is unaffected, but the V_{max} is reduced. A sample of RT would be required to carry out these experiments, along with a method of measuring the product (p. 379).

56 Membrane transport processes

56.1 *Tip:* Use Eqn [56.1] to calculate flux rates.

(a) Here the units are consistent, so no changes are required before substituting values into Eqn [56.1]
$\phi = (0.0001 \times 150) \div 50\,000 = \mathbf{3 \times 10^{-7}\,mol\,m^{-2}\,s^{-1}}$.

(b) Again, the units are consistent, so no changes are needed. $\phi = (1.65 \times 10^{-4} \times 106) \div (8.25 \times 10^{4}) = \mathbf{2.12 \times 10^{-7}\,mol\,m^{-2}\,s^{-1}}$.

(c) Here, the values must be converted to the same units, so $[C_i] = 10.5 \div 1000$ (convert from mmol to mol) $\times 1000$ (convert from dm^3 to m^3) $= 10.5\,mol\,m^{-3}$ and $M_a = 1.66 \times 10^{-9} \times 1000$ (convert from dm^3 to m^3) $= 1.66 \times 10^{-6}\,m^2\,m^{-3}$. Then, using Eqn [56.1], $\phi = (4.75 \times 10^{-5} \times 10.5) \div (1.66 \times 10^6) = 3.004\,518\,1 \times 10^{-10} = \mathbf{3.00 \times 10^{-10}\,mol\,m^{-2}\,s^{-1}}$.

56.2 *Tip:* Substitute values into Eqn [56.2] to determine passive fluxes.

(a) $J = 2 \times 10^{-7}\,(1.5 - 10) = \mathbf{-1.7 \times 10^{-6}\,mol\,m^{-2}\,s^{-1}}$ (note that the passive flux is outwards in this case, signified by the negative sign).

(b) $J = 1.6 \times 10^{-9}\,(0.03 - 8.65) = -1.3792 \times 10^{-8} = \mathbf{-1.38 \times 10^{-8}\,mol\,m^{-2}\,s^{-1}}$ (note that the passive flux is outwards in this case, signified by the negative sign).

(c) First, convert all values to the same units, e.g. $mol\,m^{-3}$ (numerically equivalent to $mmol\,dm^{-3}$) for the internal and external concentrations and $m\,s^{-1}$ ($\div 100$ to convert from $cm\,s^{-1}$) for the permeability coefficient, then substitute into Eqn [56.2]. $J = 2.6 \times 10^{-5}\,(3.45 - 0.25) = \mathbf{8.32 \times 10^{-5}\,mol\,m^{-2}\,s^{-1}}$ (in this case, the passive flux is inwardly directed, signified by the positive value for J).

56.3 *Tip:* First convert all values to the appropriate base units, for ease of comparison (see table).

Kinetic parameters for amino acid uptake into three different cell types

Cell type	V_{max} $(mol\,m^{-3}\,s^{-1})$	K_s $(mol\,m^{-3})$
A	1.52×10^{-8}	1.24×10^{-3}
B	9.6×10^{-9}	6.54×10^{-4}
C	8.4×10^{-10}	2.54×10^{-4}

(a) Cell type A has the highest maximum rate (highest value for V_{max}).

(b) Cell type C has the highest affinity (smallest value for K_s).

(c) To determine the rate of transport for each cell type at this concentration, substitute the relevant values from the table above into Eqn [56.3]. Thus, to 3 significant figures, for cell type A, $v = [(1.52 \times 10^{-8}) \times (1 \times 10^{-4})] \div [(1.24 \times 10^{-3}) + (1 \times 10^{-4})] = \mathbf{1.22 \times 10^{-9}\,mol\,m^{-2}\,s^{-1}}$, and for cell type B, $v = [(9.6 \times 10^{-9}) \times (1 \times 10^{-4})] \div [(6.54 \times 10^{-4} + 1 \times 10^{-4})] = \mathbf{1.27 \times 10^{-9}\,mol\,m^{-2}\,s^{-1}}$, and for cell type C, $v = [(8.4 \times 10^{-10}) \times (1 \times 10^{-4})] \div [(2.54 \times 10^{-4}) + (1 \times 10^{-4})] = \mathbf{2.37 \times 10^{-10}\,mol\,m^{-2}\,s^{-1}}$. Thus, the fastest rate is for cell type B.

56.4 *Tip:* Use the Nernst equation (Eqn [56.4]) to calculate transmembrane electrical potentials (don't forget to include the charge on each ion, z). From Chapter 29, the value for the gas constant, $R = 8.31443\,J\,K^{-1}\,mol^{-1}$, and Faraday's constant, $F = 9.648675 \times 10^{4}\,C\,mol^{-1}$ ($\equiv J\,V^{-1}\,mol^{-1}$, see Table 29.2). At 25 °C, $T = 273.15 + 25 = 298.15\,K$ (see Box 29.1).

(a) For K^+, $E_n = 2.303\,[(8.31443 \times 298.15) \div (+1 \times 9.648675 \times 10^4)]$ log $(10 \div 197) = -0.076\,5921\,V = \mathbf{-76.6\,mV}$. For Na^+, $E_n = 2.303\,[(8.314\,43 \times 298.15) \div (+1 \times 9.648\,675 \times 10^4)]$ log $(225 \div 8.4) = +0.084\,4874\,V = \mathbf{+84.4\,mV}$. For Cl^-, $E_n = 2.303\,[(8.314\,43 \times 298.15) \div (-1 \times 9.648\,675 \times 10^4)]$ log $(235 \div 27.3) = -0.055\,3173\,V = \mathbf{-55.3\,mV}$.

(b) The transmembrane equilibrium potential for K^+ is close to the membrane potential, suggesting electrochemical equilibrium. The equilibrium potential for Na^+ is more positive than the membrane potential, indicating that this cation is actively transported out of the cell (active efflux). The equilibrium potential for Cl^- is less negative than the membrane potential, indicating that this anion is actively accumulated within the cell. An alternative approach to this type of problem is to calculate the internal ion concentration that would be achieved by passive equilibration, by substituting the measured membrane potential and external ion concentration into Eqn [56.4], and solving for $[C_i]$.

57 Photosynthesis and respiration

57.1 *Tip:* Chapter 57 contains several definitions within the margin boxes.

(a) Net photosynthesis is the apparent (measured) rate of CO_2 uptake or O_2 production, while gross photosynthesis is the rate of CO_2 uptake or O_2 production with allowance for gas exchange due to respiration and the oxidative photosynthetic carbon cycle (photorespiration).

(b) In C_3 photosynthesis, the first stable product is phosphoglyceric acid, a C_3 compound, while in C_4 photosynthesis the early products are the C_4 acids malate or aspartate.

(c) The oxygenase function of Rubisco leads to the production of a molecule of the C_2 compound glycollic acid plus one molecule of C_3 phosphoglyceric acid, while the carboxylase function leads to the production of two molecules of phosphoglyceric acid.

(d) Coupling is the link between O_2 consumption and phosphorylation, while uncoupling refers to the extent to which these processes are not linked, e.g. as a result of the action of an 'uncoupler' (metabolic inhibitor) such as CCCP.

(e) The respiratory quotient is the ratio of CO_2 evolved to O_2 consumed (Eqn [57.11]), while the respiratory control ratio is a measure of the rate of O_2 consumption with and without ADP (see Eqn [57.12]).

57.2 *Tip:* See Box 39.1 for examples of how to use specific activity to calculate amount of substance. First, convert from amount of radioactivity (d.p.m.) to amount of substance (e.g. μmol) using the specific activity: $2808 \div 0.72 = 3900$ nmol $\div 3.9$ μmol. Next, calculate the amount per minute by dividing by the incubation time: $3.9 \div 3 = 1.3$ μmol min^{-1}. Finally, express the answer per mg chl a by taking into account the amount of chl a involved: $1.3 \div 0.29 = 4.482\,758\,6 = \underline{\mathbf{4.48\ \mu mol\ (mg\ chl\ a)^{-1}\ min^{-1}}}$.

57.3

(a) DCPIP is reduced from a blue-coloured compound (absorbing maximally towards the red end of the EMR spectrum, e.g. 600 nm) to a colourless (*leuco*) compound when it accepts electrons from photosystem II (PS II, p. 402).

(b) Simazine clearly acts as an inhibitor of photosynthetic electron transport, and this is likely to explain its herbicidal action (simazine is known to inhibit PS II).

(c) The plotted curve is shown in the first figure: drawing tangents to each curve at zero time (p. 472) gave the following initial rates: control $= 3.15 \times 10^{-3}$ s^{-1}; 1.0 nmol l^{-1} simazine $= 2.24 \times 10^{-3}$ s^{-1}; 10.0 nmol l^{-1} simazine $= 1.76 \times 10^{-3}$ s^{-1}; 100.0 nmol l^{-1} simazine $= 1.04 \times 10^{-3}$ s^{-1}. Converting these values to percentage inhibition gives the following (expressed to 3 significant figures): 1.0 nmol l^{-1} simazine $= 28.9\%$; 10.0 nmol l^{-1} simazine $= 44.1\%$;

Plot of absorbance against time for a chloroplast suspension incubated with DCPIP and various levels of simazine.

Plot of percentage inhibition caused by simazine against $\log_{10}$ simazine concentration, showing the 50% inhibition point.

100.0 nmol l^{-1} simazine $= 67.0\%$. These values are then log-transformed (p. 470) and plotted against simazine concentration (the second figure), giving a log I_{50} value of 1.15, which gives a true (antilog) estimate for the $\underline{\mathbf{I_{50}\ of\ simazine = 14.1\ nmol^{-1}}}$.

57.4 *Tip:* Typical RQ values for carbohydrates, fats and proteins are given on p. 404. Glucose is a carbohydrate, triglycerides are lipids, and casein is the major protein fraction from milk.

(a) (iii)

(b) (i)

(c) (ii)

57.5 *Tip:* Calculate the amounts of ADP and O_2 involved (in the same units) and substitute values into Eqn [57.13]. Begin by calculating the amount of ADP added to the chamber, as $25 \div 1000$ (convert from l to ml) $\times 0.05$ (account for volume used, in ml) $= 1.25 \times 10^{-3}$ mmol ($\equiv 1.25$ μmol). Next, calculate the amount of O_2 consumed within the chamber, as $218 - 174 = 44$ μmol l^{-1}, therefore $44 \div 1000$ (convert from l to ml) $\times 5$ (account for volume of chamber) $= 0.22$ μmol. Substituting these values into Eqn [57.12] gives P/O $= 1.25 \div (2 \times 0.22) = 2.84$ (to 3 significant figures). This is close to the predicted P/O value for NADH of 3, which indicates that the mitochondrial suspension shows tight coupling between O_2 uptake and ATP synthesis (ADP consumption).

Answers to study exercises

57.6 *Tip:* Substitute values into Eqn [57.14]. Thus $\Delta p = -85.6 - [59 (8.6 - 7.4)] = -156.4\,\text{mV}$. Mitochondrial Δp is usually $180–200\,\text{mV}$ (p. 406), so this value is a little low and may indicate that some of the mitochondria are damaged.

58 Mendelian genetics

58.1 The table shows the layout of the Punnett square.

Punnett square for cross RrOO × RrOo

		Parent 1	
Gametes		**RO**	**rO**
	RO	RROO	RrOO
	Ro	RROo	RrOo
	rO	RrOO	rrOO
	ro	RrOo	rrOo

(left column label: Parent 2)

Genotype ratios: RROO : RROo : 1RrOo : RrOO : RrOO : rrOo : rroo in ratio 1 : 1 : 2 : 1 : 1 : 1 : 1
Phenotype ratio: red closed : pink closed : pink open : white closed : in ratio 1 : 2 : 1

58.2 Probability of blue-eyed $= 0.25$
Probability of blonde $= 0.5$
Probability of girl $= 0.5$
Overall probability $= 0.25 \times 0.5 \times 0.5 = \underline{\textbf{0.0625}}$

58.3 Assuming normal mice are homozygous for tail presence, The approximately 1 : 1 phenotype ratio in the F_1 indicates that the tail-less phenotype is heterozygous and possibly dominant. The approximately 1 : 2 : 1 ratio of phenotypes in the F_2 generation (counting 'dead on birth' as a phenotype) also indicates that tail-less might be dominant over normal. The results could be explained if the tail-less gene is fatal when double recessive. There is no sex linkage because the ratio of males to females is roughly equivalent in all progeny phenotypes.

58.4 Use notation X = female, Y = male, X^R = red allele, X^r = white allele.
(a) Assume progeny ratio is 2 : 1 : 1, then cross must be $X^R X^r$ (red-eyed heterozygous female) × $X^R Y$ (red-eyed male), giving progeny genotypes $X^R X^R$, $X^R X^r$, $X^R Y$ and $X^r Y$ in the ratio 1 : 1 : 1 : 1 and phenotypes as observed.
(b) Assume progeny ratio is 1 : 1, then cross must be *either* $X^R X^R$ (red-eyed homozygous female) × $X^r Y$ (white-eyed male), giving progeny genotypes $X^R X^r$, $X^R Y$ in the ratio 1 : 1 and the phenotypes as observed; *or* $X^R X^R$ (red-eyed homozygous female) × $X^R Y$ (red-eyed male), giving progeny genotypes $X^R X^R$, $X^R Y$ in the ratio 1 : 1 and the phenotypes as observed.
(c) Assume progeny ratio is 1 : 1 : 1 : 1, then cross must be $X^R X^r$ (red-eyed heterozygous female) × $X^r Y$ (white-eyed male), giving progeny genotypes $X^R X^r$, $X^r X^r$, $X^R Y$ and $X^r Y$ in the ratio 1 : 1 : 1 : 1 and the phenotypes as observed.

58.5 The expected values are 137 : 274 : 137, based on a 1 : 2 : 1 ratio. The χ^2 value is $1.05 + 3.07 + 2.11 = 6.23$ (see Box 58.2 for method of working). Since this value is greater than the critical value for χ^2 for 2 degrees of freedom ($n - 1$ categories $= 3 - 1$) at $P = 0.05$ (which is 5.99, Table 58.1), the geneticist should reject the null hypothesis of a 1 : 2 : 1 outcome.

59 Bacterial and phage genetics

59.1
(a) A zygote, formed by the fusion of two gametes, contains two copies of each chromosome and is diploid, while a merozygote is a cell containing two copies of part of its genome (a partial diploid).
(b) Tranformation is the uptake and assimilation of external genetic material into the genome of a cell, while transposition is the movement of genetic material due to the action of a transposon (a small mobile DNA sequence, coding for its own movement within the genome).
(c) In generalised transduction, a suitably sized fragment of the bacterial genome is packaged inside the protein coat of a phage and then introduced into a new cell, where it may be incorporated by homologous recombination, while specialised transduction involves the inclusion of one or more bacterial genes during excision of a latent phage, followed by transfer and reintegration into a new cell.
(d) While a prototroph can grow in unsupplemented minimal medium, an auxotroph requires a specific additional organic compound in order to grow in minimal medium.
(e) HFr strains have F plasmid DNA integrated into the chromosome and show a high frequency of recombination for chromosomal genes during conjugation, while F' strains have a modified F plasmid containing one or more chromosomal genes which are transferred at very high frequency during conjugation.

59.2
(a) Ampicillin-resistant, capable of growth on lactose, and a tryptophan auxotroph, requiring tryptophan in the growth medium.
(b) Histidine auxotroph, incapable of using lactose as a carbon source for growth.
(c) Glutamine auxotroph, due to the insertional inactivation of the *gln*A gene by transposon 10.
(d) Prototroph – capable of growing in the absence of tryptophan (note that the chromosomal *trp*A gene is inactivated by Tn6, but the F' plasmid-encoded *trp*A gene will complement the inactivated chromosomal gene).
(e) The functional *gal* gene present in the $\lambda dgal$ genome would complement the chromosomal deficiency (Gal$^-$), giving a strain that would be capable of growth on lactose.

59.3 *Tip:* Look for overlapping sequences, and remember that the F plasmid DNA may integrate either way round. The sequences overlap as follows:

Strain (b) Y D F X W
Strain (a)   X W C Z A
Strain (c)   Z A E B Y

So, the complete (linear) sequence is **Y D F X W C Z A E B**, shown in circular form in the figure.

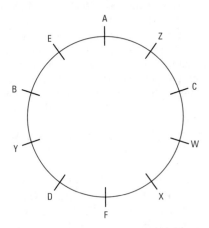

Chromosome map for study exercise 59.3 (note that the map shows only the position of each gene relative to the others, not the exact location).

59.4

(a) Medium A tests for ampicillin resistance; medium B tests for the ability to grow without added tryptophan (tryptophan prototrophy); medium C tests for the ability to grow without added histidine; medium D tests for the growth on lactose as the sole carbon and energy source (the small amounts of tryptophan and histidine would not support significant growth).

(b) For each character, the HFr strain must carry the wild-type gene and the recipient must carry a defective (mutant) form. Thus (i) the HFr donor has

Number of recombinant colonies as a function of time for an interrupted conjugation experiment (data from table in study exercise 59.4).

the phenotype Amp^r, His$^+$, Trp$^+$, Lac$^+$ and (ii) the F$^-$ recipient strain has the phenotype Amp^s His$^-$ Trp$^-$ Lac$^-$.

(c) *Tip:* Begin by plotting the number of recombinant colonies against time – extrapolation to the *x*-axis gives the time of entry for each gene – as in Fig. 59.6. This is shown in the figure here, giving the following times of entry, in minutes: **Trp = 8; His = 17; Amp = 27; Lac = 36**. This could also be represented in map form, as in the figure in exercise 59.3.

60   Molecular genetics I – fundamental principles

60.1

(a) *Tip:* Use the relationship given on p. 430, where an absorbance value of 1 corresponds to a single stranded DNA concentration of 33 μg ml^{-1}. Thus, $0.14 \times 33 = 4.62 \mu$g ml^{-1} (DNA in the spectrophotometer cuvette) $\times 100$ (to account for the 100-fold dilution step, i.e. $5 + 495 \mu l) = 462 \mu$g ml^{-1}.

(b) *Tip:* It is essential that you understand the difference between *amount* of substance and *concentration*, as discussed on p. 245, before you perform these calculations. Chapters 23 and 24 also give advice on calculations involving molar concentrations, while Chapter 29 covers units and prefixes. One approach is to divide by the M_r of the DNA probe (in this case, 24 bases $\times 325 = 7800$) to covert μg ml^{-1} to μmol ml^{-1}, thus $462 \div 7800 = 0.0592307 \mu$mol ml^{-1}, equivalent to **59.2 μmol l^{-1}** ('micromolar').

(c) The working solution of the probe is required at 100×10 pmol ml$^{-1} = 1000$ pmol ml$^{-1} \equiv 1$ nmol ml^{-1}. The reconstituted stock contains the DNA probe at a concentration of 0.0592307μmol ml^{-1} ($\equiv 59.2307$ nmol ml^{-1}). So, a dilution of 1 in 59.2 (3 significant figures) is required, for a volume of 5 ml, i.e. **take 84.4 μl of reconstituted stock and make up to a final volume of 5 ml with an appropriate buffer solution**.

60.2 *Tip:* Table 60.2 gives advice for standard polyacrylamide and agarose gels, while pulse field gel electrophoresis is covered on pp. 430–1.

(a) Use an agarose gel, e.g. at a concentration of 0.3% w/v.

(b) Use a polyacrylamide gel, e.g. at a concentration of 5% w/v.

(c) Use PACE, which is a variant of pulsed field gel electrophoresis that is able to fractionate DNA molecules of widely different sizes.

60.3 Stringency is a term used to describe the interaction between a nucleic acid probe and its target sequence – high stringency refers to conditions where the hybridisation requires exact complementarity between the two, while low stringency implies that a degree of base mismatching will be tolerated. Stability depends on the number and type of complementary base pairs that can be formed between the probe and the target sequence. The more G + C pairs (with 3 H-bonds, rather than the 2 between A-T, p. 365), the more stable the binding. Stability also increases with probe size, but decreases with increasing incubation temperature, ionic strength and the pH of the hybridisation buffer. Low stringency hybridisation is useful if you are working with a probe obtained from a species different from the source of target DNA. Stringent conditions are required when attempting to detect a single base change, e.g. in hybridisation of mutant and wild-type DNA.

60.4 *Tip:* The gel is read from top (largest fragment at 3′ end) to bottom (smallest fragment at 5′ end) – note also that the original strand has the complementary sequence to that read from the gel. The sequence from the gel is ATTGCGTATTCG, while the (complementary) sequence of the original strand is therefore TAACGCATAAGC.

61 Molecular genetics II – PCR and related applications

61.1 Insufficient Mg^{2+} can impair the polymerisation reaction, since it is an essential co-factor for thermostable DNA polymerases. Excess Mg^{2+} stabilises double stranded DNA and may prevent complete denaturation of the PCR product after each cycle, thereby reducing yield. Excess Mg^{2+} can also promote spurious annealing of primers, and this can lead to production of non-specific products (for more details, see: http://www.promega.com/guides/pcr_guide/070_04/promega.html).

61.2

(i) They should be at least 18 nucleotides long (optimally, 18–30 nucleotides).

(ii) The 3′ ends of primers should end with a G or C.

(iii) They should have similar G + C content so that they have similar annealing temperatures, ideally within 5 °C of each other, based on Eqn [61.1].

(iv) The primers should have minimal self-complementarity, and minimal complementarity to each other, so that primer dimers are not formed.

61.3 *Tip:* Use Eqn [61.1] to calculate T_m values for the primer illustrated. The number of bases is: G = 7, C = 3; A = 3; T = 5, therefore: $T_m = 4(7 + 3) + 2(3 + 5) = 56 °C$ (if the sequence is short enough, you can add up the individual 2s and 4s in your head as you work along the primer).

61.4 *Tip:* Box 61.1 covers the key aspects. Use a laminar flow hood to avoid sample contamination during processing (built-in UV lighting can be used to degrade contaminating DNA); use separate laboratories for (i) initial preparation (pre-PCR), (ii) PCR processing and (iii) storage and analysis of products (post-PCR); keep separate supplies of disposable plastic items (tips, tubes, etc.) for (i) sample preparation, (ii) PCR reagents and (iii) product analysis; autoclave all reagents, buffers and plastic items; wear disposable gloves throughout, changing them between procedures.

61.5 *Tip:* You'll need to rewrite the primer sequences in 3′ to 5′ order, to check alignment against the lower strand in the target sequence, since this runs from the 3′ to the 5′ end (in all three cases, the second of the two primers is directed towards the lower strand).

Primer pair (a) is not suitable: these oligonucleotides may lead to the formation of primer dimers (p. 438) because the two sequences partially complement one another, as follows:

```
5′-TCGCTGAAGGACATGTCG-3′
      3′-CCTGTACAGCGGATCTAGC-5′
```

The GC content of the two primers also differs (p. 438), with the upper primer containing 10 G + C and the lower primer containing 11 G + C. Ideally, they should have the same G + C content, and therefore Tm, if possible.

Primer pair (b) is also unsuitable: although their GC contents are identical, the second primer contains a single mismatch error, and thus will not hybridise perfectly with the central section of the (upper) single stranded template, as follows:

```
5′-26basesTACGGTCGAGAC[G]TAAGGA17bases-3′
     3′-ATGCCAGCTCTG[G]ATTCCT-5′
```

Also, the 3′ end of the second primer (where elongation is initiated) ends with TA. For optimal hybridisation (p. 438), it should end in either GC, CG, GG or CC.

Primer pair (c): these two primers have the same GC content, 3′ ends comprising two G or C residues, no mismatched bases and they should not hybridise to one another. They are therefore the most suited pair for the amplification of the desired DNA sequence. Note that sometimes a 'perfect' pair of primers cannot be designed because of the constraints imposed by the target DNA sequence, and high AT contents, or 3′ ends that include A or T residues have to be used.

61.6 *Tip:* Use the Web to research forensic applications of PCR and DNA testing. In this instance, the tests carried out included PCR targeted at: (i) DNA-based sex testing, to establish which bones were from males and which from females, and whether the number of each was consistent with the Tsar's family), (ii) short tandem repeat (STR) analysis, a variation of VNTR (p. 441), to establish that a single family group was involved, and (iii) mitochondrial DNA (mitDNA) analysis. Mitochondrial DNA is very useful in forensic studies as it is more stable than chromosomal DNA and can be amplified when samples are too small or too old for conventional DNA analysis. Furthermore, if no soft tissue is available, mitDNA can be extracted from solid material such as bone. Since mitDNA is inherited through the maternal line, it can be used to establish family relationships between generations, especially if it can be compared with known members of the family (in this case, the mitDNA of Prince Philip, the Duke of Edinburgh was used, as he is the grandnephew of Tsarina Alexandra). Using these techniques the FSS was able to confirm that the bones found in Yekaterinberg were from Tsar Nicholas and his family. More details, plus other examples of DNA analysis in forensic science, can be found at: http://www.forensic.gov.uk/forensic/entry.htm (look under "news and casefiles").

62 Molecular genetics III – genetic engineering techniques

62.1 *Tip:* The origins of restriction enzyme names are explained in Chapter 60 (p. 428). *Hin* dIII was the third restriction enzyme to be isolated from *Haemophilus influenzae* strain Rd, while *Eco* RI was the first isolated from *Escherichia coli* strain R. Note that in most cases, the first letter of the genus and the first two letters of the species are used to construct the first part of the restriction enzyme code, e.g. *Ava* I from *Anabaena variabilis* (Fig. 62.1).

62.2

(a) Purification step for DNA, reducing the level of most proteins and non-anionic cellular constituents.

(b) Precipitates DNA and reduces salt contamination.

(c) Degrades contaminating RNA (ribonuclease) and proteins (protease).

(d) Lysozyme digests the peptidoglycan of the bacterial cell wall and EDTA aids its access through the Gram-negative bacterial outer membrane (p. 237) to reach the peptidoglycan layer.

(e) Sodium dodecyl sulphate at high concentration solubilises membranes and causes cell lysis.

(f) NaOH aids cell lysis and disrupts macromolecules. Neutralisation with potassium acetate allows plasmid DNA to return to a soluble form, while leaving chromosomal DNA and other macromolecules as an insoluble mass.

The order of use of these reagents is: (d); (e); (f); (c); (a); (b).

62.3 First, determine the fragment sizes (in kbp) for each digest:

> *Eco* RI: 7 kbp
>
> *Hin* dIII: 7 kbp
>
> *Pvu* II: 7 kbp

The results for the individual enzymes confirm that the plasmid is cut once, creating a single linear molecule of 7 kbp (note that an intact, circular, plasmid would run further on the gel, since it would be more compact).

> *Eco* RI and *Hin* dIII: 1 and 6 kbp
>
> *Eco* RI and *Pvu* II: 3 and 4 kbp
>
> *Hin* dIII and *Pvu* II: 2 and 5 kbp
>
> *Eco* RI, *Hin* dIII and *Pvu* II: 1, 2 and 4 kbp

The approach to working out the relative locations of each restriction site is to match up the sizes of the band, or bands, that no longer appear on the gel when the enzymes are combined and then try to piece together the fragments, to see how they were combined in the intact molecule by sketching out possible configurations. The exercise is not unlike a jigsaw puzzle. The results for the paired enzyme combinations confirm that each cuts the plasmid once, since two fragments are obtained. The minimum distance between two enzymes is given by the smaller band in each case: 1 kbp between *Eco* RI and *Hin* dIII, 3 kbp between *Eco* RI and *Pvu* II and 2 kbp between *Hin* dIII and *Pvu* II. In this instance, the results when all three enzymes are combined can then be compared to those for any pair of enzymes (e.g. *Eco* RI and *Pvu* II), showing that the *Hin* dIII site must lie between *Eco* RI and *Pvu* II sites, since the 3 kbp fragment is cleaved into a 1 kbp and a 2 kbp

fragment, giving the map shown below. (Note that the results cannot tell us the *absolute* orientation of the sites, but only their relative position: a mirror image of the map shown in the figure would give the same results. Complex restriction digests are best analysed using an appropriate software package: alternatively, restriction sites can be predicted on the basis of DNA sequence information.)

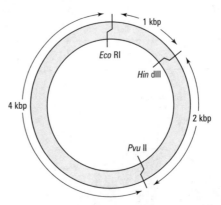

Restriction map of plasmid pRD.

62.4 *Tip:* Work through the calculation in small steps, taking into account the various volumes and dilutions used, to arrive at the correct answer. First, calculate the number of transformants in the entire sample: 180×10 (to correct for 10-fold dilution) $\div 200 \times 500$ (to convert from $200\,\mu l$ to $500\,\mu l$) $= 4500$ CFU. Next, calculate the amount of plasmid DNA (in μg) used in the procedure: $20 \times 0.1 = 2.0\,\text{ng} = 0.002\,\mu g$. Finally, divide the number of transformants by the amount of DNA, to give the answer: $4500 \div 0.002 = 2\,250\,000 = \textbf{2.25} \times \textbf{10}^{6}$ **CFU (μg DNA)$^{-1}$**. An alternative approach is to calculate the amount of plasmid DNA (in μg) present in the subsample used on the spread plate, as 0.1×20 (ng added) $\div 10$ (dilution factor) $\times 200 \div 500$ (fractional volume spread) $= 0.08\,\text{ng} = 0.000\,08\,\mu g$. Next, divide the number of transformants on the spread plate by this value to give the answer: $180 \div 0.000\,08 = \textbf{2.25} \times \textbf{10}^{6}$ **CFU (μg DNA)$^{-1}$**.

63 Using graphs

63.1

(a) Three-dimensional graph.

(b) Pie chart.

(c) Scatter diagram, possibly with an added trend line.

(d) Bar chart.

(e) Plotted curve.

63.2 *Tip:* The data must first be calculated as a proportion of the total, and then the degrees of the relevant 'slice' worked out by multiplying by 360 (the number of degrees in a circle), as shown in the table overleaf. Use a compass to make a circle for your graph, then use a protractor to mark out the number of degrees required per slice. The resulting graph should look like the figure overleaf.

Number of strains of bacteria isolated from a water sample

Bacterium	Number of strains	Proportion of total	Degrees for 'slice'
Escherichia coli	37	0.435	156.6
Aeromonas hydrophila	8	0.294	105.8
Klebsiella spp.	13	0.153	55.1
Salmonella enterica	2	0.094	33.9
Enterococcus spp.	25	0.024	8.6
Total	85	1	360

Pie chart showing the relative proportions of strains of five bacteria isolated from a water sample.

63.3 *Tip:* First decide on the class boundaries and number of classes – in this case, the values range from 8.1 to 15.1. The subdivisions shown in the table below provide eight classes, which gives a frequency distribution with a reasonable number of classes to aggregate the data sufficiently, but also provide enough detail to indicate the overall shape of the distribution. Note that Excel® also has a useful histogram function, but you will need to

Data of table in study exercise 63.6 presented as a frequency distribution

Class	Frequency
8.0–8.9	2
9.0–9.9	5
10.0–10.9	17
11.0–11.9	22
12.0–12.9	26
13.0–13.9	17
14.0–14.9	10
15.0–15.9	1

learn how to set the class boundaries (termed 'bin values') to make effective use of this function.

A histogram for these data is shown in the figure below. Your brief description should include something about the location, dispersion and shape of the distribution (see Chapter 66), for example: 'The modal class of the distribution is $12.0-12.9\,\mathrm{g\,l^{-1}}$, with a range of $7.0\,\mathrm{g\,l^{-1}}$ ($15.5-8.5\,\mathrm{g\,l^{-1}}$). The data show a slight negative skew, with 28 values in the three classes above the mode and 46 in the four classes below it'.

Frequency distribution of data of table in study exercise 63.3.

63.4 *Tip:* The Sunday newspaper supplements often analyse news stories with the aid of graphs, and might be a good source for material, as their articles are often slanted towards a particular viewpoint, and you may find that the graphical presentation has been chosen to support this.

64 Presenting data in tables

64.1 *Tip:* To convert all of the concentrations to the same units, you will need to know the relative molecular mass of each constituent (glutamate $M_r = 147.1$; proline $M_r = 115.1$; trehalose $M_r = 342.3$). We have used $\mathrm{mmol\,l^{-1}}$ in the example below, but other units would be equally valid, as long as you are consistent. Data expressed as % (w/v) were first converted to $\mathrm{g\,l^{-1}}$ (multiplied by 10), then to $\mathrm{mmol\,l^{-1}}$.

Concentrations of low molecular weight solutes in bacteria.

Bacterium	Solute concentration (mmol l⁻¹)*		
	Glutamate	Proline	Trehalose
Bacillus subtilis	52.1	39.7	<0.1
Escherichia coli	34.0	21.0	154.7
Staphylococcus aureus	15.3	NT	NT

* All values expressed to 1 decimal place.
NT = not tested.

64.2 *Tip:* Box 64.1 gives the key aspects. The following table gives one possible layout.

The principal components of a typical table

Component	Comment:
Title	Concise, self-contained description of table contents, with numbering where appropriate
Column/row headings	Identifies the content of each column and row, showing units of measurement, where appropriate
Data values	Quoted to an appropriate number of significant figures/decimal places
Footnotes	All abbreviations and other individual details must be explained
Rulings	Used to emphasise any groupings within the table, and to separate individual items

64.3

(a) **11–14 years**.

(b) *Tip:* Calculate the ratio of male:female energy requirement, in order to establish which is greatest in proportional terms, as in the following table.

Male:female energy requirements, calculated from the table in study exercise 64.3

Age	Male:female energy requirement
<1	1.0625
1–3	1.0612
4–6	1.1077
7–10	1.1233
11–14	1.2078
15–18	1.3068
19–50	1.3086
>50	1.2338

This shows that the age class where the energy requirement of males is greatest in proportion to that of females is **19–50 years**.

(c) **Birth to 10 years**.

(d) **15–18 years for males**, **11–50 years for females**.

65 Hints for solving numerical problems

65.1

(a) $[C] = A/\varepsilon l$

(b) $\varepsilon = A/[C]l$

65.2

(a) Subtract ax from both sides and then swap sides, so: **$b = y - ax$**

(b) 1. Subtract b from both sides and then swap sides, so: $ax = y - b$
2. Divide both sides by a, so: **$x = (y - b)/a$**

(c) Raise each side to the power $\frac{1}{3}$, then swap sides, so: **$y = x^{1/3}$**

(d) 1. Take logs of both sides, so: $\log x = \log(3^y)$
2. Noting $\log(3^y) = y \log 3$, substitute on right-hand side, so $\log x = y \log 3$
3. Divide both sides by $\log 3$, then swap sides, so: **$y = \log x/\log 3$**

(e) 1. Divide both sides by $1 - y$, so: $z^p + 3 = x/(1 - y)$
2. Subtract 3 from both sides, so: $z^p = x/(1 - y) - 3$
3. Raise both sides to the power $1/p$, so: **$z = ((x \div (1 - y)) - 3)^{1/p}$**

(f) 1. multiply both sides by pq, so: $zpq = (y - z)^{1/n}$
2. Raise each side to the power n, so: $zpq^n = (y - z)$
3. Take logs of both sides, so: $n\log(zpq) = \log(y - z)$
4. Hence **$n = (\log(zpq)) \div (\log(y - z))$**

65.3

(a) **215**
(b) **107 000**
(c) **0.04**
(d) **99.82**
(e) **99.90**
(f) **100.00**
(g) **6260**
(h) **130 000**
(i) **2**
(j) **5**
(k) **3**
(l) **6**
(m) **2**
(n) **5**

65.4

(a) **17.14%**
(b) **7.55%**
(c) **14.01**
(d) $100 \times (75.02 - 55.23) \div 55.23 = 35.831\,975 = \textbf{35.83\%}$

65.5

(a) (i) **0.000 000 000 000 000 000 160 219 2 C**;
(ii) **299 792 400 mws^{-1}**
(b) **4207.3**; **0.804 14**; **0.098 27**; **7.0238**; **309.09**

65.6 *Tip:* To calculate x, substitute values into Eqn [65.4].

(a) $x = (7.0 - 4.5) \div 0.02 = \textbf{125}$;
(b) $x = (15.4 - -2.6) \div -4.46 = -4.035\,874\,439 = \textbf{-4.04}$.
Tip: to calculate y, substitute values into Eqn [65.3].
(c) $y = 0.2 + (-0.63 \times 10.5) = -6.415 = \textbf{-6.42}$;
(d) $y = -1.8 + (4.1 \times 4.5) = 16.65 = \textbf{16.6}$.

66 Descriptive statistics

66.1

mean = **4.9**
median = **4**
mode = **3**
The distribution is **positively skewed**.

66.2

(a) **Range = 8**
(b) **Variance = 4.464**
(c) **Standard deviation = 2.113**

(d) **Coefficient of variation = 43.12%** (CoV = 100 × 2.113/4.9)

(e) **Standard error = 0.2728**

66.3 *Tip:* Substitute values into Eqn [66.3] to calculate the SE of each sample.

For sample A: 12.7 ÷ 3.464 101 615 = 3.666 174 209 = **3.67**.
For sample B: 14.4 ÷ 4.472 135 955 = 3.219 937 888 = **3.22**.
Thus, in absolute terms, sample B has the lower standard error (note that the higher standard deviation of sample B is more than offset by the increased number of data values). To calculate the proportional standard error, divide the SE by the mean, as follows:

For sample A: 3.666 174 209 ÷ 16.2 = 0.226 307 05 = **0.226**.
For sample B: 3.219 937 888 ÷ 13.2 = 0.243 934 688 = **0.244**.
Thus, in proportion to the mean, sample A has the lower standard error.

66.4

Larval size data (recalculated)

Replicate sample	Mean sample larval size (mm)	Sample number	Mean size × sample size
A	3.0	24	72.0
B	2.5	37	92.5
C	2.0	6	12.0
Total		67	176.5

True mean = 176.5/67 = **2.63 mm**

67 Choosing and using statistical tests

67.1 *Tip:* First calculate the standard error using Eqn [66.3], as 6.8 ÷ 4 = 1.7. Then, substitute values into Eqn [67.2] to calculate the 95% confidence limits (note that you also need the value for $t_{0.05[15]} = 2.131$). The upper limit is calculated as: 24.7 + (2.131 × 1.7) = 28.3227 = **28.3**. The lower limit is calculated as 24.7 − (2.131 × 1.7) = 21.0773 = **21.1**.

67.2 *Tip:* The variance of the data, s^2, computes as 10.543 and the mean as 3.4. Hence $s^2 \div \text{mean} = $ **3.1**, hence the data appear clumped. In biological terms this might mean that if a snail is infected once, then it has a greater chance of multiple infection. Perhaps parasite eggs are clumped in the snails' environment.

67.3 *Tip:* The calculated $t = $ **2.136** with 12 degrees of freedom; the critical value at $P = 5\%$ is 2.18 (Table 67.2); hence you would accept the null hypothesis that the samples came from the same population and hence conclude that the plant hormone had no significant effect.

67.4 *Tip:* Amino acid uptake will be the dependent (y) variable and time the independent (x) variable. From the Excel output, the coefficients are: intercept = **1.17** (to 3 significant figures) and slope (labelled as 'X variable 1') = **2.95** (to 3 significant figures), so the linear relationship has the following form: $y = 1.17 + 2.95x$. The strength of the relationship is measured by the coefficient of determination, termed 'R squared' in the Excel output. In this case, a value of **0.971** (to 3 significant figures) shows that there is a very strong fit of the y data to the trend line.

Index

Index

Index

Index